DISTRIBUTED SYSTEMS

Principles and Paradigms

Second Edition

About the Authors

Andrew S. Tanenbaum has an S.B. degree from M.I.T. and a Ph.D. from the University of California at Berkeley. He is currently a Professor of Computer Science at the Vrije Universiteit in Amsterdam, The Netherlands, where he heads the Computer Systems Group. Until stepping down in Jan. 2005, for 12 years he had been Dean of the Advanced School for Computing and Imaging, an interuniversity graduate school doing research on advanced parallel, distributed, and imaging systems.

In the past, he has done research on compilers, operating systems, networking, and local-area distributed systems. His current research focuses primarily on computer security, especially in operating systems, networks, and large wide-area distributed systems. Together, all these research projects have led to over 125 refereed papers in journals and conference proceedings and five books, which have been translated into 21 languages.

Prof. Tanenbaum has also produced a considerable volume of software. He was the principal architect of the Amsterdam Compiler Kit, a toolkit for writing portable compilers, as well as of MINIX, a small UNIX clone aimed at very high reliability. It is available for free at *www.minix3.org*. This system provided the inspiration and base on which Linux was developed. He was also one of the chief designers of *Amoeba* and *Globe*.

His Ph.D. students have gone on to greater glory after getting their degrees. He is very proud of them. In this respect he resembles a mother hen.

Prof. Tanenbaum is a Fellow of the ACM, a Fellow of the the IEEE, and a member of the Royal Netherlands Academy of Arts and Sciences. He is also winner of the 1994 ACM Karl V. Karlstrom Outstanding Educator Award, winner of the 1997 ACM/SIGCSE Award for Outstanding Contributions to Computer Science Education, and winner of the 2002 Texty award for excellence in textbooks. In 2004 he was named as one of the five new Academy Professors by the Royal Academy. His home page is at *www.cs.vu.nl/~ast*.

Maarten van Steen is a professor at the Vrije Universiteit, Amsterdam, where he teaches operating systems, computer networks, and distributed systems. He has also given various highly successful courses on computer systems related subjects to ICT professionals from industry and governmental organizations.

Prof. van Steen studied Applied Mathematics at Twente University and received a Ph.D. from Leiden University in Computer Science. After his graduate studies he went to work for an industrial research laboratory where he eventually became head of the Computer Systems Group, concentrating on programming support for parallel applications.

After five years of struggling simultaneously do research and management, he decided to return to academia, first as an assistant professor in Computer Science at the Erasmus University Rotterdam, and later as an assistant professor in Andrew Tanenbaum's group at the Vrije Universiteit Amsterdam. Going back to university was the right decision; his wife thinks so, too.

His current research concentrates on large-scale distributed systems. Part of his research focuses on Web-based systems, in particular adaptive distribution and replication in Globule, a content delivery network of which his colleague Guillaume Pierre is the chief designer. Another subject of extensive research is fully decentralized (gossip-based) peer-to-peer systems of which results have been included in Tribler, a BitTorrent application developed in collaboration with colleagues from the Technical University of Delft.

DISTRIBUTED SYSTEMS

Principles and Paradigms

Second Edition

Andrew S. Tanenbaum
Maarten Van Steen

*Vrije Universiteit
Amsterdam, The Netherlands*

PEARSON
Prentice
Hall

Upper Saddle River, NJ 07458

Library of Congress Cataloging-in-Publication Data

Tanenbaum, Andrew S.
  Distributed systems : principles and paradigms / Andrew S. Tanenbaum, Maarten Van Steen.
    p. cm.
  Includes bibliographical references and index.
  ISBN 0-13-239227-5
  1. Electronic data processing--Distributed processing. 2. Distributed operating systems (Computers) I. Steen,
Maarten van. II. Title.
  QA76.9.D5T36 2006
  005.4'476--dc22

                                                            2006024063

Vice President and Editorial Director, ECS: *Marcia J. Horton*
Executive Editor: *Tracy Dunkelberger*
Editorial Assistant: *Christianna Lee*
Associtate Editor: *Carole Snyder*
Executive Managing Editor: *Vince O'Brien*
Managing Editor: *Camille Trentacoste*
Production Editor: *Craig Little*
Director of Creative Services: *Paul Belfanti*
Creative Director: *Juan Lopez*
Art Director: *Heather Scott*
Cover Designer: *Tamara Newnam*
Art Editor: *Xiaohong Zhu*
Manufacturing Manager, ESM: *Alexis Heydt-Long*
Manufacturing Buyer: *Lisa McDowell*
Executive Marketing Manager: *Robin O'Brien*
Marketing Assistant: *Mack Patterson*

 © 2007 Pearson Education, Inc.
Pearson Prentice Hall
Pearson Education, Inc.
Upper Saddle River, NJ 07458

Pearson Prentice Hall™ is a trademark of Pearson Education, Inc.

Printed in the United States of America

10 9 8 7 6 5 4 3 2 1

ISBN: 0-13-239227-5

Pearson Education Ltd., *London*
Pearson Education Australia Pty. Ltd., *Sydney*
Pearson Education Singapore, Pte. Ltd.
Pearson Education North Asia Ltd., *Hong Kong*
Pearson Education Canada, Inc., *Toronto*
Pearson Educación de Mexico, S.A. de C.V.
Pearson Education—Japan, *Tokyo*
Pearson Education Malaysia, Pte. Ltd.
Pearson Education, Inc., *Upper Saddle River, New Jersey*

To Suzanne, Barbara, Marvin, and the memory of Bram and Sweetie π
- AST

To Mariëlle, Max, and Elke
- MvS

CONTENTS

8   FAULT TOLERANCE   321

[handwritten margin notes: Symmetric Crypt: DES. / Public-Key Crypt: RSA / Hash: MD5]

9   SECURITY   377

[handwritten margin notes: Shared secret key / scalability / key distribution Center / ticket / Public-key crypt / Digital Signature / Session Keys. / The Globus. (grid). / Control / Layering Security. / Distribution of Security (TCB, RISC) / Group. / Secure Replicated. / secret sharing / Access Control Matrix / Protection Domains / Agent / Target → JVM / Key establishment / Key distribution / Lifetime of certificate]

10 DISTRIBUTED OBJECT-BASED SYSTEMS   443

11   DISTRIBUTED FILE SYSTEMS   491

(handwritten annotations):
remote access
upload/download
File system model, file operations
file-striping.
Ivy: DHash.
Compound RPCs
Symbolic link
File Handles, Automounting

12   DISTRIBUTED WEB-BASED SYSTEMS   545

13   DISTRIBUTED COORDINATION-BASED   589
SYSTEMS

[handwritten annotations: "⇒ generative communication. Javaspace in Jini / TIB. Rendezvous"]

[handwritten annotation: "process complete → data turn into"]

14 SUGGESTIONS FOR FURTHER READING AND BIBLIOGRAPHY 623

PREFACE

Distributed systems form a rapidly changing field of computer science. Since the previous edition of this book, exciting new topics have emerged such as peer-to-peer computing and sensor networks, while others have become much more mature, like Web services and Web applications in general. Changes such as these required that we revised our original text to bring it up-to-date.

This second edition reflects a major revision in comparison to the previous one. We have added a separate chapter on architectures reflecting the progress that has been made on organizing distributed systems. Another major difference is that there is now much more material on decentralized systems, in particular peer-to-peer computing. Not only do we discuss the basic techniques, we also pay attention to their applications, such as file sharing, information dissemination, content-delivery networks, and publish/subscribe systems.

Next to these two major subjects, new subjects are discussed throughout the book. For example, we have added material on sensor networks, virtualization, server clusters, and Grid computing. Special attention is paid to self-management of distributed systems, an increasingly important topic as systems continue to scale.

Of course, we have also modernized the material where appropriate. For example, when discussing consistency and replication, we now focus on consistency models that are more appropriate for modern distributed systems rather than the original models, which were tailored to high-performance distributed computing. Likewise, we have added material on modern distributed algorithms, including GPS-based clock synchronization and localization algorithms.

Although unusual, we have nevertheless been able to *reduce* the total number of pages. This reduction is partly caused by discarding subjects such as distributed garbage collection and electronic payment protocols, and also reorganizing the last four chapters.

As in the previous edition, the book is divided into two parts. Principles of distributed systems are discussed in chapters 2–9, whereas overall approaches to how distributed applications should be developed (the paradigms) are discussed in chapters 10–13. Unlike the previous edition, however, we have decided not to discuss complete case studies in the paradigm chapters. Instead, each principle is now explained through a representative case. For example, object invocations are now discussed as a communication principle in Chap. 10 on object-based distributed systems. This approach allowed us to condense the material, but also to make it more enjoyable to read and study.

Of course, we continue to draw extensively from practice to explain what distributed systems are all about. Various aspects of real-life systems such as Web-Sphere MQ, DNS, GPS, Apache, CORBA, Ice, NFS, Akamai, TIB/Rendezvous, Jini, and many more are discussed throughout the book. These examples illustrate the thin line between theory and practice, which makes distributed systems such an exciting field.

A number of people have contributed to this book in various ways. We would especially like to thank D. Robert Adams, Arno Bakker, Coskun Bayrak, Jacques Chassin de Kergommeaux, Randy Chow, Michel Chaudron, Puneet Singh Chawla, Fabio Costa, Cong Du, Dick Epema, Kevin Fenwick, Chandana Gamage, Ali Ghodsi, Giorgio Ingargiola, Mark Jelasity, Ahmed Kamel, Gregory Kapfhammer, Jeroen Ketema, Onno Kubbe, Patricia Lago, Steve MacDonald, Michael J. McCarthy, M. Tamer Ozsu, Guillaume Pierre, Avi Shahar, Swaminathan Sivasubramanian, Chintan Shah, Ruud Stegers, Paul Tymann, Craig E. Wills, Reuven Yagel, and Dakai Zhu for reading parts of the manuscript, helping identifying mistakes in the previous edition, and offering useful comments.

Finally, we would like to thank our families. Suzanne has been through this process seventeen times now. That's a lot of times for me but also for her. Not once has she said: "Enough is enough" although surely the thought has occurred to her. Thank you. Barbara and Marvin now have a much better idea of what professors do for a living and know the difference between a good textbook and a bad one. They are now an inspiration to me to try to produce more good ones than bad ones (AST).

Because I took a sabbatical leave to update the book, the whole business of writing was also much more enjoyable for Mariëlle. She is beginning to get used to it, but continues to remain supportive while alerting me when it is indeed time to redirect attention to more important issues. I owe her many thanks. Max and Elke by now have a much better idea of what writing a book means, but compared to what they are reading themselves, find it difficult to understand what is so exciting about these strange things called distributed systems. I can't blame them (MvS).

1

INTRODUCTION

Computer systems are undergoing a revolution. From 1945, when the modern computer era began, until about 1985, computers were large and expensive. Even minicomputers cost at least tens of thousands of dollars each. As a result, most organizations had only a handful of computers, and for lack of a way to connect them, these operated independently from one another.

Starting around the the mid-1980s, however, two advances in technology began to change that situation. The first was the development of powerful microprocessors. Initially, these were 8-bit machines, but soon 16-, 32-, and 64-bit CPUs became common. Many of these had the computing power of a mainframe (i.e., large) computer, but for a fraction of the price.

The amount of improvement that has occurred in computer technology in the past half century is truly staggering and totally unprecedented in other industries. From a machine that cost 10 million dollars and executed 1 instruction per second, we have come to machines that cost 1000 dollars and are able to execute 1 billion instructions per second, a price/performance gain of 10^{13}. If cars had improved at this rate in the same time period, a Rolls Royce would now cost 1 dollar and get a billion miles per gallon. (Unfortunately, it would probably also have a 200-page manual telling how to open the door.)

The second development was the invention of high-speed computer networks. **Local-area networks** or **LANs** allow hundreds of machines within a building to be connected in such a way that small amounts of information can be transferred between machines in a few microseconds or so. Larger amounts of data can be

1

moved between machines at rates of 100 million to 10 billion bits/sec. **Wide-area networks** or **WANs** allow millions of machines all over the earth to be connected at speeds varying from 64 Kbps (kilobits per second) to gigabits per second.

The result of these technologies is that it is now not only feasible, but easy, to put together computing systems composed of large numbers of computers connected by a high-speed network. They are usually called computer networks or **distributed systems**, in contrast to the previous **centralized systems** (or **single-processor systems**) consisting of a single computer, its peripherals, and perhaps some remote terminals.

1.1 DEFINITION OF A DISTRIBUTED SYSTEM

Various definitions of distributed systems have been given in the literature, none of them satisfactory, and none of them in agreement with any of the others. For our purposes it is sufficient to give a loose characterization:

> *A distributed system is a collection of independent computers that appears to its users as a single coherent system.*

This definition has several important aspects. The first one is that a distributed system consists of components (i.e., computers) that are autonomous. A second aspect is that users (be they people or programs) think they are dealing with a single system. This means that one way or the other the autonomous components need to collaborate. How to establish this collaboration lies at the heart of developing distributed systems. Note that no assumptions are made concerning the type of computers. In principle, even within a single system, they could range from high-performance mainframe computers to small nodes in sensor networks. Likewise, no assumptions are made on the way that computers are interconnected. We will return to these aspects later in this chapter.

Instead of going further with definitions, it is perhaps more useful to concentrate on important characteristics of distributed systems. One important characteristic is that differences between the various computers and the ways in which they communicate are mostly hidden from users. The same holds for the internal organization of the distributed system. Another important characteristic is that users and applications can interact with a distributed system in a consistent and uniform way, regardless of where and when interaction takes place.

In principle, distributed systems should also be relatively easy to expand or scale. This characteristic is a direct consequence of having independent computers, but at the same time, hiding how these computers actually take part in the system as a whole. A distributed system will normally be continuously available, although perhaps some parts may be temporarily out of order. Users and applications should not notice that parts are being replaced or fixed, or that new parts are added to serve more users or applications.

In order to support heterogeneous computers and networks while offering a single-system view, distributed systems are often organized by means of a layer of software–that is, logically placed between a higher-level layer consisting of users and applications, and a layer underneath consisting of operating systems and basic communication facilities, as shown in Fig. 1-1 Accordingly, such a distributed system is sometimes called **middleware**.

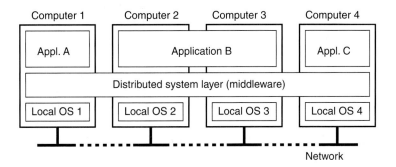

Figure 1-1. A distributed system organized as middleware. The middleware layer extends over multiple machines, and offers each application the same interface.

Fig. 1-1 shows four networked computers and three applications, of which application *B* is distributed across computers 2 and 3. Each application is offered the same interface. The distributed system provides the means for components of a single distributed application to communicate with each other, but also to let different applications communicate. At the same time, it hides, as best and reasonable as possible, the differences in hardware and operating systems from each application.

1.2 GOALS

Just because it is possible to build distributed systems does not necessarily mean that it is a good idea. After all, with current technology it is also possible to put four floppy disk drives on a personal computer. It is just that doing so would be pointless. In this section we discuss four important goals that should be met to make building a distributed system worth the effort. A distributed system should make resources easily accessible; it should reasonably hide the fact that resources are distributed across a network; it should be open; and it should be scalable.

1.2.1 Making Resources Accessible

The main goal of a distributed system is to make it easy for the users (and applications) to access remote resources, and to share them in a controlled and efficient way. Resources can be just about anything, but typical examples include things like printers, computers, storage facilities, data, files, Web pages, and networks, to name just a few. There are many reasons for wanting to share resources. One obvious reason is that of economics. For example, it is cheaper to let a printer be shared by several users in a small office than having to buy and maintain a separate printer for each user. Likewise, it makes economic sense to share costly resources such as supercomputers, high-performance storage systems, imagesetters, and other expensive peripherals.

Connecting users and resources also makes it easier to collaborate and exchange information, as is clearly illustrated by the success of the Internet with its simple protocols for exchanging files, mail, documents, audio, and video. The connectivity of the Internet is now leading to numerous virtual organizations in which geographically widely-dispersed groups of people work together by means of **groupware**, that is, software for collaborative editing, teleconferencing, and so on. Likewise, the Internet connectivity has enabled electronic commerce allowing us to buy and sell all kinds of goods without actually having to go to a store or even leave home.

However, as connectivity and sharing increase, security is becoming increasingly important. In current practice, systems provide little protection against eavesdropping or intrusion on communication. Passwords and other sensitive information are often sent as cleartext (i.e., unencrypted) through the network, or stored at servers that we can only hope are trustworthy. In this sense, there is much room for improvement. For example, it is currently possible to order goods by merely supplying a credit card number. Rarely is proof required that the customer owns the card. In the future, placing orders this way may be possible only if you can actually prove that you physically possess the card by inserting it into a card reader.

Another security problem is that of tracking communication to build up a preference profile of a specific user (Wang et al., 1998). Such tracking explicitly violates privacy, especially if it is done without notifying the user. A related problem is that increased connectivity can also lead to unwanted communication, such as electronic junk mail, often called spam. In such cases, what we may need is to protect ourselves using special information filters that select incoming messages based on their content.

1.2.2 Distribution Transparency

An important goal of a distributed system is to hide the fact that its processes and resources are physically distributed across multiple computers. A distributed system that is able to present itself to users and applications as if it were only a single computer system is said to be **transparent**. Let us first take a look at what kinds of transparency exist in distributed systems. After that we will address the more general question whether transparency is always required.

Types of Transparency

The concept of transparency can be applied to several aspects of a distributed system, the most important ones shown in Fig. 1-2.

Transparency	Description
Access	Hide differences in data representation and how a resource is accessed
Location	Hide where a resource is located
Migration	Hide that a resource may move to another location
Relocation	Hide that a resource may be moved to another location while in use
Replication	Hide that a resource is replicated
Concurrency	Hide that a resource may be shared by several competitive users
Failure	Hide the failure and recovery of a resource

Figure 1-2. Different forms of transparency in a distributed system (ISO, 1995).

Access transparency deals with hiding differences in data representation and the way that resources can be accessed by users. At a basic level, we wish to hide differences in machine architectures, but more important is that we reach agreement on how data is to be represented by different machines and operating systems. For example, a distributed system may have computer systems that run different operating systems, each having their own file-naming conventions. Differences in naming conventions, as well as how files can be manipulated, should all be hidden from users and applications.

An important group of transparency types has to do with the location of a resource. **Location transparency** refers to the fact that users cannot tell where a resource is physically located in the system. Naming plays an important role in achieving location transparency. In particular, location transparency can be achieved by assigning only logical names to resources, that is, names in which the location of a resource is not secretly encoded. An example of a such a name is the URL *http://www.prenhall.com/index.html*, which gives no clue about the location of Prentice Hall's main Web server. The URL also gives no clue as to whether *index.html* has always been at its current location or was recently moved there. Distributed systems in which resources can be moved without affecting how those resources can be accessed are said to provide **migration transparency**. Even stronger is the situation in which resources can be relocated *while* they are being accessed without the user or application noticing anything. In such cases, the system is said to support **relocation transparency**. An example of relocation transparency is when mobile users can continue to use their wireless laptops while moving from place to place without ever being (temporarily) disconnected.

As we shall see, replication plays a very important role in distributed systems. For example, resources may be replicated to increase availability or to improve performance by placing a copy close to the place where it is accessed. **Replication transparency** deals with hiding the fact that several copies of a resource exist. To hide replication from users, it is necessary that all replicas have the same name. Consequently, a system that supports replication transparency should generally support location transparency as well, because it would otherwise be impossible to refer to replicas at different locations.

We already mentioned that an important goal of distributed systems is to allow sharing of resources. In many cases, sharing resources is done in a cooperative way, as in the case of communication. However, there are also many examples of competitive sharing of resources. For example, two independent users may each have stored their files on the same file server or may be accessing the same tables in a shared database. In such cases, it is important that each user does not notice that the other is making use of the same resource. This phenomenon is called **concurrency transparency**. An important issue is that concurrent access to a shared resource leaves that resource in a consistent state. Consistency can be achieved through locking mechanisms, by which users are, in turn, given exclusive access to the desired resource. A more refined mechanism is to make use of transactions, but as we shall see in later chapters, transactions are quite difficult to implement in distributed systems.

A popular alternative definition of a distributed system, due to Leslie Lamport, is "You know you have one when the crash of a computer you've never heard of stops you from getting any work done." This description puts the finger on another important issue of distributed systems design: dealing with failures. Making a distributed system **failure transparent** means that a user does not notice that a resource (he has possibly never heard of) fails to work properly, and that the system subsequently recovers from that failure. Masking failures is one of the hardest issues in distributed systems and is even impossible when certain apparently realistic assumptions are made, as we will discuss in Chap. 8. The main difficulty in masking failures lies in the inability to distinguish between a dead resource and a painfully slow resource. For example, when contacting a busy Web server, a browser will eventually time out and report that the Web page is unavailable. At that point, the user cannot conclude that the server is really down.

Degree of Transparency

Although distribution transparency is generally considered preferable for any distributed system, there are situations in which attempting to completely hide all distribution aspects from users is not a good idea. An example is requesting your electronic newspaper to appear in your mailbox before 7 A.M. local time, as usual, while you are currently at the other end of the world living in a different time zone. Your morning paper will not be the morning paper you are used to.

Likewise, a wide-area distributed system that connects a process in San Francisco to a process in Amsterdam cannot be expected to hide the fact that Mother

Nature will not allow it to send a message from one process to the other in less than about 35 milliseconds. In practice it takes several hundreds of milliseconds using a computer network. Signal transmission is not only limited by the speed of light, but also by limited processing capacities of the intermediate switches.

There is also a trade-off between a high degree of transparency and the performance of a system. For example, many Internet applications repeatedly try to contact a server before finally giving up. Consequently, attempting to mask a transient server failure before trying another one may slow down the system as a whole. In such a case, it may have been better to give up earlier, or at least let the user cancel the attempts to make contact.

Another example is where we need to guarantee that several replicas, located on different continents, need to be consistent all the time. In other words, if one copy is changed, that change should be propagated to all copies before allowing any other operation. It is clear that a single update operation may now even take seconds to complete, something that cannot be hidden from users.

Finally, there are situations in which it is not at all obvious that hiding distribution is a good idea. As distributed systems are expanding to devices that people carry around, and where the very notion of location and context awareness is becoming increasingly important, it may be best to actually *expose* distribution rather than trying to hide it. This distribution exposure will become more evident when we discuss embedded and ubiquitous distributed systems later in this chapter. As a simple example, consider an office worker who wants to print a file from her notebook computer. It is better to send the print job to a busy nearby printer, rather than to an idle one at corporate headquarters in a different country.

There are also other arguments against distribution transparency. Recognizing that full distribution transparency is simply impossible, we should ask ourselves whether it is even wise to *pretend* that we can achieve it. It may be much better to make distribution explicit so that the user and application developer are never tricked into believing that there is such a thing as transparency. The result will be that users will much better understand the (sometimes unexpected) behavior of a distributed system, and are thus much better prepared to deal with this behavior.

The conclusion is that aiming for distribution transparency may be a nice goal when designing and implementing distributed systems, but that it should be considered together with other issues such as performance and comprehensibility. The price for not being able to achieve full transparency may be surprisingly high.

1.2.3 Openness

Another important goal of distributed systems is openness. An **open distributed system** is a system that offers services according to standard rules that describe the syntax and semantics of those services. For example, in computer networks, standard rules govern the format, contents, and meaning of messages sent and received. Such rules are formalized in protocols. In distributed systems, services are generally specified through **interfaces**, which are often described in an **Interface Definition Language** (**IDL**). Interface definitions written in an IDL nearly always capture only the syntax of services. In other words, they specify precisely the names of the functions that are available together with types of the parameters, return values, possible exceptions that can be raised, and so on. The hard part is specifying precisely what those services do, that is, the semantics of interfaces. In practice, such specifications are always given in an informal way by means of natural language.

If properly specified, an interface definition allows an arbitrary process that needs a certain interface to talk to another process that provides that interface. It also allows two independent parties to build completely different implementations of those interfaces, leading to two separate distributed systems that operate in exactly the same way. Proper specifications are complete and neutral. Complete means that everything that is necessary to make an implementation has indeed been specified. However, many interface definitions are not at all complete, so that it is necessary for a developer to add implementation-specific details. Just as important is the fact that specifications do not prescribe what an implementation should look like; they should be neutral. Completeness and neutrality are important for interoperability and portability (Blair and Stefani, 1998). **Interoperability** characterizes the extent by which two implementations of systems or components from different manufacturers can co-exist and work together by merely relying on each other's services as specified by a common standard. **Portability** characterizes to what extent an application developed for a distributed system *A* can be executed, without modification, on a different distributed system *B* that implements the same interfaces as *A*.

Another important goal for an open distributed system is that it should be easy to configure the system out of different components (possibly from different developers). Also, it should be easy to add new components or replace existing ones without affecting those components that stay in place. In other words, an open distributed system should also be **extensible**. For example, in an extensible system, it should be relatively easy to add parts that run on a different operating system, or even to replace an entire file system. As many of us know from daily practice, attaining such flexibility is easier said than done.

Separating Policy from Mechanism

To achieve flexibility in open distributed systems, it is crucial that the system is organized as a collection of relatively small and easily replaceable or adaptable components. This implies that we should provide definitions not only for the highest-level interfaces, that is, those seen by users and applications, but also definitions for interfaces to internal parts of the system and describe how those parts interact. This approach is relatively new. Many older and even contemporary systems are constructed using a monolithic approach in which components are only logically separated but implemented as one, huge program. This approach makes it hard to replace or adapt a component without affecting the entire system. Monolithic systems thus tend to be closed instead of open.

The need for changing a distributed system is often caused by a component that does not provide the optimal policy for a specific user or application. As an example, consider caching in the World Wide Web. Browsers generally allow users to adapt their caching policy by specifying the size of the cache, and whether a cached document should always be checked for consistency, or perhaps only once per session. However, the user cannot influence other caching parameters, such as how long a document may remain in the cache, or which document should be removed when the cache fills up. Also, it is impossible to make caching decisions based on the *content* of a document. For instance, a user may want to cache railroad timetables, knowing that these hardly change, but never information on current traffic conditions on the highways.

What we need is a separation between policy and mechanism. In the case of Web caching, for example, a browser should ideally provide facilities for only storing documents, and at the same time allow users to decide which documents are stored and for how long. In practice, this can be implemented by offering a rich set of parameters that the user can set (dynamically). Even better is that a user can implement his own policy in the form of a component that can be plugged into the browser. Of course, that component must have an interface that the browser can understand so that it can call procedures of that interface.

1.2.4 Scalability

Worldwide connectivity through the Internet is rapidly becoming as common as being able to send a postcard to anyone anywhere around the world. With this in mind, scalability is one of the most important design goals for developers of distributed systems.

Scalability of a system can be measured along at least three different dimensions (Neuman, 1994). First, a system can be scalable with respect to its size, meaning that we can easily add more users and resources to the system. Second, a geographically scalable system is one in which the users and resources may lie far apart. Third, a system can be administratively scalable, meaning that it can still be easy to manage even if it spans many independent administrative organizations. Unfortunately, a system that is scalable in one or more of these dimensions often exhibits some loss of performance as the system scales up.

Scalability Problems

When a system needs to scale, very different types of problems need to be solved. Let us first consider scaling with respect to size. If more users or resources need to be supported, we are often confronted with the limitations of centralized services, data, and algorithms (see Fig. 1-3). For example, many services are centralized in the sense that they are implemented by means of only a single server running on a specific machine in the distributed system. The problem with this scheme is obvious: the server can become a bottleneck as the number of users and applications grows. Even if we have virtually unlimited processing and storage capacity, communication with that server will eventually prohibit further growth.

Unfortunately, using only a single server is sometimes unavoidable. Imagine that we have a service for managing highly confidential information such as medical records, bank accounts, and so on. In such cases, it may be best to implement that service by means of a single server in a highly secured separate room, and protected from other parts of the distributed system through special network components. Copying the server to several locations to enhance performance may be out of the question as it would make the service less secure.

Concept	Example
Centralized services	A single server for all users
Centralized data	A single on-line telephone book
Centralized algorithms	Doing routing based on complete information

Figure 1-3. Examples of scalability limitations.

Just as bad as centralized services are centralized data. How should we keep track of the telephone numbers and addresses of 50 million people? Suppose that each data record could be fit into 50 characters. A single 2.5-gigabyte disk partition would provide enough storage. But here again, having a single database would undoubtedly saturate all the communication lines into and out of it. Likewise, imagine how the Internet would work if its Domain Name System (DNS) was still implemented as a single table. DNS maintains information on millions of computers worldwide and forms an essential service for locating Web servers. If each request to resolve a URL had to be forwarded to that one and only DNS server, it is clear that no one would be using the Web (which, by the way, would solve the problem).

Finally, centralized algorithms are also a bad idea. In a large distributed system, an enormous number of messages have to be routed over many lines. From a theoretical point of view, the optimal way to do this is collect complete information about the load on all machines and lines, and then run an algorithm to compute all the optimal routes. This information can then be spread around the system to improve the routing.

The trouble is that collecting and transporting all the input and output information would again be a bad idea because these messages would overload part of the network. In fact, any algorithm that operates by collecting information from all the sites, sends it to a single machine for processing, and then distributes the results should generally be avoided. Only decentralized algorithms should be used. These algorithms generally have the following characteristics, which distinguish them from centralized algorithms:

1. No machine has complete information about the system state.

2. Machines make decisions based only on local information.

3. Failure of one machine does not ruin the algorithm.

4. There is no implicit assumption that a global clock exists.

The first three follow from what we have said so far. The last is perhaps less obvious but also important. Any algorithm that starts out with: "At precisely 12:00:00 all machines shall note the size of their output queue" will fail because it is impossible to get all the clocks exactly synchronized. Algorithms should take into account the lack of exact clock synchronization. The larger the system, the larger the uncertainty. On a single LAN, with considerable effort it may be possible to get all clocks synchronized down to a few microseconds, but doing this nationally or internationally is tricky.

Geographical scalability has its own problems. One of the main reasons why it is currently hard to scale existing distributed systems that were designed for local-area networks is that they are based on **synchronous communication**. In this form of communication, a party requesting service, generally referred to as a **client**, blocks until a reply is sent back. This approach generally works fine in LANs where communication between two machines is generally at worst a few hundred microseconds. However, in a wide-area system, we need to take into account that interprocess communication may be hundreds of milliseconds, three orders of magnitude slower. Building interactive applications using synchronous communication in wide-area systems requires a great deal of care (and not a little patience).

Another problem that hinders geographical scalability is that communication in wide-area networks is inherently unreliable, and virtually always point-to-point. In contrast, local-area networks generally provide highly reliable communication facilities based on broadcasting, making it much easier to develop distributed systems. For example, consider the problem of locating a service. In a local-area system, a process can simply broadcast a message to every machine, asking if it is running the service it needs. Only those machines that have that service respond, each providing its network address in the reply message. Such a location scheme is unthinkable in a wide-area system: just imagine what would happen if we tried to locate a service this way in the Internet. Instead, special location services need to be designed, which may need to scale worldwide and be capable of servicing a billion users. We return to such services in Chap. 5.

Geographical scalability is strongly related to the problems of centralized solutions that hinder size scalability. If we have a system with many centralized components, it is clear that geographical scalability will be limited due to the performance and reliability problems resulting from wide-area communication. In addition, centralized components now lead to a waste of network resources. Imagine that a single mail server is used for an entire country. This would mean that sending an e-mail to your neighbor would first have to go to the central mail server, which may be hundreds of miles away. Clearly, this is not the way to go.

Finally, a difficult, and in many cases open question is how to scale a distributed system across multiple, independent administrative domains. A major problem that needs to be solved is that of conflicting policies with respect to resource usage (and payment), management, and security.

For example, many components of a distributed system that reside within a single domain can often be trusted by users that operate within that same domain. In such cases, system administration may have tested and certified applications, and may have taken special measures to ensure that such components cannot be tampered with. In essence, the users trust their system administrators. However, this trust does not expand naturally across domain boundaries.

If a distributed system expands into another domain, two types of security measures need to be taken. First of all, the distributed system has to protect itself against malicious attacks from the new domain. For example, users from the new domain may have only read access to the file system in its original domain. Likewise, facilities such as expensive image setters or high-performance computers may not be made available to foreign users. Second, the new domain has to protect itself against malicious attacks from the distributed system. A typical example is that of downloading programs such as applets in Web browsers. Basically, the new domain does not know behavior what to expect from such foreign code, and may therefore decide to severely limit the access rights for such code. The problem, as we shall see in Chap. 9, is how to enforce those limitations.

Scaling Techniques

Having discussed some of the scalability problems brings us to the question of how those problems can generally be solved. In most cases, scalability problems in distributed systems appear as performance problems caused by limited capacity of servers and network. There are now basically only three techniques for scaling: hiding communication latencies, distribution, and replication [see also Neuman (1994)].

Hiding communication latencies is important to achieve geographical scalability. The basic idea is simple: try to avoid waiting for responses to remote (and potentially distant) service requests as much as possible. For example, when a service has been requested at a remote machine, an alternative to waiting for a reply from the server is to do other useful work at the requester's side. Essentially, what this means is constructing the requesting application in such a way that it uses only **asynchronous communication**. When a reply comes in, the application is interrupted and a special handler is called to complete the previously-issued request. Asynchronous communication can often be used in batch-processing systems and parallel applications, in which more or less independent tasks can be scheduled for execution while another task is waiting for communication to complete. Alternatively, a new thread of control can be started to perform the request. Although it blocks waiting for the reply, other threads in the process can continue.

However, there are many applications that cannot make effective use of asynchronous communication. For example, in interactive applications when a user sends a request he will generally have nothing better to do than to wait for the answer. In such cases, a much better solution is to reduce the overall communication, for example, by moving part of the computation that is normally done at the server to the client process requesting the service. A typical case where this approach works is accessing databases using forms. Filling in forms can be done by sending a separate message for each field, and waiting for an acknowledgment from the server, as shown in Fig. 1-4(a). For example, the server may check for syntactic errors before accepting an entry. A much better solution is to ship the code for filling in the form, and possibly checking the entries, to the client, and have the client return a completed form, as shown in Fig. 1-4(b). This approach of shipping code is now widely supported by the Web in the form of Java applets and Javascript.

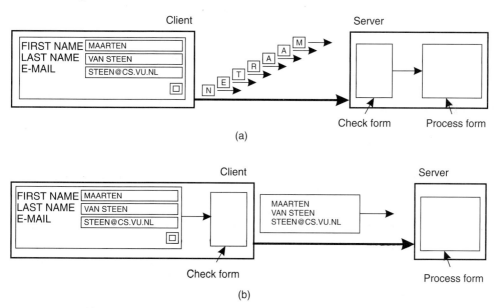

Figure 1-4. The difference between letting (a) a server or (b) a client check forms as they are being filled.

Another important scaling technique is **distribution**. Distribution involves taking a component, splitting it into smaller parts, and subsequently spreading those parts across the system. An excellent example of distribution is the Internet Domain Name System (DNS). The DNS name space is hierarchically organized into a tree of **domains**, which are divided into nonoverlapping **zones**, as shown in Fig. 1-5. The names in each zone are handled by a single name server. Without going into too many details, one can think of each path name being the name of a host in the Internet, and thus associated with a network address of that host. Basically, resolving a name means returning the network address of the associated host. Consider, for example, the name *nl.vu.cs.flits*. To resolve this name, it is first passed to the server of zone *Z1* (see Fig. 1-5) which returns the address of the server for zone *Z2*, to which the rest of name, *vu.cs.flits*, can be handed. The server for *Z2* will return the address of the server for zone *Z3*, which is capable of handling the last part of the name and will return the address of the associated host.

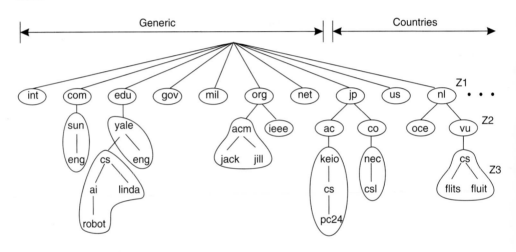

Figure 1-5. An example of dividing the DNS name space into zones.

This example illustrates how the *naming service*, as provided by DNS, is distributed across several machines, thus avoiding that a single server has to deal with all requests for name resolution.

As another example, consider the World Wide Web. To most users, the Web appears to be an enormous document-based information system in which each document has its own unique name in the form of a URL. Conceptually, it may even appear as if there is only a single server. However, the Web is physically distributed across a large number of servers, each handling a number of Web documents. The name of the server handling a document is encoded into that document's URL. It is only because of this distribution of documents that the Web has been capable of scaling to its current size.

Considering that scalability problems often appear in the form of performance degradation, it is generally a good idea to actually **replicate** components across a distributed system. Replication not only increases availability, but also helps to balance the load between components leading to better performance. Also, in geographically widely-dispersed systems, having a copy nearby can hide much of the communication latency problems mentioned before.

Caching is a special form of replication, although the distinction between the two is often hard to make or even artificial. As in the case of replication, caching results in making a copy of a resource, generally in the proximity of the client accessing that resource. However, in contrast to replication, caching is a decision made by the client of a resource, and not by the owner of a resource. Also, caching happens on demand whereas replication is often planned in advance.

There is one serious drawback to caching and replication that may adversely affect scalability. Because we now have multiple copies of a resource, modifying one copy makes that copy different from the others. Consequently, caching and replication leads to **consistency** problems.

To what extent inconsistencies can be tolerated depends highly on the usage of a resource. For example, many Web users find it acceptable that their browser returns a cached document of which the validity has not been checked for the last few minutes. However, there are also many cases in which strong consistency guarantees need to be met, such as in the case of electronic stock exchanges and auctions. The problem with strong consistency is that an update must be immediately propagated to all other copies. Moreover, if two updates happen concurrently, it is often also required that each copy is updated in the same order. Situations such as these generally require some global synchronization mechanism. Unfortunately, such mechanisms are extremely hard or even impossible to implement in a scalable way, as she insists that photons and electrical signals obey a speed limit of 187 miles/msec (the speed of light). Consequently, scaling by replication may introduce other, inherently nonscalable solutions. We return to replication and consistency in Chap. 7.

When considering these scaling techniques, one could argue that size scalability is the least problematic from a technical point of view. In many cases, simply increasing the capacity of a machine will the save the day (at least temporarily and perhaps at significant costs). Geographical scalability is a much tougher problem as Mother Nature is getting in our way. Nevertheless, practice shows that combining distribution, replication, and caching techniques with different forms of consistency will often prove sufficient in many cases. Finally, administrative scalability seems to be the most difficult one, partly also because we need to solve nontechnical problems (e.g., politics of organizations and human collaboration). Nevertheless, progress has been made in this area, by simply *ignoring* administrative domains. The introduction and now widespread use of peer-to-peer technology demonstrates what can be achieved if end users simply take over control (Aberer and Hauswirth, 2005; Lua et al., 2005; and Oram, 2001). However, let it be clear that peer-to-peer technology can at best be only a partial solution to solving administrative scalability. Eventually, it will have to be dealt with.

1.2.5 Pitfalls

It should be clear by now that developing distributed systems can be a formidable task. As we will see many times throughout this book, there are so many issues to consider at the same time that it seems that only complexity can be the result. Nevertheless, by following a number of design principles, distributed systems can be developed that strongly adhere to the goals we set out in this chapter. Many principles follow the basic rules of decent software engineering and will not be repeated here.

However, distributed systems differ from traditional software because components are dispersed across a network. Not taking this dispersion into account during design time is what makes so many systems needlessly complex and results in mistakes that need to be patched later on. Peter Deutsch, then at Sun Microsystems, formulated these mistakes as the following false assumptions that everyone makes when developing a distributed application for the first time:

1. The network is reliable.

2. The network is secure.

3. The network is homogeneous.

4. The topology does not change.

5. Latency is zero.

6. Bandwidth is infinite.

7. Transport cost is zero.

8. There is one administrator.

Note how these assumptions relate to properties that are unique to distributed systems: reliability, security, heterogeneity, and topology of the network; latency and bandwidth; transport costs; and finally administrative domains. When developing nondistributed applications, many of these issues will most likely not show up.

Most of the principles we discuss in this book relate immediately to these assumptions. In all cases, we will be discussing solutions to problems that are caused by the fact that one or more assumptions are false. For example, reliable networks simply do not exist, leading to the impossibility of achieving failure transparency. We devote an entire chapter to deal with the fact that networked communication is inherently insecure. We have already argued that distributed systems need to take heterogeneity into account. In a similar vein, when discussing replication for solving scalability problems, we are essentially tackling latency and bandwidth problems. We will also touch upon management issues at various points throughout this book, dealing with the false assumptions of zero-cost transportation and a single administrative domain.

1.3 TYPES OF DISTRIBUTED SYSTEMS

Before starting to discuss the principles of distributed systems, let us first take a closer look at the various types of distributed systems. In the following we make a distinction between distributed computing systems, distributed information systems, and distributed embedded systems.

1.3.1 Distributed Computing Systems

An important class of distributed systems is the one used for high-performance computing tasks. Roughly speaking, one can make a distinction between two subgroups. In **cluster computing** the underlying hardware consists of a collection of similar workstations or PCs, closely connected by means of a high-speed local-area network. In addition, each node runs the same operating system.

The situation becomes quite different in the case of **grid computing**. This subgroup consists of distributed systems that are often constructed as a federation of computer systems, where each system may fall under a different administrative domain, and may be very different when it comes to hardware, software, and deployed network technology.

Cluster Computing Systems

Cluster computing systems became popular when the price/performance ratio of personal computers and workstations improved. At a certain point, it became financially and technically attractive to build a supercomputer using off-the-shelf technology by simply hooking up a collection of relatively simple computers in a high-speed network. In virtually all cases, cluster computing is used for parallel programming in which a single (compute intensive) program is run in parallel on multiple machines.

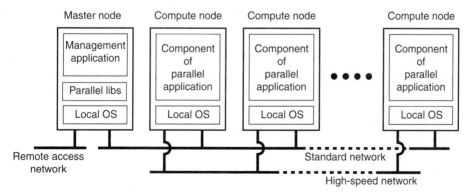

Figure 1-6. An example of a cluster computing system.

One well-known example of a cluster computer is formed by Linux-based Beowulf clusters, of which the general configuration is shown in Fig. 1-6. Each cluster consists of a collection of compute nodes that are controlled and accessed by means of a single master node. The master typically handles the allocation of nodes to a particular parallel program, maintains a batch queue of submitted jobs, and provides an interface for the users of the system. As such, the master actually runs the middleware needed for the execution of programs and management of the cluster, while the compute nodes often need nothing else but a standard operating system.

An important part of this middleware is formed by the libraries for executing parallel programs. As we will discuss in Chap. 4, many of these libraries effectively provide only advanced message-based communication facilities, but are not capable of handling faulty processes, security, etc.

As an alternative to this hierarchical organization, a symmetric approach is followed in the MOSIX system (Amar et al., 2004). MOSIX attempts to provide a **single-system image** of a cluster, meaning that to a process a cluster computer offers the ultimate distribution transparency by appearing to be a single computer. As we mentioned, providing such an image under all circumstances is impossible. In the case of MOSIX, the high degree of transparency is provided by allowing processes to dynamically and preemptively migrate between the nodes that make up the cluster. Process migration allows a user to start an application on any node (referred to as the home node), after which it can transparently move to other nodes, for example, to make efficient use of resources. We will return to process migration in Chap. 3.

Grid Computing Systems

A characteristic feature of cluster computing is its homogeneity. In most cases, the computers in a cluster are largely the same, they all have the same operating system, and are all connected through the same network. In contrast, grid computing systems have a high degree of heterogeneity: no assumptions are made concerning hardware, operating systems, networks, administrative domains, security policies, etc.

A key issue in a grid computing system is that resources from different organizations are brought together to allow the collaboration of a group of people or institutions. Such a collaboration is realized in the form of a **virtual organization**. The people belonging to the same virtual organization have access rights to the resources that are provided to that organization. Typically, resources consist of compute servers (including supercomputers, possibly implemented as cluster computers), storage facilities, and databases. In addition, special networked devices such as telescopes, sensors, etc., can be provided as well.

Given its nature, much of the software for realizing grid computing evolves around providing access to resources from different administrative domains, and to only those users and applications that belong to a specific virtual organization. For this reason, focus is often on architectural issues. An architecture proposed by Foster et al. (2001). is shown in Fig. 1-7

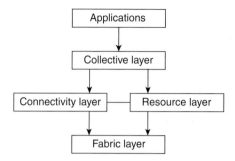

Figure 1-7. A layered architecture for grid computing systems.

The architecture consists of four layers. The lowest *fabric layer* provides interfaces to local resources at a specific site. Note that these interfaces are tailored to allow sharing of resources within a virtual organization. Typically, they will provide functions for querying the state and capabilities of a resource, along with functions for actual resource management (e.g., locking resources).

The *connectivity layer* consists of communication protocols for supporting grid transactions that span the usage of multiple resources. For example, protocols are needed to transfer data between resources, or to simply access a resource from a remote location. In addition, the connectivity layer will contain security protocols to authenticate users and resources. Note that in many cases human users are not authenticated; instead, programs acting on behalf of the users are authenticated. In this sense, delegating rights from a user to programs is an important function that needs to be supported in the connectivity layer. We return extensively to delegation when discussing security in distributed systems.

The *resource layer* is responsible for managing a single resource. It uses the functions provided by the connectivity layer and calls directly the interfaces made available by the fabric layer. For example, this layer will offer functions for obtaining configuration information on a specific resource, or, in general, to perform specific operations such as creating a process or reading data. The resource layer is thus seen to be responsible for access control, and hence will rely on the authentication performed as part of the connectivity layer.

The next layer in the hierarchy is the *collective layer*. It deals with handling access to multiple resources and typically consists of services for resource discovery, allocation and scheduling of tasks onto multiple resources, data replication, and so on. Unlike the connectivity and resource layer, which consist of a relatively small, standard collection of protocols, the collective layer may consist of many different protocols for many different purposes, reflecting the broad spectrum of services it may offer to a virtual organization.

Finally, the *application layer* consists of the applications that operate within a virtual organization and which make use of the grid computing environment.

Typically the collective, connectivity, and resource layer form the heart of what could be called a grid middleware layer. These layers jointly provide access to and management of resources that are potentially dispersed across multiple sites. An important observation from a middleware perspective is that with grid computing the notion of a site (or administrative unit) is common. This prevalence is emphasized by the gradual shift toward a **service-oriented architecture** in which sites offer access to the various layers through a collection of Web services (Joseph et al., 2004). This, by now, has led to the definition of an alternative architecture known as the **Open Grid Services Architecture** (**OGSA**). This architecture consists of various layers and many components, making it rather complex. Complexity seems to be the fate of any standardization process. Details on OGSA can be found in Foster et al. (2005).

1.3.2 Distributed Information Systems

Another important class of distributed systems is found in organizations that were confronted with a wealth of networked applications, but for which interoperability turned out to be a painful experience. Many of the existing middleware solutions are the result of working with an infrastructure in which it was easier to integrate applications into an enterprise-wide information system (Bernstein, 1996; and Alonso et al., 2004).

We can distinguish several levels at which integration took place. In many cases, a networked application simply consisted of a server running that application (often including a database) and making it available to remote programs, called **clients**. Such clients could send a request to the server for executing a specific operation, after which a response would be sent back. Integration at the lowest level would allow clients to wrap a number of requests, possibly for different servers, into a single larger request and have it executed as a **distributed transaction**. The key idea was that all, or none of the requests would be executed.

As applications became more sophisticated and were gradually separated into independent components (notably distinguishing database components from processing components), it became clear that integration should also take place by letting applications communicate directly with each other. This has now led to a huge industry that concentrates on **enterprise application integration** (**EAI**). In the following, we concentrate on these two forms of distributed systems.

Transaction Processing Systems

To clarify our discussion, let us concentrate on database applications. In practice, operations on a database are usually carried out in the form of **transactions**. Programming using transactions requires special primitives that must either be supplied by the underlying distributed system or by the language runtime system. Typical examples of transaction primitives are shown in Fig. 1-8. The exact list of primitives depends on what kinds of objects are being used in the transaction (Gray and Reuter, 1993). In a mail system, there might be primitives to send, receive, and forward mail. In an accounting system, they might be quite different. READ and WRITE are typical examples, however. Ordinary statements, procedure calls, and so on, are also allowed inside a transaction. In particular, we mention that remote procedure calls (RPCs), that is, procedure calls to remote servers, are often also encapsulated in a transaction, leading to what is known as a **transactional RPC**. We discuss RPCs extensively in Chap. 4.

Primitive	Description
BEGIN_TRANSACTION	Mark the start of a transaction
END_TRANSACTION	Terminate the transaction and try to commit
ABORT_TRANSACTION	Kill the transaction and restore the old values
READ	Read data from a file, a table, or otherwise
WRITE	Write data to a file, a table, or otherwise

Figure 1-8. Example primitives for transactions.

BEGIN_TRANSACTION and END_TRANSACTION are used to delimit the scope of a transaction. The operations between them form the body of the transaction. The characteristic feature of a transaction is either all of these operations are executed or none are executed. These may be system calls, library procedures, or bracketing statements in a language, depending on the implementation.

This all-or-nothing property of transactions is one of the four characteristic properties that transactions have. More specifically, transactions are:

1. Atomic: To the outside world, the transaction happens indivisibly.

2. Consistent: The transaction does not violate system invariants.

3. Isolated: Concurrent transactions do not interfere with each other.

4. Durable: Once a transaction commits, the changes are permanent.

These properties are often referred to by their initial letters: **ACID**.

The first key property exhibited by all transactions is that they are **atomic**. This property ensures that each transaction either happens completely, or not at all, and if it happens, it happens in a single indivisible, instantaneous action. While a transaction is in progress, other processes (whether or not they are themselves involved in transactions) cannot see any of the intermediate states.

The second property says that they are **consistent**. What this means is that if the system has certain invariants that must always hold, if they held before the transaction, they will hold afterward too. For example, in a banking system, a key invariant is the law of conservation of money. After every internal transfer, the amount of money in the bank must be the same as it was before the transfer, but for a brief moment during the transaction, this invariant may be violated. The violation is not visible outside the transaction, however.

The third property says that transactions are **isolated** or **serializable**. What it means is that if two or more transactions are running at the same time, to each of them and to other processes, the final result looks as though all transactions ran sequentially in some (system dependent) order.

The fourth property says that transactions are **durable**. It refers to the fact that once a transaction commits, no matter what happens, the transaction goes forward and the results become permanent. No failure after the commit can undo the results or cause them to be lost. (Durability is discussed extensively in Chap. 8.)

So far, transactions have been defined on a single database. A **nested transaction** is constructed from a number of subtransactions, as shown in Fig. 1-9. The top-level transaction may fork off children that run in parallel with one another, on different machines, to gain performance or simplify programming. Each of these children may also execute one or more subtransactions, or fork off its own children.

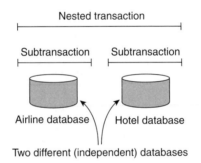

Figure 1-9. A nested transaction.

Subtransactions give rise to a subtle, but important, problem. Imagine that a transaction starts several subtransactions in parallel, and one of these commits, making its results visible to the parent transaction. After further computation, the parent aborts, restoring the entire system to the state it had before the top-level transaction started. Consequently, the results of the subtransaction that committed must nevertheless be undone. Thus the permanence referred to above applies only to top-level transactions.

Since transactions can be nested arbitrarily deeply, considerable administration is needed to get everything right. The semantics are clear, however. When any transaction or subtransaction starts, it is conceptually given a private copy of all data in the entire system for it to manipulate as it wishes. If it aborts, its private universe just vanishes, as if it had never existed. If it commits, its private universe replaces the parent's universe. Thus if a subtransaction commits and then later a new subtransaction is started, the second one sees the results produced by the first one. Likewise, if an enclosing (higher-level) transaction aborts, all its underlying subtransactions have to be aborted as well.

Nested transactions are important in distributed systems, for they provide a natural way of distributing a transaction across multiple machines. They follow a *logical* division of the work of the original transaction. For example, a transaction for planning a trip by which three different flights need to be reserved can be logically split up into three subtransactions. Each of these subtransactions can be managed separately and independent of the other two.

In the early days of enterprise middleware systems, the component that handled distributed (or nested) transactions formed the core for integrating applications at the server or database level. This component was called a **transaction processing monitor** or **TP monitor** for short. Its main task was to allow an application to access multiple server/databases by offering it a transactional programming model, as shown in Fig. 1-10.

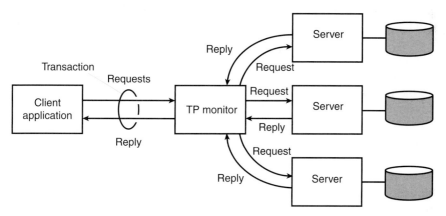

Figure 1-10. The role of a TP monitor in distributed systems.

Enterprise Application Integration

As mentioned, the more applications became decoupled from the databases they were built upon, the more evident it became that facilities were needed to integrate applications independent from their databases. In particular, application components should be able to communicate directly with each other and not merely by means of the request/reply behavior that was supported by transaction processing systems.

This need for interapplication communication led to many different communication models, which we will discuss in detail in this book (and for which reason we shall keep it brief for now). The main idea was that existing applications could directly exchange information, as shown in Fig. 1-11.

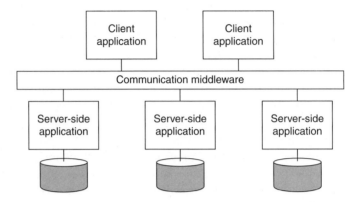

Figure 1-11. Middleware as a communication facilitator in enterprise application integration.

Several types of communication middleware exist. With **remote procedure calls (RPC)**, an application component can effectively send a request to another application component by doing a local procedure call, which results in the request being packaged as a message and sent to the callee. Likewise, the result will be sent back and returned to the application as the result of the procedure call.

As the popularity of object technology increased, techniques were developed to allow calls to remote objects, leading to what is known as **remote method invocations (RMI)**. An RMI is essentially the same as an RPC, except that it operates on objects instead of applications.

RPC and RMI have the disadvantage that the caller and callee both need to be up and running at the time of communication. In addition, they need to know exactly how to refer to each other. This tight coupling is often experienced as a serious drawback, and has led to what is known as **message-oriented middleware**, or simply **MOM**. In this case, applications simply send messages to logical contact points, often described by means of a subject. Likewise, applications can indicate their interest for a specific type of message, after which the communication middleware will take care that those messages are delivered to those applications. These so-called **publish/subscribe** systems form an important and expanding class of distributed systems. We will discuss them at length in Chap. 13.

1.3.3 Distributed Pervasive Systems

The distributed systems we have been discussing so far are largely characterized by their stability: nodes are fixed and have a more or less permanent and high-quality connection to a network. To a certain extent, this stability has been realized through the various techniques that are discussed in this book and which aim at achieving distribution transparency. For example, the wealth of techniques for masking failures and recovery will give the impression that only occasionally things may go wrong. Likewise, we have been able to hide aspects related to the actual network location of a node, effectively allowing users and applications to believe that nodes stay put.

However, matters have become very different with the introduction of mobile and embedded computing devices. We are now confronted with distributed systems in which instability is the default behavior. The devices in these, what we refer to as **distributed pervasive systems**, are often characterized by being small, battery-powered, mobile, and having only a wireless connection, although not all these characteristics apply to all devices. Moreover, these characteristics need not necessarily be interpreted as restrictive, as is illustrated by the possibilities of modern smart phones (Roussos et al., 2005).

As its name suggests, a distributed pervasive system is part of our surroundings (and as such, is generally inherently distributed). An important feature is the general lack of human administrative control. At best, devices can be configured by their owners, but otherwise they need to automatically discover their environment and "nestle in" as best as possible. This nestling in has been made more precise by Grimm et al. (2004) by formulating the following three requirements for pervasive applications:

1. Embrace contextual changes.

2. Encourage ad hoc composition.

3. Recognize sharing as the default.

Embracing contextual changes means that a device must be continuously be aware of the fact that its environment may change all the time. One of the simplest changes is discovering that a network is no longer available, for example, because a user is moving between base stations. In such a case, the application should react, possibly by automatically connecting to another network, or taking other appropriate actions.

Encouraging ad hoc composition refers to the fact that many devices in pervasive systems will be used in very different ways by different users. As a result, it should be easy to configure the suite of applications running on a device, either by the user or through automated (but controlled) interposition.

One very important aspect of pervasive systems is that devices generally join the system in order to access (and possibly provide) information. This calls for means to easily read, store, manage, and share information. In light of the intermittent and changing connectivity of devices, the space where accessible information resides will most likely change all the time.

Mascolo et al. (2004) as well as Niemela and Latvakoski (2004) came to similar conclusions: in the presence of mobility, devices should support easy and application-dependent adaptation to their local environment. They should be able to efficiently discover services and react accordingly. It should be clear from these requirements that distribution transparency is not really in place in pervasive systems. In fact, distribution of data, processes, and control is *inherent* to these systems, for which reason it may be better just to simply expose it rather than trying to hide it. Let us now take a look at some concrete examples of pervasive systems.

Home Systems

An increasingly popular type of pervasive system, but which may perhaps be the least constrained, are systems built around home networks. These systems generally consist of one or more personal computers, but more importantly integrate typical consumer electronics such as TVs, audio and video equipment, gaming devices, (smart) phones, PDAs, and other personal wearables into a single system. In addition, we can expect that all kinds of devices such as kitchen appliances, surveillance cameras, clocks, controllers for lighting, and so on, will all be hooked up into a single distributed system.

From a system's perspective there are several challenges that need to be addressed before pervasive home systems become reality. An important one is that such a system should be completely self-configuring and self-managing. It cannot be expected that end users are willing and able to keep a distributed home system up and running if its components are prone to errors (as is the case with many of today's devices.) Much has already been accomplished through the **Universal Plug and Play** (**UPnP**) standards by which devices automatically obtain IP addresses, can discover each other, etc. (UPnP Forum, 2003). However, more is needed. For example, it is unclear how software and firmware in devices can be easily updated without manual intervention, or when updates do take place, that compatibility with other devices is not violated.

Another pressing issue is managing what is known as a *"personal space."* Recognizing that a home system consists of many shared as well as personal devices, and that the data in a home system is also subject to sharing restrictions, much attention is paid to realizing such personal spaces. For example, part of Alice's personal space may consist of her agenda, family photo's, a diary, music and videos that she bought, etc. These personal assets should be stored in such a way that Alice has access to them whenever appropriate. Moreover, parts of this personal space should be (temporarily) accessible to others, for example, when she needs to make a business appointment.

Fortunately, things may become simpler. It has long been thought that the personal spaces related to home systems were inherently distributed across the various devices. Obviously, such a dispersion can easily lead to significant synchronization problems. However, problems may be alleviated due to the rapid increase in the capacity of hard disks, along with a decrease in their size. Configuring a multi-terabyte storage unit for a personal computer is not really a problem. At the same time, portable hard disks having a capacity of hundreds of gigabytes are being placed inside relatively small portable media players. With these continuously increasing capacities, we may see pervasive home systems adopt an architecture in which a single machine acts as a master (and is hidden away somewhere in the basement next to the central heating), and all other fixed devices simply provide a convenient interface for humans. Personal devices will then be crammed with daily needed information, but will never run out of storage.

However, having enough storage does not solve the problem of managing personal spaces. Being able to store huge amounts of data shifts the problem to storing *relevant* data and being able to find it later. Increasingly we will see pervasive systems, like home networks, equipped with what are called **recommenders**, programs that consult what other users have stored in order to identify similar taste, and from that subsequently derive which content to place in one's personal space. An interesting observation is that the amount of information that recommender programs need to do their work is often small enough to allow them to be run on PDAs (Miller et al., 2004).

Electronic Health Care Systems

Another important and upcoming class of pervasive systems are those related to (personal) electronic health care. With the increasing cost of medical treatment, new devices are being developed to monitor the well-being of individuals and to automatically contact physicians when needed. In many of these systems, a major goal is to prevent people from being hospitalized.

Personal health care systems are often equipped with various sensors organized in a (preferably wireless) body-area network (BAN). An important issue is that such a network should at worst only minimally hinder a person. To this end, the network should be able to operate while a person is moving, with no strings (i.e., wires) attached to immobile devices.

This requirement leads to two obvious organizations, as shown in Fig. 1-12. In the first one, a central hub is part of the BAN and collects data as needed. From time to time, this data is then offloaded to a larger storage device. The advantage of this scheme is that the hub can also manage the BAN. In the second scenario, the BAN is continuously hooked up to an external network, again through a wireless connection, to which it sends monitored data. Separate techniques will need to be deployed for managing the BAN. Of course, further connections to a physician or other people may exist as well.

From a distributed system's perspective we are immediately confronted with questions such as:

1. Where and how should monitored data be stored?

2. How can we prevent loss of crucial data?

3. What infrastructure is needed to generate and propagate alerts?

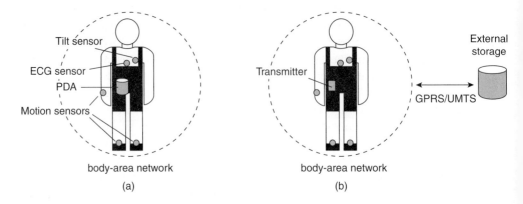

Figure 1-12. Monitoring a person in a pervasive electronic health care system, using (a) a local hub or (b) a continuous wireless connection.

4. How can physicians provide online feedback?

5. How can extreme robustness of the monitoring system be realized?

6. What are the security issues and how can the proper policies be enforced?

Unlike home systems, we cannot expect the architecture of pervasive health care systems to move toward single-server systems and have the monitoring devices operate with minimal functionality. On the contrary: for reasons of efficiency, devices and body-area networks will be required to support **in-network data processing**, meaning that monitoring data will, for example, have to be aggregated before permanently storing it or sending it to a physician. Unlike the case for distributed information systems, there is yet no clear answer to these questions.

Sensor Networks

Our last example of pervasive systems is sensor networks. These networks in many cases form part of the enabling technology for pervasiveness and we see that many solutions for sensor networks return in pervasive applications. What makes sensor networks interesting from a distributed system's perspective is that in virtually all cases they are used for processing information. In this sense, they do more than just provide communication services, which is what traditional computer networks are all about. Akyildiz et al. (2002) provide an overview from a networking perspective. A more systems-oriented introduction to sensor networks is given by Zhao and Guibas (2004). Strongly related are **mesh networks** which essentially form a collection of (fixed) nodes that communicate through wireless links. These networks may form the basis for many medium-scale distributed systems. An overview is provided in Akyildiz et al. (2005).

A sensor network typically consists of tens to hundreds or thousands of relatively small nodes, each equipped with a sensing device. Most sensor networks use wireless communication, and the nodes are often battery powered. Their limited resources, restricted communication capabilities, and constrained power consumption demand that efficiency be high on the list of design criteria.

The relation with distributed systems can be made clear by considering sensor networks as distributed databases. This view is quite common and easy to understand when realizing that many sensor networks are deployed for measurement and surveillance applications (Bonnet et al., 2002). In these cases, an operator would like to extract information from (a part of) the network by simply issuing queries such as "What is the northbound traffic load on Highway 1?" Such queries resemble those of traditional databases. In this case, the answer will probably need to be provided through collaboration of many sensors located around Highway 1, while leaving other sensors untouched.

To organize a sensor network as a distributed database, there are essentially two extremes, as shown in Fig. 1-13. First, sensors do not cooperate but simply send their data to a centralized database located at the operator's site. The other extreme is to forward queries to relevant sensors and to let each compute an answer, requiring the operator to sensibly aggregate the returned answers.

Neither of these solutions is very attractive. The first one requires that sensors send all their measured data through the network, which may waste network resources and energy. The second solution may also be wasteful as it discards the aggregation capabilities of sensors which would allow much less data to be returned to the operator. What is needed are facilities for **in-network data processing**, as we also encountered in pervasive health care systems.

In-network processing can be done in numerous ways. One obvious one is to forward a query to all sensor nodes along a tree encompassing all nodes and to subsequently aggregate the results as they are propagated back to the root, where the initiator is located. Aggregation will take place where two or more branches of the tree come to together. As simple as this scheme may sound, it introduces difficult questions:

1. How do we (dynamically) set up an efficient tree in a sensor network?

2. How does aggregation of results take place? Can it be controlled?

3. What happens when network links fail?

These questions have been partly addressed in TinyDB, which implements a declarative (database) interface to wireless sensor networks. In essence, TinyDB can use any tree-based routing algorithm. An intermediate node will collect and aggregate the results from its children, along with its own findings, and send that toward the root. To make matters efficient, queries span a period of time allowing

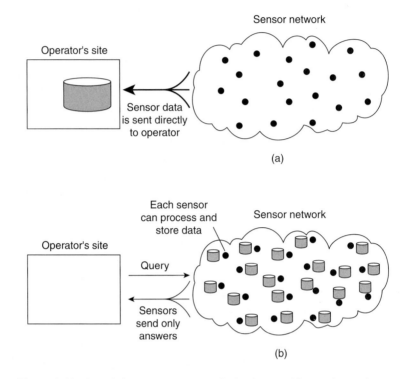

Figure 1-13. Organizing a sensor network database, while storing and processing data (a) only at the operator's site or (b) only at the sensors.

for careful scheduling of operations so that network resources and energy are optimally consumed. Details can be found in Madden et al. (2005).

However, when queries can be initiated from different points in the network, using single-rooted trees such as in TinyDB may not be efficient enough. As an alternative, sensor networks may be equipped with special nodes where results are forwarded to, as well as the queries related to those results. To give a simple example, queries and results related temperature readings are collected at a different location than those related to humidity measurements. This approach corresponds directly to the notion of publish/subscribe systems, which we will discuss extensively in Chap. 13.

1.4 SUMMARY

Distributed systems consist of autonomous computers that work together to give the appearance of a single coherent system. One important advantage is that they make it easier to integrate different applications running on different computers into a single system. Another advantage is that when properly designed, distributed systems scale well with respect to the size of the underlying network. These advantages often come at the cost of more complex software, degradation of performance, and also often weaker security. Nevertheless, there is considerable interest worldwide in building and installing distributed systems.

Distributed systems often aim at hiding many of the intricacies related to the distribution of processes, data, and control. However, this distribution transparency not only comes at a performance price, but in practical situations it can never be fully achieved. The fact that trade-offs need to be made between achieving various forms of distribution transparency is inherent to the design of distributed systems, and can easily complicate their understanding.

Matters are further complicated by the fact that many developers initially make assumptions about the underlying network that are fundamentally wrong. Later, when assumptions are dropped, it may turn out to be difficult to mask unwanted behavior. A typical example is assuming that network latency is not significant. Later, when porting an existing system to a wide-area network, hiding latencies may deeply affect the system's original design. Other pitfalls include assuming that the network is reliable, static, secure, and homogeneous.

Different types of distributed systems exist which can be classified as being oriented toward supporting computations, information processing, and pervasiveness. Distributed computing systems are typically deployed for high-performance applications often originating from the field of parallel computing. A huge class of distributed can be found in traditional office environments where we see databases playing an important role. Typically, transaction processing systems are deployed in these environments. Finally, an emerging class of distributed systems is where components are small and the system is composed in an ad hoc fashion, but most of all is no longer managed through a system administrator. This last class is typically represented by ubiquitous computing environments.

PROBLEMS

1. An alternative definition for a distributed system is that of a collection of independent computers providing the view of being a *single system*, that is, it is completely hidden from users that there even multiple computers. Give an example where this view would come in very handy.

2. What is the role of middleware in a distributed system?

3. Many networked systems are organized in terms of a back office and a front office. How does organizations match with the coherent view we demand for a distributed system?

4. Explain what is meant by (distribution) transparency, and give examples of different types of transparency.

5. Why is it sometimes so hard to hide the occurrence and recovery from failures in a distributed system?

6. Why is it not always a good idea to aim at implementing the highest degree of transparency possible?

7. What is an open distributed system and what benefits does openness provide?

8. Describe precisely what is meant by a scalable system.

9. Scalability can be achieved by applying different techniques. What are these techniques?

10. Explain what is meant by a virtual organization and give a hint on how such organizations could be implemented.

11. When a transaction is aborted, we have said that the world is restored to its previous state, as though the transaction had never happened. We lied. Give an example where resetting the world is impossible.

12. Executing nested transactions requires some form of coordination. Explain what a coordinator should actually do.

13. We argued that distribution transparency may not be in place for pervasive systems. This statement is not true for all types of transparencies. Give an example.

14. We already gave some examples of distributed pervasive systems: home systems, electronic health-care systems, and sensor networks. Extend this list with more examples.

15. **(Lab assignment)** Sketch a design for a home system consisting of a separate media server that will allow for the attachment of a wireless client. The latter is connected to (analog) audio/video equipment and transforms the digital media streams to analog output. The server runs on a separate machine, possibly connected to the Internet, but has no keyboard and/or monitor connected.

2

ARCHITECTURES

Distributed systems are often complex pieces of software of which the components are by definition dispersed across multiple machines. To master their complexity, it is crucial that these systems are properly organized. There are different ways on how to view the organization of a distributed system, but an obvious one is to make a distinction between the logical organization of the collection of software components and on the other hand the actual physical realization.

The organization of distributed systems is mostly about the software components that constitute the system. These **software architectures** tell us how the various software components are to be organized and how they should interact. In this chapter we will first pay attention to some commonly applied approaches toward organizing (distributed) computer systems.

The actual realization of a distributed system requires that we instantiate and place software components on real machines. There are many different choices that can be made in doing so. The final instantiation of a software architecture is also referred to as a **system architecture**. In this chapter we will look into traditional centralized architectures in which a single server implements most of the software components (and thus functionality), while remote clients can access that server using simple communication means. In addition, we consider decentralized architectures in which machines more or less play equal roles, as well as hybrid organizations.

As we explained in Chap. 1, an important goal of distributed systems is to separate applications from underlying platforms by providing a middleware layer.

Adopting such a layer is an important architectural decision, and its main purpose is to provide distribution transparency. However, trade-offs need to be made to achieve transparency, which has led to various techniques to make middleware adaptive. We discuss some of the more commonly applied ones in this chapter, as they affect the organization of the middleware itself.

Adaptability in distributed systems can also be achieved by having the system monitor its own behavior and taking appropriate measures when needed. This insight has led to a class of what are now referred to as **autonomic systems**. These distributed systems are frequently organized in the form of feedback control loops, which form an important architectural element during a system's design. In this chapter, we devote a section to autonomic distributed systems.

2.1 ARCHITECTURAL STYLES

We start our discussion on architectures by first considering the logical organization of distributed systems into software components, also referred to as software architecture (Bass et al., 2003). Research on software architectures has matured considerably and it is now commonly accepted that designing or adopting an architecture is crucial for the successful development of large systems.

For our discussion, the notion of an **architectural style** is important. Such a style is formulated in terms of components, the way that components are connected to each other, the data exchanged between components, and finally how these elements are jointly configured into a system. A **component** is a modular unit with well-defined required and provided interfaces that is replaceable within its environment (OMG, 2004b). As we shall discuss below, the important issue about a component for distributed systems is that it can be replaced, provided we respect its interfaces. A somewhat more difficult concept to grasp is that of a **connector**, which is generally described as a mechanism that mediates communication, coordination, or cooperation among components (Mehta et al., 2000; and Shaw and Clements, 1997). For example, a connector can be formed by the facilities for (remote) procedure calls, message passing, or streaming data.

Using components and connectors, we can come to various configurations, which, in turn have been classified into architectural styles. Several styles have by now been identified, of which the most important ones for distributed systems are:

1. Layered architectures

2. Object-based architectures

3. Data-centered architectures

4. Event-based architectures

The basic idea for the layered style is simple: components are organized in a **layered fashion** where a component at layer L_i is allowed to call components at the underlying layer L_{i-1}, but not the other way around, as shown in Fig. 2-1(a). This model has been widely adopted by the networking community; we briefly review it in Chap. 4. An key observation is that control generally flows from layer to layer: requests go down the hierarchy whereas the results flow upward.

A far looser organization is followed in **object-based architectures**, which are illustrated in Fig. 2-1(b). In essence, each object corresponds to what we have defined as a component, and these components are connected through a (remote) procedure call mechanism. Not surprisingly, this software architecture matches the client-server system architecture we described above. The layered and object-based architectures still form the most important styles for large software systems (Bass et al., 2003).

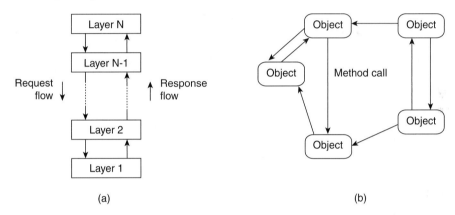

Figure 2-1. The (a) layered and (b) object-based architectural style.

Data-centered architectures evolve around the idea that processes communicate through a common (passive or active) repository. It can be argued that for distributed systems these architectures are as important as the layered and object-based architectures. For example, a wealth of networked applications have been developed that rely on a shared distributed file system in which virtually all communication takes place through files. Likewise, Web-based distributed systems, which we discuss extensively in Chap. 12, are largely data-centric: processes communicate through the use of shared Web-based data services.

In **event-based architectures**, processes essentially communicate through the propagation of events, which optionally also carry data, as shown in Fig. 2-2(a). For distributed systems, event propagation has generally been associated with what are known as **publish/subscribe systems** (Eugster et al., 2003). The basic idea is that processes publish events after which the middleware ensures that only those processes that subscribed to those events will receive them. The main advantage of event-based systems is that processes are loosely coupled. In principle, they need not explicitly refer to each other. This is also referred to as being decoupled in space, or **referentially decoupled**.

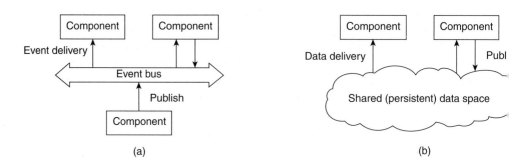

Figure 2-2. The (a) event-based and (b) shared data-space architectural style.

Event-based architectures can be combined with data-centered architectures, yielding what is also known as **shared data spaces**. The essence of shared data spaces is that processes are now also decoupled in time: they need not both be active when communication takes place. Furthermore, many shared data spaces use a SQL-like interface to the shared repository in that sense that data can be accessed using a description rather than an explicit reference, as is the case with files. We devote Chap. 13 to this architectural style.

What makes these software architectures important for distributed systems is that they all aim at achieving (at a reasonable level) distribution transparency. However, as we have argued, distribution transparency requires making trade-offs between performance, fault tolerance, ease-of-programming, and so on. As there is no single solution that will meet the requirements for all possible distributed applications, researchers have abandoned the idea that a single distributed system can be used to cover 90% of all possible cases.

2.2 SYSTEM ARCHITECTURES

Now that we have briefly discussed some common architectural styles, let us take a look at how many distributed systems are actually organized by considering where software components are placed. Deciding on software components, their interaction, and their placement leads to an instance of a software architecture, also called a **system architecture** (Bass et al., 2003). We will discuss centralized and decentralized organizations, as well as various hybrid forms.

2.2.1 Centralized Architectures

Despite the lack of consensus on many distributed systems issues, there is one issue that many researchers and practitioners agree upon: thinking in terms of *clients* that request services from *servers* helps us understand and manage the complexity of distributed systems and that is a good thing.

In the basic client-server model, processes in a distributed system are divided into two (possibly overlapping) groups. A **server** is a process implementing a specific service, for example, a file system service or a database service. A **client** is a process that requests a service from a server by sending it a request and subsequently waiting for the server's reply. This client-server interaction, also known as **request-reply behavior** is shown in Fig. 2-3

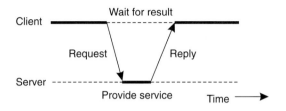

Figure 2-3. General interaction between a client and a server.

Communication between a client and a server can be implemented by means of a simple connectionless protocol when the underlying network is fairly reliable as in many local-area networks. In these cases, when a client requests a service, it simply packages a message for the server, identifying the service it wants, along with the necessary input data. The message is then sent to the server. The latter, in turn, will always wait for an incoming request, subsequently process it, and package the results in a reply message that is then sent to the client.

Using a connectionless protocol has the obvious advantage of being efficient. As long as messages do not get lost or corrupted, the request/reply protocol just sketched works fine. Unfortunately, making the protocol resistant to occasional transmission failures is not trivial. The only thing we can do is possibly let the client resend the request when no reply message comes in. The problem, however, is that the client cannot detect whether the original request message was lost, or that transmission of the reply failed. If the reply was lost, then resending a request may result in performing the operation twice. If the operation was something like "transfer $10,000 from my bank account," then clearly, it would have been better that we simply reported an error instead. On the other hand, if the operation was "tell me how much money I have left," it would be perfectly acceptable to resend the request. When an operation can be repeated multiple times without harm, it is said to be **idempotent**. Since some requests are idempotent and others are not it should be clear that there is no single solution for dealing with lost messages. We defer a detailed discussion on handling transmission failures to Chap. 8.

As an alternative, many client-server systems use a reliable connection-oriented protocol. Although this solution is not entirely appropriate in a local-area network due to relatively low performance, it works perfectly fine in wide-area systems in which communication is inherently unreliable. For example, virtually all Internet application protocols are based on reliable TCP/IP connections. In this case, whenever a client requests a service, it first sets up a connection to the server before sending the request. The server generally uses that same connection to send the reply message, after which the connection is torn down. The trouble is that setting up and tearing down a connection is relatively costly, especially when the request and reply messages are small.

Application Layering

The client-server model has been subject to many debates and controversies over the years. One of the main issues was how to draw a clear distinction between a client and a server. Not surprisingly, there is often no clear distinction. For example, a server for a distributed database may continuously act as a client because it is forwarding requests to different file servers responsible for implementing the database tables. In such a case, the database server itself essentially does no more than process queries.

However, considering that many client-server applications are targeted toward supporting user access to databases, many people have advocated a distinction between the following three levels, essentially following the layered architectural style we discussed previously:

1. The user-interface level

2. The processing level

3. The data level

The user-interface level contains all that is necessary to directly interface with the user, such as display management. The processing level typically contains the applications. The data level manages the actual data that is being acted on.

Clients typically implement the user-interface level. This level consists of the programs that allow end users to interact with applications. There is a considerable difference in how sophisticated user-interface programs are.

The simplest user-interface program is nothing more than a character-based screen. Such an interface has been typically used in mainframe environments. In those cases where the mainframe controls all interaction, including the keyboard and monitor, one can hardly speak of a client-server environment. However, in many cases, the user's terminal does some local processing such as echoing typed keystrokes, or supporting form-like interfaces in which a complete entry is to be edited before sending it to the main computer.

Nowadays, even in mainframe environments, we see more advanced user interfaces. Typically, the client machine offers at least a graphical display in which pop-up or pull-down menus are used, and of which many of the screen controls are handled through a mouse instead of the keyboard. Typical examples of such interfaces include the X-Windows interfaces as used in many UNIX environments, and earlier interfaces developed for MS-DOS PCs and Apple Macintoshes.

Modern user interfaces offer considerably more functionality by allowing applications to share a single graphical window, and to use that window to exchange data through user actions. For example, to delete a file, it is usually possible to move the icon representing that file to an icon representing a trash can. Likewise, many word processors allow a user to move text in a document to another position by using only the mouse. We return to user interfaces in Chap. 3.

Many client-server applications can be constructed from roughly three different pieces: a part that handles interaction with a user, a part that operates on a database or file system, and a middle part that generally contains the core functionality of an application. This middle part is logically placed at the processing level. In contrast to user interfaces and databases, there are not many aspects common to the processing level. Therefore, we shall give several examples to make this level clearer.

As a first example, consider an Internet search engine. Ignoring all the animated banners, images, and other fancy window dressing, the user interface of a search engine is very simple: a user types in a string of keywords and is subsequently presented with a list of titles of Web pages. The back end is formed by a huge database of Web pages that have been prefetched and indexed. The core of the search engine is a program that transforms the user's string of keywords into one or more database queries. It subsequently ranks the results into a list, and transforms that list into a series of HTML pages. Within the client-server model, this information retrieval part is typically placed at the processing level. Fig. 2-4 shows this organization.

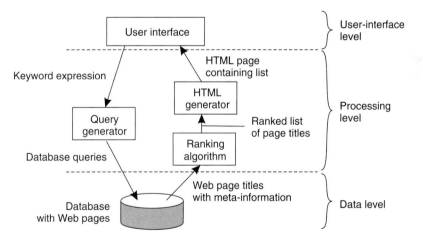

Figure 2-4. The simplified organization of an Internet search engine into three different layers.

As a second example, consider a decision support system for a stock brokerage. Analogous to a search engine, such a system can be divided into a front end implementing the user interface, a back end for accessing a database with the financial data, and the analysis programs between these two. Analysis of financial data may require sophisticated methods and techniques from statistics and artificial intelligence. In some cases, the core of a financial decision support system may even need to be executed on high-performance computers in order to achieve the throughput and responsiveness that is expected from its users.

As a last example, consider a typical desktop package, consisting of a word processor, a spreadsheet application, communication facilities, and so on. Such "office" suites are generally integrated through a common user interface that supports compound documents, and operates on files from the user's home directory. (In an office environment, this home directory is often placed on a remote file server.) In this example, the processing level consists of a relatively large collection of programs, each having rather simple processing capabilities.

The data level in the client-server model contains the programs that maintain the actual data on which the applications operate. An important property of this level is that data are often **persistent**, that is, even if no application is running, data will be stored somewhere for next use. In its simplest form, the data level consists of a file system, but it is more common to use a full-fledged database. In the client-server model, the data level is typically implemented at the server side.

Besides merely storing data, the data level is generally also responsible for keeping data consistent across different applications. When databases are being used, maintaining consistency means that metadata such as table descriptions, entry constraints and application-specific metadata are also stored at this level. For example, in the case of a bank, we may want to generate a notification when a customer's credit card debt reaches a certain value. This type of information can be maintained through a database trigger that activates a handler for that trigger at the appropriate moment.

In most business-oriented environments, the data level is organized as a relational database. Data independence is crucial here. The data are organized independent of the applications in such a way that changes in that organization do not affect applications, and neither do the applications affect the data organization. Using relational databases in the client-server model helps separate the processing level from the data level, as processing and data are considered independent.

However, relational databases are not always the ideal choice. A characteristic feature of many applications is that they operate on complex data types that are more easily modeled in terms of objects than in terms of relations. Examples of such data types range from simple polygons and circles to representations of aircraft designs, as is the case with computer-aided design (CAD) systems.

In those cases where data operations are more easily expressed in terms of object manipulations, it makes sense to implement the data level by means of an object-oriented or object-relational database. Notably the latter type has gained popularity as these databases build upon the widely dispersed relational data model, while offering the advantages that object-orientation gives.

Multitiered Architectures

The distinction into three logical levels as discussed so far, suggests a number of possibilities for physically distributing a client-server application across several machines. The simplest organization is to have only two types of machines:

1. A client machine containing only the programs implementing (part of) the user-interface level

2. A server machine containing the rest, that is the programs implementing the processing and data level

In this organization everything is handled by the server while the client is essentially no more than a dumb terminal, possibly with a pretty graphical interface. There are many other possibilities, of which we explore some of the more common ones in this section.

One approach for organizing the clients and servers is to distribute the programs in the application layers of the previous section across different machines, as shown in Fig. 2-5 [see also Umar (1997); and Jing et al. (1999)]. As a first step, we make a distinction between only two kinds of machines: client machines and server machines, leading to what is also referred to as a **(physically) two-tiered architecture**.

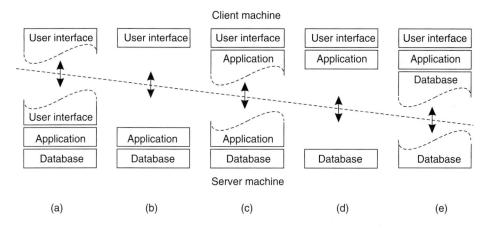

Figure 2-5. Alternative client-server organizations (a)–(e).

One possible organization is to have only the terminal-dependent part of the user interface on the client machine, as shown in Fig. 2-5(a), and give the applications remote control over the presentation of their data. An alternative is to place the entire user-interface software on the client side, as shown in Fig. 2-5(b). In such cases, we essentially divide the application into a graphical front end, which communicates with the rest of the application (residing at the server) through an application-specific protocol. In this model, the front end (the client software) does no processing other than necessary for presenting the application's interface.

Continuing along this line of reasoning, we may also move part of the application to the front end, as shown in Fig. 2-5(c). An example where this makes sense is where the application makes use of a form that needs to be filled in entirely before it can be processed. The front end can then check the correctness and consistency of the form, and where necessary interact with the user. Another example of the organization of Fig. 2-5(c), is that of a word processor in which the basic editing functions execute on the client side where they operate on locally cached, or in-memory data, but where the advanced support tools such as checking the spelling and grammar execute on the server side.

In many client-server environments, the organizations shown in Fig. 2-5(d) and Fig. 2-5(e) are particularly popular. These organizations are used where the client machine is a PC or workstation, connected through a network to a distributed file system or database. Essentially, most of the application is running on the client machine, but all operations on files or database entries go to the server. For example, many banking applications run on an end-user's machine where the user prepares transactions and such. Once finished, the application contacts the database on the bank's server and uploads the transactions for further processing. Fig. 2-5(e) represents the situation where the client's local disk contains part of the data. For example, when browsing the Web, a client can gradually build a huge cache on local disk of most recent inspected Web pages.

We note that for a few years there has been a strong trend to move away from the configurations shown in Fig. 2-5(d) and Fig. 2-5(e) in those case that client software is placed at end-user machines. In these cases, most of the processing and data storage is handled at the server side. The reason for this is simple: although client machines do a lot, they are also more problematic to manage. Having more functionality on the client machine makes client-side software more prone to errors and more dependent on the client's underlying platform (i.e., operating system and resources). From a system's management perspective, having what are called **fat clients** is not optimal. Instead the **thin clients** as represented by the organizations shown in Fig. 2-5(a)–(c) are much easier, perhaps at the cost of less sophisticated user interfaces and client-perceived performance.

Note that this trend does not imply that we no longer need distributed systems. On the contrary, what we are seeing is that server-side solutions are becoming increasingly more distributed as a single server is being replaced by multiple servers running on different machines. In particular, when distinguishing only client and server machines as we have done so far, we miss the point that a server may sometimes need to act as a client, as shown in Fig. 2-6, leading to a **(physically) three-tiered architecture**.

In this architecture, programs that form part of the processing level reside on a separate server, but may additionally be partly distributed across the client and server machines. A typical example of where a three-tiered architecture is used is

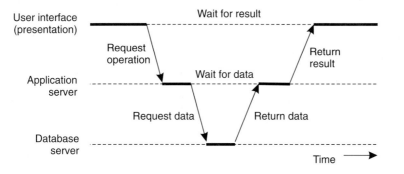

Figure 2-6. An example of a server acting as client.

in transaction processing. As we discussed in Chap. 1, a separate process, called the transaction processing monitor, coordinates all transactions across possibly different data servers.

Another, but very different example where we often see a three-tiered architecture is in the organization of Web sites. In this case, a Web server acts as an entry point to a site, passing requests to an application server where the actual processing takes place. This application server, in turn, interacts with a database server. For example, an application server may be responsible for running the code to inspect the available inventory of some goods as offered by an electronic bookstore. To do so, it may need to interact with a database containing the raw inventory data. We will come back to Web site organization in Chap. 12.

2.2.2 Decentralized Architectures

Multitiered client-server architectures are a direct consequence of dividing applications into a user-interface, processing components, and a data level. The different tiers correspond directly with the logical organization of applications. In many business environments, distributed processing is equivalent to organizing a client-server application as a multitiered architecture. We refer to this type of distribution as **vertical distribution**. The characteristic feature of vertical distribution is that it is achieved by placing *logically* different components on different machines. The term is related to the concept of **vertical fragmentation** as used in distributed relational databases, where it means that tables are split column-wise, and subsequently distributed across multiple machines (Oszu and Valduriez, 1999).

Again, from a system management perspective, having a vertical distribution can help: functions are logically and physically split across multiple machines, where each machine is tailored to a specific group of functions. However, vertical distribution is only one way of organizing client-server applications. In modern architectures, it is often the distribution of the clients and the servers that counts, which we refer to as **horizontal distribution**. In this type of distribution, a client or server may be physically split up into logically equivalent parts, but each part is operating on its own share of the complete data set, thus balancing the load. In this section we will take a look at a class of modern system architectures that support horizontal distribution, known as **peer-to-peer systems**.

From a high-level perspective, the processes that constitute a peer-to-peer system are all equal. This means that the functions that need to be carried out are represented by every process that constitutes the distributed system. As a consequence, much of the interaction between processes is symmetric: each process will act as a client and a server at the same time (which is also referred to as acting as a **servent**).

Given this symmetric behavior, peer-to-peer architectures evolve around the question how to organize the processes in an **overlay network**, that is, a network in which the nodes are formed by the processes and the links represent the possible communication channels (which are usually realized as TCP connections). In general, a process cannot communicate directly with an arbitrary other process, but is required to send messages through the available communication channels. Two types of overlay networks exist: those that are structured and those that are not. These two types are surveyed extensively in Lua et al. (2005) along with numerous examples. Aberer et al. (2005) provide a reference architecture that allows for a more formal comparison of the different types of peer-to-peer systems. A survey taken from the perspective of content distribution is provided by Androutsellis-Theotokis and Spinellis (2004).

Structured Peer-to-Peer Architectures

In a structured peer-to-peer architecture, the overlay network is constructed using a deterministic procedure. By far the most-used procedure is to organize the processes through a **distributed hash table** (**DHT**). In a DHT-based system, data items are assigned a random key from a large identifier space, such as a 128-bit or 160-bit identifier. Likewise, nodes in the system are also assigned a random number from the same identifier space. The crux of every DHT-based system is then to implement an efficient and deterministic scheme that uniquely maps the key of a data item to the identifier of a node based on some distance metric (Balakrishnan, 2003). Most importantly, when looking up a data item, the network address of the node responsible for that data item is returned. Effectively, this is accomplished by *routing* a request for a data item to the responsible node.

For example, in the Chord system (Stoica et al., 2003) the nodes are logically organized in a ring such that a data item with key k is mapped to the node with the smallest identifier $id \geq k$. This node is referred to as the *successor* of key k and denoted as *succ(k)*, as shown in Fig. 2-7. To actually look up the data item, an application running on an arbitrary node would then call the function LOOKUP(k) which would subsequently return the network address of *succ(k)*. At that point, the application can contact the node to obtain a copy of the data item.

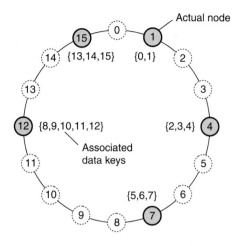

Figure 2-7. The mapping of data items onto nodes in Chord.

We will not go into algorithms for looking up a key now, but defer that discussion until Chap. 5 where we describe details of various naming systems. Instead, let us concentrate on how nodes organize themselves into an overlay network, or, in other words, **membership management**. In the following, it is important to realize that looking up a key does not follow the logical organization of nodes in the ring from Fig. 2-7. Rather, each node will maintain shortcuts to other nodes in such a way that lookups can generally be done in O(*log* (*N*)) number of steps, where *N* is the number of nodes participating in the overlay.

Now consider Chord again. When a node wants to join the system, it starts with generating a random identifier *id*. Note that if the identifier space is large enough, then provided the random number generator is of good quality, the probability of generating an identifier that is already assigned to an actual node is close to zero. Then, the node can simply do a lookup on *id*, which will return the network address of *succ(id)*. At that point, the joining node can simply contact *succ(id)* and its predecessor and insert itself in the ring. Of course, this scheme requires that each node also stores information on its predecessor. Insertion also yields that each data item whose key is now associated with node *id*, is transferred from *succ(id)*.

Leaving is just as simple: node *id* informs its departure to its predecessor and successor, and transfers its data items to *succ(id)*.

Similar approaches are followed in other DHT-based systems. As an example, consider the **Content Addressable Network (CAN)**, described in Ratnasamy et al. (2001). CAN deploys a *d*-dimensional Cartesian coordinate space, which is completely partitioned among all all the nodes that participate in the system. For purpose of illustration, let us consider only the 2-dimensional case, of which an example is shown in Fig. 2-8.

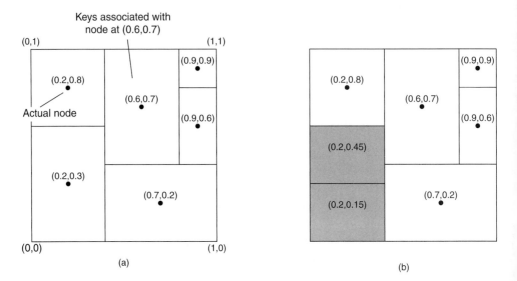

Figure 2-8. (a) The mapping of data items onto nodes in CAN. (b) Splitting a region when a node joins.

Fig. 2-8(a) shows how the two-dimensional space $[0,1] \times [0,1]$ is divided among six nodes. Each node has an associated region. Every data item in CAN will be assigned a unique point in this space, after which it is also clear which node is responsible for that data (ignoring data items that fall on the border of multiple regions, for which a deterministic assignment rule is used).

When a node P wants to join a CAN system, it picks an arbitrary point from the coordinate space and subsequently looks up the node Q in whose region that point falls. This lookup is accomplished through positioned-based routing, of which the details are deferred until later chapters. Node Q then splits its region into two halves, as shown in Fig. 2-8(b), and one half is assigned to the node P. Nodes keep track of their neighbors, that is, nodes responsible for adjacent region. When splitting a region, the joining node P can easily come to know who its new neighbors are by asking node P. As in Chord, the data items for which node P is now responsible are transferred from node Q.

Leaving is a bit more problematic in CAN. Assume that in Fig. 2-8, the node with coordinate $(0.6,0.7)$ leaves. Its region will be assigned to one of its neighbors, say the node at $(0.9,0.9)$, but it is clear that simply merging it and obtaining a rectangle cannot be done. In this case, the node at $(0.9,0.9)$ will simply take care of that region and inform the old neighbors of this fact. Obviously, this may lead to less symmetric partitioning of the coordinate space, for which reason a background process is periodically started to repartition the entire space.

Unstructured Peer-to-Peer Architectures

Unstructured peer-to-peer systems largely rely on randomized algorithms for constructing an overlay network. The main idea is that each node maintains a list of neighbors, but that this list is constructed in a more or less random way. Likewise, data items are assumed to be randomly placed on nodes. As a consequence, when a node needs to locate a specific data item, the only thing it can effectively do is flood the network with a search query (Risson and Moors, 2006). We will return to searching in unstructured overlay networks in Chap. 5, and for now concentrate on membership management.

One of the goals of many unstructured peer-to-peer systems is to construct an overlay network that resembles a **random graph**. The basic model is that each node maintains a list of c neighbors, where, ideally, each of these neighbors represents a randomly chosen *live* node from the current set of nodes. The list of neighbors is also referred to as a **partial view**. There are many ways to construct such a partial view. Jelasity et al. (2004, 2005a) have developed a framework that captures many different algorithms for overlay construction to allow for evaluations and comparison. In this framework, it is assumed that nodes regularly exchange entries from their partial view. Each entry identifies another node in the network, and has an associated age that indicates how old the reference to that node is. Two threads are used, as shown in Fig. 2-9.

The active thread takes the initiative to communicate with another node. It selects that node from its current partial view. Assuming that entries need to be *pushed* to the selected peer, it continues by constructing a buffer containing $c/2+1$ entries, including an entry identifying itself. The other entries are taken from the current partial view.

If the node is also in *pull mode* it will wait for a response from the selected peer. That peer, in the meantime, will also have constructed a buffer by means the passive thread shown in Fig. 2-9(b), whose activities strongly resemble that of the active thread.

The crucial point is the construction of a new partial view. This view, for initiating as well as for the contacted peer, will contain exactly c entries, part of which will come from received buffer. In essence, there are two ways to construct the new view. First, the two nodes may decide to discard the entries that they had sent to each other. Effectively, this means that they will *swap* part of their original views. The second approach is to discard as many *old* entries as possible. In general, it turns out that the two approaches are complementary [see Jelasity et al. (2005a) for the details]. It turns out that many membership management protocols for unstructured overlays fit this framework. There are a number of interesting observations to make.

First, let us assume that when a node wants to join it contacts an arbitrary other node, possibly from a list of well-known access points. This access point is just a regular member of the overlay, except that we can assume it to be highly

Actions by active thread (periodically repeated):

```
select a peer P from the current partial view;
if PUSH_MODE {
    mybuffer = [(MyAddress, 0)];
    permute partial view;
    move H oldest entries to the end;
    append first c/2 entries to mybuffer;
    send mybuffer to P;
} else {
    send trigger to P;
}
if PULL_MODE {
    receive P's buffer;
}
construct a new partial view from the current one and P's buffer;
increment the age of every entry in the new partial view;
```

(a)

Actions by passive thread:

```
receive buffer from any process Q;
if PULL_MODE {
    mybuffer = [(MyAddress, 0)];
    permute partial view;
    move H oldest entries to the end;
    append first c/2 entries to mybuffer;
    send mybuffer to P;
}
construct a new partial view from the current one and P's buffer;
increment the age of every entry in the new partial view;
```

(b)

Figure 2-9. (a) The steps taken by the active thread. (b) The steps take by the passive thread.

available. In this case, it turns out that protocols that use only *push mode* or only *pull mode* can fairly easily lead to disconnected overlays. In other words, groups of nodes will become isolated and will never be able to reach every other node in the network. Clearly, this is an undesirable feature, for which reason it makes more sense to let nodes actually *exchange* entries.

Second, leaving the network turns out to be a very simple operation provided the nodes exchange partial views on a regular basis. In this case, a node can simply depart without informing any other node. What will happen is that when a node P selects one of its apparent neighbors, say node Q, and discovers that Q no longer responds, it simply removes the entry from its partial view to select another peer. It turns out that when constructing a new partial view, a node follows the policy to discard as many old entries as possible, departed nodes will rapidly be forgotten. In other words, entries referring to departed nodes will automatically be quickly removed from partial views.

However, there is a price to pay when this strategy is followed. To explain, consider for a node P the set of nodes that have an entry in their partial view that refers to P. Technically, this is known as the **indegree** of a node. The higher node P's indegree is, the higher the probability that some other node will decide to contact P. In other words, there is a danger that P will become a popular node, which could easily bring it into an imbalanced position regarding workload. Systematically discarding old entries turns out to promote nodes to ones having a high indegree. There are other trade-offs in addition, for which we refer to Jelasity et al. (2005a).

Topology Management of Overlay Networks

Although it would seem that structured and unstructured peer-to-peer systems form strict independent classes, this need actually not be case [see also Castro et al. (2005)]. One key observation is that by carefully exchanging and selecting entries from partial views, it is possible to construct and maintain specific topologies of overlay networks. This topology management is achieved by adopting a two-layered approach, as shown in Fig. 2-10.

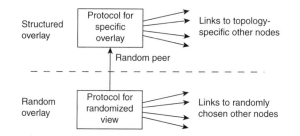

Figure 2-10. A two-layered approach for constructing and maintaining specific overlay topologies using techniques from unstructured peer-to-peer systems.

The lowest layer constitutes an unstructured peer-to-peer system in which nodes periodically exchange entries of their partial views with the aim to maintain an accurate random graph. Accuracy in this case refers to the fact that the partial view should be filled with entries referring to randomly selected *live* nodes.

The lowest layer passes its partial view to the higher layer, where an additional selection of entries takes place. This then leads to a second list of neighbors corresponding to the desired topology. Jelasity and Babaoglu (2005) propose to use a *ranking function* by which nodes are ordered according to some criterion relative to a given node. A simple ranking function is to order a set of nodes by increasing distance from a given node P. In that case, node P will gradually build up a list of its nearest neighbors, provided the lowest layer continues to pass randomly selected nodes.

As an illustration, consider a logical grid of size $N \times N$ with a node placed on each point of the grid. Every node is required to maintain a list of c nearest neighbors, where the distance between a node at (a_1, a_2) and (b_1, b_2) is defined as $d_1 + d_2$, with $d_i = min(N - |a_i - b_i|, |a_i - b_i|)$. If the lowest layer periodically executes the protocol as outlined in Fig. 2-9, the topology that will evolve is a torus, shown in Fig. 2-11.

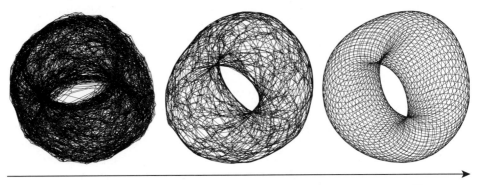

Time

Figure 2-11. Generating a specific overlay network using a two-layered unstructured peer-to-peer system [adapted with permission from Jelasity and Babaoglu (2005)].

Of course, completely different ranking functions can be used. Notably those that are related to capturing the **semantic proximity** of the data items as stored at a peer node are interesting. This proximity allows for the construction of **semantic overlay networks** that allow for highly efficient search algorithms in unstructured peer-to-peer systems. We will return to these systems in Chap. 5 when we discuss attribute-based naming.

Superpeers

Notably in unstructured peer-to-peer systems, locating relevant data items can become problematic as the network grows. The reason for this scalability problem is simple: as there is no deterministic way of routing a lookup request to a specific data item, essentially the only technique a node can resort to is flooding the request. There are various ways in which flooding can be dammed, as we will discuss in Chap. 5, but as an alternative many peer-to-peer systems have proposed to make use of special nodes that maintain an index of data items.

There are other situations in which abandoning the symmetric nature of peer-to-peer systems is sensible. Consider a collaboration of nodes that offer resources to each other. For example, in a collaborative **content delivery network (CDN)**, nodes may offer storage for hosting copies of Web pages allowing Web clients to access pages nearby, and thus to access them quickly. In this case a node P may need to seek for resources in a specific part of the network. In that case, making use of a broker that collects resource usage for a number of nodes that are in each other's proximity will allow to quickly select a node with sufficient resources.

Nodes such as those maintaining an index or acting as a broker are generally referred to as **superpeers**. As their name suggests, superpeers are often also organized in a peer-to-peer network, leading to a hierarchical organization as explained in Yang and Garcia-Molina (2003). A simple example of such an organization is shown in Fig. 2-12. In this organization, every regular peer is connected as a client to a superpeer. All communication from and to a regular peer proceeds through that peer's associated superpeer.

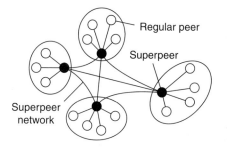

Figure 2-12. A hierarchical organization of nodes into a superpeer network.

In many cases, the client-superpeer relation is fixed: whenever a regular peer joins the network, it attaches to one of the superpeers and remains attached until it leaves the network. Obviously, it is expected that superpeers are long-lived processes with a high availability. To compensate for potential unstable behavior of a superpeer, backup schemes can be deployed, such as pairing every superpeer with another one and requiring clients to attach to both.

Having a fixed association with a superpeer may not always be the best solution. For example, in the case of file-sharing networks, it may be better for a client to attach to a superpeer that maintains an index of files that the client is generally interested in. In that case, chances are bigger that when a client is looking for a specific file, its superpeer will know where to find it. Garbacki et al. (2005) describe a relatively simple scheme in which the client-superpeer relation can change as clients discover better superpeers to associate with. In particular, a superpeer returning the result of a lookup operation is given preference over other superpeers.

As we have seen, peer-to-peer networks offer a flexible means for nodes to join and leave the network. However, with superpeer networks a new problem is introduced, namely how to select the nodes that are eligible to become superpeer.

This problem is closely related to the **leader-election problem**, which we discuss in Chap. 6, when we return to electing superpeers in a peer-to-peer network.

2.2.3 Hybrid Architectures

So far, we have focused on client-server architectures and a number of peer-to-peer architectures. Many distributed systems combine architectural features, as we already came across in superpeer networks. In this section we take a look at some specific classes of distributed systems in which client-server solutions are combined with decentralized architectures.

Edge-Server Systems

An important class of distributed systems that is organized according to a hybrid architecture is formed by **edge-server systems**. These systems are deployed on the Internet where servers are placed "at the edge" of the network. This edge is formed by the boundary between enterprise networks and the actual Internet, for example, as provided by an **Internet Service Provider (ISP)**. Likewise, where end users at home connect to the Internet through their ISP, the ISP can be considered as residing at the edge of the Internet. This leads to a general organization as shown in Fig. 2-13.

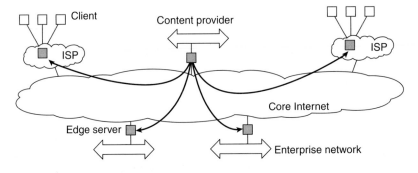

Figure 2-13. Viewing the Internet as consisting of a collection of edge servers.

End users, or clients in general, connect to the Internet by means of an edge server. The edge server's main purpose is to serve content, possibly after applying filtering and transcoding functions. More interesting is the fact that a collection of edge servers can be used to optimize content and application distribution. The basic model is that for a specific organization, one edge server acts as an origin server from which all content originates. That server can use other edge servers for replicating Web pages and such (Leff et al., 2004; Nayate et al., 2004; and Rabinovich and Spatscheck, 2002). We will return to edge-server systems in Chap. 12 when we discuss Web-based solutions.

Collaborative Distributed Systems

Hybrid structures are notably deployed in collaborative distributed systems. The main issue in many of these systems to first get started, for which often a traditional client-server scheme is deployed. Once a node has joined the system, it can use a fully decentralized scheme for collaboration.

To make matters concrete, let us first consider the BitTorrent file-sharing system (Cohen, 2003). BitTorrent is a peer-to-peer file downloading system. Its principal working is shown in Fig. 2-14 The basic idea is that when an end user is looking for a file, he downloads chunks of the file from other users until the downloaded chunks can be assembled together yielding the complete file. An important design goal was to ensure collaboration. In most file-sharing systems, a significant fraction of participants merely download files but otherwise contribute close to nothing (Adar and Huberman, 2000; Saroiu et al., 2003; and Yang et al., 2005). To this end, a file can be downloaded only when the downloading client is providing content to someone else. We will return to this "tit-for-tat" behavior shortly.

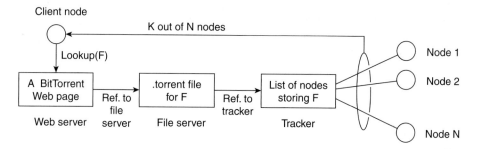

Figure 2-14. The principal working of BitTorrent [adapted with permission from Pouwelse et al. (2004)].

To download a file, a user needs to access a global directory, which is just one of a few well-known Web sites. Such a directory contains references to what are called *.torrent* files. A *.torrent* file contains the information that is needed to download a specific file. In particular, it refers to what is known as a **tracker**, which is a server that is keeping an accurate account of *active* nodes that have (chunks) of the requested file. An active node is one that is currently downloading another file. Obviously, there will be many different trackers, although there will generally be only a single tracker per file (or collection of files).

Once the nodes have been identified from where chunks can be downloaded, the downloading node effectively becomes active. At that point, it will be forced to help others, for example by providing chunks of the file it is downloading that others do not yet have. This enforcement comes from a very simple rule: if node P notices that node Q is downloading more than it is uploading, P can decide to decrease the rate at which it sends data to Q. This scheme works well provided P has something to download from Q. For this reason, nodes are often supplied with references to many other nodes putting them in a better position to trade data.

Clearly, BitTorrent combines centralized with decentralized solutions. As it turns out, the bottleneck of the system is, not surprisingly, formed by the trackers.

As another example, consider the Globule collaborative content distribution network (Pierre and van Steen, 2006). Globule strongly resembles the edge-server architecture mentioned above. In this case, instead of edge servers, end users (but also organizations) voluntarily provide enhanced Web servers that are capable of collaborating in the replication of Web pages. In its simplest form, each such server has the following components:

1. A component that can redirect client requests to other servers.

2. A component for analyzing access patterns.

3. A component for managing the replication of Web pages.

The server provided by Alice is the Web server that normally handles the traffic for Alice's Web site and is called the **origin server** for that site. It collaborates with other servers, for example, the one provided by Bob, to host the pages from Bob's site. In this sense, Globule is a decentralized distributed system. Requests for Alice's Web site are initially forwarded to her server, at which point they may be redirected to one of the other servers. Distributed redirection is also supported.

However, Globule also has a centralized component in the form of its **broker**. The broker is responsible for registering servers, and making these servers known to others. Servers communicate with the broker completely analogous to what one would expect in a client-server system. For reasons of availability, the broker can be replicated, but as we shall later in this book, this type of replication is widely applied in order to achieve reliable client-server computing.

2.3 ARCHITECTURES VERSUS MIDDLEWARE

When considering the architectural issues we have discussed so far, a question that comes to mind is where middleware fits in. As we discussed in Chap. 1, middleware forms a layer between applications and distributed platforms, as shown in Fig. 1-1. An important purpose is to provide a degree of distribution transparency, that is, to a certain extent hiding the distribution of data, processing, and control from applications.

What is comonly seen in practice is that middleware systems actually follow a specific architectural sytle. For example, many middleware solutions have adopted an object-based architectural style, such as CORBA (OMG, 2004a). Others, like TIB/Rendezvous (TIBCO, 2005) provide middleware that follows the event-based architectural style. In later chapters, we will come across more examples of architectural styles.

Having middleware molded according to a specific architectural style has the benefit that designing applications may become simpler. However, an obvious drawback is that the middleware may no longer be optimal for what an application developer had in mind. For example, CORBA initially offered only objects that could be invoked by remote clients. Later, it was felt that having only this form of interaction was too restrictive, so that other interaction patterns such as messaging were added. Obviously, adding new features can easily lead to bloated middleware solutions.

In addition, although middleware is meant to provide distribution transparency, it is generally felt that specific solutions should be adaptable to application requirements. One solution to this problem is to make several versions of a middleware system, where each version is tailored to a specific class of applications. An approach that is generally considered better is to make middleware systems such that they are easy to configure, adapt, and customize as needed by an application. As a result, systems are now being developed in which a stricter separation between policies and mechanisms is being made. This has led to several mechanisms by which the behavior of middleware can be modified (Sadjadi and McKinley, 2003). Let us take a look at some of the commonly followed approaches.

2.3.1 Interceptors

Conceptually, an **interceptor** is nothing but a software construct that will break the usual flow of control and allow other (application specific) code to be executed. To make interceptors generic may require a substantial implementation effort, as illustrated in Schmidt et al. (2000), and it is unclear whether in such cases generality should be preferred over restricted applicability and simplicity. Also, in many cases having only limited interception facilities will improve management of the software and the distributed system as a whole.

To make matters concrete, consider interception as supported in many object-based distributed systems. The basic idea is simple: an object A can call a method that belongs to an object B, while the latter resides on a different machine than A. As we explain in detail later in the book, such a remote-object invocation is carried as a three-step approach:

1. Object A is offered a local interface that is exactly the same as the interface offered by object B. A simply calls the method available in that interface.

2. The call by A is transformed into a generic object invocation, made possible through a general object-invocation interface offered by the middleware at the machine where A resides.

3. Finally, the generic object invocation is transformed into a message that is sent through the transport-level network interface as offered by A's local operating system.

This scheme is shown in Fig. 2-15.

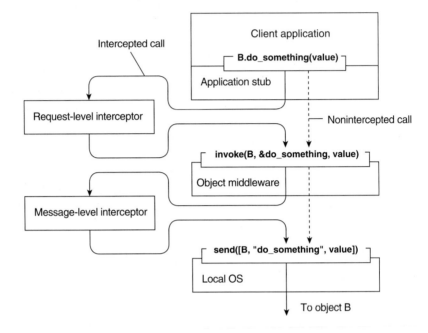

Figure 2-15. Using interceptors to handle remote-object invocations.

After the first step, the call B.do_something(value) is transformed into a generic call such as invoke(B, &do_something, value) with a reference to B's method and the parameters that go along with the call. Now imagine that object B is replicated. In that case, each replica should actually be invoked. This is a clear point where interception can help. What the **request-level interceptor** will do is simply call invoke(B, &do_something, value) for each of the replicas. The beauty of this all is that the object A need not be aware of the replication of B, but also the object middleware need not have special components that deal with this replicated call. Only the request-level interceptor, which may be *added* to the middleware needs to know about B's replication.

In the end, a call to a remote object will have to be sent over the network. In practice, this means that the messaging interface as offered by the local operating system will need to be invoked. At that level, a **message-level interceptor** may assist in transferring the invocation to the target object. For example, imagine that the parameter value actually corresponds to a huge array of data. In that case, it may be wise to fragment the data into smaller parts to have it assembled again at the destination. Such a fragmentation may improve performance or reliability. Again, the middleware need not be aware of this fragmentation; the lower-level interceptor will transparently handle the rest of the communication with the local operating system.

2.3.2 General Approaches to Adaptive Software

What interceptors actually offer is a means to adapt the middleware. The need for adaptation comes from the fact that the environment in which distributed applications are executed changes continuously. Changes include those resulting from mobility, a strong variance in the quality-of-service of networks, failing hardware, and battery drainage, amongst others. Rather than making applications responsible for reacting to changes, this task is placed in the middleware.

These strong influences from the environment have brought many designers of middleware to consider the construction of *adaptive software*. However, adaptive software has not been as successful as anticipated. As many researchers and developers consider it to be an important aspect of modern distributed systems, let us briefly pay some attention to it. McKinley et al. (2004) distinguish three basic techniques to come to software adaptation:

1. Separation of concerns

2. Computational reflection

3. Component-based design

Separating concerns relates to the traditional way of modularizing systems: separate the parts that implement functionality from those that take care of other things (known as *extra functionalities*) such as reliability, performance, security, etc. One can argue that developing middleware for distributed applications is largely about handling extra functionalities independent from applications. The main problem is that we cannot easily separate these extra functionalities by means of modularization. For example, simply putting security into a separate module is not going to work. Likewise, it is hard to imagine how fault tolerance can be isolated into a separate box and sold as an independent service. Separating and subsequently weaving these *cross-cutting* concerns into a (distributed) system is the major theme addressed by **aspect-oriented software development** (Filman et al., 2005). However, aspect orientation has not yet been successfully applied to developing large-scale distributed systems, and it can be expected that there is still a long way to go before it reaches that stage.

Computational reflection refers to the ability of a program to inspect itself and, if necessary, adapt its behavior (Kon et al., 2002). Reflection has been built into programming languages, including Java, and offers a powerful facility for runtime modifications. In addition, some middleware systems provide the means to apply reflective techniques. However, just as in the case of aspect orientation, reflective middleware has yet to prove itself as a powerful tool to manage the complexity of large-scale distributed systems. As mentioned by Blair et al. (2004), applying reflection to a broad domain of applications is yet to be done.

Finally, component-based design supports adaptation through composition. A system may either be configured statically at design time, or dynamically at runtime. The latter requires support for late binding, a technique that has been successfully applied in programming language environments, but also for operating systems where modules can be loaded and unloaded at will. Research is now well underway to allow automatically selection of the best implementation of a component during runtime (Yellin, 2003), but again, the process remains complex for distributed systems, especially when considering that replacement of one component requires knowning what the effect of that replacement on other components will be. In many cases, components are less independent as one may think.

2.3.3 Discussion

Software architectures for distributed systems, notably found as middleware, are bulky and complex. In large part, this bulkiness and complexity arises from the need to be general in the sense that distribution transparency needs to be provided. At the same time applications have specific extra-functional requirements that conflict with aiming at fully achieving this transparency. These conflicting requirements for generality and specialization have resulted in middleware solutions that are highly flexible. The price to pay, however, is complexity. For example, Zhang and Jacobsen (2004) report a 50% increase in the size of a particular software product in just four years since its introduction, whereas the total number of files for that product had tripled during the same period. Obviously, this is not an encouraging direction to pursue.

Considering that virtually all large software systems are nowadays required to execute in a networked environment, we can ask ourselves whether the complexity of distributed systems is simply an inherent feature of attempting to make distribution transparent. Of course, issues such as openness are equally important, but the need for flexibility has never been so prevalent as in the case of middleware.

Coyler et al. (2003) argue that what is needed is a stronger focus on (external) simplicity, a simpler way to construct middleware by components, and application independence. Whether any of the techniques mentioned above forms the solution is subject to debate. In particular, none of the proposed techniques so far have found massive adoption, nor have they been successfully applied to large-scale systems.

The underlying assumption is that we need *adaptive software* in the sense that the software should be allowed to change as the environment changes. However, one should question whether adapting to a changing environment is a good reason to adopt changing the software. Faulty hardware, security attacks, energy drainage, and so on, all seem to be environmental influences that can (and should) be anticipated by software.

The strongest, and certainly most valid, argument for supporting adaptive software is that many distributed systems cannot be shut down. This constraint calls for solutions to replace and upgrade components on the fly, but is not clear whether any of the solutions proposed above are the best ones to tackle this maintenance problem.

What then remains is that distributed systems should be able to react to changes in their environment by, for example, switching policies for allocating resources. All the software components to enable such an adaptation will already be in place. It is the algorithms contained in these components and which dictate the behavior that change their settings. The challenge is to let such reactive behavior take place without human intervention. This approach is seen to work better when discussing the physical organization of distributed systems when decisions are taken about where components are placed, for example. We discuss such system architectural issues next.

2.4 SELF-MANAGEMENT IN DISTRIBUTED SYSTEMS

Distributed systems—and notably their associated middleware—need to provide general solutions toward shielding undesirable features inherent to networking so that they can support as many applications as possible. On the other hand, full distribution transparency is not what most applications actually want, resulting in application-specific solutions that need to be supported as well. We have argued that, for this reason, distributed systems should be adaptive, but notably when it comes to adapting their execution behavior and not the software components they comprise.

When adaptation needs to be done automatically, we see a strong interplay between system architectures and software architectures. On the one hand, we need to organize the components of a distributed system such that monitoring and adjustments can be done, while on the other hand we need to decide where the processes are to be executed that handle the adaptation.

In this section we pay explicit attention to organizing distributed systems as high-level feedback-control systems allowing automatic adaptations to changes. This phenomenon is also known as **autonomic computing** (Kephart, 2003) or **self-star systems** (Babaoglu et al., 2005). The latter name indicates the variety by which automatic adaptations are being captured: self-managing, self-healing, self-configuring, self-optimizing, and so on. We resort simply to using the name self-managing systems as coverage of its many variants.

2.4.1 The Feedback Control Model

There are many different views on self-managing systems, but what most have in common (either explicitly or implicitly) is the assumption that adaptations take place by means of one or more **feedback control loops**. Accordingly, systems that are organized by means of such loops are referred to as **feedback control systems**. Feedback control has since long been applied in various engineering fields, and its mathematical foundations are gradually also finding their way in computing systems (Hellerstein et al., 2004; and Diao et al., 2005). For self-managing systems, the architectural issues are initially the most interesting. The basic idea behind this organization is quite simple, as shown in Fig. 2-16.

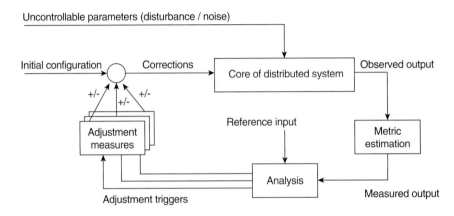

Figure 2-16. The logical organization of a feedback control system.

The core of a feedback control system is formed by the components that need to be managed. These components are assumed to be driven through controllable input parameters, but their behavior may be influenced by all kinds of *uncontrollable* input, also known as disturbance or noise input. Although disturbance will often come from the environment in which a distributed system is executing, it may well be the case that unanticipated component interaction causes unexpected behavior.

There are essentially three elements that form the feedback control loop. First, the system itself needs to be monitored, which requires that various aspects of the system need to be measured. In many cases, measuring behavior is easier said than done. For example, round-trip delays in the Internet may vary wildly, and also depend on what exactly is being measured. In such cases, accurately estimating a delay may be difficult indeed. Matters are further complicated when a node *A* needs to estimate the latency between two other completely different nodes *B* and *C*, without being able to intrude on either two nodes. For reasons as this, a feedback control loop generally contains a logical **metric estimation component**.

Another part of the feedback control loop analyzes the measurements and compares these to reference values. This **feedback analysis component** forms the heart of the control loop, as it will contain the algorithms that decide on possible adaptations.

The last group of components consist of various mechanisms to directly influence the behavior of the system. There can be many different mechanisms: placing replicas, changing scheduling priorities, switching services, moving data for reasons of availability, redirecting requests to different servers, etc. The analysis component will need to be aware of these mechanisms and their (expected) effect on system behavior. Therefore, it will trigger one or several mechanisms, to subsequently later observe the effect.

An interesting observation is that the feedback control loop also fits the manual management of systems. The main difference is that the analysis component is replaced by human administrators. However, in order to properly manage any distributed system, these administrators will need decent monitoring equipment as well as decent mechanisms to control the behavior of the system. It should be clear that properly analyzing measured data and triggering the correct actions makes the development of self-managing systems so difficult.

It should be stressed that Fig. 2-16 shows the *logical* organization of a self-managing system, and as such corresponds to what we have seen when discussing software architectures. However, the *physical* organization may be very different. For example, the analysis component may be fully distributed across the system. Likewise, taking performance measurements are usually done at each machine that is part of the distributed system. Let us now take a look at a few concrete examples on how to monitor, analyze, and correct distributed systems in an automatic fashion. These examples will also illustrate this distinction between logical and physical organization.

2.4.2 Example: Systems Monitoring with Astrolabe

As our first example, we consider Astrolabe (Van Renesse et al., 2003), which is a system that can support general monitoring of very large distributed systems. In the context of self-managing systems, Astrolabe is to be positioned as a general tool for observing systems behavior. Its output can be used to feed into an analysis component for deciding on corrective actions.

Astrolabe organizes a large collection of hosts into a hierarchy of zones. The lowest-level zones consist of just a single host, which are subsequently grouped into zones of increasing size. The top-level zone covers all hosts. Every host runs an Astrolabe process, called an *agent*, that collects information on the zones in which that host is contained. The agent also communicates with other agents with the aim to spread zone information across the entire system.

Each host maintains a set of *attributes* for collecting local information. For example, a host may keep track of specific files it stores, its resource usage, and so on. Only the attributes as maintained directly by hosts, that is, at the lowest level of the hierarchy are writable. Each zone can also have a collection of attributes, but the values of these attributes are *computed* from the values of lower level zones.

Consider the following simple example shown in Fig. 2-17 with three hosts, *A*, *B*, and *C* grouped into a zone. Each machine keeps track of its IP address, CPU load, available free memory, and the number of active processes. Each of these attributes can be directly written using local information from each host. At the zone level, only aggregated information can be collected, such as the average CPU load, or the average number of active processes.

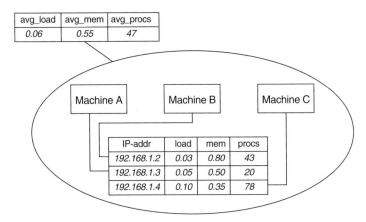

Figure 2-17. Data collection and information aggregation in Astrolabe.

Fig. 2-17 shows how the information as gathered by each machine can be viewed as a record in a database, and that these records jointly form a relation (table). This representation is done on purpose: it is the way that Astrolabe views all the collected data. However, per zone information can only be computed from the basic records as maintained by hosts.

Aggregated information is obtained by programmable aggregation functions, which are very similar to functions available in the relational database language SQL. For example, assuming that the host information from Fig. 2-17 is maintained in a local table called *hostinfo*, we could collect the average number of processes for the zone containing machines *A*, *B*, and *C*, through the simple SQL query

SELECT AVG(procs) AS avg_procs FROM hostinfo

Combined with a few enhancements to SQL, it is not hard to imagine that more informative queries can be formulated.

Queries such as these are continuously evaluated *by* each agent running on each host. Obviously, this is possible only if zone information is propagated to all nodes that comprise Astrolabe. To this end, an agent running on a host is responsible for computing parts of the tables of its associated zones. Records for which it holds no computational responsibility are occasionally sent to it through a simple, yet effective exchange procedure known as **gossiping**. Gossiping protocols will be discussed in detail in Chap. 4. Likewise, an agent will pass computed results to other agents as well.

The result of this information exchange is that eventually, all agents that needed to assist in obtaining some aggregated information will see the same result (provided that no changes occur in the meantime).

2.4.3 Example: Differentiating Replication Strategies in Globule

Let us now take a look at Globule, a collaborative content distribution network (Pierre and van Steen, 2006). Globule relies on end-user servers being placed in the Internet, and that these servers collaborate to optimize performance through replication of Web pages. To this end, each origin server (i.e., the server responsible for handling updates of a specific Web site), keeps track of access patterns on a per-page basis. Access patterns are expressed as read and write operations for a page, each operation being timestamped and logged by the origin server for that page.

In its simplest form, Globule assumes that the Internet can be viewed as an edge-server system as we explained before. In particular, it assumes that requests can always be passed through an appropriate edge server, as shown in Fig. 2-18. This simple model allows an origin server to see what would have happened if it had placed a replica on a specific edge server. On the one hand, placing a replica closer to clients would improve client-perceived latency, but this will induce traffic between the origin server and that edge server in order to keep a replica consistent with the original page.

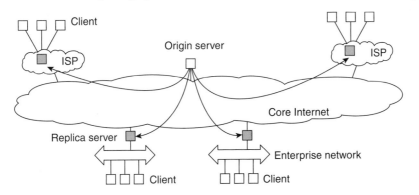

Figure 2-18. The edge-server model assumed by Globule.

When an origin server receives a request for a page, it records the IP address from where the request originated, and looks up the ISP or enterprise network associated with that request using the *WHOIS* Internet service (Deutsch et al., 1995). The origin server then looks for the nearest existing replica server that could act as edge server for that client, and subsequently computes the latency to that server along with the maximal bandwidth. In its simplest configuration, Globule assumes that the latency between the replica server and the requesting user machine is negligible, and likewise that bandwidth between the two is plentiful.

Once enough requests for a page have been collected, the origin server performs a simple "what-if analysis." Such an analysis boils down to evaluating several replication policies, where a policy describes where a specific page is replicated to, and how that page is kept consistent. Each replication policy incurs a cost that can be expressed as a simple linear function:

$$cost = (w_1 \times m_1) + (w_2 \times m_2) + \cdots + (w_n \times m_n)$$

where m_k denotes a performance metric and w_k is the weight indicating how important that metric is. Typical performance metrics are the aggregated delays between a client and a replica server when returning copies of Web pages, the total consumed bandwidth between the origin server and a replica server for keeping a replica consistent, and the number of stale copies that are (allowed to be) returned to a client (Pierre et al., 2002).

For example, assume that the typical delay between the time a client C issues a request and when that page is returned from the best replica server is d_C ms. Note that what the best replica server is, is determined by a replication policy. Let m_1 denote the aggregated delay over a given time period, that is, $m_1 = \Sigma\, d_C$. If the origin server wants to optimize client-perceived latency, it will choose a relatively high value for w_1. As a consequence, only those policies that actually minimize m_1 will show to have relatively low costs.

In Globule, an origin server regularly evaluates a few tens of replication polices using a trace-driven simulation, for each Web page separately. From these simulations, a best policy is selected and subsequently enforced. This may imply that new replicas are installed at different edge servers, or that a different way of keeping replicas consistent is chosen. The collecting of traces, the evaluation of replication policies, and the enforcement of a selected policy is all done automatically.

There are a number of subtle issues that need to be dealt with. For one thing, it is unclear how many requests need to be collected before an evaluation of the current policy can take place. To explain, suppose that at time T_i the origin server selects policy p for the next period until T_{i+1}. This selection takes place based on a series of past requests that were issued between T_{i-1} and T_i. Of course, in hindsight at time T_{i+1}, the server may come to the conclusion that it should have selected policy p^* given the actual requests that were issued between T_i and T_{i+1}. If p^* is different from p, then the selection of p at T_i was wrong.

As it turns out, the percentage of wrong predictions is dependent on the length of the series of requests (called the trace length) that are used to predict and select

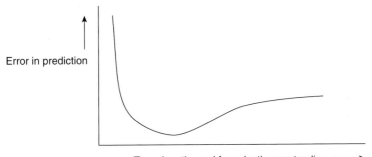

Figure 2-19. The dependency between prediction accuracy and trace length.

a next policy. This dependency is sketched in Fig. 2-19. What is seen is that the error in predicting the best policy goes up if the trace is not long enough. This is easily explained by the fact that we need enough requests to do a proper evaluation. However, the error also increases if we use too many requests. The reason for this is that a very long trace length captures so many *changes* in access patterns that predicting the best policy to follow becomes difficult, if not impossible. This phenomenon is well known and is analogous to trying to predict the weather for tomorrow by looking at what happened during the immediately preceding 100 years. A much better prediction can be made by just looking only at the recent past.

Finding the optimal trace length can be done automatically as well. We leave it as an exercise to sketch a solution to this problem.

2.4.4 Example: Automatic Component Repair Management in Jade

When maintaining clusters of computers, each running sophisticated servers, it becomes important to alleviate management problems. One approach that can be applied to servers that are built using a component-based approach, is to detect component failures and have them automatically replaced. The Jade system follows this approach (Bouchenak et al., 2005). We describe it briefly in this section.

Jade is built on the Fractal component model, a Java implementation of a framework that allows components to be added and removed at runtime (Bruneton et al., 2004). A component in Fractal can have two types of interfaces. A **server interface** is used to call methods that are implemented by that component. A **client interface** is used by a component to call other components. Components are connected to each other by **binding** interfaces. For example, a client interface of component C_1 can be bound to the server interface of component C_2. A primitive binding means that a call to a client interface directly leads to calling the bounded server interface. In the case of composite binding, the call may proceed through one or more other components, for example, because the client and server interface did not match and some kind of conversion is needed. Another reason may be that the connected components lie on different machines.

Jade uses the notion of a **repair management domain**. Such a domain consists of a number of nodes, where each node represents a server along with the components that are executed by that server. There is a separate node manager which is responsible for adding and removing nodes from the domain. The node manager may be replicated for assuring high availability.

Each node is equipped with failure detectors, which monitor the health of a node or one of its components and report any failures to the node manager. Typically, these detectors consider exceptional changes in the state of component, the usage of resources, and the actual failure of a component. Note that the latter may actually mean that a machine has crashed.

When a failure has been detected, a repair procedure is started. Such a procedure is driven by a repair policy, partly executed by the node manager. Policies are stated explicitly and are carried out depending on the detected failure. For example, suppose a node failure has been detected. In that case, the repair policy may prescribe that the following steps are to be carried out:

1. Terminate every binding between a component on a nonfaulty node, and a component on the node that just failed.

2. Request the node manager to start and add a new node to the domain.

3. Configure the new node with exactly the same components as those on the crashed node.

4. Re-establish all the bindings that were previously terminated.

In this example, the repair policy is simple and will only work when no crucial data has been lost (the crashed components are said to be **stateless**).

The approach followed by Jade is an example of self-management: upon the detection of a failure, a repair policy is automatically executed to bring the system as a whole into a state in which it was before the crash. Being a component-based system, this automatic repair requires specific support to allow components to be added and removed at runtime. In general, turning legacy applications into self-managing systems is not possible.

2.5 SUMMARY

Distributed systems can be organized in many different ways. We can make a distinction between software architecture and system architecture. The latter considers where the components that constitute a distributed system are placed across the various machines. The former is more concerned about the logical organization of the software: how do components interact, it what ways can they be structured, how can they be made independent, and so on.

A key idea when talking about architectures is architectural style. A style reflects the basic principle that is followed in organizing the interaction between the software components comprising a distributed system. Important styles include layering, object orientation, event orientation, and data-space orientation.

There are many different organizations of distributed systems. An important class is where machines are divided into clients and servers. A client sends a request to a server, who will then produce a result that is returned to the client. The client-server architecture reflects the traditional way of modularizing software in which a module calls the functions available in another module. By placing different components on different machines, we obtain a natural physical distribution of functions across a collection of machines.

Client-server architectures are often highly centralized. In decentralized architectures we often see an equal role played by the processes that constitute a distributed system, also known as peer-to-peer systems. In peer-to-peer systems, the processes are organized into an overlay network, which is a logical network in which every process has a local list of other peers that it can communicate with. The overlay network can be structured, in which case deterministic schemes can be deployed for routing messages between processes. In unstructured networks, the list of peers is more or less random, implying that search algorithms need to be deployed for locating data or other processes.

As an alternative, self-managing distributed systems have been developed. These systems, to an extent, merge ideas from system and software architectures. Self-managing systems can be generally organized as feedback-control loops. Such loops contain a monitoring component by the behavior of the distributed system is measured, an analysis component to see whether anything needs to be adjusted, and a collection of various instruments for changing the behavior. Feedback-control loops can be integrated into distributed systems at numerous places. Much research is still needed before a common understanding how such loops such be developed and deployedis reached.

PROBLEMS

1. If a client and a server are placed far apart, we may see network latency dominating overall performance. How can we tackle this problem?

2. What is a three-tiered client-server architecture?

3. What is the difference between a vertical distribution and a horizontal distribution?

4. Consider a chain of processes $P_1, P_2, ..., P_n$ implementing a multitiered client-server architecture. Process P_i is client of process P_{i+1}, and P_i will return a reply to P_{i-1} only after receiving a reply from P_{i+1}. What are the main problems with this organization when taking a look at the request-reply performance at process P_1?

5. In a structured overlay network, messages are routed according to the topology of the overlay. What is an important disadvantage of this approach?

6. Consider the CAN network from Fig. 2-8. How would you route a message from the node with coordinates (0.2,0.3) to the one with coordinates (0.9,0.6)?

7. Considering that a node in CAN knows the coordinates of its immediate neighbors, a reasonable routing policy would be to forward a message to the closest node toward the destination. How good is this policy?

8. Consider an unstructured overlay network in which each node randomly chooses c neighbors. If P and Q are both neighbors of R, what is the probability that they are also neighbors of each other?

9. Consider again an unstructured overlay network in which every node randomly chooses c neighbors. To search for a file, a node floods a request to its neighbors and requests those to flood the request once more. How many nodes will be reached?

10. Not every node in a peer-to-peer network should become superpeer. What are reasonable requirements that a superpeer should meet?

11. Consider a BitTorrent system in which each node has an outgoing link with a bandwidth capacity B_{out} and an incoming link with bandwidth capacity B_{in}. Some of these nodes (called seeds) voluntarily offer files to be downloaded by others. What is the maximum download capacity of a BitTorrent client if we assume that it can contact at most one seed at a time?

12. Give a compelling (technical) argument why the tit-for-tat policy as used in BitTorrent is far from optimal for file sharing in the Internet.

13. We gave two examples of using interceptors in adaptive middleware. What other examples come to mind?

14. To what extent are interceptors dependent on the middleware where they are deployed?

15. Modern cars are stuffed with electronic devices. Give some examples of feedback control systems in cars.

16. Give an example of a self-managing system in which the analysis component is completely distributed or even hidden.

17. Sketch a solution to automatically determine the best trace length for predicting replication policies in Globule.

18. (Lab assignment) Using existing software, design and implement a BitTorrent-based system for distributing files to many clients from a single, powerful server. Matters are simplified by using a standard Web server that can operate as tracker.

3

PROCESSES

In this chapter, we take a closer look at how the different types of processes play a crucial role in distributed systems. The concept of a process originates from the field of operating systems where it is generally defined as a program in execution. From an operating-system perspective, the management and scheduling of processes are perhaps the most important issues to deal with. However, when it comes to distributed systems, other issues turn out to be equally or more important.

For example, to efficiently organize client-server systems, it is often convenient to make use of multithreading techniques. As we discuss in the first section, a main contribution of threads in distributed systems is that they allow clients and servers to be constructed such that communication and local processing can overlap, resulting in a high level of performance.

In recent years, the concept of virtualization has gained popularity. Virtualization allows an application, and possibly also its complete environment including the operating system, to run concurrently with other applications, but highly independent of the underlying hardware and platforms, leading to a high degree of portability. Moreover, virtualization helps in isolating failures caused by errors or security problems. It is an important concept for distributed systems, and we pay attention to it in a separate section.

As we argued in Chap. 2, client-server organizations are important in distributed systems. In this chapter, we take a closer look at typical organizations of both clients and servers. We also pay attention to general design issues for servers.

An important issue, especially in wide-area distributed systems, is moving processes between different machines. Process migration or more specifically, code migration, can help in achieving scalability, but can also help to dynamically configure clients and servers. What is actually meant by code migration and what its implications are is also discussed in this chapter.

3.1 THREADS

Although processes form a building block in distributed systems, practice indicates that the granularity of processes as provided by the operating systems on which distributed systems are built is not sufficient. Instead, it turns out that having a finer granularity in the form of multiple threads of control per process makes it much easier to build distributed applications and to attain better performance. In this section, we take a closer look at the role of threads in distributed systems and explain why they are so important. More on threads and how they can be used to build applications can be found in Lewis and Berg (1998) and Stevens (1999).

3.1.1 Introduction to Threads

To understand the role of threads in distributed systems, it is important to understand what a process is, and how processes and threads relate. To execute a program, an operating system creates a number of virtual processors, each one for running a different program. To keep track of these virtual processors, the operating system has a **process table**, containing entries to store CPU register values, memory maps, open files, accounting information, privileges, etc. A **process** is often defined as a program in execution, that is, a program that is currently being executed on one of the operating system's virtual processors. An important issue is that the operating system takes great care to ensure that independent processes cannot maliciously or inadvertently affect the correctness of each other's behavior. In other words, the fact that multiple processes may be concurrently sharing the same CPU and other hardware resources is made transparent. Usually, the operating system requires hardware support to enforce this separation.

This concurrency transparency comes at a relatively high price. For example, each time a process is created, the operating system must create a complete independent address space. Allocation can mean initializing memory segments by, for example, zeroing a data segment, copying the associated program into a text segment, and setting up a stack for temporary data. Likewise, switching the CPU between two processes may be relatively expensive as well. Apart from saving the CPU context (which consists of register values, program counter, stack pointer, etc.), the operating system will also have to modify registers of the memory management unit (MMU) and invalidate address translation caches such as in the translation lookaside buffer (TLB). In addition, if the operating system supports more processes than it can simultaneously hold in main memory, it may have to swap processes between main memory and disk before the actual switch can take place.

Like a process, a thread executes its own piece of code, independently from other threads. However, in contrast to processes, no attempt is made to achieve a high degree of concurrency transparency if this would result in performance degradation. Therefore, a thread system generally maintains only the minimum information to allow a CPU to be shared by several threads. In particular, a **thread context** often consists of nothing more than the CPU context, along with some other information for thread management. For example, a thread system may keep track of the fact that a thread is currently blocked on a mutex variable, so as not to select it for execution. Information that is not strictly necessary to manage multiple threads is generally ignored. For this reason, protecting data against inappropriate access by threads within a single process is left entirely to application developers.

There are two important implications of this approach. First of all, the performance of a multithreaded application need hardly ever be worse than that of its single-threaded counterpart. In fact, in many cases, multithreading leads to a performance gain. Second, because threads are not automatically protected against each other the way processes are, development of multithreaded applications requires additional intellectual effort. Proper design and keeping things simple, as usual, help a lot. Unfortunately, current practice does not demonstrate that this principle is equally well understood.

Thread Usage in Nondistributed Systems

Before discussing the role of threads in distributed systems, let us first consider their usage in traditional, nondistributed systems. There are several benefits to multithreaded processes that have increased the popularity of using thread systems.

The most important benefit comes from the fact that in a single-threaded process, whenever a blocking system call is executed, the process as a whole is blocked. To illustrate, consider an application such as a spreadsheet program, and assume that a user continuously and interactively wants to change values. An important property of a spreadsheet program is that it maintains the functional dependencies between different cells, often from different spreadsheets. Therefore, whenever a cell is modified, all dependent cells are automatically updated. When a user changes the value in a single cell, such a modification can trigger a large series of computations. If there is only a single thread of control, computation cannot proceed while the program is waiting for input. Likewise, it is not easy to provide input while dependencies are being calculated. The easy solution is to have at least two threads of control: one for handling interaction with the user and one for updating the spreadsheet. In the mean time, a third thread could be used for backing up the spreadsheet to disk while the other two are doing their work.

Another advantage of multithreading is that it becomes possible to exploit parallelism when executing the program on a multiprocessor system. In that case, each thread is assigned to a different CPU while shared data are stored in shared main memory. When properly designed, such parallelism can be transparent: the process will run equally well on a uniprocessor system, albeit slower. Multithreading for parallelism is becoming increasingly important with the availability of relatively cheap multiprocessor workstations. Such computer systems are typically used for running servers in client-server applications.

Multithreading is also useful in the context of large applications. Such applications are often developed as a collection of cooperating programs, each to be executed by a separate process. This approach is typical for a UNIX environment. Cooperation between programs is implemented by means of interprocess communication (IPC) mechanisms. For UNIX systems, these mechanisms typically include (named) pipes, message queues, and shared memory segments [see also Stevens and Rago (2005)]. The major drawback of all IPC mechanisms is that communication often requires extensive context switching, shown at three different points in Fig. 3-1.

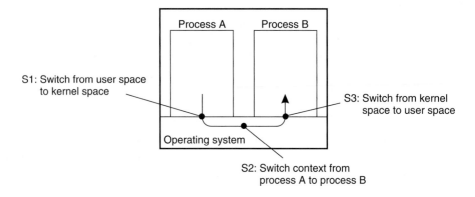

Figure 3-1. Context switching as the result of IPC.

Because IPC requires kernel intervention, a process will generally first have to switch from user mode to kernel mode, shown as $S1$ in Fig. 3-1. This requires changing the memory map in the MMU, as well as flushing the TLB. Within the kernel, a process context switch takes place ($S2$ in the figure), after which the other party can be activated by switching from kernel mode to user mode again ($S3$ in Fig. 3-1). The latter switch again requires changing the MMU map and flushing the TLB.

Instead of using processes, an application can also be constructed such that different parts are executed by separate threads. Communication between those parts is entirely dealt with by using shared data. Thread switching can sometimes be done entirely in user space, although in other implementations, the kernel is aware of threads and schedules them. The effect can be a dramatic improvement in performance.

Finally, there is also a pure software engineering reason to use threads: many applications are simply easier to structure as a collection of cooperating threads. Think of applications that need to perform several (more or less independent) tasks. For example, in the case of a word processor, separate threads can be used for handling user input, spelling and grammar checking, document layout, index generation, etc.

Thread Implementation

Threads are often provided in the form of a thread package. Such a package contains operations to create and destroy threads as well as operations on synchronization variables such as mutexes and condition variables. There are basically two approaches to implement a thread package. The first approach is to construct a thread library that is executed entirely in user mode. The second approach is to have the kernel be aware of threads and schedule them.

A user-level thread library has a number of advantages. First, it is cheap to create and destroy threads. Because all thread administration is kept in the user's address space, the price of creating a thread is primarily determined by the cost for allocating memory to set up a thread stack. Analogously, destroying a thread mainly involves freeing memory for the stack, which is no longer used. Both operations are cheap.

A second advantage of user-level threads is that switching thread context can often be done in just a few instructions. Basically, only the values of the CPU registers need to be stored and subsequently reloaded with the previously stored values of the thread to which it is being switched. There is no need to change memory maps, flush the TLB, do CPU accounting, and so on. Switching thread context is done when two threads need to synchronize, for example, when entering a section of shared data.

However, a major drawback of user-level threads is that invocation of a blocking system call will immediately block the entire process to which the thread belongs, and thus also all the other threads in that process. As we explained, threads are particularly useful to structure large applications into parts that could be logically executed at the same time. In that case, blocking on I/O should not prevent other parts to be executed in the meantime. For such applications, user-level threads are of no help.

These problems can be mostly circumvented by implementing threads in the operating system's kernel. Unfortunately, there is a high price to pay: every thread operation (creation, deletion, synchronization, etc.), will have to be carried out by the kernel, requiring a system call. Switching thread contexts may now become as expensive as switching process contexts. As a result, most of the performance benefits of using threads instead of processes then disappears.

A solution lies in a hybrid form of user-level and kernel-level threads, generally referred to as **lightweight processes** (**LWP**). An LWP runs in the context of a single (heavy-weight) process, and there can be several LWPs per process. In addition to having LWPs, a system also offers a user-level thread package, offering applications the usual operations for creating and destroying threads. In addition, the package provides facilities for thread synchronization, such as mutexes and condition variables. The important issue is that the thread package is implemented entirely in user space. In other words, all operations on threads are carried out without intervention of the kernel.

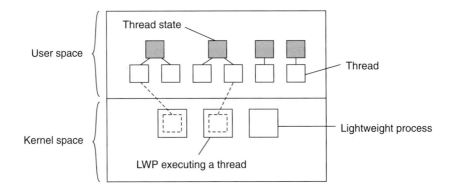

Figure 3-2. Combining kernel-level lightweight processes and user-level threads.

The thread package can be shared by multiple LWPs, as shown in Fig. 3-2. This means that each LWP can be running its own (user-level) thread. Multi-threaded applications are constructed by creating threads, and subsequently assigning each thread to an LWP. Assigning a thread to an LWP is normally implicit and hidden from the programmer.

The combination of (user-level) threads and LWPs works as follows. The thread package has a single routine to schedule the next thread. When creating an LWP (which is done by means of a system call), the LWP is given its own stack, and is instructed to execute the scheduling routine in search of a thread to execute. If there are several LWPs, then each of them executes the scheduler. The thread table, which is used to keep track of the current set of threads, is thus shared by the LWPs. Protecting this table to guarantee mutually exclusive access is done by means of mutexes that are implemented entirely in user space. In other words, synchronization between LWPs does not require any kernel support.

When an LWP finds a runnable thread, it switches context to that thread. Meanwhile, other LWPs may be looking for other runnable threads as well. If a thread needs to block on a mutex or condition variable, it does the necessary administration and eventually calls the scheduling routine. When another runnable thread has been found, a context switch is made to that thread. The beauty of all this is that the LWP executing the thread need not be informed: the context switch is implemented completely in user space and appears to the LWP as normal program code.

Now let us see what happens when a thread does a blocking system call. In that case, execution changes from user mode to kernel mode, but still continues in the context of the current LWP. At the point where the current LWP can no longer continue, the operating system may decide to switch context to another LWP, which also implies that a context switch is made back to user mode. The selected LWP will simply continue where it had previously left off.

There are several advantages to using LWPs in combination with a user-level thread package. First, creating, destroying, and synchronizing threads is relatively cheap and involves no kernel intervention at all. Second, provided that a process has enough LWPs, a blocking system call will not suspend the entire process. Third, there is no need for an application to know about the LWPs. All it sees are user-level threads. Fourth, LWPs can be easily used in multiprocessing environments, by executing different LWPs on different CPUs. This multiprocessing can be hidden entirely from the application. The only drawback of lightweight processes in combination with user-level threads is that we still need to create and destroy LWPs, which is just as expensive as with kernel-level threads. However, creating and destroying LWPs needs to be done only occasionally, and is often fully controlled by the operating system.

An alternative, but similar approach to lightweight processes, is to make use of **scheduler activations** (Anderson et al., 1991). The most essential difference between scheduler activations and LWPs is that when a thread blocks on a system call, the kernel does an *upcall* to the thread package, effectively calling the scheduler routine to select the next runnable thread. The same procedure is repeated when a thread is unblocked. The advantage of this approach is that it saves management of LWPs by the kernel. However, the use of upcalls is considered less elegant, as it violates the structure of layered systems, in which calls only to the next lower-level layer are permitted.

3.1.2 Threads in Distributed Systems

An important property of threads is that they can provide a convenient means of allowing blocking system calls without blocking the entire process in which the thread is running. This property makes threads particularly attractive to use in distributed systems as it makes it much easier to express communication in the form of maintaining multiple logical connections at the same time. We illustrate this point by taking a closer look at multithreaded clients and servers, respectively.

Multithreaded Clients

To establish a high degree of distribution transparency, distributed systems that operate in wide-area networks may need to conceal long interprocess message propagation times. The round-trip delay in a wide-area network can easily be in the order of hundreds of milliseconds, or sometimes even seconds.

The usual way to hide communication latencies is to initiate communication and immediately proceed with something else. A typical example where this happens is in Web browsers. In many cases, a Web document consists of an HTML file containing plain text along with a collection of images, icons, etc. To fetch each element of a Web document, the browser has to set up a TCP/IP connection, read the incoming data, and pass it to a display component. Setting up a connection as well as reading incoming data are inherently blocking operations. When dealing with long-haul communication, we also have the disadvantage that the time for each operation to complete may be relatively long.

A Web browser often starts with fetching the HTML page and subsequently displays it. To hide communication latencies as much as possible, some browsers start displaying data while it is still coming in. While the text is made available to the user, including the facilities for scrolling and such, the browser continues with fetching other files that make up the page, such as the images. The latter are displayed as they are brought in. The user need thus not wait until all the components of the entire page are fetched before the page is made available.

In effect, it is seen that the Web browser is doing a number of tasks simultaneously. As it turns out, developing the browser as a multithreaded client simplifies matters considerably. As soon as the main HTML file has been fetched, separate threads can be activated to take care of fetching the other parts. Each thread sets up a separate connection to the server and pulls in the data. Setting up a connection and reading data from the server can be programmed using the standard (blocking) system calls, assuming that a blocking call does not suspend the entire process. As is also illustrated in Stevens (1998), the code for each thread is the same and, above all, simple. Meanwhile, the user notices only delays in the display of images and such, but can otherwise browse through the document.

There is another important benefit to using multithreaded Web browsers in which several connections can be opened simultaneously. In the previous example, several connections were set up to the same server. If that server is heavily loaded, or just plain slow, no real performance improvements will be noticed compared to pulling in the files that make up the page strictly one after the other.

However, in many cases, Web servers have been replicated across multiple machines, where each server provides exactly the same set of Web documents. The replicated servers are located at the same site, and are known under the same name. When a request for a Web page comes in, the request is forwarded to one of the servers, often using a round-robin strategy or some other load-balancing technique (Katz et al., 1994). When using a multithreaded client, connections may be set up to different replicas, allowing data to be transferred in parallel, effectively establishing that the entire Web document is fully displayed in a much shorter time than with a nonreplicated server. This approach is possible only if the client can handle truly parallel streams of incoming data. Threads are ideal for this purpose.

Multithreaded Servers

Although there are important benefits to multithreaded clients, as we have seen, the main use of multithreading in distributed systems is found at the server side. Practice shows that multithreading not only simplifies server code considerably, but also makes it much easier to develop servers that exploit parallelism to attain high performance, even on uniprocessor systems. However, now that multiprocessor computers are widely available as general-purpose workstations, multithreading for parallelism is even more useful.

To understand the benefits of threads for writing server code, consider the organization of a file server that occasionally has to block waiting for the disk. The file server normally waits for an incoming request for a file operation, subsequently carries out the request, and then sends back the reply. One possible, and particularly popular organization is shown in Fig. 3-3. Here one thread, the **dispatcher**, reads incoming requests for a file operation. The requests are sent by clients to a well-known end point for this server. After examining the request, the server chooses an idle (i.e., blocked) **worker thread** and hands it the request.

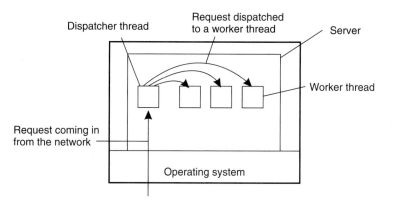

Figure 3-3. A multithreaded server organized in a dispatcher/worker model.

The worker proceeds by performing a blocking read on the *local* file system, which may cause the thread to be suspended until the data are fetched from disk. If the thread is suspended, another thread is selected to be executed. For example, the dispatcher may be selected to acquire more work. Alternatively, another worker thread can be selected that is now ready to run.

Now consider how the file server might have been written in the absence of threads. One possibility is to have it operate as a single thread. The main loop of the file server gets a request, examines it, and carries it out to completion before getting the next one. While waiting for the disk, the server is idle and does not process any other requests. Consequently, requests from other clients cannot be handled. In addition, if the file server is running on a dedicated machine, as is commonly the case, the CPU is simply idle while the file server is waiting for the disk. The net result is that many fewer requests/sec can be processed. Thus threads gain considerable performance, but each thread is programmed sequentially, in the usual way.

So far we have seen two possible designs: a multithreaded file server and a single-threaded file server. Suppose that threads are not available but the system designers find the performance loss due to single threading unacceptable. A third possibility is to run the server as a big finite-state machine. When a request comes in, the one and only thread examines it. If it can be satisfied from the cache, fine, but if not, a message must be sent to the disk.

However, instead of blocking, it records the state of the current request in a table and then goes and gets the next message. The next message may either be a request for new work or a reply from the disk about a previous operation. If it is new work, that work is started. If it is a reply from the disk, the relevant information is fetched from the table and the reply processed and subsequently sent to the client. In this scheme, the server will have to make use of nonblocking calls to send and receive.

In this design, the "sequential process" model that we had in the first two cases is lost. The state of the computation must be explicitly saved and restored in the table for every message sent and received. In effect, we are simulating threads and their stacks the hard way. The process is being operated as a finite-state machine that gets an event and then reacts to it, depending on what is in it.

Model	Characteristics
Threads	Parallelism, blocking system calls
Single-threaded process	No parallelism, blocking system calls
Finite-state machine	Parallelism, nonblocking system calls

Figure 3-4. Three ways to construct a server.

It should now be clear what threads have to offer. They make it possible to retain the idea of sequential processes that make blocking system calls (e.g., an RPC to talk to the disk) and still achieve parallelism. Blocking system calls make programming easier and parallelism improves performance. The single-threaded server retains the ease and simplicity of blocking system calls, but gives up some amount of performance. The finite-state machine approach achieves high performance through parallelism, but uses nonblocking calls, thus is hard to program. These models are summarized in Fig. 3-4.

3.2 VIRTUALIZATION

Threads and processes can be seen as a way to do more things at the same time. In effect, they allow us build (pieces of) programs that appear to be executed simultaneously. On a single-processor computer, this simultaneous execution is, of course, an illusion. As there is only a single CPU, only an instruction from a single thread or process will be executed at a time. By rapidly switching between threads and processes, the illusion of parallelism is created.

This separation between having a single CPU and being able to pretend there are more can be extended to other resources as well, leading to what is known as **resource virtualization**. This virtualization has been applied for many decades, but has received renewed interest as (distributed) computer systems have become more commonplace and complex, leading to the situation that application software is mostly always outliving its underlying systems software and hardware. In this section, we pay some attention to the role of virtualization and discuss how it can be realized.

3.2.1 The Role of Virtualization in Distributed Systems

In practice, every (distributed) computer system offers a programming interface to higher level software, as shown in Fig. 3-5(a). There are many different types of interfaces, ranging from the basic instruction set as offered by a CPU to the vast collection of application programming interfaces that are shipped with many current middleware systems. In its essence, virtualization deals with extending or replacing an existing interface so as to mimic the behavior of another system, as shown in Fig. 3-5(b). We will come to discuss technical details on virtualization shortly, but let us first concentrate on why virtualization is important for distributed systems.

One of the most important reasons for introducing virtualization in the 1970s, was to allow legacy software to run on expensive mainframe hardware. The software not only included various applications, but in fact also the operating systems they were developed for. This approach toward supporting legacy software has been successfully applied on the IBM 370 mainframes (and their successors) that offered a virtual machine to which different operating systems had been ported.

As hardware became cheaper, computers became more powerful, and the number of different operating system flavors was reducing, virtualization became less of an issue. However, matters have changed again since the late 1990s for several reasons, which we will now discuss.

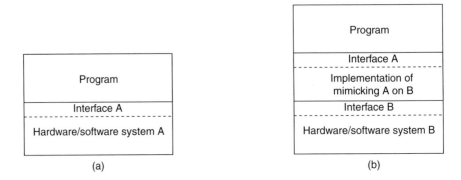

Figure 3-5. (a) General organization between a program, interface, and system. (b) General organization of virtualizing system A on top of system B.

First, while hardware and low-level systems software change reasonably fast, software at higher levels of abstraction (e.g., middleware and applications), are much more stable. In other words, we are facing the situation that legacy software cannot be maintained in the same pace as the platforms it relies on. Virtualization can help here by porting the legacy interfaces to the new platforms and thus immediately opening up the latter for large classes of existing programs.

Equally important is the fact that networking has become completely pervasive. It is hard to imagine that a modern computer is not connected to a network. In practice, this connectivity requires that system administrators maintain a large and heterogeneous collection of server computers, each one running very different applications, which can be accessed by clients. At the same time the various resources should be easily accessible to these applications. Virtualization can help a lot: the diversity of platforms and machines can be reduced by essentially letting each application run on its own virtual machine, possibly including the related libraries *and* operating system, which, in turn, run on a common platform.

This last type of virtualization provides a high degree of portability and flexibility. For example, in order to realize content delivery networks that can easily support replication of dynamic content, Awadallah and Rosenblum (2002) argue that management becomes much easier if edge servers would support virtualization, allowing a complete site, including its environment to be dynamically copied. As we will discuss later, it is primarily such portability arguments that make virtualization an important mechanism for distributed systems.

3.2.2 Architectures of Virtual Machines

There are many different ways in which virtualization can be realized in practice. An overview of these various approaches is described by Smith and Nair (2005). To understand the differences in virtualization, it is important to realize that computer systems generally offer four different types of interfaces, at four different levels:

1. An interface between the hardware and software, consisting of **machine instructions** that can be invoked by any program.

2. An interface between the hardware and software, consisting of machine instructions that can be invoked only by privileged programs, such as an operating system.

3. An interface consisting of **system calls** as offered by an operating system.

4. An interface consisting of library calls, generally forming what is known as an **application programming interface** (**API**). In many cases, the aforementioned system calls are hidden by an API.

These different types are shown in Fig. 3-6. The essence of virtualization is to mimic the behavior of these interfaces.

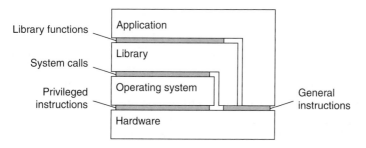

Figure 3-6. Various interfaces offered by computer systems.

Virtualization can take place in two different ways. First, we can build a runtime system that essentially provides an abstract instruction set that is to be used for executing applications. Instructions can be interpreted (as is the case for the Java runtime environment), but could also be emulated as is done for running Windows applications on UNIX platforms. Note that in the latter case, the emulator will also have to mimic the behavior of system calls, which has proven to be generally far from trivial. This type of virtualization leads to what Smith and Nair (2005) call a **process virtual machine**, stressing that virtualization is done essentially only for a single process.

An alternative approach toward virtualization is to provide a system that is essentially implemented as a layer completely shielding the original hardware, but offering the complete instruction set of that same (or other hardware) as an interface. Crucial is the fact that this interface can be offered *simultaneously* to different programs. As a result, it is now possible to have multiple, and different operating systems run independently and concurrently on the same platform. The layer is generally referred to as a **virtual machine monitor** (**VMM**). Typical examples of this approach are VMware (Sugerman et al., 2001) and Xen (Barham et al., 2003). These two different approaches are shown in Fig. 3-7.

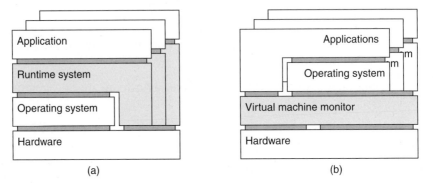

Figure 3-7. (a) A process virtual machine, with multiple instances of (application, runtime) combinations. (b) A virtual machine monitor, with multiple instances of (applications, operating system) combinations.

As argued by Rosenblum and Garfinkel (2005), VMMs will become increasingly important in the context of reliability and security for (distributed) systems. As they allow for the isolation of a complete application and its environment, a failure caused by an error or security attack need no longer affect a complete machine. In addition, as we also mentioned before, portability is greatly improved as VMMs provide a further decoupling between hardware and software, allowing a complete environment to be moved from one machine to another.

3.3 CLIENTS

In the previous chapters we discussed the client-server model, the roles of clients and servers, and the ways they interact. Let us now take a closer look at the anatomy of clients and servers, respectively. We start in this section with a discussion of clients. Servers are discussed in the next section.

3.3.1 Networked User Interfaces

A major task of client machines is to provide the means for users to interact with remote servers. There are roughly two ways in which this interaction can be supported. First, for each remote service the client machine will have a separate counterpart that can contact the service over the network. A typical example is an agenda running on a user's PDA that needs to synchronize with a remote, possibly shared agenda. In this case, an application-level protocol will handle the synchronization, as shown in Fig. 3-8(a).

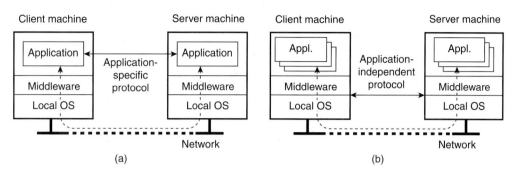

Figure 3-8. (a) A networked application with its own protocol. (b) A general solution to allow access to remote applications.

A second solution is to provide direct access to remote services by only offering a convenient user interface. Effectively, this means that the client machine is used only as a terminal with no need for local storage, leading to an application-neutral solution as shown in Fig. 3-8(b). In the case of networked user interfaces, everything is processed and stored at the server. This **thin-client approach** is receiving more attention as Internet connectivity increases, and hand-held devices are becoming more sophisticated. As we argued in the previous chapter, thin-client solutions are also popular as they ease the task of system management. Let us take a look at how networked user interfaces can be supported.

Example: The X Window System

Perhaps one of the oldest and still widely-used networked user interfaces is the **X Window system**. The X Window System, generally referred to simply as X, is used to control bit-mapped terminals, which include a monitor, keyboard, and a pointing device such as a mouse. In a sense, X can be viewed as that part of an operating system that controls the terminal. The heart of the system is formed by what we shall call the **X kernel**. It contains all the terminal-specific device drivers, and as such, is generally highly hardware dependent.

The X kernel offers a relatively low-level interface for controlling the screen, but also for capturing events from the keyboard and mouse. This interface is made available to applications as a library called *Xlib*. This general organization is shown in Fig. 3-9.

The interesting aspect of X is that the X kernel and the X applications need not necessarily reside on the same machine. In particular, X provides the **X protocol**, which is an application-level communication protocol by which an instance of *Xlib* can exchange data and events with the X kernel. For example, *Xlib* can send

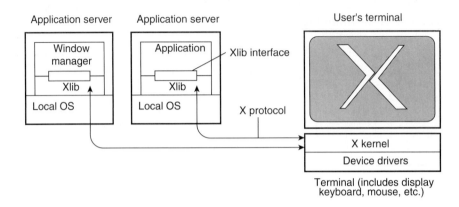

Figure 3-9. The basic organization of the X Window System.

requests to the X kernel for creating or killing a window, setting colors, and defining the type of cursor to display, among many other requests. In turn, the X kernel will react to local events such as keyboard and mouse input by sending event packets back to *Xlib*.

Several applications can communicate at the same time with the X kernel. There is one specific application that is given special rights, known as the **window manager**. This application can dictate the "look and feel" of the display as it appears to the user. For example, the window manager can prescribe how each window is decorated with extra buttons, how windows are to be placed on the display, and so. Other applications will have to adhere to these rules.

It is interesting to note how the X window system actually fits into client-server computing. From what we have described so far, it should be clear that the X kernel receives requests to manipulate the display. It gets these requests from (possibly remote) applications. In this sense, the X kernel acts as a server, while the applications play the role of clients. This terminology has been adopted by X, and although strictly speaking is correct, it can easily lead to confusion.

Thin-Client Network Computing

Obviously, applications manipulate a display using the specific display commands as offered by X. These commands are generally sent over the network where they are subsequently executed by the X kernel. By its nature, applications written for X should preferably separate application logic from user-interface commands. Unfortunately, this is often not the case. As reported by Lai and Nieh (2002), it turns out that much of the application logic and user interaction are tightly coupled, meaning that an application will send many requests to the X kernel for which it will expect a response before being able to make a next step. This synchronous behavior may adversely affect performance when operating over a wide-area network with long latencies.

There are several solutions to this problem. One is to re-engineer the implementation of the X protocol, as is done with NX (Pinzari, 2003). An important part of this work concentrates on bandwidth reduction by compressing X messages. First, messages are considered to consist of a fixed part, which is treated as an identifier, and a variable part. In many cases, multiple messages will have the same identifier in which case they will often contain similar data. This property can be used to send only the differences between messages having the same identifier.

Both the sending and receiving side maintain a local cache of which the entries can be looked up using the identifier of a message. When a message is sent, it is first looked up in the local cache. If found, this means that a previous message with the same identifier but possibly different data had been sent. In that case, differential encoding is used to send only the differences between the two. At the receiving side, the message is also looked up in the local cache, after which decoding through the differences can take place. In the cache miss, standard compression techniques are used, which generally already leads to factor four improvement in bandwidth. Overall, this technique has reported bandwidth reductions up to a factor 1000, which allows X to also run through low-bandwidth links of only 9600 kbps.

An important side effect of caching messages is that the sender and receiver have shared information on what the current status of the display is. For example, the application can request geometric information on various objects by simply requesting lookups in the local cache. Having this shared information alone already reduces the number of messages required to keep the application and the display synchronized.

Despite these improvements, X still requires having a display server running. This may be asking a lot, especially if the display is something as simple as a cell phone. One solution to keeping the software at the display very simple is to let all the processing take place at the application side. Effectively, this means that the entire display is controlled up to the pixel level at the application side. Changes in the bitmap are then sent over the network to the display, where they are immediately transferred to the local frame buffer.

This approach requires sophisticated compression techniques in order to prevent bandwidth availability to become a problem. For example, consider displaying a video stream at a rate of 30 frames per second on a 320×240 screen. Such a screen size is common for many PDAs. If each pixel is encoded by 24 bits, then without compression we would need a bandwidth of approximately 53 Mbps. Compression is clearly needed in such a case, and many techniques are currently being deployed. Note, however, that compression requires decompression at the receiver, which, in turn, may be computationally expensive without hardware support. Hardware support can be provided, but this raises the devices cost.

The drawback of sending raw pixel data in comparison to higher-level protocols such as X is that it is impossible to make any use of application semantics, as these are effectively lost at that level. Baratto et al. (2005) propose a different technique. In their solution, referred to as THINC, they provide a few high-level display commands that operate at the level of the video device drivers. These commands are thus device dependent, more powerful than raw pixel operations, but less powerful compared to what a protocol such as X offers. The result is that display servers can be much simpler, which is good for CPU usage, while at the same time application-dependent optimizations can be used to reduce bandwidth and synchronization.

In THINC, display requests from the application are intercepted and translated into the lower level commands. By intercepting application requests, THINC can make use of application semantics to decide what combination of lower level commands can be used best. Translated commands are not immediately sent out to the display, but are instead queued. By batching several commands it is possible to aggregate display commands into a single one, leading to fewer messages. For example, when a new command for drawing in a particular region of the screen effectively overwrites what a previous (and still queued) command would have established, the latter need not be sent out to the display. Finally, instead of letting the display ask for refreshments, THINC always pushes updates as they come available. This push approach saves latency as there is no need for an update request to be sent out by the display.

As it turns out, the approach followed by THINC provides better overall performance, although very much in line with that shown by NX. Details on performance comparison can be found in Baratto et al. (2005).

Compound Documents

Modern user interfaces do a lot more than systems such as X or its simple applications. In particular, many user interfaces allow applications to share a single graphical window, and to use that window to exchange data through user actions. Additional actions that can be performed by the user include what are generally called **drag-and-drop** operations, and **in-place editing**, respectively.

A typical example of drag-and-drop functionality is moving an icon representing a file A to an icon representing a trash can, resulting in the file being deleted. In this case, the user interface will need to do more than just arrange icons on the display: it will have to pass the name of the file A to the application associated with the trash can as soon as A's icon has been moved above that of the trash can application. Other examples easily come to mind.

In-place editing can best be illustrated by means of a document containing text and graphics. Imagine that the document is being displayed within a standard word processor. As soon as the user places the mouse above an image, the user interface passes that information to a drawing program to allow the user to modify the image. For example, the user may have rotated the image, which may effect the placement of the image in the document. The user interface therefore finds out what the new height and width of the image are, and passes this information to the word processor. The latter, in turn, can then automatically update the page layout of the document.

The key idea behind these user interfaces is the notion of a **compound document**, which can be defined as a collection of documents, possibly of very different kinds (like text, images, spreadsheets, etc.), which are seamlessly integrated at the user-interface level. A user interface that can handle compound documents hides the fact that different applications operate on different parts of the document. To the user, all parts are integrated in a seamless way. When changing one part affects other parts, the user interface can take appropriate measures, for example, by notifying the relevant applications.

Analogous to the situation described for the X Window System, the applications associated with a compound document do not have to execute on the client's machine. However, it should be clear that user interfaces that support compound documents may have to do a lot more processing than those that do not.

3.3.2 Client-Side Software for Distribution Transparency

Client software comprises more than just user interfaces. In many cases, parts of the processing and data level in a client-server application are executed on the client side as well. A special class is formed by embedded client software, such as for automatic teller machines (ATMs), cash registers, barcode readers, TV set-top boxes, etc. In these cases, the user interface is a relatively small part of the client software, in contrast to the local processing and communication facilities.

Besides the user interface and other application-related software, client software comprises components for achieving distribution transparency. Ideally, a client should not be aware that it is communicating with remote processes. In contrast, distribution is often less transparent to servers for reasons of performance and correctness. For example, in Chap. 6 we will show that replicated servers sometimes need to communicate in order to establish that operations are performed in a specific order at each replica.

Access transparency is generally handled through the generation of a client stub from an interface definition of what the server has to offer. The stub provides the same interface as available at the server, but hides the possible differences in machine architectures, as well as the actual communication.

There are different ways to handle location, migration, and relocation transparency. Using a convenient naming system is crucial, as we shall also see in the next chapter. In many cases, cooperation with client-side software is also important. For example, when a client is already bound to a server, the client can be directly informed when the server changes location. In this case, the client's middleware can hide the server's current geographical location from the user, and also transparently rebind to the server if necessary. At worst, the client's application may notice a temporary loss of performance.

In a similar way, many distributed systems implement replication transparency by means of client-side solutions. For example, imagine a distributed system with replicated servers, Such replication can be achieved by forwarding a request to each replica, as shown in Fig. 3-10. Client-side software can transparently collect all responses and pass a single response to the client application.

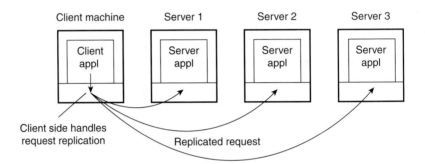

Figure 3-10. Transparent replication of a server using a client-side solution.

Finally, consider failure transparency. Masking communication failures with a server is typically done through client middleware. For example, client middleware can be configured to repeatedly attempt to connect to a server, or perhaps try another server after several attempts. There are even situations in which the client middleware returns data it had cached during a previous session, as is sometimes done by Web browsers that fail to connect to a server.

Concurrency transparency can be handled through special intermediate servers, notably transaction monitors, and requires less support from client software. Likewise, persistence transparency is often completely handled at the server.

3.4 SERVERS

Let us now take a closer look at the organization of servers. In the following pages, we first concentrate on a number of general design issues for servers, to be followed by a discussion of server clusters.

3.4.1 General Design Issues

A server is a process implementing a specific service on behalf of a collection of clients. In essence, each server is organized in the same way: it waits for an incoming request from a client and subsequently ensures that the request is taken care of, after which it waits for the next incoming request.

There are several ways to organize servers. In the case of an **iterative server**, the server itself handles the request and, if necessary, returns a response to the requesting client. A **concurrent server** does not handle the request itself, but passes it to a separate thread or another process, after which it immediately waits for the next incoming request. A multithreaded server is an example of a concurrent server. An alternative implementation of a concurrent server is to fork a new process for each new incoming request. This approach is followed in many UNIX systems. The thread or process that handles the request is responsible for returning a response to the requesting client.

Another issue is where clients contact a server. In all cases, clients send requests to an **end point**, also called a **port**, at the machine where the server is running. Each server listens to a specific end point. How do clients know the end point of a service? One approach is to globally assign end points for well-known services. For example, servers that handle Internet FTP requests always listen to TCP port 21. Likewise, an HTTP server for the World Wide Web will always listen to TCP port 80. These end points have been assigned by the Internet Assigned Numbers Authority (IANA), and are documented in Reynolds and Postel (1994). With assigned end points, the client only needs to find the network address of the machine where the server is running. As we explain in the next chapter, name services can be used for that purpose.

There are many services that do not require a preassigned end point. For example, a time-of-day server may use an end point that is dynamically assigned to it by its local operating system. In that case, a client will first have to look up the end point. One solution is to have a special daemon running on each machine that runs servers. The daemon keeps track of the current end point of each service implemented by a co-located server. The daemon itself listens to a well-known end point. A client will first contact the daemon, request the end point, and then contact the specific server, as shown in Fig. 3-11(a).

It is common to associate an end point with a specific service. However, actually implementing each service by means of a separate server may be a waste of resources. For example, in a typical UNIX system, it is common to have lots of servers running simultaneously, with most of them passively waiting until a client request comes in. Instead of having to keep track of so many passive processes, it is often more efficient to have a single **superserver** listening to each end point associated with a specific service, as shown in Fig. 3-11(b). This is the approach taken, for example, with the *inetd* daemon in UNIX. *Inetd* listens to a number of well-known ports for Internet services. When a request comes in, the daemon forks a process to take further care of the request. That process will exit after it is finished.

Another issue that needs to be taken into account when designing a server is whether and how a server can be interrupted. For example, consider a user who has just decided to upload a huge file to an FTP server. Then, suddenly realizing that it is the wrong file, he wants to interrupt the server to cancel further data

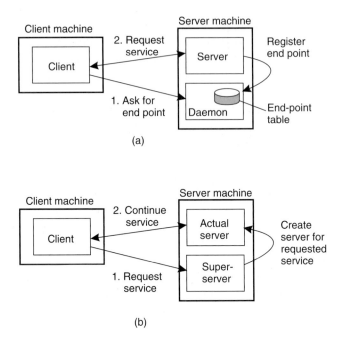

Figure 3-11. (a) Client-to-server binding using a daemon. (b) Client-to-server binding using a superserver.

transmission. There are several ways to do this. One approach that works only too well in the current Internet (and is sometimes the only alternative) is for the user to abruptly exit the client application (which will automatically break the connection to the server), immediately restart it, and pretend nothing happened. The server will eventually tear down the old connection, thinking the client has probably crashed.

A much better approach for handling communication interrupts is to develop the client and server such that it is possible to send **out-of-band** data, which is data that is to be processed by the server before any other data from that client. One solution is to let the server listen to a separate control end point to which the client sends out-of-band data, while at the same time listening (with a lower priority) to the end point through which the normal data passes. Another solution is to send out-of-band data across the same connection through which the client is sending the original request. In TCP, for example, it is possible to transmit urgent data. When urgent data are received at the server, the latter is interrupted (e.g., through a signal in UNIX systems), after which it can inspect the data and handle them accordingly.

A final, important design issue, is whether or not the server is stateless. A **stateless server** does not keep information on the state of its clients, and can change its own state without having to inform any client (Birman, 2005). A Web server, for example, is stateless. It merely responds to incoming HTTP requests, which can be either for uploading a file to the server or (most often) for fetching a file. When the request has been processed, the Web server forgets the client completely. Likewise, the collection of files that a Web server manages (possibly in cooperation with a file server), can be changed without clients having to be informed.

Note that in many stateless designs, the server actually does maintain information on its clients, but crucial is the fact that if this information is lost, it will not lead to a disruption of the service offered by the server. For example, a Web server generally logs all client requests. This information is useful, for example, to decide whether certain documents should be replicated, and where they should be replicated to. Clearly, there is no penalty other than perhaps in the form of suboptimal performance if the log is lost.

A particular form of a stateless design is where the server maintains what is known as **soft state**. In this case, the server promises to maintain state on behalf of the client, but only for a limited time. After that time has expired, the server falls back to default behavior, thereby discarding any information it kept on account of the associated client. An example of this type of state is a server promising to keep a client informed about updates, but only for a limited time. After that, the client is required to poll the server for updates. Soft-state approaches originate from protocol design in computer networks, but can be equally applied to server design (Clark, 1989; and Lui et al., 2004).

In contrast, a **stateful server** generally maintains persistent information on its clients. This means that the information needs to be explicitly deleted by the server. A typical example is a file server that allows a client to keep a local copy of a file, even for performing update operations. Such a server would maintain a table containing *(client, file)* entries. Such a table allows the server to keep track of which client currently has the update permissions on which file, and thus possibly also the most recent version of that file.

This approach can improve the performance of read and write operations as perceived by the client. Performance improvement over stateless servers is often an important benefit of stateful designs. However, the example also illustrates the major drawback of stateful servers. If the server crashes, it has to recover its table of *(client, file)* entries, or otherwise it cannot guarantee that it has processed the most recent updates on a file. In general, a stateful server needs to recover its entire state as it was just before the crash. As we discuss in Chap. 8, enabling recovery can introduce considerable complexity. In a stateless design, no special measures need to be taken at all for a crashed server to recover. It simply starts running again, and waits for client requests to come in.

Ling et al. (2004) argue that one should actually make a distinction between (temporary) **session state** and permanent state. The example above is typical for session state: it is associated with a series of operations by a single user and should be maintained for a some time, but not indefinitely. As it turns out, session state is often maintained in three-tiered client-server architectures, where the application server actually needs to access a database server through a series of queries before being able to respond to the requesting client. The issue here is that no real harm is done if session state is lost, provided that the client can simply re-issue the original request. This observation allows for simpler and less reliable storage of state.

What remains for permanent state is typically information maintained in data-bases, such as customer information, keys associated with purchased software, etc. However, for most distributed systems, maintaining session state already implies a stateful design requiring special measures when failures do happen and making explicit assumptions about the durability of state stored at the server. We will return to these matters extensively when discussing fault tolerance.

When designing a server, the choice for a stateless or stateful design should not affect the services provided by the server. For example, if files have to be opened before they can be read from, or written to, then a stateless server should one way or the other mimic this behavior. A common solution, which we discuss in more detail in Chap. 11, is that the server responds to a read or write request by first opening the referred file, then does the actual read or write operation, and immediately closes the file again.

In other cases, a server may want to keep a record on a client's behavior so that it can more effectively respond to its requests. For example, Web servers sometimes offer the possibility to immediately direct a client to his favorite pages. This approach is possible only if the server has history information on that client. When the server cannot maintain state, a common solution is then to let the client send along additional information on its previous accesses. In the case of the Web, this information is often transparently stored by the client's browser in what is called a **cookie**, which is a small piece of data containing client-specific information that is of interest to the server. Cookies are never executed by a browser; they are merely stored.

The first time a client accesses a server, the latter sends a cookie along with the requested Web pages back to the browser, after which the browser safely tucks the cookie away. Each subsequent time the client accesses the server, its cookie for that server is sent along with the request. Although in principle, this approach works fine, the fact that cookies are sent back for safekeeping by the browser is often hidden entirely from users. So much for privacy. Unlike most of grandma's cookies, these cookies should stay where they are baked.

3.4.2 Server Clusters

In Chap. 1 we briefly discussed cluster computing as one of the many appear-ances of distributed systems. We now take a closer look at the organization of server clusters, along with the salient design issues.

General Organization

Simply put, a server cluster is nothing else but a collection of machines connected through a network, where each machine runs one or more servers. The server clusters that we consider here, are the ones in which the machines are connected through a local-area network, often offering high bandwidth and low latency.

In most cases, a server cluster is logically organized into three tiers, as shown in Fig. 3-12. The first tier consists of a (logical) switch through which client requests are routed. Such a switch can vary widely. For example, transport-layer switches accept incoming TCP connection requests and pass requests on to one of servers in the cluster, as we discuss below. A completely different example is a Web server that accepts incoming HTTP requests, but that partly passes requests to application servers for further processing only to later collect results and return an HTTP response.

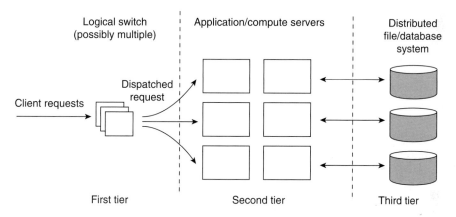

Figure 3-12. The general organization of a three-tiered server cluster.

As in any multitiered client-server architecture, many server clusters also contain servers dedicated to application processing. In cluster computing, these are typically servers running on high-performance hardware dedicated to delivering compute power. However, in the case of enterprise server clusters, it may be the case that applications need only run on relatively low-end machines, as the required compute power is not the bottleneck, but access to storage is.

This brings us the third tier, which consists of data-processing servers, notably file and database servers. Again, depending on the usage of the server cluster, these servers may be running an specialized machines, configured for high-speed disk access and having large server-side data caches.

Of course, not all server clusters will follow this strict separation. It is frequently the case that each machine is equipped with its own local storage, often integrating application and data processing in a single server leading to a two-tiered architecture. For example, when dealing with streaming media by means of a server cluster, it is common to deploy a two-tiered system architecture, where each machine acts as a dedicated media server (Steinmetz and Nahrstedt, 2004).

When a server cluster offers multiple services, it may happen that different machines run different application servers. As a consequence, the switch will have to be able to distinguish services or otherwise it cannot forward requests to the proper machines. As it turns out, many second-tier machines run only a single application. This limitation comes from dependencies on available software and hardware, but also that different applications are often managed by different administrators. The latter do not like to interfere with each other's machines.

As a consequence, we may find that certain machines are temporarily idle, while others are receiving an overload of requests. What would be useful is to temporarily migrate services to idle machines. A solution proposed in Awadallah and Rosenblum (2004), is to use virtual machines allowing a relative easy migration of code to real machines. We will return to code migration later in this chapter.

Let us take a closer look at the first tier, consisting of the switch. An important design goal for server clusters is to hide the fact that there are multiple servers. In other words, client applications running on remote machines should have no need to know anything about the internal organization of the cluster. This access transparency is invariably offered by means of a single access point, in turn implemented through some kind of hardware switch such as a dedicated machine.

The switch forms the entry point for the server cluster, offering a single network address. For scalability and availability, a server cluster may have multiple access points, where each access point is then realized by a separate dedicated machine. We consider only the case of a single access point.

A standard way of accessing a server cluster is to set up a TCP connection over which application-level requests are then sent as part of a session. A session ends by tearing down the connection. In the case of **transport-layer switches**, the switch accepts incoming TCP connection requests, and hands off such connections to one of the servers (Hunt et al, 1997; and Pai et al., 1998). The principle working of what is commonly known as **TCP handoff** is shown in Fig. 3-13.

When the switch receives a TCP connection request, it subsequently identifies the best server for handling that request, and forwards the request packet to that server. The server, in turn, will send an acknowledgment back to the requesting client, but inserting the switch's IP address as the source field of the header of the IP packet carrying the TCP segment. Note that this spoofing is necessary for the client to continue executing the TCP protocol: it is expecting an answer back from the switch, not from some arbitrary server it is has never heard of before. Clearly, a TCP-handoff implementation requires operating-system level modifications.

It can already be seen that the switch can play an important role in distributing the load among the various servers. By deciding where to forward a request to, the

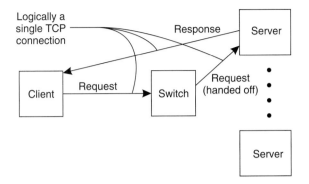

Figure 3-13. The principle of TCP handoff.

switch also decides which server is to handle further processing of the request. The simplest load-balancing policy that the switch can follow is round robin: each time it picks the next server from its list to forward a request to.

More advanced server selection criteria can be deployed as well. For example, assume multiple services are offered by the server cluster. If the switch can distinguish those services when a request comes in, it can then take informed decisions on where to forward the request to. This server selection can still take place at the transport level, provided services are distinguished by means of a port number. One step further is to have the switch actually inspect the payload of the incoming request. This method can be applied only if it is known what that payload can look like. For example, in the case of Web servers, the switch can eventually expect an HTTP request, based on which it can then decide who is to process it. We will return to such **content-aware request distribution** when we discuss Web-based systems in Chap. 12.

Distributed Servers

The server clusters discussed so far are generally rather statically configured. In these clusters, there is often an separate administration machine that keeps track of available servers, and passes this information to other machines as appropriate, such as the switch.

As we mentioned, most server clusters offer a single access point. When that point fails, the cluster becomes unavailable. To eliminate this potential problem, several access points can be provided, of which the addresses are made publicly available. For example, the **Domain Name System (DNS)** can return several addresses, all belonging to the same host name. This approach still requires clients to make several attempts if one of the addresses fails. Moreover, this does not solve the problem of requiring static access points.

Having stability, like a long-living access point, is a desirable feature from a client's and a server's perspective. On the other hand, it also desirable to have a high degree of flexibility in configuring a server cluster, including the switch. This observation has lead to a design of a **distributed server** which effectively is nothing but a possibly dynamically changing set of machines, with also possibly varying access points, but which nevertheless appears to the outside world as a single, powerful machine. The design of such a distributed server is given in Szymaniak et al. (2005). We describe it briefly here.

The basic idea behind a distributed server is that clients benefit from a robust, high-performing, stable server. These properties can often be provided by high-end mainframes, of which some have an acclaimed mean time between failure of more than 40 years. However, by grouping simpler machines transparently into a cluster, and not relying on the availability of a single machine, it may be possible to achieve a better degree of stability than by each component individually. For example, such a cluster could be dynamically configured from end-user machines, as in the case of a collaborative distributed system.

Let us concentrate on how a stable access point can be achieved in such a system. The main idea is to make use of available networking services, notably mobility support for IP version 6 (MIPv6). In MIPv6, a mobile node is assumed to have a **home network** where it normally resides and for which it has an associated stable address, known as its **home address (HoA)**. This home network has a special router attached, known as the **home agent**, which will take care of traffic to the mobile node when it is away. To this end, when a mobile node attaches to a foreign network, it will receive a temporary **care-of address (CoA)** where it can be reached. This care-of address is reported to the node's home agent who will then see to it that all traffic is forwarded to the mobile node. Note that applications communicating with the mobile node will only see the address associated with the node's home network. They will never see the care-of address.

This principle can be used to offer a stable address of a distributed server. In this case, a single unique **contact address** is initially assigned to the server cluster. The contact address will be the server's life-time address to be used in all communication with the outside world. At any time, one node in the distributed server will operate as an access point using that contact address, but this role can easily be taken over by another node. What happens is that the access point records its own address as the care-of address at the home agent associated with the distributed server. At that point, all traffic will be directed to the access point, who will then take care in distributing requests among the currently participating nodes. If the access point fails, a simple fail-over mechanism comes into place by which another access point reports a new care-of address.

This simple configuration would make the home agent as well as the access point a potential bottleneck as all traffic would flow through these two machines. This situation can be avoided by using an MIPv6 feature known as *route optimization*. Route optimization works as follows. Whenever a mobile node with home address *HA* reports its current care-of address, say *CA*, the home agent can forward *CA* to a client. The latter will then locally store the pair *(HA, CA)*. From that moment on, communication will be directly forwarded to *CA*. Although the application at the client side can still use the home address, the underlying support software for MIPv6 will translate that address to *CA* and use that instead.

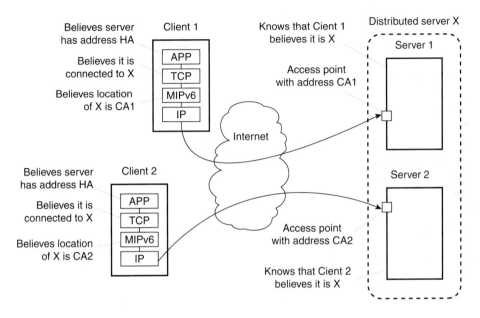

Figure 3-14. Route optimization in a distributed server.

Route optimization can be used to make different clients believe they are communicating with a single server, where, in fact, each client is communicating with a different member node of the distributed server, as shown in Fig. 3-14. To this end, when an access point of a distributed server forwards a request from client C_1 to, say node S_1 (with address CA_1), it passes enough information to S_1 to let it initiate the route optimization procedure by which eventually the client is made to believe that the care-of address is CA_1. This will allow C_1 to store the pair *(HA, CA_1)*. During this procedure, the access point (as well as the home agent) tunnel most of the traffic between C_1 and S_1. This will prevent the home agent from believing that the care-of address has changed, so that it will continue to communicate with the access point.

Of course, while this route optimization procedure is taking place, requests from other clients may still come in. These remain in a pending state at the access point until they can be forwarded. The request from another client C_2 may then be forwarded to member node S_2 (with address CA_2), allowing the latter to let client

C_2 store the pair *(HA, CA$_2$)*. As a result, different clients will be directly communicating with different members of the distributed server, where each client application still has the illusion that this server has address *HA*. The home agent continues to communicate with the access point talking to the contact address.

3.4.3 Managing Server Clusters

A server cluster should appear to the outside world as a single computer, as is indeed often the case. However, when it comes to managing a cluster, the situation changes dramatically. Several attempts have been made to ease the management of server clusters as we discuss next.

Common Approaches

By far the most common approach to managing a server cluster is to extend the traditional managing functions of a single computer to that of a cluster. In its most primitive form, this means that an administrator can log into a node from a remote client and execute local managing commands to monitor, install, and change components.

Somewhat more advanced is to hide the fact that you need to login into a node and instead provide an interface at an administration machine that allows to collect information from one or more servers, upgrade components, add and remove nodes, etc. The main advantage of the latter approach is that collective operations, which operate on a group of servers, can be more easily provided. This type of managing server clusters is widely applied in practice, exemplified by management software such as Cluster Systems Management from IBM (Hochstetler and Beringer, 2004).

However, as soon as clusters grow beyond several tens of nodes, this type of management is not the way to go. Many data centers need to manage thousands of servers, organized into many clusters but all operating collaboratively. Doing this by means of centralized administration servers is simply out of the question. Moreover, it can be easily seen that very large clusters need continuous repair management (including upgrades). To simplify matters, if p is the probability that a server is currently faulty, and we assume that faults are independent, then for a cluster of N servers to operate without a single server being faulty is $(1-p)^N$. With $p=0.001$ and $N=1000$, there is only a 36 percent chance that all the servers are correctly functioning.

As it turns out, support for very large server clusters is almost always ad hoc. There are various rules of thumb that should be considered (Brewer, 2001), but there is no systematic approach to dealing with massive systems management. Cluster management is still very much in its infancy, although it can be expected that the self-managing solutions as discussed in the previous chapter will eventually find their way in this area, after more experience with them has been gained.

Example: PlanetLab

Let us now take a closer look at a somewhat unusual cluster server. PlanetLab is a collaborative distributed system in which different organizations each donate one or more computers, adding up to a total of hundreds of nodes. Together, these computers form a 1-tier server cluster, where access, processing, and storage can all take place on each node individually. Management of PlanetLab is by necessity almost entirely distributed. Before we explain its basic principles, let us first describe the main architectural features (Peterson et al., 2005).

In PlanetLab, an organization donates one or more nodes, where each node is easiest thought of as just a single computer, although it could also be itself a cluster of machines. Each node is organized as shown in Fig. 3-15. There are two important components (Bavier et al., 2004). The first one is the virtual machine monitor (VMM), which is an enhanced Linux operating system. The enhancements mainly comprise adjustments for supporting the second component, namely **vservers**. A (Linux) vserver can best be thought of as a separate environment in which a group of processes run. Processes from different vservers are *completely* independent. They cannot directly share any resources such as files, main memory, and network connections as is normally the case with processes running on top of an operating systems. Instead, a vserver provides an environment consisting of its own collection of software packages, programs, and networking facilities. For example, a vserver may provide an environment in which a process will notice that it can make use of Python 1.5.2 in combination with an older Apache Web server, say *httpd 1.3.1*. In contrast, another vserver may support the latest versions of Python and *httpd*. In this sense, calling a vserver a "server" is a bit of a misnomer as it really only isolates groups of processes from each other. We return to vservers briefly below.

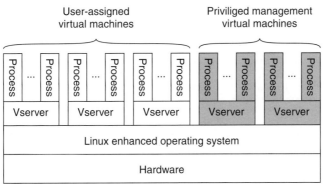

Figure 3-15. The basic organization of a PlanetLab node.

The Linux VMM ensures that vservers are separated: processes in different vservers are executed concurrently and independently, each making use only of the software packages and programs available in their own environment. The isolation between processes in different vservers is strict. For example, two processes in different vservers may have the same user ID, but this does not imply that they stem from the same user. This separation considerably eases supporting users from different organizations that want to use PlanetLab as, for example, a testbed to experiment with completely different distributed systems and applications.

To support such experimentations, PlanetLab introduces the notion of a **slice**, which is a set of vservers, each vserver running on a different node. A slice can thus be thought of as a virtual server cluster, implemented by means of a collection of virtual machines. The virtual machines in PlanetLab run on top of the Linux operating system, which has been extended with a number of kernel modules

There are several issues that make management of PlanetLab a special problem. Three salient ones are:

1. Nodes belong to different organizations. Each organization should be allowed to specify who is allowed to run applications on their nodes, and restrict resource usage appropriately.

2. There are various monitoring tools available, but they all assume a very specific combination of hardware and software. Moreover, they are all tailored to be used within a single organization.

3. Programs from different slices but running on the same node should not interfere with each other. This problem is similar to process independence in operating systems.

Let us take a look at each of these issues in more detail.

Central to managing PlanetLab resources is the **node manager**. Each node has such a manager, implemented by means of a separate vserver, whose only task is to create other vservers on the node it manages and to control resource allocation. The node manager does not make any policy decisions; it is merely a mechanism to provide the essential ingredients to get a program running on a given node.

Keeping track of resources is done by means of a resource specification, or *rspec* for short. An *rspec* specifies a time interval during which certain resources have been allocated. Resources include disk space, file descriptors, inbound and outbound network bandwidth, transport-level end points, main memory, and CPU usage. An *rspec* is identified through a globally unique 128-bit identifier known as a resource capability (*rcap*). Given an *rcap*, the node manager can look up the associated *rspec* in a local table.

Resources are bound to slices. In other words, in order to make use of resources, it is necessary to create a slice. Each slice is associated with a **service provider**, which can best be seen as an entity having an account on PlanetLab.

Every slice can then be identified by a (*principal_id*, *slice_tag*) pair, where the *principal_id* identifies the provider and *slice_tag* is an identifier chosen by the provider.

To create a new slice, each node will run a **slice creation service (SCS)**, which, in turn, can contact the node manager requesting it to create a vserver and to allocate resources. The node manager itself cannot be contacted directly over a network, allowing it to concentrate only on local resource management. In turn, the SCS will not accept slice-creation requests from just anybody. Only specific **slice authorities** are eligible for requesting the creation of a slice. Each slice authority will have access rights to a collection of nodes. The simplest model is that there is only a single slice authority that is allowed to request slice creation on all nodes.

To complete the picture, a service provider will contact a slice authority and request it to create a slice across a collection of nodes. The service provider will be known to the slice authority, for example, because it has been previously authenticated and subsequently registered as a PlanetLab user. In practice, Planet-Lab users contact a slice authority by means of a Web-based service. Further details can be found in Chun and Spalink (2003).

What this procedure reveals is that managing PlanetLab is done through intermediaries. One important class of such intermediaries is formed by slice authorities. Such authorities have obtained credentials at nodes to create slides. Obtaining these credentials has been achieved out-of-band, essentially by contacting system administrators at various sites. Obviously, this is a time-consuming process which not be carried out by end users (or, in PlanetLab terminology, service providers).

Besides slice authorities, there are also management authorities. Where a slice authority concentrates only on managing slices, a management authority is responsible for keeping an eye on nodes. In particular, it ensures that the nodes under its regime run the basic PlanetLab software and abide to the rules set out by PlanetLab. Service providers trust that a management authority provides nodes that will behave properly.

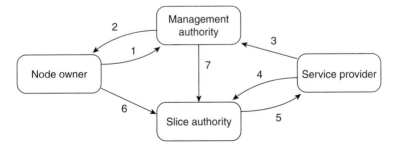

Figure 3-16. The management relationships between various PlanetLab entities.

This organization leads to the management structure shown in Fig. 3-16, described in terms of trust relationships in Peterson et al. (2005). The relations are as follows:

1. A node owner puts its node under the regime of a management authority, possibly restricting usage where appropriate.

2. A management authority provides the necessary software to add a node to PlanetLab.

3. A service provider registers itself with a management authority, trusting it to provide well-behaving nodes.

4. A service provider contacts a slice authority to create a slice on a collection of nodes.

5. The slice authority needs to authenticate the service provider.

6. A node owner provides a slice creation service for a slice authority to create slices. It essentially delegates resource management to the slice authority.

7. A management authority delegates the creation of slices to a slice authority.

These relationships cover the problem of delegating nodes in a controlled way such that a node owner can rely on a decent and secure management. The second issue that needs to be handled is monitoring. What is needed is a unified approach to allow users to see how well their programs are behaving within a specific slice.

PlanetLab follows a simple approach. Every node is equipped with a collection of sensors, each sensor being capable of reporting information such as CPU usage, disk activity, and so on. Sensors can be arbitrarily complex, but the important issue is that they always report information on a per-node basis. This information is made available by means of a Web server: every sensor is accessible through simple HTTP requests (Bavier et al., 2004).

Admittedly, this approach to monitoring is still rather primitive, but it should be seen as a basis for advanced monitoring schemes. For example, there is, in principle, no reason why Astrolabe, which we discussed in Chap. 2, cannot be used for aggregated sensor readings across multiple nodes.

Finally, to come to our third management issue, namely the protection of programs against each other, PlanetLab uses Linux virtual servers (called vservers) to isolate slices. As mentioned, the main idea of a vserver is to run applications in there own environment, which includes all files that are normally shared across a single machine. Such a separation can be achieved relatively easy by means of the UNIX chroot command, which effectively changes the root of the file system from where applications will look for files. Only the superuser can execute chroot.

Of course, more is needed. Linux virtual servers not only separate the file system, but also normally shared information on processes, network addresses, memory usage, and so on. As a consequence, a physical machine is actually partitioned into multiple units, each unit corresponding to a full-fledged Linux environment, isolated from the other parts. An overview of Linux virtual servers can be found in Potzl et al. (2005).

3.5 CODE MIGRATION

So far, we have been mainly concerned with distributed systems in which communication is limited to passing data. However, there are situations in which passing programs, sometimes even while they are being executed, simplifies the design of a distributed system. In this section, we take a detailed look at what code migration actually is. We start by considering different approaches to code migration, followed by a discussion on how to deal with the local resources that a migrating program uses. A particularly hard problem is migrating code in heterogeneous systems, which is also discussed.

3.5.1 Approaches to Code Migration

Before taking a look at the different forms of code migration, let us first consider why it may be useful to migrate code.

Reasons for Migrating Code

Traditionally, code migration in distributed systems took place in the form of **process migration** in which an entire process was moved from one machine to another (Milojicic et al., 2000). Moving a running process to a different machine is a costly and intricate task, and there had better be a good reason for doing so. That reason has always been performance. The basic idea is that overall system performance can be improved if processes are moved from heavily-loaded to lightly-loaded machines. Load is often expressed in terms of the CPU queue length or CPU utilization, but other performance indicators are used as well.

Load distribution algorithms by which decisions are made concerning the allocation and redistribution of tasks with respect to a set of processors, play an important role in compute-intensive systems. However, in many modern distributed systems, optimizing computing capacity is less an issue than, for example, trying to minimize communication. Moreover, due to the heterogeneity of the underlying platforms and computer networks, performance improvement through code migration is often based on qualitative reasoning instead of mathematical models.

Consider, as an example, a client-server system in which the server manages a huge database. If a client application needs to perform many database operations involving large quantities of data, it may be better to ship part of the client application to the server and send only the results across the network. Otherwise, the network may be swamped with the transfer of data from the server to the client. In this case, code migration is based on the assumption that it generally makes sense to process data close to where those data reside.

This same reason can be used for migrating parts of the server to the client. For example, in many interactive database applications, clients need to fill in forms that are subsequently translated into a series of database operations. Processing the form at the client side, and sending only the completed form to the server, can sometimes avoid that a relatively large number of small messages need to cross the network. The result is that the client perceives better performance, while at the same time the server spends less time on form processing and communication.

Support for code migration can also help improve performance by exploiting parallelism, but without the usual intricacies related to parallel programming. A typical example is searching for information in the Web. It is relatively simple to implement a search query in the form of a small mobile program, called a **mobile agent**, that moves from site to site. By making several copies of such a program, and sending each off to different sites, we may be able to achieve a linear speed-up compared to using just a single program instance.

Besides improving performance, there are other reasons for supporting code migration as well. The most important one is that of flexibility. The traditional approach to building distributed applications is to partition the application into different parts, and decide in advance where each part should be executed. This approach, for example, has led to the different multitiered client-server applications discussed in Chap. 2.

However, if code can move between different machines, it becomes possible to dynamically configure distributed systems. For example, suppose a server implements a standardized interface to a file system. To allow remote clients to access the file system, the server makes use of a proprietary protocol. Normally, the client-side implementation of the file system interface, which is based on that protocol, would need to be linked with the client application. This approach requires that the software be readily available to the client at the time the client application is being developed.

An alternative is to let the server provide the client's implementation no sooner than is strictly necessary, that is, when the client binds to the server. At that point, the client dynamically downloads the implementation, goes through the necessary initialization steps, and subsequently invokes the server. This principle is shown in Fig. 3-17. This model of dynamically moving code from a remote site does require that the protocol for downloading and initializing code is standardized. Also, it is necessary that the downloaded code can be executed on the client's machine. Different solutions are discussed below and in later chapters.

The important advantage of this model of dynamically downloading client-side software is that clients need not have all the software preinstalled to talk to

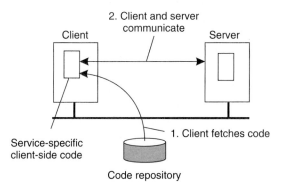

Figure 3-17. The principle of dynamically configuring a client to communicate to a server. The client first fetches the necessary software, and then invokes the server.

servers. Instead, the software can be moved in as necessary, and likewise, discarded when no longer needed. Another advantage is that as long as interfaces are standardized, we can change the client-server protocol and its implementation as often as we like. Changes will not affect existing client applications that rely on the server. There are, of course, also disadvantages. The most serious one, which we discuss in Chap. 9, has to do with security. Blindly trusting that the downloaded code implements only the advertised interface while accessing your unprotected hard disk and does not send the juiciest parts to heaven-knows-who may not always be such a good idea.

Models for Code Migration

Although code migration suggests that we move only code between machines, the term actually covers a much richer area. Traditionally, communication in distributed systems is concerned with exchanging data between processes. Code migration in the broadest sense deals with moving programs between machines, with the intention to have those programs be executed at the target. In some cases, as in process migration, the execution status of a program, pending signals, and other parts of the environment must be moved as well.

To get a better understanding of the different models for code migration, we use a framework described in Fuggetta et al. (1998). In this framework, a process consists of three segments. The *code segment* is the part that contains the set of instructions that make up the program that is being executed. The *resource segment* contains references to external resources needed by the process, such as files, printers, devices, other processes, and so on. Finally, an *execution segment* is used to store the current execution state of a process, consisting of private data, the stack, and, of course, the program counter.

The bare minimum for code migration is to provide only **weak mobility**. In this model, it is possible to transfer only the code segment, along with perhaps some initialization data. A characteristic feature of weak mobility is that a transferred program is always started from one of several predefined starting positions. This is what happens, for example, with Java applets, which always start execution from the beginning. The benefit of this approach is its simplicity. Weak mobility requires only that the target machine can execute that code, which essentially boils down to making the code portable. We return to these matters when discussing migration in heterogeneous systems.

In contrast to weak mobility, in systems that support **strong mobility** the execution segment can be transferred as well. The characteristic feature of strong mobility is that a running process can be stopped, subsequently moved to another machine, and then resume execution where it left off. Clearly, strong mobility is much more general than weak mobility, but also much harder to implement.

Irrespective of whether mobility is weak or strong, a further distinction can be made between sender-initiated and receiver-initiated migration. In **sender-initiated** migration, migration is initiated at the machine where the code currently resides or is being executed. Typically, sender-initiated migration is done when uploading programs to a compute server. Another example is sending a search program across the Internet to a Web database server to perform the queries at that server. In **receiver-initiated** migration, the initiative for code migration is taken by the target machine. Java applets are an example of this approach.

Receiver-initiated migration is simpler than sender-initiated migration. In many cases, code migration occurs between a client and a server, where the client takes the initiative for migration. Securely uploading code to a server, as is done in sender-initiated migration, often requires that the client has previously been registered and authenticated at that server. In other words, the server is required to know all its clients, the reason being is that the client will presumably want access to the server's resources such as its disk. Protecting such resources is essential. In contrast, downloading code as in the receiver-initiated case, can often be done anonymously. Moreover, the server is generally not interested in the client's resources. Instead, code migration to the client is done only for improving client-side performance. To that end, only a limited number of resources need to be protected, such as memory and network connections. We return to secure code migration extensively in Chap. 9.

In the case of weak mobility, it also makes a difference if the migrated code is executed by the target process, or whether a separate process is started. For example, Java applets are simply downloaded by a Web browser and are executed in the browser's address space. The benefit of this approach is that there is no need to start a separate process, thereby avoiding communication at the target machine. The main drawback is that the target process needs to be protected against malicious or inadvertent code executions. A simple solution is to let the operating system take care of that by creating a separate process to execute the migrated code.

Note that this solution does not solve the resource-access problems mentioned above. They still have to be dealt with.

Instead of moving a running process, also referred to as process migration, strong mobility can also be supported by remote cloning. In contrast to process migration, cloning yields an exact copy of the original process, but now running on a different machine. The cloned process is executed in parallel to the original process. In UNIX systems, remote cloning takes place by forking off a child process and letting that child continue on a remote machine. The benefit of cloning is that the model closely resembles the one that is already used in many applications. The only difference is that the cloned process is executed on a different machine. In this sense, migration by cloning is a simple way to improve distribution transparency.

The various alternatives for code migration are summarized in Fig. 3-18.

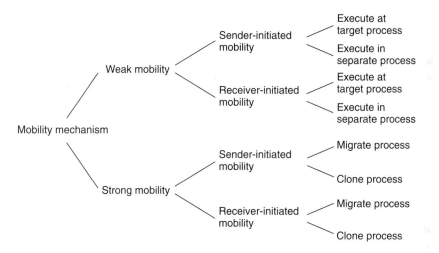

Figure 3-18. Alternatives for code migration.

3.5.2 Migration and Local Resources

So far, only the migration of the code and execution segment has been taken into account. The resource segment requires some special attention. What often makes code migration so difficult is that the resource segment cannot always be simply transferred along with the other segments without being changed. For example, suppose a process holds a reference to a specific TCP port through which it was communicating with other (remote) processes. Such a reference is held in its resource segment. When the process moves to another location, it will have to give up the port and request a new one at the destination. In other cases, transferring a reference need not be a problem. For example, a reference to a file by means of an absolute URL will remain valid irrespective of the machine where the process that holds the URL resides.

To understand the implications that code migration has on the resource segment, Fuggetta et al. (1998) distinguish three types of process-to-resource bindings. The strongest binding is when a process refers to a resource by its identifier. In that case, the process requires precisely the referenced resource, and nothing else. An example of such a **binding by identifier** is when a process uses a URL to refer to a specific Web site or when it refers to an FTP server by means of that server's Internet address. In the same line of reasoning, references to local communication end points also lead to a binding by identifier.

A weaker form of process-to-resource binding is when only the value of a resource is needed. In that case, the execution of the process would not be affected if another resource would provide that same value. A typical example of **binding by value** is when a program relies on standard libraries, such as those for programming in C or Java. Such libraries should always be locally available, but their exact location in the local file system may differ between sites. Not the specific files, but their content is important for the proper execution of the process.

Finally, the weakest form of binding is when a process indicates it needs only a resource of a specific type. This **binding by type** is exemplified by references to local devices, such as monitors, printers, and so on.

When migrating code, we often need to change the references to resources, but cannot affect the kind of process-to-resource binding. If, and exactly how a reference should be changed, depends on whether that resource can be moved along with the code to the target machine. More specifically, we need to consider the resource-to-machine bindings, and distinguish the following cases. **Unattached resources** can be easily moved between different machines, and are typically (data) files associated only with the program that is to be migrated. In contrast, moving or copying a **fastened resource** may be possible, but only at relatively high costs. Typical examples of fastened resources are local databases and complete Web sites. Although such resources are, in theory, not dependent on their current machine, it is often infeasible to move them to another environment. Finally, **fixed resources** are intimately bound to a specific machine or environment and cannot be moved. Fixed resources are often local devices. Another example of a fixed resource is a local communication end point.

Combining three types of process-to-resource bindings, and three types of resource-to-machine bindings, leads to nine combinations that we need to consider when migrating code. These nine combinations are shown in Fig. 3-19.

Let us first consider the possibilities when a process is bound to a resource by identifier. When the resource is unattached, it is generally best to move it along with the migrating code. However, when the resource is shared by other processes, an alternative is to establish a global reference, that is, a reference that can cross machine boundaries. An example of such a reference is a URL. When the resource is fastened or fixed, the best solution is also to create a global reference.

		Resource-to-machine binding		
		Unattached	Fastened	Fixed
Process-	By identifier	MV (or GR)	GR (or MV)	GR
to-resource	By value	CP (or MV,GR)	GR (or CP)	GR
binding	By type	RB (or MV,CP)	RB (or GR,CP)	RB (or GR)

GR	Establish a global systemwide reference
MV	Move the resource
CP	Copy the value of the resource
RB	Rebind process to locally-available resource

Figure 3-19. Actions to be taken with respect to the references to local resources when migrating code to another machine.

It is important to realize that establishing a global reference may be more than just making use of URLs, and that the use of such a reference is sometimes prohibitively expensive. Consider, for example, a program that generates high-quality images for a dedicated multimedia workstation. Fabricating high-quality images in real time is a compute-intensive task, for which reason the program may be moved to a high-performance compute server. Establishing a global reference to the multimedia workstation means setting up a communication path between the compute server and the workstation. In addition, there is significant processing involved at both the server and the workstation to meet the bandwidth requirements of transferring the images. The net result may be that moving the program to the compute server is not such a good idea, only because the cost of the global reference is too high.

Another example of where establishing a global reference is not always that easy is when migrating a process that is making use of a local communication end point. In that case, we are dealing with a fixed resource to which the process is bound by the identifier. There are basically two solutions. One solution is to let the process set up a connection to the source machine after it has migrated and install a separate process at the source machine that simply forwards all incoming messages. The main drawback of this approach is that whenever the source machine malfunctions, communication with the migrated process may fail. The alternative solution is to have all processes that communicated with the migrating process, change *their* global reference, and send messages to the new communication end point at the target machine.

The situation is different when dealing with bindings by value. Consider first a fixed resource. The combination of a fixed resource and binding by value occurs, for example, when a process assumes that memory can be shared between processes. Establishing a global reference in this case would mean that we need to implement a distributed form of shared memory. In many cases, this is not really a viable or efficient solution.

Fastened resources that are referred to by their value, are typically runtime libraries. Normally, copies of such resources are readily available on the target machine, or should otherwise be copied before code migration takes place. Establishing a global reference is a better alternative when huge amounts of data are to be copied, as may be the case with dictionaries and thesauruses in text processing systems.

The easiest case is when dealing with unattached resources. The best solution is to copy (or move) the resource to the new destination, unless it is shared by a number of processes. In the latter case, establishing a global reference is the only option.

The last case deals with bindings by type. Irrespective of the resource-to-machine binding, the obvious solution is to rebind the process to a locally available resource of the same type. Only when such a resource is not available, will we need to copy or move the original one to the new destination, or establish a global reference.

3.5.3 Migration in Heterogeneous Systems

So far, we have tacitly assumed that the migrated code can be easily executed at the target machine. This assumption is in order when dealing with homogeneous systems. In general, however, distributed systems are constructed on a heterogeneous collection of platforms, each having their own operating system and machine architecture. Migration in such systems requires that each platform is supported, that is, that the code segment can be executed on each platform. Also, we need to ensure that the execution segment can be properly represented at each platform.

The problems coming from heterogeneity are in many respects the same as those of portability. Not surprisingly, solutions are also very similar. For example, at the end of the 1970s, a simple solution to alleviate many of the problems of porting Pascal to different machines was to generate machine-independent intermediate code for an abstract virtual machine (Barron, 1981). That machine, of course, would need to be implemented on many platforms, but it would then allow Pascal programs to be run anywhere. Although this simple idea was widely used for some years, it never really caught on as the general solution to portability problems for other languages, notably C.

About 25 years later, code migration in heterogeneous systems is being attacked by scripting languages and highly portable languages such as Java. In essence, these solutions adopt the same approach as was done for porting Pascal. All such solutions have in common that they rely on a (process) virtual machine that either directly interprets source code (as in the case of scripting languages), or otherwise interprets intermediate code generated by a compiler (as in Java). Being in the right place at the right time is also important for language developers.

Recent developments have started to weaken the dependency on programming languages. In particular, solutions have been proposed not only to migrate processes, but to migrate entire computing environments. The basic idea is to compartmentalize the overall environment and to provide processes in the same part their own view on their computing environment.

If the compartmentalization is done properly, it becomes possible to decouple a part from the underlying system and actually migrate it to another machine. In this way, migration would actually provide a form of strong mobility for processes, as they can then be moved at any point during their execution, and continue where they left off when migration completes. Moreover, many of the intricacies related to migrating processes while they have bindings to local resources may be solved, as these bindings are in many cases simply preserved. The local resources, namely, are often part of the environment that is being migrated.

There are several reasons for wanting to migrate entire environments, but perhaps the most important one is that it allows continuation of operation while a machine needs to be shutdown. For example, in a server cluster, the systems administrator may decide to shut down or replace a machine, but will not have to stop all its running processes. Instead, it can temporarily freeze an environment, move it to another machine (where it sits next to other, existing environments), and simply unfreeze it again. Clearly, this is an extremely powerful way to manage long-running compute environments and their processes.

Let us consider one specific example of migrating virtual machines, as discussed in Clark et al. (2005). In this case, the authors concentrated on real-time migration of a virtualized operating system, typically something that would be convenient in a cluster of servers where a tight coupling is achieved through a single, shared local-area network. Under these circumstances, migration involves two major problems: migrating the entire memory image and migrating bindings to local resources.

As to the first problem, there are, in principle, three ways to handle migration (which can be combined):

1. Pushing memory pages to the new machine and resending the ones that are later modified during the migration process.

2. Stopping the current virtual machine; migrate memory, and start the new virtual machine.

3. Letting the new virtual machine pull in new pages as needed, that is, let processes start on the new virtual machine immediately and copy memory pages on demand.

The second option may lead to unacceptable downtime if the migrating virtual machine is running a live service, that is, one that offers continuous service. On the other hand, a pure on-demand approach as represented by the third option may extensively prolong the migration period, but may also lead to poor performance because it takes a long time before the working set of the migrated processes has been moved to the new machine.

As an alternative, Clark et al. (2005) propose to use a pre-copy approach which combines the first option, along with a brief stop-and-copy phase as represented by the second option. As it turns out, this combination can lead to service downtimes of 200 ms or less.

Concerning local resources, matters are simplified when dealing only with a cluster server. First, because there is a single network, the only thing that needs to be done is to announce the new network-to-MAC address binding, so that clients can contact the migrated processes at the correct network interface. Finally, if it can be assumed that storage is provided as a separate tier (like we showed in Fig. 3-12), then migrating binding to files is similarly simple.

The overall effect is that, instead of migrating processes, we now actually see that an entire operating system can be moved between machines.

3.6 SUMMARY

Processes play a fundamental role in distributed systems as they form a basis for communication between different machines. An important issue is how processes are internally organized and, in particular, whether or not they support multiple threads of control. Threads in distributed systems are particularly useful to continue using the CPU when a blocking I/O operation is performed. In this way, it becomes possible to build highly-efficient servers that run multiple threads in parallel, of which several may be blocking to wait until disk I/O or network communication completes.

Organizing a distributed application in terms of clients and servers has proven to be useful. Client processes generally implement user interfaces, which may range from very simple displays to advanced interfaces that can handle compound documents. Client software is furthermore aimed at achieving distribution transparency by hiding details concerning the communication with servers, where those servers are currently located, and whether or not servers are replicated. In addition, client software is partly responsible for hiding failures and recovery from failures.

Servers are often more intricate than clients, but are nevertheless subject to only a relatively few design issues. For example, servers can either be iterative or concurrent, implement one or more services, and can be stateless or stateful. Other design issues deal with addressing services and mechanisms to interrupt a server after a service request has been issued and is possibly already being processed.

Special attention needs to be paid when organizing servers into a cluster. A common objective is hide the internals of a cluster from the outside world. This means that the organization of the cluster should be shielded from applications. To this end, most clusters use a single entry point that can hand off messages to servers in the cluster. A challenging problem is to transparently replace this single entry point by a fully distributed solution.

An important topic for distributed systems is the migration of code between different machines. Two important reasons to support code migration are increasing performance and flexibility. When communication is expensive, we can sometimes reduce communication by shipping computations from the server to the client, and let the client do as much local processing as possible. Flexibility is increased if a client can dynamically download software needed to communicate with a specific server. The downloaded software can be specifically targeted to that server, without forcing the client to have it preinstalled.

Code migration brings along problems related to usage of local resources for which it is required that either resources are migrated as well, new bindings to local resources at the target machine are established, or for which systemwide network references are used. Another problem is that code migration requires that we take heterogeneity into account. Current practice indicates that the best solution to handle heterogeneity is to use virtual machines. These can take either the form of process virtual machines as in the case of, for example, Java, or through using virtual machine monitors that effectively allow the migration of a collection of processes along with their underlying operating system.

PROBLEMS

1. In this problem you are to compare reading a file using a single-threaded file server and a multithreaded server. It takes 15 msec to get a request for work, dispatch it, and do the rest of the necessary processing, assuming that the data needed are in a cache in main memory. If a disk operation is needed, as is the case one-third of the time, an additional 75 msec is required, during which time the thread sleeps. How many requests/sec can the server handle if it is single threaded? If it is multithreaded?

2. Would it make sense to limit the number of threads in a server process?

3. In the text, we described a multithreaded file server, showing why it is better than a single-threaded server and a finite-state machine server. Are there any circumstances in which a single-threaded server might be better? Give an example.

4. Statically associating only a single thread with a lightweight process is not such a good idea. Why not?

5. Having only a single lightweight process per process is also not such a good idea. Why not?

6. Describe a simple scheme in which there are as many lightweight processes as there are runnable threads.

7. X designates a user's terminal as hosting the server, while the application is referred to as the client. Does this make sense?

8. The X protocol suffers from scalability problems. How can these problems be tackled?

9. Proxies can support replication transparency by invoking each replica, as explained in the text. Can (the server side of) an application be subject to a replicated calls?

10. Constructing a concurrent server by spawning a process has some advantages and disadvantages compared to multithreaded servers. Mention a few.

11. Sketch the design of a multithreaded server that supports multiple protocols using sockets as its transport-level interface to the underlying operating system.

12. How can we prevent an application from circumventing a window manager, and thus being able to completely mess up a screen?

13. Is a server that maintains a TCP/IP connection to a client stateful or stateless?

14. Imagine a Web server that maintains a table in which client IP addresses are mapped to the most recently accessed Web pages. When a client connects to the server, the server looks up the client in its table, and if found, returns the registered page. Is this server stateful or stateless?

15. Strong mobility in UNIX systems could be supported by allowing a process to fork a child on a remote machine. Explain how this would work.

16. In Fig. 3-18 it is suggested that strong mobility cannot be combined with executing migrated code in a target process. Give a counterexample.

17. Consider a process P that requires access to file F which is locally available on the machine where P is currently running. When P moves to another machine, it still requires access to F. If the file-to-machine binding is fixed, how could the systemwide reference to F be implemented?

18. Describe in detail how TCP packets flow in the case of TCP handoff, along with the information on source and destination addresses in the various headers.

4

COMMUNICATION

Interprocess communication is at the heart of all distributed systems. It makes no sense to study distributed systems without carefully examining the ways that processes on different machines can exchange information. Communication in distributed systems is always based on low-level message passing as offered by the underlying network. Expressing communication through message passing is harder than using primitives based on shared memory, as available for nondistributed platforms. Modern distributed systems often consist of thousands or even millions of processes scattered across a network with unreliable communication such as the Internet. Unless the primitive communication facilities of computer networks are replaced by something else, development of large-scale distributed applications is extremely difficult.

In this chapter, we start by discussing the rules that communicating processes must adhere to, known as protocols, and concentrate on structuring those protocols in the form of layers. We then look at three widely-used models for communication: Remote Procedure Call (RPC), Message-Oriented Middleware (MOM), and data streaming. We also discuss the general problem of sending data to multiple receivers, called multicasting.

Our first model for communication in distributed systems is the remote procedure call (RPC). An RPC aims at hiding most of the intricacies of message passing, and is ideal for client-server applications.

In many distributed applications, communication does not follow the rather strict pattern of client-server interaction. In those cases, it turns out that thinking in terms of messages is more appropriate. However, the low-level communication facilities of computer networks are in many ways not suitable due to their lack of distribution transparency. An alternative is to use a high-level message-queuing model, in which communication proceeds much the same as in electronic mail systems. Message-oriented middleware (MOM) is a subject important enough to warrant a section of its own.

With the advent of multimedia distributed systems, it became apparent that many systems were lacking support for communication of continuous media, such as audio and video. What is needed is the notion of a stream that can support the continuous flow of messages, subject to various timing constraints. Streams are discussed in a separate section.

Finally, since our understanding of setting up multicast facilities has improved, novel and elegant solutions for data dissemination have emerged. We pay separate attention to this subject in the last section of this chapter.

4.1 FUNDAMENTALS

Before we start our discussion on communication in distributed systems, we first recapitulate some of the fundamental issues related to communication. In the next section we briefly discuss network communication protocols, as these form the basis for any distributed system. After that, we take a different approach by classifying the different types of communication that occurs in distributed systems.

4.1.1 Layered Protocols

Due to the absence of shared memory, all communication in distributed systems is based on sending and receiving (low level) messages. When process A wants to communicate with process B, it first builds a message in its own address space. Then it executes a system call that causes the operating system to send the message over the network to B. Although this basic idea sounds simple enough, in order to prevent chaos, A and B have to agree on the meaning of the bits being sent. If A sends a brilliant new novel written in French and encoded in IBM's EBCDIC character code, and B expects the inventory of a supermarket written in English and encoded in ASCII, communication will be less than optimal.

Many different agreements are needed. How many volts should be used to signal a 0-bit, and how many volts for a 1-bit? How does the receiver know which is the last bit of the message? How can it detect if a message has been damaged or lost, and what should it do if it finds out? How long are numbers, strings, and other data items, and how are they represented? In short, agreements are needed at a variety of levels, varying from the low-level details of bit transmission to the high-level details of how information is to be expressed.

To make it easier to deal with the numerous levels and issues involved in communication, the International Standards Organization (ISO) developed a reference model that clearly identifies the various levels involved, gives them standard names, and points out which level should do which job. This model is called the **Open Systems Interconnection Reference Model** (Day and Zimmerman, 1983), usually abbreviated as **ISO OSI** or sometimes just the **OSI model**. It should be emphasized that the protocols that were developed as part of the OSI model were never widely used and are essentially dead now. However, the underlying model itself has proved to be quite useful for understanding computer networks. Although we do not intend to give a full description of this model and all of its implications here, a short introduction will be helpful. For more details, see Tanenbaum (2003).

The OSI model is designed to allow open systems to communicate. An open system is one that is prepared to communicate with any other open system by using standard rules that govern the format, contents, and meaning of the messages sent and received. These rules are formalized in what are called **protocols**. To allow a group of computers to communicate over a network, they must all agree on the protocols to be used. A distinction is made between two general types of protocols. With **connection oriented** protocols, before exchanging data the sender and receiver first explicitly establish a connection, and possibly negotiate the protocol they will use. When they are done, they must release (terminate) the connection. The telephone is a connection-oriented communication system. With **connectionless** protocols, no setup in advance is needed. The sender just transmits the first message when it is ready. Dropping a letter in a mailbox is an example of connectionless communication. With computers, both connection-oriented and connectionless communication are common.

In the OSI model, communication is divided up into seven levels or layers, as shown in Fig. 4-1. Each layer deals with one specific aspect of the communication. In this way, the problem can be divided up into manageable pieces, each of which can be solved independent of the others. Each layer provides an interface to the one above it. The interface consists of a set of operations that together define the service the layer is prepared to offer its users.

When process A on machine 1 wants to communicate with process B on machine 2, it builds a message and passes the message to the application layer on its machine. This layer might be a library procedure, for example, but it could also be implemented in some other way (e.g., inside the operating system, on an external network processor, etc.). The application layer software then adds a **header** to the front of the message and passes the resulting message across the layer 6/7 interface to the presentation layer. The presentation layer in turn adds its own header and passes the result down to the session layer, and so on. Some layers add not only a header to the front, but also a trailer to the end. When it hits the bottom, the physical layer actually transmits the message (which by now might look as shown in Fig. 4-2) by putting it onto the physical transmission medium.

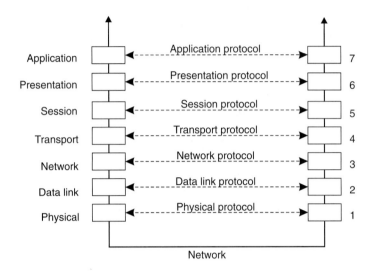

Figure 4-1. Layers, interfaces, and protocols in the OSI model.

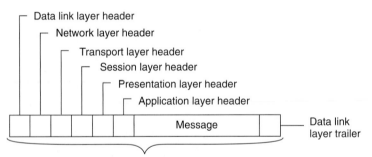

Figure 4-2. A typical message as it appears on the network.

When the message arrives at machine 2, it is passed upward, with each layer stripping off and examining its own header. Finally, the message arrives at the receiver, process *B*, which may reply to it using the reverse path. The information in the layer *n* header is used for the layer *n* protocol.

As an example of why layered protocols are important, consider communication between two companies, Zippy Airlines and its caterer, Mushy Meals, Inc. Every month, the head of passenger service at Zippy asks her secretary to contact the sales manager's secretary at Mushy to order 100,000 boxes of rubber chicken. Traditionally, the orders went via the post office. However, as the postal service deteriorated, at some point the two secretaries decided to abandon it and communicate by e-mail. They could do this without bothering their bosses, since their protocol deals with the physical transmission of the orders, not their contents.

Similarly, the head of passenger service can decide to drop the rubber chicken and go for Mushy's new special, prime rib of goat, without that decision affecting the secretaries. The thing to notice is that we have two layers here, the bosses and the secretaries. Each layer has its own protocol (subjects of discussion and technology) that can be changed independently of the other one. It is precisely this independence that makes layered protocols attractive. Each one can be changed as technology improves, without the other ones being affected.

In the OSI model, there are not two layers, but seven, as we saw in Fig. 4-1. The collection of protocols used in a particular system is called a **protocol suite** or **protocol stack**. It is important to distinguish a *reference model* from its actual *protocols*. As we mentioned, the OSI protocols were never popular. In contrast, protocols developed for the Internet, such as TCP and IP, are mostly used. In the following sections, we will briefly examine each of the OSI layers in turn, starting at the bottom. However, instead of giving examples of OSI protocols, where appropriate, we will point out some of the Internet protocols used in each layer.

Lower-Level Protocols

We start with discussing the three lowest layers of the OSI protocol suite. Together, these layers implement the basic functions that encompass a computer network.

The physical layer is concerned with transmitting the 0s and 1s. How many volts to use for 0 and 1, how many bits per second can be sent, and whether transmission can take place in both directions simultaneously are key issues in the physical layer. In addition, the size and shape of the network connector (plug), as well as the number of pins and meaning of each are of concern here.

The physical layer protocol deals with standardizing the electrical, mechanical, and signaling interfaces so that when one machine sends a 0 bit it is actually received as a 0 bit and not a 1 bit. Many physical layer standards have been developed (for different media), for example, the RS-232-C standard for serial communication lines.

The physical layer just sends bits. As long as no errors occur, all is well. However, real communication networks are subject to errors, so some mechanism is needed to detect and correct them. This mechanism is the main task of the data link layer. What it does is to group the bits into units, sometimes called **frames**, and see that each frame is correctly received.

The data link layer does its work by putting a special bit pattern on the start and end of each frame to mark them, as well as computing a **checksum** by adding up all the bytes in the frame in a certain way. The data link layer appends the checksum to the frame. When the frame arrives, the receiver recomputes the checksum from the data and compares the result to the checksum following the frame. If the two agree, the frame is considered correct and is accepted. It they disagree, the receiver asks the sender to retransmit it. Frames are assigned sequence numbers (in the header), so everyone can tell which is which.

On a LAN, there is usually no need for the sender to locate the receiver. It just puts the message out on the network and the receiver takes it off. A wide-area network, however, consists of a large number of machines, each with some number of lines to other machines, rather like a large-scale map showing major cities and roads connecting them. For a message to get from the sender to the receiver it may have to make a number of hops, at each one choosing an outgoing line to use. The question of how to choose the best path is called **routing**, and is essentially the primary task of the network layer.

The problem is complicated by the fact that the shortest route is not always the best route. What really matters is the amount of delay on a given route, which, in turn, is related to the amount of traffic and the number of messages queued up for transmission over the various lines. The delay can thus change over the course of time. Some routing algorithms try to adapt to changing loads, whereas others are content to make decisions based on long-term averages.

At present, the most widely used network protocol is the connectionless **IP** (**Internet Protocol**), which is part of the Internet protocol suite. An IP **packet** (the technical term for a message in the network layer) can be sent without any setup. Each IP packet is routed to its destination independent of all others. No internal path is selected and remembered.

Transport Protocols

The transport layer forms the last part of what could be called a basic network protocol stack, in the sense that it implements all those services that are not provided at the interface of the network layer, but which are reasonably needed to build network applications. In other words, the transport layer turns the underlying network into something that an application developer can use.

Packets can be lost on the way from the sender to the receiver. Although some applications can handle their own error recovery, others prefer a reliable connection. The job of the transport layer is to provide this service. The idea is that the application layer should be able to deliver a message to the transport layer with the expectation that it will be delivered without loss.

Upon receiving a message from the application layer, the transport layer breaks it into pieces small enough for transmission, assigns each one a sequence number, and then sends them all. The discussion in the transport layer header concerns which packets have been sent, which have been received, how many more the receiver has room to accept, which should be retransmitted, and similar topics.

Reliable transport connections (which by definition are connection oriented) can be built on top of connection-oriented or connectionless network services. In the former case all the packets will arrive in the correct sequence (if they arrive at all), but in the latter case it is possible for one packet to take a different route and arrive earlier than the packet sent before it. It is up to the transport layer software to put everything back in order to maintain the illusion that a transport connection is like a big tube—you put messages into it and they come out undamaged and in the same order in which they went in. Providing this end-to-end communication behavior is an important aspect of the transport layer.

The Internet transport protocol is called **TCP (Transmission Control Proto-col)** and is described in detail in Comer (2006). The combination TCP/IP is now used as a de facto standard for network communication. The Internet protocol suite also supports a connectionless transport protocol called **UDP** (Universal Datagram Protocol), which is essentially just IP with some minor additions. User programs that do not need a connection-oriented protocol normally use UDP.

Additional transport protocols are regularly proposed. For example, to support real-time data transfer, the **Real-time Transport Protocol (RTP)** has been de-fined. RTP is a framework protocol in the sense that it specifies packet formats for real-time data without providing the actual mechanisms for guaranteeing data delivery. In addition, it specifies a protocol for monitoring and controlling data transfer of RTP packets (Schulzrinne et al., 2003).

Higher-Level Protocols

Above the transport layer, OSI distinguished three additional layers. In prac-tice, only the application layer is ever used. In fact, in the Internet protocol suite, everything above the transport layer is grouped together. In the face of middle-ware systems, we shall see in this section that neither the OSI nor the Internet ap-proach is really appropriate.

The session layer is essentially an enhanced version of the transport layer. It provides dialog control, to keep track of which party is currently talking, and it provides synchronization facilities. The latter are useful to allow users to insert checkpoints into long transfers, so that in the event of a crash, it is necessary to go back only to the last checkpoint, rather than all the way back to the beginning. In practice, few applications are interested in the session layer and it is rarely sup-ported. It is not even present in the Internet protocol suite. However, in the con-text of developing middleware solutions, the concept of a session and its related protocols has turned out to be quite relevant, notably when defining higher-level communication protocols.

Unlike the lower layers, which are concerned with getting the bits from the sender to the receiver reliably and efficiently, the presentation layer is concerned with the meaning of the bits. Most messages do not consist of random bit strings, but more structured information such as people's names, addresses, amounts of money, and so on. In the presentation layer it is possible to define records contain-ing fields like these and then have the sender notify the receiver that a message contains a particular record in a certain format. This makes it easier for machines with different internal representations to communicate with each other.

The OSI application layer was originally intended to contain a collection of standard network applications such as those for electronic mail, file transfer, and terminal emulation. By now, it has become the container for all applications and protocols that in one way or the other do not fit into one of the underlying layers. From the perspective of the OSI reference model, virtually all distributed systems are just applications.

What is missing in this model is a clear distinction between applications, application-specific protocols, and general-purpose protocols. For example, the Internet **File Transfer Protocol** (**FTP**) (Postel and Reynolds, 1985; and Horowitz and Lunt, 1997) defines a protocol for transferring files between a client and server machine. The protocol should not be confused with the *ftp* program, which is an end-user application for transferring files and which also (not entirely by coincidence) happens to implement the Internet FTP.

Another example of a typical application-specific protocol is the **HyperText Transfer Protocol** (**HTTP**) (Fielding et al., 1999), which is designed to remotely manage and handle the transfer of Web pages. The protocol is implemented by applications such as Web browsers and Web servers. However, HTTP is now also used by systems that are not intrinsically tied to the Web. For example, Java's object-invocation mechanism uses HTTP to request the invocation of remote objects that are protected by a firewall (Sun Microsystems, 2004b).

There are also many general-purpose protocols that are useful to many applications, but which cannot be qualified as transport protocols. In many cases, such protocols fall into the category of middleware protocols, which we discuss next.

Middleware Protocols

Middleware is an application that logically lives (mostly) in the application layer, but which contains many general-purpose protocols that warrant their own layers, independent of other, more specific applications. A distinction can be made between high-level communication protocols and protocols for establishing various middleware services.

There are numerous protocols to support a variety of middleware services. For example, as we discuss in Chap. 9, there are various ways to establish authentication, that is, provide proof of a claimed identity. Authentication protocols are not closely tied to any specific application, but instead, can be integrated into a middleware system as a general service. Likewise, authorization protocols by which authenticated users and processes are granted access only to those resources for which they have authorization, tend to have a general, application-independent nature.

As another example, we shall consider a number of distributed commit protocols in Chap. 8. Commit protocols establish that in a group of processes either all processes carry out a particular operation, or that the operation is not carried out at all. This phenomenon is also referred to as **atomicity** and is widely applied in transactions. As we shall see, besides transactions, other applications, like fault-tolerant ones, can also take advantage of distributed commit protocols.

As a last example, consider a distributed locking protocol by which a resource can be protected against simultaneous access by a collection of processes that are distributed across multiple machines. We shall come across a number of such protocols in Chap. 6. Again, this is an example of a protocol that can be used to implement a general middleware service, but which, at the same time, is highly independent of any specific application.

Middleware communication protocols support high-level communication services. For example, in the next two sections we shall discuss protocols that allow a process to call a procedure or invoke an object on a remote machine in a highly transparent way. Likewise, there are high-level communication services for setting and synchronizing streams for transferring real-time data, such as needed for multimedia applications. As a last example, some middleware systems offer reliable multicast services that scale to thousands of receivers spread across a wide-area network.

Some of the middleware communication protocols could equally well belong in the transport layer, but there may be specific reasons to keep them at a higher level. For example, reliable multicasting services that guarantee scalability can be implemented only if application requirements are taken into account. Consequently, a middleware system may offer different (tunable) protocols, each in turn implemented using different transport protocols, but offering a single interface.

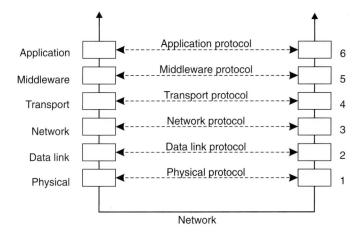

Figure 4-3. An adapted reference model for networked communication.

Taking this approach to layering leads to a slightly adapted reference model for communication, as shown in Fig. 4-3. Compared to the OSI model, the session and presentation layer have been replaced by a single middleware layer that contains application-independent protocols. These protocols do not belong in the lower layers we just discussed. The original transport services may also be offered as a middleware service, without being modified. This approach is somewhat analogous to offering UDP at the transport level. Likewise, middleware communication services may include message-passing services comparable to those offered by the transport layer.

In the remainder of this chapter, we concentrate on four high-level middleware communication services: remote procedure calls, message queuing services, support for communication of continuous media through streams, and multicasting. Before doing so, there are other general criteria for distinguishing (middleware) communication which we discuss next.

4.1.2 Types of Communication

To understand the various alternatives in communication that middleware can offer to applications, we view the middleware as an additional service in client-server computing, as shown in Fig. 4-4. Consider, for example an electronic mail system. In principle, the core of the mail delivery system can be seen as a middleware communication service. Each host runs a user agent allowing users to compose, send, and receive e-mail. A sending user agent passes such mail to the mail delivery system, expecting it, in turn, to eventually deliver the mail to the intended recipient. Likewise, the user agent at the receiver's side connects to the mail delivery system to see whether any mail has come in. If so, the messages are transferred to the user agent so that they can be displayed and read by the user.

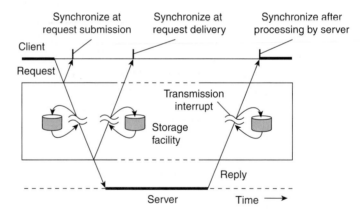

Figure 4-4. Viewing middleware as an intermediate (distributed) service in application-level communication.

An electronic mail system is a typical example in which communication is persistent. With **persistent communication**, a message that has been submitted for transmission is stored by the communication middleware as long as it takes to deliver it to the receiver. In this case, the middleware will store the message at one or several of the storage facilities shown in Fig. 4-4. As a consequence, it is not necessary for the sending application to continue execution after submitting the message. Likewise, the receiving application need not be executing when the message is submitted.

In contrast, with **transient communication**, a message is stored by the communication system only as long as the sending and receiving application are executing. More precisely, in terms of Fig. 4-4, the middleware cannot deliver a message due to a transmission interrupt, or because the recipient is currently not active, it will simply be discarded. Typically, all transport-level communication services offer only transient communication. In this case, the communication system consists traditional store-and-forward routers. If a router cannot deliver a message to the next one or the destination host, it will simply drop the message.

Besides being persistent or transient, communication can also be asynchronous or synchronous. The characteristic feature of **asynchronous communication** is that a sender continues immediately after it has submitted its message for transmission. This means that the message is (temporarily) stored immediately by the middleware upon submission. With **synchronous communication**, the sender is blocked until its request is known to be accepted. There are essentially three points where synchronization can take place. First, the sender may be blocked until the middleware notifies that it will take over transmission of the request. Second, the sender may synchronize until its request has been delivered to the intended recipient. Third, synchronization may take place by letting the sender wait until its request has been fully processed, that is, up the time that the recipient returns a response.

Various combinations of persistence and synchronization occur in practice. Popular ones are persistence in combination with synchronization at request submission, which is a common scheme for many message-queuing systems, which we discuss later in this chapter. Likewise, transient communication with synchronization after the request has been fully processed is also widely used. This scheme corresponds with remote procedure calls, which we also discuss below.

Besides persistence and synchronization, we should also make a distinction between discrete and streaming communication. The examples so far all fall in the category of discrete communication: the parties communicate by messages, each message forming a complete unit of information. In contrast, streaming involves sending multiple messages, one after the other, where the messages are related to each other by the order they are sent, or because there is a temporal relationship. We return to streaming communication extensively below.

4.2 REMOTE PROCEDURE CALL

Many distributed systems have been based on explicit message exchange between processes. However, the procedures send and receive do not conceal communication at all, which is important to achieve access transparency in distributed systems. This problem has long been known, but little was done about it until a paper by Birrell and Nelson (1984) introduced a completely different way of handling communication. Although the idea is refreshingly simple (once someone has thought of it), the implications are often subtle. In this section we will examine the concept, its implementation, its strengths, and its weaknesses.

In a nutshell, what Birrell and Nelson suggested was allowing programs to call procedures located on other machines. When a process on machine *A* calls a procedure on machine *B*, the calling process on *A* is suspended, and execution of the called procedure takes place on *B*. Information can be transported from the caller to the callee in the parameters and can come back in the procedure result. No message passing at all is visible to the programmer. This method is known as **Remote Procedure Call**, or often just **RPC**.

While the basic idea sounds simple and elegant, subtle problems exist. To start with, because the calling and called procedures run on different machines, they execute in different address spaces, which causes complications. Parameters and results also have to be passed, which can be complicated, especially if the machines are not identical. Finally, either or both machines can crash and each of the possible failures causes different problems. Still, most of these can be dealt with, and RPC is a widely-used technique that underlies many distributed systems.

4.2.1 Basic RPC Operation

We first start with discussing conventional procedure calls, and then explain how the call itself can be split into a client and server part that are each executed on different machines.

Conventional Procedure Call

To understand how RPC works, it is important first to fully understand how a conventional (i.e., single machine) procedure call works. Consider a call in C like

    count = read(fd, buf, nbytes);

where *fd* is an integer indicating a file, *buf* is an array of characters into which data are read, and *nbytes* is another integer telling how many bytes to read. If the call is made from the main program, the stack will be as shown in Fig. 4-5(a) before the call. To make the call, the caller pushes the parameters onto the stack in order, last one first, as shown in Fig. 4-5(b). (The reason that C compilers push the parameters in reverse order has to do with *printf*—by doing so, *printf* can always locate its first parameter, the format string.) After the read procedure has finished running, it puts the return value in a register, removes the return address, and transfers control back to the caller. The caller then removes the parameters from the stack, returning the stack to the original state it had before the call.

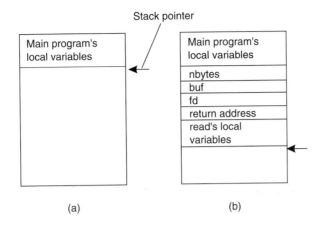

Figure 4-5. (a) Parameter passing in a local procedure call: the stack before the call to read. (b) The stack while the called procedure is active.

Several things are worth noting. For one, in C, parameters can be **call-by-value** or **call-by-reference**. A value parameter, such as *fd* or *nbytes*, is simply copied to the stack as shown in Fig. 4-5(b). To the called procedure, a value parameter is just an initialized local variable. The called procedure may modify it, but such changes do not affect the original value at the calling side.

A reference parameter in C is a pointer to a variable (i.e., the address of the variable), rather than the value of the variable. In the call to read, the second parameter is a reference parameter because arrays are always passed by reference in C. What is actually pushed onto the stack is the address of the character array. If the called procedure uses this parameter to store something into the character array, it *does* modify the array in the calling procedure. The difference between call-by-value and call-by-reference is quite important for RPC, as we shall see.

One other parameter passing mechanism also exists, although it is not used in C. It is called **call-by-copy/restore**. It consists of having the variable copied to the stack by the caller, as in call-by-value, and then copied back after the call, overwriting the caller's original value. Under most conditions, this achieves exactly the same effect as call-by-reference, but in some situations, such as the same parameter being present multiple times in the parameter list, the semantics are different. The call-by-copy/restore mechanism is not used in many languages.

The decision of which parameter passing mechanism to use is normally made by the language designers and is a fixed property of the language. Sometimes it depends on the data type being passed. In C, for example, integers and other scalar types are always passed by value, whereas arrays are always passed by reference, as we have seen. Some Ada compilers use copy/restore for **in out** parameters, but others use call-by-reference. The language definition permits either choice, which makes the semantics a bit fuzzy.

Client and Server Stubs

The idea behind RPC is to make a remote procedure call look as much as possible like a local one. In other words, we want RPC to be transparent—the calling procedure should not be aware that the called procedure is executing on a different machine or vice versa. Suppose that a program needs to read some data from a file. The programmer puts a call to read in the code to get the data. In a traditional (single-processor) system, the read routine is extracted from the library by the linker and inserted into the object program. It is a short procedure, which is generally implemented by calling an equivalent read system call. In other words, the read procedure is a kind of interface between the user code and the local operating system.

Even though read does a system call, it is called in the usual way, by pushing the parameters onto the stack, as shown in Fig. 4-5(b). Thus the programmer does not know that read is actually doing something fishy.

RPC achieves its transparency in an analogous way. When read is actually a remote procedure (e.g., one that will run on the file server's machine), a different version of read, called a **client stub**, is put into the library. Like the original one, it, too, is called using the calling sequence of Fig. 4-5(b). Also like the original one, it too, does a call to the local operating system. Only unlike the original one, it does not ask the operating system to give it data. Instead, it packs the parameters into a message and requests that message to be sent to the server as illustrated in Fig. 4-6. Following the call to send, the client stub calls receive, blocking itself until the reply comes back.

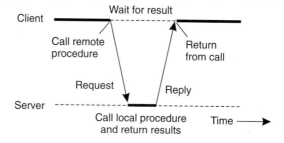

Figure 4-6. Principle of RPC between a client and server program.

When the message arrives at the server, the server's operating system passes it up to a **server stub**. A server stub is the server-side equivalent of a client stub: it is a piece of code that transforms requests coming in over the network into local procedure calls. Typically the server stub will have called receive and be blocked waiting for incoming messages. The server stub unpacks the parameters from the message and then calls the server procedure in the usual way (i.e., as in Fig. 4-5). From the server's point of view, it is as though it is being called directly by the client—the parameters and return address are all on the stack where they belong and nothing seems unusual. The server performs its work and then returns the result to the caller in the usual way. For example, in the case of read, the server will fill the buffer, pointed to by the second parameter, with the data. This buffer will be internal to the server stub.

When the server stub gets control back after the call has completed, it packs the result (the buffer) in a message and calls send to return it to the client. After that, the server stub usually does a call to receive again, to wait for the next incoming request.

When the message gets back to the client machine, the client's operating system sees that it is addressed to the client process (or actually the client stub, but the operating system cannot see the difference). The message is copied to the waiting buffer and the client process unblocked. The client stub inspects the message, unpacks the result, copies it to its caller, and returns in the usual way. When the caller gets control following the call to read, all it knows is that its data are available. It has no idea that the work was done remotely instead of by the local operating system.

This blissful ignorance on the part of the client is the beauty of the whole scheme. As far as it is concerned, remote services are accessed by making ordinary (i.e., local) procedure calls, not by calling send and receive. All the details of the message passing are hidden away in the two library procedures, just as the details of actually making system calls are hidden away in traditional libraries.

To summarize, a remote procedure call occurs in the following steps:

1. The client procedure calls the client stub in the normal way.

2. The client stub builds a message and calls the local operating system.

3. The client's OS sends the message to the remote OS.

4. The remote OS gives the message to the server stub.

5. The server stub unpacks the parameters and calls the server.

6. The server does the work and returns the result to the stub.

7. The server stub packs it in a message and calls its local OS.

8. The server's OS sends the message to the client's OS.

9. The client's OS gives the message to the client stub.

10. The stub unpacks the result and returns to the client.

The net effect of all these steps is to convert the local call by the client procedure to the client stub, to a local call to the server procedure without either client or server being aware of the intermediate steps or the existence of the network.

4.2.2 Parameter Passing

The function of the client stub is to take its parameters, pack them into a message, and send them to the server stub. While this sounds straightforward, it is not quite as simple as it at first appears. In this section we will look at some of the issues concerned with parameter passing in RPC systems.

Passing Value Parameters

Packing parameters into a message is called **parameter marshaling**. As a very simple example, consider a remote procedure, add(i, j), that takes two integer parameters i and j and returns their arithmetic sum as a result. (As a practical matter, one would not normally make such a simple procedure remote due to the overhead, but as an example it will do.) The call to add, is shown in the left-hand portion (in the client process) in Fig. 4-7. The client stub takes its two parameters and puts them in a message as indicated. It also puts the name or number of the procedure to be called in the message because the server might support several different calls, and it has to be told which one is required.

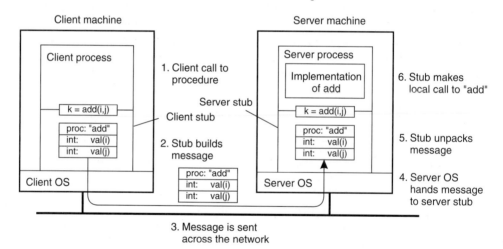

Figure 4-7. The steps involved in a doing a remote computation through RPC.

When the message arrives at the server, the stub examines the message to see which procedure is needed and then makes the appropriate call. If the server also supports other remote procedures, the server stub might have a switch statement in it to select the procedure to be called, depending on the first field of the message. The actual call from the stub to the server looks like the original client call, except that the parameters are variables initialized from the incoming message.

When the server has finished, the server stub gains control again. It takes the result sent back by the server and packs it into a message. This message is sent back back to the client stub, which unpacks it to extract the result and returns the value to the waiting client procedure.

As long as the client and server machines are identical and all the parameters and results are scalar types, such as integers, characters, and Booleans, this model works fine. However, in a large distributed system, it is common that multiple machine types are present. Each machine often has its own representation for numbers, characters, and other data items. For example, IBM mainframes use the EBCDIC character code, whereas IBM personal computers use ASCII. As a consequence, it is not possible to pass a character parameter from an IBM PC client to an IBM mainframe server using the simple scheme of Fig. 4-7: the server will interpret the character incorrectly.

Similar problems can occur with the representation of integers (one's complement versus two's complement) and floating-point numbers. In addition, an even more annoying problem exists because some machines, such as the Intel Pentium, number their bytes from right to left, whereas others, such as the Sun SPARC, number them the other way. The Intel format is called **little endian** and the SPARC format is called **big endian**, after the politicians in *Gulliver's Travels* who went to war over which end of an egg to break (Cohen, 1981). As an example, consider a procedure with two parameters, an integer and a four-character string. Each parameter requires one 32-bit word. Fig. 4-8(a) shows what the parameter portion of a message built by a client stub on an Intel Pentium might look like. The first word contains the integer parameter, 5 in this case, and the second contains the string "JILL."

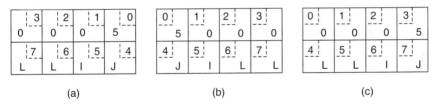

Figure 4-8. (a) The original message on the Pentium. (b) The message after receipt on the SPARC. (c) The message after being inverted. The little numbers in boxes indicate the address of each byte.

Since messages are transferred byte for byte (actually, bit for bit) over the network, the first byte sent is the first byte to arrive. In Fig. 4-8(b) we show what the message of Fig. 4-8(a) would look like if received by a SPARC, which numbers its bytes with byte 0 at the left (high-order byte) instead of at the right (low-order byte) as do all the Intel chips. When the server stub reads the parameters at addresses 0 and 4, respectively, it will find an integer equal to 83,886,080 (5×2^{24}) and a string "JILL".

One obvious, but unfortunately incorrect, approach is to simply invert the bytes of each word after they are received, leading to Fig. 4-8(c). Now the integer is 5 and the string is "LLIJ". The problem here is that integers are reversed by the different byte ordering, but strings are not. Without additional information about what is a string and what is an integer, there is no way to repair the damage.

Passing Reference Parameters

We now come to a difficult problem: How are pointers, or in general, references passed? The answer is: only with the greatest of difficulty, if at all. Remember that a pointer is meaningful only within the address space of the process in which it is being used. Getting back to our read example discussed earlier, if the second parameter (the address of the buffer) happens to be 1000 on the client, one cannot just pass the number 1000 to the server and expect it to work. Address 1000 on the server might be in the middle of the program text.

One solution is just to forbid pointers and reference parameters in general. However, these are so important that this solution is highly undesirable. In fact, it is not necessary either. In the read example, the client stub knows that the second parameter points to an array of characters. Suppose, for the moment, that it also knows how big the array is. One strategy then becomes apparent: copy the array into the message and send it to the server. The server stub can then call the server with a pointer to this array, even though this pointer has a different numerical value than the second parameter of read has. Changes the server makes using the pointer (e.g., storing data into it) directly affect the message buffer inside the server stub. When the server finishes, the original message can be sent back to the client stub, which then copies it back to the client. In effect, call-by-reference has been replaced by copy/restore. Although this is not always identical, it frequently is good enough.

One optimization makes this mechanism twice as efficient. If the stubs know whether the buffer is an input parameter or an output parameter to the server, one of the copies can be eliminated. If the array is input to the server (e.g., in a call to write) it need not be copied back. If it is output, it need not be sent over in the first place.

As a final comment, it is worth noting that although we can now handle pointers to simple arrays and structures, we still cannot handle the most general case of a pointer to an arbitrary data structure such as a complex graph. Some systems attempt to deal with this case by actually passing the pointer to the server stub and generating special code in the server procedure for using pointers. For example, a request may be sent back to the client to provide the referenced data.

Parameter Specification and Stub Generation

From what we have explained so far, it is clear that hiding a remote procedure call requires that the caller and the callee agree on the format of the messages they exchange, and that they follow the same steps when it comes to, for example, passing complex data structures. In other words, both sides in an RPC should follow the same protocol or the RPC will not work correctly.

As a simple example, consider the procedure of Fig. 4-9(a). It has three parameters, a character, a floating-point number, and an array of five integers. Assuming a word is four bytes, the RPC protocol might prescribe that we should transmit a character in the rightmost byte of a word (leaving the next 3 bytes empty), a float as a whole word, and an array as a group of words equal to the array length, preceded by a word giving the length, as shown in Fig. 4-9(b). Thus given these rules, the client stub for foobar knows that it must use the format of Fig. 4-9(b), and the server stub knows that incoming messages for foobar will have the format of Fig. 4-9(b).

foobar's local variables	
	x
y	
5	
z[0]	
z[1]	
z[2]	
z[3]	
z[4]	

```
foobar( char x; float y; int z[5] )
{
    ....
}
```

(a)   (b)

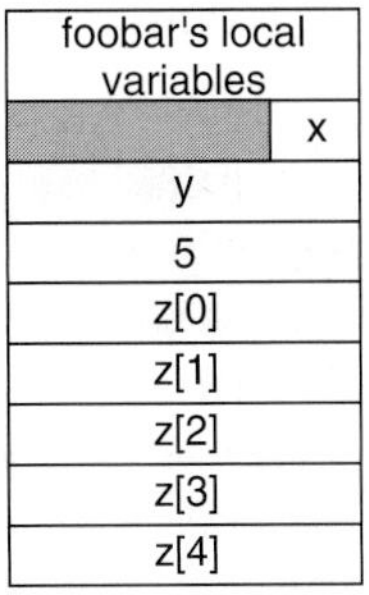

Figure 4-9. (a) A procedure. (b) The corresponding message.

Defining the message format is one aspect of an RPC protocol, but it is not sufficient. What we also need is the client and the server to agree on the representation of simple data structures, such as integers, characters, Booleans, etc. For example, the protocol could prescribe that integers are represented in two's complement, characters in 16-bit Unicode, and floats in the IEEE standard #754 format, with everything stored in little endian. With this additional information, messages can be unambiguously interpreted.

With the encoding rules now pinned down to the last bit, the only thing that remains to be done is that the caller and callee agree on the actual exchange of messages. For example, it may be decided to use a connection-oriented transport service such as TCP/IP. An alternative is to use an unreliable datagram service and let the client and server implement an error control scheme as part of the RPC protocol. In practice, several variants exist.

Once the RPC protocol has been fully defined, the client and server stubs need to be implemented. Fortunately, stubs for the same protocol but different procedures normally differ only in their interface to the applications. An interface consists of a collection of procedures that can be called by a client, and which are implemented by a server. An interface is usually available in the same programing language as the one in which the client or server is written (although this is strictly speaking, not necessary). To simplify matters, interfaces are often specified by means of an **Interface Definition Language (IDL)**. An interface specified in such an IDL is then subsequently compiled into a client stub and a server stub, along with the appropriate compile-time or run-time interfaces.

Practice shows that using an interface definition language considerably simplifies client-server applications based on RPCs. Because it is easy to fully generate client and server stubs, all RPC-based middleware systems offer an IDL to support application development. In some cases, using the IDL is even mandatory, as we shall see in later chapters.

4.2.3 Asynchronous RPC

As in conventional procedure calls, when a client calls a remote procedure, the client will block until a reply is returned. This strict request-reply behavior is unnecessary when there is no result to return, and only leads to blocking the client while it could have proceeded and have done useful work just after requesting the remote procedure to be called. Examples of where there is often no need to wait for a reply include: transferring money from one account to another, adding entries into a database, starting remote services, batch processing, and so on.

To support such situations, RPC systems may provide facilities for what are called **asynchronous RPCs**, by which a client immediately continues after issuing the RPC request. With asynchronous RPCs, the server immediately sends a reply back to the client the moment the RPC request is received, after which it calls the requested procedure. The reply acts as an acknowledgment to the client that the server is going to process the RPC. The client will continue without further blocking as soon as it has received the server's acknowledgment. Fig. 4-10(b) shows how client and server interact in the case of asynchronous RPCs. For comparison, Fig. 4-10(a) shows the normal request-reply behavior.

Asynchronous RPCs can also be useful when a reply will be returned but the client is not prepared to wait for it and do nothing in the meantime. For example, a client may want to prefetch the network addresses of a set of hosts that it expects to contact soon. While a naming service is collecting those addresses, the client may want to do other things. In such cases, it makes sense to organize the communication between the client and server through two asynchronous RPCs, as shown in Fig. 4-11. The client first calls the server to hand over a list of host names that should be looked up, and continues when the server has acknowledged the receipt of that list. The second call is done by the server, who calls the client to hand over the addresses it found. Combining two asynchronous RPCs is sometimes also referred to as a **deferred synchronous RPC**.

It should be noted that variants of asynchronous RPCs exist in which the client continues executing immediately after sending the request to the server. In

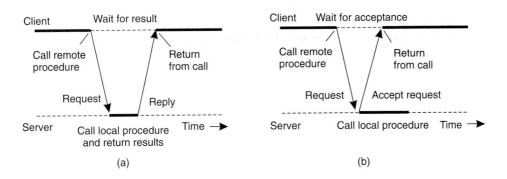

Figure 4-10. (a) The interaction between client and server in a traditional RPC. (b) The interaction using asynchronous RPC.

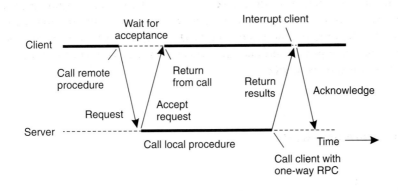

Figure 4-11. A client and server interacting through two asynchronous RPCs.

other words, the client does not wait for an acknowledgment of the server's acceptance of the request. We refer to such RPCs as **one-way RPCs**. The problem with this approach is that when reliability is not guaranteed, the client cannot know for sure whether or not its request will be processed. We return to these matters in Chap. 8. Likewise, in the case of deferred synchronous RPC, the client may poll the server to see whether the results are available yet instead of letting the server calling back the client.

4.2.4 Example: DCE RPC

Remote procedure calls have been widely adopted as the basis of middleware and distributed systems in general. In this section, we take a closer look at one specific RPC system: the **Distributed Computing Environment (DCE)**, which was developed by the Open Software Foundation (OSF), now called The Open Group. DCE RPC is not as popular as some other RPC systems, notably Sun RPC. However, DCE RPC is nevertheless representative of other RPC systems, and its specifications have been adopted in Microsoft's base system for distributed computing, DCOM (Eddon and Eddon, 1998). We start with a brief introduction to DCE, after which we consider the principal workings of DCE RPC. Detailed technical information on how to develop RPC-based applications can be found in Stevens (1999).

Introduction to DCE

DCE is a true middleware system in that it is designed to execute as a layer of abstraction between existing (network) operating systems and distributed applications. Initially designed for UNIX, it has now been ported to all major operating systems including VMS and Windows variants, as well as desktop operating systems. The idea is that the customer can take a collection of existing machines, add the DCE software, and then be able to run distributed applications, all without disturbing existing (nondistributed) applications. Although most of the DCE package runs in user space, in some configurations a piece (part of the distributed file system) must be added to the kernel. The Open Group itself only sells source code, which vendors integrate into their systems.

The programming model underlying all of DCE is the client-server model, which was extensively discussed in the previous chapter. User processes act as clients to access remote services provided by server processes. Some of these services are part of DCE itself, but others belong to the applications and are written by the applications programmers. All communication between clients and servers takes place by means of RPCs.

There are a number of services that form part of DCE itself. The **distributed file service** is a worldwide file system that provides a transparent way of accessing any file in the system in the same way. It can either be built on top of the hosts' native file systems or used instead of them. The **directory service** is used to keep track of the location of all resources in the system. These resources include machines, printers, servers, data, and much more, and they may be distributed geographically over the entire world. The directory service allows a process to ask for a resource and not have to be concerned about where it is, unless the process cares. The **security service** allows resources of all kinds to be protected, so access can be restricted to authorized persons. Finally, the **distributed time service** is a service that attempts to keep clocks on the different machines globally synchronized. As we shall see in later chapters, having some notion of global time makes it much easier to ensure consistency in a distributed system.

Goals of DCE RPC

The goals of the DCE RPC system are relatively traditional. First and foremost, the RPC system makes it possible for a client to access a remote service by simply calling a local procedure. This interface makes it possible for client (i.e., application) programs to be written in a simple way, familiar to most pro-grammers. It also makes it easy to have large volumes of existing code run in a distributed environment with few, if any, changes.

It is up to the RPC system to hide all the details from the clients, and, to some extent, from the servers as well. To start with, the RPC system can automatically locate the correct server, and subsequently set up the communication between cli-ent and server software (generally called **binding**). It can also handle the mes-sage transport in both directions, fragmenting and reassembling them as needed (e.g., if one of the parameters is a large array). Finally, the RPC system can auto-matically handle data type conversions between the client and the server, even if they run on different architectures and have a different byte ordering.

As a consequence of the RPC system's ability to hide the details, clients and servers are highly independent of one another. A client can be written in Java and a server in C, or vice versa. A client and server can run on different hardware plat-forms and use different operating systems. A variety of network protocols and data representations are also supported, all without any intervention from the cli-ent or server.

Writing a Client and a Server

The DCE RPC system consists of a number of components, including lan-guages, libraries, daemons, and utility programs, among others. Together these make it possible to write clients and servers. In this section we will describe the pieces and how they fit together. The entire process of writing and using an RPC client and server is summarized in Fig. 4-12.

In a client-server system, the glue that holds everything together is the inter-face definition, as specified in the **Interface Definition Language**, or **IDL**. It permits procedure declarations in a form closely resembling function prototypes in ANSI C. IDL files can also contain type definitions, constant declarations, and other information needed to correctly marshal parameters and unmarshal results. Ideally, the interface definition should also contain a formal definition of what the procedures do, but such a definition is beyond the current state of the art, so the interface definition just defines the syntax of the calls, not their semantics. At best the writer can add a few comments describing what the procedures do.

A crucial element in every IDL file is a globally unique identifier for the specified interface. The client sends this identifier in the first RPC message and the server verifies that it is correct. In this way, if a client inadvertently tries to bind to the wrong server, or even to an older version of the right server, the server will detect the error and the binding will not take place.

Interface definitions and unique identifiers are closely related in DCE. As illustrated in Fig. 4-12, the first step in writing a client/server application is usual-ly calling the *uuidgen* program, asking it to generate a prototype IDL file contain-ing an interface identifier guaranteed never to be used again in any interface

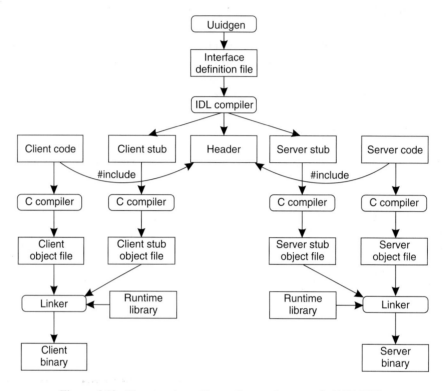

Figure 4-12. The steps in writing a client and a server in DCE RPC.

generated anywhere by *uuidgen*. Uniqueness is ensured by encoding in it the location and time of creation. It consists of a 128-bit binary number represented in the IDL file as an ASCII string in hexadecimal.

The next step is editing the IDL file, filling in the names of the remote procedures and their parameters. It is worth noting that RPC is not totally transparent—for example, the client and server cannot share global variables—but the IDL rules make it impossible to express constructs that are not supported.

When the IDL file is complete, the IDL compiler is called to process it. The output of the IDL compiler consists of three files:

1. A header file (e.g., *interface.h*, in C terms).

2. The client stub.

3. The server stub.

The header file contains the unique identifier, type definitions, constant definitions, and function prototypes. It should be included (using *#include*) in both the client and server code. The client stub contains the actual procedures that the client program will call. These procedures are the ones responsible for collecting and packing the parameters into the outgoing message and then calling the runtime system to send it. The client stub also handles unpacking the reply and returning values to the client. The server stub contains the procedures called by the runtime system on the server machine when an incoming message arrives. These, in turn, call the actual server procedures that do the work.

The next step is for the application writer to write the client and server code. Both of these are then compiled, as are the two stub procedures. The resulting client code and client stub object files are then linked with the runtime library to produce the executable binary for the client. Similarly, the server code and server stub are compiled and linked to produce the server's binary. At runtime, the client and server are started so that the application is actually executed as well.

Binding a Client to a Server

To allow a client to call a server, it is necessary that the server be registered and prepared to accept incoming calls. Registration of a server makes it possible for a client to locate the server and bind to it. Server location is done in two steps:

1. Locate the server's machine.

2. Locate the server (i.e., the correct process) on that machine.

The second step is somewhat subtle. Basically, what it comes down to is that to communicate with a server, the client needs to know an **end point**, on the server's machine to which it can send messages. An end point (also commonly known as a **port**) is used by the server's operating system to distinguish incoming messages for different processes. In DCE, a table of *(server, end point)*pairs is maintained on each server machine by a process called the **DCE daemon**. Before it becomes available for incoming requests, the server must ask the operating system for an end point. It then registers this end point with the DCE daemon. The DCE daemon records this information (including which protocols the server speaks) in the end point table for future use.

The server also registers with the directory service by providing it the network address of the server's machine and a name under which the server can be looked up. Binding a client to a server then proceeds as shown in Fig. 4-13.

Let us assume that the client wants to bind to a video server that is locally known under the name */local/multimedia/video/movies*. It passes this name to the directory server, which returns the network address of the machine running the video server. The client then goes to the DCE daemon on that machine (which has a well-known end point), and asks it to look up the end point of the video server in its end point table. Armed with this information, the RPC can now take place. On subsequent RPCs this lookup is not needed. DCE also gives clients the ability to do more sophisticated searches for a suitable server when that is needed. Secure RPC is also an option where confidentiality or data integrity is crucial.

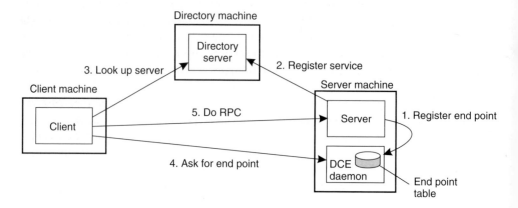

Figure 4-13. Client-to-server binding in DCE.

Performing an RPC

The actual RPC is carried out transparently and in the usual way. The client stub marshals the parameters to the runtime library for transmission using the protocol chosen at binding time. When a message arrives at the server side, it is routed to the correct server based on the end point contained in the incoming message. The runtime library passes the message to the server stub, which unmarshals the parameters and calls the server. The reply goes back by the reverse route.

DCE provides several semantic options. The default is **at-most-once operation**, in which case no call is ever carried out more than once, even in the face of system crashes. In practice, what this means is that if a server crashes during an RPC and then recovers quickly, the client does not repeat the operation, for fear that it might already have been carried out once.

Alternatively, it is possible to mark a remote procedure as **idempotent** (in the IDL file), in which case it can be repeated multiple times without harm. For example, reading a specified block from a file can be tried over and over until it succeeds. When an idempotent RPC fails due to a server crash, the client can wait until the server reboots and then try again. Other semantics are also available (but rarely used), including broadcasting the RPC to all the machines on the local network. We return to RPC semantics in Chap. 8, when discussing RPC in the presence of failures.

4.3 MESSAGE-ORIENTED COMMUNICATION

Remote procedure calls and remote object invocations contribute to hiding communication in distributed systems, that is, they enhance access transparency. Unfortunately, neither mechanism is always appropriate. In particular, when it cannot be assumed that the receiving side is executing at the time a request is issued, alternative communication services are needed. Likewise, the inherent synchronous nature of RPCs, by which a client is blocked until its request has been processed, sometimes needs to be replaced by something else.

That something else is messaging. In this section we concentrate on message-oriented communication in distributed systems by first taking a closer look at what exactly synchronous behavior is and what its implications are. Then, we discuss messaging systems that assume that parties are executing at the time of communication. Finally, we will examine message-queuing systems that allow processes to exchange information, even if the other party is not executing at the time communication is initiated.

4.3.1 Message-Oriented Transient Communication

Many distributed systems and applications are built directly on top of the simple message-oriented model offered by the transport layer. To better understand and appreciate the message-oriented systems as part of middleware solutions, we first discuss messaging through transport-level sockets.

Berkeley Sockets

Special attention has been paid to standardizing the interface of the transport layer to allow programmers to make use of its entire suite of (messaging) protocols through a simple set of primitives. Also, standard interfaces make it easier to port an application to a different machine.

As an example, we briefly discuss the **sockets interface** as introduced in the 1970s in Berkeley UNIX. Another important interface is **XTI**, which stands for the **X/Open Transport Interface**, formerly called the Transport Layer Interface (TLI), and developed by AT&T. Sockets and XTI are very similar in their model of network programming, but differ in their set of primitives.

Conceptually, a **socket** is a communication end point to which an application can write data that are to be sent out over the underlying network, and from which incoming data can be read. A socket forms an abstraction over the actual communication end point that is used by the local operating system for a specific transport protocol. In the following text, we concentrate on the socket primitives for TCP, which are shown in Fig. 4-14.

Servers generally execute the first four primitives, normally in the order given. When calling the socket primitive, the caller creates a new communication end point for a specific transport protocol. Internally, creating a communication end point means that the local operating system reserves resources to accommodate sending and receiving messages for the specified protocol.

The bind primitive associates a local address with the newly-created socket. For example, a server should bind the IP address of its machine together with a (possibly well-known) port number to a socket. Binding tells the operating system that the server wants to receive messages only on the specified address and port.

Primitive	Meaning
Socket	Create a new communication end point
Bind	Attach a local address to a socket
Listen	Announce willingness to accept connections
Accept	Block caller until a connection request arrives
Connect	Actively attempt to establish a connection
Send	Send some data over the connection
Receive	Receive some data over the connection
Close	Release the connection

Figure 4-14. The socket primitives for TCP/IP.

The listen primitive is called only in the case of connection-oriented communication. It is a nonblocking call that allows the local operating system to reserve enough buffers for a specified maximum number of connections that the caller is willing to accept.

A call to accept blocks the caller until a connection request arrives. When a request arrives, the local operating system creates a new socket with the same properties as the original one, and returns it to the caller. This approach will allow the server to, for example, fork off a process that will subsequently handle the actual communication through the new connection. The server, in the meantime, can go back and wait for another connection request on the original socket.

Let us now take a look at the client side. Here, too, a socket must first be created using the socket primitive, but explicitly binding the socket to a local address is not necessary, since the operating system can dynamically allocate a port when the connection is set up. The connect primitive requires that the caller specifies the transport-level address to which a connection request is to be sent. The client is blocked until a connection has been set up successfully, after which both sides can start exchanging information through the send and receive primitives. Finally, closing a connection is symmetric when using sockets, and is established by having both the client and server call the close primitive. The general pattern followed by a client and server for connection-oriented communication using sockets is shown in Fig. 4-15. Details about network programming using sockets and other interfaces in a UNIX environment can be found in Stevens (1998).

The Message-Passing Interface (MPI)

With the advent of high-performance multicomputers, developers have been looking for message-oriented primitives that would allow them to easily write highly efficient applications. This means that the primitives should be at a convenient level of abstraction (to ease application development), and that their

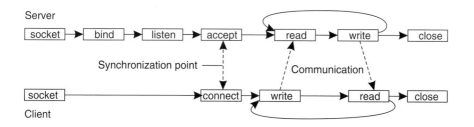

Figure 4-15. Connection-oriented communication pattern using sockets.

implementation incurs only minimal overhead. Sockets were deemed insufficient for two reasons. First, they were at the wrong level of abstraction by supporting only simple send and receive primitives. Second, sockets had been designed to communicate across networks using general-purpose protocol stacks such as TCP/IP. They were not considered suitable for the proprietary protocols developed for high-speed interconnection networks, such as those used in high-performance server clusters. Those protocols required an interface that could handle more advanced features, such as different forms of buffering and synchronization.

The result was that most interconnection networks and high-performance multicomputers were shipped with proprietary communication libraries. These libraries offered a wealth of high-level and generally efficient communication primitives. Of course, all libraries were mutually incompatible, so that application developers now had a portability problem.

The need to be hardware and platform independent eventually led to the definition of a standard for message passing, simply called the **Message-Passing Interface** or **MPI**. MPI is designed for parallel applications and as such is tailored to transient communication. It makes direct use of the underlying network. Also, it assumes that serious failures such as process crashes or network partitions are fatal and do not require automatic recovery.

MPI assumes communication takes place within a known group of processes. Each group is assigned an identifier. Each process within a group is also assigned a (local) identifier. A (*groupID*, *processID*) pair therefore uniquely identifies the source or destination of a message, and is used instead of a transport-level address. There may be several, possibly overlapping groups of processes involved in a computation and that are all executing at the same time.

At the core of MPI are messaging primitives to support transient communication, of which the most intuitive ones are summarized in Fig. 4-16.

Transient asynchronous communication is supported by means of the MPI_bsend primitive. The sender submits a message for transmission, which is generally first copied to a local buffer in the MPI runtime system. When the message has been copied, the sender continues. The local MPI runtime system will remove the message from its local buffer and take care of transmission as soon as a receiver has called a receive primitive.

Primitive	Meaning
MPI_bsend	Append outgoing message to a local send buffer
MPI_send	Send a message and wait until copied to local or remote buffer
MPI_ssend	Send a message and wait until receipt starts
MPI_sendrecv	Send a message and wait for reply
MPI_isend	Pass reference to outgoing message, and continue
MPI_issend	Pass reference to outgoing message, and wait until receipt starts
MPI_recv	Receive a message; block if there is none
MPI_irecv	Check if there is an incoming message, but do not block

Figure 4-16. Some of the most intuitive message-passing primitives of MPI.

There is also a blocking send operation, called MPI_send, of which the semantics are implementation dependent. The primitive MPI_send may either block the caller until the specified message has been copied to the MPI runtime system at the sender's side, or until the receiver has initiated a receive operation. Synchronous communication by which the sender blocks until its request is accepted for further processing is available through the MPI_ssend primitive. Finally, the strongest form of synchronous communication is also supported: when a sender calls MPI_sendrecv, it sends a request to the receiver and blocks until the latter returns a reply. Basically, this primitive corresponds to a normal RPC.

Both MPI_send and MPI_ssend have variants that avoid copying messages from user buffers to buffers internal to the local MPI runtime system. These variants correspond to a form of asynchronous communication. With MPI_isend, a sender passes a pointer to the message after which the MPI runtime system takes care of communication. The sender immediately continues. To prevent overwriting the message before communication completes, MPI offers primitives to check for completion, or even to block if required. As with MPI_send, whether the message has actually been transferred to the receiver or that it has merely been copied by the local MPI runtime system to an internal buffer is left unspecified.

Likewise, with MPI_issend, a sender also passes only a pointer to the MPI runtime system. When the runtime system indicates it has processed the message, the sender is then guaranteed that the receiver has accepted the message and is now working on it.

The operation MPI_recv is called to receive a message; it blocks the caller until a message arrives. There is also an asynchronous variant, called MPI_irecv, by which a receiver indicates that is prepared to accept a message. The receiver can check whether or not a message has indeed arrived, or block until one does.

The semantics of MPI communication primitives are not always straightforward, and different primitives can sometimes be interchanged without affecting the correctness of a program. The official reason why so many different forms of communication are supported is that it gives implementers of MPI systems enough possibilities for optimizing performance. Cynics might say the committee could not make up its collective mind, so it threw in everything. MPI has been designed for high-performance parallel applications, which makes it easier to understand its diversity in different communication primitives.

More on MPI can be found in Gropp et al. (1998b) The complete reference in which the over 100 functions in MPI are explained in detail, can be found in Snir et al. (1998) and Gropp et al. (1998a)

4.3.2 Message-Oriented Persistent Communication

We now come to an important class of message-oriented middleware services, generally known as **message-queuing systems**, or just **Message-Oriented Middleware** (**MOM**). Message-queuing systems provide extensive support for persistent asynchronous communication. The essence of these systems is that they offer intermediate-term storage capacity for messages, without requiring either the sender or receiver to be active during message transmission. An important difference with Berkeley sockets and MPI is that message-queuing systems are typically targeted to support message transfers that are allowed to take minutes instead of seconds or milliseconds. We first explain a general approach to message-queuing systems, and conclude this section by comparing them to more traditional systems, notably the Internet e-mail systems.

Message-Queuing Model

The basic idea behind a message-queuing system is that applications communicate by inserting messages in specific queues. These messages are forwarded over a series of communication servers and are eventually delivered to the destination, even if it was down when the message was sent. In practice, most communication servers are directly connected to each other. In other words, a message is generally transferred directly to a destination server. In principle, each application has its own private queue to which other applications can send messages. A queue can be read only by its associated application, but it is also possible for multiple applications to share a single queue.

An important aspect of message-queuing systems is that a sender is generally given only the guarantees that its message will eventually be inserted in the recipient's queue. No guarantees are given about when, or even if the message will actually be read, which is completely determined by the behavior of the recipient.

These semantics permit communication loosely-coupled in time. There is thus no need for the receiver to be executing when a message is being sent to its queue. Likewise, there is no need for the sender to be executing at the moment its message is picked up by the receiver. The sender and receiver can execute completely independently of each other. In fact, once a message has been deposited in a queue, it will remain there until it is removed, irrespective of whether its sender or receiver is executing. This gives us four combinations with respect to the execution mode of the sender and receiver, as shown in Fig. 4-17.

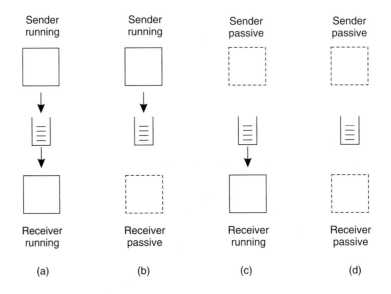

Figure 4-17. Four combinations for loosely-coupled communications using queues.

In Fig. 4-17(a), both the sender and receiver execute during the entire transmission of a message. In Fig. 4-17(b), only the sender is executing, while the receiver is passive, that is, in a state in which message delivery is not possible. Nevertheless, the sender can still send messages. The combination of a passive sender and an executing receiver is shown in Fig. 4-17(c). In this case, the receiver can read messages that were sent to it, but it is not necessary that their respective senders are executing as well. Finally, in Fig. 4-17(d), we see the situation that the system is storing (and possibly transmitting) messages even while sender and receiver are passive.

Messages can, in principle, contain any data. The only important aspect from the perspective of middleware is that messages are properly addressed. In practice, addressing is done by providing a systemwide unique name of the destination queue. In some cases, message size may be limited, although it is also possible that the underlying system takes care of fragmenting and assembling large messages in a way that is completely transparent to applications. An effect of this approach is that the basic interface offered to applications can be extremely simple, as shown in Fig. 4-18.

The put primitive is called by a sender to pass a message to the underlying system that is to be appended to the specified queue. As we explained, this is a

Primitive	Meaning
Put	Append a message to a specified queue
Get	Block until the specified queue is nonempty, and remove the first message
Poll	Check a specified queue for messages, and remove the first. Never block
Notify	Install a handler to be called when a message is put into the specified queue

Figure 4-18. Basic interface to a queue in a message-queuing system.

nonblocking call. The get primitive is a blocking call by which an authorized process can remove the longest pending message in the specified queue. The process is blocked only if the queue is empty. Variations on this call allow searching for a specific message in the queue, for example, using a priority, or a matching pattern. The nonblocking variant is given by the poll primitive. If the queue is empty, or if a specific message could not be found, the calling process simply continues.

Finally, most queuing systems also allow a process to install a handler as a *callback function*, which is automatically invoked whenever a message is put into the queue. Callbacks can also be used to automatically start a process that will fetch messages from the queue if no process is currently executing. This approach is often implemented by means of a daemon on the receiver's side that continuously monitors the queue for incoming messages and handles accordingly.

General Architecture of a Message-Queuing System

Let us now take a closer look at what a general message-queuing system looks like. One of the first restrictions that we make is that messages can be put only into queues that are *local* to the sender, that is, queues on the same machine, or no worse than on a machine nearby such as on the same LAN that can be efficiently reached through an RPC. Such a queue is called the **source queue**. Likewise, messages can be read only from local queues. However, a message put into a queue will contain the specification of a **destination queue** to which it should be transferred. It is the responsibility of a message-queuing system to provide queues to senders and receivers and take care that messages are transferred from their source to their destination queue.

It is important to realize that the collection of queues is distributed across multiple machines. Consequently, for a message-queuing system to transfer messages, it should maintain a mapping of queues to network locations. In practice, this means that it should maintain a (possibly distributed) database of **queue names** to network locations, as shown in Fig. 4-19. Note that such a mapping is completely analogous to the use of the Domain Name System (DNS) for e-mail in the Internet. For example, when sending a message to the logical *mail* address *steen@cs.vu.nl*, the mailing system will query DNS to find the *network* (i.e., IP) address of the recipient's mail server to use for the actual message transfer.

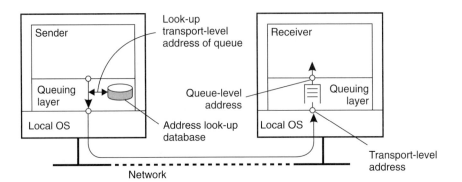

Figure 4-19. The relationship between queue-level addressing and network-level addressing.

Queues are managed by **queue managers**. Normally, a queue manager inter-acts directly with the application that is sending or receiving a message. However, there are also special queue managers that operate as routers, or **relays**: they forward incoming messages to other queue managers. In this way, a message-queuing system may gradually grow into a complete, application-level, **overlay network**, on top of an existing computer network. This approach is similar to the construction of the early MBone over the Internet, in which ordinary user processes were configured as multicast routers. As it turns out, multicasting through overlay networks is still important as we will discuss later in this chapter.

Relays can be convenient for a number of reasons. For example, in many message-queuing systems, there is no general naming service available that can dynamically maintain queue-to-location mappings. Instead, the topology of the queuing network is static, and each queue manager needs a copy of the queue-to-location mapping. It is needless to say that in large-scale queuing systems, this approach can easily lead to network-management problems.

One solution is to use a few routers that know about the network topology. When a sender A puts a message for destination B in its local queue, that message is first transferred to the nearest router, say R1, as shown in Fig. 4-20. At that point, the router knows what to do with the message and forwards it in the direction of B. For example, R1 may derive from B's name that the message should be forwarded to router R2. In this way, only the routers need to be updated when queues are added or removed, while every other queue manager has to know only where the nearest router is.

Relays can thus generally help build scalable message-queuing systems. However, as queuing networks grow, it is clear that the manual configuration of networks will rapidly become completely unmanageable. The only solution is to adopt dynamic routing schemes as is done for computer networks. In that respect, it is somewhat surprising that such solutions are not yet integrated into some of the popular message-queuing systems.

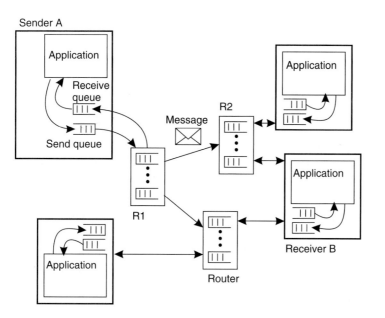

Figure 4-20. The general organization of a message-queuing system with routers.

Another reason why relays are used is that they allow for secondary processing of messages. For example, messages may need to be logged for reasons of security or fault tolerance. A special form of relay that we discuss in the next section is one that acts as a gateway, transforming messages into a format that can be understood by the receiver.

Finally, relays can be used for multicasting purposes. In that case, an incoming message is simply put into each send queue.

Message Brokers

An important application area of message-queuing systems is integrating existing and new applications into a single, coherent distributed information system. Integration requires that applications can understand the messages they receive. In practice, this requires the sender to have its outgoing messages in the same format as that of the receiver.

The problem with this approach is that each time an application is added to the system that requires a separate message format, each potential receiver will have to be adjusted in order to produce that format.

An alternative is to agree on a common message format, as is done with traditional network protocols. Unfortunately, this approach will generally not work for message-queuing systems. The problem is the level of abstraction at which these systems operate. A common message format makes sense only if the collection of processes that make use of that format indeed have enough in common. If the collection of applications that make up a distributed information system is highly diverse (which it often is), then the best common format may well be no more than a sequence of bytes.

Although a few common message formats for specific application domains have been defined, the general approach is to learn to live with different formats, and try to provide the means to make conversions as simple as possible. In message-queuing systems, conversions are handled by special nodes in a queuing network, known as **message brokers**. A message broker acts as an application-level gateway in a message-queuing system. Its main purpose is to convert incoming messages so that they can be understood by the destination application. Note that to a message-queuing system, a message broker is just another application, as shown in Fig. 4-21. In other words, a message broker is generally not considered to be an integral part of the queuing system.

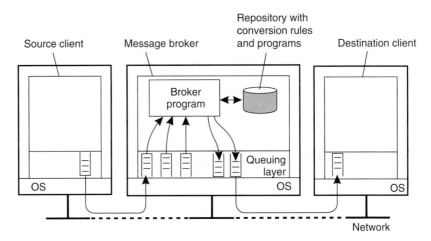

Figure 4-21. The general organization of a message broker in a message-queuing system.

A message broker can be as simple as a reformatter for messages. For example, assume an incoming message contains a table from a database, in which records are separated by a special *end-of-record* delimiter and fields within a record have a known, fixed length. If the destination application expects a different delimiter between records, and also expects that fields have variable lengths, a message broker can be used to convert messages to the format expected by the destination.

In a more advanced setting, a message broker may act as an application-level gateway, such as one that handles the conversion between two different database applications. In such cases, frequently it cannot be guaranteed that all information contained in the incoming message can actually be transformed into something appropriate for the outgoing message.

However, more common is the use of a message broker for advanced **enter-prise application integration** (**EAI**) as we discussed in Chap. 1. In this case, rather than (only) converting messages, a broker is responsible for matching applications based on the messages that are being exchanged. In such a model, called **publish/subscribe**, applications send messages in the form of *publishing*. In particular, they may publish a message on topic *X*, which is then sent to the broker. Applications that have stated their interest in messages on topic *X*, that is, who have *subscribed* to those messages, will then receive these messages from the broker. More advanced forms of mediation are also possible, but we will defer further discussion until Chap. 13.

At the heart of a message broker lies a repository of rules and programs that can transform a message of type *T1* to one of type *T2*. The problem is defining the rules and developing the programs. Most message broker products come with sophisticated development tools, but the bottom line is still that the repository needs to be filled by experts. Here we see a perfect example where commercial products are often misleadingly said to provide "intelligence," where, in fact, the only intelligence is to be found in the heads of those experts.

A Note on Message-Queuing Systems

Considering what we have said about message-queuing systems, it would appear that they have long existed in the form of implementations for e-mail services. E-mail systems are generally implemented through a collection of mail servers that store and forward messages on behalf of the users on hosts directly connected to the server. Routing is generally left out, as e-mail systems can make direct use of the underlying transport services. For example, in the mail protocol for the Internet, SMTP (Postel, 1982), a message is transferred by setting up a direct TCP connection to the destination mail server.

What makes e-mail systems special compared to message-queuing systems is that they are primarily aimed at providing direct support for end users. This explains, for example, why a number of groupware applications are based directly on an e-mail system (Khoshafian and Buckiewicz 1995). In addition, e-mail systems may have very specific requirements such as automatic message filtering, support for advanced messaging databases (e.g., to easily retrieve previously stored messages), and so on.

General message-queuing systems are not aimed at supporting only end users. An important issue is that they are set up to enable persistent communication between processes, regardless of whether a process is running a user application, handling access to a database, performing computations, and so on. This approach leads to a different set of requirements for message-queuing systems than pure e-mail systems. For example, e-mail systems generally need not provide guaranteed message delivery, message priorities, logging facilities, efficient multicasting, load balancing, fault tolerance, and so on for general usage.

General-purpose message-queuing systems, therefore, have a wide range of applications, including e-mail, workflow, groupware, and batch processing. However, as we have stated before, the most important application area is the integration of a (possibly widely-dispersed) collection of databases and applications into a federated information system (Hohpe and Woolf, 2004). For example, a query expanding several databases may need to be split into subqueries that are forwarded to individual databases. Message-queuing systems assist by providing the basic means to package each subquery into a message and routing it to the appropriate database. Other communication facilities we have discussed in this chapter are far less appropriate.

4.3.3 Example: IBM's WebSphere Message-Queuing System

To help understand how message-queuing systems work in practice, let us take a look at one specific system, namely the message-queuing system that is part of IBM's WebSphere product. Formerly known as MQSeries, it is now referred to as **WebSphere MQ**. There is a wealth of documentation on WebSphere MQ, and in the following we can only resort to the basic principles. Many architectural details concerning message-queuing networks can be found in IBM (2005b, 2005d). Programming message-queuing networks is not something that can be learned on a Sunday afternoon, and MQ's programming guide (IBM, 2005a) is a good example showing that going from principles to practice may require substantial effort.

Overview

The basic architecture of an MQ queuing network is quite straightforward, and is shown in Fig. 4-22. All queues are managed by **queue managers**. A queue manager is responsible for removing messages from its send queues, and forwarding those to other queue managers. Likewise, a queue manager is responsible for handling incoming messages by picking them up from the underlying network and subsequently storing each message in the appropriate input queue. To give an impression of what messaging can mean: a message has a maximum default size of 4 MB, but this can be increased up to 100 MB. A queue is normally restricted to 2 GB of data, but depending on the underlying operating system, this maximum can be easily set higher.

Queue managers are pairwise connected through **message channels**, which are an abstraction of transport-level connections. A message channel is a unidirectional, reliable connection between a sending and a receiving queue manager, through which queued messages are transported. For example, an Internet-based message channel is implemented as a TCP connection. Each of the two ends of a message channel is managed by a **message channel agent** (**MCA**). A sending MCA is basically doing nothing else than checking send queues for a message, wrapping it into a transport-level packet, and sending it along the connection to its associated receiving MCA. Likewise, the basic task of a receiving MCA is listening for an incoming packet, unwrapping it, and subsequently storing the unwrapped message into the appropriate queue.

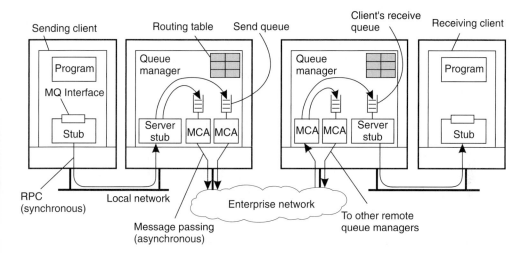

Figure 4-22. General organization of IBM's message-queuing system.

Queue managers can be linked into the same process as the application for which it manages the queues. In that case, the queues are hidden from the application behind a standard interface, but effectively can be directly manipulated by the application. An alternative organization is one in which queue managers and applications run on separate machines. In that case, the application is offered the same interface as when the queue manager is colocated on the same machine. However, the interface is implemented as a proxy that communicates with the queue manager using traditional RPC-based synchronous communication. In this way, MQ basically retains the model that only queues local to an application can be accessed.

Channels

An important component of MQ is formed by the message channels. Each message channel has exactly one associated send queue from which it fetches the messages it should transfer to the other end. Transfer along the channel can take place only if both its sending and receiving MCA are up and running. Apart from starting both MCAs manually, there are several alternative ways to start a channel, some of which we discuss next.

One alternative is to have an application directly start its end of a channel by activating the sending or receiving MCA. However, from a transparency point of view, this is not a very attractive alternative. A better approach to start a *sending* MCA is to configure the channel's send queue to set off a trigger when a message is first put into the queue. That trigger is associated with a handler to start the sending MCA so that it can remove messages from the send queue.

Another alternative is to start an MCA over the network. In particular, if one side of a channel is already active, it can send a control message requesting that the other MCA to be started. Such a control message is sent to a daemon listening to a well-known address on the same machine as where the other MCA is to be started.

Channels are stopped automatically after a specified time has expired during which no more messages were dropped into the send queue.

Each MCA has a set of associated attributes that determine the overall behavior of a channel. Some of the attributes are listed in Fig. 4-23. Attribute values of the sending and receiving MCA should be compatible and perhaps negotiated first before a channel can be set up. For example, both MCAs should obviously support the same transport protocol. An example of a nonnegotiable attribute is whether or not messages are to be delivered in the same order as they are put into the send queue. If one MCA wants FIFO delivery, the other must comply. An example of a negotiable attribute value is the maximum message length, which will simply be chosen as the minimum value specified by either MCA.

Attribute	Description
Transport type	Determines the transport protocol to be used
FIFO delivery	Indicates that messages are to be delivered in the order they are sent
Message length	Maximum length of a single message
Setup retry count	Specifies maximum number of retries to start up the remote MCA
Delivery retries	Maximum times MCA will try to put received message into queue

Figure 4-23. Some attributes associated with message channel agents.

Message Transfer

To transfer a message from one queue manager to another (possibly remote) queue manager, it is necessary that each message carries its destination address, for which a transmission header is used. An address in MQ consists of two parts. The first part consists of the name of the queue manager to which the message is to be delivered. The second part is the name of the destination queue resorting under that manager to which the message is to be appended.

Besides the destination address, it is also necessary to specify the route that a message should follow. Route specification is done by providing the name of the local send queue to which a message is to be appended. Thus it is not necessary to provide the full route in a message. Recall that each message channel has exactly one send queue. By telling to which send queue a message is to be appended, we efectively specify to which queue manager a message is to be forwarded.

In most cases, routes are explicitly stored inside a queue manager in a routing table. An entry in a routing table is a pair (*destQM*, *sendQ*), where *destQM* is the name of the destination queue manager, and *sendQ* is the name of the local send queue to which a message for that queue manager should be appended. (A routing table entry is called an alias in MQ.)

It is possible that a message needs to be transferred across multiple queue managers before reaching its destination. Whenever such an intermediate queue manager receives the message, it simply extracts the name of the destination queue manager from the message header, and does a routing-table look-up to find the local send queue to which the message should be appended.

It is important to realize that each queue manager has a systemwide unique name that is effectively used as an identifier for that queue manager. The problem with using these names is that replacing a queue manager, or changing its name, will affect all applications that send messages to it. Problems can be alleviated by using a **local alias** for queue manager names. An alias defined within a queue manager *M1* is another name for a queue manager *M2*, but which is available only to applications interfacing to *M1*. An alias allows the use of the same (logical) name for a queue, even if the queue manager of that queue changes. Changing the name of a queue manager requires that we change its alias in all queue managers. However, applications can be left unaffected.

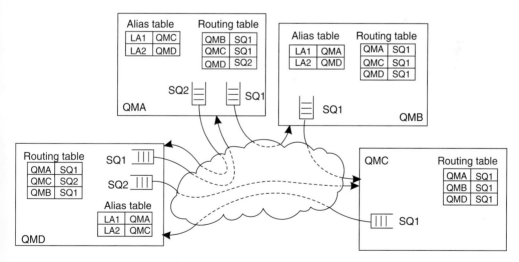

Figure 4-24. The general organization of an MQ queuing network using routing tables and aliases.

The principle of using routing tables and aliases is shown in Fig. 4-24. For example, an application linked to queue manager *QMA* can refer to a remote queue manager using the local alias *LA1*. The queue manager will first look up the actual destination in the alias table to find it is queue manager *QMC*. The route to *QMC* is found in the routing table, which states that messages for *QMC* should be appended to the outgoing queue *SQ1*, which is used to transfer messages to queue manager *QMB*. The latter will use its routing table to forward the message to *QMC*.

Following this approach of routing and aliasing leads to a programming interface that, fundamentally, is relatively simple, called the **Message Queue Interface** (**MQI**). The most important primitives of MQI are summarized in Fig. 4-25.

Primitive	Description
MQopen	Open a (possibly remote) queue
MQclose	Close a queue
MQput	Put a message into an opened queue
MQget	Get a message from a (local) queue

Figure 4-25. Primitives available in the message-queuing interface.

To put messages into a queue, an application calls the MQopen primitive, specifying a destination queue in a specific queue manager. The queue manager can be named using the locally-available alias. Whether the destination queue is actually remote or not is completely transparent to the application. MQopen should also be called if the application wants to get messages from its local queue. Only local queues can be opened for reading incoming messages. When an application is finished with accessing a queue, it should close it by calling MQclose.

Messages can be written to, or read from, a queue using MQput and MQget, respectively. In principle, messages are removed from a queue on a priority basis. Messages with the same priority are removed on a first-in, first-out basis, that is, the longest pending message is removed first. It is also possible to request for specific messages. Finally, MQ provides facilities to signal applications when messages have arrived, thus avoiding that an application will continuously have to poll a message queue for incoming messages.

Managing Overlay Networks

From the description so far, it should be clear that an important part of managing MQ systems is connecting the various queue managers into a consistent overlay network. Moreover, this network needs to be maintained over time. For small networks, this maintenance will not require much more than average administrative work, but matters become complicated when message queuing is used to integrate and disintegrate large existing systems.

A major issue with MQ is that overlay networks need to be manually adminis-trated. This administration not only involves creating channels between queue managers, but also filling in the routing tables. Obviously, this can grow into a nightmare. Unfortunately, management support for MQ systems is advanced only in the sense that an administrator can set virtually every possible attribute, and tweak any thinkable configuration. However, the bottom line is that channels and routing tables need to be manually maintained.

At the heart of overlay management is the **channel control function** com-ponent, which logically sits between message channel agents. This component allows an operator to monitor exactly what is going on at two end points of a channel. In addition, it is used to create channels and routing tables, but also to manage the queue managers that host the message channel agents. In a way, this approach to overlay management strongly resembles the management of cluster servers where a single administration server is used. In the latter case, the server essentially offers only a remote shell to each machine in the cluster, along with a few collective operations to handle groups of machines. The good news about dis-tributed-systems management is that it offers lots of opportunities if you are look-ing for an area to explore new solutions to serious problems.

4.4 STREAM-ORIENTED COMMUNICATION

Communication as discussed so far has concentrated on exchanging more-or-less independent and complete units of information. Examples include a request for invoking a procedure, the reply to such a request, and messages exchanged be-tween applications as in message-queuing systems. The characteristic feature of this type of communication is that it does not matter at what particular point in time communication takes place. Although a system may perform too slow or too fast, timing has no effect on correctness.

There are also forms of communication in which timing plays a crucial role. Consider, for example, an audio stream built up as a sequence of 16-bit samples, each representing the amplitude of the sound wave as is done through Pulse Code Modulation (PCM). Also assume that the audio stream represents CD quality, meaning that the original sound wave has been sampled at a frequency of 44,100 Hz. To reproduce the original sound, it is essential that the samples in the audio stream are played out in the order they appear in the stream, but also at intervals of exactly $1/44,100$ sec. Playing out at a different rate will produce an incorrect version of the original sound.

The question that we address in this section is which facilities a distributed system should offer to exchange time-dependent information such as audio and video streams. Various network protocols that deal with stream-oriented commu-nication are discussed in Halsall (2001). Steinmetz and Nahrstedt (2004) provide an overall introduction to multimedia issues, part of which forms stream-oriented communication. Query processing on data streams is discussed in Babcock et al. (2002).

4.4.1 Support for Continuous Media

Support for the exchange of time-dependent information is often formulated as support for continuous media. A medium refers to the means by which information is conveyed. These means include storage and transmission media, presentation media such as a monitor, and so on. An important type of medium is the way that information is *represented*. In other words, how is information encoded in a computer system? Different representations are used for different types of information. For example, text is generally encoded as ASCII or Unicode. Images can be represented in different formats such as GIF or JPEG. Audio streams can be encoded in a computer system by, for example, taking 16-bit samples using PCM.

In **continuous (representation) media**, the temporal relationships between different data items are fundamental to correctly interpreting what the data actually means. We already gave an example of reproducing a sound wave by playing out an audio stream. As another example, consider motion. Motion can be represented by a series of images in which successive images must be displayed at a uniform spacing T in time, typically 30–40 msec per image. Correct reproduction requires not only showing the stills in the correct order, but also at a constant frequency of $1/T$ images per second.

In contrast to continuous media, **discrete (representation) media**, is characterized by the fact that temporal relationships between data items are *not* fundamental to correctly interpreting the data. Typical examples of discrete media include representations of text and still images, but also object code or executable files.

Data Stream

To capture the exchange of time-dependent information, distributed systems generally provide support for **data streams**. A data stream is nothing but a sequence of data units. Data streams can be applied to discrete as well as continuous media. For example, UNIX pipes or TCP/IP connections are typical examples of (byte-oriented) discrete data streams. Playing an audio file typically requires setting up a continuous data stream between the file and the audio device.

Timing is crucial to continuous data streams. To capture timing aspects, a distinction is often made between different transmission modes. In **asynchronous transmission mode** the data items in a stream are transmitted one after the other, but there are no further timing constraints on when transmission of items should take place. This is typically the case for discrete data streams. For example, a file can be transferred as a data stream, but it is mostly irrelevant exactly when the transfer of each item completes.

In **synchronous transmission mode**, there is a maximum end-to-end delay defined for each unit in a data stream. Whether a data unit is transferred much faster than the maximum tolerated delay is not important. For example, a sensor may sample temperature at a certain rate and pass it through a network to an operator. In that case, it may be important that the end-to-end propagation time through the network is guaranteed to be lower than the time interval between taking samples, but it cannot do any harm if samples are propagated much faster than necessary.

Finally, in **isochronous transmission mode**, it is necessary that data units are transferred on time. This means that data transfer is subject to a maximum *and* minimum end-to-end delay, also referred to as bounded (delay) jitter. Isochronous transmission mode is particularly interesting for distributed multimedia systems, as it plays a crucial role in representing audio and video. In this chapter, we consider only continuous data streams using isochronous transmission, which we will refer to simply as streams.

Streams can be simple or complex. A **simple stream** consists of only a single sequence of data, whereas a **complex stream** consists of several related simple streams, called **substreams**. The relation between the substreams in a complex stream is often also time dependent. For example, stereo audio can be transmitted by means of a complex stream consisting of two substreams, each used for a single audio channel. It is important, however, that those two substreams are continuously synchronized. In other words, data units from each stream are to be communicated pairwise to ensure the effect of stereo. Another example of a complex stream is one for transmitting a movie. Such a stream could consist of a single video stream, along with two streams for transmitting the sound of the movie in stereo. A fourth stream might contain subtitles for the deaf, or a translation into a different language than the audio. Again, synchronization of the substreams is important. If synchronization fails, reproduction of the movie fails. We return to stream synchronization below.

From a distributed systems perspective, we can distinguish several elements that are needed for supporting streams. For simplicity, we concentrate on streaming stored data, as opposed to streaming live data. In the latter case, data is captured in real time and sent over the network to recipients. The main difference between the two is that streaming live data leaves less opportunities for tuning a stream. Following Wu et al. (2001), we can then sketch a general client-server architecture for supporting continuous multimedia streams as shown in Fig. 4-26.

This general architecture reveals a number of important issues that need to be dealt with. In the first place, the multimedia data, notably video and to a lesser extent audio, will need to be compressed substantially in order to reduce the required storage and especially the network capacity. More important from the perspective of communication are controlling the quality of the transmission and synchronization issues. We discuss these issues next.

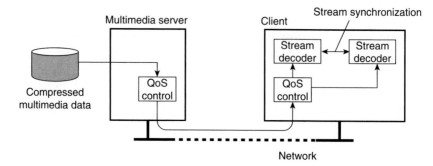

Figure 4-26. A general architecture for streaming stored multimedia data over a network.

4.4.2 Streams and Quality of Service

Timing (and other nonfunctional) requirements are generally expressed as **Quality of Service (QoS)** requirements. These requirements describe what is needed from the underlying distributed system and network to ensure that, for example, the temporal relationships in a stream can be preserved. QoS for continuous data streams mainly concerns timeliness, volume, and reliability. In this section we take a closer look at QoS and its relation to setting up a stream.

Much has been said about how to specify required QoS (see, e.g., Jin and Nahrstedt, 2004). From an application's perspective, in many cases it boils down to specifying a few important properties (Halsall, 2001):

1. The required bit rate at which data should be transported.

2. The maximum delay until a session has been set up (i.e., when an application can start sending data).

3. The maximum end-to-end delay (i.e., how long it will take until a data unit makes it to a recipient).

4. The maximum delay variance, or jitter.

5. The maximum round-trip delay.

It should be noted that many refinements can be made to these specifications, as explained, for example, by Steinmetz and Nahrstadt (2004). However, when dealing with stream-oriented communication that is based on the Internet protocol stack, we simply have to live with the fact that the basis of communication is formed by an extremely simple, best-effort datagram service: IP. When the going gets tough, as may easily be the case in the Internet, the specification of IP allows a protocol implementation to drop packets whenever it sees fit. Many, if not all distributed systems that support stream-oriented communication, are currently built on top of the Internet protocol stack. So much for QoS specifications. (Actually, IP does provide some QoS support, but it is rarely implemented.)

Enforcing QoS

Given that the underlying system offers only a best-effort delivery service, a distributed system can try to conceal as much as possible of the *lack* of quality of service. Fortunately, there are several mechanisms that it can deploy.

First, the situation is not really so bad as sketched so far. For example, the Internet provides a means for differentiating classes of data by means of its **differentiated services**. A sending host can essentially mark outgoing packets as belonging to one of several classes, including an **expedited forwarding** class that essentially specifies that a packet should be forwarded by the current router with absolute priority (Davie et al., 2002). In addition, there is also an **assured forwarding** class, by which traffic is divided into four subclasses, along with three ways to drop packets if the network gets congested. Assured forwarding therefore effectively defines a range of priorities that can be assigned to packets, and as such allows applications to differentiate time-sensitive packets from noncritical ones.

Besides these network-level solutions, a distributed system can also help in getting data across to receivers. Although there are generally not many tools available, one that is particularly useful is to use buffers to reduce jitter. The principle is simple, as shown in Fig. 4-27. Assuming that packets are delayed with a certain variance when transmitted over the network, the receiver simply stores them in a buffer for a maximum amount of time. This will allow the receiver to pass packets to the application at a regular rate, knowing that there will always be enough packets entering the buffer to be played back at that rate.

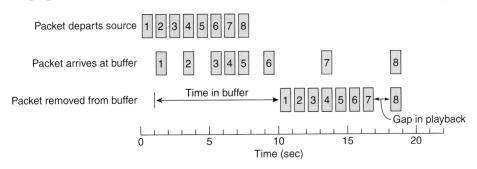

Figure 4-27. Using a buffer to reduce jitter.

Of course, things may go wrong, as is illustrated by packet #8 in Fig. 4-27. The size of the receiver's buffer corresponds to 9 seconds of packets to pass to the application. Unfortunately, packet #8 took 11 seconds to reach the receiver, at which time the buffer will have been completely emptied. The result is a gap in the playback at the application. The only solution is to increase the buffer size. The obvious drawback is that the delay at which the receiving application can start playing back the data contained in the packets increases as well.

Other techniques can be used as well. Realizing that we are dealing with an underlying best-effort service also means that packets may be lost. To compensate for this loss in quality of service, we need to apply error correction techniques (Perkins et al., 1998; and Wah et al., 2000). Requesting the sender to retransmit a missing packet is generally out of the question, so that **forward error correction** (**FEC**) needs to be applied. A well-known technique is to encode the outgoing packets in such a way that any k out of n received packets is enough to reconstruct k correct packets.

One problem that may occur is that a single packet contains multiple audio and video frames. As a consequence, when a packet is lost, the receiver may actually perceive a large gap when playing out frames. This effect can be somewhat circumvented by interleaving frames, as shown in Fig. 4-28. In this way, when a packet is lost, the resulting gap in successive frames is distributed over time. Note, however, that this approach does require a larger receive buffer in comparison to noninterleaving, and thus imposes a higher start delay for the receiving application. For example, when considering Fig. 4-28(b), to play the first four frames, the receiver will need to have four packets delivered, instead of only one packet in comparison to noninterleaved transmission.

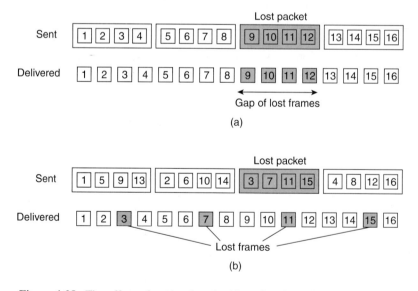

Figure 4-28. The effect of packet loss in (a) noninterleaved transmission and (b) interleaved transmission.

4.4.3 Stream Synchronization

An important issue in multimedia systems is that different streams, possibly in the form of a complex stream, are mutually synchronized. Synchronization of streams deals with maintaining temporal relations between streams. Two types of synchronization occur.

The simplest form of synchronization is that between a discrete data stream and a continuous data stream. Consider, for example, a slide show on the Web that has been enhanced with audio. Each slide is transferred from the server to the client in the form of a discrete data stream. At the same time, the client should play out a specific (part of an) audio stream that matches the current slide that is also fetched from the server. In this case, the audio stream is to be synchronized with the presentation of slides.

A more demanding type of synchronization is that between continuous data streams. A daily example is playing a movie in which the video stream needs to be synchronized with the audio, commonly referred to as lip synchronization. Another example of synchronization is playing a stereo audio stream consisting of two substreams, one for each channel. Proper play out requires that the two substreams are tightly synchronized: a difference of more than 20 µsec can distort the stereo effect.

Synchronization takes place at the level of the data units of which a stream is made up. In other words, we can synchronize two streams only between data units. The choice of what exactly a data unit is depends very much on the level of abstraction at which a data stream is viewed. To make things concrete, consider again a CD-quality (single-channel) audio stream. At the finest granularity, such a stream appears as a sequence of 16-bit samples. With a sampling frequency of 44,100 Hz, synchronization with other audio streams could, in theory, take place approximately every 23 µsec. For high-quality stereo effects, it turns out that synchronization at this level is indeed necessary.

However, when we consider synchronization between an audio stream and a video stream for lip synchronization, a much coarser granularity can be taken. As we explained, video frames need to be displayed at a rate of 25 Hz or more. Taking the widely-used NTSC standard of 29.97 Hz, we could group audio samples into logical units that last as long as a video frame is displayed (33 msec). With an audio sampling frequency of 44,100 Hz, an audio data unit can thus be as large as 1470 samples, or 11,760 bytes (assuming each sample is 16 bits). In practice, larger units lasting 40 or even 80 msec can be tolerated (Steinmetz, 1996).

Synchronization Mechanisms

Let us now see how synchronization is actually done. Two issues need to be distinguished: (1) the basic mechanisms for synchronizing two streams, and (2) the distribution of those mechanisms in a networked environment.

Synchronization mechanisms can be viewed at several different levels of abstraction. At the lowest level, synchronization is done explicitly by operating on the data units of simple streams. This principle is shown in Fig. 4-29. In essence, there is a process that simply executes read and write operations on several simple streams, ensuring that those operations adhere to specific timing and synchronization constraints.

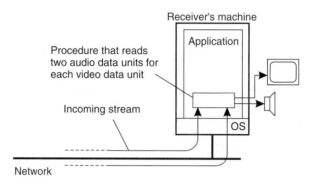

Figure 4-29. The principle of explicit synchronization on the level data units.

For example, consider a movie that is presented as two input streams. The video stream contains uncompressed low-quality images of 320×240 pixels, each encoded by a single byte, leading to video data units of 76,800 bytes each. Assume that images are to be displayed at 30 Hz, or one image every 33 msec. The audio stream is assumed to contain audio samples grouped into units of 11760 bytes, each corresponding to 33 ms of audio, as explained above. If the input process can handle 2.5 MB/sec, we can achieve lip synchronization by simply alternating between reading an image and reading a block of audio samples every 33 ms.

The drawback of this approach is that the application is made completely responsible for implementing synchronization while it has only low-level facilities available. A better approach is to offer an application an interface that allows it to more easily control streams and devices. Returning to our example, assume that the video display has a control interface that allows it to specify the rate at which images should be displayed. In addition, the interface offers the facility to register a user-defined handler that is called each time k new images have arrived. An analogous interface is offered by the audio device. With these control interfaces, an application developer can write a simple monitor program consisting of two handlers, one for each stream, that jointly check if the video and audio stream are sufficiently synchronized, and if necessary, adjust the rate at which video or audio units are presented.

This last example is illustrated in Fig. 4-30, and is typical for many multimedia middleware systems. In effect, multimedia middleware offers a collection of interfaces for controlling audio and video streams, including interfaces for controlling devices such as monitors, cameras, microphones, etc. Each device and stream has its own high-level interfaces, including interfaces for notifying an application when some event occurred. The latter are subsequently used to write handlers for synchronizing streams. Examples of such interfaces are given in Blair and Stefani (1998).

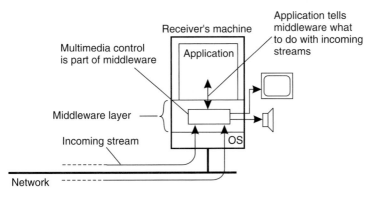

Figure 4-30. The principle of synchronization as supported by high-level interfaces.

The distribution of synchronization mechanisms is another issue that needs to be looked at. First, the receiving side of a complex stream consisting of substreams that require synchronization, needs to know exactly what to do. In other words, it must have a complete *synchronization specification* locally available. Common practice is to provide this information implicitly by multiplexing the different streams into a single stream containing all data units, including those for synchronization.

This latter approach to synchronization is followed for MPEG streams. The **MPEG (Motion Picture Experts Group)** standards form a collection of algorithms for compressing video and audio. Several MPEG standards exist. MPEG-2, for example, was originally designed for compressing broadcast quality video into 4 to 6 Mbps. In MPEG-2, an unlimited number of continuous and discrete streams can be merged into a single stream. Each input stream is first turned into a stream of packets that carry a timestamp based on a 90-kHz system clock. These streams are subsequently multiplexed into a **program stream** then consisting of variable-length packets, but which have in common that they all have the same time base. The receiving side demultiplexes the stream, again using the timestamps of each packet as the basic mechanism for interstream synchronization.

Another important issue is whether synchronization should take place at the sending or the receiving side. If the sender handles synchronization, it may be possible to merge streams into a single stream with a different type of data unit. Consider again a stereo audio stream consisting of two substreams, one for each channel. One possibility is to transfer each stream independently to the receiver and let the latter synchronize the samples pairwise. Obviously, as each substream may be subject to different delays, synchronization can be extremely difficult. A better approach is to merge the two substreams at the sender. The resulting stream consists of data units consisting of pairs of samples, one for each channel. The receiver now merely has to read in a data unit, and split it into a left and right sample. Delays for both channels are now identical.

4.5 MULTICAST COMMUNICATION

An important topic in communication in distributed systems is the support for sending data to multiple receivers, also known as multicast communication. For many years, this topic has belonged to the domain of network protocols, where numerous proposals for network-level and transport-level solutions have been implemented and evaluated (Janic, 2005; and Obraczka, 1998). A major issue in all solutions was setting up the communication paths for information dissemination. In practice, this involved a huge management effort, in many cases requiring human intervention. In addition, as long as there is no convergence of proposals, ISPs have shown to be reluctant to support multicasting (Diot et al., 2000).

With the advent of peer-to-peer technology, and notably structured overlay management, it became easier to set up communication paths. As peer-to-peer solutions are typically deployed at the application layer, various application-level multicasting techniques have been introduced. In this section, we will take a brief look at these techniques.

Multicast communication can also be accomplished in other ways than setting up explicit communication paths. As we also explore in this section, gossip-based information dissemination provides simple (yet often less efficient) ways for multicasting.

4.5.1 Application-Level Multicasting

The basic idea in application-level multicasting is that nodes organize into an overlay network, which is then used to disseminate information to its members. An important observation is that network routers are not involved in group membership. As a consequence, the connections between nodes in the overlay network may cross several physical links, and as such, routing messages within the overlay may not be optimal in comparison to what could have been achieved by network-level routing.

A crucial design issue is the construction of the overlay network. In essence, there are two approaches (El-Sayed, 2003). First, nodes may organize themselves directly into a tree, meaning that there is a unique (overlay) path between every pair of nodes. An alternative approach is that nodes organize into a mesh network in which every node will have multiple neighbors and, in general, there exist multiple paths between every pair of nodes. The main difference between the two is that the latter generally provides higher robustness: if a connection breaks (e.g., because a node fails), there will still be an opportunity to disseminate information without having to immediately reorganize the entire overlay network.

To make matters concrete, let us consider a relatively simple scheme for constructing a multicast tree in Chord, which we described in Chap. 2. This scheme was originally proposed for Scribe (Castro et al., 2002) which is an application-level multicasting scheme built on top of Pastry (Rowstron and Druschel, 2001). The latter is also a DHT-based peer-to-peer system.

Assume a node wants to start a multicast session. To this end, it simply generates a multicast identifier, say *mid* which is just a randomly-chosen 160-bit key. It then looks up *succ(mid)*, which is the node responsible for that key, and promotes it to become the root of the multicast tree that will be used to sending data to interested nodes. In order to join the tree, a node P simply executes the operation LOOKUP(mid) having the effect that a lookup message with the request to join the multicast group *mid* will be routed from P to *succ(mid)*. As we mentioned before, the routing algorithm itself will be explained in detail in Chap. 5.

On its way toward the root, the join request will pass several nodes. Assume it first reaches node Q. If Q had never seen a join request for *mid* before, it will become a **forwarder** for that group. At that point, P will become a child of Q whereas the latter will continue to forward the join request to the root. If the next node on the root, say R is also not yet a forwarder, it will become one and record Q as its child and continue to send the join request.

On the other hand, if Q (or R) is already a forwarder for *mid*, it will also record the previous sender as its child (i.e., P or Q, respectively), but there will not be a need to send the join request to the root anymore, as Q (or R) will already be a member of the multicast tree.

Nodes such as P that have explicitly requested to join the multicast tree are, by definition, also forwarders. The result of this scheme is that we construct a multicast tree across the overlay network with two types of nodes: pure forwarders that act as helpers, and nodes that are also forwarders, but have explicitly requested to join the tree. Multicasting is now simple: a node merely sends a multicast message toward the root of the tree by again executing the LOOKUP(mid) operation, after which that message can be sent along the tree.

We note that this high-level description of multicasting in Scribe does not do justice to its original design. The interested reader is therefore encouraged to take a look at the details, which can be found in Castro et al. (2002).

Overlay Construction

From the high-level description given above, it should be clear that although building a tree by itself is not that difficult once we have organized the nodes into an overlay, building an efficient tree may be a different story. Note that in our description so far, the selection of nodes that participate in the tree does not take into account any performance metrics: it is purely based on the (logical) routing of messages through the overlay.

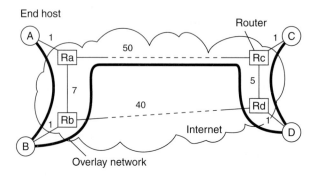

Figure 4-31. The relation between links in an overlay and actual network-level routes.

To understand the problem at hand, take a look at Fig. 4-31 which shows a small set of four nodes that are organized in a simple overlay network, with node *A* forming the root of a multicast tree. The costs for traversing a physical link are also shown. Now, whenever *A* multicasts a message to the other nodes, it is seen that this message will traverse each of the links *<B, Rb>*, *<Ra, Rb>*, *<Rc, Rd>*, and *<D, Rd>* twice. The overlay network would have been more efficient if we had not constructed an overlay link from *B* to *D*, but instead from *A* to *C*. Such a configuration would have saved the double traversal across links *<Ra, Rb>* and *<Rc, Rd>*.

The quality of an application-level multicast tree is generally measured by three different metrics: link stress, stretch, and tree cost. **Link stress** is defined per link and counts how often a packet crosses the same link (Chu et al., 2002). A link stress greater than 1 comes from the fact that although at a logical level a packet may be forwarded along two different connections, part of those connections may actually correspond to the same physical link, as we showed in Fig. 4-31.

The **stretch** or **Relative Delay Penalty** (**RDP**) measures the ratio in the delay between two nodes in the overlay, and the delay that those two nodes would experience in the underlying network. For example, in the overlay network, messages from *B* to *C* follow the route $B \rightarrow Rb \rightarrow Ra \rightarrow Rc \rightarrow C$, having a total cost of 59 units. However, messages would have been routed in the underlying network along the path $B \rightarrow Rb \rightarrow Rd \rightarrow Rc \rightarrow C$, with a total cost of 47 units, leading to a stretch of 1.255. Obviously, when constructing an overlay network, the goal is to minimize the aggregated stretch, or similarly, the average RDP measured over all node pairs.

Finally, the **tree cost** is a global metric, generally related to minimizing the aggregated link costs. For example, if the cost of a link is taken to be the delay between its two end nodes, then optimizing the tree cost boils down to finding a minimal spanning tree in which the total time for disseminating information to all nodes is minimal.

To simplify matters somewhat, assume that a multicast group has an associated and well-known node that keeps track of the nodes that have joined the tree. When a new node issues a join request, it contacts this **rendezvous node** to obtain a (potentially partial) list of members. The goal is to select the best member that can operate as the new node's parent in the tree. Who should it select? There are many alternatives and different proposals often follow very different solutions.

Consider, for example, a multicast group with only a single source. In this case, the selection of the best node is obvious: it should be the source (because in that case we can be assured that the stretch will be equal to 1). However, in doing so, we would introduce a star topology with the source in the middle. Although simple, it is not difficult to imagine the source may easily become overloaded. In other words, selection of a node will generally be constrained in such a way that only those nodes may be chosen who have k or less neighbors, with k being a design parameter. This constraint severely complicates the tree-establishment algorithm, as a good solution may require that part of the existing tree is reconfigured.

Tan et al. (2003) provide an extensive overview and evaluation of various solutions to this problem. As an illustration, let us take a closer look at one specific family, known as **switch-trees** (Helder and Jamin, 2002). The basic idea is simple. Assume we already have a multicast tree with a single source as root. In this tree, a node P can switch parents by dropping the link to its current parent in favor of a link to another node. The only constraints imposed on switching links is that the new parent can never be a member of the subtree rooted at P (as this would partition the tree and create a loop), and that the new parent will not have too many immediate children. The latter is needed to limit the load of forwarding messages by any single node.

There are different criteria for deciding to switch parents. A simple one is to optimize the route to the source, effectively minimizing the delay when a message is to be multicast. To this end, each node regularly receives information on other nodes (we will explain one specific way of doing this below). At that point, the node can evaluate whether another node would be a better parent in terms of delay along the route to the source, and if so, initiates a switch.

Another criteria could be whether the delay to the potential other parent is lower than to the current parent. If every node takes this as a criterion, then the aggregated delays of the resulting tree should ideally be minimal. In other words, this is an example of optimizing the cost of the tree as we explained above. However, more information would be needed to construct such a tree, but as it turns out, this simple scheme is a reasonable heuristic leading to a good approximation of a minimal spanning tree.

As an example, consider the case where a node P receives information on the neighbors of its parent. Note that the neighbors consist of P's grandparent, along with the other siblings of P's parent. Node P can then evaluate the delays to each of these nodes and subsequently choose the one with the lowest delay, say Q, as its new parent. To that end, it sends a switch request to Q. To prevent loops from being formed due to concurrent switching requests, a node that has an outstanding switch request will simply refuse to process any incoming requests. In effect, this leads to a situation where only completely independent switches can be carried out simultaneously. Furthermore, P will provide Q with enough information to allow the latter to conclude that both nodes have the same parent, or that Q is the grandparent.

An important problem that we have not yet addressed is node failure. In the case of switch-trees, a simple solution is proposed: whenever a node notices that its parent has failed, it simply attaches itself to the root. At that point, the optimization protocol can proceed as usual and will eventually place the node at a good point in the multicast tree. Experiments described in Helder and Jamin (2002) show that the resulting tree is indeed close to a minimal spanning one.

4.5.2 Gossip-Based Data Dissemination

An increasingly important technique for disseminating information is to rely on *epidemic behavior*. Observing how diseases spread among people, researchers have since long investigated whether simple techniques could be developed for spreading information in very large-scale distributed systems. The main goal of these **epidemic protocols** is to rapidly propagate information among a large collection of nodes using only local information. In other words, there is no central component by which information dissemination is coordinated.

To explain the general principles of these algorithms, we assume that all updates for a specific data item are initiated at a single node. In this way, we simply avoid write-write conflicts. The following presentation is based on the classical paper by Demers et al. (1987) on epidemic algorithms. A recent overview of epidemic information dissemination can be found in Eugster at el. (2004).

Information Dissemination Models

As the name suggests, epidemic algorithms are based on the theory of epidemics, which studies the spreading of infectious diseases. In the case of large-scale distributed systems, instead of spreading diseases, they spread information. Research on epidemics for distributed systems also aims at a completely different goal: whereas health organizations will do their utmost best to prevent infectious diseases from spreading across large groups of people, designers of epidemic algorithms for distributed systems will try to "infect" all nodes with new information as fast as possible.

Using the terminology from epidemics, a node that is part of a distributed system is called **infected** if it holds data that it is willing to spread to other nodes. A node that has not yet seen this data is called **susceptible**. Finally, an updated node that is not willing or able to spread its data is said to be **removed**. Note that we assume we can distinguish old from new data, for example, because it has been timestamped or versioned. In this light, nodes are also said to spread updates.

A popular propagation model is that of **anti-entropy**. In this model, a node P picks another node Q at random, and subsequently exchanges updates with Q. There are three approaches to exchanging updates:

1. P only pushes its own updates to Q

2. P only pulls in new updates from Q

3. P and Q send updates to each other (i.e., a push-pull approach)

When it comes to rapidly spreading updates, only pushing updates turns out to be a bad choice. Intuitively, this can be understood as follows. First, note that in a pure push-based approach, updates can be propagated only by infected nodes. However, if many nodes are infected, the probability of each one selecting a susceptible node is relatively small. Consequently, chances are that a particular node remains susceptible for a long period simply because it is not selected by an infected node.

In contrast, the pull-based approach works much better when many nodes are infected. In that case, spreading updates is essentially triggered by susceptible nodes. Chances are large that such a node will contact an infected one to subsequently pull in the updates and become infected as well.

It can be shown that if only a single node is infected, updates will rapidly spread across all nodes using either form of anti-entropy, although push-pull remains the best strategy (Jelasity et al., 2005a). Define a **round** as spanning a period in which every node will at least once have taken the initiative to exchange updates with a randomly chosen other node. It can then be shown that the number of rounds to propagate a single update to all nodes takes $O(log(N))$ rounds, where N is the number of nodes in the system. This indicates indeed that propagating updates is fast, but above all scalable.

One specific variant of this approach is called **rumor spreading**, or simply **gossiping**. It works as follows. If node P has just been updated for data item x, it contacts an arbitrary other node Q and tries to push the update to Q. However, it is possible that Q was already updated by another node. In that case, P may lose interest in spreading the update any further, say with probability $1/k$. In other words, it then becomes removed.

Gossiping is completely analogous to real life. When Bob has some hot news to spread around, he may phone his friend Alice telling her all about it. Alice, like Bob, will be really excited to spread the gossip to her friends as well. However, she will become disappointed when phoning a friend, say Chuck, only to hear that the news has already reached him. Chances are that she will stop phoning other friends, for what good is it if they already know?

Gossiping turns out to be an excellent way of rapidly spreading news. However, it cannot guarantee that all nodes will actually be updated (Demers et al., 1987). It can be shown that when there is a large number of nodes that participate in the epidemics, the fraction s of nodes that will remain ignorant of an update, that is, remain susceptible, satisfies the equation:

$$s = e^{-(k+1)(1-s)}$$

Fig. 4-32 shows $ln(s)$ as a function of k. For example, if $k = 4$, $ln(s) = -4.97$, so that s is less than 0.007, meaning that less than 0.7% of the nodes remain susceptible. Nevertheless, special measures are needed to guarantee that those nodes will also be updated. Combining anti-entropy with gossiping will do the trick.

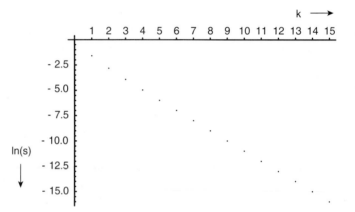

Figure 4-32. The relation between the fraction s of update-ignorant nodes and the parameter k in pure gossiping. The graph displays $ln(s)$ as a function of k.

One of the main advantages of epidemic algorithms is their scalability, due to the fact that the number of synchronizations between processes is relatively small compared to other propagation methods. For wide-area systems, Lin and Marzullo (1999) show that it makes sense to take the actual network topology into account to achieve better results. In their approach, nodes that are connected to only a few other nodes are contacted with a relatively high probability. The underlying assumption is that such nodes form a bridge to other remote parts of the network; therefore, they should be contacted as soon as possible. This approach is referred to as **directional gossiping** and comes in different variants.

This problem touches upon an important assumption that most epidemic solutions make, namely that a node can randomly select any other node to gossip with. This implies that, in principle, the complete set of nodes should be known to each member. In a large system, this assumption can never hold.

Fortunately, there is no need to have such a list. As we explained in Chap. 2, maintaining a partial view that is more or less continuously updated will organize the collection of nodes into a random graph. By regularly updating the partial view of each node, random selection is no longer a problem.

Removing Data

Epidemic algorithms are extremely good for spreading updates. However, they have a rather strange side-effect: spreading the *deletion* of a data item is hard. The essence of the problem lies in the fact that deletion of a data item destroys all information on that item. Consequently, when a data item is simply removed from a node, that node will eventually receive old copies of the data item and interpret those as updates on something it did not have before.

The trick is to record the deletion of a data item as just another update, and keep a record of that deletion. In this way, old copies will not be interpreted as something new, but merely treated as versions that have been updated by a delete operation. The recording of a deletion is done by spreading **death certificates**.

Of course, the problem with death certificates is that they should eventually be cleaned up, or otherwise each node will gradually build a huge local database of historical information on deleted data items that is otherwise not used. Demers et al. (1987) propose to use what they call dormant death certificates. Each death certificate is timestamped when it is created. If it can be assumed that updates propagate to all nodes within a known finite time, then death certificates can be removed after this maximum propagation time has elapsed.

However, to provide hard guarantees that deletions are indeed spread to all nodes, only a very few nodes maintain dormant death certificates that are never thrown away. Assume node P has such a certificate for data item x. If by any chance an obsolete update for x reaches P, P will react by simply spreading the death certificate for x again.

Applications

To finalize this presentation, let us take a look at some interesting applications of epidemic protocols. We already mentioned spreading updates, which is perhaps the most widely-deployed application. Also, in Chap. 2 we discussed how providing positioning information about nodes can assist in constructing specific topologies. In the same light, gossiping can be used to discover nodes that have a few outgoing wide-area links, to subsequently apply directional gossiping as we mentioned above.

Another interesting application area is simply collecting, or actually aggregating information (Jelasity et al., 2005b). Consider the following information exchange. Every node i initially chooses an arbitrary number, say x_i. When node i contacts node j, they each update their value as:

$$x_i, x_j \leftarrow (x_i + x_j) / 2$$

Obviously, after this exchange, both i and j will have the same value. In fact, it is not difficult to see that eventually all nodes will have the same value, namely the average of all initial values. Propagation speed is again exponential.

What use does computing the average have? Consider the situation that all nodes i have set x_i to zero, except for x_1, which has set it to 1:

$$x_i \leftarrow \begin{cases} 1 & \text{if } i = 1 \\ 0 & \text{if } i > 1 \end{cases}$$

If there N nodes, then eventually each node will compute the average, which is $1/N$. As a consequence, every node i can estimate the size of the system as being $1/x_i$. This information alone can be used to dynamically adjust various system parameters. For example, the size of the partial view (i.e., the number of neighbors that each nodes keeps track of) should be dependent on the total number of participating nodes. Knowing this number will allow a node to dynamically adjust the size of its partial view. Indeed, this can be viewed as a property of self-management.

Computing the average may prove to be difficult when nodes regularly join and leave the system. One practical solution to this problem is to introduce epochs. Assuming that node 1 is stable, it simply starts a new epoch now and then. When node i sees a new epoch for the first time, it resets its own variable x_i to zero and starts computing the average again.

Of course, other results can also be computed. For example, instead of having a fixed node (x_1) start the computation of the average, we can easily pick a random node as follows. Every node i initially sets x_i to a random number from the same interval, say $[0,1]$, and also stores it permanently as m_i. Upon an exchange between nodes i and j, each change their value to:

$$x_i, x_j \leftarrow max(x_i, x_j)$$

Each node i for which $m_i < x_i$ will lose the competition for being the initiator in starting the computation of the average. In the end, there will be a single winner. Of course, although it is easy to conclude that a node has lost, it is much more difficult to decide that it has won, as it remains uncertain whether all results have come in. The solution to this problem is to be optimistic: a node always assumes it is the winner until proven otherwise. At that point, it simply resets the variable it is using for computing the average to zero. Note that by now, several different computations (in our example computing a maximum and computing an average) may be executing concurrently.

4.6 SUMMARY

Having powerful and flexible facilities for communication between processes is essential for any distributed system. In traditional network applications, communication is often based on the low-level message-passing primitives offered by the transport layer. An important issue in middleware systems is to offer a higher level of abstraction that will make it easier to express communication between processes than the support offered by the interface to the transport layer.

One of the most widely used abstractions is the Remote Procedure Call (RPC). The essence of an RPC is that a service is implemented by means of a procedure, of which the body is executed at a server. The client is offered only the signature of the procedure, that is, the procedure's name along with its parameters. When the client calls the procedure, the client-side implementation, called a stub, takes care of wrapping the parameter values into a message and sending that to the server. The latter calls the actual procedure and returns the results, again in a message. The client's stub extracts the result values from the return message and passes it back to the calling client application.

RPCs offer synchronous communication facilities, by which a client is blocked until the server has sent a reply. Although variations of either mechanism exist by which this strict synchronous model is relaxed, it turns out that general-purpose, high-level message-oriented models are often more convenient.

In message-oriented models, the issues are whether or not communication is persistent, and whether or not communication is synchronous. The essence of persistent communication is that a message that is submitted for transmission, is stored by the communication system as long as it takes to deliver it. In other words, neither the sender nor the receiver needs to be up and running for message transmission to take place. In transient communication, no storage facilities are offered, so that the receiver must be prepared to accept the message when it is sent.

In asynchronous communication, the sender is allowed to continue immediately after the message has been submitted for transmission, possibly before it has even been sent. In synchronous communication, the sender is blocked at least until a message has been received. Alternatively, the sender may be blocked until message delivery has taken place or even until the receiver has responded as with RPCs.

Message-oriented middleware models generally offer persistent asynchronous communication, and are used where RPCs are not appropriate. They are often used to assist the integration of (widely-dispersed) collections of databases into large-scale information systems. Other applications include e-mail and workflow.

A very different form of communication is that of streaming, in which the issue is whether or not two successive messages have a temporal relationship. In continuous data streams, a maximum end-to-end delay is specified for each message. In addition, it is also required that messages are sent subject to a minimum end-to-end delay. Typical examples of such continuous data streams are video and audio streams. Exactly what the temporal relations are, or what is expected from the underlying communication subsystem in terms of quality of service is often difficult to specify and to implement. A complicating factor is the role of jitter. Even if the average performance is acceptable, substantial variations in delivery time may lead to unacceptable performance.

Finally, an important class of communication protocols in distributed systems is multicasting. The basic idea is to disseminate information from one sender to multiple receivers. We have discussed two different approaches. First, multicasting can be achieved by setting up a tree from the sender to the receivers. Considering that it is now well understood how nodes can self-organize into peer-to-peer system, solutions have also appeared to dynamically set up trees in a decentralized fashion.

Another important class of dissemination solutions deploys epidemic protocols. These protocols have proven to be very simple, yet extremely robust. Apart from merely spreading messages, epidemic protocols can also be efficiently deployed for aggregating information across a large distributed system.

PROBLEMS

1. In many layered protocols, each layer has its own header. Surely it would be more efficient to have a single header at the front of each message with all the control in it than all these separate headers. Why is this not done?

2. Why are transport-level communication services often inappropriate for building distributed applications?

3. A reliable multicast service allows a sender to reliably pass messages to a collection of receivers. Does such a service belong to a middleware layer, or should it be part of a lower-level layer?

4. Consider a procedure *incr* with two integer parameters. The procedure adds one to each parameter. Now suppose that it is called with the same variable twice, for example, as *incr(i, i)*. If *i* is initially 0, what value will it have afterward if call-by-reference is used? How about if copy/restore is used?

5. C has a construction called a union, in which a field of a record (called a struct in C) can hold any one of several alternatives. At run time, there is no sure-fire way to tell which one is in there. Does this feature of C have any implications for remote procedure call? Explain your answer.

6. One way to handle parameter conversion in RPC systems is to have each machine send parameters in its native representation, with the other one doing the translation, if need be. The native system could be indicated by a code in the first byte. However, since locating the first byte in the first word is precisely the problem, can this work?

7. Assume a client calls an asynchronous RPC to a server, and subsequently waits until the server returns a result using another asynchronous RPC. Is this approach the same as letting the client execute a normal RPC? What if we replace the asynchronous RPCs with asynchronous RPCs?

8. Instead of letting a server register itself with a daemon as in DCE, we could also choose to always assign it the same end point. That end point can then be used in references to objects in the server's address space. What is the main drawback of this scheme?

9. Would it be useful also to make a distinction between static and dynamic RPCs?

10. Describe how connectionless communication between a client and a server proceeds when using sockets.

11. Explain the difference between the primitives MPI_bsend and MPI_isend in MPI.

12. Suppose that you could make use of only transient asynchronous communication primitives, including only an asynchronous receive primitive. How would you implement primitives for transient *synchronous* communication?

13. Suppose that you could make use of only transient synchronous communication primitives. How would you implement primitives for transient *asynchronous* communication?

14. Does it make sense to implement persistent asynchronous communication by means of RPCs?

15. In the text we stated that in order to automatically start a process to fetch messages from an input queue, a daemon is often used that monitors the input queue. Give an alternative implementation that does not make use of a daemon.

16. Routing tables in IBM WebSphere, and in many other message-queuing systems, are configured manually. Describe a simple way to do this automatically.

17. With persistent communication, a receiver generally has its own local buffer where messages can be stored when the receiver is not executing. To create such a buffer, we may need to specify its size. Give an argument why this is preferable, as well as one against specification of the size.

18. Explain why transient synchronous communication has inherent scalability problems, and how these could be solved.

19. Give an example where multicasting is also useful for discrete data streams.

20. Suppose that in a sensor network measured temperatures are not timestamped by the sensor, but are immediately sent to the operator. Would it be enough to guarantee only a maximum end-to-end delay?

21. How could you guarantee a maximum end-to-end delay when a collection of computers is organized in a (logical or physical) ring?

22. How could you guarantee a minimum end-to-end delay when a collection of computers is organized in a (logical or physical) ring?

23. Despite that multicasting is technically feasible, there is very little support to deploy it in the Internet. The answer to this problem is to be sought in down-to-earth business models: no one really knows how to make money out of multicasting. What scheme can you invent?

24. Normally, application-level multicast trees are optimized with respect stretch, which is measured in terms of delay or hop counts. Give an example where this metric could lead to very poor trees.

25. When searching for files in an unstructured peer-to-peer system, it may help to restrict the search to nodes that have files similar to yours. Explain how gossiping can help to find those nodes.

5

NAMING

Names play a very important role in all computer systems. They are used to share resources, to uniquely identify entities, to refer to locations, and more. An important issue with naming is that a name can be resolved to the entity it refers to. Name resolution thus allows a process to access the named entity. To resolve names, it is necessary to implement a naming system. The difference between naming in distributed systems and nondistributed systems lies in the way naming systems are implemented.

In a distributed system, the implementation of a naming system is itself often distributed across multiple machines. How this distribution is done plays a key role in the efficiency and scalability of the naming system. In this chapter, we concentrate on three different, important ways that names are used in distributed systems.

First, after discussing some general issues with respect to naming, we take a closer look at the organization and implementation of human-friendly names. Typical examples of such names include those for file systems and the World Wide Web. Building worldwide, scalable naming systems is a primary concern for these types of names.

Second, names are used to locate entities in a way that is independent of their current location. As it turns out, naming systems for human-friendly names are not particularly suited for supporting this type of tracking down entities. Most names do not even hint at the entity's location. Alternative organizations are needed, such as those being used for mobile telephony where names are location-independent identifiers, and those for distributed hash tables.

Finally, humans often prefer to describe entities by means of various characteristics, leading to a situation in which we need to resolve a description by means of attributes to an entity adhering to that description. This type of name resolution is notoriously difficult and we will pay separate attention to it.

5.1 NAMES, IDENTIFIERS, AND ADDRESSES

Let us start by taking a closer look at what a name actually is. A name in a distributed system is a string of bits or characters that is used to refer to an entity. An entity in a distributed system can be practically anything. Typical examples include resources such as hosts, printers, disks, and files. Other well-known examples of entities that are often explicitly named are processes, users, mailboxes, newsgroups, Web pages, graphical windows, messages, network connections, and so on.

Entities can be operated on. For example, a resource such as a printer offers an interface containing operations for printing a document, requesting the status of a print job, and the like. Furthermore, an entity such as a network connection may provide operations for sending and receiving data, setting quality-of-service parameters, requesting the status, and so forth.

To operate on an entity, it is necessary to access it, for which we need an **access point**. An access point is yet another, but special, kind of entity in a distributed system. The name of an access point is called an **address**. The address of an access point of an entity is also simply called an address of that entity.

An entity can offer more than one access point. As a comparison, a telephone can be viewed as an access point of a person, whereas the telephone number corresponds to an address. Indeed, many people nowadays have several telephone numbers, each number corresponding to a point where they can be reached. In a distributed system, a typical example of an access point is a host running a specific server, with its address formed by the combination of, for example, an IP address and port number (i.e., the server's transport-level address).

An entity may change its access points in the course of time. For example, when a mobile computer moves to another location, it is often assigned a different IP address than the one it had before. Likewise, when a person moves to another city or country, it is often necessary to change telephone numbers as well. In a similar fashion, changing jobs or Internet Service Providers, means changing your e-mail address.

An address is thus just a special kind of name: it refers to an access point of an entity. Because an access point is tightly associated with an entity, it would seem convenient to use the address of an access point as a regular name for the associated entity. Nevertheless, this is hardly ever done as such naming is generally very inflexible and often human unfriendly.

For example, it is not uncommon to regularly reorganize a distributed system, so that a specific server is now running on a different host than previously. The old machine on which the server used to be running may be reassigned to a completely different server. In other words, an entity may easily change an access point, or an access point may be reassigned to a different entity. If an address is used to refer to an entity, we will have an invalid reference the instant the access point changes or is reassigned to another entity. Therefore, it is much better to let a service be known by a separate name independent of the address of the associated server.

Likewise, if an entity offers more than one access point, it is not clear which address to use as a reference. For instance, many organizations distribute their Web service across several servers. If we would use the addresses of those servers as a reference for the Web service, it is not obvious which address should be chosen as the best one. Again, a much better solution is to have a single name for the Web service independent from the addresses of the different Web servers.

These examples illustrate that a name for an entity that is independent from its addresses is often much easier and more flexible to use. Such a name is called **location independent**.

In addition to addresses, there are other types of names that deserve special treatment, such as names that are used to uniquely identify an entity. A true **identifier** is a name that has the following properties (Wieringa and de Jonge, 1995):

1. An identifier refers to at most one entity.

2. Each entity is referred to by at most one identifier.

3. An identifier always refers to the same entity (i.e., it is never reused).

By using identifiers, it becomes much easier to unambiguously refer to an entity. For example, assume two processes each refer to an entity by means of an identifier. To check if the processes are referring to the same entity, it is sufficient to test if the two identifiers are equal. Such a test would not be sufficient if the two processes were using regular, nonunique, nonidentifying names. For example, the name "John Smith" cannot be taken as a unique reference to just a single person.

Likewise, if an address can be reassigned to a different entity, we cannot use an address as an identifier. Consider the use of telephone numbers, which are reasonably stable in the sense that a telephone number for some time refers to the same person or organization. However, using a telephone number as an identifier will not work, as it can be reassigned in the course of time. Consequently, Bob's new bakery may be receiving phone calls for Alice's old antique store for a long time. In this case, it would have been better to use a true identifier for Alice instead of her phone number.

Addresses and identifiers are two important types of names that are each used for very different purposes. In many computer systems, addresses and identifiers are represented in machine-readable form only, that is, in the form of bit strings. For example, an Ethernet address is essentially a random string of 48 bits. Likewise, memory addresses are typically represented as 32-bit or 64-bit strings.

Another important type of name is that which is tailored to be used by humans, also referred to as **human-friendly names**. In contrast to addresses and identifiers, a human-friendly name is generally represented as a character string. These names appear in many different forms. For example, files in UNIX systems have character-string names that can be as long as 255 characters, and which are defined entirely by the user. Similarly, DNS names are represented as relatively simple case-insensitive character strings.

Having names, identifiers, and addresses brings us to the central theme of this chapter: how do we resolve names and identifiers to addresses? Before we go into various solutions, it is important to realize that there is often a close relationship between name resolution in distributed systems and message routing. In principle, a naming system maintains a **name-to-address binding** which in its simplest form is just a table of *(name, address)* pairs. However, in distributed systems that span large networks and for which many resources need to be named, a centralized table is not going to work.

Instead, what often happens is that a name is decomposed into several parts such as *ftp.cs.vu.nl* and that name resolution takes place through a recursive lookup of those parts. For example, a client needing to know the address of the FTP server named by *ftp.cs.vu.nl* would first resolve *nl* to find the server *NS(nl)* responsible for names that end with *nl*, after which the rest of the name is passed to server *NS(nl)*. This server may then resolve the name *vu* to the server *NS(vu.nl)* responsible for names that end with *vu.nl* who can further handle the remaining name *ftp.cs*. Eventually, this leads to routing the name resolution request as:

$$NS(.) \;\rightarrow\; NS(nl) \;\rightarrow\; NS(vu.nl) \;\rightarrow\; \text{address of } ftp.cs.vu.nl$$

where *NS(.)* denotes the server that can return the address of *NS(nl)*, also known as the **root server**. *NS(vu.nl)* will return the actual address of the FTP server. It is interesting to note that the boundaries between name resolution and message routing are starting to blur.

In the following sections we will consider three different classes of naming systems. First, we will take a look at how identifiers can be resolved to addresses. In this case, we will also see an example where name resolution is actually indistinguishable from message routing. After that, we consider human-friendly names and descriptive names (i.e., entities that are described by a collection of names).

5.2 FLAT NAMING

Above, we explained that identifiers are convenient to uniquely represent entities. In many cases, identifiers are simply random bit strings, which we conveniently refer to as unstructured, or flat names. An important property of such a name is that it does not contain any information whatsoever on how to locate the access point of its associated entity. In the following, we will take a look at how flat names can be resolved, or, equivalently, how we can locate an entity when given only its identifier.

5.2.1 Simple Solutions

We first consider two simple solutions for locating an entity. Both solutions are applicable only to local-area networks. Nevertheless, in that environment, they often do the job well, making their simplicity particularly attractive.

Broadcasting and Multicasting

Consider a distributed system built on a computer network that offers efficient broadcasting facilities. Typically, such facilities are offered by local-area networks in which all machines are connected to a single cable or the logical equivalent thereof. Also, local-area wireless networks fall into this category.

Locating an entity in such an environment is simple: a message containing the identifier of the entity is broadcast to each machine and each machine is requested to check whether it has that entity. Only the machines that can offer an access point for the entity send a reply message containing the address of that access point.

This principle is used in the Internet **Address Resolution Protocol** (**ARP**) to find the data-link address of a machine when given only an IP address (Plummer, 1982). In essence, a machine broadcasts a packet on the local network asking who is the owner of a given IP address. When the message arrives at a machine, the receiver checks whether it should listen to the requested IP address. If so, it sends a reply packet containing, for example, its Ethernet address.

Broadcasting becomes inefficient when the network grows. Not only is network bandwidth wasted by request messages, but, more seriously, too many hosts may be interrupted by requests they cannot answer. One possible solution is to switch to multicasting, by which only a restricted group of hosts receives the request. For example, Ethernet networks support data-link level multicasting directly in hardware.

Multicasting can also be used to locate entities in point-to-point networks. For example, the Internet supports network-level multicasting by allowing hosts to join a specific multicast group. Such groups are identified by a multicast address. When a host sends a message to a multicast address, the network layer provides a best-effort service to deliver that message to all group members. Efficient implementations for multicasting in the Internet are discussed in Deering and Cheriton (1990) and Deering et al. (1996).

A multicast address can be used as a general location service for multiple entities. For example, consider an organization where each employee has his or her own mobile computer. When such a computer connects to the locally available network, it is dynamically assigned an IP address. In addition, it joins a specific multicast group. When a process wants to locate computer A, it sends a "where is A?" request to the multicast group. If A is connected, it responds with its current IP address.

Another way to use a multicast address is to associate it with a replicated entity, and to use multicasting to locate the *nearest* replica. When sending a request to the multicast address, each replica responds with its current (normal) IP address. A crude way to select the nearest replica is to choose the one whose reply comes in first. We will discuss other ones in later chapters. As it turns out, selecting a nearest replica is generally not that easy.

Forwarding Pointers

Another popular approach to locating mobile entities is to make use of forwarding pointers (Fowler, 1985). The principle is simple: when an entity moves from A to B, it leaves behind in A a reference to its new location at B. The main advantage of this approach is its simplicity: as soon as an entity has been located, for example by using a traditional naming service, a client can look up the current address by following the chain of forwarding pointers.

There are also a number of important drawbacks. First, if no special measures are taken, a chain for a highly mobile entity can become so long that locating that entity is prohibitively expensive. Second, all intermediate locations in a chain will have to maintain their part of the chain of forwarding pointers as long as needed. A third (and related) drawback is the vulnerability to broken links. As soon as any forwarding pointer is lost (for whatever reason) the entity can no longer be reached. An important issue is, therefore, to keep chains relatively short, and to ensure that forwarding pointers are robust.

To better understand how forwarding pointers work, consider their use with respect to remote objects: objects that can be accessed by means of a remote procedure call. Following the approach in **SSP chains** (Shapiro et al., 1992), each forwarding pointer is implemented as a *(client stub, server stub)* pair as shown in Fig. 5-1. (We note that in Shapiro's original terminology, a server stub was called a scion, leading to *(stub,scion)* pairs, which explains its name.) A server stub contains either a local reference to the actual object or a local reference to a remote client stub for that object.

Whenever an object moves from address space A to B, it leaves behind a client stub in its place in A and installs a server stub that refers to it in B. An interesting aspect of this approach is that migration is completely transparent to a client. The only thing the client sees of an object is a client stub. How, and to which location that client stub forwards its invocations, are hidden from the client. Also note that this use of forwarding pointers is not like looking up an address. Instead, a client's request is forwarded along the chain to the actual object.

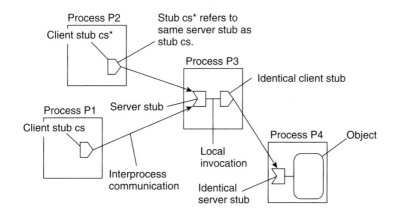

Figure 5-1. The principle of forwarding pointers using *(client stub, server stub)* pairs.

To short-cut a chain of *(client stub, server stub)* pairs, an object invocation carries the identification of the client stub from where that invocation was initiated. A client-stub identification consists of the client's transport-level address, combined with a locally generated number to identify that stub. When the invocation reaches the object at its current location, a response is sent back to the client stub where the invocation was initiated (often without going back up the chain). The current location is piggybacked with this response, and the client stub adjusts its companion server stub to the one in the object's current location. This principle is shown in Fig. 5-2.

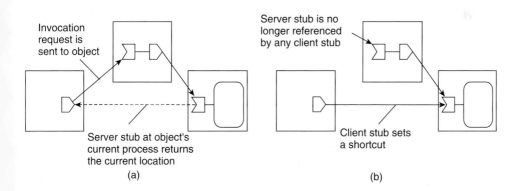

Figure 5-2. Redirecting a forwarding pointer by storing a shortcut in a client stub.

There is a trade-off between sending the response directly to the initiating client stub, or along the reverse path of forwarding pointers. In the former case, communication is faster because fewer processes may need to be passed. On the other hand, only the initiating client stub can be adjusted, whereas sending the response along the reverse path allows adjustment of all intermediate stubs.

When a server stub is no longer referred to by any client, it can be removed. This by itself is strongly related to distributed garbage collection, a generally far from trivial problem that we will not further discuss here. The interested reader is referred to Abdullahi and Ringwood (1998), Plainfosse and Shapiro (1995), and Veiga and Ferreira (2005).

Now suppose that process P_1 in Fig. 5-1 passes its reference to object O to process P_2. Reference passing is done by installing a copy p' of client stub p in the address space of process P_2. Client stub p' refers to the same server stub as p, so that the forwarding invocation mechanism works the same as before.

Problems arise when a process in a chain of *(client stub, server stub)* pairs crashes or becomes otherwise unreachable. Several solutions are possible. One possibility, as followed in Emerald (Jul et al., 1988) and in the LII system (Black and Artsy, 1990), is to let the machine where an object was created (called the object's **home location**), always keep a reference to its current location. That reference is stored and maintained in a fault-tolerant way. When a chain is broken, the object's home location is asked where the object is now. To allow an object's home location to change, a traditional naming service can be used to record the current home location. Such home-based approaches are discussed next.

5.2.2 Home-Based Approaches

The use of broadcasting and forwarding pointers imposes scalability problems. Broadcasting or multicasting is difficult to implement efficiently in large-scale networks whereas long chains of forwarding pointers introduce performance problems and are susceptible to broken links.

A popular approach to supporting mobile entities in large-scale networks is to introduce a **home location**, which keeps track of the current location of an entity. Special techniques may be applied to safeguard against network or process failures. In practice, the home location is often chosen to be the place where an entity was created.

The home-based approach is used as a fall-back mechanism for location services based on forwarding pointers, as discussed above. Another example where the home-based approach is followed is in Mobile IP (Johnson et al., 2004), which we briefly explained in Chap. 3. Each mobile host uses a fixed IP address. All communication to that IP address is initially directed to the mobile host's **home agent**. This home agent is located on the local-area network corresponding to the network address contained in the mobile host's IP address. In the case of IPv6, it is realized as a network-layer component. Whenever the mobile host moves to another network, it requests a temporary address that it can use for communication. This **care-of address** is registered at the home agent.

When the home agent receives a packet for the mobile host, it looks up the host's current location. If the host is on the current local network, the packet is simply forwarded. Otherwise, it is tunneled to the host's current location, that is, wrapped as data in an IP packet and sent to the care-of address. At the same time, the sender of the packet is informed of the host's current location. This principle is shown in Fig. 5-3. Note that the IP address is effectively used as an identifier for the mobile host.

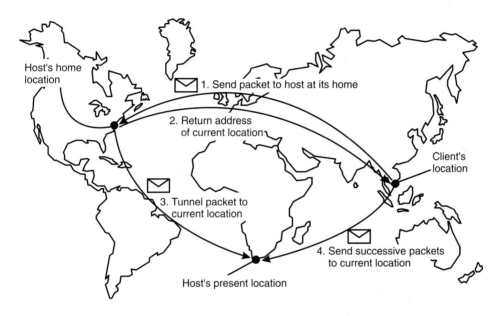

Figure 5-3. The principle of Mobile IP.

Fig. 5-3 also illustrates another drawback of home-based approaches in large-scale networks. To communicate with a mobile entity, a client first has to contact the home, which may be at a completely different location than the entity itself. The result is an increase in communication latency.

A drawback of the home-based approach is the use of a fixed home location. For one thing, it must be ensured that the home location always exists. Otherwise, contacting the entity will become impossible. Problems are aggravated when a long-lived entity decides to move permanently to a completely different part of the network than where its home is located. In that case, it would have been better if the home could have moved along with the host.

A solution to this problem is to register the home at a traditional naming service and to let a client first look up the location of the home. Because the home location can be assumed to be relatively stable, that location can be effectively cached after it has been looked up.

5.2.3 Distributed Hash Tables

Let us now take a closer look at recent developments on how to resolve an i-dentifier to the address of the associated entity. We have already mentioned distributed hash tables a number of times, but have deferred discussion on how they actually work. In this section we correct this situation by first considering the Chord system as an easy-to-explain DHT-based system. In its simplest form, DHT-based systems do not consider network proximity at all. This negligence may easily lead to performance problems. We also discuss solutions for network-aware systems.

General Mechanism

Various DHT-based systems exist, of which a brief overview is given in Balakrishnan et al. (2003). The Chord system (Stoica et al., 2003) is representative for many of them, although there are subtle important differences that influence their complexity in maintenance and lookup protocols. As we explained briefly in Chap. 2, Chord uses an m-bit identifier space to assign randomly-chosen identifiers to nodes as well as keys to specific entities. The latter can be virtually anything: files, processes, etc. The number m of bits is usually 128 or 160, depending on which hash function is used. An entity with key k falls under the jurisdiction of the node with the smallest identifier $id \geq k$. This node is referred to as the *successor* of k and denoted as *succ(k)*.

The main issue in DHT-based systems is to efficiently resolve a key k to the address of *succ(k)*. An obvious nonscalable approach is let each node p keep track of the successor *succ(p+1)* as well as its predecessor *pred(p)*. In that case, whenever a node p receives a request to resolve key k, it will simply forward the request to one of its two neighbors—whichever one is appropriate—unless $pred(p) < k \leq p$ in which case node p should return its own address to the process that initiated the resolution of key k.

Instead of this linear approach toward key lookup, each Chord node maintains a **finger table** of at most m entries. If FT_p denotes the finger table of node p, then

$$FT_p[i] = succ(p+2^{i-1})$$

Put in other words, the i-th entry points to the first node succeeding p by at least 2^{i-1}. Note that these references are actually short-cuts to existing nodes in the i-dentifier space, where the short-cutted distance from node p increases exponentially as the index in the finger table increases. To look up a key k, node p will then immediately forward the request to node q with index j in p's finger table where:

$$q = FT_p[j] \leq k < FT_p[j+1]$$

(For clarity, we ignore modulo arithmetic.)

To illustrate this lookup, consider resolving $k = 26$ from node 1 as shown Fig. 5-4. First, node 1 will look up $k = 26$ in its finger table to discover that this value is larger than $FT_1[5]$, meaning that the request will be forwarded to node $18 = FT_1[5]$. Node 18, in turn, will select node 20, as $FT_{18}[2] < k \leq FT_{18}[3]$. Finally, the request is forwarded from node 20 to node 21 and from there to node 28, which is responsible for $k = 26$. At that point, the address of node 28 is returned to node 1 and the key has been resolved. For similar reasons, when node 28 is requested to resolve the key $k = 12$, a request will be routed as shown by the dashed line in Fig. 5-4. It can be shown that a lookup will generally require $O(log(N))$ steps, with N being the number of nodes in the system.

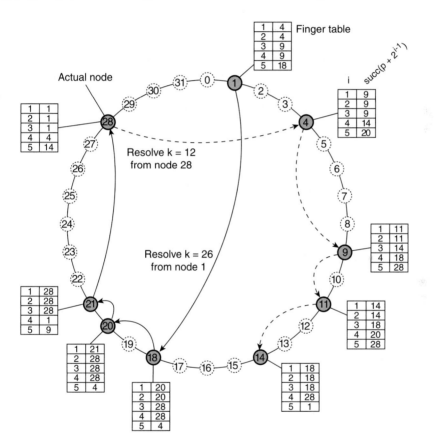

Figure 5-4. Resolving key 26 from node 1 and key 12 from node 28 in a Chord system.

In large distributed systems the collection of participating nodes can be expected to change all the time. Not only will nodes join and leave voluntarily, we also need to consider the case of nodes failing (and thus effectively leaving the system), to later recover again (at which point they join again).

Joining a DHT-based system such as Chord is relatively simple. Suppose node p wants to join. It simply contacts an arbitrary node in the existing system and requests a lookup for $succ(p+1)$. Once this node has been identified, p can insert itself into the ring. Likewise, leaving can be just as simple. Note that nodes also keep track of their predecessor.

Obviously, the complexity comes from keeping the finger tables up-to-date. Most important is that for every node q, $FT_q[1]$ is correct as this entry refers to the next node in the ring, that is, the successor of $q+1$. In order to achieve this goal, each node q regularly runs a simple procedure that contacts $succ(q+1)$ and requests to return $pred(succ(q+1))$. If $q = pred(succ(q+1))$ then q knows its information is consistent with that of its successor. Otherwise, if q's successor has updated its predecessor, then apparently a new node p had entered the system, with $q < p \leq succ(q+1)$, so that q will adjust $FT_q[1]$ to p. At that point, it will also check whether p has recorded q as its predecessor. If not, another adjustment of $FT_q[1]$ is needed.

In a similar way, to update a finger table, node q simply needs to find the successor for $k = q + 2^{i-1}$ for each entry i. Again, this can be done by issuing a request to resolve $succ(k)$. In Chord, such requests are issued regularly by means of a background process.

Likewise, each node q will regularly check whether its predecessor is alive. If the predecessor has failed, the only thing that q can do is record the fact by setting $pred(q)$ to "unknown". On the other hand, when node q is updating its link to the next known node in the ring, and finds that the predecessor of $succ(q+1)$ has been set to "unknown," it will simply notify $succ(q+1)$ that it suspects it to be the predecessor. By and large, these simple procedures ensure that a Chord system is generally consistent, only perhaps with exception of a few nodes. The details can be found in Stoica et al. (2003).

Exploiting Network Proximity

One of the potential problems with systems such as Chord is that requests may be routed erratically across the Internet. For example, assume that node 1 in Fig. 5-4 is placed in Amsterdam, The Netherlands; node 18 in San Diego, California; node 20 in Amsterdam again; and node 21 in San Diego. The result of resolving key 26 will then incur three wide-area message transfers which arguably could have been reduced to at most one. To minimize these pathological cases, designing a DHT-based system requires taking the underlying network into account.

Castro et al. (2002b) distinguish three different ways for making a DHT-based system aware of the underlying network. In the case of **topology-based assignment of node identifiers** the idea is to assign identifiers such that two nearby nodes will have identifiers that are also close to each other. It is not difficult to imagine that this approach may impose severe problems in the case of relatively simple systems such as Chord. In the case where node identifiers are sampled from a one-dimensional space, mapping a logical ring to the Internet is far from trivial. Moreover, such a mapping can easily expose correlated failures: nodes on the same enterprise network will have identifiers from a relatively small interval. When that network becomes unreachable, we suddenly have a gap in the otherwise uniform distribution of identifiers.

With **proximity routing**, nodes maintain a list of alternatives to forward a request to. For example, instead of having only a single successor, each node in Chord could equally well keep track of r successors. In fact, this redundancy can be applied for every entry in a finger table. For node p, $FT_p[i]$ points to the first node in the range $[p+2^{i-1}, p+2^i-1]$. There is no reason why p cannot keep track of r nodes in that range: if needed, each one of them can be used to route a lookup request for a key $k > p+2^i-1$. In that case, when choosing to forward a lookup request, a node can pick one of the r successors that is closest to itself, but also satisfies the constraint that the identifier of the chosen node should be smaller than that of the requested key. An additional advantage of having multiple successors for every table entry is that node failures need not immediately lead to failures of lookups, as multiple routes can be explored.

Finally, in **proximity neighbor selection** the idea is to optimize routing tables such that the nearest node is selected as neighbor. This selection works only when there are more nodes to choose from. In Chord, this is normally not the case. However, in other protocols such as Pastry (Rowstron and Druschel, 2001), when a node joins it receives information about the current overlay from multiple other nodes. This information is used by the new node to construct a routing table. Obviously, when there are alternative nodes to choose from, proximity neighbor selection will allow the joining node to choose the best one.

Note that it may not be that easy to draw a line between proximity routing and proximity neighbor selection. In fact, when Chord is modified to include r successors for each finger table entry, proximity neighbor selection resorts to identifying the closest r neighbors, which comes very close to proximity routing as we just explained (Dabek at al., 2004b).

Finally, we also note that a distinction can be made between **iterative** and **recursive lookups**. In the former case, a node that is requested to look up a key will return the network address of the next node found to the requesting process. The process will then request that next node to take another step in resolving the key. An alternative, and essentially the way that we have explained it so far, is to let a node forward a lookup request to the next node. Both approaches have their advantages and disadvantages, which we explore later in this chapter.

5.2.4 Hierarchical Approaches

In this section, we first discuss a general approach to a hierarchical location scheme, after which a number of optimizations are presented. The approach we present is based on the Globe location service, described in detail in Ballintijn

(2003). An overview can be found in van Steen et al. (1998b). This is a general-purpose location service that is representative of many hierarchical location services proposed for what are called Personal Communication Systems, of which a general overview can be found in Pitoura and Samaras (2001).

In a hierarchical scheme, a network is divided into a collection of **domains**. There is a single top-level domain that spans the entire network. Each domain can be subdivided into multiple, smaller subdomains. A lowest-level domain, called a **leaf domain**, typically corresponds to a local-area network in a computer network or a cell in a mobile telephone network.

Each domain D has an associated directory node *dir(D)* that keeps track of the entities in that domain. This leads to a tree of directory nodes. The directory node of the top-level domain, called the **root (directory) node**, knows about all entities. This general organization of a network into domains and directory nodes is illustrated in Fig. 5-5.

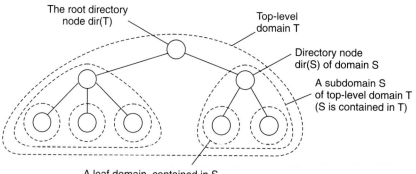

Figure 5-5. Hierarchical organization of a location service into domains, each having an associated directory node.

To keep track of the whereabouts of an entity, each entity currently located in a domain D is represented by a **location record** in the directory node *dir(D)*. A location record for entity E in the directory node N for a leaf domain D contains the entity's current address in that domain. In contrast, the directory node N' for the next higher-level domain D' that contains D, will have a location record for E containing only a pointer to N. Likewise, the parent node of N' will store a location record for E containing only a pointer to N'. Consequently, the root node will have a location record for each entity, where each location record stores a pointer to the directory node of the next lower-level subdomain where that record's associated entity is currently located.

An entity may have multiple addresses, for example if it is replicated. If an entity has an address in leaf domain D_1 and D_2 respectively, then the directory node of the smallest domain containing both D_1 and D_2, will have two pointers, one for each subdomain containing an address. This leads to the general organization of the tree as shown in Fig. 5-6.

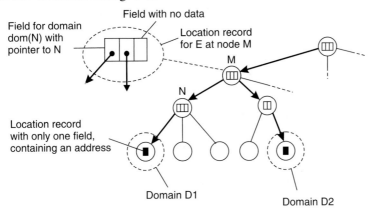

Figure 5-6. An example of storing information of an entity having two addresses in different leaf domains.

Let us now consider how a lookup operation proceeds in such a hierarchical location service. As is shown in Fig. 5-7, a client wishing to locate an entity E, issues a lookup request to the directory node of the leaf domain D in which the client resides. If the directory node does not store a location record for the entity, then the entity is currently not located in D. Consequently, the node forwards the request to its parent. Note that the parent node represents a larger domain than its child. If the parent also has no location record for E, the lookup request is forwarded to a next level higher, and so on.

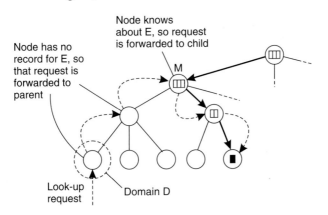

Figure 5-7. Looking up a location in a hierarchically organized location service.

As soon as the request reaches a directory node M that stores a location record for entity E, we know that E is somewhere in the domain *dom(M)* represented by node M. In Fig. 5-7, M is shown to store a location record containing a pointer to one of its subdomains. The lookup request is then forwarded to the directory node of that subdomain, which in turn forwards it further down the tree, until the request finally reaches a leaf node. The location record stored in the leaf node will contain the address of E in that leaf domain. This address can then be returned to the client that initially requested the lookup to take place.

An important observation with respect to hierarchical location services is that the lookup operation exploits locality. In principle, the entity is searched in a gradually increasing ring centered around the requesting client. The search area is expanded each time the lookup request is forwarded to a next higher-level directory node. In the worst case, the search continues until the request reaches the root node. Because the root node has a location record for each entity, the request can then simply be forwarded along a downward path of pointers to one of the leaf nodes.

Update operations exploit locality in a similar fashion, as shown in Fig. 5-8. Consider an entity E that has created a replica in leaf domain D for which it needs to insert its address. The insertion is initiated at the leaf node $dir(D)$ of D which immediately forwards the insert request to its parent. The parent will forward the insert request as well, until it reaches a directory node M that already stores a location record for E.

Node M will then store a pointer in the location record for E, referring to the child node from where the insert request was forwarded. At that point, the child node creates a location record for E, containing a pointer to the next lower-level node from where the request came. This process continues until we reach the leaf node from which the insert was initiated. The leaf node, finally, creates a record with the entity's address in the associated leaf domain.

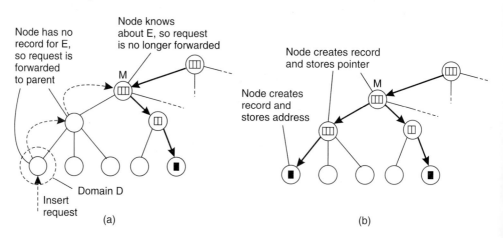

Figure 5-8. (a) An insert request is forwarded to the first node that knows about entity E. (b) A chain of forwarding pointers to the leaf node is created.

Inserting an address as just described leads to installing the chain of pointers in a top-down fashion starting at the lowest-level directory node that has a location record for entity E. An alternative is to create a location record before passing the insert request to the parent node. In other words, the chain of pointers is constructed from the bottom up. The advantage of the latter is that an address becomes available for lookups as soon as possible. Consequently, if a parent node is temporarily unreachable, the address can still be looked up within the domain represented by the current node.

A delete operation is analogous to an insert operation. When an address for entity E in leaf domain D needs to be removed, directory node $dir(D)$ is requested to remove that address from its location record for E. If that location record becomes empty, that is, it contains no other addresses for E in D, the record can be removed. In that case, the parent node of $dir(D)$ wants to remove its pointer to $dir(D)$. If the location record for E at the parent now also becomes empty, that record should be removed as well and the next higher-level directory node should be informed. Again, this process continues until a pointer is removed from a location record that remains nonempty afterward or until the root is reached.

5.3 STRUCTURED NAMING

Flat names are good for machines, but are generally not very convenient for humans to use. As an alternative, naming systems generally support structured names that are composed from simple, human-readable names. Not only file naming, but also host naming on the Internet follow this approach. In this section, we concentrate on structured names and the way that these names are resolved to addresses.

5.3.1 Name Spaces

Names are commonly organized into what is called a **name space**. Name spaces for structured names can be represented as a labeled, directed graph with two types of nodes. A **leaf node** represents a named entity and has the property that it has no outgoing edges. A leaf node generally stores information on the entity it is representing—for example, its address—so that a client can access it. Alternatively, it can store the state of that entity, such as in the case of file systems in which a leaf node actually contains the complete file it is representing. We return to the contents of nodes below.

In contrast to a leaf node, a **directory node** has a number of outgoing edges, each labeled with a name, as shown in Fig. 5-9. Each node in a naming graph is considered as yet another entity in a distributed system, and, in particular, has an associated identifier. A directory node stores a table in which an outgoing edge is represented as a pair *(edge label, node identifier)*. Such a table is called a **directory table**.

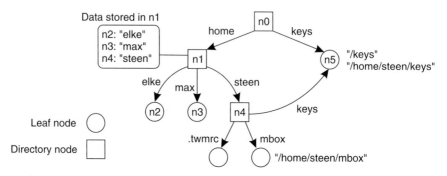

Figure 5-9. A general naming graph with a single root node.

The naming graph shown in Fig. 5-9 has one node, namely n_0, which has only outgoing and no incoming edges. Such a node is called the **root (node)** of the naming graph. Although it is possible for a naming graph to have several root nodes, for simplicity, many naming systems have only one. Each path in a naming graph can be referred to by the sequence of labels corresponding to the edges in that path, such as

   N:<label-1, label-2, ..., label-n>

where *N* refers to the first node in the path. Such a sequence is called a **path name**. If the first node in a path name is the root of the naming graph, it is called an **absolute path name**. Otherwise, it is called a **relative path name**.

It is important to realize that names are always organized in a name space. As a consequence, a name is always defined relative only to a directory node. In this sense, the term "absolute name" is somewhat misleading. Likewise, the difference between global and local names can often be confusing. A **global name** is a name that denotes the same entity, no matter where that name is used in a system. In other words, a global name is always interpreted with respect to the same directory node. In contrast, a **local name** is a name whose interpretation depends on where that name is being used. Put differently, a local name is essentially a relative name whose directory in which is contained is (implicitly) known. We return to these issues later when we discuss name resolution.

This description of a naming graph comes close to what is implemented in many file systems. However, instead of writing the sequence of edge labels to represent a path name, path names in file systems are generally represented as a single string in which the labels are separated by a special separator character, such as a slash ("/"). This character is also used to indicate whether a path name is absolute. For example, in Fig. 5-9, instead of using n_0:*<home, steen, mbox>*, that is, the actual path name, it is common practice to use its string representation */home/steen/mbox*. Note also that when there are several paths that lead to the same node, that node can be represented by different path names. For example, node n_5 in Fig. 5-9 can be referred to by */home/steen/keys* as well as */keys*. The string representation of path names can be equally well applied to naming graphs other than those used for only file systems. In Plan 9 (Pike et al., 1995), all resources, such as processes, hosts, I/O devices, and network interfaces, are named in the same fashion as traditional files. This approach is analogous to implementing a single naming graph for all resources in a distributed system.

There are many different ways to organize a name space. As we mentioned, most name spaces have only a single root node. In many cases, a name space is also strictly hierarchical in the sense that the naming graph is organized as a tree. This means that each node except the root has exactly one incoming edge; the root has no incoming edges. As a consequence, each node also has exactly one associated (absolute) path name.

The naming graph shown in Fig. 5-9 is an example of *directed acyclic graph*. In such an organization, a node can have more than one incoming edge, but the graph is not permitted to have a cycle. There are also name spaces that do not have this restriction.

To make matters more concrete, consider the way that files in a traditional UNIX file system are named. In a naming graph for UNIX, a directory node represents a file directory, whereas a leaf node represents a file. There is a single root directory, represented in the naming graph by the root node. The implementation of the naming graph is an integral part of the complete implementation of the file system. That implementation consists of a contiguous series of blocks from a logical disk, generally divided into a boot block, a superblock, a series of index nodes (called inodes), and file data blocks. See also Crowley (1997), Silberschatz et al. (2005), and Tanenbaum and Woodhull (2006). This organization is shown in Fig. 5-10.

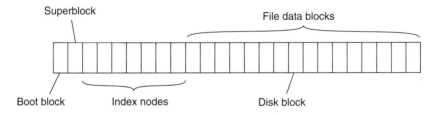

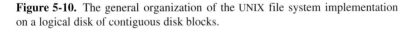

Figure 5-10. The general organization of the UNIX file system implementation on a logical disk of contiguous disk blocks.

The boot block is a special block of data and instructions that are automatically loaded into main memory when the system is booted. The boot block is used to load the operating system into main memory.

The superblock contains information on the entire file system, such as its size, which blocks on disk are not yet allocated, which inodes are not yet used, and so on. Inodes are referred to by an index number, starting at number zero, which is reserved for the inode representing the root directory.

Each inode contains information on where the data of its associated file can be found on disk. In addition, an inode contains information on its owner, time of creation and last modification, protection, and the like. Consequently, when given the index number of an inode, it is possible to access its associated file. Each directory is implemented as a file as well. This is also the case for the root directory, which contains a mapping between file names and index numbers of inodes. It is thus seen that the index number of an inode corresponds to a node identifier in the naming graph.

5.3.2 Name Resolution

Name spaces offer a convenient mechanism for storing and retrieving information about entities by means of names. More generally, given a path name, it should be possible to look up any information stored in the node referred to by that name. The process of looking up a name is called **name resolution**.

To explain how name resolution works, let us consider a path name such as N:<$label_1, label_2, ..., label_n$>. Resolution of this name starts at node N of the naming graph, where the name $label_1$ is looked up in the directory table, and which returns the identifier of the node to which $label_1$ refers. Resolution then continues at the identified node by looking up the name $label_2$ in its directory table, and so on. Assuming that the named path actually exists, resolution stops at the last node referred to by $label_n$, by returning the content of that node.

A name lookup returns the identifier of a node from where the name resolution process continues. In particular, it is necessary to access the directory table of the identified node. Consider again a naming graph for a UNIX file system. As mentioned, a node identifier is implemented as the index number of an inode. Accessing a directory table means that first the inode has to be read to find out where the actual data are stored on disk, and then subsequently to read the data blocks containing the directory table.

Closure Mechanism

Name resolution can take place only if we know how and where to start. In our example, the starting node was given, and we assumed we had access to its directory table. Knowing how and where to start name resolution is generally referred to as a **closure mechanism**. Essentially, a closure mechanism deals with selecting the initial node in a name space from which name resolution is to start (Radia, 1989). What makes closure mechanisms sometimes hard to understand is that they are necessarily partly implicit and may be very different when comparing them to each other.

For example, name resolution in the naming graph for a UNIX file system makes use of the fact that the inode of the root directory is the first inode in the logical disk representing the file system. Its actual byte offset is calculated from the values in other fields of the superblock, together with hard-coded information in the operating system itself on the internal organization of the superblock.

To make this point clear, consider the string representation of a file name such as */home/steen/mbox*. To resolve this name, it is necessary to already have access to the directory table of the root node of the appropriate naming graph. Being a root node, the node itself cannot have been looked up unless it is implemented as a different node in a another naming graph, say G. But in that case, it would have been necessary to already have access to the root node of G. Consequently, resolving a file name requires that some mechanism has already been implemented by which the resolution process can start.

A completely different example is the use of the string "0031204430784". Many people will not know what to do with these numbers, unless they are told that the sequence is a telephone number. That information is enough to start the resolution process, in particular, by dialing the number. The telephone system subsequently does the rest.

As a last example, consider the use of global and local names in distributed systems. A typical example of a local name is an environment variable. For example, in UNIX systems, the variable named *HOME* is used to refer to the home directory of a user. Each user has its own copy of this variable, which is initialized to the global, systemwide name corresponding to the user's home directory. The closure mechanism associated with environment variables ensures that the name of the variable is properly resolved by looking it up in a user-specific table.

Linking and Mounting

Strongly related to name resolution is the use of **aliases**. An alias is another name for the same entity. An environment variable is an example of an alias. In terms of naming graphs, there are basically two different ways to implement an alias. The first approach is to simply allow multiple absolute paths names to refer to the same node in a naming graph. This approach is illustrated in Fig. 5-9, in which node n_5 can be referred to by two different path names. In UNIX terminology, both path names */keys* and */home/steen/keys* in Fig. 5-9 are called **hard links** to node n_5.

The second approach is to represent an entity by a leaf node, say N, but instead of storing the address or state of that entity, the node stores an absolute path name. When first resolving an absolute path name that leads to N, name resolution will return the path name stored in N, at which point it can continue with resolving that new path name. This principle corresponds to the use of **symbolic links** in

UNIX file systems, and is illustrated in Fig. 5-11. In this example, the path name */home/steen/keys*, which refers to a node containing the absolute path name */keys*, is a symbolic link to node n_5.

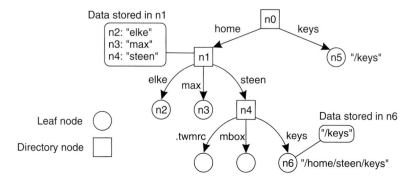

Figure 5-11. The concept of a symbolic link explained in a naming graph.

Name resolution as described so far takes place completely within a single name space. However, name resolution can also be used to merge different name spaces in a transparent way. Let us first consider a mounted file system. In terms of our naming model, a mounted file system corresponds to letting a directory node store the identifier of a directory node from a *different* name space, which we refer to as a foreign name space. The directory node storing the node identifier is called a **mount point**. Accordingly, the directory node in the foreign name space is called a **mounting point**. Normally, the mounting point is the root of a name space. During name resolution, the mounting point is looked up and resolution proceeds by accessing its directory table.

The principle of mounting can be generalized to other name spaces as well. In particular, what is needed is a directory node that acts as a mount point and stores all the necessary information for identifying and accessing the mounting point in the foreign name space. This approach is followed in many distributed file systems.

Consider a collection of name spaces that is distributed across different machines. In particular, each name space is implemented by a different server, each possibly running on a separate machine. Consequently, if we want to mount a foreign name space NS_2 into a name space NS_1, it may be necessary to communicate over a network with the server of NS_2, as that server may be running on a different machine than the server for NS_1. To mount a foreign name space in a distributed system requires at least the following information:

1. The name of an access protocol.

2. The name of the server.

3. The name of the mounting point in the foreign name space.

Note that each of these names needs to be resolved. The name of an access protocol needs to be resolved to the implementation of a protocol by which communication with the server of the foreign name space can take place. The name of the server needs to be resolved to an address where that server can be reached. As the last part in name resolution, the name of the mounting point needs to be resolved to a node identifier in the foreign name space.

In nondistributed systems, none of the three points may actually be needed. For example, in UNIX, there is no access protocol and no server. Also, the name of the mounting point is not necessary, as it is simply the root directory of the foreign name space.

The name of the mounting point is to be resolved by the server of the foreign name space. However, we also need name spaces and implementations for the access protocol and the server name. One possibility is to represent the three names listed above as a URL.

To make matters concrete, consider a situation in which a user with a laptop computer wants to access files that are stored on a remote file server. The client machine and the file server are both configured with Sun's **Network File System** (**NFS**), which we will discuss in detail in Chap. 11. NFS is a distributed file system that comes with a protocol that describes precisely how a client can access a file stored on a (remote) NFS file server. In particular, to allow NFS to work across the Internet, a client can specify exactly which file it wants to access by means of an NFS URL, for example, *nfs://flits.cs.vu.nl//home/steen*. This URL names a file (which happens to be a directory) called */home/steen* on an NFS file server *flits.cs.vu.nl*, which can be accessed by a client by means of the NFS protocol (Shepler et al., 2003).

The name *nfs* is a well-known name in the sense that worldwide agreement exists on how to interpret that name. Given that we are dealing with a URL, the name *nfs* will be resolved to an implementation of the NFS protocol. The server name is resolved to its address using DNS, which is discussed in a later section. As we said, */home/steen* is resolved by the server of the foreign name space.

The organization of a file system on the client machine is partly shown in Fig. 5-12. The root directory has a number of user-defined entries, including a subdirectory called */remote*. This subdirectory is intended to include mount points for foreign name spaces such as the user's home directory at the Vrije Universiteit. To this end, a directory node named */remote/vu* is used to store the URL *nfs://flits.cs.vu.nl//home/steen*.

Now consider the name */remote/vu/mbox*. This name is resolved by starting in the root directory on the client's machine and continues until the node */remote/vu* is reached. The process of name resolution then continues by returning the URL *nfs://flits.cs.vu.nl//home/steen*, in turn leading the client machine to contact the file server *flits.cs.vu.nl* by means of the NFS protocol, and to subsequently access directory */home/steen*. Name resolution can then be continued by reading the file named *mbox* in that directory, after which the resolution process stops.

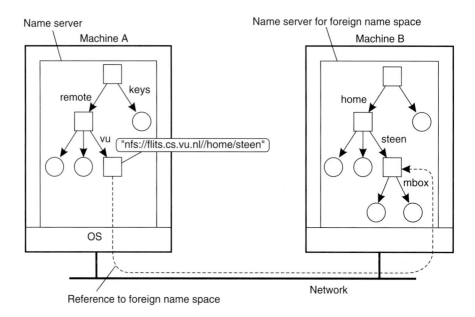

Figure 5-12. Mounting remote name spaces through a specific access protocol.

Distributed systems that allow mounting a remote file system as just described allow a client machine to, for example, execute the following commands:

```
cd  /remote/vu
ls  −l
```

which subsequently lists the files in the directory */home/steen* on the remote file server. The beauty of all this is that the user is spared the details of the actual access to the remote server. Ideally, only some loss in performance is noticed compared to accessing locally-available files. In effect, to the client it appears that the name space rooted on the local machine, and the one rooted at */home/steen* on the remote machine, form a single name space.

5.3.3 The Implementation of a Name Space

A name space forms the heart of a naming service, that is, a service that allows users and processes to add, remove, and look up names. A naming service is implemented by name servers. If a distributed system is restricted to a local-area network, it is often feasible to implement a naming service by means of only a single name server. However, in large-scale distributed systems with many entities, possibly spread across a large geographical area, it is necessary to distribute the implementation of a name space over multiple name servers.

Name Space Distribution

Name spaces for a large-scale, possibly worldwide distributed system, are usually organized hierarchically. As before, assume such a name space has only a single root node. To effectively implement such a name space, it is convenient to partition it into logical layers. Cheriton and Mann (1989) distinguish the following three layers.

The **global layer** is formed by highest-level nodes, that is, the root node and other directory nodes logically close to the root, namely its children. Nodes in the global layer are often characterized by their stability, in the sense that directory tables are rarely changed. Such nodes may represent organizations, or groups of organizations, for which names are stored in the name space.

The **administrational layer** is formed by directory nodes that together are managed within a single organization. A characteristic feature of the directory nodes in the administrational layer is that they represent groups of entities that belong to the same organization or administrational unit. For example, there may be a directory node for each department in an organization, or a directory node from which all hosts can be found. Another directory node may be used as the starting point for naming all users, and so forth. The nodes in the administrational layer are relatively stable, although changes generally occur more frequently than to nodes in the global layer.

Finally, the **managerial layer** consists of nodes that may typically change regularly. For example, nodes representing hosts in the local network belong to this layer. For the same reason, the layer includes nodes representing shared files such as those for libraries or binaries. Another important class of nodes includes those that represent user-defined directories and files. In contrast to the global and administrational layer, the nodes in the managerial layer are maintained not only by system administrators, but also by individual end users of a distributed system.

To make matters more concrete, Fig. 5-13 shows an example of the partitioning of part of the DNS name space, including the names of files within an organization that can be accessed through the Internet, for example, Web pages and transferable files. The name space is divided into nonoverlapping parts, called **zones** in DNS (Mockapetris, 1987). A zone is a part of the name space that is implemented by a separate name server. Some of these zones are illustrated in Fig. 5-13.

If we take a look at availability and performance, name servers in each layer have to meet different requirements. High availability is especially critical for name servers in the global layer. If a name server fails, a large part of the name space will be unreachable because name resolution cannot proceed beyond the failing server.

Performance is somewhat subtle. Due to the low rate of change of nodes in the global layer, the results of lookup operations generally remain valid for a long time. Consequently, those results can be effectively cached (i.e., stored locally) by

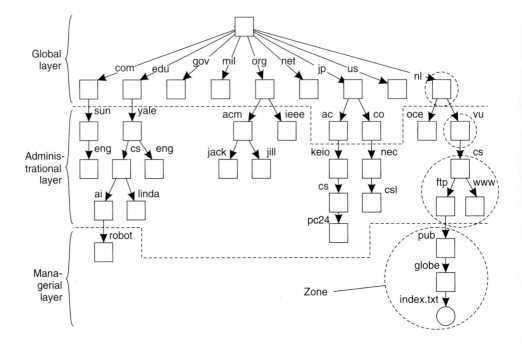

Figure 5-13. An example partitioning of the DNS name space, including Internet-accessible files, into three layers.

the clients. The next time the same lookup operation is performed, the results can be retrieved from the client's cache instead of letting the name server return the results. As a result, name servers in the global layer do not have to respond quickly to a single lookup request. On the other hand, throughput may be important, especially in large-scale systems with millions of users.

The availability and performance requirements for name servers in the global layer can be met by replicating servers, in combination with client-side caching. As we discuss in Chap. 7, updates in this layer generally do not have to come into effect immediately, making it much easier to keep replicas consistent.

Availability for a name server in the administrational layer is primarily important for clients in the same organization as the name server. If the name server fails, many resources within the organization become unreachable because they cannot be looked up. On the other hand, it may be less important that resources in an organization are temporarily unreachable for users outside that organization.

With respect to performance, name servers in the administrational layer have similar characteristics as those in the global layer. Because changes to nodes do not occur all that often, caching lookup results can be highly effective, making performance less critical. However, in contrast to the global layer, the administrational layer should take care that lookup results are returned within a few milliseconds, either directly from the server or from the client's local cache. Likewise, updates should generally be processed quicker than those of the global layer. For example, it is unacceptable that an account for a new user takes hours to become effective.

These requirements can often be met by using high-performance machines to run name servers. In addition, client-side caching should be applied, combined with replication for increased overall availability.

Availability requirements for name servers at the managerial level are generally less demanding. In particular, it often suffices to use a single (dedicated) machine to run name servers at the risk of temporary unavailability. However, performance is crucial. Users expect operations to take place immediately. Because updates occur regularly, client-side caching is often less effective, unless special measures are taken, which we discuss in Chap. 7.

Item	Global	Administrational	Managerial
Geographical scale of network	Worldwide	Organization	Department
Total number of nodes	Few	Many	Vast numbers
Responsiveness to lookups	Seconds	Milliseconds	Immediate
Update propagation	Lazy	Immediate	Immediate
Number of replicas	Many	None or few	None
Is client-side caching applied?	Yes	Yes	Sometimes

Figure 5-14. A comparison between name servers for implementing nodes from a large-scale name space partitioned into a global layer, an administrational layer, and a managerial layer.

A comparison between name servers at different layers is shown in Fig. 5-14. In distributed systems, name servers in the global and administrational layer are the most difficult to implement. Difficulties are caused by replication and caching, which are needed for availability and performance, but which also introduce consistency problems. Some of the problems are aggravated by the fact that caches and replicas are spread across a wide-area network, which introduces long communication delays thereby making synchronization even harder. Replication and caching are discussed extensively in Chap. 7.

Implementation of Name Resolution

The distribution of a name space across multiple name servers affects the implementation of name resolution. To explain the implementation of name resolution in large-scale name services, we assume for the moment that name servers are not replicated and that no client-side caches are used. Each client has access to a local **name resolver**, which is responsible for ensuring that the name resolution process is carried out. Referring to Fig. 5-13, assume the (absolute) path name

  root:*<nl, vu, cs, ftp, pub, globe, index.html>*

is to be resolved. Using a URL notation, this path name would correspond to *ftp://ftp.cs.vu.nl/pub/globe/index.html*. There are now two ways to implement name resolution.

In **iterative name resolution**, a name resolver hands over the complete name to the root name server. It is assumed that the address where the root server can be contacted is well known. The root server will resolve the path name as far as it can, and return the result to the client. In our example, the root server can resolve only the label *nl*, for which it will return the address of the associated name server.

At that point, the client passes the remaining path name (i.e., *nl*:*<vu, cs, ftp, pub, globe, index.html>*) to that name server. This server can resolve only the label *vu*, and returns the address of the associated name server, along with the remaining path name *vu*:*<cs, ftp, pub, globe, index.html>*.

The client's name resolver will then contact this next name server, which responds by resolving the label *cs*, and subsequently also *ftp*, returning the address of the FTP server along with the path name *ftp*:*<pub, globe, index.html>*. The client then contacts the FTP server, requesting it to resolve the last part of the original path name. The FTP server will subsequently resolve the labels *pub*, *globe*, and *index.html*, and transfer the requested file (in this case using FTP). This process of iterative name resolution is shown in Fig. 5-15. (The notation #*<cs>* is used to indicate the address of the server responsible for handling the node referred to by *<cs>*.)

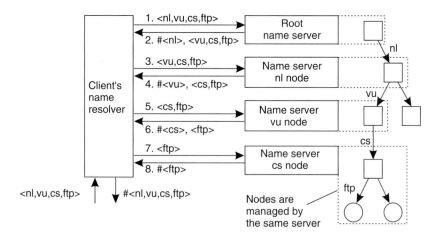

Figure 5-15. The principle of iterative name resolution.

In practice, the last step, namely contacting the FTP server and requesting it to transfer the file with path name *ftp:<pub, globe, index.html>*, is carried out separately by the client process. In other words, the client would normally hand only the path name *root:<nl, vu, cs, ftp>* to the name resolver, from which it would expect the address where it can contact the FTP server, as is also shown in Fig. 5-15.

An alternative to iterative name resolution is to use recursion during name resolution. Instead of returning each intermediate result back to the client's name resolver, with **recursive name resolution**, a name server passes the result to the next name server it finds. So, for example, when the root name server finds the address of the name server implementing the node named *nl*, it requests that name server to resolve the path name *nl:<vu, cs, ftp, pub, globe, index.html>*. Using recursive name resolution as well, this next server will resolve the complete path and eventually return the file *index.html* to the root server, which, in turn, will pass that file to the client's name resolver.

Recursive name resolution is shown in Fig. 5-16. As in iterative name resolution, the last resolution step (contacting the FTP server and asking it to transfer the indicated file) is generally carried out as a separate process by the client.

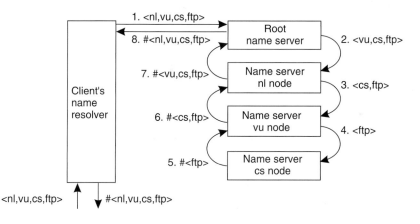

Figure 5-16. The principle of recursive name resolution.

The main drawback of recursive name resolution is that it puts a higher performance demand on each name server. Basically, a name server is required to handle the complete resolution of a path name, although it may do so in cooperation with other name servers. This additional burden is generally so high that name servers in the global layer of a name space support only iterative name resolution.

There are two important advantages to recursive name resolution. The first advantage is that caching results is more effective compared to iterative name resolution. The second advantage is that communication costs may be reduced. To explain these advantages, assume that a client's name resolver will accept path names referring only to nodes in the global or administrational layer of the name space. To resolve that part of a path name that corresponds to nodes in the managerial layer, a client will separately contact the name server returned by its name resolver, as we discussed above.

Recursive name resolution allows each name server to gradually learn the address of each name server responsible for implementing lower-level nodes. As a result, caching can be effectively used to enhance performance. For example, when the root server is requested to resolve the path name *root:<nl, vu, cs, ftp>*, it will eventually get the address of the name server implementing the node referred to by that path name. To come to that point, the name server for the *nl* node has to look up the address of the name server for the *vu* node, whereas the latter has to look up the address of the name server handling the *cs* node.

Because changes to nodes in the global and administrational layer do not occur often, the root name server can effectively cache the returned address. Moreover, because the address is also returned, by recursion, to the name server responsible for implementing the *vu* node and to the one implementing the *nl* node, it might as well be cached at those servers too.

Likewise, the results of intermediate name lookups can also be returned and cached. For example, the server for the *nl* node will have to look up the address of the *vu* node server. That address can be returned to the root server when the *nl* server returns the result of the original name lookup. A complete overview of the resolution process, and the results that can be cached by each name server is shown in Fig. 5-17.

Server for node	Should resolve	Looks up	Passes to child	Receives and caches	Returns to requester
cs	<ftp>	#<ftp>	—	—	#<ftp>
vu	<cs,ftp>	#<cs>	<ftp>	#<ftp>	#<cs> #<cs, ftp>
nl	<vu,cs,ftp>	#<vu>	<cs,ftp>	#<cs> #<cs,ftp>	#<vu> #<vu,cs> #<vu,cs,ftp>
root	<nl,vu,cs,ftp>	#<nl>	<vu,cs,ftp>	#<vu> #<vu,cs> #<vu,cs,ftp>	#<nl> #<nl,vu> #<nl,vu,cs> #<nl,vu,cs,ftp>

Figure 5-17. Recursive name resolution of *<nl, vu, cs, ftp>*. Name servers cache intermediate results for subsequent lookups.

The main benefit of this approach is that, eventually, lookup operations can be handled quite efficiently. For example, suppose that another client later requests resolution of the path name *root*:*<nl, vu, cs, flits>*. This name is passed to the root, which can immediately forward it to the name server for the *cs* node, and request it to resolve the remaining path name *cs*:*<flits>*.

With iterative name resolution, caching is necessarily restricted to the client's name resolver. Consequently, if a client *A* requests the resolution of a name, and another client *B* later requests that same name to be resolved, name resolution will have to pass through the same name servers as was done for client *A*. As a compromise, many organizations use a local, intermediate name server that is shared by all clients. This local name server handles all naming requests and caches results. Such an intermediate server is also convenient from a management point of view. For example, only that server needs to know where the root name server is located; other machines do not require this information.

The second advantage of recursive name resolution is that it is often cheaper with respect to communication. Again, consider the resolution of the path name *root*:*<nl, vu, cs, ftp>* and assume the client is located in San Francisco. Assuming that the client knows the address of the server for the *nl* node, with recursive name resolution, communication follows the route from the client's host in San Francisco to the *nl* server in The Netherlands, shown as *R* 1 in Fig. 5-18. From there on, communication is subsequently needed between the *nl* server and the name server of the Vrije Universiteit on the university campus in Amsterdam, The Netherlands. This communication is shown as *R* 2. Finally, communication is needed between the *vu* server and the name server in the Computer Science Department, shown as *R* 3. The route for the reply is the same, but in the opposite direction. Clearly, communication costs are dictated by the message exchange between the client's host and the *nl* server.

In contrast, with iterative name resolution, the client's host has to communicate separately with the *nl* server, the *vu* server, and the *cs* server, of which the total costs may be roughly three times that of recursive name resolution. The arrows in Fig. 5-18 labeled *I* 1, *I* 2, and *I* 3 show the communication path for iterative name resolution.

5.3.4 Example: The Domain Name System

One of the largest distributed naming services in use today is the Internet Domain Name System (DNS). DNS is primarily used for looking up IP addresses of hosts and mail servers. In the following pages, we concentrate on the organization of the DNS name space, and the information stored in its nodes. Also, we take a closer look at the actual implementation of DNS. More information can be found in Mockapetris (1987) and Albitz and Liu (2001). A recent assessment of DNS, notably concerning whether it still fits the needs of the current Internet, can be found in Levien (2005). From this report, one can draw the somewhat surprising conclusion that even after more than 30 years, DNS gives no indication that it

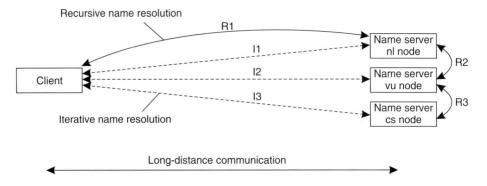

Figure 5-18. The comparison between recursive and iterative name resolution with respect to communication costs.

needs to be replaced. We would argue that the main cause lies in the designer's deep understanding of how to keep matters simple. Practice in other fields of distributed systems indicates that not many are gifted with such an understanding.

The DNS Name Space

The DNS name space is hierarchically organized as a rooted tree. A label is a case-insensitive string made up of alphanumeric characters. A label has a maximum length of 63 characters; the length of a complete path name is restricted to 255 characters. The string representation of a path name consists of listing its labels, starting with the rightmost one, and separating the labels by a dot ("."). The root is represented by a dot. So, for example, the path name *root:<nl, vu, cs, flits>*, is represented by the string *flits.cs.vu.nl.*, which includes the rightmost dot to indicate the root node. We generally omit this dot for readability.

Because each node in the DNS name space has exactly one incoming edge (with the exception of the root node, which has no incoming edges), the label attached to a node's incoming edge is also used as the name for that node. A subtree is called a **domain**; a path name to its root node is called a **domain name**. Note that, just like a path name, a domain name can be either absolute or relative.

The contents of a node is formed by a collection of **resource records**. There are different types of resource records. The major ones are shown in Fig. 5-19.

A node in the DNS name space often will represent several entities at the same time. For example, a domain name such as *vu.nl* is used to represent a domain and a zone. In this case, the domain is implemented by means of several (nonoverlapping) zones.

An *SOA* (start of authority) resource record contains information such as an e-mail address of the system administrator responsible for the represented zone, the name of the host where data on the zone can be fetched, and so on.

Type of record	Associated entity	Description
SOA	Zone	Holds information on the represented zone
A	Host	Contains an IP address of the host this node represents
MX	Domain	Refers to a mail server to handle mail addressed to this node
SRV	Domain	Refers to a server handling a specific service
NS	Zone	Refers to a name server that implements the represented zone
CNAME	Node	Symbolic link with the primary name of the represented node
PTR	Host	Contains the canonical name of a host
HINFO	Host	Holds information on the host this node represents
TXT	Any kind	Contains any entity-specific information considered useful

Figure 5-19. The most important types of resource records forming the contents of nodes in the DNS name space.

An *A* (address) record, represents a particular host in the Internet. The *A* record contains an IP address for that host to allow communication. If a host has several IP addresses, as is the case with multi-homed machines, the node will contain an *A* record for each address.

Another type of record is the *MX* (mail exchange) record, which is like a symbolic link to a node representing a mail server. For example, the node representing the domain *cs.vu.nl* has an *MX* record containing the name *zephyr.cs.vu.nl*, which refers to a mail server. That server will handle all incoming mail addressed to users in the *cs.vu.nl* domain. There may be several *MX* records stored in a node.

Related to *MX* records are *SRV* records, which contain the name of a server for a specific service. *SRV* records are defined in Gulbrandsen (2000). The service itself is identified by means of a name along with the name of a protocol. For example, the Web server in the *cs.vu.nl* domain could be named by means of an *SRV* record such as *_http._tcp.cs.vu.nl*. This record would then refer to the actual name of the server (which is *soling.cs.vu.nl*). An important advantage of SRV records is that clients need no longer know the DNS name of the host providing a specific service. Instead, only service names need to be standardized, after which the providing host can be looked up.

Nodes that represent a zone, contain one or more *NS* (name server) records. Like *MX* records, an *NS* record contains the name of a name server that implements the zone represented by the node. In principle, each node in the name space can store an *NS* record referring to the name server that implements it. However, as we discuss below, the implementation of the DNS name space is such that only nodes representing zones need to store *NS* records.

DNS distinguishes aliases from what are called **canonical names**. Each host is assumed to have a canonical, or primary name. An alias is implemented by means of node storing a *CNAME* record containing the canonical name of a host. The name of the node storing such a record is thus the same as a symbolic link, as was shown in Fig. 5-11.

DNS maintains an inverse mapping of IP addresses to host names by means of *PTR* (pointer) records. To accommodate the lookups of host names when given only an IP address, DNS maintains a domain named *in-addr.arpa*, which contains nodes that represent Internet hosts and which are named by the IP address of the represented host. For example, host *www.cs.vu.nl* has IP address 130.37.20.20. DNS creates a node named *20.20.37.130.in-addr.arpa*, which is used to store the canonical name of that host (which happens to be *soling.cs.vu.nl*) in a *PTR* record.

The last two record types are *HINFO* records and *TXT* records. An *HINFO* (host info) record is used to store additional information on a host such as its machine type and operating system. In a similar fashion, *TXT* records are used for any other kind of data that a user finds useful to store about the entity represented by the node.

DNS Implementation

In essence, the DNS name space can be divided into a global layer and an administrational layer as shown in Fig. 5-13. The managerial layer, which is generally formed by local file systems, is formally not part of DNS and is therefore also not managed by it.

Each zone is implemented by a name server, which is virtually always replicated for availability. Updates for a zone are normally handled by the primary name server. Updates take place by modifying the DNS database local to the primary server. Secondary name servers do not access the database directly, but, instead, request the primary server to transfer its content. The latter is called a **zone transfer** in DNS terminology.

A DNS database is implemented as a (small) collection of files, of which the most important one contains all the resource records for *all* the nodes in a particular zone. This approach allows nodes to be simply identified by means of their domain name, by which the notion of a node identifier reduces to an (implicit) index into a file.

To better understand these implementation issues, Fig. 5-20 shows a small part of the file that contains most of the information for the *cs.vu.nl* domain (the file has been edited for simplicity). The file shows the contents of several nodes that are part of the *cs.vu.nl* domain, where each node is identified by means of its domain name.

The node *cs.vu.nl* represents the domain as well as the zone. Its *SOA* resource record contains specific information on the validity of this file, which will not concern us further. There are four name servers for this zone, referred to by their canonical host names in the *NS* records. The *TXT* record is used to give some additional information on this zone, but cannot be automatically processed by any name server. Furthermore, there is a single mail server that can handle incoming mail addressed to users in this domain. The number preceding the name of a mail server specifies a selection priority. A sending mail server should always first attempt to contact the mail server with the lowest number.

Name	Record type	Record value
cs.vu.nl.	SOA	star.cs.vu.nl. hostmaster.cs.vu.nl. 2005092900 7200 3600 2419200 3600
cs.vu.nl.	TXT	"Vrije Universiteit - Math. & Comp. Sc."
cs.vu.nl.	MX	1 mail.few.vu.nl.
cs.vu.nl.	NS	ns.vu.nl.
cs.vu.nl.	NS	top.cs.vu.nl.
cs.vu.nl.	NS	solo.cs.vu.nl.
cs.vu.nl.	NS	star.cs.vu.nl.
star.cs.vu.nl.	A	130.37.24.6
star.cs.vu.nl.	A	192.31.231.42
star.cs.vu.nl.	MX	1 star.cs.vu.nl.
star.cs.vu.nl.	MX	666 zephyr.cs.vu.nl.
star.cs.vu.nl.	HINFO	"Sun" "Unix"
zephyr.cs.vu.nl.	A	130.37.20.10
zephyr.cs.vu.nl.	MX	1 zephyr.cs.vu.nl.
zephyr.cs.vu.nl.	MX	2 tornado.cs.vu.nl.
zephyr.cs.vu.nl.	HINFO	"Sun" "Unix"
ftp.cs.vu.nl.	CNAME	soling.cs.vu.nl.
www.cs.vu.nl.	CNAME	soling.cs.vu.nl.
soling.cs.vu.nl.	A	130.37.20.20
soling.cs.vu.nl.	MX	1 soling.cs.vu.nl.
soling.cs.vu.nl.	MX	666 zephyr.cs.vu.nl.
soling.cs.vu.nl.	HINFO	"Sun" "Unix"
vucs-das1.cs.vu.nl.	PTR	0.198.37.130.in-addr.arpa.
vucs-das1.cs.vu.nl.	A	130.37.198.0
inkt.cs.vu.nl.	HINFO	"OCE" "Proprietary"
inkt.cs.vu.nl.	A	192.168.4.3
pen.cs.vu.nl.	HINFO	"OCE" "Proprietary"
pen.cs.vu.nl.	A	192.168.4.2
localhost.cs.vu.nl.	A	127.0.0.1

Figure 5-20. An excerpt from the DNS database for the zone *cs.vu.nl*.

The host *star.cs.vu.nl* operates as a name server for this zone. Name servers are critical to any naming service. What can be seen about this name server is that additional robustness has been created by giving two separate network interfaces, each represented by a separate *A* resource record. In this way, the effects of a broken network link can be somewhat alleviated as the server will remain accessible.

The next four lines (for *zephyr.cs.vu.nl*) give the necessary information about one of the department's mail servers. Note that this mail server is also backed up by another mail server, whose path is *tornado.cs.vu.nl*.

The next six lines show a typical configuration in which the department's Web server, as well as the department's FTP server are implemented by a single machine, called *soling.cs.vu.nl*. By executing both servers on the same machine (and essentially using that machine only for Internet services and not anything else), system management becomes easier. For example, both servers will have the same view of the file system, and for efficiency, part of the file system may be implemented on *soling.cs.vu.nl*. This approach is often applied in the case of WWW and FTP services.

The following two lines show information on one of the department's older server clusters. In this case, it tells us that the address *130.37.198.0* is associated with the host name *vucs-das1.cs.vu.nl*.

The next four lines show information on two major printers connected to the local network. Note that addresses in the range *192.168.0.0* to *192.168.255.255* are private: they can be accessed only from inside the local network and are not accessible from an arbitrary Internet host.

Name	Record type	Record value
cs.vu.nl.	NS	solo.cs.vu.nl.
cs.vu.nl.	NS	star.cs.vu.nl.
cs.vu.nl.	NS	ns.vu.nl.
cs.vu.nl.	NS	top.cs.vu.nl.
ns.vu.nl.	A	130.37.129.4
top.cs.vu.nl.	A	130.37.20.4
solo.cs.vu.nl.	A	130.37.20.5
star.cs.vu.nl.	A	130.37.24.6
star.cs.vu.nl.	A	192.31.231.42

Figure 5-21. Part of the description for the *vu.nl* domain which contains the *cs.vu.nl* domain.

Because the *cs.vu.nl* domain is implemented as a single zone, Fig. 5-20 does not include references to other zones. The way to refer to nodes in a subdomain that are implemented in a different zone is shown in Fig. 5-21. What needs to be done is to specify a name server for the subdomain by simply giving its domain name and IP address. When resolving a name for a node that lies in the *cs.vu.nl* domain, name resolution will continue at a certain point by reading the DNS database stored by the name server for the *cs.vu.nl* domain.

Decentralized DNS Implementations

The implementation of DNS we described so far is the standard one. It follows a hierarchy of servers with 13 well-known root servers and ending in millions of servers at the leaves. An important observation is that higher-level nodes receive many more requests than lower-level nodes. Only by caching the name-to-address bindings of these higher levels is it possible to avoid sending requests to them and thus swamping them.

These scalability problems can be avoided altogether with fully decentralized solutions. In particular, we can compute the hash of a DNS name, and subsequently take that hash as a key value to be looked up in a distributed hash table or a hierarchical location service with a fully partitioned root node. The obvious drawback of this approach is that we lose the structure of the original name. This loss may prevent efficient implementations of, for example, finding all children in a specific domain.

On the other hand, there are many advantages to mapping DNS to a DHT-based implementation, notably its scalability. As argued by Walfish et al. (2004), when there is a need for many names, using identifiers as a semantic-free way of accessing data will allow different systems to make use of a single naming system. The reason is simple: by now it is well understood how a huge collection of (flat) names can be efficiently supported. What needs to be done is to maintain the mapping of identifier-to-name information, where in this case a name may come from the DNS space, be a URL, and so on. Using identifiers can be made easier by letting users or organizations use a strict local name space. The latter is completely analogous to maintaining a private setting of environment variables on a computer.

Mapping DNS onto DHT-based peer-to-peer systems has been explored in CoDoNS (Ramasubramanian and Sirer, 2004a). They used a DHT-based system in which the prefixes of keys are used to route to a node. To explain, consider the case that each digit from an identifier is taken from the set $\{\ 0, ..., b-1\ \}$, where b is the base number. For example, in Chord, $b = 2$. If we assume that $b = 4$, then consider a node whose identifier is 3210. In their system, this node is assumed to keep a routing table of nodes having the following identifiers:

n_0:   a node whose identifier has prefix 0
n_1:   a node whose identifier has prefix 1
n_2:   a node whose identifier has prefix 2
n_{30}:   a node whose identifier has prefix 30
n_{31}:   a node whose identifier has prefix 31
n_{33}:   a node whose identifier has prefix 33
n_{320}:   a node whose identifier has prefix 320
n_{322}:   a node whose identifier has prefix 322
n_{323}:   a node whose identifier has prefix 323

Node 3210 is responsible for handling keys that have prefix 321. If it receives a lookup request for key 3123, it will forward it to node n_{31}, which, in turn, will see whether it needs to forward it to a node whose identifier has prefix 312. (We should note that each node maintains two other lists that it can use for routing if it misses an entry in its routing table.) Details of this approach can be found for Pastry (Rowstron and Druschel, 2001) and Tapestry (Zhao et al., 2004).

Returning to CoDoNS, a node responsible for key k stores the DNS resource records associated with domain name that hashes to k. The interesting part, however, is that CoDoNS attempts to minimize the number of hops in routing a request by replicating resource records. The principle strategy is simple: node 3210 will replicate its content to nodes having prefix 321. Such a replication will reduce each routing path ending in node 3210 by one hop. Of course, this replication can be applied again to all nodes having prefix 32, and so on.

When a DNS record gets replicated to all nodes with i matching prefixes, it is said to be replicated at level i. Note that a record replicated at level i (generally) requires i lookup steps to be found. However, there is a trade-off between the level of replication and the use of network and node resources. What CoDoNS does is replicate to the extent that the resulting aggregate lookup latency is less than a given constant C.

More specifically, think for a moment about the frequency distribution of the queries. Imagine ranking the lookup queries by how often a specific key is requested putting the most requested key in first position. The distribution of the lookups is said to be **Zipf-like** if the frequency of the n-th ranked item is proportional to $1/n^{\alpha}$, with α close to 1. George Zipf was a Harvard linguist who discovered this distribution while studying word-use frequencies in a natural language. However, as it turns out, it also applies among many other things, to the population of cities, size of earthquakes, top-income distributions, revenues of corporations, and, perhaps no longer surprisingly, DNS queries (Jung et al., 2002).

Now, if x_i is the fraction of most popular records that are to be replicated at level i, then Ramasubramanian and Sirer (2004b) show that x_i can be expressed by the following formula (for our purposes, only the fact that this formula exists is actually important; we will see how to use it shortly):

$$x_i = \left[\frac{d^i(\log N - C)}{1 + d + \cdots + d^{\log N - 1}} \right]^{\frac{1}{(1-\alpha)}} \quad with \ d = b^{(1-\alpha)/\alpha}$$

where N is the number of nodes in the network and α is the parameter in the Zipf distribution.

This formula allows to take informed decisions on which DNS records should be replicated. To make matters concrete, consider the case that $b = 32$ and $\alpha = 0.9$. Then, in a network with 10,000 nodes and 1,000,000 DNS records, and trying to achieve an average of $C=1$ hop only when doing a lookup, we will have that $x_0 = 0.0000701674$, meaning that only the 70 most popular DNS records should be replicated everywhere. Likewise, with $x_1 = 0.00330605$, the 3306 next most popular records should be replicated at level 1. Of course, it is required that $x_i < 1$. In this example, $x_2 = 0.155769$ and $x_3 > 1$, so that only the next most popular 155,769 records get replicated and all the others or not. Nevertheless, on average, a single hop is enough to find a requested DNS record.

5.4 ATTRIBUTE-BASED NAMING

Flat and structured names generally provide a unique and location-independent way of referring to entities. Moreover, structured names have been partly designed to provide a human-friendly way to name entities so that they can be conveniently accessed. In most cases, it is assumed that the name refers to only a single entity. However, location independence and human friendliness are not the only criterion for naming entities. In particular, as more information is being made available it becomes important to effectively search for entities. This approach requires that a user can provide merely a description of what he is looking for.

There are many ways in which descriptions can be provided, but a popular one in distributed systems is to describe an entity in terms of (*attribute, value*) pairs, generally referred to as **attribute-based naming**. In this approach, an entity is assumed to have an associated collection of attributes. Each attribute says something about that entity. By specifying which values a specific attribute should have, a user essentially constrains the set of entities that he is interested in. It is up to the naming system to return one or more entities that meet the user's description. In this section we take a closer look at attribute-based naming systems.

5.4.1 Directory Services

Attribute-based naming systems are also known as **directory services**, whereas systems that support structured naming are generally called **naming systems**. With directory services, entities have a set of associated attributes that can be used for searching. In some cases, the choice of attributes can be relatively simple. For example, in an e-mail system, messages can be tagged with attributes for the sender, recipient, subject, and so on. However, even in the case of e-mail, matters become difficult when other types of descriptors are needed, as is illustrated by the difficulty of developing filters that will allow only certain messages (based on their descriptors) to be passed through.

What it all boils down to is that designing an appropriate set of attributes is not trivial. In most cases, attribute design has to be done manually. Even if there is consensus on the set of attributes to use, practice shows that setting the values consistently by a diverse group of people is a problem by itself, as many will have experienced when accessing music and video databases on the Internet.

To alleviate some of these problems, research has been conducted on unifying the ways that resources can be described. In the context of distributed systems, one particularly relevant development is the **resource description framework (RDF)**. Fundamental to the RDF model is that resources are described as triplets consisting of a subject, a predicate, and an object. For example, (*Person, name, Alice*) describes a resource *Person* whose *name* is *Alice*. In RDF, each subject, predicate, or object can be a resource itself. This means that *Alice* may be implemented as reference to a file that can be subsequently retrieved. In the case of a predicate, such a resource could contain a textual description of that predicate. Of course, resources associated with subjects and objects could be anything. References in RDF are essentially URLs.

If resource descriptions are stored, it becomes possible to query that storage in a way that is common for many attributed-based naming systems. For example, an application could ask for the information associated with a person named Alice. Such a query would return a reference to the person resource associated with Alice. This resource can then subsequently be fetched by the application. More information on RDF can be found in Manola and Miller (2004).

In this example, the resource descriptions are stored at a central location. There is no reason why the resources should reside at the same location as well. However, not having the descriptions in the same place may incur a serious performance problem. Unlike structured naming systems, looking up values in an attribute-based naming system essentially requires an exhaustive search through all descriptors. When considering performance, such a search is less of problem within a single data store, but separate techniques need to be applied when the data is distributed across multiple, potentially dispersed computers. In the following, we will take a look at different approaches to solving this problem in distributed systems.

5.4.2 Hierarchical Implementations: LDAP

A common approach to tackling distributed directory services is to combine structured naming with attribute-based naming. This approach has been widely adopted, for example, in Microsoft's Active Directory service and other systems. Many of these systems use, or rely on the **lightweight directory access protocol** commonly referred simply as **LDAP**. The LDAP directory service has been derived from OSI's X.500 directory service. As with many OSI services, the quality of their associated implementations hindered widespread use, and simplifications were needed to make it useful. Detailed information on LDAP can be found in Arkills (2003).

Conceptually, an LDAP directory service consists of a number of records, usually referred to as directory entries. A directory entry is comparable to a resource record in DNS. Each record is made up of a collection of (*attribute, value*) pairs, where each attribute has an associated type. A distinction is made between single-valued attributes and multiple-valued attributes. The latter typically represent arrays and lists. As an example, a simple directory entry identifying the network addresses of some general servers from Fig. 5-20 is shown in Fig. 5-22.

Attribute	Abbr.	Value
Country	C	NL
Locality	L	Amsterdam
Organization	O	Vrije Universiteit
OrganizationalUnit	OU	Comp. Sc.
CommonName	CN	Main server
Mail_Servers	—	137.37.20.3, 130.37.24.6, 137.37.20.10
FTP_Server	—	130.37.20.20
WWW_Server	—	130.37.20.20

Figure 5-22. A simple example of an LDAP directory entry using LDAP naming conventions.

In our example, we have used a naming convention described in the LDAP standards, which applies to the first five attributes. The attributes *Organization* and *OrganizationUnit* describe, respectively, the organization and the department associated with the data that are stored in the record. Likewise, the attributes *Locality* and *Country* provide additional information on where the entry is stored. The *CommonName* attribute is often used as an (ambiguous) name to identify an entry within a limited part of the directory. For example, the name "Main server" may be enough to find our example entry given the specific values for the other four attributes *Country*, *Locality*, *Organization*, and *OrganizationalUnit*. In our example, only attribute *Mail_Servers* has multiple values associated with it. All other attributes have only a single value.

The collection of all directory entries in an LDAP directory service is called a **directory information base** (**DIB**). An important aspect of a DIB is that each record is uniquely named so that it can be looked up. Such a globally unique name appears as a sequence of naming attributes in each record. Each naming attribute is called a **relative distinguished name**, or **RDN** for short. In our example in Fig. 5-22, the first five attributes are all naming attributes. Using the conventional abbreviations for representing naming attributes in LDAP, as shown in Fig. 5-22, the attributes *Country*, *Organization*, and *OrganizationalUnit* could be used to form the globally unique name

/C=NL/O=Vrije Universiteit/OU=Comp. Sc.

analogous to the DNS name *nl.vu.cs*.

As in DNS, the use of globally unique names by listing RDNs in sequence, leads to a hierarchy of the collection of directory entries, which is referred to as a

directory information tree (DIT). A DIT essentially forms the naming graph of an LDAP directory service in which each node represents a directory entry. In addition, a node may also act as a directory in the traditional sense, in that there may be several children for which the node acts as parent. To explain, consider the naming graph as partly shown in Fig. 5-23(a). (Recall that labels are associated with edges.)

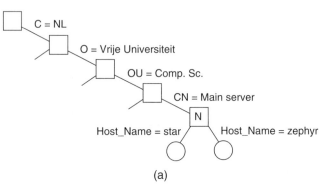

(a)

Attribute	Value	Attribute	Value
Country	NL	Country	NL
Locality	Amsterdam	Locality	Amsterdam
Organization	Vrije Universiteit	Organization	Vrije Universiteit
OrganizationalUnit	Comp. Sc.	OrganizationalUnit	Comp. Sc.
CommonName	Main server	CommonName	Main server
Host_Name	star	Host_Name	zephyr
Host_Address	192.31.231.42	Host_Address	137.37.20.10

(b)

Figure 5-23. (a) Part of a directory information tree. (b) Two directory entries having *Host_Name* as RDN.

Node *N* corresponds to the directory entry shown in Fig. 5-22. At the same time, this node acts as a parent to a number of other directory entries that have an additional naming attribute *Host_Name* that is used as an RDN. For example, such entries may be used to represent hosts as shown in Fig. 5-23(b).

A node in an LDAP naming graph can thus simultaneously represent a directory in the traditional sense as we discussed previously, as well as an LDAP record. This distinction is supported by two different lookup operations. The read operation is used to read a single record given its path name in the DIT. In contrast, the list operation is used to list the names of all outgoing edges of a given node in the DIT. Each name corresponds to a child node of the given node. Note that the list operation does not return any records; it merely returns names. In other words, calling read with as input the name

　　/C=NL/O=Vrije Universiteit/OU=Comp. Sc./CN=Main server

will return the record shown in Fig. 5-22, whereas calling list will return the names *star* and *zephyr* from the entries shown in Fig. 5-23(b) as well as the names of other hosts that have been registered in a similar way.

　　Implementing an LDAP directory service proceeds in much the same way as implementing a naming service such as DNS, except that LDAP supports more lookup operations as we will discuss shortly. When dealing with a large-scale directory, the DIT is usually partitioned and distributed across several servers, known as **directory service agents** (**DSA**). Each part of a partitioned DIT thus corresponds to a zone in DNS. Likewise, each DSA behaves very much the same as a normal name server, except that it implements a number of typical directory services, such as advanced search operations.

　　Clients are represented by what are called **directory user agents**, or simply **DUA**s. A DUA is similar to a name resolver in structured-naming services. A DUA exchanges information with a DSA according to a standardized access protocol.

　　What makes an LDAP implementation different from a DNS implementation are the facilities for searching through a DIB. In particular, facilities are provided to search for a directory entry given a set of criteria that attributes of the searched entries should meet. For example, suppose that we want a list of all main servers at the Vrije Universiteit. Using the notation defined in Howes (1997), such a list can be returned using a search operation such as

　　answer = search("&(C=NL)(O=Vrije Universiteit)(OU=*)(CN=Main server)")

In this example, we have specified that the place to look for main servers is the organization named *Vrije Universiteit* in country *NL*, but that we are not interested in a particular organizational unit. However, each returned result should have the *CN* attribute equal to *Main server*.

　　As we already mentioned, searching in a directory service is generally an expensive operation. For example, to find all main servers at the Vrije Universiteit requires searching all entries at each department and combining the results in a single answer. In other words, we will generally need to access several leaf nodes of a DIT in order to get an answer. In practice, this also means that several DSAs need to be accessed. In contrast, naming services can often be implemented in such a way that a lookup operation requires accessing only a single leaf node.

　　This whole setup of LDAP can be taken one step further by allowing several trees to co-exist, while also being linked to each other. This approach is followed in Microsoft's Active Directory leading to a *forest* of LDAP domains (Allen and Lowe-Norris, 2003). Obviously, searching in such an organization can be overwhelmingly complex. To circumvent some of the scalability problems, Active

Directory usually assumes there is a global index server (called a global catalog) that can be searched first. The index will indicate which LDAP domains need to be searched further.

Although LDAP by itself already exploits hierarchy for scalability, it is common to combine LDAP with DNS. For example, every tree in LDAP needs to be accessible at the root (known in Active Directory as a domain controller). The root is often known under a DNS name, which, in turn, can be found through an appropriate SRV record as we explained above.

LDAP typically represents a standard way of supporting attribute-based naming. Other recent directory services following this more traditional approach have been developed as well, notably in the context of grid computing and Web services. One specific example is the **universal directory and discovery integration** or simply **UDDI**.

These services assume an implementation in which one, or otherwise only a few nodes cooperate to maintain a simple distributed database. From a technological point of view, there is no real novelty here. Likewise, there is also nothing really new to report when it comes to introducing terminology, as can be readily observed when going through the hundreds of pages of the UDDI specifications (Clement et al., 2004). The fundamental scheme is always the same: scalability is achieved by making several of these databases accessible to applications, which are then responsible for querying each database separately and aggregating the results. So much for middleware support.

5.4.3 Decentralized Implementations

With the advent of peer-to-peer systems, researchers have also been looking for solutions for decentralized attribute-based naming systems. The key issue here is that *(attribute, value)* pairs need to be efficiently mapped so that searching can be done efficiently, that is, by avoiding an exhaustive search through the entire attribute space. In the following we will take a look at several ways how to establish such a mapping.

Mapping to Distributed Hash Tables

Let us first consider the case where *(attribute, value)* pairs need to be supported by a DHT-based system. First, assume that queries consist of a conjunction of pairs as with LDAP, that is, a user specifies a list of attributes, along with the unique value he wants to see for every respective attribute. The main advantage of this type of query is that no ranges need to be supported. Range queries may significantly increase the complexity of mapping pairs to a DHT.

Single-valued queries are supported in the INS/Twine system (Balazinska et al., 2002). Each entity (referred to as a resource) is assumed to be described by means of possibly hierarchically organized attributes such as shown in Fig. 5-24.

Each such description is translated into an **attribute-value tree** (**AVTree**) which is then used as the basis for an encoding that maps well onto a DHT-based system.

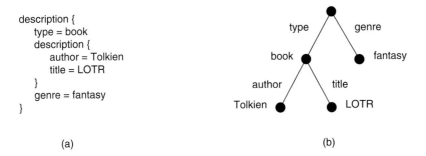

(a)   (b)

Figure 5-24. (a) A general description of a resource. (b) Its representation as an AVTree.

The main issue is to transform the AVTrees into a collection of keys that can be looked up in a DHT system. In this case, every path originating in the root is assigned a unique hash value, where a path description starts with a link (representing an attribute), and ends either in a node (value), or another link. Taking Fig. 5-24(b) as our example, the following hashes of all such paths are considered:

h_1:   hash(type-book)
h_2:   hash(type-book-author)
h_3:   hash(type-book-author-Tolkien)
h_4:   hash(type-book-title)
h_5:   hash(type-book-title-LOTR)
h_6:   hash(genre-fantasy)

A node responsible for hash value h_i will keep (a reference to) the actual resource. In our example, this may lead to six nodes storing information on Tolkien's Lord of the Rings. However, the benefit of this redundancy is that it will allow supporting partial queries. For example, consider a query such as "Return books written by Tolkien." This query is translated into the AVTree shown in Fig. 5-25 leading to computing the following three hashes:

h_1:   hash(type-book)
h_2:   hash(type-book-author)
h_3:   hash(type-book-author-Tolkien)

These values will be sent to nodes that store information on Tolkien's books, and will at least return Lord of the Rings. Note that a hash such as h_1 is rather general and will be generated often. These type of hashes can be filtered out of the system. Moreover, it is not difficult to see that only the most specific hashes need to be evaluated. Further details can be found in Balzinska et al. (2002).

Now let's take a look at another type of query, namely those that can contain range specifications for attribute values. For example, someone looking for a

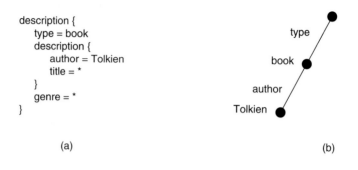

```
description {
    type = book
    description {
        author = Tolkien
        title = *
    }
    genre = *
}
```

(a)   (b)

Figure 5-25. (a) The resource description of a query. (b) Its representation as an AVTree.

house will generally want to specify that the price must fall within a specific range. Again, several solutions have been proposed and we will come across some of them when discussing publish/subscribe systems in Chap. 13. Here, we discuss a solution adopted in the SWORD resource discovery system (Oppenheimer et al., 2005).

In SWORD, (*attribute, value*) pairs as provided by a resource description are first transformed into a key for a DHT. Note that these pairs always contain a single value; only queries may contain value ranges for attributes. When computing the hash, the name of the attribute and its value are kept separate. In other words, specific bits in the resulting key will identify the attribute name, while others identify its value. In addition, the key will contain a number of random bits to guarantee uniqueness among all keys that need to be generated.

In this way, the space of attributes is conveniently partitioned: if n bits are reserved to code attribute names, 2^n different server groups can be used, one group for each attribute name. Likewise, by using m bits to encode values, a further partitioning per server group can be applied to store specific (*attribute, value*) pairs. DHTs are used only for distributing attribute names.

For each attribute name, the possible range of its value is partitioned into subranges and a single server is assigned to each subrange. To explain, consider a resource description with two attributes: a_1 taking values in the range [1..10] and a_2 taking values in the range [101...200]. Assume there are two servers for a_1: s_{11} takes care of recording values of a_1 in [1..5], and s_{12} for values in [6..10]. Likewise, server s_{21} records values for a_2 in range [101..150] and server s_{22} for values in [151..200]. Then, when the resource gets values ($a_1 = 7, a_2 = 175$), server s_{12} *and* server s_{22} will have to be informed.

The advantage of this scheme is that range queries can be easily supported. When a query is issued to return resources that have a_2 lying between 165 and 189, the query can be forwarded to server s_{22} who can then return the resources that match the query range. The drawback, however, is that updates need to be sent to multiple servers. Moreover, it is not immediately clear how well the load is balanced between the various servers. In particular, if certain range queries turn out to be very popular, specific servers will receive a high fraction of all queries. How this load-balancing problem can be tackled for DHT-based systems is discussed in Bharambe at al. (2004).

Semantic Overlay Networks

The decentralized implementations of attribute-based naming already show an increasing degree of autonomy of the various nodes. The system is less sensitive to nodes joining and leaving in comparison to, for example, distributed LDAP-based systems. This degree of autonomy is further increased when nodes have descriptions of resources that are there to be discovered by others. In other words, there is no a priori deterministic scheme by which (*attribute, value*) pairs are spread across a collection of nodes.

Not having such a scheme forces nodes to discover where requested resources are. Such a discovery is typical for unstructured overlay networks, which we already discussed in Chap. 2. In order to make searching efficient, it is important that a node has references to others that can most likely answer its queries. If we make the assumption that queries originating from node P are strongly related to the resources that P has, then we are seeking to provide P with a collection of links to *semantically proximal* neighbors. Recall that such a list is also known as a **partial view**. Semantical proximity can be defined in different ways, but it boils down to keeping track of nodes with similar resources. The nodes and these links will then form what is known as a **semantic overlay network**.

A common approach to semantic overlay networks is to assume that there is commonality in the meta information maintained at each node. In other words, the resources stored at each node are described using the same collection of attributes, or, more precisely, the same data schema (Crespo and Garcia-Molina, 2003). Having such a schema will allow defining specific similarity functions between nodes. Each node will then keep only links to the K most similar neighbors and query those nodes first when looking for specific data. Note that this approach makes sense only if we can generally assume that a query initiated at a node relates to the content stored at that node.

Unfortunately, assuming commonality in data schemas is generally wrong. In practice, the meta information on resources is highly inconsistent across different nodes and reaching consensus and what and how to describe resources is close to impossible. For this reason, semantic overlay networks will generally need to find different ways to define similarity.

One approach is to forget about attributes altogether and consider only very simple descriptors such as file names. Passively constructing an overlay can be done by keeping track of which nodes respond positively to file searches. For example, Sripanidkulchai et al. (2003) first send a query to a node's semantic neighbors, but if the requested file is not there a (limited) broadcast is then done. Of course, such a broadcast may lead to an update of the semantic-neighbors list. As a note, it is interesting to see that if a node requests its semantic neighbors to forward a query to *their* semantic neighbors, that the effect is minimal (Handrukande et al., 2004). This phenomenon can be explained by what is known as the **small-world effect** which essentially states that the friends of Alice are also each other's friends (Watts, 1999).

A more proactive approach toward constructing a semantic-neighbor list is proposed by Voulgaris and van Steen (2005) who use a simple **semantic proximity function** defined on the file lists FL_P and FL_Q of two nodes P and Q, respectively. This function simply counts the number of common files in FL_P and FL_Q. The goal is then to optimize the proximity function by letting a node keep a list of only those neighbors that have the most files in common with it.

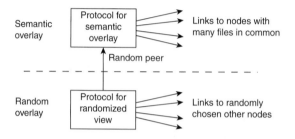

Figure 5-26. Maintaining a semantic overlay through gossiping.

To this end, a two-layered gossiping scheme is deployed as shown in Fig. 5-26. The bottom layer consists of an epidemic protocol that aims at maintaining a partial view of uniform randomly-selected nodes. There are different ways to achieve this as we explained in Chap. 2 [see also Jelasity et al. (2005a)]. The top layer maintains a list of semantically proximal neighbors through gossiping. To initiate an exchange, an node P can randomly select a neighbor Q from its current list, but the trick is to let P send only those entries that are semantically closest to Q. In turn, when P receives entries from Q, it will eventually keep a partial view consisting only of the semantically closest nodes. As it turns out, the partial views as maintained by the top layer will rapidly converge to an optimum.

As will have become clear by now, semantic overlay networks are closely related to decentralized searching. An extensive overview of searching in all kinds of peer-to-peer systems is discussed in Risson and Moors (2006).

5.5 SUMMARY

Names are used to refer to entities. Essentially, there are three types of names. An address is the name of an access point associated with an entity, also simply called the address of an entity. An identifier is another type of name. It has three properties: each entity is referred to by exactly one identifier, an identifier refers to only one entity, and is never assigned to another entity. Finally, human-friendly names are targeted to be used by humans and as such are represented as character strings. Given these types, we make a distinction between flat naming, structured naming, and attribute-based naming.

Systems for flat naming essentially need to resolve an identifier to the address of its associated entity. This locating of an entity can be done in different ways. The first approach is to use broadcasting or multicasting. The identifier of the entity is broadcast to every process in the distributed system. The process offering an access point for the entity responds by providing an address for that access point. Obviously, this approach has limited scalability.

A second approach is to use forwarding pointers. Each time an entity moves to a next location, it leaves behind a pointer telling where it will be next. Locating the entity requires traversing the path of forwarding pointers. To avoid large chains of pointers, it is important to reduce chains periodically

A third approach is to allocate a home to an entity. Each time an entity moves to another location, it informs its home where it is. Locating an entity proceeds by first asking its home for the current location.

A fourth approach is to organize all nodes into a structured peer-to-peer system, and systematically assign nodes to entities taking their respective identifiers into account. By subsequently devising a routing algorithm by which lookup requests are moved toward the node responsible for a given entity, efficient and robust name resolution is possible.

A fifth approach is to build a hierarchical search tree. The network is divided into nonoverlapping domains. Domains can be grouped into higher-level (nonoverlapping) domains, and so on. There is a single top-level domain that covers the entire network. Each domain at every level has an associated directory node. If an entity is located in a domain D, the directory node of the next higher-level domain will have a pointer to D. A lowest-level directory node stores the address of the entity. The top-level directory node knows about all entities.

Structured names are easily organized in a name space. A name space can be represented by a naming graph in which a node represents a named entity and the label on an edge represents the name under which that entity is known. A node having multiple outgoing edges represents a collection of entities and is also known as a context node or directory. Large-scale naming graphs are often organized as rooted acyclic directed graphs.

Naming graphs are convenient to organize human-friendly names in a structured way. An entity can be referred to by a path name. Name resolution is the process of traversing the naming graph by looking up the components of a path name, one at a time. A large-scale naming graph is implemented by distributing its nodes across multiple name servers. When resolving a path name by traversing the naming graph, name resolution continues at the next name server as soon as a node is reached implemented by that server.

More problematic are attribute-based naming schemes in which entities are described by a collection of (*attribute, value*) pairs. Queries are also formulated as such pairs, essentially requiring an exhaustive search through all descriptors. Such a search is only feasible when the descriptors are stored in a single database. However, alternative solutions have been devised by which the pairs are mapped onto DHT-based systems, essentially leading to a distribution of the collection of entity descriptors.

Related to attribute-based naming is to gradually replace name resolution by distributed search techniques. This approach is followed in semantic overlay networks, in which nodes maintain a local list of other nodes that have semantically similar content. These semantic lists allow for efficient search to take place by which first the immediate neighbors are queried, and only after that has had no success will a (limited) broadcast be deployed.

PROBLEMS

1. Give an example of where an address of an entity E needs to be further resolved into another address to actually access E.

2. Would you consider a URL such as *http://www.acme.org/index.html* to be location independent? What about *http://www.acme.nl/index.html*?

3. Give some examples of true identifiers.

4. Is an identifier allowed to contain information on the entity it refers to?

5. Outline an efficient implementation of globally unique identifiers.

6. Consider the Chord system as shown in Fig. 5-4 and assume that node 7 has just joined the network. What would its finger table be and would there be any changes to other finger tables?

7. Consider a Chord DHT-based system for which k bits of an m-bit identifier space have been reserved for assigning to superpeers. If identifiers are randomly assigned, how many superpeers can one expect to have in an N-node system?

8. If we insert a node into a Chord system, do we need to instantly update all the finger tables?

9. What is a major drawback of recursive lookups when resolving a key in a DHT-based system?

10. A special form of locating an entity is called anycasting, by which a service is identified by means of an IP address (see, for example, RFC 1546). Sending a request to an anycast address, returns a response from a server implementing the service identified

by that anycast address. Outline the implementation of an anycast service based on the hierarchical location service described in Sec. 5.2.4.

11. Considering that a two-tiered home-based approach is a specialization of a hierarchical location service, where is the root?

12. Suppose that it is known that a specific mobile entity will almost never move outside domain D, and if it does, it can be expected to return soon. How can this information be used to speed up the lookup operation in a hierarchical location service?

13. In a hierarchical location service with a depth of k, how many location records need to be updated at most when a mobile entity changes its location?

14. Consider an entity moving from location A to B, while passing several intermediate locations where it will reside for only a relatively short time. When arriving at B, it settles down for a while. Changing an address in a hierarchical location service may still take a relatively long time to complete, and should therefore be avoided when visiting an intermediate location. How can the entity be located at an intermediate location?

15. The root node in hierarchical location services may become a potential bottleneck. How can this problem be effectively circumvented?

16. Give an example of how the closure mechanism for a URL could work.

17. Explain the difference between a hard link and a soft link in UNIX systems. Are there things that can be done with a hard link that cannot be done with a soft link or vice versa?

18. High-level name servers in DNS, that is, name servers implementing nodes in the DNS name space that are close to the root, generally do not support recursive name resolution. Can we expect much performance improvement if they did?

19. Explain how DNS can be used to implement a home-based approach to locating mobile hosts.

20. How is a mounting point looked up in most UNIX systems?

21. Consider a distributed file system that uses per-user name spaces. In other words, each user has his own, private name space. Can names from such name spaces be used to share resources between two different users?

22. Consider DNS. To refer to a node N in a subdomain implemented as a different zone than the current domain, a name server for that zone needs to be specified. Is it always necessary to include a resource record for that server's address, or is it sometimes sufficient to provide only its domain name?

23. Counting common files is a rather naive way of defining semantic proximity. Assume you were to build semantic overlay networks based on text documents, what other semantic proximity function can you think of?

24. **(Lab assignment)** Set up your own DNS server. Install BIND on either a Windows or UNIX machine and configure it for a few simple names. Test your configuration using tools such as the Domain Information Groper (DIG). Make sure your DNS database includes records for name servers, mail servers, and standard servers. Note that if you

are running BIND on a machine with host name *HOSTNAME*, you should be able to resolve names of the form *RESOURCE-NAME.HOSTNAME* .

6

SYNCHRONIZATION

In the previous chapters, we have looked at processes and communication between processes. While communication is important, it is not the entire story. Closely related is how processes cooperate and synchronize with one another. Cooperation is partly supported by means of naming, which allows processes to at least share resources, or entities in general.

In this chapter, we mainly concentrate on how processes can synchronize. For example, it is important that multiple processes do not simultaneously access a shared resource, such as printer, but instead cooperate in granting each other temporary exclusive access. Another example is that multiple processes may sometimes need to agree on the ordering of events, such as whether message *m1* from process *P* was sent before or after message *m2* from process *Q*.

As it turns out, synchronization in distributed systems is often much more difficult compared to synchronization in uniprocessor or multiprocessor systems. The problems and solutions that are discussed in this chapter are, by their nature, rather general, and occur in many different situations in distributed systems.

We start with a discussion of the issue of synchronization based on actual time, followed by synchronization in which only relative ordering matters rather than ordering in absolute time.

In many cases, it is important that a group of processes can appoint one process as a coordinator, which can be done by means of election algorithms. We discuss various election algorithms in a separate section.

Distributed algorithms come in all sorts and flavors and have been developed for very different types of distributed systems. Many examples (and further references) can be found in Andrews (2000) and Guerraoui and Rodrigues (2006). More formal approaches to a wealth of algorithms can be found in text books from Attiya and Welch (2004), Lynch (1996), and (Tel, 2000).

6.1 CLOCK SYNCHRONIZATION

In a centralized system, time is unambiguous. When a process wants to know the time, it makes a system call and the kernel tells it. If process A asks for the time, and then a little later process B asks for the time, the value that B gets will be higher than (or possibly equal to) the value A got. It will certainly not be lower. In a distributed system, achieving agreement on time is not trivial.

Just think, for a moment, about the implications of the lack of global time on the UNIX *make* program, as a single example. Normally, in UNIX, large programs are split up into multiple source files, so that a change to one source file only requires one file to be recompiled, not all the files. If a program consists of 100 files, not having to recompile everything because one file has been changed greatly increases the speed at which programmers can work.

The way *make* normally works is simple. When the programmer has finished changing all the source files, he runs *make*, which examines the times at which all the source and object files were last modified. If the source file *input.c* has time 2151 and the corresponding object file *input.o* has time 2150, *make* knows that *input.c* has been changed since *input.o* was created, and thus *input.c* must be recompiled. On the other hand, if *output.c* has time 2144 and *output.o* has time 2145, no compilation is needed. Thus *make* goes through all the source files to find out which ones need to be recompiled and calls the compiler to recompile them.

Now imagine what could happen in a distributed system in which there were no global agreement on time. Suppose that *output.o* has time 2144 as above, and shortly thereafter *output.c* is modified but is assigned time 2143 because the clock on its machine is slightly behind, as shown in Fig. 6-1. *Make* will not call the compiler. The resulting executable binary program will then contain a mixture of object files from the old sources and the new sources. It will probably crash and the programmer will go crazy trying to understand what is wrong with the code.

There are many more examples where an accurate account of time is needed. The example above can easily be reformulated to file timestamps in general. In addition, think of application domains such as financial brokerage, security auditing, and collaborative sensing, and it will become clear that accurate timing is important. Since time is so basic to the way people think and the effect of not having all the clocks synchronized can be so dramatic, it is fitting that we begin our study of synchronization with the simple question: Is it possible to synchronize all the clocks in a distributed system? The answer is surprisingly complicated.

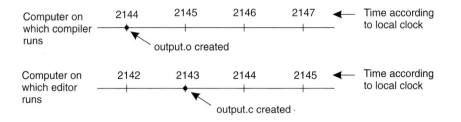

Figure 6-1. When each machine has its own clock, an event that occurred after another event may nevertheless be assigned an earlier time.

6.1.1 Physical Clocks

Nearly all computers have a circuit for keeping track of time. Despite the widespread use of the word "clock" to refer to these devices, they are not actually clocks in the usual sense. **Timer** is perhaps a better word. A computer timer is usually a precisely machined quartz crystal. When kept under tension, quartz crystals oscillate at a well-defined frequency that depends on the kind of crystal, how it is cut, and the amount of tension. Associated with each crystal are two registers, a **counter** and a **holding register**. Each oscillation of the crystal decrements the counter by one. When the counter gets to zero, an interrupt is generated and the counter is reloaded from the holding register. In this way, it is possible to program a timer to generate an interrupt 60 times a second, or at any other desired frequency. Each interrupt is called one **clock tick**.

When the system is booted, it usually asks the user to enter the date and time, which is then converted to the number of ticks after some known starting date and stored in memory. Most computers have a special battery-backed up CMOS RAM so that the date and time need not be entered on subsequent boots. At every clock tick, the interrupt service procedure adds one to the time stored in memory. In this way, the (software) clock is kept up to date.

With a single computer and a single clock, it does not matter much if this clock is off by a small amount. Since all processes on the machine use the same clock, they will still be internally consistent. For example, if the file *input.c* has time 2151 and file *input.o* has time 2150, *make* will recompile the source file, even if the clock is off by 2 and the true times are 2153 and 2152, respectively. All that really matters are the relative times.

As soon as multiple CPUs are introduced, each with its own clock, the situation changes radically. Although the frequency at which a crystal oscillator runs is usually fairly stable, it is impossible to guarantee that the crystals in different computers all run at exactly the same frequency. In practice, when a system has *n* computers, all *n* crystals will run at slightly different rates, causing the (software) clocks gradually to get out of synch and give different values when read out. This difference in time values is called **clock skew**. As a consequence of this clock skew, programs that expect the time associated with a file, object, process, or message to be correct and independent of the machine on which it was generated (i.e., which clock it used) can fail, as we saw in the *make* example above.

In some systems (e.g., real-time systems), the actual clock time is important. Under these circumstances, external physical clocks are needed. For reasons of efficiency and redundancy, multiple physical clocks are generally considered desirable, which yields two problems: (1) How do we synchronize them with real-world clocks, and (2) How do we synchronize the clocks with each other?

Before answering these questions, let us digress slightly to see how time is actually measured. It is not nearly as easy as one might think, especially when high accuracy is required. Since the invention of mechanical clocks in the 17th century, time has been measured astronomically. Every day, the sun appears to rise on the eastern horizon, then climbs to a maximum height in the sky, and finally sinks in the west. The event of the sun's reaching its highest apparent point in the sky is called the **transit of the sun**. This event occurs at about noon each day. The interval between two consecutive transits of the sun is called the **solar day**. Since there are 24 hours in a day, each containing 3600 seconds, the **solar second** is defined as exactly 1/86400th of a solar day. The geometry of the mean solar day calculation is shown in Fig. 6-2.

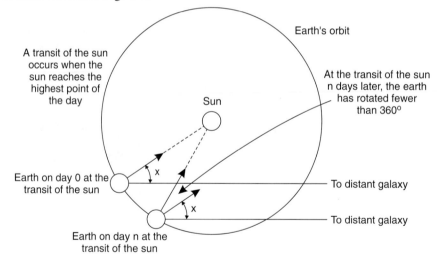

Figure 6-2. Computation of the mean solar day.

In the 1940s, it was established that the period of the earth's rotation is not constant. The earth is slowing down due to tidal friction and atmospheric drag. Based on studies of growth patterns in ancient coral, geologists now believe that 300 million years ago there were about 400 days per year. The length of the year (the time for one trip around the sun) is not thought to have changed; the day has simply become longer. In addition to this long-term trend, short-term variations in the length of the day also occur, probably caused by turbulence deep in the earth's core of molten iron. These revelations led astronomers to compute the length of the day by measuring a large number of days and taking the average before dividing by 86,400. The resulting quantity was called the **mean solar second**.

With the invention of the atomic clock in 1948, it became possible to measure time much more accurately, and independent of the wiggling and wobbling of the earth, by counting transitions of the cesium 133 atom. The physicists took over the job of timekeeping from the astronomers and defined the second to be the time it takes the cesium 133 atom to make exactly 9,192,631,770 transitions. The choice of 9,192,631,770 was made to make the atomic second equal to the mean solar second in the year of its introduction. Currently, several laboratories around the world have cesium 133 clocks. Periodically, each laboratory tells the Bureau International de l'Heure (BIH) in Paris how many times its clock has ticked. The BIH averages these to produce **International Atomic Time**, which is abbreviated **TAI**. Thus TAI is just the mean number of ticks of the cesium 133 clocks since midnight on Jan. 1, 1958 (the beginning of time) divided by 9,192,631,770.

Although TAI is highly stable and available to anyone who wants to go to the trouble of buying a cesium clock, there is a serious problem with it; 86,400 TAI seconds is now about 3 msec less than a mean solar day (because the mean solar day is getting longer all the time). Using TAI for keeping time would mean that over the course of the years, noon would get earlier and earlier, until it would eventually occur in the wee hours of the morning. People might notice this and we could have the same kind of situation as occurred in 1582 when Pope Gregory XIII decreed that 10 days be omitted from the calendar. This event caused riots in the streets because landlords demanded a full month's rent and bankers a full month's interest, while employers refused to pay workers for the 10 days they did not work, to mention only a few of the conflicts. The Protestant countries, as a matter of principle, refused to have anything to do with papal decrees and did not accept the Gregorian calendar for 170 years.

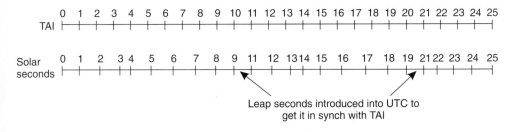

Figure 6-3. TAI seconds are of constant length, unlike solar seconds. Leap seconds are introduced when necessary to keep in phase with the sun.

BIH solves the problem by introducing **leap seconds** whenever the discrepancy between TAI and solar time grows to 800 msec. The use of leap seconds is illustrated in Fig. 6-3. This correction gives rise to a time system based on constant TAI seconds but which stays in phase with the apparent motion of the sun. It is called **Universal Coordinated Time**, but is abbreviated as **UTC**. UTC is the basis of all modern civil timekeeping. It has essentially replaced the old standard, Greenwich Mean Time, which is astronomical time.

Most electric power companies synchronize the timing of their 60-Hz or 50-Hz clocks to UTC, so when BIH announces a leap second, the power companies raise their frequency to 61 Hz or 51 Hz for 60 or 50 sec, to advance all the clocks in their distribution area. Since 1 sec is a noticeable interval for a computer, an operating system that needs to keep accurate time over a period of years must have special software to account for leap seconds as they are announced (unless they use the power line for time, which is usually too crude). The total number of leap seconds introduced into UTC so far is about 30.

To provide UTC to people who need precise time, the National Institute of Standard Time (NIST) operates a shortwave radio station with call letters WWV from Fort Collins, Colorado. WWV broadcasts a short pulse at the start of each UTC second. The accuracy of WWV itself is about ±1 msec, but due to random atmospheric fluctuations that can affect the length of the signal path, in practice the accuracy is no better than ±10 msec. In England, the station MSF, operating from Rugby, Warwickshire, provides a similar service, as do stations in several other countries.

Several earth satellites also offer a UTC service. The Geostationary Environment Operational Satellite can provide UTC accurately to 0.5 msec, and some other satellites do even better.

Using either shortwave radio or satellite services requires an accurate knowledge of the relative position of the sender and receiver, in order to compensate for the signal propagation delay. Radio receivers for WWV, GEOS, and the other UTC sources are commercially available.

6.1.2 Global Positioning System

As a step toward actual clock synchronization problems, we first consider a related problem, namely determining one's geographical position anywhere on Earth. This positioning problem is by itself solved through a highly specific, dedicated distributed system, namely **GPS**, which is an acronym for **global positioning system**. GPS is a satellite-based distributed system that was launched in 1978. Although it has been used mainly for military applications, in recent years it has found its way to many civilian applications, notably for traffic navigation. However, many more application domains exist. For example, GPS phones now allow to let callers track each other's position, a feature which may show to be extremely handy when you are lost or in trouble. This principle can easily be applied to tracking other things as well, including pets, children, cars, boats, and so on. An excellent overview of GPS is provided by Zogg (2002).

GPS uses 29 satellites each circulating in an orbit at a height of approximately 20,000 km. Each satellite has up to four atomic clocks, which are regularly cali-brated from special stations on Earth. A satellite continuously broadcasts its posi-tion, and time stamps each message with its local time. This broadcasting allows every receiver on Earth to accurately compute its own position using, in principle, only three satellites. To explain, let us first assume that all clocks, including the receiver's, are synchronized.

In order to compute a position, consider first the two-dimensional case, as shown in Fig. 6-4, in which two satellites are drawn, along with the circles repres-enting points at the same distance from each respective satellite. The y-axis represents the height, while the x-axis represents a straight line along the Earth's surface at sea level. Ignoring the highest point, we see that the intersection of the two circles is a unique point (in this case, perhaps somewhere up a mountain).

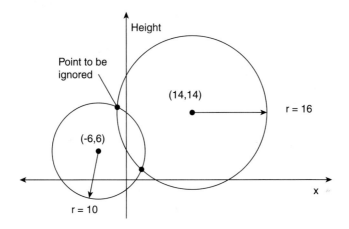

Figure 6-4. Computing a position in a two-dimensional space.

This principle of intersecting circles can be expanded to three dimensions, meaning that we need three satellites to determine the longitude, latitude, and alti-tude of a receiver on Earth. This positioning is all fairly straightforward, but mat-ters become complicated when we can no longer assume that all clocks are per-fectly synchronized.

There are two important real-world facts that we need to take into account:

1. It takes a while before data on a satellite's position reaches the re-ceiver.

2. The receiver's clock is generally not in synch with that of a satellite.

Assume that the timestamp from a satellite is completely accurate. Let Δ_r denote the deviation of the receiver's clock from the actual time. When a message is received from satellite i with timestamp T_i, then the measured delay Δ_i by the receiver consists of two components: the actual delay, along with its own deviation:

$$\Delta_i = (T_{now} - T_i) + \Delta_r$$

As signals travel with the speed of light, c, the measured distance of the satellite is clearly $c\,\Delta_i$. With

$$d_i = c\,(T_{now} - T_i)$$

being the real distance between the receiver and the satellite, the measured distance can be rewritten to $d_i + c\,\Delta_r$. The real distance is simply computed as:

$$d_i = \sqrt{(x_i - x_r)^2 + (y_i - y_r)^2 + (z_i - z_r)^2}$$

where x_i, y_i, and z_i denote the coordinates of satellite i. What we see now is that if we have four satellites, we get four equations in four unknowns, allowing us to solve the coordinates x_r, y_r, and z_r for the receiver, but also Δ_r. In other words, a GPS measurement will also give an account of the actual time. Later in this chapter we will return to determining positions following a similar approach.

So far, we have assumed that measurements are perfectly accurate. Of course, they are not. For one thing, GPS does not take leap seconds into account. In other words, there is a systematic deviation from UTC, which by January 1, 2006 is 14 seconds. Such an error can be easily compensated for in software. However, there are many other sources of errors, starting with the fact that the atomic clocks in the satellites are not always in perfect synch, the position of a satellite is not known precisely, the receiver's clock has a finite accuracy, the signal propagation speed is not constant (as signals slow down when entering, e.g., the ionosphere), and so on. Moreover, we all know that the earth is not a perfect sphere, leading to further corrections.

By and large, computing an accurate position is far from a trivial undertaking and requires going down into many gory details. Nevertheless, even with relatively cheap GPS receivers, positioning can be precise within a range of 1–5 meters. Moreover, professional receivers (which can easily be hooked up in a computer network) have a claimed error of less than 20–35 nanoseconds. Again, we refer to the excellent overview by Zogg (2002) as a first step toward getting acquainted with the details.

6.1.3 Clock Synchronization Algorithms

If one machine has a WWV receiver, the goal becomes keeping all the other machines synchronized to it. If no machines have WWV receivers, each machine keeps track of its own time, and the goal is to keep all the machines together as well as possible. Many algorithms have been proposed for doing this synchronization. A survey is given in Ramanathan et al. (1990).

All the algorithms have the same underlying model of the system. Each machine is assumed to have a timer that causes an interrupt H times a second. When this timer goes off, the interrupt handler adds 1 to a software clock that keeps track of the number of ticks (interrupts) since some agreed-upon time in the past. Let us call the value of this clock C. More specifically, when the UTC time is t, the value of the clock on machine p is $C_p(t)$. In a perfect world, we would have $C_p(t) = t$ for all p and all t. In other words, $C'_p(t) = dC/dt$ ideally should be 1. $C'_p(t)$ is called the **frequency** of p's clock at time t. The **skew** of the clock is defined as $C'_p(t) - 1$ and denotes the extent to which the frequency differs from that of a perfect clock. The **offset** relative to a specific time t is $C_p(t) - t$.

Real timers do not interrupt exactly H times a second. Theoretically, a timer with $H = 60$ should generate 216,000 ticks per hour. In practice, the relative error obtainable with modern timer chips is about 10^{-5}, meaning that a particular machine can get a value in the range 215,998 to 216,002 ticks per hour. More precisely, if there exists some constant ρ such that

$$1 - \rho \le \frac{dC}{dt} \le 1 + \rho$$

the timer can be said to be working within its specification. The constant ρ is specified by the manufacturer and is known as the **maximum drift rate**. Note that the maximum drift rate specifies to what extent a clock's skew is allowed to fluctuate. Slow, perfect, and fast clocks are shown in Fig. 6-5.

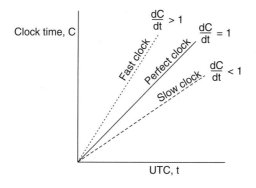

Figure 6-5. The relation between clock time and UTC when clocks tick at different rates.

If two clocks are drifting from UTC in the opposite direction, at a time Δt after they were synchronized, they may be as much as $2\rho\,\Delta t$ apart. If the operating system designers want to guarantee that no two clocks ever differ by more than δ, clocks must be resynchronized (in software) at least every $\delta/2\rho$ seconds. The various algorithms differ in precisely how this resynchronization is done.

Network Time Protocol

A common approach in many protocols and originally proposed by Cristian (1989) is to let clients contact a time server. The latter can accurately provide the current time, for example, because it is equipped with a WWV receiver or an accurate clock. The problem, of course, is that when contacting the server, message delays will have outdated the reported time. The trick is to find a good estimation for these delays. Consider the situation sketched in Fig. 6-6.

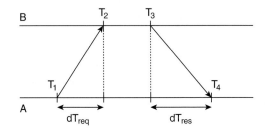

Figure 6-6. Getting the current time from a time server.

In this case, A will send a request to B, timestamped with value T_1. B, in turn, will record the time of receipt T_2 (taken from its own local clock), and returns a response timestamped with value T_3, and piggybacking the previously recorded value T_2. Finally, A records the time of the response's arrival, T_4. Let us assume that the propagation delays from A to B is roughly the same as B to A, meaning that $T_2 - T_1 \approx T_4 - T_3$. In that case, A can estimate its offset relative to B as

$$\theta = T_3 - \frac{(T_2 - T_1) + (T_4 - T_3)}{2} = \frac{(T_2 - T_1) + (T_3 - T_4)}{2}$$

Of course, time is not allowed to run backward. If A's clock is fast, $\theta < 0$, meaning that A should, in principle, set its clock backward. This is not allowed as it could cause serious problems such as an object file compiled just after the clock change having a time earlier than the source which was modified just before the clock change.

Such a change must be introduced gradually. One way is as follows. Suppose that the timer is set to generate 100 interrupts per second. Normally, each interrupt would add 10 msec to the time. When slowing down, the interrupt routine adds only 9 msec each time until the correction has been made. Similarly, the clock can be advanced gradually by adding 11 msec at each interrupt instead of jumping it forward all at once.

In the case of the **network time protocol (NTP)**, this protocol is set up pairwise between servers. In other words, B will also probe A for its current time. The offset θ is computed as given above, along with the estimation δ for the delay:

$$\delta = \frac{(T_2 - T_1) + (T_4 - T_3)}{2}$$

Eight pairs of (θ, δ) values are buffered, finally taking the minimal value found for δ as the best estimation for the delay between the two servers, and subsequently the associated value θ as the most reliable estimation of the offset.

Applying NTP symmetrically should, in principle, also let B adjust its clock to that of A. However, if B's clock is known to be more accurate, then such an adjustment would be foolish. To solve this problem, NTP divides servers into strata. A server with a **reference clock** such as a WWV receiver or an atomic clock, is known to be a **stratum-1 server** (the clock itself is said to operate at stratum 0). When A contacts B, it will only adjust its time if its own stratum level is higher than that of B. Moreover, after the synchronization, A's stratum level will become one higher than that of B. In other words, if B is a stratum-k server, then A will become a stratum-$(k+1)$ server if its original stratum level was already larger than k. Due to the symmetry of NTP, if A's stratum level was *lower* than that of B, B will adjust itself to A.

There are many important features about NTP, of which many relate to identifying and masking errors, but also security attacks. NTP is described in Mills (1992) and is known to achieve (worldwide) accuracy in the range of 1–50 msec. The newest version (NTPv4) was initially documented only by means of its implementation, but a detailed description can now be found in Mills (2006).

The Berkeley Algorithm

In many algorithms such as NTP, the time server is passive. Other machines periodically ask it for the time. All it does is respond to their queries. In Berkeley UNIX, exactly the opposite approach is taken (Gusella and Zatti, 1989). Here the time server (actually, a time daemon) is active, polling every machine from time to time to ask what time it is there. Based on the answers, it computes an average time and tells all the other machines to advance their clocks to the new time or slow their clocks down until some specified reduction has been achieved. This method is suitable for a system in which no machine has a WWV receiver. The time daemon's time must be set manually by the operator periodically. The method is illustrated in Fig. 6-7.

In Fig. 6-7(a), at 3:00, the time daemon tells the other machines its time and asks for theirs. In Fig. 6-7(b), they respond with how far ahead or behind the time daemon they are. Armed with these numbers, the time daemon computes the average and tells each machine how to adjust its clock [see Fig. 6-7(c)].

Note that for many purposes, it is sufficient that all machines agree on the same time. It is not essential that this time also agrees with the real time as announced on the radio every hour. If in our example of Fig. 6-7 the time daemon's clock would never be manually calibrated, no harm is done provided

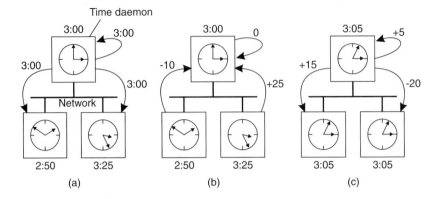

Figure 6-7. (a) The time daemon asks all the other machines for their clock values. (b) The machines answer. (c) The time daemon tells everyone how to adjust their clock.

none of the other nodes communicates with external computers. Everyone will just happily agree on a current time, without that value having any relation with reality.

Clock Synchronization in Wireless Networks

An important advantage of more traditional distributed systems is that we can easily and efficiently deploy time servers. Moreover, most machines can contact each other, allowing for a relatively simple dissemination of information. These assumptions are no longer valid in many wireless networks, notably sensor networks. Nodes are resource constrained, and multihop routing is expensive. In addition, it is often important to optimize algorithms for energy consumption. These and other observations have led to the design of very different clock synchronization algorithms for wireless networks. In the following, we consider one specific solution. Sivrikaya and Yener (2004) provide a brief overview of other solutions. An extensive survey can be found in Sundararaman et al. (2005).

Reference broadcast synchronization (RBS) is a clock synchronization protocol that is quite different from other proposals (Elson et al., 2002). First, the protocol does not assume that there is a single node with an accurate account of the actual time available. Instead of aiming to provide all nodes UTC time, it aims at merely internally synchronizing the clocks, just as the Berkeley algorithm does. Second, the solutions we have discussed so far are designed to bring the sender and receiver into synch, essentially following a two-way protocol. RBS deviates from this pattern by letting only the receivers synchronize, keeping the sender out of the loop.

In RBS, a sender broadcasts a reference message that will allow its receivers to adjust their clocks. A key observation is that in a sensor network the time to propagate a signal to other nodes is roughly constant, provided no multi-hop routing is assumed. Propagation time in this case is measured from the moment that a message leaves the network interface of the sender. As a consequence, two important sources for variation in message transfer no longer play a role in estimating delays: the time spent to construct a message, and the time spent to access the network. This principle is shown in Fig. 6-8.

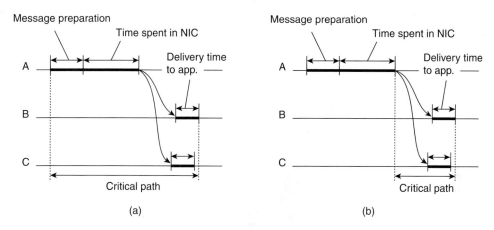

Figure 6-8. (a) The usual critical path in determining network delays. (b) The critical path in the case of RBS.

Note that in protocols such as NTP, a timestamp is added to the message before it is passed on the network interface. Furthermore, as wireless networks are based on a contention protocol, there is generally no saying how long it will take before a message can actually be transmitted. These factors of nondeterminism are eliminated in RBS. What remains is the delivery time at the receiver, but this time varies considerably less than the network-access time.

The idea underlying RBS is simple: when a node broadcasts a reference message m, each node p simply records the time $T_{p,m}$ that it received m. Note that $T_{p,m}$ is read from p's local clock. Ignoring clock skew, two nodes p and q can exchange each other's delivery times in order to estimate their mutual, relative offset:

$$Offset\,[p,q\,] = \frac{\sum_{k=1}^{M}(T_{p,k} - T_{q,k})}{M}$$

where M is the total number of reference messages sent. This information is important: node p will know the value of q's clock relative to its own value. Moreover, if it simply stores these offsets, there is no need to adjust its own clock, which saves energy.

Unfortunately, clocks can drift apart. The effect is that simply computing the average offset as done above will not work: the last values sent are simply less accurate than the first ones. Moreover, as time goes by, the offset will presumably increase. Elson et al. use a very simple algorithm to compensate for this: instead of computing an average they apply standard linear regression to compute the offset as a function:

$$Offset [p,q](t) = \alpha t + \beta$$

The constants α and β are computed from the pairs $(T_{p,k}, T_{q,k})$. This new form will allow a much more accurate computation of q's current clock value by node p, and vice versa.

6.2 LOGICAL CLOCKS

So far, we have assumed that clock synchronization is naturally related to real time. However, we have also seen that it may be sufficient that every node agrees on a current time, without that time necessarily being the same as the real time. We can go one step further. For running *make*, for example, it is adequate that two nodes agree that *input.o* is outdated by a new version of *input.c*. In this case, keeping track of each other's events (such as a producing a new version of *input.c*) is what matters. For these algorithms, it is conventional to speak of the clocks as **logical clocks**.

In a classic paper, Lamport (1978) showed that although clock synchronization is possible, it need not be absolute. If two processes do not interact, it is not necessary that their clocks be synchronized because the lack of synchronization would not be observable and thus could not cause problems. Furthermore, he pointed out that what usually matters is not that all processes agree on exactly what time it is, but rather that they agree on the order in which events occur. In the *make* example, what counts is whether *input.c* is older or newer than *input.o*, not their absolute creation times.

In this section we will discuss Lamport's algorithm, which synchronizes logical clocks. Also, we discuss an extension to Lamport's approach, called vector timestamps.

6.2.1 Lamport's Logical Clocks

To synchronize logical clocks, Lamport defined a relation called **happens-before**. The expression $a \rightarrow b$ is read "*a* happens before *b*" and means that all processes agree that first event *a* occurs, then afterward, event *b* occurs. The happens-before relation can be observed directly in two situations:

1. If *a* and *b* are events in the same process, and *a* occurs before *b*, then $a \rightarrow b$ is true.

2. If *a* is the event of a message being sent by one process, and *b* is the event of the message being received by another process, then $a \rightarrow b$

is also true. A message cannot be received before it is sent, or even at the same time it is sent, since it takes a finite, nonzero amount of time to arrive.

Happens-before is a transitive relation, so if $a \rightarrow b$ and $b \rightarrow c$, then $a \rightarrow c$. If two events, x and y, happen in different processes that do not exchange messages (not even indirectly via third parties), then $x \rightarrow y$ is not true, but neither is $y \rightarrow x$. These events are said to be **concurrent**, which simply means that nothing can be said (or need be said) about when the events happened or which event happened first.

What we need is a way of measuring a notion of time such that for every event, a, we can assign it a time value $C(a)$ on which all processes agree. These time values must have the property that if $a \rightarrow b$, then $C(a) < C(b)$. To rephrase the conditions we stated earlier, if a and b are two events within the same process and a occurs before b, then $C(a) < C(b)$. Similarly, if a is the sending of a message by one process and b is the reception of that message by another process, then $C(a)$ and $C(b)$ must be assigned in such a way that everyone agrees on the values of $C(a)$ and $C(b)$ with $C(a) < C(b)$. In addition, the clock time, C, must always go forward (increasing), never backward (decreasing). Corrections to time can be made by adding a positive value, never by subtracting one.

Now let us look at the algorithm Lamport proposed for assigning times to events. Consider the three processes depicted in Fig. 6-9(a). The processes run on different machines, each with its own clock, running at its own speed. As can be seen from the figure, when the clock has ticked 6 times in process P_1, it has ticked 8 times in process P_2 and 10 times in process P_3. Each clock runs at a constant rate, but the rates are different due to differences in the crystals.

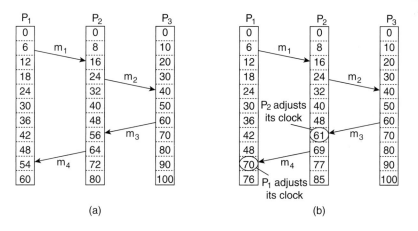

(a)   (b)

Figure 6-9. (a) Three processes, each with its own clock. The clocks run at different rates. (b) Lamport's algorithm corrects the clocks.

At time 6, process P_1 sends message m_1 to process P_2. How long this message takes to arrive depends on whose clock you believe. In any event, the clock in process P_2 reads 16 when it arrives. If the message carries the starting time, 6, in it, process P_2 will conclude that it took 10 ticks to make the journey. This value is certainly possible. According to this reasoning, message m_2 from P_2 to R takes 16 ticks, again a plausible value.

Now consider message m_3. It leaves process P_3 at 60 and arrives at P_2 at 56. Similarly, message m_4 from P_2 to P_1 leaves at 64 and arrives at 54. These values are clearly impossible. It is this situation that must be prevented.

Lamport's solution follows directly from the happens-before relation. Since m_3 left at 60, it must arrive at 61 or later. Therefore, each message carries the sending time according to the sender's clock. When a message arrives and the receiver's clock shows a value prior to the time the message was sent, the receiver fast forwards its clock to be one more than the sending time. In Fig. 6-9(b) we see that m_3 now arrives at 61. Similarly, m_4 arrives at 70.

To prepare for our discussion on vector clocks, let us formulate this procedure more precisely. At this point, it is important to distinguish three different layers of software as we already encountered in Chap. 1: the network, a middleware layer, and an application layer, as shown in Fig. 6-10. What follows is typically part of the middleware layer.

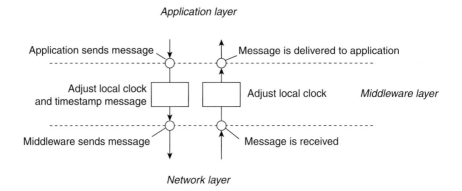

Figure 6-10. The positioning of Lamport's logical clocks in distributed systems.

To implement Lamport's logical clocks, each process P_i maintains a *local* counter C_i. These counters are updated as follows steps (Raynal and Singhal, 1996):

1. Before executing an event (i.e., sending a message over the network, delivering a message to an application, or some other internal event), P_i executes $C_i \leftarrow C_i + 1$.

2. When process P_i sends a message m to P_j, it sets m's timestamp $ts(m)$ equal to C_i after having executed the previous step.

3. Upon the receipt of a message m, process P_j adjusts its own local counter as $C_j \leftarrow \max\{C_j, ts(m)\}$, after which it then executes the first step and delivers the message to the application.

In some situations, an additional requirement is desirable: no two events ever occur at exactly the same time. To achieve this goal, we can attach the number of the process in which the event occurs to the low-order end of the time, separated by a decimal point. For example, an event at time 40 at process P_i will be time-stamped with $40.i$.

Note that by assigning the event time $C(a) \leftarrow C_i(a)$ if a happened at process P_i at time $C_i(a)$, we have a distributed implementation of the global time value we were initially seeking for.

Example: Totally Ordered Multicasting

As an application of Lamport's logical clocks, consider the situation in which a database has been replicated across several sites. For example, to improve query performance, a bank may place copies of an account database in two different cities, say New York and San Francisco. A query is always forwarded to the nearest copy. The price for a fast response to a query is partly paid in higher update costs, because each update operation must be carried out at each replica.

In fact, there is a more stringent requirement with respect to updates. Assume a customer in San Francisco wants to add $100 to his account, which currently contains $1,000. At the same time, a bank employee in New York initiates an update by which the customer's account is to be increased with 1 percent interest. Both updates should be carried out at both copies of the database. However, due to communication delays in the underlying network, the updates may arrive in the order as shown in Fig. 6-11.

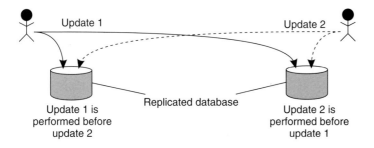

Figure 6-11. Updating a replicated database and leaving it in an inconsistent state.

The customer's update operation is performed in San Francisco before the interest update. In contrast, the copy of the account in the New York replica is first updated with the 1 percent interest, and after that with the $100 deposit. Consequently, the San Francisco database will record a total amount of $1,111, whereas the New York database records $1,110.

The problem that we are faced with is that the two update operations should have been performed in the same order at each copy. Although it makes a difference whether the deposit is processed before the interest update or the other way around, which order is followed is not important from a consistency point of view. The important issue is that both copies should be exactly the same. In general, situations such as these require a **totally-ordered multicast**, that is, a multicast operation by which all messages are delivered in the same order to each receiver. Lamport's logical clocks can be used to implement totally-ordered multicasts in a completely distributed fashion.

Consider a group of processes multicasting messages to each other. Each message is always timestamped with the current (logical) time of its sender. When a message is multicast, it is conceptually also sent to the sender. In addition, we assume that messages from the same sender are received in the order they were sent, and that no messages are lost.

When a process receives a message, it is put into a local queue, ordered according to its timestamp. The receiver multicasts an acknowledgment to the other processes. Note that if we follow Lamport's algorithm for adjusting local clocks, the timestamp of the received message is lower than the timestamp of the acknowledgment. The interesting aspect of this approach is that all processes will eventually have the same copy of the local queue (provided no messages are removed).

A process can deliver a queued message to the application it is running only when that message is at the head of the queue and has been acknowledged by each other process. At that point, the message is removed from the queue and handed over to the application; the associated acknowledgments can simply be removed. Because each process has the same copy of the queue, all messages are delivered in the same order everywhere. In other words, we have established totally-ordered multicasting.

As we shall see in later chapters, totally-ordered multicasting is an important vehicle for replicated services where the replicas are kept consistent by letting them execute the same operations in the same order everywhere. As the replicas essentially follow the same transitions in the same finite state machine, it is also known as **state machine replication** (Schneider, 1990).

6.2.2 Vector Clocks

Lamport's logical clocks lead to a situation where all events in a distributed system are totally ordered with the property that if event a happened before event b, then a will also be positioned in that ordering before b, that is, $C(a) < C(b)$.

However, with Lamport clocks, nothing can be said about the relationship between two events a and b by merely comparing their time values $C(a)$ and $C(b)$, respectively, In other words, if $C(a) < C(b)$, then this does not necessarily imply that a indeed happened before b. Something more is needed for that.

To explain, consider the messages as sent by the three processes shown in Fig. 6-12. Denote by $T_{snd}(m_i)$ the logical time at which message m_i was sent, and likewise, by $T_{rcv}(m_i)$ the time of its receipt. By construction, we know that for each message $T_{snd}(m_i) < T_{rcv}(m_i)$. But what can we conclude in general from $T_{rcv}(m_i) < T_{snd}(m_j)$?

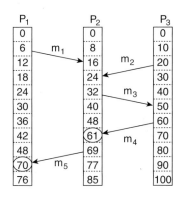

Figure 6-12. Concurrent message transmission using logical clocks.

In the case for which $m_i = m_1$ and $m_j = m_3$, we know that these values correspond to events that took place at process P_2, meaning that m_3 was indeed sent after the receipt of message m_1. This may indicate that the sending of message m_3 depended on what was received through message m_1. However, we also know that $T_{rcv}(m_1) < T_{snd}(m_2)$. However, the sending of m_2 has nothing to do with the receipt of m_1.

The problem is that Lamport clocks do not capture **causality**. Causality can be captured by means of **vector clocks**. A vector clock $VC(a)$ assigned to an event a has the property that if $VC(a) < VC(b)$ for some event b, then event a is known to causally precede event b. Vector clocks are constructed by letting each process P_i maintain a vector VC_i with the following two properties:

1. $VC_i[i]$ is the number of events that have occurred so far at P_i. In other words, $VC_i[i]$ is the local logical clock at process P_i.

2. If $VC_i[j] = k$ then P_i knows that k events have occurred at P_j. It is thus P_i's knowledge of the local time at P_j.

The first property is maintained by incrementing $VC_i[i]$ at the occurrence of each new event that happens at process P_i. The second property is maintained by piggybacking vectors along with messages that are sent. In particular, the following steps are performed:

1. Before executing an event (i.e., sending a message over the network, delivering a message to an application, or some other internal event), P_i executes $VC_i[i] \leftarrow VC_i[i] + 1$.

2. When process P_i sends a message m to P_j, it sets m's (vector) timestamp $ts(m)$ equal to VC_i after having executed the previous step.

3. Upon the receipt of a message m, process P_j adjusts its own vector by setting $VC_j[k] \leftarrow \max\{VC_j[k], ts(m)[k]\}$ for each k, after which it executes the first step and delivers the message to the application.

Note that if an event a has timestamp $ts(a)$, then $ts(a)[i]-1$ denotes the number of events processed at P_i that causally precede a. As a consequence, when P_j receives a message from P_i with timestamp $ts(m)$, it knows about the number of events that have occurred at P_i that causally preceded the sending of m. More important, however, is that P_j is also told how many events at *other* processes have taken place before P_i sent message m. In other words, timestamp $ts(m)$ tells the receiver how many events in other processes have preceded the sending of m, and on which m may causally depend.

Enforcing Causal Communication

Using vector clocks, it is now possible to ensure that a message is delivered only if all messages that causally precede it have also been received as well. To enable such a scheme, we will assume that messages are multicast within a group of processes. Note that this **causally-ordered multicasting** is weaker than the totally-ordered multicasting we discussed earlier. Specifically, if two messages are not in any way related to each other, we do not care in which order they are delivered to applications. They may even be delivered in different order at different locations.

Furthermore, we assume that clocks are only adjusted when sending and receiving messages. In particular, upon sending a message, process P_i will only increment $VC_i[i]$ by 1. When it receives a message m with timestamp $ts(m)$, it only adjusts $VC_i[k]$ to $\max\{VC_i[k], ts(m)[k]\}$ for each k.

Now suppose that P_j receives a message m from P_i with (vector) timestamp $ts(m)$. The delivery of the message to the application layer will then be delayed until the following two conditions are met:

1. $ts(m)[i] = VC_j[i]+1$

2. $ts(m)[k] \leq VC_j[k]$ for all $k \neq i$

The first condition states that m is the next message that P_j was expecting from process P_i. The second condition states that P_j has seen all the messages that have been seen by P_i when it sent message m. Note that there is no need for process P_j to delay the delivery of its own messages.

As an example, consider three processes P_0, P_1, and P_2 as shown in Fig. 6-13. At local time $(1,0,0)$, P_1 sends message m to the other two processes. After its receipt by P_1, the latter decides to send $m*$, which arrives at P_2 sooner than m. At that point, the delivery of $m*$ is delayed by P_2 until m has been received and delivered to P_2's application layer.

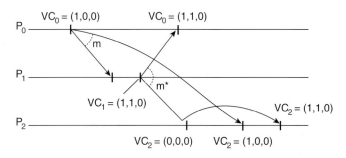

Figure 6-13. Enforcing causal communication.

A Note on Ordered Message Delivery

Some middleware systems, notably ISIS and its successor Horus (Birman and van Renesse, 1994), provide support for totally-ordered and causally-ordered (reliable) multicasting. There has been some controversy whether such support should be provided as part of the message-communication layer, or whether applications should handle ordering (see, e.g., Cheriton and Skeen, 1993; and Birman, 1994). Matters have not been settled, but more important is that the arguments still hold today.

There are two main problems with letting the middleware deal with message ordering. First, because the middleware cannot tell what a message actually contains, only *potential* causality is captured. For example, two messages from the same sender that are completely independent will always be marked as causally related by the middleware layer. This approach is overly restrictive and may lead to efficiency problems.

A second problem is that not all causality may be captured. Consider an electronic bulletin board. Suppose Alice posts an article. If she then phones Bob telling about what she just wrote, Bob may post another article as a reaction without having seen Alice's posting on the board. In other words, there is a causality between Bob's posting and that of Alice due to *external* communication. This causality is not captured by the bulletin board system.

In essence, ordering issues, like many other application-specific communication issues, can be adequately solved by looking at the application for which communication is taking place. This is also known as the **end-to-end argument** in systems design (Saltzer et al., 1984). A drawback of having only application-level solutions is that a developer is forced to concentrate on issues that do not immediately relate to the core functionality of the application. For example, ordering may not be the most important problem when developing a messaging system such as an electronic bulletin board. In that case, having an underlying communication layer handle ordering may turn out to be convenient. We will come across the end-to-end argument a number of times, notably when dealing with security in distributed systems.

6.3 MUTUAL EXCLUSION

Fundamental to distributed systems is the concurrency and collaboration among multiple processes. In many cases, this also means that processes will need to simultaneously access the same resources. To prevent that such concurrent accesses corrupt the resource, or make it inconsistent, solutions are needed to grant mutual exclusive access by processes. In this section, we take a look at some of the more important distributed algorithms that have been proposed. A recent survey of distributed algorithms for mutual exclusion is provided by Saxena and Rai (2003). Older, but still relevant is Velazquez (1993).

6.3.1 Overview

Distributed mutual exclusion algorithms can be classified into two different categories. In **token-based solutions** mutual exclusion is achieved by passing a special message between the processes, known as a **token**. There is only one token available and who ever has that token is allowed to access the shared resource. When finished, the token is passed on to a next process. If a process having the token is not interested in accessing the resource, it simply passes it on.

Token-based solutions have a few important properties. First, depending on the how the processes are organized, they can fairly easily ensure that every process will get a chance at accessing the resource. In other words, they avoid **starvation**. Second, **deadlocks** by which several processes are waiting for each other to proceed, can easily be avoided, contributing to their simplicity. Unfortunately, the main drawback of token-based solutions is a rather serious one: when the token is lost (e.g., because the process holding it crashed), an intricate distributed procedure needs to be started to ensure that a new token is created, but above all, that it is also the only token.

As an alternative, many distributed mutual exclusion algorithms follow a **permission-based approach**. In this case, a process wanting to access the resource first requires the permission of other processes. There are many different ways toward granting such a permission and in the sections that follow we will consider a few of them.

6.3.2 A Centralized Algorithm

The most straightforward way to achieve mutual exclusion in a distributed system is to simulate how it is done in a one-processor system. One process is elected as the coordinator. Whenever a process wants to access a shared resource, it sends a request message to the coordinator stating which resource it wants to access and asking for permission. If no other process is currently accessing that resource, the coordinator sends back a reply granting permission, as shown in Fig. 6-14(a). When the reply arrives, the requesting process can go ahead.

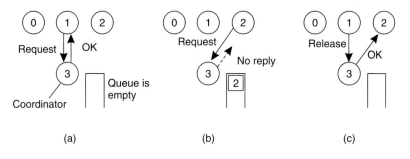

(a)   (b)   (c)

Figure 6-14. (a) Process 1 asks the coordinator for permission to access a shared resource. Permission is granted. (b) Process 2 then asks permission to access the same resource. The coordinator does not reply. (c) When process 1 releases the resource, it tells the coordinator, which then replies to 2.

Now suppose that another process, 2 in Fig. 6-14(b), asks for permission to access the resource. The coordinator knows that a different process is already at the resource, so it cannot grant permission. The exact method used to deny permission is system dependent. In Fig. 6-14(b), the coordinator just refrains from replying, thus blocking process 2, which is waiting for a reply. Alternatively, it could send a reply saying "permission denied." Either way, it queues the request from 2 for the time being and waits for more messages.

When process 1 is finished with the resource, it sends a message to the coordinator releasing its exclusive access, as shown in Fig. 6-14(c). The coordinator takes the first item off the queue of deferred requests and sends that process a grant message. If the process was still blocked (i.e., this is the first message to it), it unblocks and accesses the resource. If an explicit message has already been sent denying permission, the process will have to poll for incoming traffic or block later. Either way, when it sees the grant, it can go ahead as well.

It is easy to see that the algorithm guarantees mutual exclusion: the coordinator only lets one process at a time to the resource. It is also fair, since requests are granted in the order in which they are received. No process ever waits forever (no starvation). The scheme is easy to implement, too, and requires only three messages per use of resource (request, grant, release). It's simplicity makes an attractive solution for many practical situations.

The centralized approach also has shortcomings. The coordinator is a single point of failure, so if it crashes, the entire system may go down. If processes normally block after making a request, they cannot distinguish a dead coordinator from "permission denied" since in both cases no message comes back. In addition, in a large system, a single coordinator can become a performance bottleneck. Nevertheless, the benefits coming from its simplicity outweigh in many cases the potential drawbacks. Moreover, distributed solutions are not necessarily better, as our next example illustrates.

6.3.3 A Decentralized Algorithm

Having a single coordinator is often a poor approach. Let us take a look at fully decentralized solution. Lin et al. (2004) propose to use a voting algorithm that can be executed using a DHT-based system. In essence, their solution extends the central coordinator in the following way. Each resource is assumed to be replicated n times. Every replica has its own coordinator for controlling the access by concurrent processes.

However, whenever a process wants to access the resource, it will simply need to get a majority vote from $m > n/2$ coordinators. Unlike in the centralized scheme discussed before, we assume that when a coordinator does not give permission to access a resource (which it will do when it had granted permission to another process), it will tell the requester.

This scheme essentially makes the original centralized solution less vulnerable to failures of a single coordinator. The assumption is that when a coordinator crashes, it recovers quickly but will have forgotten any vote it gave before it crashed. Another way of viewing this is that a coordinator resets itself at arbitrary moments. The risk that we are taking is that a reset will make the coordinator forget that it had previously granted permission to some process to access the resource. As a consequence, it may incorrectly grant this permission again to another process after its recovery.

Let p be the probability that a coordinator resets during a time interval Δt. The probability $P[k]$ that k out of m coordinators reset during the same interval is then

$$P[k] = \begin{bmatrix} m \\ k \end{bmatrix} p^k (1-p)^{m-k}$$

Given that at least $2m - n$ coordinators need to reset in order to violate the correctness of the voting mechanism, the probability that such a violation occurs is then $\sum_{k=2m-n}^{n} P[k]$. To give an impression of what this could mean, assume that we are dealing with a DHT-based system in which each node participates for about 3 hours in a row. Let Δt be 10 seconds, which is considered to be a conservative value for a single process to want to access a shared resource. (Different mechanisms are needed for very long allocations.) With $n = 32$ and $m = 0.75n$, the probability of violating correctness is less than 10^{-40}. This probability is surely smaller than the availability of any resource.

To implement this scheme, Lin et al. (2004) use a DHT-based system in which a resource is replicated n times. Assume that the resource is known under its unique name *rname*. We can then assume that the i-th replica is named *rname-i* which is then used to compute a unique key using a known hash function. As a consequence, every process can generate the n keys given a resource's name, and subsequently lookup each node responsible for a replica (and controlling access to that replica).

If permission to access the resource is denied (i.e., a process gets less than m votes), it is assumed that it will back off for a randomly-chosen time, and make a next attempt later. The problem with this scheme is that if many nodes want to access the same resource, it turns out that the utilization rapidly drops. In other words, there are so many nodes competing to get access that eventually no one is able to get enough votes leaving the resource unused. A solution to solve this problem can be found in Lin et al. (2004).

6.3.4 A Distributed Algorithm

To many, having a probabilistically correct algorithm is just not good enough. So researchers have looked for deterministic distributed mutual exclusion algorithms. Lamport's 1978 paper on clock synchronization presented the first one. Ricart and Agrawala (1981) made it more efficient. In this section we will describe their method.

Ricart and Agrawala's algorithm requires that there be a total ordering of all events in the system. That is, for any pair of events, such as messages, it must be unambiguous which one actually happened first. Lamport's algorithm presented in Sec. 6.2.1 is one way to achieve this ordering and can be used to provide timestamps for distributed mutual exclusion.

The algorithm works as follows. When a process wants to access a shared resource, it builds a message containing the name of the resource, its process number, and the current (logical) time. It then sends the message to all other processes, conceptually including itself. The sending of messages is assumed to be reliable; that is, no message is lost.

When a process receives a request message from another process, the action it takes depends on its own state with respect to the resource named in the message. Three different cases have to be clearly distinguished:

1. If the receiver is not accessing the resource and does not want to access it, it sends back an *OK* message to the sender.

2. If the receiver already has access to the resource, it simply does not reply. Instead, it queues the request.

3. If the receiver wants to access the resource as well but has not yet done so, it compares the timestamp of the incoming message with the one contained in the message that it has sent everyone. The lowest one wins. If the incoming message has a lower timestamp, the receiver sends back an *OK* message. If its own message has a lower timestamp, the receiver queues the incoming request and sends nothing.

After sending out requests asking permission, a process sits back and waits until everyone else has given permission. As soon as all the permissions are in, it may go ahead. When it is finished, it sends *OK* messages to all processes on its queue and deletes them all from the queue.

Let us try to understand why the algorithm works. If there is no conflict, it clearly works. However, suppose that two processes try to simultaneously access the resource, as shown in Fig. 6-15(a).

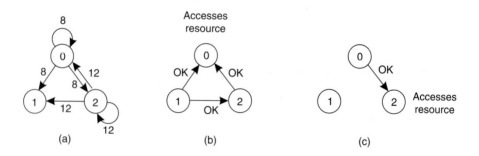

Figure 6-15. (a) Two processes want to access a shared resource at the same moment. (b) Process 0 has the lowest timestamp, so it wins. (c) When process 0 is done, it sends an *OK* also, so 2 can now go ahead.

Process 0 sends everyone a request with timestamp 8, while at the same time, process 2 sends everyone a request with timestamp 12. Process 1 is not interested in the resource, so it sends *OK* to both senders. Processes 0 and 2 both see the conflict and compare timestamps. Process 2 sees that it has lost, so it grants permission to 0 by sending *OK*. Process 0 now queues the request from 2 for later processing and access the resource, as shown in Fig. 6-15(b). When it is finished, it removes the request from 2 from its queue and sends an *OK* message to process 2, allowing the latter to go ahead, as shown in Fig. 6-15(c). The algorithm works because in the case of a conflict, the lowest timestamp wins and everyone agrees on the ordering of the timestamps.

Note that the situation in Fig. 6-15 would have been essentially different if process 2 had sent its message earlier in time so that process 0 had gotten it and granted permission before making its own request. In this case, 2 would have noticed that it itself had already access to the resource at the time of the request, and queued it instead of sending a reply.

As with the centralized algorithm discussed above, mutual exclusion is guaranteed without deadlock or starvation. The number of messages required per entry is now $2(n-1)$, where the total number of processes in the system is n. Best of all, no single point of failure exists.

Unfortunately, the single point of failure has been replaced by n points of failure. If any process crashes, it will fail to respond to requests. This silence will be interpreted (incorrectly) as denial of permission, thus blocking all subsequent attempts by all processes to enter all critical regions. Since the probability of one of the n processes failing is at least n times as large as a single coordinator failing, we have managed to replace a poor algorithm with one that is more than n times worse and requires much more network traffic as well.

The algorithm can be patched up by the same trick that we proposed earlier. When a request comes in, the receiver always sends a reply, either granting or denying permission. Whenever either a request or a reply is lost, the sender times out and keeps trying until either a reply comes back or the sender concludes that the destination is dead. After a request is denied, the sender should block waiting for a subsequent *OK* message.

Another problem with this algorithm is that either a multicast communication primitive must be used, or each process must maintain the group membership list itself, including processes entering the group, leaving the group, and crashing. The method works best with small groups of processes that never change their group memberships.

Finally, recall that one of the problems with the centralized algorithm is that making it handle all requests can lead to a bottleneck. In the distributed algorithm, *all* processes are involved in *all* decisions concerning accessing the shared resource. If one process is unable to handle the load, it is unlikely that forcing everyone to do exactly the same thing in parallel is going to help much.

Various minor improvements are possible to this algorithm. For example, getting permission from everyone is really overkill. All that is needed is a method to prevent two processes from accessing the resource at the same time. The algorithm can be modified to grant permission when it has collected permission from a simple majority of the other processes, rather than from all of them. Of course, in this variation, after a process has granted permission to one process, it cannot grant the same permission to another process until the first one has finished.

Nevertheless, this algorithm is slower, more complicated, more expensive, and less robust that the original centralized one. Why bother studying it under these conditions? For one thing, it shows that a distributed algorithm is at least possible, something that was not obvious when we started. Also, by pointing out the shortcomings, we may stimulate future theoreticians to try to produce algorithms that are actually useful. Finally, like eating spinach and learning Latin in high school, some things are said to be good for you in some abstract way. It may take some time to discover exactly what.

6.3.5 A Token Ring Algorithm

A completely different approach to deterministically achieving mutual exclusion in a distributed system is illustrated in Fig. 6-16. Here we have a bus network, as shown in Fig. 6-16(a), (e.g., Ethernet), with no inherent ordering of the processes. In software, a logical ring is constructed in which each process is assigned a position in the ring, as shown in Fig. 6-16(b). The ring positions may be allocated in numerical order of network addresses or some other means. It does not matter what the ordering is. All that matters is that each process knows who is next in line after itself.

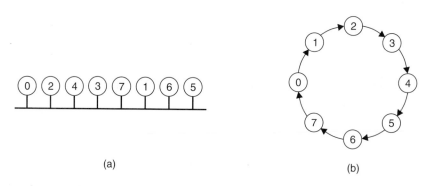

(a)   (b)

Figure 6-16. (a) An unordered group of processes on a network. (b) A logical ring constructed in software.

When the ring is initialized, process 0 is given a **token**. The token circulates around the ring. It is passed from process k to process $k+1$ (modulo the ring size) in point-to-point messages. When a process acquires the token from its neighbor, it checks to see if it needs to access the shared resource. If so, the process goes ahead, does all the work it needs to, and releases the resources. After it has finished, it passes the token along the ring. It is not permitted to immediately enter the resource again using the same token.

If a process is handed the token by its neighbor and is not interested in the resource, it just passes the token along. As a consequence, when no processes need the resource, the token just circulates at high speed around the ring.

The correctness of this algorithm is easy to see. Only one process has the token at any instant, so only one process can actually get to the resource. Since the token circulates among the processes in a well-defined order, starvation cannot occur. Once a process decides it wants to have access to the resource, at worst it will have to wait for every other process to use the resource.

As usual, this algorithm has problems too. If the token is ever lost, it must be regenerated. In fact, detecting that it is lost is difficult, since the amount of time between successive appearances of the token on the network is unbounded. The fact that the token has not been spotted for an hour does not mean that it has been lost; somebody may still be using it.

The algorithm also runs into trouble if a process crashes, but recovery is easier than in the other cases. If we require a process receiving the token to acknowledge receipt, a dead process will be detected when its neighbor tries to give it the token and fails. At that point the dead process can be removed from the group, and the token holder can throw the token over the head of the dead process to the next member down the line, or the one after that, if necessary. Of course, doing so requires that everyone maintain the current ring configuration.

6.3.6 A Comparison of the Four Algorithms

A brief comparison of the four mutual exclusion algorithms we have looked at is instructive. In Fig. 6-17 we have listed the algorithms and three key properties: the number of messages required for a process to access and release a shared resource, the delay before access can occur (assuming messages are passed sequentially over a network), and some problems associated with each algorithm.

Algorithm	Messages per entry/exit	Delay before entry (in message times)	Problems
Centralized	3	2	Coordinator crash
Decentralized	3mk, k = 1,2,...	2 m	Starvation, low efficiency
Distributed	2 (n − 1)	2 (n − 1)	Crash of any process
Token ring	1 to ∞	0 to n − 1	Lost token, process crash

Figure 6-17. A comparison of three mutual exclusion algorithms.

The centralized algorithm is simplest and also most efficient. It requires only three messages to enter and leave a critical region: a request, a grant to enter, and a release to exit. In the decentralized case, we see that these messages need to be carried out for each of the m coordinators, but now it is possible that several attempts need to be made (for which we introduce the variable k). The distributed algorithm requires $n - 1$ request messages, one to each of the other processes, and an additional $n - 1$ grant messages, for a total of $2(n - 1)$. (We assume that only point-to-point communication channels are used.) With the token ring algorithm, the number is variable. If every process constantly wants to enter a critical region, then each token pass will result in one entry and exit, for an average of one message per critical region entered. At the other extreme, the token may sometimes circulate for hours without anyone being interested in it. In this case, the number of messages per entry into a critical region is unbounded.

The delay from the moment a process needs to enter a critical region until its actual entry also varies for the three algorithms. When the time using a resource is short, the dominant factor in the delay is the actual mechanism for accessing a resource. When resources are used for a long time period, the dominant factor is waiting for everyone else to take their turn. In Fig. 6-17 we show the former case. It takes only two message times to enter a critical region in the centralized case, but $3mk$ times for the decentralized case, where k is the number of attempts that need to be made. Assuming that messages are sent one after the other, $2(n-1)$ message times are needed in the distributed case. For the token ring, the time varies from 0 (token just arrived) to $n-1$ (token just departed).

Finally, all algorithms except the decentralized one suffer badly in the event of crashes. Special measures and additional complexity must be introduced to avoid having a crash bring down the entire system. It is ironic that the distributed algorithms are even more sensitive to crashes than the centralized one. In a system that is designed to be fault tolerant, none of these would be suitable, but if crashes are very infrequent, they might do. The decentralized algorithm is less sensitive to crashes, but processes may suffer from starvation and special measures are needed to guarantee efficiency.

6.4 GLOBAL POSITIONING OF NODES

When the number of nodes in a distributed system grows, it becomes increasingly difficult for any node to keep track of the others. Such knowledge may be important for executing distributed algorithms such as routing, multicasting, data placement, searching, and so on. We have already seen different examples in which large collections of nodes are organized into specific topologies that facilitate the efficient execution of such algorithms. In this section, we take a look at another organization that is related to timing issues.

In **geometric overlay networks** each node is given a position in an m-dimensional geometric space, such that the distance between two nodes in that space reflects a real-world performance metric. The simplest, and most applied example, is where distance corresponds to internode latency. In other words, given two nodes P and Q, then the distance $d(P,Q)$ reflects how long it would take for a message to travel from P to Q and *vice versa*.

There are many applications of geometric overlay networks. Consider the situation where a Web site at server O has been replicated to multiple servers $S_1,...,S_k$ on the Internet. When a client C requests a page from O, the latter may decide to redirect that request to the server closest to C, that is, the one that will give the best response time. If the geometric location of C is known, as well as those of each replica server, O can then simply pick that server S_i for which $d(C,S_i)$ is minimal. Note that such a selection requires only local processing at O. In other words, there is, for example, no need to sample all the latencies between C and each of the replica servers.

Another example, which we will work out in detail in the following chapter, is optimal replica placement. Consider again a Web site that has gathered the positions of its clients. If the site were to replicate its content to K servers, it can compute the K best positions where to place replicas such that the average client-to-replica response time is minimal. Performing such computations is almost trivially feasible if clients and servers have geometric positions that reflect internode latencies.

As a last example, consider **position-based routing** (Araujo and Rodrigues, 2005; and Stojmenovic, 2002). In such schemes, a message is forwarded to its destination using only positioning information. For example, a naive routing algorithm to let each node forward a message to the neighbor closest to the destination. Although it can be easily shown that this specific algorithm need not converge, it illustrates that only local information is used to take a decision. There is no need to propagate link information or such to all nodes in the network, as is the case with conventional routing algorithms.

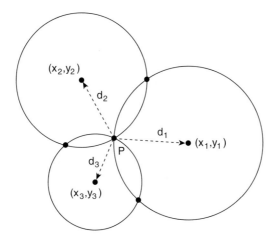

Figure 6-18. Computing a node's position in a two-dimensional space.

Theoretically, positioning a node in an m-dimensional geometric space requires $m+1$ distance measures to nodes with known positions. This can be easily seen by considering the case $m = 2$, as shown in Fig. 6-18. Assuming that node P wants to compute its own position, it contacts three other nodes with known positions and measures its distance to each of them. Contacting only one node would tell P about the circle it is located on; contacting only two nodes would tell it about the position of the intersection of two circles (which generally consists of two points); a third node would subsequently allow P to compute is actual location.

Just as in GPS, node P can compute is own coordinates (x_P, y_P) by solving the three equations with the two unknowns x_P and y_P:

$$d_i = \sqrt{(x_i - x_P)^2 + (y_i - y_P)^2} \qquad (i=1,2,3)$$

As said, d_i generally corresponds to measuring the latency between P and the node at (x_i, y_i). This latency can be estimated as being half the round-trip delay, but it should be clear that its value will be different over time. The effect is a different positioning whenever P would want to recompute its position. Moreover, if other nodes would use P's current position to compute their own coordinates, then it should be clear that the error in positioning P will affect the accuracy of the positioning of other nodes.

Moreover, it should also be clear that measured distances by different nodes will generally not even be consistent. For example, assume we are computing distances in a one-dimensional space as shown in Fig. 6-19. In this example, we see that although R measures its distance to Q as 2.0, and $d(P,Q)$ has been measured to be 1.0, when R measures $d(P,R)$ it finds 3.2, which is clearly inconsistent with the other two measurements.

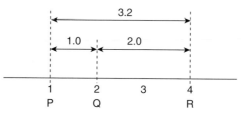

Figure 6-19. Inconsistent distance measurements in a one-dimensional space.

Fig. 6-19 also suggests how this situation can be improved. In our simple example, we could solve the inconsistencies by merely computing positions in a two-dimensional space. This by itself, however, is not a general solution when dealing with many measurements. In fact, considering that Internet latency measurements may violate the **triangle inequality**, it is generally impossible to resolve inconsistencies completely. The triangle inequality states that in a geometric space, for any arbitrary three nodes P, Q, and R it must always be true that $d(P,R) \leq d(P,Q) + d(Q,R)$.

There are various ways to approach these issues. One approach, proposed by Ng and Zhang (2002) is to use L special nodes $b_1, \ldots, b_L$, known as **landmarks**. Landmarks measure their pairwise latencies $d(b_i, b_j)$ and subsequently let a central node compute the coordinates for each landmark. To this end, the central node seeks to minimize the following aggregated error function:

$$\sum_{i=1}^{L} \sum_{j=i+1}^{L} \left[\frac{d(b_i,b_j) - \hat{d}(b_i,b_j)}{d(b_i,b_j)} \right]^2$$

where $\hat{d}(b_i,b_j)$ corresponds to the *geometric distance*, that is, the distance after nodes b_i and b_j have been positioned.

The hidden parameter in minimizing the aggregated error function is the dimension m. Obviously, we have that $L > m$, but nothing prevents us from choosing a value for m that is much smaller than L. In that case, a node P measures its distance to each of the L landmarks and computes its coordinates by minimizing

$$\sum_{i=1}^{L} \left[\frac{d(b_i,P) - \hat{d}(b_i,P)}{d(b_i,P)} \right]^2$$

As it turns out, with well-chosen landmarks, m can be as small as 6 or 7, with $\hat{d}(P,Q)$ being no more than a factor 2 different from the actual latency $d(P,Q)$ for arbitrary nodes P and Q (Szyamniak et al., 2004).

Another way to tackle this problem is to view the collection of nodes as a huge system in which nodes are attached to each other through springs. In this case, $| d(P,Q) - \hat{d}(P,Q) |$ indicates to what extent nodes P and Q are displaced relative to the situation in which the system of springs would be at rest. By letting each node (slightly) change its position, it can be shown that the system will eventually converge to an optimal organization in which the aggregated error is minimal. This approach is followed in Vivaldi, of which the details can be found in Dabek et al. (2004a).

6.5 ELECTION ALGORITHMS

Many distributed algorithms require one process to act as coordinator, initiator, or otherwise perform some special role. In general, it does not matter which process takes on this special responsibility, but one of them has to do it. In this section we will look at algorithms for electing a coordinator (using this as a generic name for the special process).

If all processes are exactly the same, with no distinguishing characteristics, there is no way to select one of them to be special. Consequently, we will assume that each process has a unique number, for example, its network address (for simplicity, we will assume one process per machine). In general, election algorithms attempt to locate the process with the highest process number and designate it as coordinator. The algorithms differ in the way they do the location.

Furthermore, we also assume that every process knows the process number of every other process. What the processes do not know is which ones are currently up and which ones are currently down. The goal of an election algorithm is to ensure that when an election starts, it concludes with all processes agreeing on who the new coordinator is to be. There are many algorithms and variations, of which several important ones are discussed in the text books by Lynch (1996) and Tel (2000), respectively.

6.5.1 Traditional Election Algorithms

We start with taking a look at two traditional election algorithms to give an impression what whole groups of researchers have been doing in the past decades. In subsequent sections, we pay attention to new applications of the election problem.

The Bully Algorithm

As a first example, consider the **bully algorithm** devised by Garcia-Molina (1982). When any process notices that the coordinator is no longer responding to requests, it initiates an election. A process, P, holds an election as follows:

1. P sends an *ELECTION* message to all processes with higher numbers.

2. If no one responds, P wins the election and becomes coordinator.

3. If one of the higher-ups answers, it takes over. P's job is done.

At any moment, a process can get an *ELECTION* message from one of its lower-numbered colleagues. When such a message arrives, the receiver sends an *OK* message back to the sender to indicate that he is alive and will take over. The receiver then holds an election, unless it is already holding one. Eventually, all processes give up but one, and that one is the new coordinator. It announces its victory by sending all processes a message telling them that starting immediately it is the new coordinator.

If a process that was previously down comes back up, it holds an election. If it happens to be the highest-numbered process currently running, it will win the election and take over the coordinator's job. Thus the biggest guy in town always wins, hence the name "bully algorithm."

In Fig. 6-20 we see an example of how the bully algorithm works. The group consists of eight processes, numbered from 0 to 7. Previously process 7 was the coordinator, but it has just crashed. Process 4 is the first one to notice this, so it sends *ELECTION* messages to all the processes higher than it, namely 5, 6, and 7, as shown in Fig. 6-20(a). Processes 5 and 6 both respond with *OK*, as shown in

Fig. 6-20(b). Upon getting the first of these responses, 4 knows that its job is over. It knows that one of these bigwigs will take over and become coordinator. It just sits back and waits to see who the winner will be (although at this point it can make a pretty good guess).

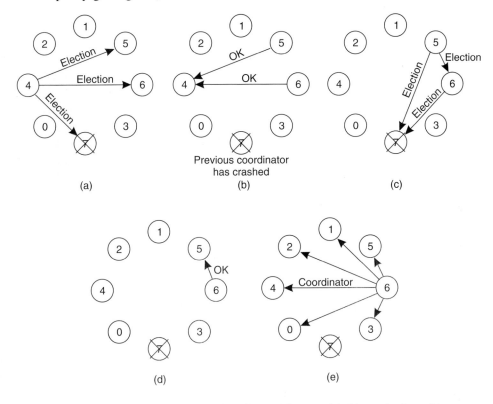

Figure 6-20. The bully election algorithm. (a) Process 4 holds an election. (b) Processes 5 and 6 respond, telling 4 to stop. (c) Now 5 and 6 each hold an election. (d) Process 6 tells 5 to stop. (e) Process 6 wins and tells everyone.

In Fig. 6-20(c), both 5 and 6 hold elections, each one only sending messages to those processes higher than itself. In Fig. 6-20(d) process 6 tells 5 that it will take over. At this point 6 knows that 7 is dead and that it (6) is the winner. If there is state information to be collected from disk or elsewhere to pick up where the old coordinator left off, 6 must now do what is needed. When it is ready to take over, 6 announces this by sending a *COORDINATOR* message to all running processes. When 4 gets this message, it can now continue with the operation it was trying to do when it discovered that 7 was dead, but using 6 as the coordinator this time. In this way the failure of 7 is handled and the work can continue.

If process 7 is ever restarted, it will just send all the others a *COORDINATOR* message and bully them into submission.

A Ring Algorithm

Another election algorithm is based on the use of a ring. Unlike some ring algorithms, this one does not use a token. We assume that the processes are physically or logically ordered, so that each process knows who its successor is. When any process notices that the coordinator is not functioning, it builds an *ELECTION* message containing its own process number and sends the message to its successor. If the successor is down, the sender skips over the successor and goes to the next member along the ring, or the one after that, until a running process is located. At each step along the way, the sender adds its own process number to the list in the message effectively making itself a candidate to be elected as coordinator.

Eventually, the message gets back to the process that started it all. That process recognizes this event when it receives an incoming message containing its own process number. At that point, the message type is changed to *COORDINATOR* and circulated once again, this time to inform everyone else who the coordinator is (the list member with the highest number) and who the members of the new ring are. When this message has circulated once, it is removed and everyone goes back to work.

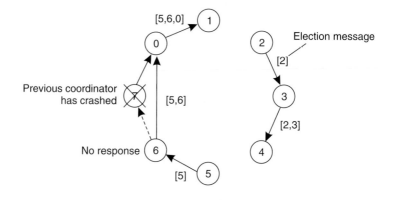

Figure 6-21. Election algorithm using a ring.

In Fig. 6-21 we see what happens if two processes, 2 and 5, discover simultaneously that the previous coordinator, process 7, has crashed. Each of these builds an *ELECTION* message and and each of them starts circulating its message, independent of the other one. Eventually, both messages will go all the way around, and both 2 and 5 will convert them into *COORDINATOR* messages, with exactly the same members and in the same order. When both have gone around again, both will be removed. It does no harm to have extra messages circulating; at worst it consumes a little bandwidth, but this not considered wasteful.

6.5.2 Elections in Wireless Environments

Traditional election algorithms are generally based on assumptions that are not realistic in wireless environments. For example, they assume that message passing is reliable and that the topology of the network does not change. These assumptions are false in most wireless environments, especially those for mobile ad hoc networks.

Only few protocols for elections have been developed that work in ad hoc networks. Vasudevan et al. (2004) propose a solution that can handle failing nodes and partitioning networks. An important property of their solution is that the *best* leader can be elected rather than just a random as was more or less the case in the previously discussed solutions. Their protocol works as follows. To simplify our discussion, we concentrate only on ad hoc networks and ignore that nodes can move.

Consider a wireless ad hoc network. To elect a leader, any node in the network, called the source, can initiate an election by sending an *ELECTION* message to its immediate neighbors (i.e., the nodes in its range). When a node receives an *ELECTION* for the first time, it designates the sender as its parent, and subsequently sends out an *ELECTION* message to all its immediate neighbors, except for the parent. When a node receives an *ELECTION* message from a node other than its parent, it merely acknowledges the receipt.

When node R has designated node Q as its parent, it forwards the *ELECTION* message to its immediate neighbors (excluding Q) and waits for acknowledgments to come in before acknowledging the *ELECTION* message from Q. This waiting has an important consequence. First, note that neighbors that have already selected a parent will immediately respond to R. More specifically, if all neighbors already have a parent, R is a leaf node and will be able to report back to Q quickly. In doing so, it will also report information such as its battery lifetime and other resource capacities.

This information will later allow Q to compare R's capacities to that of other downstream nodes, and select the best eligible node for leadership. Of course, Q had sent an *ELECTION* message only because its own parent P had done so as well. In turn, when Q eventually acknowledges the *ELECTION* message previously sent by P, it will pass the most eligible node to P as well. In this way, the source will eventually get to know which node is best to be selected as leader, after which it will broadcast this information to all other nodes.

This process is illustrated in Fig. 6-22. Nodes have been labeled a to j, along with their capacity. Node a initiates an election by broadcasting an *ELECTION* message to nodes b and j, as shown in Fig. 6-22(b). After that step, *ELECTION* messages are propagated to all nodes, ending with the situation shown in Fig. 6-22(e), where we have omitted the last broadcast by nodes f and i. From there on, each node reports to its parent the node with the best capacity, as shown in Fig. 6-22(f). For example, when node g receives the acknowledgments from its

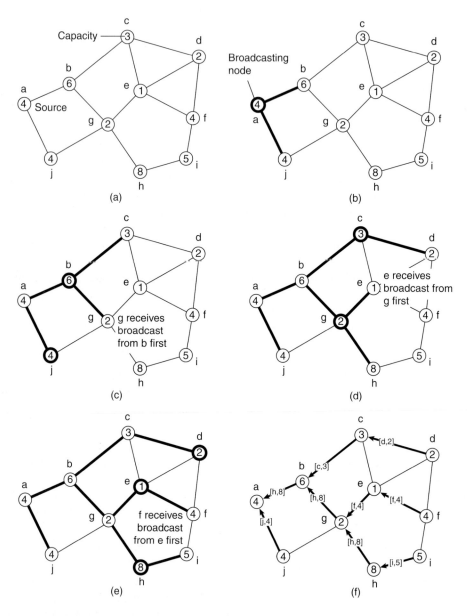

Figure 6-22. Election algorithm in a wireless network, with node *a* as the source. (a) Initial network. (b)–(e) The build-tree phase (last broadcast step by nodes f and i not shown). (f) Reporting of best node to source.

children *e* and *h*, it will notice that *h* is the best node, propagating [*h*, 8] to its own parent, node *b*. In the end, the source will note that *h* is the best leader and will broadcast this information to all other nodes.

When multiple elections are initiated, each node will decide to join only one election. To this end, each source tags its *ELECTION* message with a unique identifier. Nodes will participate only in the election with the highest identifier, stopping any running participation in other elections.

With some minor adjustments, the protocol can be shown to operate also when the network partitions, and when nodes join and leave. The details can be found in Vasudevan et al. (2004).

6.5.3 Elections in Large-Scale Systems

The algorithms we have been discussing so far generally apply to relatively small distributed systems. Moreover, the algorithms concentrate on the selection of only a single node. There are situations when several nodes should actually be selected, such as in the case of **superpeers** in peer-to-peer networks, which we discussed in Chap. 2. In this section, we concentrate specifically on the problem of selecting superpeers.

Lo et al. (2005) identified the following requirements that need to be met for superpeer selection:

1. Normal nodes should have low-latency access to superpeers.

2. Superpeers should be evenly distributed across the overlay network.

3. There should be a predefined portion of superpeers relative to the total number of nodes in the overlay network.

4. Each superpeer should not need to serve more than a fixed number of normal nodes.

Fortunately, these requirements are relatively easy to meet in most peer-to-peer systems, given the fact that the overlay network is either structured (as in DHT-based systems), or randomly unstructured (as, for example, can be realized with gossip-based solutions). Let us take a look at solutions proposed by Lo et al. (2005).

In the case of DHT-based systems, the basic idea is to reserve a fraction of the identifier space for superpeers. Recall that in DHT-based systems each node receives a random and uniformly assigned m-bit identifier. Now suppose we reserve the first (i.e., leftmost) k bits to identify superpeers. For example, if we need N superpeers, then the first $\lceil \log_2(N) \rceil$ bits of any *key* can be used to identify these nodes.

To explain, assume we have a (small) Chord system with $m = 8$ and $k = 3$. When looking up the node responsible for a specific key p, we can first decide to route the lookup request to the node responsible for the pattern

p AND 11100000

which is then treated as the superpeer. Note that each node *id* can check whether it is a superpeer by looking up

id AND 11100000

to see if this request is routed to itself. Provided node identifiers are uniformly assigned to nodes, it can be seen that with a total of N nodes the number of superpeers is, on average, equal $2^{k-m}N$.

A completely different approach is based on positioning nodes in an *m*-dimensional geometric space as we discussed above. In this case, assume we need to place N superpeers *evenly* throughout the overlay. The basic idea is simple: a total of N tokens are spread across N randomly-chosen nodes. No node can hold more than one token. Each token represents a repelling force by which another token is inclined to move away. The net effect is that if all tokens exert the same repulsion force, they will move away from each other and spread themselves evenly in the geometric space.

This approach requires that nodes holding a token learn about other tokens. To this end, Lo et al. propose to use a gossiping protocol by which a token's force is disseminated throughout the network. If a node discovers that the total forces that are acting on it exceed a threshold, it will move the token in the direction of the combined forces, as shown in Fig. 6-23.

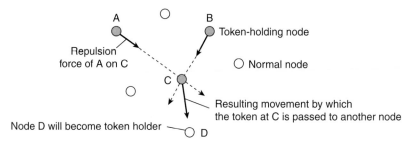

Figure 6-23. Moving tokens in a two-dimensional space using repulsion forces.

When a token is held by a node for a given amount of time, that node will promote itself to superpeer.

6.6 SUMMARY

Strongly related to communication between processes is the issue of how processes in distributed systems synchronize. Synchronization is all about doing the right thing at the right time. A problem in distributed systems, and computer networks in general, is that there is no notion of a globally shared clock. In other words, processes on different machines have their own idea of what time it is.

There are various way to synchronize clocks in a distributed system, but all methods are essentially based on exchanging clock values, while taking into account the time it takes to send and receive messages. Variations in communication delays and the way those variations are dealt with, largely determine the accuracy of clock synchronization algorithms.

Related to these synchronization problems is positioning nodes in a geometric overlay. The basic idea is to assign each node coordinates from an m-dimensional space such that the geometric distance can be used as an accurate measure for the latency between two nodes. The method of assigning coordinates strongly resembles the one applied in determining the location and time in GPS.

In many cases, knowing the absolute time is not necessary. What counts is that related events at different processes happen in the correct order. Lamport showed that by introducing a notion of logical clocks, it is possible for a collection of processes to reach global agreement on the correct ordering of events. In essence, each event e, such as sending or receiving a message, is assigned a globally unique logical timestamp $C(e)$ such that when event a happened before b, $C(a) < C(b)$. Lamport timestamps can be extended to vector timestamps: if $C(a) < C(b)$, we even know that event a causally preceded b.

An important class of synchronization algorithms is that of distributed mutual exclusion. These algorithms ensure that in a distributed collection of processes, at most one process at a time has access to a shared resource. Distributed mutual exclusion can easily be achieved if we make use of a coordinator that keeps track of whose turn it is. Fully distributed algorithms also exist, but have the drawback that they are generally more susceptible to communication and process failures.

Synchronization between processes often requires that one process acts as a coordinator. In those cases where the coordinator is not fixed, it is necessary that processes in a distributed computation decide on who is going to be that coordinator. Such a decision is taken by means of election algorithms. Election algorithms are primarily used in cases where the coordinator can crash. However, they can also be applied for the selection of superpeers in peer-to-peer systems.

PROBLEMS

1. Name at least three sources of delay that can be introduced between WWV broadcasting the time and the processors in a distributed system setting their internal clocks.

2. Consider the behavior of two machines in a distributed system. Both have clocks that are supposed to tick 1000 times per millisecond. One of them actually does, but the other ticks only 990 times per millisecond. If UTC updates come in once a minute, what is the maximum clock skew that will occur?

3. One of the modern devices that have (silently) crept into distributed systems are GPS receivers. Give examples of distributed applications that can use GPS information.

4. When a node synchronizes its clock to that of another node, it is generally a good idea to take previous measurements into account as well. Why? Also, give an example of how such past readings could be taken into account.

5. Add a new message to Fig. 6-9 that is concurrent with message A, that is, it neither happens before A nor happens after A.

6. To achieve totally-ordered multicasting with Lamport timestamps, is it strictly necessary that each message is acknowledged?

7. Consider a communication layer in which messages are delivered only in the order that they were sent. Give an example in which even this ordering is unnecessarily restrictive.

8. Many distributed algorithms require the use of a coordinating process. To what extent can such algorithms actually be considered distributed? Discuss.

9. In the centralized approach to mutual exclusion (Fig. 6-14), upon receiving a message from a process releasing its exclusive access to the resources it was using, the coordinator normally grants permission to the first process on the queue. Give another possible algorithm for the coordinator.

10. Consider Fig. 6-14 again. Suppose that the coordinator crashes. Does this always bring the system down? If not, under what circumstances does this happen? Is there any way to avoid the problem and make the system able to tolerate coordinator crashes?

11. Ricart and Agrawala's algorithm has the problem that if a process has crashed and does not reply to a request from another process to access a resources, the lack of response will be interpreted as denial of permission. We suggested that all requests be answered immediately to make it easy to detect crashed processes. Are there any circumstances where even this method is insufficient? Discuss.

12. How do the entries in Fig. 6-17 change if we assume that the algorithms can be implemented on a LAN that supports hardware broadcasts?

13. A distributed system may have multiple, independent resources. Imagine that process 0 wants to access resource A and process 1 wants to access resource B. Can Ricart and Agrawala's algorithm lead to deadlocks? Explain your answer.

14. Suppose that two processes detect the demise of the coordinator simultaneously and both decide to hold an election using the bully algorithm. What happens?

15. In Fig. 6-21 we have two *ELECTION* messages circulating simultaneously. While it does no harm to have two of them, it would be more elegant if one could be killed off. Devise an algorithm for doing this without affecting the operation of the basic election algorithm.

16. **(Lab assignment)** UNIX systems provide many facilities to keep computers in synch, notably the combination of the *crontab* tool (which allows to automatically schedule operations) and various synchronization commands are powerful. Configure a UNIX system that keeps the local time accurate with in the range of a single second. Likewise, configure an automatic backup facility by which a number of crucial files are automatically transferred to a remote machine once every 5 minutes. Your solution should be efficient when it comes to bandwidth usage.

7

CONSISTENCY AND REPLICATION

An important issue in distributed systems is the replication of data. Data are generally replicated to enhance reliability or improve performance. One of the major problems is keeping replicas consistent. Informally, this means that when one copy is updated we need to ensure that the other copies are updated as well; otherwise the replicas will no longer be the same. In this chapter, we take a detailed look at what consistency of replicated data actually means and the various ways that consistency can be achieved.

We start with a general introduction discussing why replication is useful and how it relates to scalability. We then continue by focusing on what consistency actually means. An important class of what are known as consistency models assumes that multiple processes simultaneously access shared data. Consistency for these situations can be formulated with respect to what processes can expect when reading and updating the shared data, knowing that others are accessing that data as well.

Consistency models for shared data are often hard to implement efficiently in large-scale distributed systems. Moreover, in many cases simpler models can be used, which are also often easier to implement. One specific class is formed by client-centric consistency models, which concentrate on consistency from the perspective of a single (possibly mobile) client. Client-centric consistency models are discussed in a separate section.

Consistency is only half of the story. We also need to consider how consistency is actually implemented. There are essentially two, more or less independent, issues we need to consider. First of all, we start with concentrating on managing replicas, which takes into account not only the placement of replica servers, but also how content is distributed to these servers.

The second issue is how replicas are kept consistent. In most cases, applications require a strong form of consistency. Informally, this means that updates are to be propagated more or less immediately between replicas. There are various alter/natives for implementing strong consistency, which are discussed in a separate section. Also, attention is paid to caching protocols, which form a special case of consistency protocols.

7.1 INTRODUCTION

In this section, we start with discussing the important reasons for wanting to replicate data in the first place. We concentrate on replication as a technique for achieving scalability, and motivate why reasoning about consistency is so important.

7.1.1 Reasons for Replication

There are two primary reasons for replicating data: reliability and performance. First, data are replicated to increase the reliability of a system. If a file system has been replicated it may be possible to continue working after one replica crashes by simply switching to one of the other replicas. Also, by maintaining multiple copies, it becomes possible to provide better protection against corrupted data. For example, imagine there are three copies of a file and every read and write operation is performed on each copy. We can safeguard ourselves against a single, failing write operation, by considering the value that is returned by at least two copies as being the correct one.

The other reason for replicating data is performance. Replication for performance is important when the distributed system needs to scale in numbers and geographical area. Scaling in numbers occurs, for example, when an increasing number of processes needs to access data that are managed by a single server. In that case, performance can be improved by replicating the server and subsequently dividing the work.

Scaling with respect to the size of a geographical area may also require replication. The basic idea is that by placing a copy of data in the proximity of the process using them, the time to access the data decreases. As a consequence, the performance as perceived by that process increases. This example also illustrates that the benefits of replication for performance may be hard to evaluate. Although a client process may perceive better performance, it may also be the case that more network bandwidth is now consumed keeping all replicas up to date.

If replication helps to improve reliability and performance, who could be against it? Unfortunately, there is a price to be paid when data are replicated. The problem with replication is that having multiple copies may lead to consistency problems. Whenever a copy is modified, that copy becomes different from the rest. Consequently, modifications have to be carried out on all copies to ensure consistency. Exactly when and how those modifications need to be carried out determines the price of replication.

To understand the problem, consider improving access times to Web pages. If no special measures are taken, fetching a page from a remote Web server may sometimes even take seconds to complete. To improve performance, Web browsers often locally store a copy of a previously fetched Web page (i.e., they **cache** a Web page). If a user requires that page again, the browser automatically returns the local copy. The access time as perceived by the user is excellent. However, if the user always wants to have the latest version of a page, he may be in for bad luck. The problem is that if the page has been modified in the meantime, modifications will not have been propagated to cached copies, making those copies out-of-date.

One solution to the problem of returning a stale copy to the user is to forbid the browser to keep local copies in the first place, effectively letting the server be fully in charge of replication. However, this solution may still lead to poor access times if no replica is placed near the user. Another solution is to let the Web server invalidate or update each cached copy, but this requires that the server keeps track of all caches and sending them messages. This, in turn, may degrade the overall performance of the server. We return to performance versus scalability issues below.

7.1.2 Replication as Scaling Technique

Replication and caching for performance are widely applied as scaling techniques. Scalability issues generally appear in the form of performance problems. Placing copies of data close to the processes using them can improve performance through reduction of access time and thus solve scalability problems.

A possible trade-off that needs to be made is that keeping copies up to date may require more network bandwidth. Consider a process P that accesses a local replica N times per second, whereas the replica itself is updated M times per second. Assume that an update completely refreshes the previous version of the local replica. If $N \ll M$, that is, the access-to-update ratio is very low, we have the situation where many updated versions of the local replica will never be accessed by P, rendering the network communication for those versions useless. In this case, it may have been better not to install a local replica close to P, or to apply a different strategy for updating the replica. We return to these issues below.

A more serious problem, however, is that keeping multiple copies consistent may itself be subject to serious scalability problems. Intuitively, a collection of copies is consistent when the copies are always the same. This means that a read operation performed at any copy will always return the same result. Consequently, when an update operation is performed on one copy, the update should be propagated to all copies before a subsequent operation takes place, no matter at which copy that operation is initiated or performed.

This type of consistency is sometimes informally (and imprecisely) referred to as tight consistency as provided by what is also called synchronous replication. (In the next section, we will provide precise definitions of consistency and introduce a range of consistency models.) The key idea is that an update is performed at all copies as a single atomic operation, or transaction. Unfortunately, implementing atomicity involving a large number of replicas that may be widely dispersed across a large-scale network is inherently difficult when operations are also required to complete quickly.

Difficulties come from the fact that we need to synchronize all replicas. In essence, this means that all replicas first need to reach agreement on when exactly an update is to be performed locally. For example, replicas may need to decide on a global ordering of operations using Lamport timestamps, or let a coordinator assign such an order. Global synchronization simply takes a lot of communication time, especially when replicas are spread across a wide-area network.

We are now faced with a dilemma. On the one hand, scalability problems can be alleviated by applying replication and caching, leading to improved performance. On the other hand, to keep all copies consistent generally requires global synchronization, which is inherently costly in terms of performance. The cure may be worse than the disease.

In many cases, the only real solution is to loosen the consistency constraints. In other words, if we can relax the requirement that updates need to be executed as atomic operations, we may be able to avoid (instantaneous) global synchronizations, and may thus gain performance. The price paid is that copies may not always be the same everywhere. As it turns out, to what extent consistency can be loosened depends highly on the access and update patterns of the replicated data, as well as on the purpose for which those data are used.

In the following sections, we first consider a range of consistency models by providing precise definitions of what consistency actually means. We then continue with our discussion of the different ways to implement consistency models through what are called distribution and consistency protocols. Different approaches to classifying consistency and replication can be found in Gray et al. (1996) and Wiesmann et al. (2000).

7.2 DATA-CENTRIC CONSISTENCY MODELS

Traditionally, consistency has been discussed in the context of read and write operations on shared data, available by means of (distributed) shared memory, a (distributed) shared database, or a (distributed) file system. In this section, we use the broader term **data store**. A data store may be physically distributed across multiple machines. In particular, each process that can access data from the store is assumed to have a local (or nearby) copy available of the entire store. Write operations are propagated to the other copies, as shown in Fig. 7-1. A data operation is classified as a write operation when it changes the data, and is otherwise classified as a read operation.

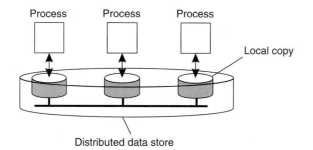

Figure 7-1. The general organization of a logical data store, physically distributed and replicated across multiple processes.

A **consistency model** is essentially a contract between processes and the data store. It says that if processes agree to obey certain rules, the store promises to work correctly. Normally, a process that performs a read operation on a data item, expects the operation to return a value that shows the results of the last write operation on that data.

In the absence of a global clock, it is difficult to define precisely which write operation is the last one. As an alternative, we need to provide other definitions, leading to a range of consistency models. Each model effectively restricts the values that a read operation on a data item can return. As is to be expected, the ones with major restrictions are easy to use, for example when developing applications, whereas those with minor restrictions are sometimes difficult. The trade-off is, of course, that the easy-to-use models do not perform nearly as well as the difficult ones. Such is life.

7.2.1 Continuous Consistency

From what we have discussed so far, it should be clear that there is no such thing as a best solution to replicating data. Replicating data poses consistency problems that cannot be solved efficiently in a general way. Only if we loosen consistency can there be hope for attaining efficient solutions. Unfortunately, there are also no general rules for loosening consistency: exactly what can be tolerated is highly dependent on applications.

There are different ways for applications to specify what inconsistencies they can tolerate. Yu and Vahdat (2002) take a general approach by distinguishing three independent axes for defining inconsistencies: deviation in numerical values between replicas, deviation in staleness between replicas, and deviation with respect to the ordering of update operations. They refer to these deviations as forming **continuous consistency** ranges.

Measuring inconsistency in terms of numerical deviations can be used by applications for which the data have numerical semantics. One obvious example is the replication of records containing stock market prices. In this case, an application may specify that two copies should not deviate more than $0.02, which would be an *absolute numerical deviation*. Alternatively, a *relative numerical deviation* could be specified, stating that two copies should differ by no more than, for example, 0.5%. In both cases, we would see that if a stock goes up (and one of the replicas is immediately updated) without violating the specified numerical deviations, replicas would still be considered to be mutually consistent.

Numerical deviation can also be understood in terms of the number of updates that have been applied to a given replica, but have not yet been seen by others. For example, a Web cache may not have seen a batch of operations carried out by a Web server. In this case, the associated deviation in the *value* is also referred to as its *weight*.

Staleness deviations relate to the last time a replica was updated. For some applications, it can be tolerated that a replica provides old data as long as it is not *too* old. For example, weather reports typically stay reasonably accurate over some time, say a few hours. In such cases, a main server may receive timely updates, but may decide to propagate updates to the replicas only once in a while.

Finally, there are classes of applications in which the ordering of updates are allowed to be different at the various replicas, as long as the differences remain bounded. One way of looking at these updates is that they are applied tentatively to a local copy, awaiting global agreement from all replicas. As a consequence, some updates may need to be rolled back and applied in a different order before becoming permanent. Intuitively, ordering deviations are much harder to grasp than the other two consistency metrics. We will provide examples below to clarify matters.

The Notion of a Conit

To define inconsistencies, Yu and Vahdat introduce a consistency unit, abbreviated to **conit**. A conit specifies the unit over which consistency is to be measured. For example, in our stock-exchange example, a conit could be defined as a record representing a single stock. Another example is an individual weather report.

To give an example of a conit, and at the same time illustrate numerical and ordering deviations, consider the two replicas as shown in Fig. 7-2. Each replica i maintains a two-dimensional vector clock VC_i, just like the ones we described in

Chap. 6. We use the notation t,i to express an operation that was carried out by replica i at (its) logical time t.

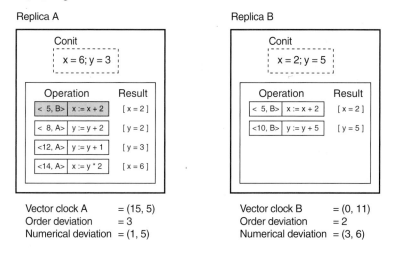

Figure 7-2. An example of keeping track of consistency deviations [adapted from (Yu and Vahdat, 2002)].

In this example we see two replicas that operate on a conit containing the data items x and y. Both variables are assumed to have been initialized to 0. Replica A received the operation

$$5,B : x \leftarrow x + 2$$

from replica B and has made it permanent (i.e., the operation has been committed at A and cannot be rolled back). Replica A has three tentative update operations: $8,A$, $12,A$, and $14,A$, which brings its ordering deviation to 3. Also note that due to the last operation $14,A$, A's vector clock becomes (15,5).

The only operation from B that A has not yet seen is $10,B$, bringing its numerical deviation with respect to operations to 1. In this example, the weight of this deviation can be expressed as the maximum difference between the (committed) values of x and y at A, and the result from operations at B not seen by A. The committed value at A is $(x,y) = (2,0)$, whereas the—for A unseen—operation at B yields a difference of $y = 5$.

A similar reasoning shows that B has two tentative update operations: $5,B$ and $10,B$, which means it has an ordering deviation of 2. Because B has not yet seen a single operation from A, its vector clock becomes (0,11). The numerical deviation is 3 with a total weight of 6. This last value comes from the fact B's committed value is $(x,y) = (0,0)$, whereas the tentative operations at A will already bring x to 6.

Note that there is a trade-off between maintaining fine-grained and coarse-grained conits. If a conit represents a lot of data, such as a complete database, then updates are aggregated for all the data in the conit. As a consequence, this may bring replicas sooner in an inconsistent state. For example, assume that in Fig. 7-3 two replicas may differ in no more than one outstanding update. In that case, when the data items in Fig. 7-3(a) have each been updated once at the first replica, the second one will need to be updated as well. This is not the case when choosing a smaller conit, as shown in Fig. 7-3(b). There, the replicas are still considered to be up to date. This problem is particularly important when the data items contained in a conit are used completely independently, in which case they are said to **falsely share** the conit.

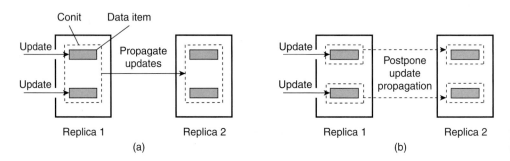

Figure 7-3. Choosing the appropriate granularity for a conit. (a) Two updates lead to update propagation. (b) No update propagation is needed (yet).

Unfortunately, making conits very small is not a good idea, for the simple reason that the total number of conits that need to be managed grows as well. In other words, there is an overhead related to managing the conits that needs to be taken into account. This overhead, in turn, may adversely affect overall performance, which has to be taken into account.

Although from a conceptual point of view conits form an attractive means for capturing consistency requirements, there are two important issues that need to be dealt with before they can be put to practical use. First, in order to enforce consistency we need to have protocols. Protocols for continuous consistency are discussed later in this chapter.

A second issue is that program developers must specify the consistency requirements for their applications. Practice indicates that obtaining such requirements may be extremely difficult. Programmers are generally not used to handling replication, let alone understanding what it means to provide detailed information on consistency. Therefore, it is mandatory that there are simple and easy-to-understand programming interfaces.

Continuous consistency can be implemented as a toolkit which appears to programmers as just another library that they link with their applications. A conit is simply declared alongside an update of a data item. For example, the fragment of pseudocode

```
AffectsConit(ConitQ, 1, 1);
append message m to queue Q;
```

states that appending a message to queue Q belongs to a conit named "ConitQ." Likewise, operations may now also be declared as being dependent on conits:

```
DependsOnConit(ConitQ, 4, 0, 60);
read message m from head of queue Q;
```

In this case, the call to DependsOnConit() specifies that the numerical deviation, ordering deviation, and staleness should be limited to the values 4, 0, and 60 (seconds), respectively. This can be interpreted as that there should be at most 4 unseen update operations at other replicas, there should be no tentative local updates, and the local copy of Q should have been checked for staleness no more than 60 seconds ago. If these requirements are not fulfilled, the underlying middleware will attempt to bring the local copy of Q to a state such that the read operation can be carried out.

7.2.2 Consistent Ordering of Operations

Besides continuous consistency, there is a huge body of work on data-centric consistency models from the past decades. An important class of models comes from the field of concurrent programming. Confronted with the fact that in parallel and distributed computing multiple processes will need to share resources and access these resources simultaneously, researchers have sought to express the semantics of concurrent accesses when shared resources are replicated. This has led to at least one important consistency model that is widely used. In the following, we concentrate on what is known as sequential consistency, and we will also discuss a weaker variant, namely causal consistency.

The models that we discuss in this section all deal with consistently ordering operations on shared, replicated data. In principle, the models augment those of continuous consistency in the sense that when tentative updates at replicas need to be committed, replicas will need to reach agreement on a global ordering of those updates. In other words, they need to agree on a consistent ordering of those updates. The consistency models we discuss next are all about reaching such consistent orderings.

Sequential Consistency

In the following, we will use a special notation in which we draw the operations of a process along a time axis. The time axis is always drawn horizontally, with time increasing from left to right. The symbols

$$W_i(x)a \text{ and } R_i(x)b$$

mean that a write by process P_i to data item x with the value a and a read from that item by P_i returning b have been done, respectively. We assume that each data item is initially *NIL*. When there is no confusion concerning which process is accessing data, we omit the index from the symbols W and R.

Figure 7-4. Behavior of two processes operating on the same data item. The horizontal axis is time.

As an example, in Fig. 7-4 P_1 does a write to a data item x, modifying its value to a. Note that, in principle, this operation $W_1(x)a$ is first performed on a copy of the data store that is local to P_1, and is then subsequently propagated to the other local copies. In our example, P_2 later reads the value *NIL*, and some time after that a (from its local copy of the store). What we are seeing here is that it took some time to propagate the update of x to P_2, which is perfectly acceptable.

Sequential consistency is an important data-centric consistency model, which was first defined by Lamport (1979) in the context of shared memory for multiprocessor systems. In general, a data store is said to be sequentially consistent when it satisfies the following condition:

> *The result of any execution is the same as if the (read and write) operations by all processes on the data store were executed in some sequential order and the operations of each individual process appear in this sequence in the order specified by its program.*

What this definition means is that when processes run concurrently on (possibly) different machines, any valid interleaving of read and write operations is acceptable behavior, but *all processes see the same interleaving of operations*. Note that nothing is said about time; that is, there is no reference to the "most recent" write operation on a data item. Note that in this context, a process "sees" writes from all processes but only its own reads.

That time does not play a role can be seen from Fig. 7-5. Consider four processes operating on the same data item x. In Fig. 7-5(a) process P_1 first performs $W(x)a$ to x. Later (in absolute time), process P_2 also performs a write operation, by setting the value of x to b. However, both processes P_3 and P_4 *first* read value b, and later value a. In other words, the write operation of process P_2 appears to have taken place before that of P_1.

In contrast, Fig. 7-5(b) violates sequential consistency because not all processes see the same interleaving of write operations. In particular, to process P_3, it appears as if the data item has first been changed to b, and later to a. On the other hand, P_4 will conclude that the final value is b.

To make the notion of sequential consistency more concrete, consider three concurrently-executing processes P_1, P_2, and P_3, shown in Fig. 7-6 (Dubois et al., 1988). The data items in this example are formed by the three integer variables x, y, and z, which are stored in a (possibly distributed) shared sequentially consistent

P1: W(x)a			
P2:	W(x)b		
P3:		R(x)b	R(x)a
P4:			R(x)b R(x)a

(a)

P1: W(x)a			
P2:	W(x)b		
P3:		R(x)b	R(x)a
P4:			R(x)a R(x)b

(b)

Figure 7-5. (a) A sequentially consistent data store. (b) A data store that is not sequentially consistent.

Process P1	**Process P2**	**Process P3**
x ← 1;	y ← 1;	z ← 1;
print(y, z);	print(x, z);	print(x, y);

Figure 7-6. Three concurrently-executing processes.

data store. We assume that each variable is initialized to 0. In this example, an assignment corresponds to a write operation, whereas a print statement corresponds to a simultaneous read operation of its two arguments. All statements are assumed to be indivisible.

Various interleaved execution sequences are possible. With six independent statements, there are potentially 720 (6!) possible execution sequences, although some of these violate program order. Consider the 120 (5!) sequences that begin with $x \leftarrow 1$. Half of these have *print*(x,z) before $y \leftarrow 1$ and thus violate program order. Half also have *print*(x,y) before $z \leftarrow 1$ and also violate program order. Only 1/4 of the 120 sequences, or 30, are valid. Another 30 valid sequences are possible starting with $y \leftarrow 1$ and another 30 can begin with $z \leftarrow 1$, for a total of 90 valid execution sequences. Four of these are shown in Fig. 7-7.

In Fig. 7-7(a), the three processes are run in order, first P_1, then P_2, then P_3. The other three examples demonstrate different, but equally valid, interleavings of the statements in time. Each of the three processes prints two variables. Since the only values each variable can take on are the initial value (0), or the assigned value (1), each process produces a 2-bit string. The numbers after *Prints* are the actual outputs that appear on the output device.

If we concatenate the output of P_1, P_2, and P_3 in that order, we get a 6-bit string that characterizes a particular interleaving of statements. This is the string listed as the *Signature* in Fig. 7-7. Below we will characterize each ordering by its signature rather than by its printout.

Not all 64 signature patterns are allowed. As a trivial example, 000000 is not permitted, because that would imply that the print statements ran before the assignment statements, violating the requirement that statements are executed in

x ← 1;	x ← 1;	y ← 1;	y ← 1;
print(y, z);	y ← 1;	z ← 1;	x ← 1;
y ← 1;	print(x, z);	print(x, y);	z ← 1;
print(x, z);	print(y, z);	print(x, z);	print(x, z);
z ← 1;	z ← 1;	x ← 1;	print(y, z);
print(x, y);	print(x, y);	print(y, z);	print(x, y);

Prints: 001011	Prints: 101011	Prints: 010111	Prints: 111111
Signature: 001011	Signature: 101011	Signature: 110101	Signature: 111111

(a)	(b)	(c)	(d)

Figure 7-7. Four valid execution sequences for the processes of Fig. 7-6. The vertical axis is time.

program order. A more subtle example is 001001. The first two bits, 00, mean that y and z were both 0 when P_1 did its printing. This situation occurs only when P_1 executes both statements before P_2 or P_3 starts. The next two bits, 10, mean that P_2 must run after P_1 has started but before P_3 has started. The last two bits, 01, mean that P_3 must complete before P_1 starts, but we have already seen that P_1 must go first. Therefore, 001001 is not allowed.

In short, the 90 different valid statement orderings produce a variety of different program results (less than 64, though) that are allowed under the assumption of sequential consistency. The contract between the processes and the distributed shared data store is that the processes must accept all of these as valid results. In other words, the processes must accept the four results shown in Fig. 7-7 and all the other valid results as proper answers, and must work correctly if any of them occurs. A program that works for some of these results and not for others violates the contract with the data store and is incorrect.

Causal Consistency

The **causal consistency** model (Hutto and Ahamad, 1990) represents a weakening of sequential consistency in that it makes a distinction between events that are potentially causally related and those that are not. We already came across causality when discussing vector timestamps in the previous chapter. If event b is caused or influenced by an earlier event a, causality requires that everyone else first see a, then see b.

Consider a simple interaction by means of a distributed shared database. Suppose that process P_1 writes a data item x. Then P_2 reads x and writes y. Here the reading of x and the writing of y are potentially causally related because the computation of y may have depended on the value of x as read by P_2 (i.e., the value written by P_1).

On the other hand, if two processes spontaneously and simultaneously write two different data items, these are not causally related. Operations that are not causally related are said to be **concurrent**.

For a data store to be considered causally consistent, it is necessary that the store obeys the following condition:

> *Writes that are potentially causally related must be seen by all processes in the same order. Concurrent writes may be seen in a different order on different machines.*

As an example of causal consistency, consider Fig. 7-8. Here we have an event sequence that is allowed with a causally-consistent store, but which is forbidden with a sequentially-consistent store or a strictly consistent store. The thing to note is that the writes $W_2(x)b$ and $W_1(x)c$ are concurrent, so it is not required that all processes see them in the same order.

P1:	W(x)a			W(x)c		
P2:		R(x)a	W(x)b			
P3:		R(x)a			R(x)c	R(x)b
P4:		R(x)a			R(x)b	R(x)c

Figure 7-8. This sequence is allowed with a causally-consistent store, but not with a sequentially consistent store.

Now consider a second example. In Fig. 7-9(a) we have $W_2(x)b$ potentially depending on $W_1(x)a$ because the b may be a result of a computation involving the value read by $R_2(x)a$. The two writes are causally related, so all processes must see them in the same order. Therefore, Fig. 7-9(a) is incorrect. On the other hand, in Fig. 7-9(b) the read has been removed, so $W_1(x)a$ and $W_2(x)b$ are now concurrent writes. A causally-consistent store does not require concurrent writes to be globally ordered, so Fig. 7-9(b) is correct. Note that Fig. 7-9(b) reflects a situation that would not be acceptable for a sequentially consistent store.

P1: W(x)a				
P2:	R(x)a	W(x)b		
P3:			R(x)b	R(x)a
P4:			R(x)a	R(x)b

(a)

P1: W(x)a				
P2:		W(x)b		
P3:			R(x)b	R(x)a
P4:			R(x)a	R(x)b

(b)

Figure 7-9. (a) A violation of a causally-consistent store. (b) A correct sequence of events in a causally-consistent store.

Implementing causal consistency requires keeping track of which processes have seen which writes. It effectively means that a dependency graph of which operation is dependent on which other operations must be constructed and maintained. One way of doing this is by means of vector timestamps, as we discussed in the previous chapter. We return to the use of vector timestamps to capture causality later in this chapter.

Grouping Operations

Sequential and causal consistency are defined at the level read and write operations. This level of granularity is for historical reasons: these models have initially been developed for shared-memory multiprocessor systems and were actually implemented at the hardware level.

The fine granularity of these consistency models in many cases did not match the granularity as provided by applications. What we see there is that concurrency between programs sharing data is generally kept under control through synchronization mechanisms for mutual exclusion and transactions. Effectively, what happens is that at the program level read and write operations are bracketed by the pair of operations ENTER_CS and LEAVE_CS where "CS" stands for critical section. As we explained in Chap. 6, the synchronization between processes takes place by means of these two operations. In terms of our distributed data store, this means that a process that has successfully executed ENTER_CS will be ensured that the data in its local store is up to date. At that point, it can safely execute a series of read and write operations on that store, and subsequently wrap things up by calling LEAVE_CS.

In essence, what happens is that within a program the data that are operated on by a series of read and write operations are protected against concurrent accesses that would lead to seeing something else than the result of executing the series as a whole. Put differently, the bracketing turns the series of read and write operations into an atomically executed unit, thus raising the level of granularity.

In order to reach this point, we do need to have precise semantics concerning the operations ENTER_CS and LEAVE_CS. These semantics can be formulated in terms of shared **synchronization variables**. There are different ways to use these variables. We take the general approach in which each variable has some associated data, which could amount to the complete set of shared data. We adopt the convention that when a process enters its critical section it should *acquire* the relevant synchronization variables, and likewise when it leaves the critical section, it *releases* these variables. Note that the data in a process' critical section may be associated to different synchronization variables.

Each synchronization variable has a current owner, namely, the process that last acquired it. The owner may enter and exit critical sections repeatedly without having to send any messages on the network. A process not currently owning a synchronization variable but wanting to acquire it has to send a message to the current owner asking for ownership and the current values of the data associated with that synchronization variable. It is also possible for several processes to simultaneously own a synchronization variable in nonexclusive mode, meaning that they can read, but not write, the associated data.

We now demand that the following criteria are met (Bershad et al., 1993):

1. *An acquire access of a synchronization variable is not allowed to perform with respect to a process until all updates to the guarded shared data have been performed with respect to that process.*

2. *Before an exclusive mode access to a synchronization variable by a process is allowed to perform with respect to that process, no other process may hold the synchronization variable, not even in nonexclusive mode.*

3. *After an exclusive mode access to a synchronization variable has been performed, any other process' next nonexclusive mode access to that synchronization variable may not be performed until it has performed with respect to that variable's owner.*

The first condition says that when a process does an acquire, the acquire may not complete (i.e., return control to the next statement) until all the guarded shared data have been brought up to date. In other words, at an acquire, all remote changes to the guarded data must be made visible.

The second condition says that before updating a shared data item, a process must enter a critical section in exclusive mode to make sure that no other process is trying to update the shared data at the same time.

The third condition says that if a process wants to enter a critical region in nonexclusive mode, it must first check with the owner of the synchronization variable guarding the critical region to fetch the most recent copies of the guarded shared data.

Fig. 7-10 shows an example of what is known as **entry consistency**. Instead of operating on the entire shared data, in this example we associate locks with each data item. In this case, P_1 does an acquire for x, changes x once, after which it also does an acquire for y. Process P_2 does an acquire for x but not for y, so that it will read value a for x, but may read *NIL* for y. Because process P_3 first does an acquire for y, it will read the value b when y is released by P_1.

P1:	Acq(Lx) W(x)a Acq(Ly) W(y)b Rel(Lx) Rel(Ly)		
P2:		Acq(Lx) R(x)a	R(y) NIL
P3:		Acq(Ly) R(y)b	

Figure 7-10. A valid event sequence for entry consistency.

One of the programming problems with entry consistency is properly associating data with synchronization variables. One straightforward approach is to explicitly tell the middleware which data are going to be accessed, as is generally done by declaring which database tables will be affected by a transaction. In an object-based approach, we could implicitly associate a unique synchronization variable with each declared object, effectively serializing all invocations to such objects.

Consistency versus Coherence

At this point, it is useful to clarify the difference between two closely related concepts. The models we have discussed so far all deal with the fact that a number of processes execute read and write operations on a set of data items. A **consistency model** describes what can be expected with respect to that set when multiple processes concurrently operate on that data. The set is then said to be consistent if it adheres to the rules described by the model.

Where data consistency is concerned with a set of data items, **coherence models** describe what can be expected to only a single data item (Cantin et al., 2005). In this case, we assume that a data item is replicated at several places; it is said to be coherent when the various copies abide to the rules as defined by its associated coherence model. A popular model is that of sequential consistency, but now applied to only a single data item. In effect, it means that in the case of concurrent writes, all processes will eventually see the same order of updates taking place.

7.3 CLIENT-CENTRIC CONSISTENCY MODELS

The consistency models described in the previous section aim at providing a systemwide consistent view on a data store. An important assumption is that concurrent processes may be simultaneously updating the data store, and that it is necessary to provide consistency in the face of such concurrency. For example, in the case of object-based entry consistency, the data store guarantees that when an object is called, the calling process is provided with a copy of the object that reflects all changes to the object that have been made so far, possibly by other processes. During the call, it is also guaranteed that no other process can interfere—that is, mutual exclusive access is provided to the calling process.

Being able to handle concurrent operations on shared data while maintaining sequential consistency is fundamental to distributed systems. For performance reasons, sequential consistency may possibly be guaranteed only when processes use synchronization mechanisms such as transactions or locks.

In this section, we take a look at a special class of distributed data stores. The data stores we consider are characterized by the lack of simultaneous updates, or when such updates happen, they can easily be resolved. Most operations involve reading data. These data stores offer a very weak consistency model, called eventual consistency. By introducing special client-centric consistency models, it turns out that many inconsistencies can be hidden in a relatively cheap way.

7.3.1 Eventual Consistency

To what extent processes actually operate in a concurrent fashion, and to what extent consistency needs to be guaranteed, may vary. There are many examples in which concurrency appears only in a restricted form. For example, in many database systems, most processes hardly ever perform update operations; they mostly read data from the database. Only one, or very few processes perform update operations. The question then is how fast updates should be made available to only-reading processes.

As another example, consider a worldwide naming system such as DNS. The DNS name space is partitioned into domains, where each domain is assigned to a naming authority, which acts as owner of that domain. Only that authority is allowed to update its part of the name space. Consequently, conflicts resulting from two operations that both want to perform an update on the same data (i.e., **write-write conflicts**), never occur. The only situation that needs to be handled are **read-write conflicts**, in which one process wants to update a data item while another is concurrently attempting to read that item. As it turns out, it is often acceptable to propagate an update in a lazy fashion, meaning that a reading process will see an update only after some time has passed since the update took place.

Yet another example is the World Wide Web. In virtually all cases, Web pages are updated by a single authority, such as a webmaster or the actual owner of the page. There are normally no write-write conflicts to resolve. On the other hand, to improve efficiency, browsers and Web proxies are often configured to keep a fetched page in a local cache and to return that page upon the next request.

An important aspect of both types of Web caches is that they may return out-of-date Web pages. In other words, the cached page that is returned to the requesting client is an older version compared to the one available at the actual Web server. As it turns out, many users find this inconsistency acceptable (to a certain degree).

These examples can be viewed as cases of (large-scale) distributed and replicated databases that tolerate a relatively high degree of inconsistency. They have in common that if no updates take place for a long time, all replicas will gradually become consistent. This form of consistency is called **eventual consistency**.

Data stores that are eventually consistent thus have the property that in the absence of updates, all replicas converge toward identical copies of each other. Eventual consistency essentially requires only that updates are guaranteed to propagate to all replicas. Write-write conflicts are often relatively easy to solve when assuming that only a small group of processes can perform updates. Eventual consistency is therefore often cheap to implement.

Eventual consistent data stores work fine as long as clients always access the same replica. However, problems arise when different replicas are accessed over a short period of time. This is best illustrated by considering a mobile user accessing a distributed database, as shown in Fig. 7-11.

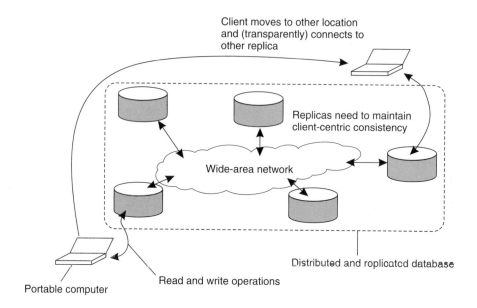

Figure 7-11. The principle of a mobile user accessing different replicas of a distributed database.

The mobile user accesses the database by connecting to one of the replicas in a transparent way. In other words, the application running on the user's portable computer is unaware on which replica it is actually operating. Assume the user performs several update operations and then disconnects again. Later, he accesses the database again, possibly after moving to a different location or by using a different access device. At that point, the user may be connected to a different replica than before, as shown in Fig. 7-11. However, if the updates performed previously have not yet been propagated, the user will notice inconsistent behavior. In particular, he would expect to see all previously made changes, but instead, it appears as if nothing at all has happened.

This example is typical for eventually-consistent data stores and is caused by the fact that users may sometimes operate on different replicas. The problem can be alleviated by introducing **client-centric consistency**. In essence, client-centric consistency provides guarantees *for a single client* concerning the consistency of accesses to a data store by that client. No guarantees are given concerning concurrent accesses by different clients.

Client-centric consistency models originate from the work on Bayou [see, for example Terry et al. (1994) and Terry et al., 1998)]. Bayou is a database system developed for mobile computing, where it is assumed that network connectivity is unreliable and subject to various performance problems. Wireless networks and networks that span large areas, such as the Internet, fall into this category.

Bayou essentially distinguishes four different consistency models. To explain these models, we again consider a data store that is physically distributed across multiple machines. When a process accesses the data store, it generally connects to the locally (or nearest) available copy, although, in principle, any copy will do just fine. All read and write operations are performed on that local copy. Updates are eventually propagated to the other copies. To simplify matters, we assume that data items have an associated owner, which is the only process that is permitted to modify that item. In this way, we avoid write-write conflicts.

Client-centric consistency models are described using the following notations. Let $x_i[t]$ denote the version of data item x at local copy L_i at time t. Version $x_i[t]$ is the result of a series of write operations at L_i that took place since initialization. We denote this set as $WS(x_i[t])$. If operations in $WS(x_i[t_1])$ have also been performed at local copy L_j at a later time t_2, we write $WS(x_i[t_1];x_j[t_2])$. If the ordering of operations or the timing is clear from the context, the time index will be omitted.

7.3.2 Monotonic Reads

The first client-centric consistency model is that of monotonic reads. A data store is said to provide **monotonic-read consistency** if the following condition holds:

If a process reads the value of a data item x, any successive read operation on x by that process will always return that same value or a more recent value.

In other words, monotonic-read consistency guarantees that if a process has seen a value of x at time t, it will never see an older version of x at a later time.

As an example where monotonic reads are useful, consider a distributed e-mail database. In such a database, each user's mailbox may be distributed and replicated across multiple machines. Mail can be inserted in a mailbox at any location. However, updates are propagated in a lazy (i.e., on demand) fashion. Only when a copy needs certain data for consistency are those data propagated to that copy. Suppose a user reads his mail in San Francisco. Assume that only reading mail does not affect the mailbox, that is, messages are not removed, stored in subdirectories, or even tagged as having already been read, and so on. When the user later flies to New York and opens his mailbox again, monotonic-read consistency guarantees that the messages that were in the mailbox in San Francisco will also be in the mailbox when it is opened in New York.

Using a notation similar to that for data-centric consistency models, monotonic-read consistency can be graphically represented as shown in Fig. 7-12. Along the vertical axis, two different local copies of the data store are shown, L_1 and L_2. Time is shown along the horizontal axis as before. In all cases, we are interested in the operations carried out by a single process P. These specific operations are shown in boldface are connected by a dashed line representing the order in which they are carried out by P.

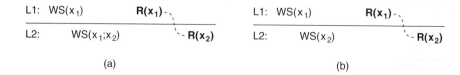

(a)   (b)

Figure 7-12. The read operations performed by a single process P at two different local copies of the same data store. (a) A monotonic-read consistent data store. (b) A data store that does not provide monotonic reads.

In Fig. 7-12(a), process P first performs a read operation on x at L_1, returning the value of x_1 (at that time). This value results from the write operations in $WS(x_1)$ performed at L_1. Later, P performs a read operation on x at L_2, shown as $R(x_2)$. To guarantee monotonic-read consistency, all operations in $WS(x_1)$ should have been propagated to L_2 before the second read operation takes place. In other words, we need to know for sure that $WS(x_1)$ is part of $WS(x_2)$, which is expressed as $WS(x_1;x_2)$.

In contrast, Fig. 7-12(b) shows a situation in which monotonic-read consistency is not guaranteed. After process P has read x_1 at L_1, it later performs the operation $R(x_2)$ at L_2. However, only the write operations in $WS(x_2)$ have been performed at L_2. No guarantees are given that this set also contains all operations contained in $WS(x_1)$.

7.3.3 Monotonic Writes

In many situations, it is important that write operations are propagated in the correct order to all copies of the data store. This property is expressed in monotonic-write consistency. In a **monotonic-write consistent** store, the following condition holds:

> *A write operation by a process on a data item x is completed before any successive write operation on x by the same process.*

Thus completing a write operation means that the copy on which a successive operation is performed reflects the effect of a previous write operation by the same process, no matter where that operation was initiated. In other words, a write operation on a copy of item x is performed only if that copy has been brought up to date by means of any preceding write operation, which may have taken place on other copies of x. If need be, the new write must wait for old ones to finish.

Note that monotonic-write consistency resembles data-centric FIFO consistency. The essence of FIFO consistency is that write operations by the same process are performed in the correct order everywhere. This ordering constraint also applies to monotonic writes, except that we are now considering consistency only for a single process instead of for a collection of concurrent processes.

Bringing a copy of x up to date need not be necessary when each write operation completely overwrites the present value of x. However, write operations are often performed on only part of the state of a data item. Consider, for example, a software library. In many cases, updating such a library is done by replacing one or more functions, leading to a next version. With monotonic-write consistency, guarantees are given that if an update is performed on a copy of the library, all preceding updates will be performed first. The resulting library will then indeed become the most recent version and will include all updates that have led to previous versions of the library.

Monotonic-write consistency is shown in Fig. 7-13. In Fig. 7-13(a), process P performs a write operation on x at local copy L_1, presented as the operation $W(x_1)$. Later, P performs another write operation on x, but this time at L_2, shown as $W(x_2)$. To ensure monotonic-write consistency, it is necessary that the previous write operation at L_1 has already been propagated to L_2. This explains operation $W(x_1)$ at L_2, and why it takes place before $W(x_2)$.

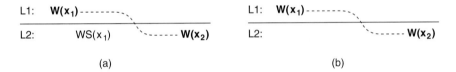

(a)   (b)

Figure 7-13. The write operations performed by a single process P at two different local copies of the same data store. (a) A monotonic-write consistent data store. (b) A data store that does not provide monotonic-write consistency.

In contrast, Fig. 7-13(b) shows a situation in which monotonic-write consistency is not guaranteed. Compared to Fig. 7-13(a), what is missing is the propagation of $W(x_1)$ to copy L_2. In other words, no guarantees can be given that the copy of x on which the second write is being performed has the same or more recent value at the time $W(x_1)$ completed at L_1.

Note that, by the definition of monotonic-write consistency, write operations by the same process are performed in the same order as they are initiated. A somewhat weaker form of monotonic writes is one in which the effects of a write operation are seen only if all preceding writes have been carried out as well, but perhaps not in the order in which they have been originally initiated. This consistency is applicable in those cases in which write operations are commutative, so that ordering is really not necessary. Details are found in Terry et al. (1994).

7.3.4 Read Your Writes

A client-centric consistency model that is closely related to monotonic reads is as follows. A data store is said to provide **read-your-writes consistency**, if the following condition holds:

The effect of a write operation by a process on data item x will always be seen by a successive read operation on x by the same process.

In other words, a write operation is always completed before a successive read operation by the same process, no matter where that read operation takes place.

The absence of read-your-writes consistency is sometimes experienced when updating Web documents and subsequently viewing the effects. Update operations frequently take place by means of a standard editor or word processor, which saves the new version on a file system that is shared by the Web server. The user's Web browser accesses that same file, possibly after requesting it from the local Web server. However, once the file has been fetched, either the server or the browser often caches a local copy for subsequent accesses. Consequently, when the Web page is updated, the user will not see the effects if the browser or the server returns the cached copy instead of the original file. Read-your-writes consistency can guarantee that if the editor and browser are integrated into a single program, the cache is invalidated when the page is updated, so that the updated file is fetched and displayed.

Similar effects occur when updating passwords. For example, to enter a digital library on the Web, it is often necessary to have an account with an accompanying password. However, changing a password make take some time to come into effect, with the result that the library may be inaccessible to the user for a few minutes. The delay can be caused because a separate server is used to manage passwords and it may take some time to subsequently propagate (encrypted) passwords to the various servers that constitute the library.

Fig. 7-14(a) shows a data store that provides read-your-writes consistency. Note that Fig. 7-14(a) is very similar to Fig. 7-12(a), except that consistency is now determined by the last write operation by process P, instead of its last read.

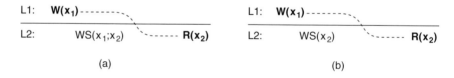

(a) (b)

Figure 7-14. (a) A data store that provides read-your-writes consistency. (b) A data store that does not.

In Fig. 7-14(a), process P performed a write operation $W(x_1)$ and later a read operation at a different local copy. Read-your-writes consistency guarantees that the effects of the write operation can be seen by the succeeding read operation. This is expressed by $WS(x_1;x_2)$, which states that $W(x_1)$ is part of $WS(x_2)$. In contrast, in Fig. 7-14(b), $W(x_1)$ has been left out of $WS(x_2)$, meaning that the effects of the previous write operation by process P have not been propagated to L_2.

7.3.5 Writes Follow Reads

The last client-centric consistency model is one in which updates are propagated as the result of previous read operations. A data store is said to provide **writes-follow-reads** consistency, if the following holds.

A write operation by a process on a data item x following a previous read operation on x by the same process is guaranteed to take place on the same or a more recent value of x that was read.

In other words, any successive write operation by a process on a data item x will be performed on a copy of x that is up to date with the value most recently read by that process.

Writes-follow-reads consistency can be used to guarantee that users of a network newsgroup see a posting of a reaction to an article only after they have seen the original article (Terry et al., 1994). To understand the problem, assume that a user first reads an article A. Then, he reacts by posting a response B. By requiring writes-follow-reads consistency, B will be written to any copy of the newsgroup only after A has been written as well. Note that users who only read articles need not require any specific client-centric consistency model. The writes-follows-reads consistency assures that reactions to articles are stored at a local copy only if the original is stored there as well.

L1:	$WS(x_1)$	$R(x_1)$-		L1:	$WS(x_1)$	$R(x_1)$-
L2:	$WS(x_1;x_2)$	$- W(x_2)$		L2:	$WS(x_2)$	$- W(x_2)$

| (a) | (b) |

Figure 7-15. (a) A writes-follow-reads consistent data store. (b) A data store that does not provide writes-follow-reads consistency.

This consistency model is shown in Fig. 7-15. In Fig. 7-15(a), a process reads x at local copy L_1. The write operations that led to the value just read, also appear in the write set at L_2, where the same process later performs a write operation. (Note that other processes at L_2 see those write operations as well.) In contrast, no guarantees are given that the operation performed at L_2, as shown in Fig. 7-15(b), are performed on a copy that is consistent with the one just read at L_1.

We will return to client-centric consistency models when we discuss implementations later on in this chapter.

7.4 REPLICA MANAGEMENT

A key issue for any distributed system that supports replication is to decide where, when, and by whom replicas should be placed, and subsequently which mechanisms to use for keeping the replicas consistent. The placement problem itself should be split into two subproblems: that of placing *replica servers*, and that of placing *content*. The difference is a subtle but important one and the two issues are often not clearly separated. Replica-server placement is concerned with finding the best locations to place a server that can host (part of) a data store. Content placement deals with finding the best servers for placing content. Note that this often means that we are looking for the optimal placement of only a single data item. Obviously, before content placement can take place, replica servers will have to be placed first. In the following, take a look at these two different placement problems, followed by a discussion on the basic mechanisms for managing the replicated content.

7.4.1 Replica-Server Placement

The placement of replica servers is not an intensively studied problem for the simple reason that it is often more of a management and commercial issue than an optimization problem. Nonetheless, analysis of client and network properties are useful to come to informed decisions.

There are various ways to compute the best placement of replica servers, but all boil down to an optimization problem in which the best K out of N locations need to be selected $(K < N)$. These problems are known to be computationally complex and can be solved only through heuristics. Qiu et al. (2001) take the distance between clients and locations as their starting point. Distance can be measured in terms of latency or bandwidth. Their solution selects one server at a time such that the average distance between that server and its clients is minimal given that already k servers have been placed (meaning that there are $N - k$ locations left).

As an alternative, Radoslavov et al. (2001) propose to ignore the position of clients and only take the topology of the Internet as formed by the autonomous systems. An **autonomous system** (**AS**) can best be viewed as a network in which the nodes all run the same routing protocol and which is managed by a single organization. As of January 2006, there were just over 20,000 ASes. Radoslavov et al. first consider the largest AS and place a server on the router with the largest number of network interfaces (i.e., links). This algorithm is then repeated with the second largest AS, and so on.

As it turns out, client-unaware server placement achieves similar results as client-aware placement, under the assumption that clients are uniformly distributed across the Internet (relative to the existing topology). To what extent this assumption is true is unclear. It has not been well studied.

One problem with these algorithms is that they are computationally expensive. For example, both the previous algorithms have a complexity that is higher than $O(N^2)$, where N is the number of locations to inspect. In practice, this means that for even a few thousand locations, a computation may need to run for tens of minutes. This may be unacceptable, notably when there are **flash crowds** (a sudden burst of requests for one specific site, which occur regularly on the Internet). In that case, quickly determining where replica servers are needed is essential, after which a specific one can be selected for content placement.

Szymaniak et al. (2006) have developed a method by which a region for placing replicas can be quickly identified. A region is identified to be a collection of nodes accessing the same content, but for which the internode latency is low. The goal of the algorithm is first to select the most demanding regions—that is, the one with the most nodes—and then to let one of the nodes in such a region act as replica server.

To this end, nodes are assumed to be positioned in an m-dimensional geometric space, as we discussed in the previous chapter. The basic idea is to identify the K largest clusters and assign a node from each cluster to host replicated content. To identify these clusters, the entire space is partitioned into cells. The K most dense cells are then chosen for placing a replica server. A cell is nothing but an m-dimensional hypercube. For a two-dimensional space, this corresponds to a rectangle.

Obviously, the cell size is important, as shown in Fig. 7-16. If cells are chosen too large, then multiple clusters of nodes may be contained in the same cell. In that case, too few replica servers for those clusters would be chosen. On the other hand, choosing small cells may lead to the situation that a single cluster is spread across a number of cells, leading to choosing too many replica servers.

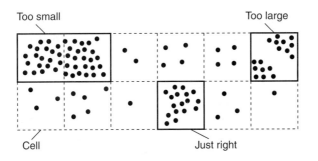

Figure 7-16. Choosing a proper cell size for server placement.

As it turns out, an appropriate cell size can be computed as a simple function of the average distance between two nodes and the number of required replicas. With this cell size, it can be shown that the algorithm performs as well as the close-to-optimal one described in Qiu et al. (2001), but having a much lower complexity: $O(N \times \max\{log(N), K\})$. To give an impression what this result means:

experiments show that computing the 20 best replica locations for a collection of 64,000 nodes is approximately 50,000 times faster. As a consequence, replica-server placement can now be done in real time.

7.4.2 Content Replication and Placement

Let us now move away from server placement and concentrate on content placement. When it comes to content replication and placement, three different types of replicas can be distinguished logically organized as shown in Fig. 7-17.

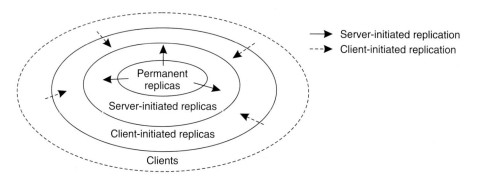

Figure 7-17. The logical organization of different kinds of copies of a data store into three concentric rings.

Permanent Replicas

Permanent replicas can be considered as the initial set of replicas that constitute a distributed data store. In many cases, the number of permanent replicas is small. Consider, for example, a Web site. Distribution of a Web site generally comes in one of two forms. The first kind of distribution is one in which the files that constitute a site are replicated across a limited number of servers at a single location. Whenever a request comes in, it is forwarded to one of the servers, for instance, using a round-robin strategy.

The second form of distributed Web sites is what is called **mirroring**. In this case, a Web site is copied to a limited number of servers, called **mirror sites**, which are geographically spread across the Internet. In most cases, clients simply choose one of the various mirror sites from a list offered to them. Mirrored Web sites have in common with cluster-based Web sites that there are only a few number of replicas, which are more or less statically configured.

Similar static organizations also appear with distributed databases (Oszu and Valduriez, 1999). Again, the database can be distributed and replicated across a number of servers that together form a cluster of servers, often referred to as a **shared-nothing architecture**, emphasizing that neither disks nor main memory are shared by processors. Alternatively, a database is distributed and possibly replicated across a number of geographically dispersed sites. This architecture is generally deployed in federated databases (Sheth and Larson, 1990).

Server-Initiated Replicas

In contrast to permanent replicas, server-initiated replicas are copies of a data store that exist to enhance performance and which are created at the initiative of the (owner of the) data store. Consider, for example, a Web server placed in New York. Normally, this server can handle incoming requests quite easily, but it may happen that over a couple of days a sudden burst of requests come in from an unexpected location far from the server. In that case, it may be worthwhile to install a number of temporary replicas in regions where requests are coming from.

The problem of dynamically placing replicas is also being addressed in Web hosting services. These services offer a (relatively static) collection of servers spread across the Internet that can maintain and provide access to Web files belonging to third parties. To provide optimal facilities such hosting services can dynamically replicate files to servers where those files are needed to enhance performance, that is, close to demanding (groups of) clients. Sivasubramanian et al. (2004b) provide an in-depth overview of replication in Web hosting services to which we will return in Chap. 12.

Given that the replica servers are already in place, deciding where to place content is easier than in the case of server placement. An approach to dynamic replication of files in the case of a Web hosting service is described in Rabinovich et al. (1999). The algorithm is designed to support Web pages for which reason it assumes that updates are relatively rare compared to read requests. Using files as the unit of data, the algorithm works as follows.

The algorithm for dynamic replication takes two issues into account. First, replication can take place to reduce the load on a server. Second, specific files on a server can be migrated or replicated to servers placed in the proximity of clients that issue many requests for those files. In the following pages, we concentrate only on this second issue. We also leave out a number of details, which can be found in Rabinovich et al. (1999).

Each server keeps track of access counts per file, and where access requests come from. In particular, it is assumed that, given a client C, each server can determine which of the servers in the Web hosting service is closest to C. (Such information can be obtained, for example, from routing databases.) If client C_1 and client C_2 share the same "closest" server P, all access requests for file F at server Q from C_1 and C_2 are jointly registered at Q as a single access count $cnt_Q(P,F)$. This situation is shown in Fig. 7-18.

When the number of requests for a specific file F at server S drops below a deletion threshold $del(S,F)$, that file can be removed from S. As a consequence, the number of replicas of that file is reduced, possibly leading to higher work

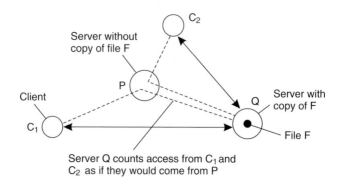

Figure 7-18. Counting access requests from different clients.

loads at other servers. Special measures are taken to ensure that at least one copy of each file continues to exist.

A replication threshold $rep(S,F)$, which is always chosen higher than the deletion threshold, indicates that the number of requests for a specific file is so high that it may be worthwhile replicating it on another server. If the number of requests lie somewhere between the deletion and replication threshold, the file is allowed only to be migrated. In other words, in that case it is important to at least keep the number of replicas for that file the same.

When a server Q decides to reevaluate the placement of the files it stores, it checks the access count for each file. If the total number of access requests for F at Q drops below the deletion threshold $del(Q,F)$, it will delete F unless it is the last copy. Furthermore, if for some server P, $cnt_Q(P,F)$ exceeds more than half of the total requests for F at Q, server P is requested to take over the copy of F. In other words, server Q will attempt to migrate F to P.

Migration of file F to server P may not always succeed, for example, because P is already heavily loaded or is out of disk space. In that case, Q will attempt to replicate F on other servers. Of course, replication can take place only if the total number of access requests for F at Q exceeds the replication threshold $rep(Q,F)$. Server Q checks all other servers in the Web hosting service, starting with the one farthest away. If, for some server R, $cnt_Q(R,F)$ exceeds a certain fraction of all requests for F at Q, an attempt is made to replicate F to R.

Server-initiated replication continues to increase in popularity in time, especially in the context of Web hosting services such as the one just described. Note that as long as guarantees can be given that each data item is hosted by at least one server, it may suffice to use only server-initiated replication and not have any permanent replicas. Nevertheless, permanent replicas are still often useful as a back-up facility, or to be used as the only replicas that are allowed to be changed to guarantee consistency. Server-initiated replicas are then used for placing read-only copies close to clients.

Client-Initiated Replicas

An important kind of replica is the one initiated by a client. Client-initiated replicas are more commonly known as (**client**) **caches**. In essence, a cache is a local storage facility that is used by a client to temporarily store a copy of the data it has just requested. In principle, managing the cache is left entirely to the client. The data store from where the data had been fetched has nothing to do with keeping cached data consistent. However, as we shall see, there are many occasions in which the client can rely on participation from the data store to inform it when cached data has become stale.

Client caches are used only to improve access times to data. Normally, when a client wants access to some data, it connects to the nearest copy of the data store from where it fetches the data it wants to read, or to where it stores the data it had just modified. When most operations involve only reading data, performance can be improved by letting the client store requested data in a nearby cache. Such a cache could be located on the client's machine, or on a separate machine in the same local-area network as the client. The next time that same data needs to be read, the client can simply fetch it from this local cache. This scheme works fine as long as the fetched data have not been modified in the meantime.

Data are generally kept in a cache for a limited amount of time, for example, to prevent extremely stale data from being used, or simply to make room for other data. Whenever requested data can be fetched from the local cache, a **cache hit** is said to have occurred. To improve the number of cache hits, caches can be shared between clients. The underlying assumption is that a data request from client C_1 may also be useful for a request from another nearby client C_2.

Whether this assumption is correct depends very much on the type of data store. For example, in traditional file systems, data files are rarely shared at all (see, e.g., Muntz and Honeyman, 1992; and Blaze, 1993) rendering a shared cache useless. Likewise, it turns out that using Web caches to share data is also losing some ground, partly also because of the improvement in network and server performance. Instead, server-initiated replication schemes are becoming more effective.

Placement of client caches is relatively simple: a cache is normally placed on the same machine as its client, or otherwise on a machine shared by clients on the same local-area network. However, in some cases, extra levels of caching are introduced by system administrators by placing a shared cache between a number of departments or organizations, or even placing a shared cache for an entire region such as a province or country.

Yet another approach is to place (cache) servers at specific points in a wide-area network and let a client locate the nearest server. When the server is located, it can be requested to hold copies of the data the client was previously fetching from somewhere else, as described in Noble et al. (1999). We will return to caching later in this chapter when discussing consistency protocols.

7.4.3 Content Distribution

Replica management also deals with propagation of (updated) content to the relevant replica servers. There are various trade-offs to make, which we discuss next.

State versus Operations

An important design issue concerns what is actually to be propagated. Basically, there are three possibilities:

1. Propagate only a notification of an update.

2. Transfer data from one copy to another.

3. Propagate the update operation to other copies.

Propagating a notification is what **invalidation protocols** do. In an invalidation protocol, other copies are informed that an update has taken place and that the data they contain are no longer valid. The invalidation may specify which part of the data store has been updated, so that only part of a copy is actually invalidated. The important issue is that no more than a notification is propagated. Whenever an operation on an invalidated copy is requested, that copy generally needs to be updated first, depending on the specific consistency model that is to be supported.

The main advantage of invalidation protocols is that they use little network bandwidth. The only information that needs to be transferred is a specification of which data are no longer valid. Such protocols generally work best when there are many update operations compared to read operations, that is, the read-to-write ratio is relatively small.

Consider, for example, a data store in which updates are propagated by sending the modified data to all replicas. If the size of the modified data is large, and updates occur frequently compared to read operations, we may have the situation that two updates occur after one another without any read operation being performed between them. Consequently, propagation of the first update to all replicas is effectively useless, as it will be overwritten by the second update. Instead, sending a notification that the data have been modified would have been more efficient.

Transferring the modified data among replicas is the second alternative, and is useful when the read-to-write ratio is relatively high. In that case, the probability that an update will be effective in the sense that the modified data will be read before the next update takes place is high. Instead of propagating modified data, it is also possible to log the changes and transfer only those logs to save bandwidth. In addition, transfers are often aggregated in the sense that multiple modifications are packed into a single message, thus saving communication overhead.

The third approach is not to transfer any data modifications at all, but to tell each replica which update operation it should perform (and sending only the parameter values that those operations need). This approach, also referred to as **active replication**, assumes that each replica is represented by a process capable of "actively" keeping its associated data up to date by performing operations (Schneider, 1990). The main benefit of active replication is that updates can often be propagated at minimal bandwidth costs, provided the size of the parameters associated with an operation are relatively small. Moreover, the operations can be of arbitrary complexity, which may allow further improvements in keeping replicas consistent. On the other hand, more processing power may be required by each replica, especially in those cases when operations are relatively complex.

Pull versus Push Protocols

Another design issue is whether updates are pulled or pushed. In a **push-based approach**, also referred to as **server-based protocols**, updates are propagated to other replicas without those replicas even asking for the updates. Push-based approaches are often used between permanent and server-initiated replicas, but can also be used to push updates to client caches. Server-based protocols are applied when replicas generally need to maintain a relatively high degree of consistency. In other words, replicas need to be kept identical.

This need for a high degree of consistency is related to the fact that permanent and server-initiated replicas, as well as large shared caches, are often shared by many clients, which, in turn, mainly perform read operations. Consequently, the read-to-update ratio at each replica is relatively high. In these cases, push-based protocols are efficient in the sense that every pushed update can be expected to be of use for one or more readers. In addition, push-based protocols make consistent data immediately available when asked for.

In contrast, in a **pull-based approach**, a server or client requests another server to send it any updates it has at that moment. Pull-based protocols, also called **client-based protocols**, are often used by client caches. For example, a common strategy applied to Web caches is first to check whether cached data items are still up to date. When a cache receives a request for items that are still locally available, the cache checks with the original Web server whether those data items have been modified since they were cached. In the case of a modification, the modified data are first transferred to the cache, and then returned to the requesting client. If no modifications took place, the cached data are returned. In other words, the client polls the server to see whether an update is needed.

A pull-based approach is efficient when the read-to-update ratio is relatively low. This is often the case with (nonshared) client caches, which have only one client. However, even when a cache is shared by many clients, a pull-based approach may also prove to be efficient when the cached data items are rarely shared. The main drawback of a pull-based strategy in comparison to a push-based approach is that the response time increases in the case of a cache miss.

When comparing push-based and pull-based solutions, there are a number of trade-offs to be made, as shown in Fig. 7-19. For simplicity, consider a client-server system consisting of a single, nondistributed server, and a number of client processes, each having their own cache.

Issue	Push-based	Pull-based
State at server	List of client replicas and caches	None
Messages sent	Update (and possibly fetch update later)	Poll and update
Response time at client	Immediate (or fetch-update time)	Fetch-update time

Figure 7-19. A comparison between push-based and pull-based protocols in the case of multiple-client, single-server systems.

An important issue is that in push-based protocols, the server needs to keep track of all client caches. Apart from the fact that stateful servers are often less fault tolerant, as we discussed in Chap. 3, keeping track of all client caches may introduce a considerable overhead at the server. For example, in a push-based approach, a Web server may easily need to keep track of tens of thousands of client caches. Each time a Web page is updated, the server will need to go through its list of client caches holding a copy of that page, and subsequently propagate the update. Worse yet, if a client purges a page due to lack of space, it has to inform the server, leading to even more communication.

The messages that need to be sent between a client and the server also differ. In a push-based approach, the only communication is that the server sends updates to each client. When updates are actually only invalidations, additional communication is needed by a client to fetch the modified data. In a pull-based approach, a client will have to poll the server, and, if necessary, fetch the modified data.

Finally, the response time at the client is also different. When a server pushes modified data to the client caches, it is clear that the response time at the client side is zero. When invalidations are pushed, the response time is the same as in the pull-based approach, and is determined by the time it takes to fetch the modified data from the server.

These trade-offs have lead to a hybrid form of update propagation based on leases. A **lease** is a promise by the server that it will push updates to the client for a specified time. When a lease expires, the client is forced to poll the server for updates and pull in the modified data if necessary. An alternative is that a client requests a new lease for pushing updates when the previous lease expires.

Leases were originally introduced by Gray and Cheriton (1989). They provide a convenient mechanism for dynamically switching between a push-based and pull-based strategy. Duvvuri et al. (2003) describe a flexible lease system that allows the expiration time to be dynamically adapted depending on different lease criteria. They distinguish the following three types of leases. (Note that in all cases, updates are pushed by the server as long as the lease has not expired.)

First, age-based leases are given out on data items depending on the last time the item was modified. The underlying assumption is that data that have not been modified for a long time can be expected to remain unmodified for some time yet to come. This assumption has shown to be reasonable in the case of Web-based data. By granting long-lasting leases to data items that are expected to remain unmodified, the number of update messages can be strongly reduced compared to the case where all leases have the same expiration time.

Another lease criterion is how often a specific client requests its cached copy to be updated. With renewal-frequency-based leases, a server will hand out a long-lasting lease to a client whose cache often needs to be refreshed. On the other hand, a client that asks only occasionally for a specific data item will be handed a short-term lease for that item. The effect of this strategy is that the server essentially keeps track only of those clients where its data are popular; moreover, those clients are offered a high degree of consistency.

The last criterion is that of state-space overhead at the server. When the server realizes that it is gradually becoming overloaded, it lowers the expiration time of new leases it hands out to clients. The effect of this strategy is that the server needs to keep track of fewer clients as leases expire more quickly. In other words, the server dynamically switches to a more stateless mode of operation, thereby offloading itself so that it can handle requests more efficiently.

Unicasting versus Multicasting

Related to pushing or pulling updates is deciding whether unicasting or multicasting should be used. In unicast communication, when a server that is part of the data store sends its update to N other servers, it does so by sending N separate messages, one to each server. With multicasting, the underlying network takes care of sending a message efficiently to multiple receivers.

In many cases, it is cheaper to use available multicasting facilities. An extreme situation is when all replicas are located in the same local-area network and that hardware broadcasting is available. In that case, broadcasting or multicasting a message is no more expensive than a single point-to-point message. Unicasting updates would then be less efficient.

Multicasting can often be efficiently combined with a push-based approach to propagating updates. When the two are carefully integrated, a server that decides to push its updates to a number of other servers simply uses a single multicast group to send its updates. In contrast, with a pull-based approach, it is generally only a single client or server that requests its copy to be updated. In that case, unicasting may be the most efficient solution.

7.5 CONSISTENCY PROTOCOLS

So far, we have mainly concentrated on various consistency models and general design issues for consistency protocols. In this section, we concentrate on the actual implementation of consistency models by taking a look at several consistency protocols. A **consistency protocol** describes an implementation of a specific consistency model. We follow the organization of our discussion on consistency models by first taking a look at data-centric models, followed by protocols for client-centric models.

7.5.1 Continuous Consistency

As part of their work on continuous consistency, Yu and Vahdat have developed a number of protocols to tackle the three forms of consistency. In the following, we briefly consider a number of solutions, omitting details for clarity.

Bounding Numerical Deviation

We first concentrate on one solution for keeping the numerical deviation within bounds. Again, our purpose is not to go into all the details for each protocol, but rather to give the general idea. Details for bounding numerical deviation can be found in Yu and Vahdat (2000b).

We concentrate on writes to a single data item x. Each write $W(x)$ has an associated weight that represents the numerical value by which x is updated, denoted as $weight(W(x))$, or simply $weight(W)$. For simplicity, we assume that $weight(W) > 0$. Each write W is initially submitted to one out of the N available replica servers, in which case that server becomes the write's origin, denoted as $origin(W)$. If we consider the system at a specific moment in time we will see several submitted writes that still need to be propagated to all servers. To this end, each server S_i will keep track of a log L_i of writes that it has performed on its own local copy of x.

Let $TW[i,j]$ be the writes executed by server S_i that originated from server S_j:

$$TW[i,j] = \sum \{weight(W) | origin(W) = S_j \ \& \ W \in L_i\}$$

Note that $TW[i,i]$ represents the aggregated writes submitted to S_i. Our goal is for any time t, to let the current value v_i at server S_i deviate within bounds from the actual value $v(t)$ of x. This actual value is completely determined by all submitted writes. That is, if $v(0)$ is the initial value of x, then

$$v(t) = v(0) + \sum_{k=1}^{N} TW[k,k]$$

and

$$v_i = v(0) + \sum_{k=1}^{N} TW[i,k]$$

Note that $v_i \leq v(t)$. Let us concentrate only on absolute deviations. In particular, for every server S_i, we associate an upperbound δ_i such that we need to enforce:

$$v(t) - v_i \leq \delta_i$$

Writes submitted to a server S_i will need to be propagated to all other servers. There are different ways in which this can be done, but typically an epidemic protocol will allow rapid dissemination of updates. In any case, when a server S_i propagates a write originating from S_j to S_k, the latter will be able to learn about the value $TW[i,j]$ at the time the write was sent. In other words, S_k can maintain a **view** $TW_k[i,j]$ of what it believes S_i will have as value for $TW[i,j]$. Obviously,

$$0 \leq TW_k[i,j] \leq TW[i,j] \leq TW[j,j]$$

The whole idea is that when server S_k notices that S_i has not been keeping in the right pace with the updates that have been submitted to S_k, it forwards writes from its log to S_i. This forwarding effectively *advances* the view $TW_k[i,k]$ that S_k has of $TW[i,k]$, making the deviation $TW[i,k] - TW_k[i,k]$ smaller. In particular, S_k advances its view on $TW[i,k]$ when an application submits a new write that would increase $TW[k,k] - TW_k[i,k]$ beyond $\delta_i / (N-1)$. We leave it as an exercise to show that advancement always ensures that $v(t) - v_i \leq \delta_i$.

Bounding Staleness Deviations

There are many ways to keep the staleness of replicas within specified bounds. One simple approach is to let server S_k keep a real-time vector clock RVC_k where $RVC_k[i] = T(i)$ means that S_k has seen all writes that have been submitted to S_i up to time $T(i)$. In this case, we assume that each submitted write is timestamped by its origin server, and that $T(i)$ denotes the time *local to S_i*.

If the clocks between the replica servers are loosely synchronized, then an acceptable protocol for bounding staleness would be the following. Whenever server S_k notes that $T(k) - RVC_k[i]$ is about to exceed a specified limit, it simply starts pulling in writes that originated from S_i with a timestamp later than $RVC_k[i]$.

Note that in this case a replica server is responsible for keeping its copy of x up to date regarding writes that have been issued elsewhere. In contrast, when maintaining numerical bounds, we followed a push approach by letting an origin server keep replicas up to date by forwarding writes. The problem with pushing writes in the case of staleness is that no guarantees can be given for consistency when it is unknown in advance what the maximal propagation time will be. This situation is somewhat improved by pulling in updates, as multiple servers can help to keep a server's copy of x fresh (up to date).

Bounding Ordering Deviations

Recall that ordering deviations in continuous consistency are caused by the fact that a replica server tentatively applies updates that have been submitted to it. As a result, each server will have a local queue of tentative writes for which the actual order in which they are to be applied to the local copy of x still needs to be determined. The ordering deviation is bounded by specifying the maximal length of the queue of tentative writes.

As a consequence, detecting when ordering consistency needs to be enforced is simple: when the length of this local queue exceeds a specified maximal length. At that point, a server will no longer accept any newly submitted writes, but will instead attempt to commit tentative writes by negotiating with other servers in which order its writes should be executed. In other words, we need to enforce a globally consistent ordering of tentative writes. There are many ways in doing this, but it turns out that so-called primary-based or quorum-based protocols are used in practice. We discuss these protocols next.

7.5.2 Primary-Based Protocols

In practice, we see that distributed applications generally follow consistency models that are relatively easy to understand. These models include those for bounding staleness deviations, and to a lesser extent also those for bounding numerical deviations. When it comes to models that handle consistent ordering of operations, sequential consistency, notably those in which operations can be grouped through locking or transactions are popular.

As soon as consistency models become slightly difficult to understand for application developers, we see that they are ignored even if performance could be improved. The bottom line is that if the semantics of a consistency model are not intuitively clear, application developers will have a hard time building correct applications. Simplicity is appreciated (and perhaps justifiably so).

In the case of sequential consistency, it turns out that primary-based protocols prevail. In these protocols, each data item x in the data store has an associated primary, which is responsible for coordinating write operations on x. A distinction can be made as to whether the primary is fixed at a remote server or if write operations can be carried out locally after moving the primary to the process where the write operation is initiated. Let us take a look at this class of protocols.

Remote-Write Protocols

The simplest primary-based protocol that supports replication is the one in which all write operations need to be forwarded to a fixed single server. Read operations can be carried out locally. Such schemes are also known as **primary-backup protocols** (Budhiraja et al., 1993). A primary-backup protocol works as shown in Fig. 7-20. A process wanting to perform a write operation on data item

x, forwards that operation to the primary server for x. The primary performs the update on its local copy of x, and subsequently forwards the update to the backup servers. Each backup server performs the update as well, and sends an acknowledgment back to the primary. When all backups have updated their local copy, the primary sends an acknowledgment back to the initial process.

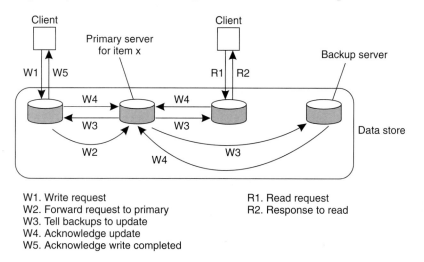

W1. Write request
W2. Forward request to primary
W3. Tell backups to update
W4. Acknowledge update
W5. Acknowledge write completed

R1. Read request
R2. Response to read

Figure 7-20. The principle of a primary-backup protocol.

A potential performance problem with this scheme is that it may take a relatively long time before the process that initiated the update is allowed to continue. In effect, an update is implemented as a blocking operation. An alternative is to use a nonblocking approach. As soon as the primary has updated its local copy of x, it returns an acknowledgment. After that, it tells the backup servers to perform the update as well. Nonblocking primary-backup protocols are discussed in Budhiraja and Marzullo (1992).

The main problem with nonblocking primary-backup protocols has to do with fault tolerance. In a blocking scheme, the client process knows for sure that the update operation is backed up by several other servers. This is not the case with a nonblocking solution. The advantage, of course, is that write operations may speed up considerably. We will return to fault tolerance issues extensively in the next chapter.

Primary-backup protocols provide a straightforward implementation of sequential consistency, as the primary can order all incoming writes in a globally unique time order. Evidently, all processes see all write operations in the same order, no matter which backup server they use to perform read operations. Also, with blocking protocols, processes will always see the effects of their most recent write operation (note that this cannot be guaranteed with a nonblocking protocol without taking special measures).

Local-Write Protocols

A variant of primary-backup protocols is one in which the primary copy migrates between processes that wish to perform a write operation. As before, whenever a process wants to update data item x, it locates the primary copy of x, and subsequently moves it to its own location, as shown in Fig. 7-21. The main advantage of this approach is that multiple, successive write operations can be carried out locally, while reading processes can still access their local copy. However, such an improvement can be achieved only if a nonblocking protocol is followed by which updates are propagated to the replicas after the primary has finished with locally performing the updates.

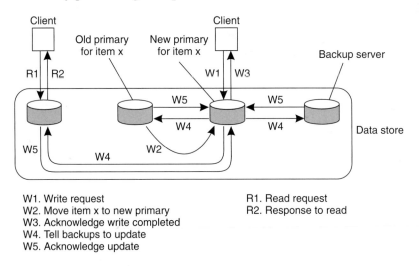

W1. Write request
W2. Move item x to new primary
W3. Acknowledge write completed
W4. Tell backups to update
W5. Acknowledge update

R1. Read request
R2. Response to read

Figure 7-21. Primary-backup protocol in which the primary migrates to the process wanting to perform an update.

This primary-backup local-write protocol can also be applied to mobile computers that are able to operate in disconnected mode. Before disconnecting, the mobile computer becomes the primary server for each data item it expects to update. While being disconnected, all update operations are carried out locally, while other processes can still perform read operations (but no updates). Later, when connecting again, updates are propagated from the primary to the backups, bringing the data store in a consistent state again. We will return to operating in disconnected mode in Chap. 11 when we discuss distributed file systems.

As a last variant of this scheme, nonblocking local-write primary-based protocols are also used for distributed file systems in general. In this case, there may be a fixed central server through which normally all write operations take place, as in the case of remote-write primary backup. However, the server temporarily allows one of the replicas to perform a series of local updates, as this may considerably speed up performance. When the replica server is done, the updates are propagated to the central server, from where they are then distributed to the other replica servers.

7.5.3 Replicated-Write Protocols

In replicated-write protocols, write operations can be carried out at multiple replicas instead of only one, as in the case of primary-based replicas. A distinction can be made between active replication, in which an operation is forwarded to all replicas, and consistency protocols based on majority voting.

Active Replication

In active replication, each replica has an associated process that carries out update operations. In contrast to other protocols, updates are generally propagated by means of the write operation that causes the update. In other words, the operation is sent to each replica. However, it is also possible to send the update, as discussed before.

One problem with active replication is that operations need to be carried out in the same order everywhere. Consequently, what is needed is a totally-ordered multicast mechanism. Such a multicast can be implemented using Lamport's logical clocks, as discussed in the previous chapter. Unfortunately, this implementation of multicasting does not scale well in large distributed systems. As an alternative, total ordering can be achieved using a central coordinator, also called a **sequencer**. One approach is to first forward each operation to the sequencer, which assigns it a unique sequence number and subsequently forwards the operation to all replicas. Operations are carried out in the order of their sequence number. Clearly, this implementation of totally-ordered multicasting strongly resembles primary-based consistency protocols.

Note that using a sequencer does not solve the scalability problem. In fact, if totally-ordered multicasting is needed, a combination of symmetric multicasting using Lamport timestamps and sequencers may be necessary. Such a solution is described in Rodrigues et al. (1996).

Quorum-Based Protocols

A different approach to supporting replicated writes is to use **voting** as originally proposed by Thomas (1979) and generalized by Gifford (1979). The basic idea is to require clients to request and acquire the permission of multiple servers before either reading or writing a replicated data item.

As a simple example of how the algorithm works, consider a distributed file system and suppose that a file is replicated on N servers. We could make a rule stating that to update a file, a client must first contact at least half the servers plus one (a majority) and get them to agree to do the update. Once they have agreed, the file is changed and a new version number is associated with the new file. The version number is used to identify the version of the file and is the same for all the newly updated files.

To read a replicated file, a client must also contact at least half the servers plus one and ask them to send the version numbers associated with the file. If all the version numbers are the same, this must be the most recent version because an attempt to update only the remaining servers would fail because there are not enough of them.

For example, if there are five servers and a client determines that three of them have version 8, it is impossible that the other two have version 9. After all, any successful update from version 8 to version 9 requires getting three servers to agree to it, not just two.

Gifford's scheme is actually somewhat more general than this. In it, to read a file of which N replicas exist, a client needs to assemble a **read quorum**, an arbitrary collection of any N_R servers, or more. Similarly, to modify a file, a **write quorum** of at least N_W servers is required. The values of N_R and N_W are subject to the following two constraints:

1. $N_R + N_W > N$

2. $N_W > N/2$

The first constraint is used to prevent read-write conflicts, whereas the second prevents write-write conflicts. Only after the appropriate number of servers has agreed to participate can a file be read or written.

To see how this algorithm works, consider Fig. 7-22(a), which has $N_R = 3$ and $N_W = 10$. Imagine that the most recent write quorum consisted of the 10 servers C through L. All of these get the new version and the new version number. Any subsequent read quorum of three servers will have to contain at least one member of this set. When the client looks at the version numbers, it will know which is most recent and take that one.

In Fig. 7-22(b) and (c), we see two more examples. In Fig. 7-22(b) a write-write conflict may occur because $N_W \leq N/2$. In particular, if one client chooses $\{A,B,C,E,F,G\}$ as its write set and another client chooses $\{D,H,I,J,K,L\}$ as its write set, then clearly we will run into trouble as the two updates will both be accepted without detecting that they actually conflict.

The situation shown in Fig. 7-22(c) is especially interesting because it sets N_R to one, making it possible to read a replicated file by finding any copy and using it. The price paid for this good read performance, however, is that write updates need to acquire all copies. This scheme is generally referred to as **Read-One, Write-All (ROWA)**. There are several variations of quorum-based replication protocols. A good overview is presented in Jalote (1994).

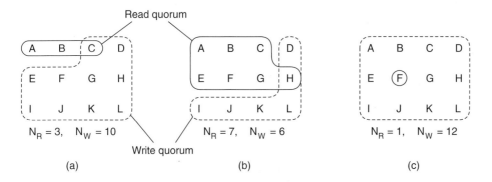

Figure 7-22. Three examples of the voting algorithm. (a) A correct choice of read and write set. (b) A choice that may lead to write-write conflicts. (c) A correct choice, known as ROWA (read one, write all).

7.5.4 Cache-Coherence Protocols

Caches form a special case of replication, in the sense that they are generally controlled by clients instead of servers. However, cache-coherence protocols, which ensure that a cache is consistent with the server-initiated replicas are, in principle, not very different from the consistency protocols discussed so far.

There has been much research in the design and implementation of caches, especially in the context of shared-memory multiprocessor systems. Many solutions are based on support from the underlying hardware, for example, by assuming that snooping or efficient broadcasting can be done. In the context of middleware-based distributed systems that are built on top of general-purpose operating systems, software-based solutions to caches are more interesting. In this case, two separate criteria are often maintained to classify caching protocols (Min and Baer, 1992; Lilja, 1993; and Tartalja and Milutinovic, 1997).

First, caching solutions may differ in their **coherence detection strategy**, that is, *when* inconsistencies are actually detected. In static solutions, a compiler is assumed to perform the necessary analysis prior to execution, and to determine which data may actually lead to inconsistencies because they may be cached. The compiler simply inserts instructions that avoid inconsistencies. Dynamic solutions are typically applied in the distributed systems studied in this book. In these solutions, inconsistencies are detected at runtime. For example, a check is made with the server to see whether the cached data have been modified since they were cached.

In the case of distributed databases, dynamic detection-based protocols can be further classified by considering exactly when during a transaction the detection is done. Franklin et al. (1997) distinguish the following three cases. First, when during a transaction a cached data item is accessed, the client needs to verify whether that data item is still consistent with the version stored at the (possibly replicated) server. The transaction cannot proceed to use the cached version until its consistency has been definitively validated.

A second, optimistic, approach is to let the transaction proceed while verification is taking place. In this case, it is assumed that the cached data were up to date when the transaction started. If that assumption later proves to be false, the transaction will have to abort.

The third approach is to verify whether the cached data are up to date only when the transaction commits. This approach is comparable to the optimistic concurrency control scheme discussed in the previous chapter. In effect, the transaction just starts operating on the cached data and hopes for the best. After all the work has been done, accessed data are verified for consistency. When stale data were used, the transaction is aborted.

Another design issue for cache-coherence protocols is the **coherence enforcement strategy**, which determines *how* caches are kept consistent with the copies stored at servers. The simplest solution is to disallow shared data to be cached at all. Instead, shared data are kept only at the servers, which maintain consistency using one of the primary-based or replication-write protocols discussed above. Clients are allowed to cache only private data. Obviously, this solution can offer only limited performance improvements.

When shared data can be cached, there are two approaches to enforce cache coherence. The first is to let a server send an invalidation to all caches whenever a data item is modified. The second is to simply propagate the update. Most caching systems use one of these two schemes. Dynamically choosing between sending invalidations or updates is sometimes supported in client-server databases (Franklin et al., 1997).

Finally, we also need to consider what happens when a process modifies cached data. When read-only caches are used, update operations can be performed only by servers, which subsequently follow some distribution protocol to ensure that updates are propagated to caches. In many cases, a pull-based approach is followed. In this case, a client detects that its cache is stale, and requests a server for an update.

An alternative approach is to allow clients to directly modify the cached data, and forward the update to the servers. This approach is followed in **write-through caches**, which are often used in distributed file systems. In effect, write-through caching is similar to a primary-based local-write protocol in which the client's cache has become a temporary primary. To guarantee (sequential) consistency, it is necessary that the client has been granted exclusive write permissions, or otherwise write-write conflicts may occur.

Write-through caches potentially offer improved performance over other schemes as all operations can be carried out locally. Further improvements can be made if we delay the propagation of updates by allowing multiple writes to take place before informing the servers. This leads to what is known as a **write-back cache**, which is, again, mainly applied in distributed file systems.

7.5.5 Implementing Client-Centric Consistency

For our last topic on consistency protocols, let us draw our attention to implementing client-centric consistency. Implementing client-centric consistency is relatively straightforward if performance issues are ignored. In the following pages, we first describe such an implementation, followed by a description of a more realistic implementation.

A Naive Implementation

In a naive implementation of client-centric consistency, each write operation W is assigned a globally unique identifier. Such an identifier is assigned by the server to which the write had been submitted. As in the case of continuous consistency, we refer to this server as the origin of W. Then, for each client, we keep track of two sets of writes. The read set for a client consists of the writes relevant for the read operations performed by a client. Likewise, the write set consists of the (identifiers of the) writes performed by the client.

Monotonic-read consistency is implemented as follows. When a client performs a read operation at a server, that server is handed the client's read set to check whether all the identified writes have taken place locally. (The size of such a set may introduce a performance problem, for which a solution is discussed below.) If not, it contacts the other servers to ensure that it is brought up to date before carrying out the read operation. Alternatively, the read operation is forwarded to a server where the write operations have already taken place. After the read operation is performed, the write operations that have taken place at the selected server and which are relevant for the read operation are added to the client's read set.

Note that it should be possible to determine exactly where the write operations identified in the read set have taken place. For example, the write identifier could include the identifier of the server to which the operation was submitted. That server is required to, for example, log the write operation so that it can be replayed at another server. In addition, write operations should be performed in the order they were submitted. Ordering can be achieved by letting the client generate a globally unique sequence number that is included in the write identifier. If each data item can be modified only by its owner, the latter can supply the sequence number.

Monotonic-write consistency is implemented analogous to monotonic reads. Whenever a client initiates a new write operation at a server, the server is handed over the client's write set. (Again, the size of the set may be prohibitively large in the face of performance requirements. An alternative solution is discussed below.) It then ensures that the identified write operations are performed first and in the correct order. After performing the new operation, that operation's write identifier is added to the write set. Note that bringing the current server up to date with the client's write set may introduce a considerable increase in the client's response time since the client then wait for the operation to fully complete.

Likewise, read-your-writes consistency requires that the server where the read operation is performed has seen all the write operations in the client's write set. The writes can simply be fetched from other servers before the read operation is performed, although this may lead to a poor response time. Alternatively, the client-side software can search for a server where the identified write operations in the client's write set have already been performed.

Finally, writes-follow-reads consistency can be implemented by first bringing the selected server up to date with the write operations in the client's read set, and then later adding the identifier of the write operation to the write set, along with the identifiers in the read set (which have now become relevant for the write operation just performed).

Improving Efficiency

It is easy to see that the read set and write set associated with each client can become very large. To keep these sets manageable, a client's read and write operations are grouped into sessions. A **session** is typically associated with an application: it is opened when the application starts and is closed when it exits. However, sessions may also be associated with applications that are temporarily exited, such as user agents for e-mail. Whenever a client closes a session, the sets are simply cleared. Of course, if a client opens a session that it never closes, the associated read and write sets can still become very large.

The main problem with the naive implementation lies in the representation of the read and write sets. Each set consists of a number of identifiers for write operations. Whenever a client forwards a read or write request to a server, a set of identifiers is handed to the server as well to see whether all write operations relevant to the request have been carried out by that server.

This information can be more efficiently represented by means of vector timestamps as follows. First, whenever a server accepts a new write operation W, it assigns that operation a globally unique identifier along with a timestamp $ts(W)$. A subsequent write operation submitted to that server is assigned a higher-valued timestamp. Each server S_i maintains a vector timestamp WVC_i, where $WVC_i[j]$ is equal to the timestamp of the most recent write operation originating from S_j that has been processed by S_i. For clarity, assume that for each server, writes from S_j are processed in the order that they were submitted.

Whenever a client issues a request to perform a read or write operation O at a specific server, that server returns its current timestamp along with the results of O. Read and write sets are subsequently represented by vector timestamps. More specifically, for each session A, we construct a vector timestamp SVC_A with $SVC_A[i]$ set equal to the maximum timestamp of all write operations in A that originate from server S_i:

$$SVC_A[j] = \max\{\ ts(W)\ |\ W \in A\ \&\ origin(W) = S_j\ \}$$

In other words, the timestamp of a session always represents the latest write operations that have been seen by the applications that are being executed as part of that session. The compactness is obtained by representing all observed write operations originating from the same server through a single timestamp.

As an example, suppose a client, as part of session A, logs in at server S_i. To that end, it passes SVC_A to S_i. Assume that $SVC_A[j] > WVC_i[j]$. What this means is that S_i has not yet seen all the writes originating from S_j that the client has seen. Depending on the required consistency, server S_i may now have to fetch these writes before being able to consistently report back to the client. Once the operation has been performed, server S_i will return its current timestamp WVC_i. At that point, SVC_A is adjusted to:

$$SVC_A[j] \leftarrow \max\{\ SVC_A[j], WVC_i[j]\}$$

Again, we see how vector timestamps can provide an elegant and compact way of representing history in a distributed system.

7.6 SUMMARY

There are primarily two reasons for replicating data: improving the reliability of a distributed system and improving performance. Replication introduces a consistency problem: whenever a replica is updated, that replica becomes different from the others. To keep replicas consistent, we need to propagate updates in such a way that temporary inconsistencies are not noticed. Unfortunately, doing so may severely degrade performance, especially in large-scale distributed systems.

The only solution to this problem is to relax consistency somewhat. Different consistency models exist. For continuous consistency, the goal is set to bounds to numerical deviation between replicas, staleness deviation, and deviations in the ordering of operations.

Numerical deviation refers to the value by which replicas may be different. This type of deviation is highly application dependent, but can, for example, be used in replication of stocks. Staleness deviation refers to the time by which a replica is still considered to be consistent, despite that updates may have taken place some time ago. Staleness deviation is often used for Web caches. Finally, ordering deviation refers to the maximum number of tentative writes that may be outstanding at any server without having synchronized with the other replica servers.

Consistent ordering of operations has since long formed the basis for many consistency models. Many variations exist, but only a few seem to prevail among application developers. Sequential consistency essentially provides the semantics that programmers expect in concurrent programming: all write operations are seen by everyone in the same order. Less used, but still relevant, is causal consistency, which reflects that operations that are potentially dependent on each other are carried out in the order of that dependency.

Weaker consistency models consider series of read and write operations. In particular, they assume that each series is appropriately "bracketed" by accompanying operations on synchronization variables, such as locks. Although this requires explicit effort from programmers, these models are generally easier to implement in an efficient way than, for example, pure sequential consistency.

As opposed to these data-centric models, researchers in the field of distributed databases for mobile users have defined a number of client-centric consistency models. Such models do not consider the fact that data may be shared by several users, but instead, concentrate on the consistency that an individual client should be offered. The underlying assumption is that a client connects to different replicas in the course of time, but that such differences should be made transparent. In essence, client-centric consistency models ensure that whenever a client connects to a new replica, that replica is brought up to date with the data that had been manipulated by that client before, and which may possibly reside at other replica sites.

To propagate updates, different techniques can be applied. A distinction needs to be made concerning *what* is exactly propagated, to *where* updates are propagated, and *by whom* propagation is initiated. We can decide to propagate notifications, operations, or state. Likewise, not every replica always needs to be updated immediately. Which replica is updated at which time depends on the distribution protocol. Finally, a choice can be made whether updates are pushed to other replicas, or that a replica pulls in updates from another replica.

Consistency protocols describe specific implementations of consistency models. With respect to sequential consistency and its variants, a distinction can be made between primary-based protocols and replicated-write protocols. In primary-based protocols, all update operations are forwarded to a primary copy that subsequently ensures the update is properly ordered and forwarded. In replicated-write protocols, an update is forwarded to several replicas at the same time. In that case, correctly ordering operations often becomes more difficult.

PROBLEMS

1. Access to shared Java objects can be serialized by declaring its methods as being synchronized. Is this enough to guarantee serialization when such an object is replicated?

2. Explain in your own words what the main reason is for actually considering weak consistency models.

3. Explain how replication in DNS takes place, and why it actually works so well.

4. During the discussion of consistency models, we often referred to the contract between the software and data store. Why is such a contract needed?

5. Given the replicas in Fig. 7-2, what would need to be done to finalize the values in the conit such that both A and B see the same result?

6. In Fig. 7-7, is 001110 a legal output for a sequentially consistent memory? Explain your answer.

7. It is often argued that weak consistency models impose an extra burden for programmers. To what extent is this statement actually true?

8. Does totally-ordered multicasting by means of a sequencer and for the sake of consistency in active replication, violate the end-to-end argument in system design?

9. What kind of consistency would you use to implement an electronic stock market? Explain your answer.

10. Consider a personal mailbox for a mobile user, implemented as part of a wide-area distributed database. What kind of client-centric consistency would be most appropriate?

11. Describe a simple implementation of read-your-writes consistency for displaying Web pages that have just been updated.

12. To make matters simple, we assumed that there were no write-write conflicts in Bayou. Of course, this is an unrealistic assumption. Explain how conflicts may happen.

13. When using a lease, is it necessary that the clocks of a client and the server, respectively, are tightly synchronized?

14. We have stated that totally-ordered multicasting using Lamport's logical clocks does not scale. Explain why.

15. Show that, in the case of continuous consistency, having a server S_k advance its view $TW_k(i,k)$ whenever it receives a fresh update that would increase $TW(k,k) - TW_k(i,k)$ beyond $\delta_i / N - 1$), ensures that $v(t) - v_i \leq \delta_i$.

16. For continuous consistency, we have assumed that each write only increases the value of data item x. Sketch a solution in which it is also possible to decrease x's value.

17. Consider a nonblocking primary-backup protocol used to guarantee sequential consistency in a distributed data store. Does such a data store always provide read-your-writes consistency?

18. For active replication to work in general, it is necessary that all operations be carried out in the same order at each replica. Is this ordering always necessary?

19. To implement totally-ordered multicasting by means of a sequencer, one approach is to first forward an operation to the sequencer, which then assigns it a unique number and subsequently multicasts the operation. Mention two alternative approaches, and compare the three solutions.

20. A file is replicated on 10 servers. List all the combinations of read quorum and write quorum that are permitted by the voting algorithm.

21. State-based leases are used to offload a server by letting it allow to keep track of as few clients as needed. Will this approach necessarily lead to better performance?

22. **(Lab assignment)** For this exercise, you are to implement a simple system that supports multicast RPC. We assume that there are multiple, replicated servers and that each client communicates with a server through an RPC. However, when dealing with replication, a client will need to send an RPC request to each replica. Program the client such that to the application it appears as if a single RPC is sent. Assume you are replicating for performance, but that servers are susceptible to failures.

8

FAULT TOLERANCE

A characteristic feature of distributed systems that distinguishes them from single-machine systems is the notion of partial failure. A partial failure may happen when one component in a distributed system fails. This failure may affect the proper operation of other components, while at the same time leaving yet other components totally unaffected. In contrast, a failure in nondistributed systems is often total in the sense that it affects all components, and may easily bring down the entire system.

An important goal in distributed systems design is to construct the system in such a way that it can automatically recover from partial failures without seriously affecting the overall performance. In particular, whenever a failure occurs, the distributed system should continue to operate in an acceptable way while repairs are being made, that is, it should tolerate faults and continue to operate to some extent even in their presence.

In this chapter, we take a closer look at techniques for making distributed systems fault tolerant. After providing some general background on fault tolerance, we will look at process resilience and reliable multicasting. Process resilience incorporates techniques by which one or more processes can fail without seriously disturbing the rest of the system. Related to this issue is reliable multicasting, by which message transmission to a collection of processes is guaranteed to succeed. Reliable multicasting is often necessary to keep processes synchronized.

Atomicity is a property that is important in many applications. For example, in distributed transactions, it is necessary to guarantee that every operation in a transaction is carried out or none of them are. Fundamental to atomicity in distributed systems is the notion of distributed commit protocols, which are discussed in a separate section in this chapter.

Finally, we will examine how to recover from a failure. In particular, we consider when and how the state of a distributed system should be saved to allow recovery to that state later on.

8.1 INTRODUCTION TO FAULT TOLERANCE

Fault tolerance has been subject to much research in computer science. In this section, we start with presenting the basic concepts related to processing failures, followed by a discussion of failure models. The key technique for handling failures is redundancy, which is also discussed. For more general information on fault tolerance in distributed systems, see, for example Jalote (1994) or (Shooman, 2002).

8.1.1 Basic Concepts

To understand the role of fault tolerance in distributed systems we first need to take a closer look at what it actually means for a distributed system to tolerate faults. Being fault tolerant is strongly related to what are called **dependable systems**. Dependability is a term that covers a number of useful requirements for distributed systems including the following (Kopetz and Verissimo, 1993):

1. Availability

2. Reliability

3. Safety

4. Maintainability

Availability is defined as the property that a system is ready to be used immediately. In general, it refers to the probability that the system is operating correctly at any given moment and is available to perform its functions on behalf of its users. In other words, a highly available system is one that will most likely be working at a given instant in time.

Reliability refers to the property that a system can run continuously without failure. In contrast to availability, reliability is defined in terms of a time interval instead of an instant in time. A highly-reliable system is one that will most likely continue to work without interruption during a relatively long period of time. This is a subtle but important difference when compared to availability. If a system goes down for one millisecond every hour, it has an availability of over 99.9999 percent, but is still highly unreliable. Similarly, a system that never crashes but is shut down for two weeks every August has high reliability but only 96 percent availability. The two are not the same.

Safety refers to the situation that when a system temporarily fails to operate correctly, nothing catastrophic happens. For example, many process control systems, such as those used for controlling nuclear power plants or sending people into space, are required to provide a high degree of safety. If such control systems temporarily fail for only a very brief moment, the effects could be disastrous. Many examples from the past (and probably many more yet to come) show how hard it is to build safe systems.

Finally, **maintainability** refers to how easy a failed system can be repaired. A highly maintainable system may also show a high degree of availability, especially if failures can be detected and repaired automatically. However, as we shall see later in this chapter, automatically recovering from failures is easier said than done.

Often, dependable systems are also required to provide a high degree of security, especially when it comes to issues such as integrity. We will discuss security in the next chapter.

A system is said to **fail** when it cannot meet its promises. In particular, if a distributed system is designed to provide its users with a number of services, the system has failed when one or more of those services cannot be (completely) provided. An **error** is a part of a system's state that may lead to a failure. For example, when transmitting packets across a network, it is to be expected that some packets have been damaged when they arrive at the receiver. Damaged in this context means that the receiver may incorrectly sense a bit value (e.g., reading a 1 instead of a 0), or may even be unable to detect that something has arrived.

The cause of an error is called a **fault**. Clearly, finding out what caused an error is important. For example, a wrong or bad transmission medium may easily cause packets to be damaged. In this case, it is relatively easy to remove the fault. However, transmission errors may also be caused by bad weather conditions such as in wireless networks. Changing the weather to reduce or prevent errors is a bit trickier.

Building dependable systems closely relates to controlling faults. A distinction can be made between preventing, removing, and forecasting faults (Avizienis et al., 2004). For our purposes, the most important issue is **fault tolerance**, meaning that a system can provide its services even in the presence of faults. In other words, the system can tolerate faults and continue to operate normally.

Faults are generally classified as transient, intermittent, or permanent. **Transient faults** occur once and then disappear. If the operation is repeated, the fault goes away. A bird flying through the beam of a microwave transmitter may cause lost bits on some network (not to mention a roasted bird). If the transmission times out and is retried, it will probably work the second time.

An **intermittent fault** occurs, then vanishes of its own accord, then reappears, and so on. A loose contact on a connector will often cause an intermittent fault.

Intermittent faults cause a great deal of aggravation because they are difficult to diagnose. Typically, when the fault doctor shows up, the system works fine.

A **permanent fault** is one that continues to exist until the faulty component is replaced. Burnt-out chips, software bugs, and disk head crashes are examples of permanent faults.

8.1.2 Failure Models

A system that fails is not adequately providing the services it was designed for. If we consider a distributed system as a collection of servers that communicate with one another and with their clients, not adequately providing services means that servers, communication channels, or possibly both, are not doing what they are supposed to do. However, a malfunctioning server itself may not always be the fault we are looking for. If such a server depends on other servers to adequately provide its services, the cause of an error may need to be searched for somewhere else.

Such dependency relations appear in abundance in distributed systems. A failing disk may make life difficult for a file server that is designed to provide a highly available file system. If such a file server is part of a distributed database, the proper working of the entire database may be at stake, as only part of its data may be accessible.

To get a better grasp on how serious a failure actually is, several classification schemes have been developed. One such scheme is shown in Fig. 8-1, and is based on schemes described in Cristian (1991) and Hadzilacos and Toueg (1993).

Type of failure	Description
Crash failure	A server halts, but is working correctly until it halts
Omission failure	A server fails to respond to incoming requests
Receive omission	A server fails to receive incoming messages
Send omission	A server fails to send messages
Timing failure	A server's response lies outside the specified time interval
Response failure	A server's response is incorrect
Value failure	The value of the response is wrong
State transition failure	The server deviates from the correct flow of control
Arbitrary failure	A server may produce arbitrary responses at arbitrary times

Figure 8-1. Different types of failures.

A **crash failure** occurs when a server prematurely halts, but was working correctly until it stopped. An important aspect of crash failures is that once the server has halted, nothing is heard from it anymore. A typical example of a crash failure is an operating system that comes to a grinding halt, and for which there is only one solution: reboot it. Many personal computer systems suffer from crash failures so often that people have come to expect them to be normal. Consequently, moving the reset button from the back of a cabinet to the front was done for good reason. Perhaps one day it can be moved to the back again, or even removed altogether.

An **omission failure** occurs when a server fails to respond to a request. Several things might go wrong. In the case of a receive omission failure, possibly the server never got the request in the first place. Note that it may well be the case that the connection between a client and a server has been correctly established, but that there was no thread listening to incoming requests. Also, a receive omission failure will generally not affect the current state of the server, as the server is unaware of any message sent to it.

Likewise, a send omission failure happens when the server has done its work, but somehow fails in sending a response. Such a failure may happen, for example, when a send buffer overflows while the server was not prepared for such a situation. Note that, in contrast to a receive omission failure, the server may now be in a state reflecting that it has just completed a service for the client. As a consequence, if the sending of its response fails, the server has to be prepared for the client to reissue its previous request.

Other types of omission failures not related to communication may be caused by software errors such as infinite loops or improper memory management by which the server is said to "hang."

Another class of failures is related to timing. **Timing failures** occur when the response lies outside a specified real-time interval. As we saw with isochronous data streams in Chap. 4, providing data too soon may easily cause trouble for a recipient if there is not enough buffer space to hold all the incoming data. More common, however, is that a server responds too late, in which case a *performance failure* is said to occur.

A serious type of failure is a **response failure**, by which the server's response is simply incorrect. Two kinds of response failures may happen. In the case of a value failure, a server simply provides the wrong reply to a request. For example, a search engine that systematically returns Web pages not related to any of the search terms used, has failed.

The other type of response failure is known as a **state transition failure**. This kind of failure happens when the server reacts unexpectedly to an incoming request. For example, if a server receives a message it cannot recognize, a state transition failure happens if no measures have been taken to handle such messages. In particular, a faulty server may incorrectly take default actions it should never have initiated.

The most serious are **arbitrary failures**, also known as **Byzantine failures**. In effect, when arbitrary failures occur, clients should be prepared for the worst. In particular, it may happen that a server is producing output it should never have produced, but which cannot be detected as being incorrect Worse yet a faulty server may even be maliciously working together with other servers to produce intentionally wrong answers. This situation illustrates why security is also considered an important requirement when talking about dependable systems. The term "Byzantine" refers to the Byzantine Empire, a time (330–1453) and place (the Balkans and modern Turkey) in which endless conspiracies, intrigue, and untruthfulness were alleged to be common in ruling circles. Byzantine faults were first analyzed by Pease et al. (1980) and Lamport et al. (1982). We return to such failures below.

Arbitrary failures are closely related to crash failures. The definition of crash failures as presented above is the most benign way for a server to halt. They are also referred to as **fail-stop failures**. In effect, a fail-stop server will simply stop producing output in such a way that its halting can be detected by other processes. In the best case, the server may have been so friendly to announce it is about to crash; otherwise it simply stops.

Of course, in real life, servers halt by exhibiting omission or crash failures, and are not so friendly as to announce in advance that they are going to stop. It is up to the other processes to decide that a server has prematurely halted. However, in such **fail-silent systems**, the other process may incorrectly conclude that a server has halted. Instead, the server may just be unexpectedly slow, that is, it is exhibiting performance failures.

Finally, there are also occasions in which the server is producing random output, but this output can be recognized by other processes as plain junk. The server is then exhibiting arbitrary failures, but in a benign way. These faults are also referred to as being **fail-safe**.

8.1.3 Failure Masking by Redundancy

If a system is to be fault tolerant, the best it can do is to try to hide the occurrence of failures from other processes. The key technique for masking faults is to use redundancy. Three kinds are possible: information redundancy, time redundancy, and physical redundancy [see also Johnson (1995)]. With information redundancy, extra bits are added to allow recovery from garbled bits. For example, a Hamming code can be added to transmitted data to recover from noise on the transmission line.

With time redundancy, an action is performed, and then, if need be, it is performed again. Transactions (see Chap. 1) use this approach. If a transaction aborts, it can be redone with no harm. Time redundancy is especially helpful when the faults are transient or intermittent.

With physical redundancy, extra equipment or processes are added to make it possible for the system as a whole to tolerate the loss or malfunctioning of some components. Physical redundancy can thus be done either in hardware or in software. For example, extra processes can be added to the system so that if a small number of them crash, the system can still function correctly. In other words, by replicating processes, a high degree of fault tolerance may be achieved. We return to this type of software redundancy below.

Physical redundancy is a well-known technique for providing fault tolerance. It is used in biology (mammals have two eyes, two ears, two lungs, etc.), aircraft (747s have four engines but can fly on three), and sports (multiple referees in case one misses an event). It has also been used for fault tolerance in electronic circuits for years; it is illustrative to see how it has been applied there. Consider, for example, the circuit of Fig. 8-2(a). Here signals pass through devices A, B, and C, in sequence. If one of them is faulty, the final result will probably be incorrect.

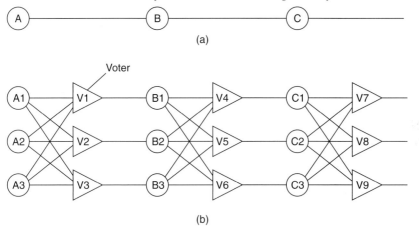

Figure 8-2. Triple modular redundancy.

In Fig. 8-2(b), each device is replicated three times. Following each stage in the circuit is a triplicated voter. Each voter is a circuit that has three inputs and one output. If two or three of the inputs are the same, the output is equal to that input. If all three inputs are different, the output is undefined. This kind of design is known as **TMR** (**Triple Modular Redundancy**).

Suppose that element A_2 fails. Each of the voters, V_1, V_2, and V_3 gets two good (identical) inputs and one rogue input, and each of them outputs the correct value to the second stage. In essence, the effect of A_2 failing is completely masked, so that the inputs to B_1, B_2, and B_3 are exactly the same as they would have been had no fault occurred.

Now consider what happens if B_3 and C_1 are also faulty, in addition to A_2. These effects are also masked, so the three final outputs are still correct.

At first it may not be obvious why three voters are needed at each stage. After all, one voter could also detect and pass though the majority view. However, a voter is also a component and can also be faulty. Suppose, for example, that voter V_1 malfunctions. The input to B_1 will then be wrong, but as long as everything else works, B_2 and B_3 will produce the same output and V_4, V_5, and V_6 will all produce the correct result into stage three. A fault in V_1 is effectively no different than a fault in B_1. In both cases B_1 produces incorrect output, but in both cases it is voted down later and the final result is still correct.

Although not all fault-tolerant distributed systems use TMR, the technique is very general, and should give a clear feeling for what a fault-tolerant system is, as opposed to a system whose individual components are highly reliable but whose organization cannot tolerate faults (i.e., operate correctly even in the presence of faulty components). Of course, TMR can be applied recursively, for example, to make a chip highly reliable by using TMR inside it, unknown to the designers who use the chip, possibly in their own circuit containing multiple copies of the chips along with voters.

8.2 PROCESS RESILIENCE

Now that the basic issues of fault tolerance have been discussed, let us concentrate on how fault tolerance can actually be achieved in distributed systems. The first topic we discuss is protection against process failures, which is achieved by replicating processes into groups. In the following pages, we consider the general design issues of process groups, and discuss what a fault-tolerant group actually is. Also, we look at how to reach agreement within a process group when one or more of its members cannot be trusted to give correct answers.

8.2.1 Design Issues

The key approach to tolerating a faulty process is to organize several identical processes into a group. The key property that all groups have is that when a message is sent to the group itself, all members of the group receive it. In this way, if one process in a group fails, hopefully some other process can take over for it (Guerraoui and Schiper, 1997).

Process groups may be dynamic. New groups can be created and old groups can be destroyed. A process can join a group or leave one during system operation. A process can be a member of several groups at the same time. Consequently, mechanisms are needed for managing groups and group membership.

Groups are roughly analogous to social organizations. Alice might be a member of a book club, a tennis club, and an environmental organization. On a particular day, she might receive mailings (messages) announcing a new birthday cake cookbook from the book club, the annual Mother's Day tennis tournament from the tennis club, and the start of a campaign to save the Southern groundhog from the environmental organization. At any moment, she is free to leave any or all of these groups, and possibly join other groups.

The purpose of introducing groups is to allow processes to deal with collections of processes as a single abstraction. Thus a process can send a message to a group of servers without having to know who they are or how many there are or where they are, which may change from one call to the next.

Flat Groups versus Hierarchical Groups

An important distinction between different groups has to do with their internal structure. In some groups, all the processes are equal. No one is boss and all decisions are made collectively. In other groups, some kind of hierarchy exists. For example, one process is the coordinator and all the others are workers. In this model, when a request for work is generated, either by an external client or by one of the workers, it is sent to the coordinator. The coordinator then decides which worker is best suited to carry it out, and forwards it there. More complex hierarchies are also possible, of course. These communication patterns are illustrated in Fig. 8-3.

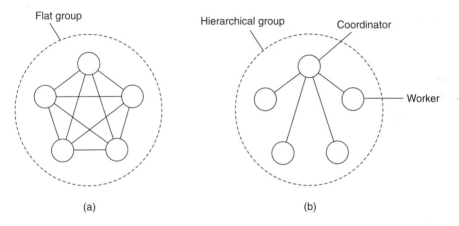

Figure 8-3. (a) Communication in a flat group. (b) Communication in a simple hierarchical group.

Each of these organizations has its own advantages and disadvantages. The flat group is symmetrical and has no single point of failure. If one of the processes crashes, the group simply becomes smaller, but can otherwise continue. A disadvantage is that decision making is more complicated. For example, to decide anything, a vote often has to be taken, incurring some delay and overhead.

The hierarchical group has the opposite properties. Loss of the coordinator brings the entire group to a grinding halt, but as long as it is running, it can make decisions without bothering everyone else.

Group Membership

When group communication is present, some method is needed for creating and deleting groups, as well as for allowing processes to join and leave groups. One possible approach is to have a **group server** to which all these requests can be sent. The group server can then maintain a complete data base of all the groups and their exact membership. This method is straightforward, efficient, and fairly easy to implement. Unfortunately, it shares a major disadvantage with all centralized techniques: a single point of failure. If the group server crashes, group management ceases to exist. Probably most or all groups will have to be reconstructed from scratch, possibly terminating whatever work was going on.

The opposite approach is to manage group membership in a distributed way. For example, if (reliable) multicasting is available, an outsider can send a message to all group members announcing its wish to join the group .

Ideally, to leave a group, a member just sends a goodbye message to everyone. In the context of fault tolerance, assuming fail-stop semantics is generally not appropriate. The trouble is, there is no polite announcement that a process crashes as there is when a process leaves voluntarily. The other members have to discover this experimentally by noticing that the crashed member no longer responds to anything. Once it is certain that the crashed member is really down (and not just slow), it can be removed from the group.

Another knotty issue is that leaving and joining have to be synchronous with data messages being sent. In other words, starting at the instant that a process has joined a group, it must receive all messages sent to that group. Similarly, as soon as a process has left a group, it must not receive any more messages from the group, and the other members must not receive any more messages from it. One way of making sure that a join or leave is integrated into the message stream at the right place is to convert this operation into a sequence of messages sent to the whole group.

One final issue relating to group membership is what to do if so many machines go down that the group can no longer function at all. Some protocol is needed to rebuild the group. Invariably, some process will have to take the initiative to start the ball rolling, but what happens if two or three try at the same time? The protocol must to be able to withstand this.

8.2.2 Failure Masking and Replication

Process groups are part of the solution for building fault-tolerant systems. In particular, having a group of identical processes allows us to mask one or more faulty processes in that group. In other words, we can replicate processes and organize them into a group to replace a single (vulnerable) process with a (fault tolerant) group. As discussed in the previous chapter, there are two ways to approach such replication: by means of primary-based protocols, or through replicated-write protocols.

Primary-based replication in the case of fault tolerance generally appears in the form of a primary-backup protocol. In this case, a group of processes is organized in a hierarchical fashion in which a primary coordinates all write operations. In practice, the primary is fixed, although its role can be taken over by one of the backups, if need be. In effect, when the primary crashes, the backups execute some election algorithm to choose a new primary.

As we explained in the previous chapter, replicated-write protocols are used in the form of active replication, as well as by means of quorum-based protocols. These solutions correspond to organizing a collection of identical processes into a flat group. The main advantage is that such groups have no single point of failure, at the cost of distributed coordination.

An important issue with using process groups to tolerate faults is how much replication is needed. To simplify our discussion, let us consider only replicated-write systems. A system is said to be **k fault tolerant** if it can survive faults in k components and still meet its specifications. If the components, say processes, fail silently, then having $k + 1$ of them is enough to provide k fault tolerance. If k of them simply stop, then the answer from the other one can be used.

On the other hand, if processes exhibit Byzantine failures, continuing to run when sick and sending out erroneous or random replies, a minimum of $2k + 1$ processors are needed to achieve k fault tolerance. In the worst case, the k failing processes could accidentally (or even intentionally) generate the same reply. However, the remaining $k + 1$ will also produce the same answer, so the client or voter can just believe the majority.

Of course, in theory it is fine to say that a system is k fault tolerant and just let the $k + 1$ identical replies outvote the k identical replies, but in practice it is hard to imagine circumstances in which one can say with certainty that k processes can fail but $k + 1$ processes cannot fail. Thus even in a fault-tolerant system some kind of statistical analysis may be needed.

An implicit precondition for this model to be relevant is that all requests arrive at all servers in the same order, also called the **atomic multicast problem**. Actually, this condition can be relaxed slightly, since reads do not matter and some writes may commute, but the general problem remains. Atomic multicasting is discussed in detail in a later section.

8.2.3 Agreement in Faulty Systems

Organizing replicated processes into a group helps to increase fault tolerance. As we mentioned, if a client can base its decisions through a voting mechanism, we can even tolerate that k out of $2k + 1$ processes are lying about their result. The assumption we are making, however, is that processes do not team up to produce a wrong result.

In general, matters become more intricate if we demand that a process group reaches an agreement, which is needed in many cases. Some examples are: electing a coordinator, deciding whether or not to commit a transaction, dividing up tasks among workers, and synchronization, among numerous other possibilities. When the communication and processes are all perfect, reaching such agreement is often straightforward, but when they are not, problems arise.

The general goal of distributed agreement algorithms is to have all the non-faulty processes reach consensus on some issue, and to establish that consensus within a finite number of steps. The problem is complicated by the fact that different assumptions about the underlying system require different solutions, assuming solutions even exist. Turek and Shasha (1992) distinguish the following cases,

1. Synchronous versus asynchronous systems. A system is **synchronous** if and only if the processes are known to operate in a lock-step mode. Formally, this means that there should be some constant $c \geq 1$, such that if any processor has taken $c + 1$ steps, every other process has taken at least 1 step. A system that is not synchronous is said to be **asynchronous.**

2. Communication delay is bounded or not. Delay is bounded if and only if we know that every message is delivered with a globally and predetermined maximum time.

3. Message delivery is ordered or not. In other words, we distinguish the situation where messages from the same sender are delivered in the order that they were sent, from the situation in which we do not have such guarantees.

4. Message transmission is done through unicasting or multicasting.

As it turns out, reaching agreement is only possible for the situations shown in Fig. 8-4. In all other cases, it can be shown that no solution exists. Note that most distributed systems in practice assume that processes behave asynchronously, message transmission is unicast, and communication delays are unbounded. As a consequence, we need to make use of ordered (reliable) message delivery, such as provided as by TCP. Fig. 8-4 illustrates the nontrivial nature of distributed agreement when processes may fail.

The problem was originally studied by Lamport et al. (1982) and is also known as the **Byzantine agreement problem**, referring to the numerous wars in which several armies needed to reach agreement on, for example, troop strengths while being faced with traitorous generals, conniving lieutenants, and so on. Consider the following solution, described in Lamport et al. (1982). In this case, we assume that processes are synchronous, messages are unicast while preserving ordering, and communication delay is bounded. We assume that there are N processes, where each process i will provide a value v_i to the others. The goal is let each process construct a vector V of length N, such that if process i is nonfaulty, $V[i] = v_i$. Otherwise, $V[i]$ is undefined. We assume that there are at most k faulty processes.

In Fig. 8-5 we illustrate the working of the algorithm for the case of $N = 4$ and $k = 1$. For these parameters, the algorithm operates in four steps. In step 1, every

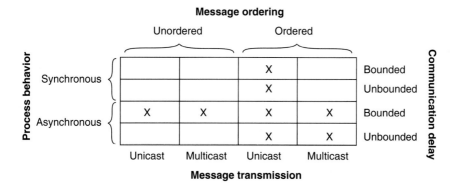

Figure 8-4. Circumstances under which distributed agreement can be reached.

nonfaulty process i sends v_i to every other process using reliable unicasting. Faulty processes may send anything. Moreover, because we are using multicasting, they may send different values to different processes. Let $v_i = i$. In Fig. 8-5(a) we see that process 1 reports 1, process 2 reports 2, process 3 lies to everyone, giving x, y, and z, respectively, and process 4 reports a value of 4. In step 2, the results of the announcements of step 1 are collected together in the form of the vectors of Fig. 8-5(b).

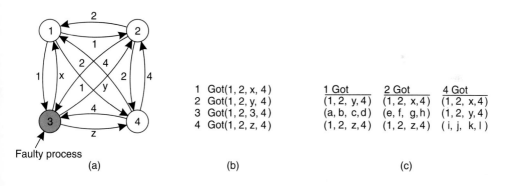

Figure 8-5. The Byzantine agreement problem for three nonfaulty and one faulty process. (a) Each process sends their value to the others. (b) The vectors that each process assembles based on (a). (c) The vectors that each process receives in step 3.

Step 3 consists of every process passing its vector from Fig. 8-5(b) to every other process. In this way, every process gets three vectors, one from every other process. Here, too, process 3 lies, inventing 12 new values, a through l. The results of step 3 are shown in Fig. 8-5(c). Finally, in step 4, each process examines the ith element of each of the newly received vectors. If any value has a majority, that value is put into the result vector. If no value has a majority, the corresponding element of the result vector is marked *UNKNOWN*. From Fig. 8-5(c) we see that 1, 2, and 4 all come to agreement on the values for v_1, v_2, and v_4, which is the correct result. What these processes conclude regarding v_3 cannot be decided, but is also irrelevant. The goal of Byzantine agreement is that consensus is reached on the value for the nonfaulty processes only.

Now let us revisit this problem for $N = 3$ and $k = 1$, that is, only two nonfaulty process and one faulty one, as illustrated in Fig. 8-6. Here we see that in Fig. 8-6(c) neither of the correctly behaving processes sees a majority for element 1, element 2, or element 3, so all of them are marked *UNKNOWN*. The algorithm has failed to produce agreement.

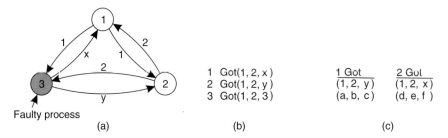

Figure 8-6. The same as Fig. 8-5, except now with two correct process and one faulty process.

In their paper, Lamport et al. (1982) proved that in a system with k faulty processes, agreement can be achieved only if $2k + 1$ correctly functioning processes are present, for a total of $3k + 1$. Put in slightly different terms, agreement is possible only if *more* than two-thirds of the processes are working properly.

Another way of looking at this problem, is as follows. Basically, what we need to achieve is a majority vote among a group of nonfaulty processes regardless of whether there are also faulty ones among their midsts. If there are k faulty processes, we need to ensure that their vote, along with that of any correct process who have been mislead by the faulty ones, still corresponds to the majority vote of the nonfaulty processes. With $2k + 1$ nonfaulty processes, this can be achieved by requiring that agreement is reached only if more than two-thirds of the votes are the same. In other words, if more than two-thirds of the processes agree on the same decision, this decision corresponds to the same majority vote by the group of nonfaulty processes.

However, reaching agreement can be even worse. Fischer et al. (1985) proved that in a distributed system in which messages cannot be guaranteed to be delivered within a known, finite time, no agreement is possible if even one process is faulty (albeit if that one process fails silently). The problem with such systems is that arbitrarily slow processes are indistinguishable from crashed ones (i.e., you cannot tell the dead from the living). Many other theoretical results are known about when agreement is possible and when it is not. Surveys of these results are given in Barborak et al. (1993) and Turek and Shasha (1992).

It should also be noted that the schemes described so far assume that nodes are either Byzantine, or collaborative. The latter cannot always be simply assumed when processes are from different administrative domains. In that case, they will more likely exhibit *rational* behavior, for example, by reporting timeouts when doing so is cheaper than executing an update operation. How to deal with these cases is not trivial. A first step toward a solution is captured in the form of **BAR fault tolerance**, which stands for Byzantine, Altruism, and Rationality. BAR fault tolerance is described in Aiyer et al. (2005).

8.2.4 Failure Detection

It may have become clear from our discussions so far that in order to properly mask failures, we generally need to detect them as well. Failure detection is one of the cornerstones of fault tolerance in distributed systems. What it all boils down to is that for a group of processes, nonfaulty members should be able to decide who is still a member, and who is not. In other words, we need to be able to detect when a member has failed.

When it comes to detecting process failures, there are essentially only two mechanisms. Either processes actively send "are you alive?" messages to each other (for which they obviously expect an answer), or passively wait until messages come in from different processes. The latter approach makes sense only when it can be guaranteed that there is enough communication between processes. In practice, actively **pinging** processes is usually followed.

There has been a huge body of theoretical work on failure detectors. What it all boils down to is that a timeout mechanism is used to check whether a process has failed. In real settings, there are two major problems with this approach. First, due to unreliable networks, simply stating that a process has failed because it does not return an answer to a ping message may be wrong. In other words, it is quite easy to generate false positives. If a false positive has the effect that a perfectly healthy process is removed from a membership list, then clearly we are doing something wrong.

Another serious problem is that timeouts are just plain crude. As noticed by Birman (2005), there is hardly any work on building proper failure detection subsystems that take more into account than only the lack of a reply to a single message. This statement is even more evident when looking at industry-deployed distributed systems.

There are various issues that need to be taken into account when designing a failure detection subsystem [see also Zhuang et al. (2005)]. For example, failure detection can take place through gossiping in which each node regularly announces to its neighbors that it is still up and running. As we mentioned, an alternative is to let nodes actively probe each other.

Failure detection can also be done as a side-effect of regularly exchanging information with neighbors, as is the case with gossip-based information dissemination (which we discussed in Chap. 4). This approach is essentially also adopted in Obduro (Vogels, 2003): processes periodically gossip their service availability. This information is gradually disseminated through the network by gossiping. Eventually, every process will know about every other process, but more importantly, will have enough information locally available to decide whether a process has failed or not. A member for which the availability information is old, will presumably have failed.

Another important issue is that a failure detection subsystem should ideally be able to distinguish network failures from node failures. One way of dealing with this problem is not to let a single node decide whether one of its neighbors has crashed. Instead, when noticing a timeout on a ping message, a node requests other neighbors to see whether they can reach the presumed failing node. Of course, positive information can also be shared: if a node is still alive, that information can be forwarded to other interested parties (who may be detecting a link failure to the suspected node).

This brings us to another key issue: when a member failure is detected, how should other nonfaulty processes be informed? One simple, and somewhat radical approach is the one followed in FUSE (Dunagan et al., 2004). In FUSE, processes can be joined in a group that spans a wide-area network. The group members create a spanning tree that is used for monitoring member failures. Members send ping messages to their neighbors. When a neighbor does not respond, the pinging node immediately switches to a state in which it will also no longer respond to pings from other nodes. By recursion, it is seen that a single node failure is rapidly promoted to a group failure notification. FUSE does not suffer a lot from link failures for the simple reason that it relies on point-to-point TCP connections between group members.

8.3 RELIABLE CLIENT-SERVER COMMUNICATION

In many cases, fault tolerance in distributed systems concentrates on faulty processes. However, we also need to consider communication failures. Most of the failure models discussed previously apply equally well to communication channels. In particular, a communication channel may exhibit crash, omission, timing, and arbitrary failures. In practice, when building reliable communication channels, the focus is on masking crash and omission failures. Arbitrary failures may occur in the form of duplicate messages, resulting from the fact that in a computer network messages may be buffered for a relatively long time, and are reinjected into the network after the original sender has already issued a retransmission [see, for example, Tanenbaum, 2003)].

8.3.1 Point-to-Point Communication

In many distributed systems, reliable point-to-point communication is established by making use of a reliable transport protocol, such as TCP. TCP masks omission failures, which occur in the form of lost messages, by using acknowledgments and retransmissions. Such failures are completely hidden from a TCP client.

However, crash failures of connections are not masked. A crash failure may occur when (for whatever reason) a TCP connection is abruptly broken so that no more messages can be transmitted through the channel. In most cases, the client is informed that the channel has crashed by raising an exception. The only way to mask such failures is to let the distributed system attempt to automatically set up a new connection, by simply resending a connection request. The underlying assumption is that the other side is still, or again, responsive to such requests.

8.3.2 RPC Semantics in the Presence of Failures

Let us now take a closer look at client-server communication when using high-level communication facilities such as Remote Procedure Calls (RPCs). The goal of RPC is to hide communication by making remote procedure calls look just like local ones. With a few exceptions, so far we have come fairly close. Indeed, as long as both client and server are functioning perfectly, RPC does its job well. The problem comes about when errors occur. It is then that the differences between local and remote calls are not always easy to mask.

To structure our discussion, let us distinguish between five different classes of failures that can occur in RPC systems, as follows:

1. The client is unable to locate the server.

2. The request message from the client to the server is lost.

3. The server crashes after receiving a request.

4. The reply message from the server to the client is lost.

5. The client crashes after sending a request.

Each of these categories poses different problems and requires different solutions.

Client Cannot Locate the Server

To start with, it can happen that the client cannot locate a suitable server. All servers might be down, for example. Alternatively, suppose that the client is compiled using a particular version of the client stub, and the binary is not used for a considerable period of time. In the meantime, the server evolves and a new version of the interface is installed; new stubs are generated and put into use. When the client is eventually run, the binder will be unable to match it up with a server and will report failure. While this mechanism is used to protect the client from accidentally trying to talk to a server that may not agree with it in terms of what parameters are required or what it is supposed to do, the problem remains of how should this failure be dealt with.

One possible solution is to have the error raise an **exception**. In some languages, (e.g., Java), programmers can write special procedures that are invoked upon specific errors, such as division by zero. In C, signal handlers can be used for this purpose. In other words, we could define a new signal type *SIGNO-SERVER*, and allow it to be handled in the same way as other signals.

This approach, too, has drawbacks. To start with, not every language has exceptions or signals. Another point is that having to write an exception or signal handler destroys the transparency we have been trying to achieve. Suppose that you are a programmer and your boss tells you to write the sum procedure. You smile and tell her it will be written, tested, and documented in five minutes. Then she mentions that you also have to write an exception handler as well, just in case the procedure is not there today. At this point it is pretty hard to maintain the illusion that remote procedures are no different from local ones, since writing an exception handler for "Cannot locate server" would be a rather unusual request in a single-processor system. So much for transparency.

Lost Request Messages

The second item on the list is dealing with lost request messages. This is the easiest one to deal with: just have the operating system or client stub start a timer when sending the request. If the timer expires before a reply or acknowledgment comes back, the message is sent again. If the message was truly lost, the server will not be able to tell the difference between the retransmission and the original, and everything will work fine. Unless, of course, so many request messages are lost that the client gives up and falsely concludes that the server is down, in which case we are back to "Cannot locate server." If the request was not lost, the only thing we need to do is let the server be able to detect it is dealing with a retransmission. Unfortunately, doing so is not so simple, as we explain when discussing lost replies.

Server Crashes

The next failure on the list is a server crash. The normal sequence of events at a server is shown in Fig. 8-7(a). A request arrives, is carried out, and a reply is sent. Now consider Fig. 8-7(b). A request arrives and is carried out, just as before, but the server crashes before it can send the reply. Finally, look at Fig. 8-7(c). Again a request arrives, but this time the server crashes before it can even be carried out. And, of course, no reply is sent back.

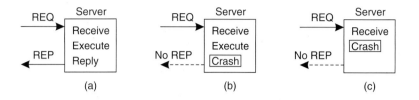

Figure 8-7. A server in client-server communication. (a) The normal case. (b) Crash after execution. (c) Crash before execution.

The annoying part of Fig. 8-7 is that the correct treatment differs for (b) and (c). In (b) the system has to report failure back to the client (e.g., raise an exception), whereas in (c) it can just retransmit the request. The problem is that the client's operating system cannot tell which is which. All it knows is that its timer has expired.

Three schools of thought exist on what to do here (Spector, 1982). One philosophy is to wait until the server reboots (or rebind to a new server) and try the operation again. The idea is to keep trying until a reply has been received, then give it to the client. This technique is called **at least once semantics** and guarantees that the RPC has been carried out at least one time, but possibly more.

The second philosophy gives up immediately and reports back failure. This way is called **at-most-once semantics** and guarantees that the RPC has been carried out at most one time, but possibly none at all.

The third philosophy is to guarantee nothing. When a server crashes, the client gets no help and no promises about what happened. The RPC may have been carried out anywhere from zero to a large number of times. The main virtue of this scheme is that it is easy to implement.

None of these are terribly attractive. What one would like is **exactly once semantics**, but in general, there is no way to arrange this. Imagine that the remote operation consists of printing some text, and that the server sends a completion message to the client when the text is printed. Also assume that when a client issues a request, it receives an acknowledgment that the request has been delivered to the server. There are two strategies the server can follow. It can either send a completion message just before it actually tells the printer to do its work, or after the text has been printed.

Assume that the server crashes and subsequently recovers. It announces to all clients that it has just crashed but is now up and running again. The problem is that the client does not know whether its request to print some text will actually be carried out.

There are four strategies the client can follow. First, the client can decide to *never* reissue a request, at the risk that the text will not be printed. Second, it can decide to *always* reissue a request, but this may lead to its text being printed twice. Third, it can decide to reissue a request only if it did not yet receive an acknowledgment that its print request had been delivered to the server. In that case, the client is counting on the fact that the server crashed before the print request could be delivered. The fourth and last strategy is to reissue a request only if it has received an acknowledgment for the print request.

With two strategies for the server, and four for the client, there are a total of eight combinations to consider. Unfortunately, no combination is satisfactory. To explain, note that there are three events that can happen at the server: send the completion message (M), print the text (P), and crash (C). These events can occur in six different orderings:

1. $M \to P \to C$: A crash occurs after sending the completion message and printing the text.

2. $M \to C(\to P)$: A crash happens after sending the completion message, but before the text could be printed.

3. $P \to M \to C$: A crash occurs after sending the completion message and printing the text.

4. $P \to C(\to M)$: The text printed, after which a crash occurs before the completion message could be sent.

5. $C(\to P \to M)$: A crash happens before the server could do anything.

6. $C(\to M \to P)$: A crash happens before the server could do anything.

The parentheses indicate an event that can no longer happen because the server already crashed. Fig. 8-8 shows all possible combinations. As can be readily verified, there is no combination of client strategy and server strategy that will work correctly under all possible event sequences. The bottom line is that the client can never know whether the server crashed just before or after having the text printed.

Client	Server					
	Strategy M → P			Strategy P → M		
Reissue strategy	MPC	MC(P)	C(MP)	PMC	PC(M)	C(PM)
Always	DUP	OK	OK	DUP	DUP	OK
Never	OK	ZERO	ZERO	OK	OK	ZERO
Only when ACKed	DUP	OK	ZERO	DUP	OK	ZERO
Only when not ACKed	OK	ZERO	OK	OK	DUP	OK

OK   =   Text is printed once
DUP   =   Text is printed twice
ZERO =   Text is not printed at all

Figure 8-8. Different combinations of client and server strategies in the presence of server crashes.

In short, the possibility of server crashes radically changes the nature of RPC and clearly distinguishes single-processor systems from distributed systems. In the former case, a server crash also implies a client crash, so recovery is neither possible nor necessary. In the latter it is both possible and necessary to take action.

Lost Reply Messages

Lost replies can also be difficult to deal with. The obvious solution is just to rely on a timer again that has been set by the client's operating system. If no reply is forthcoming within a reasonable period, just send the request once more. The trouble with this solution is that the client is not really sure why there was no answer. Did the request or reply get lost, or is the server merely slow? It may make a difference.

In particular, some operations can safely be repeated as often as necessary with no damage being done. A request such as asking for the first 1024 bytes of a file has no side effects and can be executed as often as necessary without any harm being done. A request that has this property is said to be **idempotent**.

Now consider a request to a banking server asking to transfer a million dollars from one account to another. If the request arrives and is carried out, but the reply is lost, the client will not know this and will retransmit the message. The bank server will interpret this request as a new one, and will carry it out too. Two million dollars will be transferred. Heaven forbid that the reply is lost 10 times. Transferring money is not idempotent.

One way of solving this problem is to try to structure all the requests in an idempotent way. In practice, however, many requests (e.g., transferring money) are inherently nonidempotent, so something else is needed. Another method is to have the client assign each request a sequence number. By having the server keep track of the most recently received sequence number from each client that is using it, the server can tell the difference between an original request and a retransmission and can refuse to carry out any request a second time. However, the server will still have to send a response to the client. Note that this approach does require that the server maintains administration on each client. Furthermore, it is not clear how long to maintain this administration. An additional safeguard is to have a bit in the message header that is used to distinguish initial requests from retransmissions (the idea being that it is always safe to perform an original request; retransmissions may require more care).

Client Crashes

The final item on the list of failures is the client crash. What happens if a client sends a request to a server to do some work and crashes before the server replies? At this point a computation is active and no parent is waiting for the result. Such an unwanted computation is called an **orphan**.

Orphans can cause a variety of problems that can interfere with normal operation of the system. As a bare minimum, they waste CPU cycles. They can also lock files or otherwise tie up valuable resources. Finally, if the client reboots and does the RPC again, but the reply from the orphan comes back immediately afterward, confusion can result.

What can be done about orphans? Nelson (1981) proposed four solutions. In solution 1, before a client stub sends an RPC message, it makes a log entry telling what it is about to do. The log is kept on disk or some other medium that survives crashes. After a reboot, the log is checked and the orphan is explicitly killed off. This solution is called **orphan extermination**.

The disadvantage of this scheme is the horrendous expense of writing a disk record for every RPC. Furthermore, it may not even work, since orphans themselves may do RPCs, thus creating **grandorphans** or further descendants that are difficult or impossible to locate. Finally, the network may be partitioned, due to a failed gateway, making it impossible to kill them, even if they can be located. All in all, this is not a promising approach.

In solution 2, called **reincarnation**, all these problems can be solved without the need to write disk records. The way it works is to divide time up into sequentially numbered epochs. When a client reboots, it broadcasts a message to all machines declaring the start of a new epoch. When such a broadcast comes in, all remote computations on behalf of that client are killed. Of course, if the network is partitioned, some orphans may survive. Fortunately, however, when they report back, their replies will contain an obsolete epoch number, making them easy to detect.

Solution 3 is a variant on this idea, but somewhat less draconian. It is called **gentle reincarnation**. When an epoch broadcast comes in, each machine checks to see if it has any remote computations running locally, and if so, tries its best to locate their owners. Only if the owners cannot be located anywhere is the computation killed.

Finally, we have solution 4, **expiration**, in which each RPC is given a standard amount of time, T, to do the job. If it cannot finish, it must explicitly ask for another quantum, which is a nuisance. On the other hand, if after a crash the client waits a time T before rebooting, all orphans are sure to be gone. The problem to be solved here is choosing a reasonable value of T in the face of RPCs with wildly differing requirements.

In practice, all of these methods are crude and undesirable. Worse yet, killing an orphan may have unforeseen consequences. For example, suppose that an orphan has obtained locks on one or more files or data base records. If the orphan is suddenly killed, these locks may remain forever. Also, an orphan may have already made entries in various remote queues to start up other processes at some future time, so even killing the orphan may not remove all traces of it. Conceivably, it may even started again, with unforeseen consequences. Orphan elimination is discussed in more detail by Panzieri and Shrivastava (1988).

8.4 RELIABLE GROUP COMMUNICATION

Considering how important process resilience by replication is, it is not surprising that reliable multicast services are important as well. Such services guarantee that messages are delivered to all members in a process group. Unfortunately, reliable multicasting turns out to be surprisingly tricky. In this section, we take a closer look at the issues involved in reliably delivering messages to a process group.

8.4.1 Basic Reliable-Multicasting Schemes

Although most transport layers offer reliable point-to-point channels, they rarely offer reliable communication to a collection of processes. The best they can offer is to let each process set up a point-to-point connection to each other process it wants to communicate with. Obviously, such an organization is not very efficient as it may waste network bandwidth. Nevertheless, if the number of processes is small, achieving reliability through multiple reliable point-to-point channels is a simple and often straightforward solution.

To go beyond this simple case, we need to define precisely what reliable multicasting is. Intuitively, it means that a message that is sent to a process group should be delivered to each member of that group. However, what happens if during communication a process joins the group? Should that process also receive the message? Likewise, we should also determine what happens if a (sending) process crashes during communication.

To cover such situations, a distinction should be made between reliable communication in the presence of faulty processes, and reliable communication when processes are assumed to operate correctly. In the first case, multicasting is considered to be reliable when it can be guaranteed that all nonfaulty group members receive the message. The tricky part is that agreement should be reached on what the group actually looks like before a message can be delivered, in addition to various ordering constraints. We return to these matters when we discussw atomic multicasts below.

The situation becomes simpler if we assume agreement exists on who is a member of the group and who is not. In particular, if we assume that processes do not fail, and processes do not join or leave the group while communication is going on, reliable multicasting simply means that every message should be delivered to each current group member. In the simplest case, there is no requirement that all group members receive messages in the same order, but sometimes this feature is needed.

This weaker form of reliable multicasting is relatively easy to implement, again subject to the condition that the number of receivers is limited. Consider the case that a single sender wants to multicast a message to multiple receivers.

Assume that the underlying communication system offers only unreliable multi-casting, meaning that a multicast message may be lost part way and delivered to some, but not all, of the intended receivers.

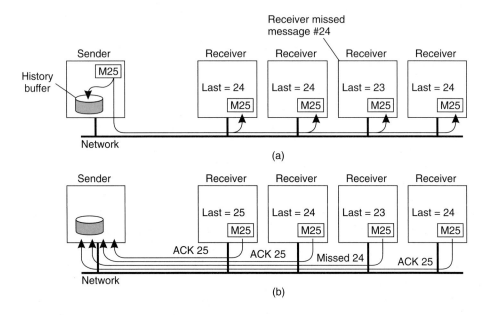

Figure 8-9. A simple solution to reliable multicasting when all receivers are known and are assumed not to fail. (a) Message transmission. (b) Reporting feedback.

A simple solution is shown in Fig. 8-9. The sending process assigns a sequence number to each message it multicasts. We assume that messages are received in the order they are sent. In this way, it is easy for a receiver to detect it is missing a message. Each multicast message is stored locally in a history buffer at the sender. Assuming the receivers are known to the sender, the sender simply keeps the message in its history buffer until each receiver has returned an acknowledgment. If a receiver detects it is missing a message, it may return a negative acknowledgment, requesting the sender for a retransmission. Alternatively, the sender may automatically retransmit the message when it has not received all acknowledgments within a certain time.

There are various design trade-offs to be made. For example, to reduce the number of messages returned to the sender, acknowledgments could possibly be piggybacked with other messages. Also, retransmitting a message can be done using point-to-point communication to each requesting process, or using a single multicast message sent to all processes. A extensive and detailed survey of total-order broadcasts can be found in Defago et al. (2004).

8.4.2 Scalability in Reliable Multicasting

The main problem with the reliable multicast scheme just described is that it cannot support large numbers of receivers. If there are N receivers, the sender must be prepared to accept at least N acknowledgments. With many receivers, the sender may be swamped with such feedback messages, which is also referred to as a feedback implosion. In addition, we may also need to take into account that the receivers are spread across a wide-area network.

One solution to this problem is not to have receivers acknowledge the receipt of a message. Instead, a receiver returns a feedback message only to inform the sender it is missing a message. Returning only such negative acknowledgments can be shown to generally scale better [see, for example, Towsley et al. (1997)], but no hard guarantees can be given that feedback implosions will never happen.

Another problem with returning only negative acknowledgments is that the sender will, in theory, be forced to keep a message in its history buffer forever. Because the sender can never know if a message has been correctly delivered to all receivers, it should always be prepared for a receiver requesting the retransmission of an old message. In practice, the sender will remove a message from its history buffer after some time has elapsed to prevent the buffer from overflowing. However, removing a message is done at the risk of a request for a retransmission not being honored.

Several proposals for scalable reliable multicasting exist. A comparison between different schemes can be found in Levine and Garcia-Luna-Aceves (1998). We now briefly discuss two very different approaches that are representative of many existing solutions.

Nonhierarchical Feedback Control

The key issue to scalable solutions for reliable multicasting is to reduce the number of feedback messages that are returned to the sender. A popular model that has been applied to several wide-area applications is **feedback suppression**. This scheme underlies the **Scalable Reliable Multicasting (SRM)** protocol developed by Floyd et al. (1997) and works as follows.

First, in SRM, receivers never acknowledge the successful delivery of a multicast message, but instead, report only when they are missing a message. How message loss is detected is left to the application. Only negative acknowledgments are returned as feedback. Whenever a receiver notices that it missed a message, it *multicasts* its feedback to the rest of the group.

Multicasting feedback allows another group member to suppress its own feedback. Suppose several receivers missed message m. Each of them will need to return a negative acknowledgment to the sender, S, so that m can be retransmitted. However, if we assume that retransmissions are always multicast to the entire group, it is sufficient that only a single request for retransmission reaches S.

For this reason, a receiver R that did not receive message m schedules a feedback message with some random delay. That is, the request for retransmission is not sent until some random time has elapsed. If, in the meantime, another request for retransmission for m reaches R, R will suppress its own feedback, knowing that m will be retransmitted shortly. In this way, ideally, only a single feedback message will reach S, which in turn subsequently retransmits m. This scheme is shown in Fig. 8-10.

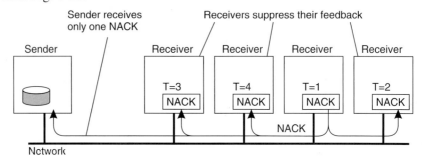

Figure 8-10. Several receivers have scheduled a request for retransmission, but the first retransmission request leads to the suppression of others.

Feedback suppression has shown to scale reasonably well, and has been used as the underlying mechanism for a number of collaborative Internet applications, such as a shared whiteboard. However, the approach also introduces a number of serious problems. First, ensuring that only one request for retransmission is returned to the sender requires a reasonably accurate scheduling of feedback messages at each receiver. Otherwise, many receivers will still return their feedback at the same time. Setting timers accordingly in a group of processes that is dispersed across a wide-area network is not that easy.

Another problem is that multicasting feedback also interrupts those processes to which the message has been successfully delivered. In other words, other receivers are forced to receive and process messages that are useless to them. The only solution to this problem is to let receivers that have not received message m join a separate multicast group for m, as explained in Kasera et al. (1997). Unfortunately, this solution requires that groups can be managed in a highly efficient manner, which is hard to accomplish in a wide-area system. A better approach is therefore to let receivers that tend to miss the same messages team up and share the same multicast channel for feedback messages and retransmissions. Details on this approach are found in Liu et al. (1998).

To enhance the scalability of SRM, it is useful to let receivers assist in local recovery. In particular, if a receiver to which message m has been successfully delivered, receives a request for retransmission, it can decide to multicast m even before the retransmission request reaches the original sender. Further details can be found in Floyd et al. (1997) and Liu et al. (1998).

Hierarchical Feedback Control

Feedback suppression as just described is basically a nonhierarchical solution. However, achieving scalability for very large groups of receivers requires that hierarchical approaches are adopted. In essence, a hierarchical solution to reliable multicasting works as shown in Fig. 8-11.

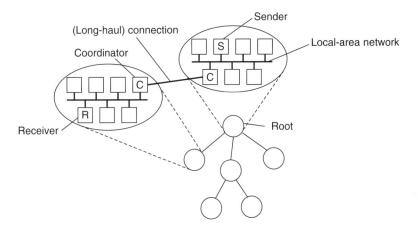

Figure 8-11. The essence of hierarchical reliable multicasting. Each local coordinator forwards the message to its children and later handles retransmission requests.

To simplify matters, assume there is only a single sender that needs to multicast messages to a very large group of receivers. The group of receivers is partitioned into a number of subgroups, which are subsequently organized into a tree. The subgroup containing the sender forms the root of the tree. Within each subgroup, any reliable multicasting scheme that works for small groups can be used.

Each subgroup appoints a local coordinator, which is responsible for handling retransmission requests of receivers contained in its subgroup. The local coordinator will thus have its own history buffer. If the coordinator itself has missed a message m, it asks the coordinator of the parent subgroup to retransmit m. In a scheme based on acknowledgments, a local coordinator sends an acknowledgment to its parent if it has received the message. If a coordinator has received acknowledgments for message m from all members in its subgroup, as well as from its children, it can remove m from its history buffer.

The main problem with hierarchical solutions is the construction of the tree. In many cases, a tree needs to be constructed dynamically. One approach is to make use of the multicast tree in the underlying network, if there is one. In principle, the approach is then to enhance each multicast router in the network layer in such a way that it can act as a local coordinator in the way just described. Unfortunately, as a practical matter, such adaptations to existing computer networks are not easy to do. For these reasons, application-level multicasting solutions as we discussed in Chap. 4 have gained popularity.

In conclusion, building reliable multicast schemes that can scale to a large number of receivers spread across a wide-area network, is a difficult problem. No single best solution exists, and each solution introduces new problems.

8.4.3 Atomic Multicast

Let us now return to the situation in which we need to achieve reliable multicasting in the presence of process failures. In particular, what is often needed in a distributed system is the guarantee that a message is delivered to either all processes or to none at all. In addition, it is generally also required that all messages are delivered in the same order to all processes. This is also known as the **atomic multicast problem**.

To see why atomicity is so important, consider a replicated database constructed as an application on top of a distributed system. The distributed system offers reliable multicasting facilities. In particular, it allows the construction of process groups to which messages can be reliably sent. The replicated database is therefore constructed as a group of processes, one process for each replica. Update operations are always multicast to all replicas and subsequently performed locally. In other words, we assume that an active-replication protocol is used.

Suppose that now that a series of updates is to be performed, but that during the execution of one of the updates, a replica crashes. Consequently, that update is lost for that replica but on the other hand, it is correctly performed at the other replicas.

When the replica that just crashed recovers, at best it can recover to the same state it had before the crash; however, it may have missed several updates. At that point, it is essential that it is brought up to date with the other replicas. Bringing the replica into the same state as the others requires that we know exactly which operations it missed, and in which order these operations are to be performed.

Now suppose that the underlying distributed system supported atomic multicasting. In that case, the update operation that was sent to all replicas just before one of them crashed is either performed at all nonfaulty replicas, or by none at all. In particular, with atomic multicasting, the operation can be performed by all correctly operating replicas only if they have reached agreement on the group membership. In other words, the update is performed if the remaining replicas have agreed that the crashed replica no longer belongs to the group.

When the crashed replica recovers, it is now forced to join the group once more. No update operations will be forwarded until it is registered as being a member again. Joining the group requires that its state is brought up to date with the rest of the group members. Consequently, atomic multicasting ensures that nonfaulty processes maintain a consistent view of the database, and forces reconciliation when a replica recovers and rejoins the group.

Virtual Synchrony

Reliable multicast in the presence of process failures can be accurately defined in terms of process groups and changes to group membership. As we did earlier, we make a distinction between *receiving* and *delivering* a message. In particular, we again adopt a model in which the distributed system consists of a communication layer, as shown in Fig. 8-12. Within this communication layer, messages are sent and received. A received message is locally buffered in the communication layer until it can be delivered to the application that is logically placed at a higher layer.

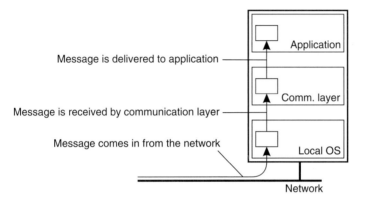

Figure 8-12. The logical organization of a distributed system to distinguish between message receipt and message delivery.

The whole idea of atomic multicasting is that a multicast message *m* is uniquely associated with a list of processes to which it should be delivered. This delivery list corresponds to a **group view**, namely, the view on the set of processes contained in the group, which the sender had at the time message *m* was multicast. An important observation is that each process on that list has the same view. In other words, they should all agree that *m* should be delivered to each one of them and to no other process.

Now suppose that the message *m* is multicast at the time its sender has group view *G*. Furthermore, assume that while the multicast is taking place, another process joins or leaves the group. This change in group membership is naturally announced to all processes in *G*. Stated somewhat differently, a **view change** takes place by multicasting a message *vc* announcing the joining or leaving of a process. We now have two multicast messages simultaneously in transit: *m* and *vc*. What we need to guarantee is that *m* is either delivered to all processes in *G* before each one of them is delivered message *vc*, or *m* is not delivered at all. Note that this requirement is somewhat comparable to totally-ordered multicasting, which we discussed in Chap. 6.

A question that quickly comes to mind is that if *m* is not delivered to any process, how can we speak of a *reliable* multicast protocol? In principle, there is only one case in which delivery of *m* is allowed to fail: when the group membership change is the result of the sender of *m* crashing. In that case, either all members of *G* should hear the abort of the new member, or none. Alternatively, *m* may be ignored by each member, which corresponds to the situation that the sender crashed before *m* was sent.

This stronger form of reliable multicast guarantees that a message multicast to group view *G* is delivered to each nonfaulty process in *G*. If the sender of the message crashes during the multicast, the message may either be delivered to all remaining processes, or ignored by each of them. A reliable multicast with this property is said to be **virtually synchronous** (Birman and Joseph, 1987).

Consider the four processes shown in Fig. 8-13. At a certain point in time, process P_1 joins the group, which then consists of P_1, P_2, P_3, and P_4. After some messages have been multicast, P_3 crashes. However, before crashing, it succeeded in multicasting a message to process P_2 and P_4, but not to P_1. However, virtual synchrony guarantees that the message is not delivered at all, effectively establishing the situation that the message was never sent before P_3 crashed.

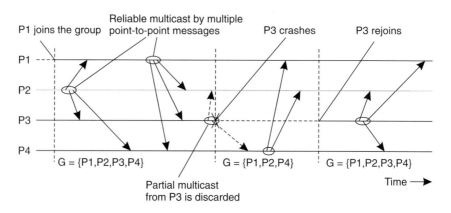

Figure 8-13. The principle of virtual synchronous multicast.

After P_3 has been removed from the group, communication proceeds between the remaining group members. Later, when P_3 recovers, it can join the group again, after its state has been brought up to date.

The principle of virtual synchrony comes from the fact that all multicasts take place between view changes. Put somewhat differently, a view change acts as a barrier across which no multicast can pass. In a sense, it is comparable to the use of a synchronization variable in distributed data stores as discussed in the previous chapter. All multicasts that are in transit while a view change takes place are completed before the view change comes into effect. The implementation of virtual synchrony is not trivial as we will discuss in detail below.

Message Ordering

Virtual synchrony allows an application developer to think about multicasts as taking place in epochs that are separated by group membership changes. However, nothing has yet been said concerning the ordering of multicasts. In general, four different orderings are distinguished:

1. Unordered multicasts

2. FIFO-ordered multicasts

3. Causally-ordered multicasts

4. Totally-ordered multicasts

A **reliable, unordered multicast** is a virtually synchronous multicast in which no guarantees are given concerning the order in which received messages are delivered by different processes. To explain, assume that reliable multicasting is supported by a library providing a send and a receive primitive. The receive operation blocks the calling process until a message is delivered to it.

Process P1	Process P2	Process P3
sends m1	receives m1	receives m2
sends m2	receives m2	receives m1

Figure 8-14. Three communicating processes in the same group. The ordering of events per process is shown along the vertical axis.

Now suppose a sender P_1 multicasts two messages to a group while two other processes in that group are waiting for messages to arrive, as shown in Fig. 8-14. Assuming that processes do not crash or leave the group during these multicasts, it is possible that the communication layer at P_2 first receives message m_1 and then m_2. Because there are no message-ordering constraints, the messages may be delivered to P_2 in the order that they are received. In contrast, the communication layer at P_3 may first receive message m_2 followed by m_1, and delivers these two in this same order to P_3.

In the case of **reliable FIFO-ordered multicasts**, the communication layer is forced to deliver incoming messages from the same process in the same order as they have been sent. Consider the communication within a group of four processes, as shown in Fig. 8-15. With FIFO ordering, the only thing that matters is that message m_1 is always delivered before m_2, and, likewise, that message m_3 is always delivered before m_4. This rule has to be obeyed by all processes in the group. In other words, when the communication layer at P_3 receives m_2 first, it will wait with delivery to P_3 until it has received and delivered m_1.

Process P1	Process P2	Process P3	Process P4
sends m1	receives m1	receives m3	sends m3
sends m2	receives m3	receives m1	sends m4
	receives m2	receives m2	
	receives m4	receives m4	

Figure 8-15. Four processes in the same group with two different senders, and a possible delivery order of messages under FIFO-ordered multicasting.

However, there is no constraint regarding the delivery of messages sent by different processes. In other words, if process P_2 receives m_1 before m_3, it may deliver the two messages in that order. Meanwhile, process P_3 may have received m_3 before receiving m_1. FIFO ordering states that P_3 may deliver m_3 before m_1, although this delivery order is different from that of P_2.

Finally, **reliable causally-ordered multicast** delivers messages so that potential causality between different messages is preserved. In other words, if a message m_1 causally precedes another message m_2, regardless of whether they were multicast by the same sender, then the communication layer at each receiver will always deliver m_2 after it has received and delivered m_1. Note that causally-ordered multicasts can be implemented using vector timestamps as discussed in Chap. 6.

Besides these three orderings, there may be the additional constraint that message delivery is to be totally ordered as well. **Total-ordered delivery** means that regardless of whether message delivery is unordered, FIFO ordered, or causally ordered, it is required additionally that when messages are delivered, they are delivered in the same order to all group members.

For example, with the combination of FIFO and totally-ordered multicast, processes P_2 and P_3 in Fig. 8-15 may both first deliver message m_3 and then message m_1. However, if P_2 delivers m_1 before m_3, while P_3 delivers m_3 before delivering m_1, they would violate the total-ordering constraint. Note that FIFO ordering should still be respected. In other words, m_2 should be delivered after m_1 and, accordingly, m_4 should be delivered after m_3.

Virtually synchronous reliable multicasting offering totally-ordered delivery of messages is called **atomic multicasting**. With the three different message ordering constraints discussed above, this leads to six forms of reliable multicasting as shown in Fig. 8-16 (Hadzilacos and Toueg, 1993).

Implementing Virtual Synchrony

Let us now consider a possible implementation of a virtually synchronous reliable multicast. An example of such an implementation appears in Isis, a fault-tolerant distributed system that has been in practical use in industry for several

Multicast	Basic Message Ordering	Total-Ordered Delivery?
Reliable multicast	None	No
FIFO multicast	FIFO-ordered delivery	No
Causal multicast	Causal-ordered delivery	No
Atomic multicast	None	Yes
FIFO atomic multicast	FIFO-ordered delivery	Yes
Causal atomic multicast	Causal-ordered delivery	Yes

Figure 8-16. Six different versions of virtually synchronous reliable multicasting.

years. We will focus on some of the implementation issues of this technique as described in Birman et al. (1991).

Reliable multicasting in Isis makes use of available reliable point-to-point communication facilities of the underlying network, in particular, TCP. Multicasting a message m to a group of processes is implemented by reliably sending m to each group member. As a consequence, although each transmission is guaranteed to succeed, there are no guarantees that *all* group members receive m. In particular, the sender may fail before having transmitted m to each member.

Besides reliable point-to-point communication, Isis also assumes that messages from the same source are received by a communication layer in the order they were sent by that source. In practice, this requirement is solved by using TCP connections for point-to-point communication.

The main problem that needs to be solved is to guarantee that all messages sent to view G are delivered to all nonfaulty processes in G before the next group membership change takes place. The first issue that needs to be taken care of is making sure that each process in G has received all messages that were sent to G. Note that because the sender of a message m to G may have failed before completing its multicast, there may indeed be processes in G that will never receive m. Because the sender has crashed, these processes should get m from somewhere else. How a process detects it is missing a message is explained next.

The solution to this problem is to let every process in G keep m until it knows for sure that all members in G have received it. If m has been received by all members in G, m is said to be **stable**. Only stable messages are allowed to be delivered. To ensure stability, it is sufficient to select an arbitrary (operational) process in G and request it to send m to all other processes.

To be more specific, assume the current view is G_i, but that it is necessary to install the next view G_{i+1}. Without loss of generality, we may assume that G_i and G_{i+1} differ by at most one process. A process P notices the view change when it receives a view-change message. Such a message may come from the process wanting to join or leave the group, or from a process that had detected the failure of a process in G_i that is now to be removed, as shown in Fig. 8-17(a).

When a process P receives the view-change message for G_{i+1}, it first forwards a copy of any unstable message from G_i it still has to every process in G_{i+1}, and subsequently marks it as being stable. Recall that Isis assumes point-to-point communication is reliable, so that forwarded messages are never lost. Such forwarding guarantees that all messages in G_i that have been received by at least one process are received by all nonfaulty processes in G_i. Note that it would also have been sufficient to elect a single coordinator to forward unstable messages.

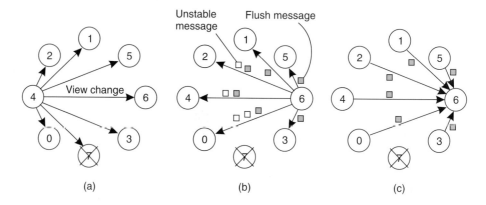

Figure 8-17. (a) Process 4 notices that process 7 has crashed and sends a view change. (b) Process 6 sends out all its unstable messages, followed by a flush message. (c) Process 6 installs the new view when it has received a flush message from everyone else.

To indicate that P no longer has any unstable messages and that it is prepared to install G_{i+1} as soon as the other processes can do that as well, it multicasts a **flush message** for G_{i+1}, as shown in Fig. 8-17(b). After P has received a flush message for G_{i+1} from each other process, it can safely install the new view [shown in Fig. 8-17(c)].

When a process Q receives a message m that was sent in G_i, and Q still believes the current view is G_i, it delivers m taking any additional message-ordering constraints into account. If it had already received m, it considers the message to be a duplicate and further discards it.

Because process Q will eventually receive the view-change message for G_{i+1}, it will also first forward any of its unstable messages and subsequently wrap things up by sending a flush message for G_{i+1}. Note that due to the message ordering underlying the communication layer, a flush message from a process is always received after the receipt of an unstable message from that same process.

The major flaw in the protocol described so far is that it cannot deal with process failures while a new view change is being announced. In particular, it assumes that until the new view G_{i+1} has been installed by each member in G_{i+1}, no process in G_{i+1} will fail (which would lead to a next view G_{i+2}). This problem is solved by announcing view changes for any view G_{i+k} even while previous changes have not yet been installed by all processes. The details are left as an exercise for the reader.

8.5 DISTRIBUTED COMMIT

The atomic multicasting problem discussed in the previous section is an example of a more general problem, known as **distributed commit**. The distributed commit problem involves having an operation being performed by each member of a process group, or none at all. In the case of reliable multicasting, the operation is the delivery of a message. With distributed transactions, the operation may be the commit of a transaction at a single site that takes part in the transaction. Other examples of distributed commit, and how it can be solved are discussed in Tanisch (2000).

Distributed commit is often established by means of a coordinator. In a simple scheme, this coordinator tells all other processes that are also involved, called participants, whether or not to (locally) perform the operation in question. This scheme is referred to as a **one-phase commit protocol**. It has the obvious drawback that if one of the participants cannot actually perform the operation, there is no way to tell the coordinator. For example, in the case of distributed transactions, a local commit may not be possible because this would violate concurrency control constraints.

In practice, more sophisticated schemes are needed, the most common one being the two-phase commit protocol, which is discussed in detail below. The main drawback of this protocol is that it cannot efficiently handle the failure of the coordinator. To that end, a three-phase protocol has been developed, which we also discuss.

8.5.1 Two-Phase Commit

The original **two-phase commit protocol (2PC)** is due to Gray (1978) Without loss of generality, consider a distributed transaction involving the participation of a number of processes each running on a different machine. Assuming that no failures occur, the protocol consists of the following two phases, each consisting of two steps [see also Bernstein et al. (1987)]:

1. The coordinator sends a *VOTE_REQUEST* message to all participants.

2. When a participant receives a *VOTE_REQUEST* message, it returns either a *VOTE_COMMIT* message to the coordinator telling the coordinator that it is prepared to locally commit its part of the transaction, or otherwise a *VOTE_ABORT* message.

3. The coordinator collects all votes from the participants. If all participants have voted to commit the transaction, then so will the coordinator. In that case, it sends a *GLOBAL_COMMIT* message to all participants. However, if one participant had voted to abort the transaction, the coordinator will also decide to abort the transaction and multicasts a *GLOBAL_ABORT* message.

4. Each participant that voted for a commit waits for the final reaction by the coordinator. If a participant receives a *GLOBAL_COMMIT* message, it locally commits the transaction. Otherwise, when receiving a *GLOBAL_ABORT* message, the transaction is locally aborted as well.

The first phase is the voting phase, and consists of steps 1 and 2. The second phase is the decision phase, and consists of steps 3 and 4. These four steps are shown as finite state diagrams in Fig. 8-18.

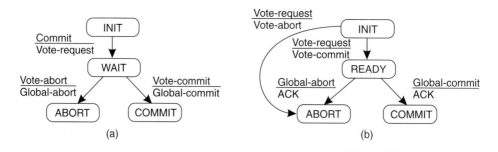

Figure 8-18. (a) The finite state machine for the coordinator in 2PC. (b) The finite state machine for a participant.

Several problems arise when this basic 2PC protocol is used in a system where failures occur. First, note that the coordinator as well as the participants have states in which they block waiting for incoming messages. Consequently, the protocol can easily fail when a process crashes for other processes may be indefinitely waiting for a message from that process. For this reason, timeout mechanism are used. These mechanisms are explained in the following pages.

When taking a look at the finite state machines in Fig. 8-18, it can be seen that there are a total of three states in which either a coordinator or participant is blocked waiting for an incoming message. First, a participant may be waiting in its *INIT* state for a *VOTE_REQUEST* message from the coordinator. If that message is not received after some time, the participant will simply decide to locally abort the transaction, and thus send a *VOTE_ABORT* message to the coordinator.

Likewise, the coordinator can be blocked in state *WAIT*, waiting for the votes of each participant. If not all votes have been collected after a certain period of

time, the coordinator should vote for an abort as well, and subsequently send
GLOBAL_ABORT to all participants.

Finally, a participant can be blocked in state *READY*, waiting for the global
vote as sent by the coordinator. If that message is not received within a given
time, the participant cannot simply decide to abort the transaction. Instead, it must
find out which message the coordinator actually sent. The simplest solution to this
problem is to let each participant block until the coordinator recovers again.

A better solution is to let a participant P contact another participant Q to see if
it can decide from Q's current state what it should do. For example, suppose that
Q had reached state *COMMIT*. This is possible only if the coordinator had sent a
GLOBAL_COMMIT message to Q just before crashing. Apparently, this message
had not yet been sent to P. Consequently, P may now also decide to locally commit. Likewise, if Q is in state *ABORT*, P can safely abort as well.

Now suppose that Q is still in state *INIT*. This situation can occur when the
coordinator has sent a *VOTE_REQUEST* to all participants, but this message has
reached P (which subsequently responded with a *VOTE_COMMIT* message), but
has not reached Q. In other words, the coordinator had crashed while multicasting
VOTE_REQUEST. In this case, it is safe to abort the transaction: both P and Q
can make a transition to state *ABORT*.

The most difficult situation occurs when Q is also in state *READY*, waiting for
a response from the coordinator. In particular, if it turns out that all participants
are in state *READY*, no decision can be taken. The problem is that although all
participants are willing to commit, they still need the coordinator's vote to reach
the final decision. Consequently, the protocol blocks until the coordinator recovers.

The various options are summarized in Fig. 8-19.

State of Q	Action by P
COMMIT	Make transition to COMMIT
ABORT	Make transition to ABORT
INIT	Make transition to ABORT
READY	Contact another participant

Figure 8-19. Actions taken by a participant P when residing in state *READY*
and having contacted another participant Q.

To ensure that a process can actually recover, it is necessary that it saves its
state to persistent storage. (How saving data can be done in a fault-tolerant way is
discussed later in this chapter.) For example, if a participant was in state *INIT*, it
can safely decide to locally abort the transaction when it recovers, and then
inform the coordinator. Likewise, when it had already taken a decision such as

when it crashed while being in either state *COMMIT* or *ABORT*, it is in order to recover to that state again, and retransmit its decision to the coordinator.

Problems arise when a participant crashed while residing in state *READY*. In that case, when recovering, it cannot decide on its own what it should do next, that is, commit or abort the transaction. Consequently, it is forced to contact other participants to find what it should do, analogous to the situation when it times out while residing in state *READY* as described above.

The coordinator has only two critical states it needs to keep track of. When it starts the 2PC protocol, it should record that it is entering state *WAIT* so that it can possibly retransmit the *VOTE_REQUEST* message to all participants after recovering. Likewise, if it had come to a decision in the second phase, it is sufficient if that decision has been recorded so that it can be retransmitted when recovering.

An outline of the actions that are executed by the coordinator is given in Fig. 8-20. The coordinator starts by multicasting a *VOTE_REQUEST* to all participants in order to collect their votes. It subsequently records that it is entering the *WAIT* state, after which it waits for incoming votes from participants.

Actions by coordinator:

```
write START_2PC to local log;
multicast VOTE_REQUEST to all participants;
while not all votes have been collected {
        wait for any incoming vote;
        if timeout {
            write GLOBAL_ABORT to local log;
            multicast GLOBAL_ABORT to all participants;
            exit;
        }
        record vote;
}
if all participants sent VOTE_COMMIT and coordinator votes COMMIT {
        write GLOBAL_COMMIT to local log;
        multicast GLOBAL_COMMIT to all participants;
} else {
        write GLOBAL_ABORT to local log;
        multicast GLOBAL_ABORT to all participants;
}
```

Figure 8-20. Outline of the steps taken by the coordinator in a two-phase commit protocol.

If not all votes have been collected but no more votes are received within a given time interval prescribed in advance, the coordinator assumes that one or more participants have failed. Consequently, it should abort the transaction and multicasts a *GLOBAL_ABORT* to the (remaining) participants.

If no failures occur, the coordinator will eventually have collected all votes. If all participants as well as the coordinator vote to commit, *GLOBAL_COMMIT* is first logged and subsequently sent to all processes. Otherwise, the coordinator multicasts a *GLOBAL_ABORT* (after recording it in the local log).

Fig. 8-21(a) shows the steps taken by a participant. First, the process waits for a vote request from the coordinator. Note that this waiting can be done by a separate thread running in the process's address space. If no message comes in, the transaction is simply aborted. Apparently, the coordinator had failed.

After receiving a vote request, the participant may decide to vote for committing the transaction for which it first records its decision in a local log, and then informs the coordinator by sending a *VOTE_COMMIT* message. The participant must then wait for the global decision. Assuming this decision (which again should come from the coordinator) comes in on time, it is simply written to the local log, after which it can be carried out.

However, if the participant times out while waiting for the coordinator's decision to come in, it executes a termination protocol by first multicasting a *DECISION_REQUEST* message to the other processes, after which it subsequently blocks while waiting for a response. When a response comes in (possibly from the coordinator, which is assumed to eventually recover), the participant writes the decision to its local log and handles it accordingly.

Each participant should be prepared to accept requests for a global decision from other participants. To that end, assume each participant starts a separate thread, executing concurrently with the main thread of the participant as shown in Fig. 8-21(b). This thread blocks until it receives a decision request. It can only be of help to anther process if its associated participant has already reached a final decision. In other words, if *GLOBAL_COMMIT* or *GLOBAL_ABORT* had been written to the local log, it is certain that the coordinator had at least sent its decision to this process. In addition, the thread may also decide to send a *GLOBAL_ABORT* when its associated participant is still in state *INIT*, as discussed previously. In all other cases, the receiving thread cannot help, and the requesting participant will not be responded to.

What is seen is that it may be possible that a participant will need to block until the coordinator recovers. This situation occurs when all participants have received and processed the *VOTE_REQUEST* from the coordinator, while in the meantime, the coordinator crashed. In that case, participants cannot cooperatively decide on the final action to take. For this reason, 2PC is also referred to as a **blocking commit protocol**.

There are several solutions to avoid blocking. One solution, described by Babaoglu and Toueg (1993), is to use a multicast primitive by which a receiver immediately multicasts a received message to all other processes. It can be shown that this approach allows a participant to reach a final decision, even if the coordinator has not yet recovered. Another solution is the three-phase commit protocol, which is the last topic of this section and is discussed next.

Actions by participant:

```
write INIT to local log;
wait for VOTE_REQUEST from coordinator;
if timeout {
    write VOTE_ABORT to local log;
    exit;
}
if participant votes COMMIT {
    write VOTE_COMMIT to local log;
    send VOTE_COMMIT to coordinator;
    wait for DECISION from coordinator;
    if timeout {
        multicast DECISION_REQUEST to other participants;
        wait until DECISION is received; /* remain blocked */
        write DECISION to local log;
    }
    if DECISION == GLOBAL_COMMIT
        write GLOBAL_COMMIT to local log;
    else if DECISION == GLOBAL_ABORT
        write GLOBAL_ABORT to local log;
} else {
    write VOTE_ABORT to local log;
    send VOTE_ABORT to coordinator;
}
```

(a)

Actions for handling decision requests: /* executed by separate thread */

```
while true {
    wait until any incoming DECISION_REQUEST is received; /* remain blocked */
    read most recently recorded STATE from the local log;
    if STATE == GLOBAL_COMMIT
        send GLOBAL_COMMIT to requesting participant;
    else if STATE == INIT or STATE == GLOBAL_ABORT
        send GLOBAL_ABORT to requesting participant;
    else
        skip; /* participant remains blocked */
}
```

(b)

Figure 8-21. (a) The steps taken by a participant process in 2PC. (b) The steps for handling incoming decision requests.

8.5.2 Three-Phase Commit

A problem with the two-phase commit protocol is that when the coordinator has crashed, participants may not be able to reach a final decision. Consequently, participants may need to remain blocked until the coordinator recovers. Skeen (1981) developed a variant of 2PC, called the **three-phase commit protocol** (**3PC**), that avoids blocking processes in the presence of fail-stop crashes. Although 3PC is widely referred to in the literature, it is not applied often in practice as the conditions under which 2PC blocks rarely occur. We discuss the protocol, as it provides further insight into solving fault-tolerance problems in distributed systems.

Like 2PC, 3PC is also formulated in terms of a coordinator and a number of participants. Their respective finite state machines are shown in Fig. 8-22. The essence of the protocol is that the states of the coordinator and each participant satisfy the following two conditions:

1. There is no single state from which it is possible to make a transition directly to either a *COMMIT* or an *ABORT* state.

2. There is no state in which it is not possible to make a final decision, and from which a transition to a *COMMIT* state can be made.

It can be shown that these two conditions are necessary and sufficient for a commit protocol to be nonblocking (Skeen and Stonebraker, 1983).

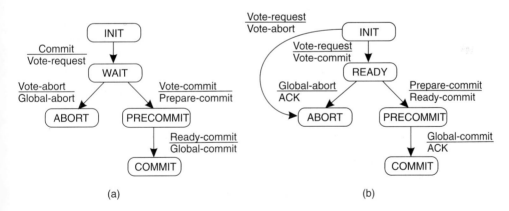

(a)   (b)

Figure 8-22. (a) The finite state machine for the coordinator in 3PC. (b) The finite state machine for a participant.

The coordinator in 3PC starts with sending a *VOTE_REQUEST* message to all participants, after which it waits for incoming responses. If any participant votes to abort the transaction, the final decision will be to abort as well, so the coordinator sends *GLOBAL_ABORT*. However, when the transaction can be committed, a

PREPARE_COMMIT message is sent. Only after each participant has acknowledged it is now prepared to commit, will the coordinator send the final GLOBAL_COMMIT message by which the transaction is actually committed.

Again, there are only a few situations in which a process is blocked while waiting for incoming messages. First, if a participant is waiting for a vote request from the coordinator while residing in state *INIT*, it will eventually make a transition to state *ABORT*, thereby assuming that the coordinator has crashed. This situation is identical to that in 2PC. Analogously, the coordinator may be in state *WAIT*, waiting for the votes from participants. On a timeout, the coordinator will conclude that a participant crashed, and will thus abort the transaction by multicasting a *GLOBAL_ABORT* message.

Now suppose the coordinator is blocked in state *PRECOMMIT*. On a timeout, it will conclude that one of the participants had crashed, but that participant is known to have voted for committing the transaction. Consequently, the coordinator can safely instruct the operational participants to commit by multicasting a *GLOBAL_COMMIT* message. In addition, it relies on a recovery protocol for the crashed participant to eventually commit its part of the transaction when it comes up again.

A participant *P* may block in the *READY* state or in the *PRECOMMIT* state. On a timeout, *P* can conclude only that the coordinator has failed, so that it now needs to find out what to do next. As in 2PC, if *P* contacts any other participant that is in state *COMMIT* (or *ABORT*), *P* should move to that state as well. In addition, if all participants are in state *PRECOMMIT*, the transaction can be safely committed.

Again analogous to 2PC, if another participant *Q* is still in the *INIT* state, the transaction can safely be aborted. It is important to note that *Q* can be in state *INIT* only if no other participant is in state *PRECOMMIT*. A participant can reach *PRECOMMIT* only if the coordinator had reached state *PRECOMMIT* before crashing, and has thus received a vote to commit from each participant. In other words, no participant can reside in state *INIT* while another participant is in state *PRECOMMIT*.

If each of the participants that *P* can contact is in state *READY* (and they together form a majority), the transaction should be aborted. The point to note is that another participant may have crashed and will later recover. However, neither *P*, nor any other of the operational participants knows what the state of the crashed participant will be when it recovers. If the process recovers to state *INIT*, then deciding to abort the transaction is the only correct decision. At worst, the process may recover to state *PRECOMMIT*, but in that case, it cannot do any harm to still abort the transaction.

This situation is the major difference with 2PC, where a crashed participant could recover to a *COMMIT* state while all the others were still in state *READY*. In that case, the remaining operational processes could not reach a final decision and would have to wait until the crashed process recovered. With 3PC, if any operational process is in its *READY* state, no crashed process will recover to a state other than *INIT*, *ABORT*, or *PRECOMMIT*. For this reason, surviving processes can always come to a final decision.

Finally, if the processes that *P* can reach are in state *PRECOMMIT* (and they form a majority), then it is safe to commit the transaction. Again, it can be shown that in this case, all other processes will either be in state *READY* or at least, will recover to state *READY*, *PRECOMMIT*, or *COMMIT* when they had crashed.

Further details on 3PC can be found in Bernstein et al. (1987) and Chow and Johnson (1997).

8.6 RECOVERY

So far, we have mainly concentrated on algorithms that allow us to tolerate faults. However, once a failure has occurred, it is essential that the process where the failure happened can recover to a correct state. In what follows, we first concentrate on what it actually means to recover to a correct state, and subsequently when and how the state of a distributed system can be recorded and recovered to, by means of checkpointing and message logging.

8.6.1 Introduction

Fundamental to fault tolerance is the recovery from an error. Recall that an error is that part of a system that may lead to a failure. The whole idea of error recovery is to replace an erroneous state with an error-free state. There are essentially two forms of error recovery.

In **backward recovery**, the main issue is to bring the system from its present erroneous state back into a previously correct state. To do so, it will be necessary to record the system's state from time to time, and to restore such a recorded state when things go wrong. Each time (part of) the system's present state is recorded, a **checkpoint** is said to be made.

Another form of error recovery is **forward recovery**. In this case, when the system has entered an erroneous state, instead of moving back to a previous, checkpointed state, an attempt is made to bring the system in a correct new state from which it can continue to execute. The main problem with forward error recovery mechanisms is that it has to be known in advance which errors may occur. Only in that case is it possible to correct those errors and move to a new state.

The distinction between backward and forward error recovery is easily explained when considering the implementation of reliable communication. The common approach to recover from a lost packet is to let the sender retransmit that packet. In effect, packet retransmission establishes that we attempt to go back to a previous, correct state, namely the one in which the packet that was lost is being sent. Reliable communication through packet retransmission is therefore an example of applying backward error recovery techniques.

An alternative approach is to use a method known as **erasure correction**. In this approach, a missing packet is constructed from other, successfully delivered packets. For example, in an (n,k) block erasure code, a set of k *source packets* is encoded into a set of n *encoded packets*, such that *any* set of k encoded packets is enough to reconstruct the original k source packets. Typical values are $k=16$ or $k=32$, and $k<n\leq2k$ [see, for example, Rizzo (1997)]. If not enough packets have yet been delivered, the sender will have to continue transmitting packets until a previously lost packet can be constructed. Erasure correction is a typical example of a forward error recovery approach.

By and large, backward error recovery techniques are widely applied as a general mechanism for recovering from failures in distributed systems. The major benefit of backward error recovery is that it is a generally applicable method independent of any specific system or process. In other words, it can be integrated into (the middleware layer) of a distributed system as a general-purpose service.

However, backward error recovery also introduces some problems (Singhal and Shivaratri, 1994). First, restoring a system or process to a previous state is generally a relatively costly operation in terms of performance. As will be discussed in succeeding sections, much work generally needs to be done to recover from, for example, a process crash or site failure. A potential way out of this problem, is to devise very cheap mechanisms by which components are simply rebooted. We will return to this approach below.

Second, because backward error recovery mechanisms are independent of the distributed application for which they are actually used, no guarantees can be given that once recovery has taken place, the same or similar failure will not happen again. If such guarantees are needed, handling errors often requires that the application gets into the loop of recovery. In other words, full-fledged failure transparency can generally not be provided by backward error recovery mechanisms.

Finally, although backward error recovery requires checkpointing, some states can simply never be rolled back to. For example, once a (possibly malicious) person has taken the $1,000 that suddenly came rolling out of the incorrectly functioning automated teller machine, there is only a small chance that money will be stuffed back in the machine. Likewise, recovering to a previous state in most UNIX systems after having enthusiastically typed

```
rm –fr *
```

but from the wrong working directory, may turn a few people pale. Some things are simply irreversible.

Checkpointing allows the recovery to a previous correct state. However, taking a checkpoint is often a costly operation and may have a severe performance penalty. As a consequence, many fault-tolerant distributed systems combine checkpointing with **message logging**. In this case, after a checkpoint has been taken, a process logs its messages before sending them off (called **sender-based logging**). An alternative solution is to let the receiving process first log an incoming message before delivering it to the application it is executing. This scheme is also referred to as **receiver-based logging**. When a receiving process crashes, it is necessary to restore the most recently checkpointed state, and from there on *replay* the messages that have been sent. Consequently, combining checkpoints with message logging makes it possible to restore a state that lies beyond the most recent checkpoint without the cost of checkpointing.

Another important distinction between checkpointing and schemes that additionally use logs follows. In a system where only checkpointing is used, processes will be restored to a checkpointed state. From there on, their behavior may be different than it was before the failure occurred. For example, because communication times are not deterministic, messages may now be delivered in a different order, in turn leading to different reactions by the receivers. However, if message logging takes place, an actual replay of the events that happened since the last checkpoint takes place. Such a replay makes it easier to interact with the outside world.

For example, consider the case that a failure occurred because a user provided erroneous input. If only checkpointing is used, the system would have to take a checkpoint before accepting the user's input in order to recover to exactly the same state. With message logging, an older checkpoint can be used, after which a replay of events can take place up to the point that the user should provide input. In practice, the combination of having fewer checkpoints and message logging is more efficient than having to take many checkpoints.

Stable Storage

To be able to recover to a previous state, it is necessary that information needed to enable recovery is safely stored. Safely in this context means that recovery information survives process crashes and site failures, but possibly also various storage media failures. Stable storage plays an important role when it comes to recovery in distributed systems. We discuss it briefly here.

Storage comes in three categories. First there is ordinary RAM memory, which is wiped out when the power fails or a machine crashes. Next there is disk storage, which survives CPU failures but which can be lost in disk head crashes.

Finally, there is also **stable storage**, which is designed to survive anything except major calamities such as floods and earthquakes. Stable storage can be implemented with a pair of ordinary disks, as shown in Fig. 8-23(a). Each block on drive 2 is an exact copy of the corresponding block on drive 1. When a block is updated, first the block on drive 1 is updated and verified, then the same block on drive 2 is done.

Suppose that the system crashes after drive 1 is updated but before the update on drive 2, as shown in Fig. 8-23(b). Upon recovery, the disk can be compared

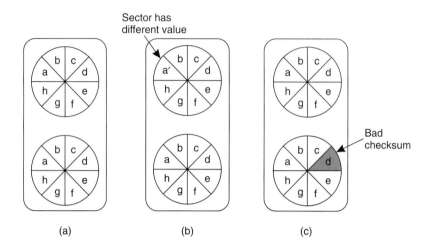

Figure 8-23. (a) Stable storage. (b) Crash after drive 1 is updated. (c) Bad spot.

block for block. Whenever two corresponding blocks differ, it can be assumed that drive 1 is the correct one (because drive 1 is always updated before drive 2), so the new block is copied from drive 1 to drive 2. When the recovery process is complete, both drives will again be identical.

Another potential problem is the spontaneous decay of a block. Dust particles or general wear and tear can give a previously valid block a sudden checksum error, without cause or warning, as shown in Fig. 8-23(c). When such an error is detected, the bad block can be regenerated from the corresponding block on the other drive.

As a consequence of its implementation, stable storage is well suited to applications that require a high degree of fault tolerance, such as atomic transactions. When data are written to stable storage and then read back to check that they have been written correctly, the chance of them subsequently being lost is extremely small.

In the next two sections we go into further details concerning checkpoints and message logging. Elnozahy et al. (2002) provide a survey of checkpointing and logging in distributed systems. Various algorithmic details can be found in Chow and Johnson (1997).

8.6.2 Checkpointing

In a fault-tolerant distributed system, backward error recovery requires that the system regularly saves its state onto stable storage. In particular, we need to record a consistent global state, also called a **distributed snapshot**. In a distributed snapshot, if a process P has recorded the receipt of a message, then there should also be a process Q that has recorded the sending of that message. After all, it must have come from somewhere.

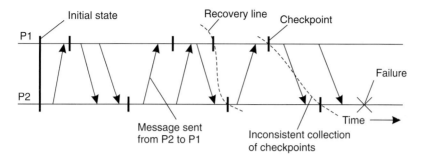

Figure 8-24. A recovery line.

In backward error recovery schemes, each process saves its state from time to time to a locally-available stable storage. To recover after a process or system failure requires that we construct a consistent global state from these local states. In particular, it is best to recover to the *most recent* distributed snapshot, also referred to as a **recovery line**. In other words, a recovery line corresponds to the most recent consistent collection of checkpoints, as shown in Fig. 8-24.

Independent Checkpointing

Unfortunately, the distributed nature of checkpointing (in which each process simply records its local state from time to time in an uncoordinated fashion) may make it difficult to find a recovery line. To discover a recovery line requires that each process is rolled back to its most recently saved state. If these local states jointly do not form a distributed snapshot, further rolling back is necessary. Below, we will describe a way to find a recovery line. This process of a cascaded rollback may lead to what is called the **domino effect** and is shown in Fig. 8-25.

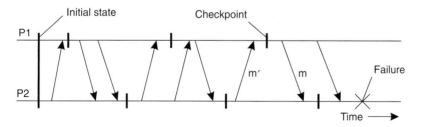

Figure 8-25. The domino effect.

When process P_2 crashes, we need to restore its state to the most recently saved checkpoint. As a consequence, process P_1 will also need to be rolled back.

Unfortunately, the two most recently saved local states do not form a consistent global state: the state saved by P_2 indicates the receipt of a message m, but no other process can be identified as its sender. Consequently, P_2 needs to be rolled back to an earlier state.

However, the next state to which P_2 is rolled back also cannot be used as part of a distributed snapshot. In this case, P_1 will have recorded the receipt of message m', but there is no recorded event of this message being sent. It is therefore necessary to also roll P_1 back to a previous state. In this example, it turns out that the recovery line is actually the initial state of the system.

As processes take local checkpoints independent of each other, this method is also referred to as **independent checkpointing**. An alternative solution is to globally coordinate checkpointing, as we discuss below, but coordination requires global synchronization, which may introduce performance problems. Another disadvantage of independent checkpointing is that each local storage needs to be cleaned up periodically, for example, by running a special distributed garbage collector. However, the main disadvantage lies in computing the recovery line.

Implementing independent checkpointing requires that dependencies are recorded in such a way that processes can jointly roll back to a consistent global state. To that end, let $CP_i(m)$ denote the m-th checkpoint taken by process P_i. Also, let $INT_i(m)$ denote the interval between checkpoints $CP_i(m-1)$ and $CP_i(m)$.

When process P_i sends a message in interval $INT_i(m)$, it piggybacks the pair (i,m) to the receiving process. When process P_j receives a message in interval $INT_j(n)$, along with the pair of indices (i,m), it then records the dependency $INT_i(m) \rightarrow INT_j(n)$. Whenever P_j takes checkpoint $CP_j(n)$, it additionally writes this dependency to its local stable storage, along with the rest of the recovery information that is part of $CP_j(n)$.

Now suppose that at a certain moment, process P_1 is required to roll back to checkpoint $CP_i(m-1)$. To ensure global consistency, we need to ensure that all processes that have received messages from P_i and were sent in interval $INT_i(m)$, are rolled back to a checkpointed state preceding the receipt of such messages. In particular, process P_j in our example, will need to be rolled back at least to checkpoint $CP_j(n-1)$. If $CP_j(n-1)$ does not lead to a globally consistent state, further rolling back may be necessary.

Calculating the recovery line requires an analysis of the interval dependencies recorded by each process when a checkpoint was taken. Without going into any further details, it turns out that such calculations are fairly complex and do not justify the need for independent checkpointing in comparison to coordinated checkpointing. In addition, as it turns out, it is often not the coordination between processes that is the dominating performance factor, but the overhead as the result of having to save the state to local stable storage. Therefore, coordinated checkpointing, which is much simpler than independent checkpointing, is often more popular, and will presumably stay so even when systems grow to much larger sizes (Elnozahy and Planck, 2004).

Coordinated Checkpointing

As its name suggests, in **coordinated checkpointing** all processes synchronize to jointly write their state to local stable storage. The main advantage of coordinated checkpointing is that the saved state is automatically globally consistent, so that cascaded rollbacks leading to the domino effect are avoided. The distributed snapshot algorithm discussed in Chap. 6 can be used to coordinate checkpointing. This algorithm is an example of nonblocking checkpoint coordination.

A simpler solution is to use a two-phase blocking protocol. A coordinator first multicasts a *CHECKPOINT_REQUEST* message to all processes. When a process receives such a message, it takes a local checkpoint, queues any subsequent message handed to it by the application it is executing, and acknowledges to the coordinator that it is has taken a checkpoint. When the coordinator has received an acknowledgment from all processes, it multicasts a *CHECKPOINT_DONE* message to allow the (blocked) processes to continue.

It is easy to see that this approach will also lead to a globally consistent state, because no incoming message will ever be registered as part of a checkpoint. The reason for this is that any message that follows a request for taking a checkpoint is not considered to be part of the local checkpoint. At the same time, outgoing messages (as handed to the checkpointing process by the application it is running), are queued locally until the *CHECKPOINT_DONE* message is received.

An improvement to this algorithm is to multicast a checkpoint request only to those processes that depend on the recovery of the coordinator, and ignore the other processes. A process is dependent on the coordinator if it has received a message that is directly or indirectly causally related to a message that the coordinator had sent since the last checkpoint. This leads to the notion of an **incremental snapshot**.

To take an incremental snapshot, the coordinator multicasts a checkpoint request only to those processes it had sent a message to since it last took a checkpoint. When a process P receives such a request, it forwards the request to all those processes to which P itself had sent a message since the last checkpoint, and so on. A process forwards the request only once. When all processes have been identified, a second multicast is used to actually trigger checkpointing and to let the processes continue where they had left off.

8.6.3 Message Logging

Considering that checkpointing is an expensive operation, especially concerning the operations involved in writing state to stable storage, techniques have been sought to reduce the number of checkpoints, but still enable recovery. An important technique in distributed systems is logging messages.

The basic idea underlying message logging is that if the transmission of messages can be *replayed*, we can still reach a globally consistent state but without having to restore that state from stable storage. Instead, a checkpointed state is taken as a starting point, and all messages that have been sent since are simply retransmitted and handled accordingly.

This approach works fine under the assumption of what is called a **piecewise deterministic model**. In such a model, the execution of each process is assumed to take place as a series of intervals in which events take place. These events are the same as those discussed in the context of Lamport's happened-before relationship in Chap. 6. For example, an event may be the execution of an instruction, the sending of a message, and so on. Each interval in the piecewise deterministic model is assumed to start with a nondeterministic event, such as the receipt of a message. However, from that moment on, the execution of the process is completely deterministic. An interval ends with the last event before a nondeterministic event occurs.

In effect, an interval can be replayed with a known result, that is, in a completely deterministic way, provided it is replayed starting with the same nondeterministic event as before. Consequently, if we record all nondeterministic events in such a model, it becomes possible to completely replay the entire execution of a process in a deterministic way.

Considering that message logs are necessary to recover from a process crash so that a globally consistent state is restored, it becomes important to know precisely when messages are to be logged. Following the approach described by Alvisi and Marzullo (1998), it turns out that many existing message-logging schemes can be easily characterized, if we concentrate on how they deal with orphan processes.

An **orphan process** is a process that survives the crash of another process, but whose state is inconsistent with the crashed process after its recovery. As an example, consider the situation shown in Fig. 8-26. Process Q receives messages m_1 and m_2 from process P and R, respectively, and subsequently sends a message m_3 to R. However, in contrast to all other messages, message m_2 is not logged. If process Q crashes and later recovers again, only the logged messages required for the recovery of Q are replayed, in our example, m_1. Because m_2 was not logged, its transmission will not be replayed, meaning that the transmission of m_3 also may not take place. Fig. 8-26.

However, the situation after the recovery of Q is inconsistent with that before its recovery. In particular, R holds a message (m_3) that was sent before the crash, but whose receipt and delivery do not take place when replaying what had happened before the crash. Such inconsistencies should obviously be avoided.

Characterizing Message-Logging Schemes

To characterize different message-logging schemes, we follow the approach described in Alvisi and Marzullo (1998). Each message m is considered to have a header that contains all information necessary to retransmit m, and to properly

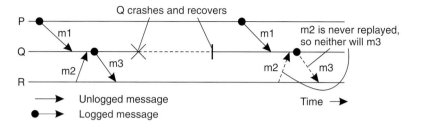

Figure 8-26. Incorrect replay of messages after recovery, leading to an orphan process.

handle it. For example, each header will identify the sender and the receiver, but also a sequence number to recognize it as a duplicate. In addition, a delivery number may be added to decide when exactly it should be handed over to the receiving application.

A message is said to be **stable** if it can no longer be lost, for example, because it has been written to stable storage. Stable messages can thus be used for recovery by replaying their transmission.

Each message m leads to a set $DEP(m)$ of processes that depend on the delivery of m. In particular, $DEP(m)$ consists of those processes to which m has been delivered. In addition, if another message m' is causally dependent on the delivery of m, and m' has been delivered to a process Q, then Q will also be contained in $DEP(m)$. Note that m' is causally dependent on the delivery of m, if it were sent by the same process that previously delivered m, or which had delivered another message that was causally dependent on the delivery of m.

The set $COPY(m)$ consists of those processes that have a copy of m, but not (yet) in their local stable storage. When a process Q delivers message m, it also becomes a member of $COPY(m)$. Note that $COPY(m)$ consists of those processes that could hand over a copy of m that can be used to replay the transmission of m. If all these processes crash, replaying the transmission of m is clearly not feasible.

Using these notations, it is now easy to define precisely what an orphan process is. Suppose that in a distributed system some processes have just crashed. Let Q be one of the surviving processes. Process Q is an orphan process if there is a message m, such that Q is contained in $DEP(m)$, while at the same time every process in $COPY(m)$ has crashed. In other words, an orphan process appears when it is dependent on m, but there is no way to replay m's transmission.

To avoid orphan processes, we thus need to ensure that if each process in $COPY(m)$ crashed, then no surviving process is left in $DEP(m)$. In other words, all processes in $DEP(m)$ should have crashed as well. This condition can be enforced if we can guarantee that whenever a process becomes a member of $DEP(m)$, it also becomes a member of $COPY(m)$. In other words, whenever a process becomes dependent on the delivery of m, it will always keep a copy of m.

There are essentially two approaches that can now be followed. The first approach is represented by what are called **pessimistic logging protocols**. These protocols take care that for each *nonstable* message m, there is at most one process dependent on m. In other words, pessimistic logging protocols ensure that each nonstable message m is delivered to at most one process. Note that as soon as m is delivered to, say process P, P becomes a member of $COPY(m)$.

The worst that can happen is that process P crashes without m ever having been logged. With pessimistic logging, P is not allowed to send any messages after the delivery of m without first having ensured that m has been written to stable storage. Consequently, no other processes will ever become dependent on the delivery of m to P, without having the possibility of replaying the transmission of m. In this way, orphan processes are always avoided.

In contrast, in an **optimistic logging protocol**, the actual work is done *after* a crash occurs. In particular, assume that for some message m, each process in $COPY(m)$ has crashed. In an optimistic approach, any orphan process in $DEP(m)$ is rolled back to a state in which it no longer belongs to $DEP(m)$. Clearly, optimistic logging protocols need to keep track of dependencies, which complicates their implementation.

As pointed out in Elnozahy et al. (2002), pessimistic logging is so much simpler than optimistic approaches, that it is the preferred way of message logging in practical distributed systems design.

8.6.4 Recovery-Oriented Computing

A related way of handling recovery is essentially to start over again. The underlying principle toward this way of masking failures is that it may be much cheaper to optimize for recovery, then it is aiming for systems that are free from failures for a long time. This approach is also referred to as **recovery-oriented computing** (Candea et al., 2004a).

There are different flavors of recovery-oriented computing. One flavor is to simply reboot (part of a system) and has been explored to restart Internet servers (Candea et al., 2004b, 2006). In order to be able reboot only a part of the system, it is crucial the fault is properly localized. At that point, rebooting simply means deleting all instances of the identified components, along with the threads operating on them, and (often) to just restart the associated requests. Note that fault localization itself may be a nontrivial exercise (Steinder and Sethi, 2004).

To enable rebooting as a practical recovery technique requires that components are largely decoupled in the sense that there are few or no dependencies between different components. If there are strong dependencies, then fault localization and analysis may still require that a complete server needs to be restarted at which point applying traditional recovery techniques as the ones we just discussed may be more efficient.

Another flavor of recovery-oriented computing is to apply checkpointing and recovery techniques, but to continue execution in a changed environment. The basic idea here is that many failures can be simply avoided if programs are given some more buffer space, memory is zeroed before allocated, changing the ordering of message delivery (as long as this does not affect semantics), and so on (Qin et al., 2005). The key idea is to tackle software failures (whereas many of the techniques discussed so far are aimed at, or are based on hardware failures). Because software execution is highly deterministic, changing an execution environment may save the day, but, of course, without repairing anything.

8.7 SUMMARY

Fault tolerance is an important subject in distributed systems design. Fault tolerance is defined as the characteristic by which a system can mask the occurrence and recovery from failures. In other words, a system is fault tolerant if it can continue to operate in the presence of failures.

Several types of failures exist. A crash failure occurs when a process simply halts. An omission failure occurs when a process does not respond to incoming requests. When a process responds too soon or too late to a request, it is said to exhibit a timing failure. Responding to an incoming request, but in the wrong way, is an example of a response failure. The most difficult failures to handle are those by which a process exhibits any kind of failure, called arbitrary or Byzantine failures.

Redundancy is the key technique needed to achieve fault tolerance. When applied to processes, the notion of process groups becomes important. A process group consists of a number of processes that closely cooperate to provide a service. In fault-tolerant process groups, one or more processes can fail without affecting the availability of the service the group implements. Often, it is necessary that communication within the group be highly reliable, and adheres to stringent ordering and atomicity properties in order to achieve fault tolerance.

Reliable group communication, also called reliable multicasting, comes in different forms. As long as groups are relatively small, it turns out that implementing reliability is feasible. However, as soon as very large groups need to be supported, scalability of reliable multicasting becomes problematic. The key issue in achieving scalability is to reduce the number of feedback messages by which receivers report the (un)successful receipt of a multicasted message.

Matters become worse when atomicity is to be provided. In atomic multicast protocols, it is essential that each group member have the same view concerning to which members a multicasted message has been delivered. Atomic multicasting can be precisely formulated in terms of a virtual synchronous execution model. In essence, this model introduces boundaries between which group membership does not change and which messages are reliably transmitted. A message can never cross a boundary.

Group membership changes are an example where each process needs to agree on the same list of members. Such agreement can be reached by means of a commit protocol, of which the two-phase commit protocol is the most widely applied. In a two-phase commit protocol, a coordinator first checks whether all processes agree to perform the same operation (i.e., whether they all agree to commit), and in a second round, multicasts the outcome of that poll. A three-phase commit protocol is used to handle the crash of the coordinator without having to block all processes to reach agreement until the coordinator recovers.

Recovery in fault-tolerant systems is invariably achieved by checkpointing the state of the system on a regular basis. Checkpointing is completely distributed. Unfortunately, taking a checkpoint is an expensive operation. To improve performance, many distributed systems combine checkpointing with message logging. By logging the communication between processes, it becomes possible to replay the execution of the system after a crash has occurred.

PROBLEMS

1. Dependable systems are often required to provide a high degree of security. Why?

2. What makes the fail-stop model in the case of crash failures so difficult to implement?

3. Consider a Web browser that returns an outdated cached page instead of a more recent one that had been updated at the server. Is this a failure, and if so, what kind of failure?

4. Can the model of triple modular redundancy described in the text handle Byzantine failures?

5. How many failed elements (devices plus voters) can Fig. 8-2 handle? Give an example of the worst case that can be masked.

6. Does TMR generalize to five elements per group instead of three? If so, what properties does it have?

7. For each of the following applications, do you think at-least-once semantics or at-most-once semantics is best? Discuss.

   (a) Reading and writing files from a file server.
   (b) Compiling a program.
   (c) Remote banking.

8. With asynchronous RPCs, a client is blocked until its request has been *accepted* by the server. To what extent do failures affect the semantics of asynchronous RPCs?

9. Give an example in which group communication requires no message ordering at all.

10. In reliable multicasting, is it always necessary that the communication layer keeps a copy of a message for retransmission purposes?

11. To what extent is scalability of atomic multicasting important?

12. In the text, we suggest that atomic multicasting can save the day when it comes to performing updates on an agreed set of processes. To what extent can we guarantee that each update is actually performed?

13. Virtual synchrony is analogous to weak consistency in distributed data stores, with group view changes acting as synchronization points. In this context, what would be the analog of strong consistency?

14. What are the permissible delivery orderings for the combination of FIFO and total-ordered multicasting in Fig. 8-15?

15. Adapt the protocol for installing a next view G_{i+1} in the case of virtual synchrony so that it can tolerate process failures.

16. In the two-phase commit protocol, why can blocking never be completely eliminated, even when the participants elect a new coordinator?

17. In our explanation of three-phase commit, it appears that committing a transaction is based on majority voting. Is this true?

18. In a piecewise deterministic execution model, is it sufficient to log only messages, or do we need to log other events as well?

19. Explain how the write-ahead log in distributed transactions can be used to recover from failures.

20. Does a stateless server need to take checkpoints?

21. Receiver-based message logging is generally considered better than sender-based logging. Why?

9

SECURITY

The last principle of distributed systems that we discuss is security. Security is by no means the least important principle. However, one could argue that it is one of the most difficult principles, as security needs to be pervasive throughout a system. A single design flaw with respect to security may render all security measures useless. In this chapter, we concentrate on the various mechanisms that are generally incorporated in distributed systems to support security.

We start with introducing the basic issues of security. Building all kinds of security mechanisms into a system does not really make sense unless it is known how those mechanisms are to be used, and against what. This requires that we know about the security policy that is to be enforced. The notion of a security policy, along with some general design issues for mechanisms that help enforce such policies, are discussed first. We also briefly touch upon the necessary cryptography.

Security in distributed systems can roughly be divided into two parts. One part concerns the communication between users or processes, possibly residing on different machines. The principal mechanism for ensuring secure communication is that of a secure channel. Secure channels, and more specifically, authentication, message integrity, and confidentiality, are discussed in a separate section.

The other part concerns authorization, which deals with ensuring that a process gets only those access rights to the resources in a distributed system it is entitled to. Authorization is covered in a separate section dealing with access control. In addition to traditional access control mechanisms, we also focus on access control when we have to deal with mobile code such as agents.

Secure channels and access control require mechanisms to distribute crypto-graphic keys, but also mechanisms to add and remove users from a system. These topics are covered by what is known as security management. In a separate section, we discuss issues dealing with managing cryptographic keys, secure group management, and handing out certificates that prove the owner is entitled to access specified resources.

9.1 INTRODUCTION TO SECURITY

We start our description of security in distributed systems by taking a look at some general security issues. First, it is necessary to define what a secure system is. We distinguish security *policies* from security *mechanisms*, and take a look at the Globus wide-area system for which a security policy has been explicitly formulated. Our second concern is to consider some general design issues for secure systems. Finally, we briefly discuss some cryptographic algorithms, which play a key role in the design of security protocols.

9.1.1 Security Threats, Policies, and Mechanisms

Security in a computer system is strongly related to the notion of dependability. Informally, a dependable computer system is one that we justifiably trust to deliver its services (Laprie, 1995). As mentioned in Chap. 7, dependability includes availability, reliability, safety, and maintainability. However, if we are to put our trust in a computer system, then confidentiality and integrity should also be taken into account. **Confidentiality** refers to the property of a computer system whereby its information is disclosed only to authorized parties. **Integrity** is the characteristic that alterations to a system's assets can be made only in an authorized way. In other words, improper alterations in a secure computer system should be detectable and recoverable. Major assets of any computer system are its hardware, software, and data.

Another way of looking at security in computer systems is that we attempt to protect the services and data it offers against **security threats**. There are four types of security threats to consider (Pfleeger, 2003):

1. Interception

2. Interruption

3. Modification

4. Fabrication

The concept of interception refers to the situation that an unauthorized party has gained access to a service or data. A typical example of interception is where communication between two parties has been overheard by someone else. Interception also happens when data are illegally copied, for example, after breaking into a person's private directory in a file system.

An example of interruption is when a file is corrupted or lost. More generally interruption refers to the situation in which services or data become unavailable, unusable, destroyed, and so on. In this sense, denial of service attacks by which someone maliciously attempts to make a service inaccessible to other parties is a security threat that classifies as interruption.

Modifications involve unauthorized changing of data or tampering with a service so that it no longer adheres to its original specifications. Examples of modifications include intercepting and subsequently changing transmitted data, tampering with database entries, and changing a program so that it secretly logs the activities of its user.

Fabrication refers to the situation in which additional data or activity are generated that would normally not exist. For example, an intruder may attempt to add an entry into a password file or database. Likewise, it is sometimes possible to break into a system by replaying previously sent messages. We shall come across such examples later in this chapter.

Note that interruption, modification, and fabrication can each be seen as a form of data falsification.

Simply stating that a system should be able to protect itself against all possible security threats is not the way to actually build a secure system. What is first needed is a description of security requirements, that is, a security policy. A **security policy** describes precisely which actions the entities in a system are allowed to take and which ones are prohibited. Entities include users, services, data, machines, and so on. Once a security policy has been laid down, it becomes possible to concentrate on the **security mechanisms** by which a policy can be enforced. Important security mechanisms are:

1. Encryption

2. Authentication

3. Authorization

4. Auditing

Encryption is fundamental to computer security. Encryption transforms data into something an attacker cannot understand. In other words, encryption provides a means to implement data confidentiality. In addition, encryption allows us to check whether data have been modified. It thus also provides support for integrity checks.

Authentication is used to verify the claimed identity of a user, client, server, host, or other entity. In the case of clients, the basic premise is that before a service starts to perform any work on behalf of a client, the service must learn the client's identity (unless the service is available to all). Typically, users are authenticated by means of passwords, but there are many other ways to authenticate clients.

After a client has been authenticated, it is necessary to check whether that client is authorized to perform the action requested. Access to records in a medical database is a typical example. Depending on who accesses the database, permission may be granted to read records, to modify certain fields in a record, or to add or remove a record.

Auditing tools are used to trace which clients accessed what, and which way. Although auditing does not really provide any protection against security threats, audit logs can be extremely useful for the analysis of a security breach, and subsequently taking measures against intruders. For this reason, attackers are generally keen not to leave any traces that could eventually lead to exposing their identity. In this sense, logging accesses makes attacking sometimes a riskier business.

Example: The Globus Security Architecture

The notion of security policy and the role that security mechanisms play in distributed systems for enforcing such policies is often best explained by taking a look at a concrete example. Consider the security policy defined for the Globus wide-area system (Chervenak et al., 2000). Globus is a system supporting large-scale distributed computations in which many hosts, files, and other resources are simultaneously used for doing a computation. Such environments are also referred to as computational grids (Foster and Kesselman, 2003). Resources in these grids are often located in different administrative domains that may be located in different parts of the world.

Because users and resources are vast in number and widely spread across different administrative domains, security is essential. To devise and properly use security mechanisms, it is necessary to understand what exactly needs to be protected, and what the assumptions are with respect to security. Simplifying matters somewhat, the security policy for Globus entails the following eight statements, which we explain below (Foster et al., 1998):

1. The environment consists of multiple administrative domains.

2. Local operations (i.e., operations that are carried out only within a single domain) are subject to a local domain security policy only.

3. Global operations (i.e., operations involving several domains) require the initiator to be known in each domain where the operation is carried out.

4. Operations between entities in different domains require mutual authentication.

5. Global authentication replaces local authentication.

6. Controlling access to resources is subject to local security only.

7. Users can delegate rights to processes.

8. A group of processes in the same domain can share credentials.

Globus assumes that the environment consists of multiple administrative domains, where each domain has its own local security policy. It is assumed that local policies cannot be changed just because the domain participates in Globus, nor can the overall policy of Globus override local security decisions. Consequently, security in Globus will restrict itself to operations that affect multiple domains.

Related to this issue is that Globus assumes that operations that are entirely local to a domain are subject only to that domain's security policy. In other words, if an operation is initiated and carried out within a single domain, all security issues will be carried out using local security measures only. Globus will not impose additional measures.

The Globus security policy states that requests for operations can be initiated either globally or locally. The initiator, be it a user or process acting on behalf of a user, must be locally known within each domain where that operation is carried out. For example, a user may have a global name that is mapped to domain-specific local names. How exactly that mapping takes place is left to each domain.

An important policy statement is that operations between entities in different domains require mutual authentication. This means, for example, that if a user in one domain makes use of a service from another domain, then the identity of the user will have to be verified. Equally important is that the user will have to be assured that he is using a service he thinks he is using. We return to authentication, extensively, later in this chapter.

The above two policy issues are combined into the following security requirement. If the identity of a user has been verified, and that user is also known locally in a domain, then he can act as being authenticated for that local domain. This means that Globus requires that its systemwide authentication measures are sufficient to consider that a user has already been authenticated for a remote domain (where that user is known) when accessing resources in that domain. Additional authentication by that domain should not be necessary.

Once a user (or process acting on behalf of a user) has been authenticated, it is still necessary to verify the exact access rights with respect to resources. For example, a user wanting to modify a file will first have to be authenticated, after which it can be checked whether or not that user is actually permitted to modify the file. The Globus security policy states that such access control decisions are made entirely local within the domain where the accessed resource is located.

To explain the seventh statement, consider a mobile agent in Globus that carries out a task by initiating several operations in different domains, one after another. Such an agent may take a long time to complete its task. To avoid having to communicate with the user on whose behalf the agent is acting, Globus requires that processes can be delegated a subset of the user's rights. As a consequence, by authenticating an agent and subsequently checking its rights, Globus should be able to allow an agent to initiate an operation without having to contact the agent's owner.

As a final policy statement, Globus requires that groups of processes running with a single domain and acting on behalf of the same user may share a single set of credentials. As will be explained below, credentials are needed for authentication. This statement essentially opens the road to scalable solutions for authentication by not demanding that each process carries its own unique set of credentials.

The Globus security policy allows its designers to concentrate on developing an overall solution for security. By assuming each domain enforces its own security policy, Globus concentrates only on security threats involving multiple domains. In particular, the security policy indicates that the important design issues are the representation of a user in a remote domain, and the allocation of resources from a remote domain to a user or his representative. What Globus therefore primarily needs, are mechanisms for cross-domain authentication, and making a user known in remote domains.

For this purpose, two types of representatives are introduced. A **user proxy** is a process that is given permission to act on behalf of a user for a limited period of time. Resources are represented by resource proxies. A **resource proxy** is a process running within a specific domain that is used to translate global operations on a resource into local operations that comply with that particular domain's security policy. For example, a user proxy typically communicates with a resource proxy when access to that resource is required.

The Globus security architecture essentially consists of entities such as users, user proxies, resource proxies, and general processes. These entities are located in domains and interact with each other. In particular, the security architecture defines four different protocols, as illustrated in Fig. 9-1 [see also Foster et al. (1998)].

The first protocol describes precisely how a user can create a user proxy and delegate rights to that proxy. In particular, in order to let the user proxy act on behalf of its user, the user gives the proxy an appropriate set of credentials.

The second protocol specifies how a user proxy can request the allocation of a resource in a remote domain. In essence, the protocol tells a resource proxy to create a process in the remote domain after mutual authentication has taken place. That process represents the user (just as the user proxy did), but operates in the same domain as the requested resource. The process is given access to the resource subject to the access control decisions local to that domain.

A process created in a remote domain may initiate additional computations in other domains. Consequently, a protocol is needed to allocate resources in a remote domain as requested by a process other than a user proxy. In the Globus system, this type of allocation is done via the user proxy, by letting a process have its

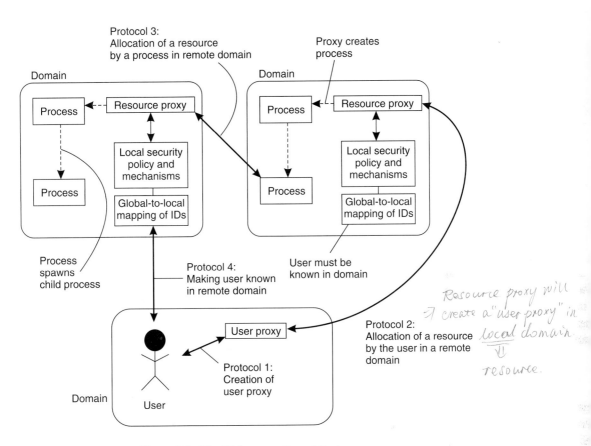

Figure 9-1. The Globus security architecture.

associated user proxy request the allocation of resources, essentially following the second protocol.

The fourth and last protocol in the Globus security architecture is the way a user can make himself known in a domain. Assuming that a user has an account in a domain, what needs to be established is that the systemwide credentials as held by a user proxy are automatically converted to credentials that are recognized by the specific domain. The protocol prescribes how the mapping between the global credentials and the local ones can be registered by the user in a mapping table local to that domain.

Specific details of each protocol are described in Foster et al. (1998). The important issue here is that the Globus security architecture reflects its security policy as stated above. The mechanisms used to implement that architecture, in particular the above mentioned protocols, are common to many distributed systems, and are discussed extensively in this chapter. The main difficulty in designing secure distributed systems is not so much caused by security mechanisms, but by deciding on how those mechanisms are to be used to enforce a security policy. In the next section, we consider some of these design decisions.

9.1.2 Design Issues

A distributed system, or any computer system for that matter, must provide security services by which a wide range of security policies can be implemented. There are a number of important design issues that need to be taken into account when implementing general-purpose security services. In the following pages, we discuss three of these issues: focus of control, layering of security mechanisms, and simplicity [see also Gollmann (2006)].

Focus of Control

When considering the protection of a (possibly distributed) application, there are essentially three different approaches that can be followed, as shown in Fig. 9-2. The first approach is to concentrate directly on the protection of the data that is associated with the application. By direct, we mean that irrespective of the various operations that can possibly be performed on a data item, the primary concern is to ensure data integrity. Typically, this type of protection occurs in database systems in which various integrity constraints can be formulated that are automatically checked each time a data item is modified [see, for example, Doorn and Rivero (2002)].

The second approach is to concentrate on protection by specifying exactly which operations may be invoked, and by whom, when certain data or resources are to be accessed. In this case, the focus of control is strongly related to access control mechanisms, which we discuss extensively later in this chapter. For example, in an object-based system, it may be decided to specify for each method that is made available to clients which clients are permitted to invoke that method. Alternatively, access control methods can be applied to an entire interface offered by an object, or to the entire object itself. This approach thus allows for various granularities of access control.

A third approach is to focus directly on users by taking measures by which only specific people have access to the application, irrespective of the operations they want to carry out. For example, a database in a bank may be protected by denying access to anyone except the bank's upper management and people specifically authorized to access it. As another example, in many universities, certain data and applications are restricted to be used by faculty and staff members only, whereas access by students is not allowed. In effect, control is focused on defining **roles** that users have, and once a user's role has been verified, access to a resource is either granted or denied. As part of designing a secure system, it is thus necessary to define roles that people may have, and provide mechanisms to support role-based access control. We return to roles later in this chapter.

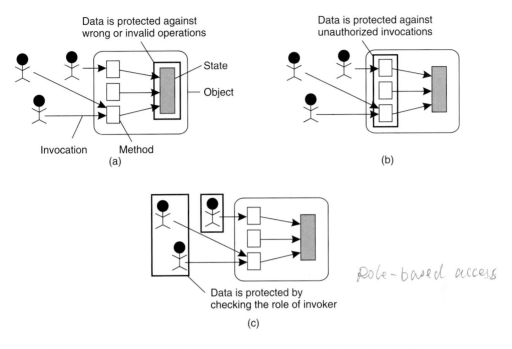

Figure 9-2. Three approaches for protection against security threats. (a) Protection against invalid operations (b) Protection against unauthorized invocations. (c) Protection against unauthorized users.

Layering of Security Mechanisms

An important issue in designing secure systems is to decide at which level security mechanisms should be placed. A level in this context is related to the logical organization of a system into a number of layers. For example, computer networks are often organized into layers following some reference model, as we discussed in Chap. 4. In Chap. 1, we introduced the organization of distributed systems consisting of separate layers for applications, middleware, operating system services, and the operating system kernel. Combining the layered organization of computer networks and distributed systems, leads roughly to what is shown in Fig. 9-3.

In essence, Fig. 9-3 separates general-purpose services from communication services. This separation is important for understanding the layering of security in distributed systems and, in particular, the notion of trust. The difference between trust and security is important. A system is either secure or it is not (taking various probabilistic measures into account), but whether a client considers a system to be secure is a matter of trust (Bishop, 2003). Security is technical; trust is emotional. In which layer security mechanisms are placed depends on the trust a client has in how secure the services are in a particular layer.

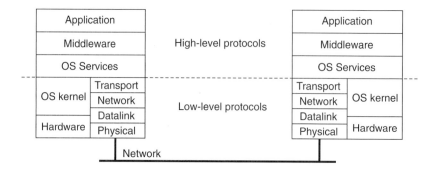

Figure 9-3. The logical organization of a distributed system into several layers.

As an example, consider an organization located at different sites that are connected through a communication service such as **Switched Multi-megabit Data Service (SMDS)**. An SMDS network can be thought of as a link-level backbone connecting various local-area networks at possibly geographically dispersed sites, as shown in Fig. 9-4.

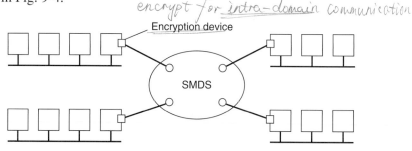

Figure 9-4. Several sites connected through a wide-area backbone service.

Security can be provided by placing encryption devices at each SMDS router, as also shown in Fig. 9-4. These devices automatically encrypt and decrypt packets that are sent between sites, but do not otherwise provide secure communication between hosts at the same site. If Alice at site *A* sends a message to Bob at site *B*, and she is worried about her message being intercepted, she must at least trust the encryption of intersite traffic to work properly. This means, for example, that she must trust the system administrators at both sites to have taken the proper measures against tampering with the devices.

Now suppose that Alice does not trust the security of intersite traffic. She may then decide to take her own measures by using a transport-level security service such as SSL. SSL stands for **Secure Sockets Layer** and can be used to securely send messages across a TCP connection. We will discuss the details of SSL later Chap. 12 when discussing Web-based systems. The important thing to observe here is that SSL allows Alice to set up a secure connection to Bob. All transport-level messages will be encrypted—and at the SMDS level as well, but that is of no concern to Alice. In this case, Alice will have to put her trust into SSL. In other words, she believes that SSL is secure.

In distributed systems, security mechanisms are often placed in the middleware layer. If Alice does not trust SSL, she may want to use a local secure RPC service. Again, she will have to trust this RPC service to do what it promises, such as not leaking information or properly authenticating clients and servers.

provide service beyond those provided by OS as to enable communi...

Security services that are placed in the middleware layer of a distributed system can be trusted only if the services they rely on to be secure are indeed secure. For example, if a secure RPC service is partly implemented by means of SSL, then trust in the RPC service depends on how much trust one has in SSL. If SSL is not trusted, then there can be no trust in the security of the RPC service.

Distribution of Security Mechanisms

Dependencies between services regarding trust lead to the notion of a **Trusted Computing Base (TCB)**. A TCB is the set of all security mechanisms in a (distributed) computer system that are needed to enforce a security policy, and that thus need to be trusted. The smaller the TCB, the better. If a distributed system is built as middleware on an existing network operating system, its security may depend on the security of the underlying local operating systems. In other words, the TCB in a distributed system may include the local operating systems at various hosts.

Consider a file server in a distributed file system. Such a server may need to rely on the various protection mechanisms offered by its local operating system. Such mechanisms include not only those for protecting files against accesses by processes other than the file server, but also mechanisms to protect the file server from being maliciously brought down.

Middleware-based distributed systems thus require trust in the existing local operating systems they depend on. If such trust does not exist, then part of the functionality of the local operating systems may need to be incorporated into the distributed system itself. Consider a microkernel operating system, in which most operating-system services run as normal user processes. In this case, the file system, for instance, can be entirely replaced by one tailored to the specific needs of a distributed system, including its various security measures.

Consistent with this approach is to separate security services from other types of services by distributing services across different machines depending on amount of security required. For example, for a secure distributed file system, it may be possible to isolate the file server from clients by placing the server on a machine with a trusted operating system, possibly running a dedicated secure file system. Clients and their applications are placed on untrusted machines.

This separation effectively reduces the TCB to a relatively small number of machines and software components. By subsequently protecting those machines against security attacks from the outside, overall trust in the security of the distributed system can be increased. Preventing clients and their applications direct access to critical services is followed in the **Reduced Interfaces for Secure System Components** (**RISSC**) approach, as described in Neumann (1995). In the RISSC approach, any security-critical server is placed on a separate machine isolated from end-user systems using low-level secure network interfaces, as shown in Fig. 9-5. Clients and their applications run on different machines and can access the secured server only through these network interfaces.

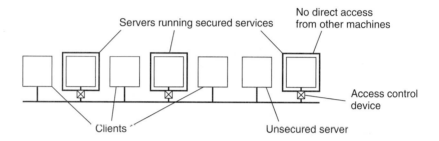

Figure 9-5. The principle of RISSC as applied to secure distributed systems.

Simplicity

Another important design issue related to deciding in which layer to place security mechanisms is that of simplicity. Designing a secure computer system is generally considered a difficult task. Consequently, if a system designer can use a few, simple mechanisms that are easily understood and trusted to work, the better it is.

Unfortunately, simple mechanisms are not always sufficient for implementing security policies. Consider once again the situation in which Alice wants to send a message to Bob as discussed above. Link-level encryption is a simple and easy-to-understand mechanism to protect against interception of intersite message traffic. However, much more is needed if Alice wants to be sure that only Bob will receive her messages. In that case, user-level authentication services are needed, and Alice may need to be aware of how such services work in order to put her trust in it. User-level authentication may therefore require at least a notion of cryptographic keys and awareness of mechanisms such as certificates, despite the fact that many security services are highly automated and hidden from users.

In other cases, the application itself is inherently complex and introducing security only makes matters worse. An example application domain involving complex security protocols (as we discuss later in this chapter) is that of digital payment systems. The complexity of digital payment protocols is often caused by the fact that multiple parties need to communicate to make a payment. In these cases, it is important that the underlying mechanisms that are used to implement the protocols are relatively simple and easy to understand. Simplicity will contribute to the trust that end users will put into the application and, more importantly, will contribute to convincing the designers that the system has no security holes.

9.1.3 Cryptography

Fundamental to security in distributed systems is the use of cryptographic techniques. The basic idea of applying these techniques is simple. Consider a sender S wanting to transmit message m to a receiver R. To protect the message against security threats, the sender first **encrypts** it into an unintelligible message m', and subsequently sends m' to R. R, in turn, must **decrypt** the received message into its original form m.

Encryption and decryption are accomplished by using cryptographic methods parameterized by keys, as shown in Fig. 9-6. The original form of the message that is sent is called the **plaintext**, shown as P in Fig. 9-6; the encrypted form is referred to as the **ciphertext**, illustrated as C.

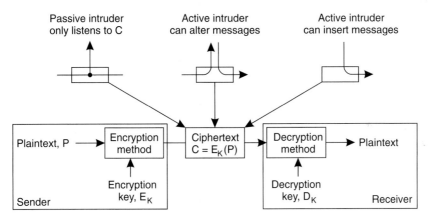

Figure 9-6. Intruders and eavesdroppers in communication.

To describe the various security protocols that are used in building security services for distributed systems, it is useful to have a notation to relate plaintext, ciphertext, and keys. Following the common notational conventions, we will use $C = E_K(P)$ to denote that the ciphertext C is obtained by encrypting the plaintext P using key K. Likewise, $P = D_K(C)$ is used to express the decryption of the ciphertext C using key K, resulting in the plaintext P.

Returning to our example shown in Fig. 9-6, while transferring a message as ciphertext C, there are three different attacks that we need to protect against, and for which encryption helps. First, an **intruder** may intercept the message without either the sender or receiver being aware that eavesdropping is happening. Of course, if the transmitted message has been encrypted in such a way that it cannot be easily decrypted without having the proper key, interception is useless: the intruder will see only unintelligible data. (By the way, the fact alone that a message is being transmitted may sometimes be enough for an intruder to draw conclusions. For example, if during a world crisis the amount of traffic into the White House suddenly drops dramatically while the amount of traffic going into a certain mountain in Colorado increases by the same amount, there may be useful information in knowing that.)

The second type of attack that needs to be dealt with is that of modifying the message. Modifying plaintext is easy; modifying ciphertext that has been properly encrypted is much more difficult because the intruder will first have to decrypt the message before he can meaningfully modify it. In addition, he will also have to properly encrypt it again or otherwise the receiver may notice that the message has been tampered with.

The third type of attack is when an intruder inserts encrypted messages into the communication system, attempting to make R believe these messages came from S. Again, as we shall see later in this chapter, encryption can help protect against such attacks. Note that if an intruder can modify messages, he can also insert messages.

There is a fundamental distinction between different cryptographic systems, based on whether or not the encryption and decryption key are the same. In a **symmetric cryptosystem**, the same key is used to encrypt and decrypt a message. In other words,

$$P = D_K(E_K(P))$$

Symmetric cryptosystems are also referred to as secret-key or shared-key systems, because the sender and receiver are required to share the same key, and to ensure that protection works, this shared key must be kept secret; no one else is allowed to see the key. We will use the notation $K_{A,B}$ to denote a key shared by A and B.

In an **asymmetric cryptosystem**, the keys for encryption and decryption are different, but together form a unique pair. In other words, there is a separate key K_E for encryption and one for decryption, K_D, such that

$$P = D_{K_D}(E_{K_E}(P))$$

One of the keys in an asymmetric cryptosystem is kept private; the other is made public. For this reason, asymmetric cryptosystems are also referred to as **public-key systems**. In what follows, we use the notation K_A^+ to denote a public key belonging to A, and K_A^- as its corresponding private key.

Anticipating the detailed discussions on security protocols later in this chapter, which one of the encryption or decryption keys that is actually made public depends on how the keys are used. For example, if Alice wants to send a confidential message to Bob, she should use Bob's public key to encrypt the message. Because Bob is the only one holding the private decryption key, he is also the only person that can decrypt the message.

On the other hand, suppose that Bob wants to know for sure that the message he just received actually came from Alice. In that case, Alice can keep her encryption key private to encrypt the messages she sends. If Bob can successfully decrypt a message using Alice's public key (and the plaintext in the message has enough information to make it meaningful to Bob), he knows that message must have come from Alice, because the decryption key is uniquely tied to the encryption key. We return to such algorithms in detail below.

One final application of cryptography in distributed systems is the use of **hash functions**. A hash function H takes a message m of arbitrary length as input and produces a bit string h having a fixed length as output:

$$h = H(m)$$

A hash h is somewhat comparable to the extra bits that are appended to a message in communication systems to allow for error detection, such a cyclic-redundancy check (CRC).

Hash functions that are used in cryptographic systems have a number of essential properties. First, they are **one-way functions**, meaning that it is computationally infeasible to find the input m that corresponds to a known output h. On the other hand, computing h from m is easy. Second, they have the **weak collision resistance** property, meaning that given an input m and its associated output $h = H(m)$, it is computationally infeasible to find another, different input $m' \neq m$, such that $H(m) = H(m')$. Finally, cryptographic hash functions also have the **strong collision resistance** property, which means that, when given only H, it is computationally infeasible to find any two different input values m and m', such that $H(m) = H(m')$.

Similar properties must apply to any encryption function E and the keys that are used. Furthermore, for any encryption function E, it should be computationally infeasible to find the key K when given the plaintext P and associated ciphertext $C = E_K(P)$. Likewise, analogous to collision resistance, when given a plaintext P and a key K, it should be effectively impossible to find another key K' such that $E_K(P) = E_{K'}(P)$.

The art and science of devising algorithms for cryptographic systems has a long and fascinating history (Kahn, 1967), and building secure systems is often surprisingly difficult, or even impossible (Schneier, 2000). It is beyond the scope of this book to discuss any of these algorithms in detail. However, to give some impression of cryptography in computer systems, we will now briefly present three representative algorithms. Detailed information on these and other cryptographic algorithms can be found in Ferguson and Schneier (2003), Menezes et al., (1996), and Schneier (1996).

Before we go into the details of the various protocols, Fig. 9-7 summarizes the notation and abbreviations we use in the mathematical expressions to follow.

Notation	Description
$K_{A,B}$	Secret key shared by A and B
K_A^+	Public key of A
K_A^-	Private key of A

Figure 9-7. Notation used in this chapter.

Symmetric Cryptosystems: DES

Our first example of a cryptographic algorithm is the **Data Encryption Standard** (**DES**), which is used for symmetric cryptosystems. DES is designed to operate on 64-bit blocks of data. A block is transformed into an encrypted (64 bit) block of output in 16 rounds, where each round uses a different 48-bit key for encryption. Each of these 16 keys is derived from a 56-bit master key, as shown in Fig. 9-8(a). Before an input block starts its 16 rounds of encryption, it is first subject to an initial permutation, of which the inverse is later applied to the encrypted output leading to the final output block.

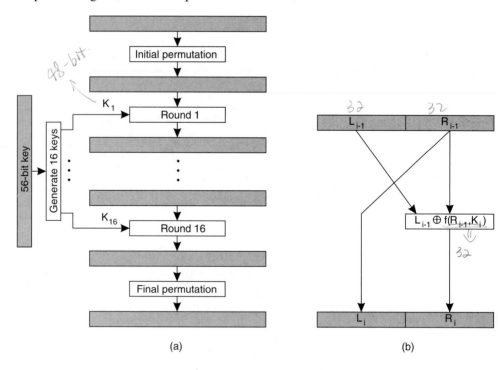

(a)   (b)

Figure 9-8. (a) The principle of DES. (b) Outline of one encryption round.

Each encryption round i takes the 64-bit block produced by the previous round $i - 1$ as its input, as shown in Fig. 9-8(b). The 64 bits are split into a left part L_{i-1} and a right part R_{i-1}, each containing 32 bits. The right part is used for the left part in the next round, that is, $L_i = R_{i-1}$.

The hard work is done in the mangler function f. This function takes a 32-bit block R_{i-1} as input, together with a 48-bit key K_i, and produces a 32-bit block that is XORed with L_{i-1} to produce R_i. (XOR is an abbreviation for the exclusive or operation.) The mangler function first expands R_{i-1} to a 48-bit block and XORs it with K_i. The result is partitioned into eight chunks of six bits each. Each chunk is then fed into a different **S-box**, which is an operation that substitutes each of the 64 possible 6-bit inputs into one of 16 possible 4-bit outputs. The eight output chunks of four bits each are then combined into a 32-bit value and permuted again.

[handwritten margin notes: $48 = 6\text{-bit} \times 8$. $6\text{-bit} \xrightarrow{S\text{-box}} 4\text{-bit}$. (diff 6-bit can generate same 4-bit)]

[handwritten: $8 \times 4\text{-bit} = 32\text{-bit}$]

The 48-bit key K_i for round i is derived from the 56-bit master key as follows. First, the master key is permuted and divided into two 28-bit halves. For each round, each half is first rotated one or two bits to the left, after which 24 bits are extracted. Together with 24 bits from the other rotated half, a 48-bit key is constructed. The details of one encryption round are shown in Fig. 9-9.

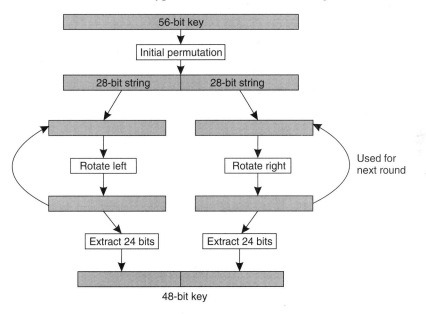

Figure 9-9. Details of per-round key generation in DES.

The principle of DES is quite simple, but the algorithm is difficult to break using analytical methods. Using a brute-force attack by simply searching for a key that will do the job has become easy as has been demonstrated a number of times. However, using DES three times in a special encrypt-decrypt-encrypt mode with different keys, also known as **Triple DES** is much more safe and is still often used [see also Barker (2004)].

What makes DES difficult to attack by analysis is that the rationale behind the design has never been explained in public. For example, it is known that taking other S-boxes than are currently used in the standard, makes the algorithm substantially easier to break (see Pfleeger, 2003 for a brief analysis of DES). A rationale for the design and use of the S-boxes was published only after "new" attack models had been devised in the 1990s. DES proved to be quite resistant to these attacks, and its designers revealed that the newly devised models were already known to them when they developed DES in 1974 (Coppersmith, 1994).

DES has been used as a standard encryption technique for years, but is currently in the process of being replaced by the Rijndael algorithm blocks of 128 bits. There are also variants with larger keys and larger data blocks. The algorithm has been designed to be fast enough so that it can even be implemented on smart cards, which form an increasingly important application area for cryptography.

Public-Key Cryptosystems: RSA

Our second example of a cryptographic algorithm is very widely used for public-key systems: **RSA**, named after its inventors: Rivest, Shamir, and Adleman (1978). The security of RSA comes from the fact that no methods are known to efficiently find the **prime factors** of large numbers. It can be shown that each integer can be written as the product of prime numbers. For example, 2100 can be written as

$$2100 = 2 \times 2 \times 3 \times 5 \times 5 \times 7$$

making 2, 3, 5, and 7 the prime factors in 2100. In RSA, the private and public keys are constructed from very large prime numbers (consisting of hundreds of decimal digits). As it turns out, breaking RSA is equivalent to finding those two prime numbers. So far, this has shown to be computationally infeasible despite mathematicians working on the problem for centuries.

Generating the private and public keys requires four steps:

1. Choose two very large prime numbers, p and q.

2. Compute $n = p \times q$ and $z = (p - 1) \times (q - 1)$.

3. Choose a number d that is relatively prime to z.

4. Compute the number e such that $e \times d = 1 \bmod z$.

One of the numbers, say d, can subsequently be used for decryption, whereas e is used for encryption. Only one of these two is made public, depending on what the algorithm is being used for.

⟨e,n⟩ = public key.
⟨d,n⟩ = private key.

Let us consider the case that Alice wants to keep the messages she sends to Bob confidential. In other words, she wants to ensure that no one but Bob can intercept and read her messages to him. RSA considers each message m to be just a string of bits. Each message is first divided into fixed-length blocks, where each block m_i, interpreted as a binary number, should lie in the interval $0 \leq m_i < n$.

To encrypt message m, the sender calculates for each block m_i the value $c_i = m_i^e \ (mod \ n)$, which is then sent to the receiver. Decryption at the receiver's side takes place by computing $m_i = c_i^d \ (mod \ n)$. Note that for the encryption, both e and n are needed, whereas decryption requires knowing the values d and n.

When comparing RSA to symmetric cryptosystems such as DES, RSA has the drawback of being computationally more complex. As it turns out, encrypting messages using RSA is approximately 100–1000 times slower than DES, depending on the implementation technique used. As a consequence, many cryptographic systems use RSA to exchange only shared keys in a secure way, but much less for actually encrypting "normal" data. We will see examples of the combination of these two techniques later in succeeding sections.

Hash Functions: MD5

As a last example of a widely-used cryptographic algorithm, we take a look at MD5 (Rivest, 1992). **MD5** is a hash function for computing a 128-bit, fixed length **message digest** from an arbitrary length binary input string. The input string is first padded to a total length of 448 bits (modulo 512), after which the length of the original bit string is added as a 64-bit integer. In effect, the input is converted to a series of 512-bit blocks.

The structure of the algorithm is shown in Fig. 9-10. Starting with some constant 128-bit value, the algorithm proceeds in k phases, where k is the number of 512-bit blocks comprising the padded message. During each phase, a 128-bit digest is computed out of a 512-bit block of data coming from the padded message, and the 128-bit digest computed in the preceding phase.

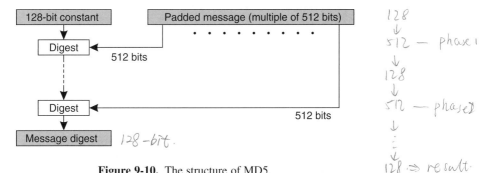

128
↓
512 — phase 1
↓
128
↓
512 — phase 2
↓
⋮
↓
128 ⇒ result

128-bit.

Figure 9-10. The structure of MD5.

A phase in MD5 consists of four rounds of computations, where each round uses one of the following four functions:

$$F(x,y,z) = (x \text{ } AND \text{ } y) \text{ } OR \text{ } ((NOT \text{ } x) \text{ } AND \text{ } z)$$
$$G(x,y,z) = (x \text{ } AND \text{ } z) \text{ } OR \text{ } (y \text{ } AND \text{ } (NOT \text{ } z))$$
$$H(x,y,z) = x \text{ } XOR \text{ } y \text{ } XOR \text{ } z$$
$$I(x,y,z) \text{ } = y \text{ } XOR \text{ } (x \text{ } OR \text{ } (NOT \text{ } z))$$

Each of these functions operates on 32-bit variables x, y, and z. To illustrate how these functions are used, consider a 512-bit block b from the padded message that is being processed during phase k. Block b is divided into 16 32-bit subblocks $b_0, b_1, ..., b_{15}$. During the first round, function F is used to change four variables (denoted as p, q, r, and s, respectively) in 16 iterations as shown in Fig. 9-11 These variables are carried to each next round, and after a phase has finished, passed on to the next phase. There are a total of 64 predefined constants C_i. The notation $x \lll n$ is used to denote a *left rotate*: the bits in x are shifted n positions to the left, where the bit shifted off the left is placed in the rightmost position.

Iterations 1–8	Iterations 9–16
$p \leftarrow (p + F(q,r,s) + b_0 + C_1) \lll 7$	$p \leftarrow (p + F(q,r,s) + b_8 + C_9) \lll 7$
$s \leftarrow (s + F(p,q,r) + b_1 + C_2) \lll 12$	$s \leftarrow (s + F(p,q,r) + b_9 + C_{10}) \lll 12$
$r \leftarrow (r + F(s,p,q) + b_2 + C_3) \lll 17$	$r \leftarrow (r + F(s,p,q) + b_{10} + C_{11}) \lll 17$
$q \leftarrow (q + F(r,s,p) + b_3 + C_4) \lll 22$	$q \leftarrow (q + F(r,s,p) + b_{11} + C_{12}) \lll 22$
$p \leftarrow (p + F(q,r,s) + b_4 + C_5) \lll 7$	$p \leftarrow (p + F(q,r,s) + b_{12} + C_{13}) \lll 7$
$s \leftarrow (s + F(p,q,r) + b_5 + C_6) \lll 12$	$s \leftarrow (s + F(p,q,r) + b_{13} + C_{14}) \lll 12$
$r \leftarrow (r + F(s,p,q) + b_6 + C_7) \lll 17$	$r \leftarrow (r + F(s,p,q) + b_{14} + C_{15}) \lll 17$
$q \leftarrow (q + F(r,s,p) + b_7 + C_8) \lll 22$	$q \leftarrow (q + F(r,s,p) + b_{15} + C_{16}) \lll 22$

Figure 9-11. The 16 iterations during the first round in a phase in MD5.

The second round uses the function G in a similar fashion, whereas H and I are used in the third and fourth round, respectively. Each step thus consists of 64 iterations, after which the next phase is started, but now with the values that p, q, r, and s have at that point.

9.2 SECURE CHANNELS

In the preceding chapters, we have frequently used the client-server model as a convenient way to organize a distributed system. In this model, servers may possibly be distributed and replicated, but also act as clients with respect to other servers. When considering security in distributed systems, it is once again useful to think in terms of clients and servers. In particular, making a distributed system secure essentially boils down to two predominant issues. The first issue is how to make the communication between clients and servers secure. Secure communication requires authentication of the communicating parties. In many cases it also requires ensuring message integrity and possibly confidentiality as well. As part of this problem, we also need to consider protecting the communication within a group of servers.

The second issue is that of authorization: once a server has accepted a request from a client, how can it find out whether that client is authorized to have that request carried out? Authorization is related to the problem of controlling access to resources, which we discuss extensively in the next section. In this section, we concentrate on protecting the communication within a distributed system.

The issue of protecting communication between clients and servers, can be thought of in terms of setting up a **secure channel** between communicating parties (Voydock and Kent, 1983). A secure channel protects senders and receivers against interception, modification, and fabrication of messages. It does not also necessarily protect against interruption. Protecting messages against interception is done by ensuring confidentiality: the secure channel ensures that its messages cannot be eavesdropped by intruders. Protecting against modification and fabrication by intruders is done through protocols for mutual authentication and message integrity. In the following pages, we first discuss various protocols that can be used for authentication, using symmetric as well as public-key cryptosystems. A detailed description of the logics underlying authentication can be found in Lampson et al. (1992). We discuss confidentiality and message integrity separately.

9.2.1 Authentication

Before going into the details of various authentication protocols, it is worthwhile noting that authentication and message integrity cannot do without each other. Consider, for example, a distributed system that supports authentication of two communicating parties, but does not provide mechanisms to ensure message integrity. In such a system, Bob may know for sure that Alice is the sender of a message m. However, if Bob cannot be given guarantees that m has not been modified during transmission, what use is it to him to know that Alice sent (the original version of) m?

Likewise, suppose that only message integrity is supported, but no mechanisms exist for authentication. When Bob receives a message stating that he has just won $1,000,000 in the lottery, how happy can he be if he cannot verify that the message was sent by the organizers of that lottery?

Consequently, authentication and message integrity should go together. In many protocols, the combination works roughly as follows. Again, assume that Alice and Bob want to communicate, and that Alice takes the initiative in setting up a channel. Alice starts by sending a message to Bob, or otherwise to a trusted third party who will help set up the channel. Once the channel has been set up,

Alice knows for sure that she is talking to Bob, and Bob knows for sure he is talking to Alice, they can exchange messages.

To subsequently ensure integrity of the data messages that are exchanged after authentication has taken place, it is common practice to use secret-key cryptography by means of session keys. A **session key** is a shared (secret) key that is used to encrypt messages for integrity and possibly also confidentiality. Such a key is generally used only for as long as the channel exists. When the channel is closed, its associated session key is discarded (or actually, securely destroyed). We return to session keys below.

Authentication Based on a Shared Secret Key

Let us start by taking a look at an authentication protocol based on a secret key that is already shared between Alice and Bob. How the two actually managed to obtain a shared key in a secure way is discussed later in this chapter. In the description of the protocol, Alice and Bob are abbreviated by A and B, respectively, and their shared key is denoted as $K_{A,B}$. The protocol takes a common approach whereby one party challenges the other to a response that can be correct only if the other knows the shared secret key. Such solutions are also known as **challenge-response protocols**.

In the case of authentication based on a shared secret key, the protocol proceeds as shown in Fig. 9-12. First, Alice sends her identity to Bob (message 1), indicating that she wants to set up a communication channel between the two. Bob subsequently sends a challenge R_B to Alice, shown as message 2. Such a challenge could take the form of a random number. Alice is required to encrypt the challenge with the secret key $K_{A,B}$ that she shares with Bob, and return the encrypted challenge to Bob. This response is shown as message 3 in Fig. 9-12 containing $K_{A,B}(R_B)$.

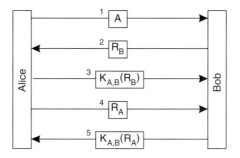

Figure 9-12. Authentication based on a shared secret key.

When Bob receives the response $K_{A,B}(R_B)$ to his challenge R_B, he can decrypt the message using the shared key again to see if it contains R_B. If so, he then knows that Alice is on the other side, for who else could have encrypted R_B with

$K_{A,B}$ in the first place? In other words, Bob has now verified that he is indeed talking to Alice. However, note that Alice has not yet verified that it is indeed Bob on the other side of the channel. Therefore, she sends a challenge R_A (message 4), which Bob responds to by returning $K_{A,B}(R_A)$, shown as message 5. When Alice decrypts it with $K_{A,B}$ and sees her R_A, she knows she is talking to Bob.

One of the harder issues in security is designing protocols that actually work. To illustrate how easily things can go wrong, consider an "optimization" of the authentication protocol in which the number of messages has been reduced from five to three, as shown in Fig. 9-13. The basic idea is that if Alice eventually wants to challenge Bob anyway, she might as well send a challenge along with her identity when setting up the channel. Likewise, Bob returns his response to that challenge, along with his own challenge in a single message.

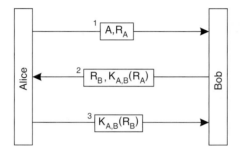

Figure 9-13. Authentication based on a shared secret key, but using three instead of five messages.

sending the challenge back.

Unfortunately, this protocol no longer works. It can easily be defeated by what is known as a **reflection attack**. To explain how such an attack works, consider an intruder called Chuck, whom we denote as C in our protocols. Chuck's goal is to set up a channel with Bob so that Bob believes he is talking to Alice. Chuck can establish this if he responds correctly to a challenge sent by Bob, for instance, by returning the encrypted version of a number that Bob sent. Without knowledge of $K_{A,B}$, only Bob can do such an encryption, and this is precisely what Chuck tricks Bob into doing.

The attack is illustrated in Fig. 9-14. Chuck starts out by sending a message containing Alice's identity A, along with a challenge R_C. Bob returns his challenge R_B and the response $K_{A,B}(R_C)$ in a single message. At that point, Chuck would need to prove he knows the secret key by returning $K_{A,B}(R_B)$ to Bob. Unfortunately, he does not have $K_{A,B}$. Instead, what he does is attempt to set up a second channel to let Bob do the encryption for him.

Therefore, Chuck sends A and R_B in a single message as before, but now pretends that he wants a second channel. This is shown as message 3 in Fig. 9-14. Bob, not recognizing that he, himself, had used R_B before as a challenge, responds with $K_{A,B}(R_B)$ and another challenge R_{B2}, shown as message 4. At that point,

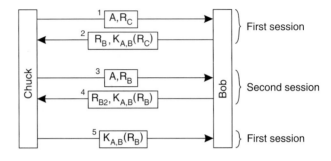

Figure 9-14. The reflection attack.

Chuck has $K_{A,B}(R_B)$ and finishes setting up the first session by returning message 5 containing the response $K_{A,B}(R_B)$, which was originally requested from the challenge sent in message 2.

  As explained in Kaufman et al. (2003), one of the mistakes made during the adaptation of the original protocol was that the two parties in the new version of the protocol were using the same challenge in two different runs of the protocol. A better design is to always use different challenges for the initiator and for the responder. For example, if Alice always uses an odd number and Bob an even number, Bob would have recognized that something fishy was going on when receiving R_B in message 3 in Fig. 9-14. (Unfortunately, this solution is subject to other attacks, notably the one known as the "man-in-the-middle-attack," which is explained in Ferguson and Schneier, 2003). In general, letting the two parties setting up a secure channel do a number of things identically is not a good idea.

  Another principle that is violated in the adapted protocol is that Bob gave away valuable information in the form of the response $K_{A,B}(R_C)$ without knowing for sure to whom he was giving it. This principle was not violated in the original protocol, in which Alice first needed to prove her identity, after which Bob was willing to pass her encrypted information.

  There are other principles that developers of cryptographic protocols have gradually come to learn over the years, and we will present some of them when discussing other protocols below. One important lesson is that designing security protocols that do what they are supposed to do is often much harder than it looks. Also, tweaking an existing protocol to improve its performance, can easily affect its correctness as we demonstrated above. More on design principles for protocols can be found in Abadi and Needham (1996).

Authentication Using a Key Distribution Center

  One of the problems with using a shared secret key for authentication is scalability. If a distributed system contains N hosts, and each host is required to share a secret key with each of the other $N - 1$ hosts, the system as a whole needs to manage $N(N-1)/2$ keys, and each host has to manage $N-1$ keys. For large N, this will lead to problems. An alternative is to use a centralized approach by means of a **Key Distribution Center** (**KDC**). This KDC shares a secret key with each of the hosts, but no pair of hosts is required to have a shared secret key as well. In other words, using a KDC requires that we manage N keys instead of $N(N-1)/2$, which is clearly an improvement.

If Alice wants to set up a secure channel with Bob, she can do so with the help of a (trusted) KDC. The whole idea is that the KDC hands out a key to both Alice and Bob that they can use for communication, shown in Fig. 9-15.

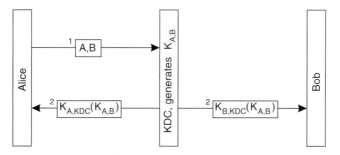

Figure 9-15. The principle of using a KDC.

Alice first sends a message to the KDC, telling it that she wants to talk to Bob. The KDC returns a message containing a shared secret key $K_{A,B}$ that she can use. The message is encrypted with the secret key $K_{A,KDC}$ that Alice shares with the KDC. In addition, the KDC sends $K_{A,B}$ also to Bob, but now encrypted with the secret key $K_{B,KDC}$ it shares with Bob.

The main drawback of this approach is that Alice may want to start setting up a secure channel with Bob even before Bob had received the shared key from the KDC. In addition, the KDC is required to get Bob into the loop by passing him the key. These problems can be circumvented if the KDC just passes $K_{B,KDC}(K_{A,B})$ back to Alice, and lets her take care of connecting to Bob. This leads to the protocol shown in Fig. 9-16. The message $K_{B,KDC}(K_{A,B})$ is also known as a **ticket**. It is Alice's job to pass this ticket to Bob. Note that Bob is still the only one that can make sensible use of the ticket, as he is the only one besides the KDC who knows how to decrypt the information it contains.

The protocol shown in Fig. 9-16 is actually a variant of a well-known example of an authentication protocol using a KDC, known as the **Needham-Schroeder authentication protocol**, named after its inventors (Needham and Schroeder, 1978). A different variant of the protocol is being used in the Kerberos system, which we describe later. The Needham-Schroeder protocol, shown in Fig. 9-17, is a multiway challenge-response protocol and works as follows.

When Alice wants to set up a secure channel with Bob, she sends a request to the KDC containing a challenge R_A, along with her identity A and, of course, that

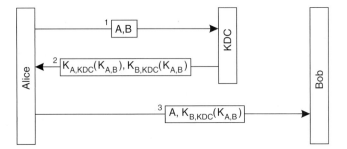

Figure 9-16. Using a ticket and letting Alice set up a connection to Bob.

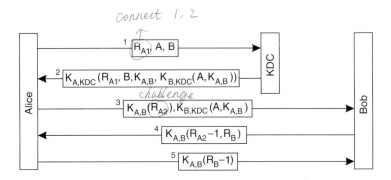

Figure 9-17. The Needham-Schroeder authentication protocol.

of Bob. The KDC responds by giving her the ticket $K_{B,KDC}(K_{A,B})$, along with the secret key $K_{A,B}$ that she can subsequently share with Bob.

The challenge R_{A1} that Alice sends to the KDC along with her request to set up a channel to Bob is also known as a nonce. A **nonce** is a random number that is used only once, such as one chosen from a very large set. The main purpose of a nonce is to uniquely relate two messages to each other, in this case message 1 and message 2. In particular, by including R_{A1} again in message 2, Alice will know for sure that message 2 is sent as a response to message 1, and that it is not, for example, a replay of an older message.

To understand the problem at hand, assume that we did not use nonces, and that Chuck has stolen one of Bob's old keys, say $K_{B,KDC}^{old}$. In addition, Chuck has intercepted an old response $K_{A,KDC}(B, K_{A,B}, K_{B,KDC}^{old}(A, K_{A,B}))$ that the KDC had returned to a previous request from Alice to talk to Bob. Meanwhile, Bob will have negotiated a new shared secret key with the KDC. However, Chuck patiently waits until Alice again requests to set up a secure channel with Bob. At that point, he replays the old response, and fools Alice into making her believe she is talking to Bob, because he can decrypt the ticket and prove he knows the shared secret key $K_{A,B}$. Clearly this is unacceptable and must be defended against.

By including a nonce, such an attack is impossible, because replaying an older message will immediately be discovered. In particular, the nonce in the response message will not match the nonce in the original request.

Message 2 also contains B, the identity of Bob. By including B, the KDC protects Alice against the following attack. Suppose that B was left out of message 2. In that case, Chuck could modify message 1 by replacing the identity of Bob with his own identity, say C. The KDC would then think Alice wants to set up a secure channel to Chuck, and responds accordingly. As soon as Alice wants to contact Bob, Chuck intercepts the message and fools Alice into believing she is talking to Bob. By copying the identity of the other party from message 1 to message 2, Alice will immediately detect that her request had been modified.

After the KDC has passed the ticket to Alice, the secure channel between Alice and Bob can be set up. Alice starts with sending message 3, which contains the ticket to Bob, and a challenge R_{A2} encrypted with the shared key $K_{A,B}$ that the KDC had just generated. Bob then decrypts the ticket to find the shared key, and returns a response $R_{A2} - 1$ along with a challenge R_B for Alice.

The following remark regarding message 4 is in order. In general, by returning $R_{A2} - 1$ and not just R_{A2}, Bob not only proves he knows the shared secret key, but also that he has actually decrypted the challenge. Again, this ties message 4 to message 3 in the same way that the nonce R_A tied message 2 to message 1. The protocol is thus more protected against replays.

However, in this special case, it would have been sufficient to just return $K_{A,B}(R_{A2}, R_B)$, for the simple reason that this message has not yet been used anywhere in the protocol before. $K_{A,B}(R_{A2}, R_B)$ already proves that Bob has been capable of decrypting the challenge sent in message 3. Message 4 as shown in Fig. 9-17 is due to historical reasons.

The Needham-Schroeder protocol as presented here still has the weak point that if Chuck ever got a hold of an old key $K_{A,B}$, he could replay message 3 and get Bob to set up a channel. Bob will then believe he is talking to Alice, while, in fact, Chuck is at the other end. In this case, we need to relate message 3 to message 1, that is, make the key dependent on the initial request from Alice to set up a channel with Bob. The solution is shown in Fig. 9-18.

The trick is to incorporate a nonce in the request sent by Alice to the KDC. However, the nonce has to come from Bob: this assures Bob that whoever wants to set up a secure channel with him, will have gotten the appropriate information from the KDC. Therefore, Alice first requests Bob to send her a nonce R_{B1}, encrypted with the key shared between Bob and the KDC. Alice incorporates this nonce in her request to the KDC, which will then subsequently decrypt it and put the result in the generated ticket. In this way, Bob will know for sure that the session key is tied to the original request from Alice to talk to Bob.

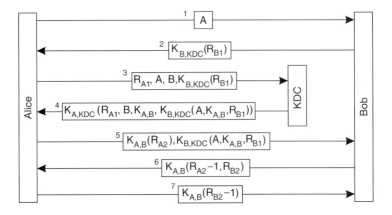

Figure 9-18. Protection against malicious reuse of a previously generated session key in the Needham-Schroeder protocol.

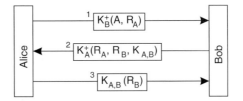

Figure 9-19. Mutual authentication in a public-key cryptosystem.

Authentication Using Public-Key Cryptography

Let us now look at authentication with a public-key cryptosystem that does not require a KDC. Again, consider the situation that Alice wants to set up a secure channel to Bob, and that both are in the possession of each other's public key. A typical authentication protocol based on public-key cryptography is shown in Fig. 9-19, which we explain next.

Alice starts with sending a challenge R_A to Bob encrypted with his public key K_B^+. It is Bob's job to decrypt the message and return the challenge to Alice. Because Bob is the only person that can decrypt the message (using the private key that is associated with the public key Alice used), Alice will know that she is talking to Bob. Note that it is important that Alice is guaranteed to be using Bob's public key, and not the public key of someone impersonating Bob. How such guarantees can be given is discussed later in this chapter.

When Bob receives Alice's request to set up a channel, he returns the decrypted challenge, along with his own challenge R_B to authenticate Alice. In addition, he generates a session key $K_{A,B}$ that can be used for further communication. Bob's response to Alice's challenge, his own challenge, and the session key are put into a message encrypted with the public key K_A^+ belonging to Alice, shown as message 2 in Fig. 9-19. Only Alice will be capable of decrypting this message using the private key K_A^- associated with K_A^+.

Alice, finally, returns her response to Bob's challenge using the session key $K_{A,B}$ generated by Bob. In that way, she will have proven that she could decrypt message 2, and thus that she is actually Alice to whom Bob is talking.

9.2.2 Message Integrity and Confidentiality

(it is indeed sent by A.)   *modification*   *interception (no one be B can decrypt)*

Besides authentication, a secure channel should also provide guarantees for message integrity and confidentiality. Message integrity means that messages are protected against surreptitious modification; confidentiality ensures that messages cannot be intercepted and read by eavesdroppers. Confidentiality is easily established by simply encrypting a message before sending it. Encryption can take place either through a secret key shared with the receiver or alternatively by using the receiver's public key. However, protecting a message against modifications is somewhat more complicated, as we discuss next.

Digital Signatures

Message integrity often goes beyond the actual transfer through a secure channel. Consider the situation in which Bob has just sold Alice a collector's item of some phonograph record for $500. The whole deal was done through e-mail. In the end, Alice sends Bob a message confirming that she will buy the record for $500. In addition to authentication, there are at least two issues that need to be taken care of regarding the integrity of the message.

1. Alice needs to be assured that Bob will not maliciously change the $500 mentioned in her message into something higher, and claim she promised more than $500.

2. Bob needs to be assured that Alice cannot deny ever having sent the message, for example, because she had second thoughts.

These two issues can be dealt with if Alice digitally signs the message in such a way that her signature is uniquely tied to its content. The unique association between a message and its signature prevents that modifications to the message will go unnoticed. In addition, if Alice's signature can be verified to be genuine, she cannot later repudiate the fact that she signed the message.

There are several ways to place digital signatures. One popular form is to use a public-key cryptosystem such as RSA, as shown in Fig. 9-20. When Alice sends a message m to Bob, she encrypts it with her *private* key K_A^-, and sends it off to Bob. If she also wants to keep the message content a secret, she can use Bob's public key and send $K_B^+(m, K_A^-(m))$, which combines m and the version signed by Alice.

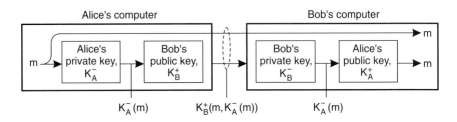

Figure 9-20. Digital signing a message using public-key cryptography.

When the message arrives at Bob, he can decrypt it using Alice's public key. If he can be assured that the public key is indeed owned by Alice, then decrypting the signed version of m and successfully comparing it to m can mean only that it came from Alice. Alice is protected against any malicious modifications to m by Bob, because Bob will always have to prove that the modified version of m was also signed by Alice. In other words, the decrypted message alone essentially never counts as proof. It is also in Bob's own interest to keep the signed version of m to protect himself against repudiation by Alice.

There are a number of problems with this scheme, although the protocol in itself is correct. First, the validity of Alice's signature holds only as long as Alice's private key remains a secret. If Alice wants to bail out of the deal even after sending Bob her confirmation, she could claim that her private key was stolen before the message was sent.

Another problem occurs when Alice decides to change her private key. Doing so may in itself be not such a bad idea, as changing keys from time to time generally helps against intrusion. However, once Alice has changed her key, her statement sent to Bob becomes worthless. What may be needed in such cases is a central authority that keeps track of when keys are changed, in addition to using timestamps when signing messages.

Another problem with this scheme is that Alice encrypts the entire message with her private key. Such an encryption may be costly in terms of processing requirements (or even mathematically infeasible as we assume that the message interpreted as a binary number is bounded by a predefined maximum), and is actually unnecessary. Recall that we need to uniquely associate a signature with a only specific message. A cheaper and arguably more elegant scheme is to use a message digest.

As we explained, a message digest is a fixed-length bit string h that has been computed from an arbitrary-length message m by means of a cryptographic hash function H. If m is changed to m', its hash $H(m')$ will be different from $h = H(m)$ so that it can easily be detected that a modification has taken place.

To digitally sign a message, Alice can first compute a message digest and subsequently encrypt the digest with her private key, as shown in Fig. 9-21. The encrypted digest is sent along with the message to Bob. Note that the message itself is sent as plaintext: everyone is allowed to read it. If confidentiality is required, then the message should also be encrypted with Bob's public key.

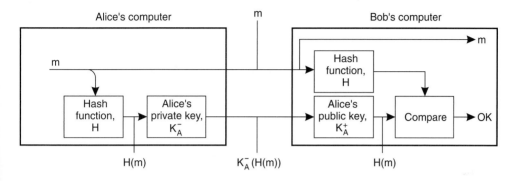

Figure 9-21. Digitally signing a message using a message digest.

When Bob receives the message and its encrypted digest, he need merely decrypt the digest with Alice's public key, and separately calculate the message digest. If the digest calculated from the received message and the decrypted digest match, Bob knows the message has been signed by Alice.

Session Keys

During the establishment of a secure channel, after the authentication phase has completed, the communicating parties generally use a unique shared session key for confidentiality. The session key is safely discarded when the channel is no longer used. An alternative would have been to use the same keys for confidentiality as those that are used for setting up the secure channel. However, there are a number of important benefits to using session keys (Kaufman et al., 2003).

First, when a key is used often, it becomes easier to reveal it. In a sense, cryptographic keys are subject to "wear and tear" just like ordinary keys. The basic idea is that if an intruder can intercept a lot of data that have been encrypted using the same key, it becomes possible to mount attacks to find certain characteristics of the keys used, and possibly reveal the plaintext or the key itself. For this reason, it is much safer to use the authentication keys as little as possible. In addition, such keys are often exchanged using some relatively time-expensive out-of-band mechanism such as regular mail or telephone. Exchanging keys that way should be kept to a minimum.

Another important reason for generating a unique key for each secure channel is to ensure protection against replay attacks as we have come across previously a number of times. By using a unique session key each time a secure channel is set up, the communicating parties are at least protected against replaying an entire session. To protect replaying individual messages from a previous session, additional measures are generally needed such as including timestamps or sequence numbers as part of the message content.

Suppose that message integrity and confidentiality were achieved by using the same key used for session establishment. In that case, whenever the key is compromised, an intruder may be able to decrypt messages transferred during an old conversation, clearly not a desirable feature. Instead, it is much safer to use per-session keys, because if such a key is compromised, at worst, only a single session is affected. Messages sent during other sessions stay confidential.

Related to this last point is that Alice may want to exchange some confidential data with Bob, but she does not trust him so much that she would give him information in the form of data that have been encrypted with long-lasting keys. She may want to reserve such keys for highly-confidential messages that she exchanges with parties she really trusts. In such cases, using a relatively cheap session key to talk to Bob is sufficient.

By and large, authentication keys are often established in such a way that replacing them is relatively expensive. Therefore, the combination of such long-lasting keys with the much cheaper and more temporary session keys is often a good choice for implementing secure channels for exchanging data.

9.2.3 Secure Group Communication

So far, we have concentrated on setting up a secure communication channel between two parties. In distributed systems, however, it is often necessary to enable secure communication between more than just two parties. A typical example is that of a replicated server for which all communication between the replicas should be protected against modification, fabrication, and interception, just as in the case of two-party secure channels. In this section, we take a closer look at secure group communication.

Confidential Group Communication

First, consider the problem of protecting communication between a group of N users against eavesdropping. To ensure confidentiality, a simple scheme is to let all group members share the same secret key, which is used to encrypt and decrypt all messages transmitted between group members. Because the secret key in this scheme is shared by all members, it is necessary that all members are trusted to indeed keep the key a secret. This prerequisite alone makes the use of a single shared secret key for confidential group communication more vulnerable to attacks compared to two-party secure channels.

An alternative solution is to use a separate shared secret key between each pair of group members. As soon as one member turns out to be leaking information, the others can simply stop sending messages to that member, but still use the keys they were using to communicate with each other. However, instead of having to maintain one key, it is now necessary to maintain $N(N-1)/2$ keys, which may be a difficult problem by itself.

Using a public-key cryptosystem can improve matters. In that case, each member has its own *(public key, private key)* pair, in which the public key can be used by all members for sending confidential messages. In this case, a total of N key pairs are needed. If one member ceases to be trustworthy, it is simply removed from the group without having been able to compromise the other keys.

Secure Replicated Servers

Now consider a completely different problem: a client issues a request to a group of replicated servers. The servers may have been replicated for reasons of fault tolerance or performance, but in any case, the client expects the response to be trustworthy. In other words, regardless of whether the group of servers is subject to Byzantine failures as we discussed in the previous chapter, a client expects that the returned response has not been subject to a security attack. Such an attack could happen if one or more servers had been successfully corrupted by an intruder.

A solution to protect the client against such attacks is to collect the responses from all servers and authenticate each one of them. If a majority exists among the responses from the noncorrupted (i.e., authenticated) servers, the client can trust the response to be correct as well. Unfortunately, this approach reveals the replication of the servers, thus violating replication transparency.

Reiter et al. (1994) proposes a solution to a secure, replicated server in which replication transparency is maintained. The advantage of their scheme is that because clients are unaware of the actual replicas, it becomes much easier to add or remove replicas in a secure way. We return to managing secure groups below when discussing key management.

The essence of secure and transparent replicated servers lies in what is known as **secret sharing**. When multiple users (or processes) share a secret, none of them knows the entire secret. Instead, the secret can be revealed only if they all get together. Such schemes can be extremely useful. Consider, for example, launching a nuclear missile. Such an act generally requires the authorization of at least two people. Each of them holds a private key that should be used in combination with the other to actually launch a missile. Using only a single key will not do.

In the case of secure, replicated servers, what we are seeking is a solution by which at most k out of the N servers can produce an incorrect answer, and of those k servers, at most $c \leq k$ have actually been corrupted by an intruder. Note that this requirement makes the service itself k fault tolerant as discussed in the previous chapter. The difference lies in the fact that we now classify a maliciously corrupted server as being faulty.

Now consider the situation in which the servers are actively replicated. In other words, a request is sent to all servers simultaneously, and subsequently handled by each of them. Each server produces a response that it returns to the client. For a securely replicated group of servers, we require that each server accompanies its response with a digital signature. If r_i is the response from server S_i, let $md(r_i)$ denote the message digest computed by server S_i. This digest is signed with server S_i's private key K_i^-.

Suppose that we want to protect the client against at most c corrupted servers. In other words, the server group should be able to tolerate corruption by at most c servers, and still be capable of producing a response that the client can put its trust in. If the signatures of the individual servers could be combined in such a way that at least $c + 1$ signatures are needed to construct a *valid* signature for the response, then this would solve our problem. In other words, we want to let the replicated servers generate a secret valid signature with the property that c corrupted servers alone are not enough to produce that signature.

As an example, consider a group of five replicated servers that should be able to tolerate two corrupted servers, and still produce a response that a client can trust. Each server S_i sends its response r_i to the client, along with its signature $sig(S_i, r_i) = K_i^-(md(r_i))$. Consequently, the client will eventually have received five triplets $<r_i, md(r_i), sig(S_i, r_i)>$ from which it should derive the correct response. This situation is shown in Fig. 9-22.

Each digest $md(r_i)$ is also calculated by the client. If r_i is incorrect, then normally this can be detected by computing $K_i^+(K_i^-(md(r_i)))$. However, this method can no longer be applied, because no individual server can be trusted. Instead, the client uses a special, publicly-known decryption function D, which takes a set $V = \{sig(S, r), sig(S', r'), sig(S'', r'')\}$ of *three* signatures as input, and produces a single digest as output:

$$d_{out} = D(V) = D(sig(S, r), sig(S', r'), sig(S'', r''))$$

For details on D, see Reiter (1994). There are $5!/(3!2!)=10$ possible combinations of three signatures that the client can use as input for D. If one of these combinations produces a correct digest $md(r_i)$ for some response r_i, then the client can consider r_i as being correct. In particular, it can trust that the response has been produced by at least three honest servers.

To improve replication transparency, Reiter and Birman let each server S_i broadcast a message containing its response r_i to the other servers, along with the associated signature $sig(S_i, r_i)$. When a server has received at least $c + 1$ of such messages, including its own message, it attempts to compute a valid signature for one of the responses. If this succeeds for, say, response r and the set V of $c + 1$ signatures, the server sends r and V as a single message to the client. The client

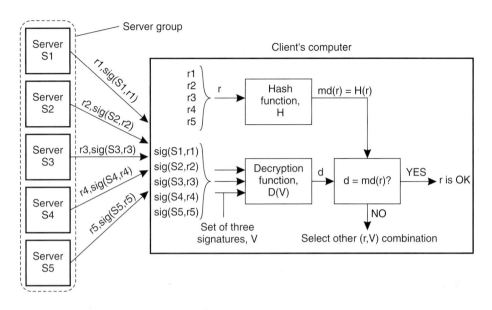

Figure 9-22. Sharing a secret signature in a group of replicated servers.

can subsequently verify the correctness of r by checking its signature, that is, whether $md(r) = D(V)$.

What we have just described is also known as an **(m,n)-threshold scheme** with, in our example, $m = c + 1$ and $n = N$, the number of servers. In an (m,n)-threshold scheme, a message has been divided into n pieces, known as **shadows**, since any m shadows can be used to reconstruct the original message, but using $m - 1$ or fewer messages cannot. There are several ways to construct (m,n)-threshold schemes. Details can be found in Schneier (1996).

9.2.4 Example: Kerberos

It should be clear by now that incorporating security into distributed systems is not trivial. Problems are caused by the fact that the entire system must be secure; if some part is insecure, the whole system may be compromised. To assist the construction of distributed systems that can enforce a myriad of security policies, a number of supporting systems have been developed that can be used as a basis for further development. An important system that is widely used is **Kerberos** (Steiner et al., 1988; and Kohl and Neuman, 1994).

Kerberos was developed at M.I.T. and is based on the Needham-Schroeder authentication protocol we described earlier. There are currently two different versions of Kerberos in use, version 4 (V4) and version 5 (V5). Both versions are conceptually similar, with V5 being much more flexible and scalable. A detailed description of V5 can be found in Neuman et al. (2005), whereas practical information on running Kerberos is described by Garman (2003).

Kerberos can be viewed as a security system that assists clients in setting up a secure channel with any server that is part of a distributed system. Security is based on shared secret keys. There are two different components. The **Authentication Server** (**AS**) is responsible for handling a login request from a user. The AS authenticates a user and provides a key that can be used to set up secure channels with servers. Setting up secure channels is handled by a **Ticket Granting Service** (**TGS**). The TGS hands out special messages, known as **tickets**, that are used to convince a server that the client is really who he or she claims to be. We give concrete examples of tickets below.

Let us take a look at how Alice logs onto a distributed system that uses Kerberos and how she can set up a secure channel with server Bob. For Alice to log onto the system, she can use any workstation available. The workstation sends her name in plaintext to the AS, which returns a session key $K_{A,TGS}$ and a ticket that she will need to hand over to the TGS.

The ticket that is returned by the AS contains the identity of Alice, along with a generated secret key that Alice and the TGS can use to communicate with each other. The ticket itself will be handed over to the TGS by Alice. Therefore, it is important that no one but the TGS can read it. For this reason, the ticket is encrypted with the secret key $K_{AS,TGS}$ shared between the AS and the TGS.

This part of the login procedure is shown as messages 1, 2, and 3 in Fig. 9-23. Message 1 is not really a message, but corresponds to Alice typing in her login name at a workstation. Message 2 contains that name and is sent to the AS. Message 3 contains the session key $K_{A,TGS}$ and the ticket $K_{AS,TGS}(A, K_{A,TGS})$. To ensure privacy, message 3 is encrypted with the secret key $K_{A,AS}$ shared between Alice and the AS.

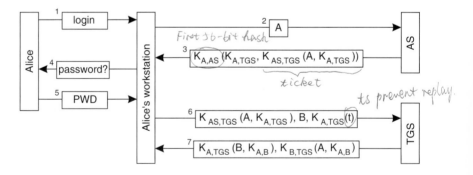

Figure 9-23. Authentication in Kerberos.

When the workstation receives the response from the AS, it prompts Alice for her password (shown as message 4), which it uses to subsequently generate the shared key $K_{A,AS}$. (It is relatively simple to take a character string password, apply a cryptographic hash, and then take the first 56 bits as the secret key.) Note that this approach not only has the advantage that Alice's password is never sent as plaintext across the network, but also that the workstation does not even have to temporarily store it. Moreover, as soon as it has generated the shared key $K_{A,AS}$, the workstation will find the session key $K_{A,TGS}$, and can forget about Alice's password and use only the shared secret $K_{A,AS}$.

After this part of the authentication has taken place, Alice can consider herself logged into the system through the current workstation. The ticket received from the AS is stored temporarily (typically for 8–24 hours), and will be used for accessing remote services. Of course, if Alice leaves her workstation, she should destroy any cached tickets. If she wants to talk to Bob, she requests the TGS to generate a session key for Bob, shown as message 6 in Fig. 9-23. The fact that Alice has the ticket $K_{AS,TGS}(A, K_{A,TGS})$ proves that she is Alice. The TGS responds with a session key $K_{A,B}$, again encapsulated in a ticket that Alice will later have to pass to Bob.

Message 6 also contains a timestamp, t, encrypted with the secret key shared between Alice and the TGS. This timestamp is used to prevent Chuck from maliciously replaying message 6 again, and trying to set up a channel to Bob. The TGS will verify the timestamp before returning a ticket to Alice. If it differs more than a few minutes from the current time, the request for a ticket is rejected.

This scheme establishes what is known as **single sign-on**. As long as Alice does not change workstations, there is no need for her to authenticate herself to any other server that is part of the distributed system. This feature is important when having to deal with many different services that are spread across multiple machines. In principle, servers in a way have delegated client authentication to the AS and TGS, and will accept requests from any client that has a valid ticket. Of course, services such as remote login will require that the associated user has an account, but this is independent from authentication through Kerberos.

Setting up a secure channel with Bob is now straightforward, and is shown in Fig. 9-24. First, Alice sends to Bob a message containing the ticket she got from the TGS, along with an encrypted timestamp. When Bob decrypts the ticket, he notices that Alice is talking to him, because only the TGS could have constructed the ticket. He also finds the secret key $K_{A,B}$, allowing him to verify the timestamp. At that point, Bob knows he is talking to Alice and not someone maliciously replaying message 1. By responding with $K_{A,B}(t + 1)$, Bob proves to Alice that he is indeed Bob.

9.3 ACCESS CONTROL

In the client-server model, which we have used so far, once a client and a server have set up a secure channel, the client can issue requests that are to be carried out by the server. Requests involve carrying out operations on resources that

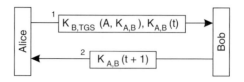

Figure 9-24. Setting up a secure channel in Kerberos.

are controlled by the server. A general situation is that of an object server that has a number of objects under its control. A request from a client generally involves invoking a method of a specific object. Such a request can be carried out only if the client has sufficient **access rights** for that invocation.

Formally, verifying access rights is referred to as **access control**, whereas **authorization** is about granting access rights. The two terms are strongly related to each other and are often used in an interchangeable way. There are many ways to achieve access control. We start with discussing some of the general issues, concentrating on different models for handling access control. One important way of actually controlling access to resources is to build a firewall that protects applications or even an entire network. Firewalls are discussed separately. With the advent of code mobility, access control could no longer be done using only the traditional methods. Instead, new techniques had to be devised, which are also discussed in this section.

9.3.1 General Issues in Access Control

In order to understand the various issues involved in access control, the simple model shown in Fig. 9-25 is generally adopted. It consists of **subjects** that issue a request to access an **object**. An object is very much like the objects we have been discussing so far. It can be thought of as encapsulating its own state and implementing the operations on that state. The operations of an object that subjects can request to be carried out are made available through interfaces. Subjects can best be thought of as being processes acting on behalf of users, but can also be objects that need the services of other objects in order to carry out their work.

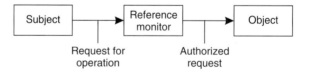

Figure 9-25. General model of controlling access to objects.

Controlling the access to an object is all about protecting the object against invocations by subjects that are not allowed to have specific (or even any) of the methods carried out. Also, protection may include object management issues, such as creating, renaming, or deleting objects. Protection is often enforced by a program called a **reference monitor**. A reference monitor records which subject may do what, and decides whether a subject is allowed to have a specific operation carried out. This monitor is called (e.g., by the underlying trusted operating system) each time an object is invoked. Consequently, it is extremely important that the reference monitor is itself tamperproof: an attacker must not be able to fool around with it.

Access Control Matrix

A common approach to modeling the access rights of subjects with respect to objects is to construct an **access control matrix**. Each subject is represented by a row in this matrix; each object is represented by a column. If the matrix is denoted M, then an entry $M[s,o]$ lists precisely which operations subject s can request to be carried out on object o. In other words, whenever a subject s requests the invocation of method m of object o, the reference monitor should check whether m is listed in $M[s,o]$. If m is not listed in $M[s,o]$, the invocation fails.

Considering that a system may easily need to support thousands of users and millions of objects that require protection, implementing an access control matrix as a true matrix is not the way to go. Many entries in the matrix will be empty: a single subject will generally have access to relatively few objects. Therefore, other, more efficient ways are followed to implement an access control matrix.

One widely-applied approach is to have each object maintain a list of the access rights of subjects that want to access the object. In essence, this means that the matrix is distributed column-wise across all objects, and that empty entries are left out. This type of implementation leads to what is called an **Access Control List** (ACL). Each object is assumed to have its own associated ACL.

Another approach is to distribute the matrix row-wise by giving each subject a list of **capabilities** it has for each object. In other words, a capability corresponds to an entry in the access control matrix. Not having a capability for a specific object means that the subject has no access rights for that object.

A capability can be compared to a ticket: its holder is given certain rights that are associated with that ticket. It is also clear that a ticket should be protected against modifications by its holder. One approach that is particularly suited in distributed systems and which has been applied extensively in Amoeba (Tanenbaum et al., 1990), is to protect (a list of) capabilities with a signature. We return to these and other matters later when discussing security management.

The difference between how ACLs and capabilities are used to protect the access to an object is shown in Fig. 9-26. Using ACLs, when a client sends a request to a server, the server's reference monitor will check whether it knows the client and if that client is known and allowed to have the requested operation carried out, as shown in Fig. 9-26(a).

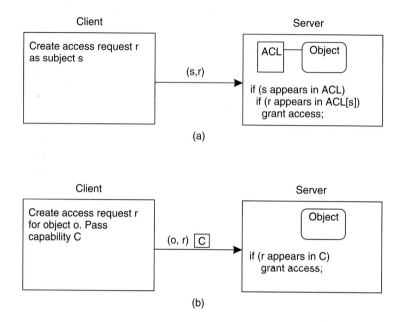

Figure 9-26. Comparison between ACLs and capabilities for protecting objects. (a) Using an ACL. (b) Using capabilities.

However, when using capabilities, a client simply sends its request to the server. The server is not interested in whether it knows the client; the capability says enough. Therefore, the server need only check whether the capability is valid and whether the requested operation is listed in the capability. This approach to protecting objects by means of capabilities is shown in Fig. 9-26(b).

Protection Domains

ACLs and capabilities help in efficiently implementing an access control matrix by ignoring all empty entries. Nevertheless, an ACL or a capability list can still become quite large if no further measures are taken.

One general way of reducing ACLs is to make use of protection domains. Formally, a **protection domain** is a set of *(object, access rights)* pairs. Each pair specifies for a given object exactly which operations are allowed to be carried out (Saltzer and Schroeder, 1975). Requests for carrying out an operation are always issued within a domain. Therefore, whenever a subject requests an operation to be carried out at an object, the reference monitor first looks up the protection domain associated with that request. Then, given the domain, the reference monitor can subsequently check whether the request is allowed to be carried out. Different uses of protection domains exist.

One approach is to construct **groups** of users. Consider, for example, a Web page on a company's internal intranet. Such a page should be available to every employee, but otherwise to no one else. Instead of adding an entry for each possible employee to the ACL for that Web page, it may be decided to have a separate group *Employee* containing all current employees. Whenever a user accesses the Web page, the reference monitor need only check whether that user is an employee. Which users belong to the group *Employee* is kept in a separate list (which, of course, is protected against unauthorized access).

Matters can be made more flexible by introducing hierarchical groups. For example, if an organization has three different branches at, say, Amsterdam, New York, and San Francisco, it may want to subdivide its *Employee* group into subgroups, one for each city, leading to an organization as shown in Fig. 9-27.

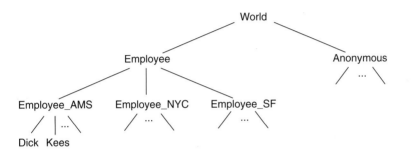

Figure 9-27. The hierarchical organization of protection domains as groups of users.

Accessing Web pages of the organization's intranet should be permitted by all employees. However, changing for example Web pages associated with the Amsterdam branch should be permitted only by a subset of employees in Amsterdam. If user Dick from Amsterdam wants to read a Web page from the intranet, the reference monitor needs to first look up the subsets *Employee_AMS*, *Employee_NYC*, and *Employee_SF* that jointly comprise the set *Employee*. It then has to check if one of these sets contains Dick. The advantage of having hierarchical groups is that managing group membership is relatively easy, and that very large groups can be constructed efficiently. An obvious disadvantage is that looking up a member can be quite costly if the membership database is distributed.

Instead of letting the reference monitor do all the work, an alternative is to let each subject carry a **certificate** listing the groups it belongs to. So, whenever Dick wants to read a Web page from the company's intranet, he hands over his certificate to the reference monitor stating that he is a member of *Employee_AMS*. To guarantee that the certificate is genuine and has not been tampered with, it should be protected by means of, for example, a digital signature. Certificates are seen to be comparable to capabilities. We return to these issues later.

Related to having groups as protection domains, it is also possible to implement protection domains as **roles**. In role-based access control, a user always logs into the system with a specific role, which is often associated with a function the user has in an organization (Sandhu et al., 1996). A user may have several functions. For example, Dick could simultaneously be head of a department, manager of a project, and member of a personnel search committee. Depending on the role he takes when logging in, he may be assigned different privileges. In other words, his role determines the protection domain (i.e., group) in which he will operate.

When assigning roles to users and requiring that users take on a specific role when logging in, it should also be possible for users to change their roles if necessary. For example, it may be required to allow Dick as head of the department to occasionally change to his role of project manager. Note that such changes are difficult to express when implementing protection domains only as groups.

Besides using protection domains, efficiency can be further improved by (hierarchically) grouping objects based on the operations they provide. For example, instead of considering individual objects, objects are grouped according to the interfaces they provide, possibly using subtyping [also referred to as interface inheritance, see Gamma et al. (1994)] to achieve a hierarchy. In this case, when a subject requests an operation to be carried out at an object, the reference monitor looks up to which interface the operation for that object belongs. It then checks whether the subject is allowed to call an operation belonging to that interface, rather than if it can call the operation for the specific object.

Combining protection domains and grouping of objects is also possible. Using both techniques, along with specific data structures and restricted operations on objects, Gladney (1997) describes how to implement ACLs for very large collections of objects that are used in digital libraries.

9.3.2 Firewalls

So far, we have shown how protection can be established using cryptographic techniques, combined with some implementation of an access control matrix. These approaches work fine as long as all communicating parties play according to the same set of rules. Such rules may be enforced when developing a stand-alone distributed system that is isolated from the rest of the world. However, matters become more complicated when outsiders are allowed to access the resources controlled by a distributed system. Examples of such accesses including sending mail, downloading files, uploading tax forms, and so on.

To protect resources under these circumstances, a different approach is needed. In practice, what happens is that external access to any part of a distributed system is controlled by a special kind of reference monitor known as a **firewall** (Cheswick and Bellovin, 2000; and Zwicky et al., 2000). Essentially, a firewall disconnects any part of a distributed system from the outside world, as shown in Fig. 9-28. All outgoing, but especially all incoming packets are routed through a special computer and inspected before they are passed. Unauthorized traffic is discarded and not allowed to continue. An important issue is that the firewall itself should be heavily protected against any kind of security threat: it should never fail.

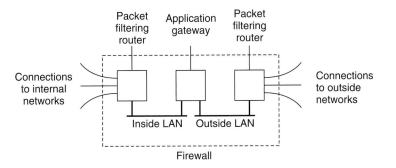

Figure 9-28. A common implementation of a firewall.

Firewalls essentially come in two different flavors that are often combined. An important type of firewall is a **packet-filtering gateway**. This type of firewall operates as a router and makes decisions as to whether or not to pass a network packet based on the source and destination address as contained in the packet's header. Typically, the packet-filtering gateway shown on the outside LAN in Fig. 9-28 would protect against incoming packets, whereas the one on the inside LAN would filter outgoing packets.

For example, to protect an internal Web server against requests from hosts that are not on the internal network, a packet-filtering gateway could decide to drop all incoming packets addressed to the Web server.

More subtle is the situation in which a company's network consists of multiple local-area networks connected, for example, through an SMDS network as we discussed before. Each LAN can be protected by means of a packet-filtering gateway, which is configured to pass incoming traffic only if it originated from a host on one of the other LANs. In this way, a private virtual network can be set up.

The other type of firewall is an **application-level gateway**. In contrast to a packet-filtering gateway, which inspects only the header of network packets, this type of firewall actually inspects the content of an incoming or outgoing message. A typical example is a mail gateway that discards incoming or outgoing mail exceeding a certain size. More sophisticated mail gateways exist that are, for example, capable of filtering spam e-mail.

Another example of an application-level gateway is one that allows external access to a digital library server, but will supply only abstracts of documents. If an external user wants more, an electronic payment protocol is started. Users inside the firewall have direct access to the library service.

A special kind of application-level gateway is what is known as a **proxy gateway**. This type of firewall works as a front end to a specific kind of application, and ensures that only those messages are passed that meet certain criteria. Consider, for example, surfing the Web. As we discuss in the next section, many Web pages contain scripts or applets that are to be executed in a user's browser. To prevent such code to be downloaded to the inside LAN, all Web traffic could be directed through a Web proxy gateway. This gateway accepts regular HTTP requests, either from inside or outside the firewall. In other words, it appears to its users as a normal Web server. However, it filters all incoming and outgoing traffic, either by discarding certain requests and pages, or modifying pages when they contain executable code.

9.3.3 Secure Mobile Code

As we discussed in Chap. 3, an important development in modern distributed systems is the ability to migrate code between hosts instead of just migrating passive data. However, mobile code introduces a number of serious security threats. For one thing, when sending an agent across the Internet, its owner will want to protect it against malicious hosts that try to steal or modify information carried by the agent.

Another issue is that hosts need to be protected against malicious agents. Most users of distributed systems will not be experts in systems technology and have no way of telling whether the program they are fetching from another host can be trusted not to corrupt their computer. In many cases it may be difficult even for an expert to detect that a program is actually being downloaded at all.

Unless security measures are taken, once a malicious program has settled itself in a computer, it can easily corrupt its host. We are faced with an access control problem: the program should not be allowed unauthorized access to the host's resources. As we shall see, protecting a host against downloaded malicious programs is not always easy. The problem is not so much as to avoid downloading of programs. Instead, what we are looking for is supporting mobile code that we can allow access to local resources in a flexible, yet fully controlled manner.

Protecting an Agent

Before we take a look at protecting a computer system against downloaded malicious code, let us first take a look at the opposite situation. Consider a mobile agent that is roaming a distributed system on behalf of a user. Such an agent may be searching for the cheapest airplane ticket from Nairobi to Malindi, and has been authorized by its owner to make a reservation as soon as it found a flight. For this purpose, the agent may carry an electronic credit card.

Obviously, we need protection here. Whenever the agent moves to a host, that host should not be allowed to steal the agent's credit card information. Also, the agent should be protected against modifications that make the owner pay much more than actually is needed. For example, if Chuck's Cheaper Charters can see that the agent has not yet visited its cheaper competitor Alice Airlines, Chuck should be prevented from changing the agent so that it will not visit Alice Airlines' host. Other examples that require protection of an agent against attacks from a hostile host include maliciously destroying an agent, or tampering with an agent such that it will attack or steal from its owner when it returns.

Unfortunately, fully protecting an agent against all kinds of attacks is impossible (Farmer et al., 1996). This impossibility is primarily caused by the fact that no hard guarantees can be given that a host will do what it promises. An alternative approach is therefore to organize agents in such a way that modifications can at least be detected. This approach has been followed in the Ajanta system (Karnik and Tripathi, 2001). Ajanta provides three mechanisms that allow an agent's owner to detect that the agent has been tampered with: read-only state, append-only logs, and selective revealing of state to certain servers.

The **read-only state** of an Ajanta agent consists of a collection of data items that is signed by the agent's owner. Signing takes place when the agent is constructed and initialized before it is sent off to other hosts. The owner first constructs a message digest, which it subsequently encrypts with its private key. When the agent arrives at a host, that host can easily detect whether the read-only state has been tampered with by verifying the state against the signed message digest of the original state.

To allow an agent to collect information while moving between hosts, Ajanta provides secure **append-only logs**. These logs are characterized by the fact that data can only be appended to the log; there is no way that data can be removed or modified without the owner being able to detect this. Using an append-only log works as follows. Initially, the log is empty and has only an associated checksum C_{init} calculated as $C_{init} = K_{owner}^{+}(N)$, where K_{owner}^{+} is the public key of the agent's owner, and N is a secret nonce known only to the owner.

When the agent moves to a server S that wants to hand it some data X, S appends X to the log then signs X with its signature $sig(S,X)$, and calculates a checksum:

$$C_{new} = K_{owner}^{+}(C_{old}, sig(S,X), S)$$

where C_{old} is the checksum that was used previously.

When the agent comes back to its owner, the owner can easily verify whether the log has been tampered with. The owner starts reading the log at the end by successively computing $K_{owner}^{-}(C)$ on the checksum C. Each iteration returns a checksum C_{next} for the next iteration, along with $sig(S,X)$ and S for some server S. The owner can then verify whether or not the then-last element in the log matches $sig(S,X)$. If so, the element is removed and processed, after which the next iteration step is taken. The iteration stops when the initial checksum is reached, or when the owner notices that the log as been tampered with because a signature does not match.

Finally, Ajanta supports **selective revealing** of state by providing an array of data items, where each entry is intended for a designated server. Each entry is encrypted with the designated server's public key to ensure confidentiality. The entire array is signed by the agent's owner to ensure integrity of the array as a whole. In other words, if *any* entry is modified by a malicious host, any of the designated servers will notice and can take appropriate action.

Besides protecting an agent against malicious hosts, Ajanta also provides various mechanisms to protect hosts against malicious agents. As we discuss next, many of these mechanisms are also supplied by other systems that support mobile code. Further information on Ajanta can be found in Tripathi et al. (1999).

Protecting the Target

Although protecting mobile code against a malicious host is important, more attention has been paid to protecting hosts against malicious mobile code. If sending an agent into the outside world is considered too dangerous, a user will generally have alternatives to get the job done for which the agent was intended. However, there are often no alternatives to letting an agent into your system, other than locking it out completely. Therefore, if it is once decided that the agent can come in, the user needs full control over what the agent can do.

As we just discussed, although protecting an agent from modification may be impossible, at least it is possible for the agent's owner to detect that modifications have been made. At worst, the owner will have to discard the agent when it returns, but otherwise no harm will have been done. However, when dealing with malicious incoming agents, simply detecting that your resources have been harassed is too late. Instead, it is essential to protect all resources against unauthorized access by downloaded code.

One approach to protection is to construct a sandbox. A **sandbox** is a technique by which a downloaded program is executed in such a way that each of its instructions can be fully controlled. If an attempt is made to execute an instruction that has been forbidden by the host, execution of the program will be stopped. Likewise, execution is halted when an instruction accesses certain registers or areas in memory that the host has not allowed.

Implementing a sandbox is not easy. One approach is to check the executable code when it is downloaded, and to insert additional instructions for situations that can be checked only at runtime (Wahbe et al., 1993). Fortunately, matters become much simpler when dealing with interpreted code. Let us briefly consider the approach taken in Java [see also MacGregor et al. (1998)]. Each Java program consists of a number of classes from which objects are created. There are no global variables and functions; everything has to be declared as part of a class. Program execution starts at a method called main. A Java program is compiled to a set of instructions that are interpreted by what is called the **Java Virtual Machine (JVM)**. For a client to download and execute a compiled Java program, it is therefore necessary that the client process is running the JVM. The JVM will subsequently handle the actual execution of the downloaded program by interpreting each of its instructions, starting at the instructions that comprise main.

In a Java sandbox, protection starts by ensuring that the component that handles the transfer of a program to the client machine can be trusted. Downloading in Java is taken care of by a set of **class loaders**. Each class loader is responsible for fetching a specified class from a server and installing it in the client's address space so that the JVM can create objects from it. Because a class loader is just another Java class, it is possible that a downloaded program contains its own class loaders. The first thing that is handled by a sandbox is that exclusively trusted class loaders are used. In particular, a Java program is not allowed to create its own class loaders by which it could circumvent the way class loading is normally handled.

The second component of a Java sandbox consists of a **byte code verifier**, which checks whether a downloaded class obeys the security rules of the sandbox. In particular, the verifier checks that the class contains no illegal instructions or instructions that could somehow corrupt the stack or memory. Not all classes are checked, as shown in Fig. 9-29; only the ones that are downloaded from an external server to the client. Classes that are located on the client's machine are generally trusted, although their integrity could also be easily verified.

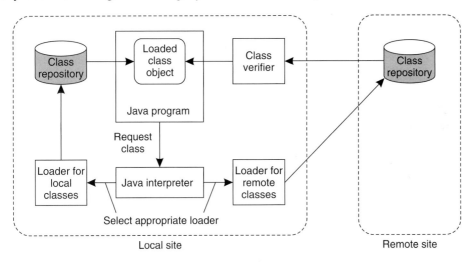

Figure 9-29. The organization of a Java sandbox.

Finally, when a class has been securely downloaded and verified, the JVM can instantiate objects from it and execute those object's methods. To further prevent objects from unauthorized access to the client's resources, a **security manager** is used to perform various checks at runtime. Java programs intended to be downloaded are forced to make use of the security manager; there is no way they can circumvent it. This means, for example, that any I/O operation is vetted for validity and will not be carried out if the security manager says "no." The security manager thus plays the role of a reference monitor we discussed earlier.

A typical security manager will disallow many operations to be carried out. For example, virtually all security managers deny access to local files and allow a program only to set up a connection to the server from where it came. Manipulating the JVM is obviously not allowed as well. However, a program is permitted to access the graphics library for display purposes and to catch events such as moving the mouse or clicking its buttons.

The original Java security manager implemented a rather strict security policy in which it made no distinction between different downloaded programs, or even programs from different servers. In many cases, the initial Java sandbox model was overly restricted and more flexibility was required. Below, we discuss an alternative approach that is currently followed.

An approach in line with sandboxing, but which offers somewhat more flexibility, is to create a playground for downloaded mobile code (Malkhi and Reiter, 2000). A **playground** is a separate, designated machine exclusively reserved for running mobile code. Resources local to the playground, such as files or network connections to external servers are available to programs executing in the playground, subject to normal protection mechanisms. However, resources local to other machines are physically disconnected from the playground and cannot be accessed by downloaded code. Users on these other machines can access the playground in a traditional way, for example, by means of RPCs. However, no mobile code is ever downloaded to machines not in the playground. This distinction between a sandbox and a playground is shown in Fig. 9-30.

dedicated machine.

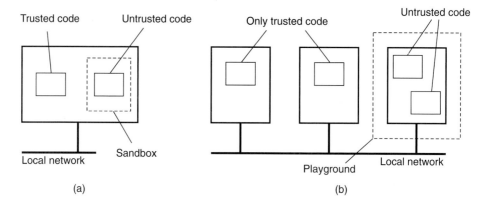

Figure 9-30. (a) A sandbox. (b) A playground.

A next step toward increased flexibility is to require that each downloaded program can be authenticated, and to subsequently enforce a specific security policy based on where the program came from. Demanding that programs can be authenticated is relatively easy: mobile code can be signed, just like any other document. This **code-signing** approach is often applied as an alternative to sandboxing as well. In effect, only code from trusted servers is accepted.

However, the difficult part is enforcing a security policy. Wallach et al. (1997) propose three mechanisms in the case of Java programs. The first approach is based on the use of object references as capabilities. To access a local resource such as a file, a program must have been given a reference to a specific object that handles file operations when it was downloaded. If no such reference is given, there is no way that files can be accessed. This principle is shown in Fig. 9-31.

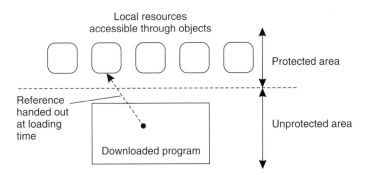

Figure 9-31. The principle of using Java object references as capabilities.

All interfaces to objects that implement the file system are initially hidden from the program by simply not handing out any references to these interfaces. Java's strong type checking ensures that it is impossible to construct a reference to one of these interfaces at runtime. In addition, we can use the property of Java to keep certain variables and methods completely internal to a class. In particular, a program can be prevented from instantiating its own file-handling objects, by essentially hiding the operation that creates new objects from a given class. (In Java terminology, a constructor is made private to its associated class.)

The second mechanism for enforcing a security policy is **(extended) stack introspection**. In essence, any call to a method m of a local resource is preceded by a call to a special procedure enable_privilege that checks whether the caller is authorized to invoke m on that resource. If the invocation is authorized, the caller is given temporary privileges for the duration of the call. Before returning control to the invoker when m is finished, the special procedure disable_privilege is invoked to disable these privileges.

To enforce calls to enable_privilege and disable_privilege, a developer of interfaces to local resources could be required to insert these calls in the appropriate places. However, it is much better to let the Java interpreter handle the calls automatically. This is the standard approach followed in, for example, Web browsers for dealing with Java applets. An elegant solution is as follows. Whenever an

enable/disable for every local resource invoked

invocation to a local resource is made, the Java interpreter automatically calls enable_privilege, which subsequently checks whether the call is permitted. If so, a call to disable_privilege is pushed on the stack to ensure that privileges are disabled when the method call returns. This approach prevents malicious programmers from circumventing the rules.

if no such en/dis, the invocation is not allowed

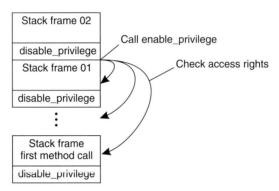

Figure 9-32. The principle of stack introspection.

Another important advantage of using the stack is that it enables a much better way of checking privileges. Suppose that a program invokes a local object $O1$, which, in turn, invokes object $O2$. Although $O1$ may have permission to invoke $O2$, if the invoker of $O1$ is not trusted to invoke a specific method belonging to $O2$, then this chain of invocations should not be allowed. Stack introspection makes it easy to check such chains, as the interpreter need merely inspect each stack frame starting at the top to see if there is a frame having the right privileges enabled (in which case the call is permitted), or if there is a frame that explicitly forbids access to the current resource (in which case the call is immediately terminated). This approach is shown in Fig. 9-32.

In essence, stack introspection allows for the attachment of privileges to classes or methods, and the checking of those privileges for each caller separately. In this way, it is possible to implement class-based protection domains, as is explained in detail in Gong and Schemers (1998).

The third approach to enforcing a security policy is by means of **name space management**. The idea is put forth below. To give programs access to local resources, they first need to attain access by including the appropriate files that contain the classes implementing those resources. Inclusion requires that a name is given to the interpreter, which then resolves it to a class, which is subsequently loaded at runtime. To enforce a security policy for a specific downloaded program, the same name can be resolved to different classes, depending on where the downloaded program came from. Typically, name resolution is handled by class loaders, which need to be adapted to implement this approach. Details of how this can be done can be found in Wallach et al. (1997).

how names are resolved into runtime classes

The approach described so far associates privileges with classes or methods based on where a downloaded program came from. By virtue of the Java interpreter, it is possible to enforce security policies through the mechanisms described above. In this sense, the security architecture becomes highly language dependent, and will need to be developed anew for other languages. Language-independent solutions, such as, for example, described in Jaeger et al. (1999), require a more general approach to enforcing security, and are also harder to implement. In these cases, support is needed from a secure operating system that is aware of downloaded mobile code and which enforces all calls to local resources to run through the kernel where subsequent checking is done.

9.3.4 Denial of Service

Access control is generally about carefully ensuring that resources are accessed only by authorized processes. A particularly annoying type of attack that is related to access control is maliciously preventing authorized processes from accessing resources. Defenses against such **denial-of-service (DoS) attacks** are becoming increasingly important as distributed systems are opened up through the Internet. Where DoS attacks that come from one or a few sources can often be handled quite effectively, matters become much more difficult when having to deal with **distributed denial of service (DDoS)**.

In DDoS attacks, a huge collection of processes jointly attempt to bring down a networked service. In these cases, we often see that the attackers have succeeded in hijacking a large group of machines which unknowingly participate in the attack. Specht and Lee (2004) distinguish two types of attacks: those aimed at bandwidth depletion and those aimed at resource depletion.

Bandwidth depletion can be accomplished by simply sending many messages to a single machine. The effect is that normal messages will hardly be able to reach the receiver. Resource depletion attacks concentrate on letting the receiver use up resources on otherwise useless messages. A well-known resource-depletion attack is TCP SYN-flooding. In this case, the attacker attempts to initiate a huge amount of connections (i.e., send SYN packets as part of the three-way handshake), but will otherwise never respond to acknowledgments from the receiver.

There is no single method to protect against DDoS attacks. One problem is that attackers make use of innocent victims by secretly installing software on their machines. In these cases, the only solution is to have machines continuously monitor their state by checking files for pollution. Considering the ease by which a virus can spread over the Internet, relying only on this countermeasure is not feasible.

Much better is to continuously monitor network traffic, for example, starting at the egress routers where packets leave an organization's network. Experience shows that by dropping packets whose source address does not belong to the organization's network we can prevent a lot of havoc. In general, the more packets can be filtered close to the sources, the better.

Alternatively, it is also possible to concentrate on ingress routers, that is, where traffic flows into an organization's network. The problem is that detecting an attack at an ingress router is too late as the network will probably already be unreachable for regular traffic. Better is to have routers further in the Internet, such as in the networks of ISPs, start dropping packets when they suspect that an attack is going on. This approach is followed by Gil and Poletto (2001), where a router will drop packets when it notices that the rate between the number of packets *to* a specific node is disproportionate to the number of packets *from* that node.

In general, a myriad of techniques need to be deployed, whereas new attacks continue to emerge. A practical overview of the state-of-the-art in denial-of-service attacks and solutions can be found in Mirkovic et al. (2005); a detailed taxonomy is presented in Mirkovic and Reiher (2004).

9.4 SECURITY MANAGEMENT

So far, we have considered secure channels and access control, but have hardly touched upon the issue how, for example, keys are obtained. In this section, we take a closer look at security management. In particular, we distinguish three different subjects. First, we need to consider the general management of cryptographic keys, and especially the means by which public keys are distributed. As it turns out, certificates play an important role here.

Second, we discuss the problem of securely managing a group of servers by concentrating on the problem of adding a new group member that is trusted by the current members. Clearly, in the face of distributed and replicated services, it is important that security is not compromised by admitting a malicious process to a group.

Third, we pay attention to authorization management by looking at capabilities and what are known as attribute certificates. An important issue in distributed systems with respect to authorization management is that one process can delegate some or all of its access rights to another process. Delegating rights in a secure way has its own subtleties as we also discuss in this section.

9.4.1 Key Management

So far, we have described various cryptographic protocols in which we (implicitly) assumed that various keys were readily available. For example, in the case of public-key cryptosystems, we assumed that a sender of a message had the public key of the receiver at its disposal so that it could encrypt the message to ensure confidentiality. Likewise, in the case of authentication using a key distribution center (KDC), we assumed each party already shared a secret key with the KDC.

However, establishing and distributing keys is not a trivial matter. For example, distributing secret keys by means of an unsecured channel is out of the question and in many cases we need to resort to out-of-band methods. Also, mechanisms are needed to revoke keys, that is, prevent a key from being used after it has been compromised or invalidated. For example, revocation is necessary when a key has been compromised.

Key Establishment

Let us start with considering how session keys can be established. When Alice wants to set up a secure channel with Bob, she may first use Bob's public key to initiate communication as shown in Fig. 9-19. If Bob accepts, he can subsequently generate the session key and return it to Alice encrypted with Alice's public key. By encrypting the shared session key before its transmission, it can be safely passed across the network.

A similar scheme can be used to generate and distribute a session key when Alice and Bob already share a secret key. However, both methods require that the communicating parties already have the means available to establish a secure channel. In other words, some form of key establishment and distribution must already have taken place. The same argument applies when a shared secret key is established by means of a trusted third party, such as a KDC.

An elegant and widely-applied scheme for establishing a shared key across an insecure channel is the **Diffie-Hellman key exchange** (Diffie and Hellman, 1976). The protocol works as follows. Suppose that Alice and Bob want to establish a shared secret key. The first requirement is that they agree on two large numbers, n and g that are subject to a number of mathematical properties (which we do not discuss here). Both n and g can be made public; there is no need to hide them from outsiders. Alice picks a large random number, say x, which she keeps secret. Likewise, Bob picks his own secret large number, say y. At this point there is enough information to construct a secret key, as shown in Fig. 9-33.

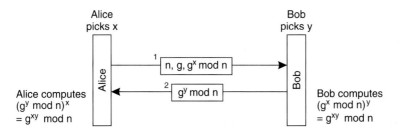

Figure 9-33. The principle of Diffie-Hellman key exchange.

Alice starts by sending $g^x \bmod n$ to Bob, along with n and g. It is important to note that this information can be sent as plaintext, as it is virtually impossible to compute x given $g^x \ mod \ n$. When Bob receives the message, he subsequently cal-culates $(g^x \ mod \ n)^y$ which is mathematically equal to $g^{xy} \ mod \ n$. In addition, he sends $g^y \ mod \ n$ to Alice, who can then compute $(g^y \ mod \ n)^x = g^{xy} \ mod \ n$. Conse-quently, both Alice and Bob, and only those two, will now have the shared secret key $g^{xy} \ mod \ n$. Note that neither of them needed to make their private number (x and y, respectively), known to the other.

Diffie-Hellman can be viewed as a public-key cryptosystem. In the case of Alice, x is her private key, whereas $g^x \ mod \ n$ is her public key. As we discuss next, securely distributing the public key is essential to making Diffie-Hellman work in practice.

Key Distribution

One of the more difficult parts in key management is the actual distribution of initial keys. In a symmetric cryptosystem, the initial shared secret key must be communicated along a secure channel that provides authentication as well as con-fidentiality, as shown in Fig. 9-34(a). If there are no keys available to Alice and Bob to set up such a secure channel, it is necessary to distribute the key out-of-band. In other words, Alice and Bob will have to get in touch with each other using some other communication means than the network. For example, one of them may phone the other, or send the key on a floppy disk using snail mail.

In the case of a public-key cryptosystem, we need to distribute the public key in such a way that the receivers can be sure that the key is indeed paired to a claimed private key. In other words, as shown in Fig. 9-34(b), although the public key itself may be sent as plaintext, it is necessary that the channel through which it is sent can provide authentication. The private key, of course, needs to be sent across a secure channel providing authentication as well as confidentiality.

When it comes to key distribution, the authenticated distribution of public keys is perhaps the most interesting. In practice, public-key distribution takes place by means of **public-key certificates**. Such a certificate consists of a public key together with a string identifying the entity to which that key is associated. The entity could be a user, but also a host or some special device. The public key and identifier have together been signed by a **certification authority**, and this sig-nature has been placed on the certificate as well. (The identity of the certification authority is naturally part of the certificate.) Signing takes place by means of a private key K_{CA}^- that belongs to the certification authority. The corresponding public key K_{CA}^+ is assumed to be well known. For example, the public keys of var-ious certification authorities are built into most Web browsers and shipped with the binaries.

Using a public-key certificate works as follows. Assume that a client wishes to ascertain that the public key found in the certificate indeed belongs to the iden-tified entity. It then uses the public key of the associated certification authority to verify the certificate's signature. If the signature on the certificate matches the

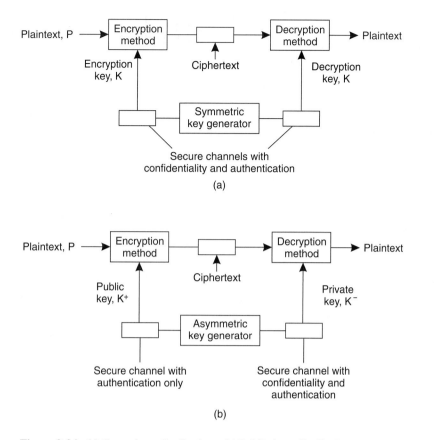

Figure 9-34. (a) Secret-key distribution. (b) Public-key distribution [see also Menezes et al. (1996)].

(public key, identifier)-pair, the client accepts that the public key indeed belongs to the identified entity.

It is important to note that by accepting the certificate as being in order, the client actually trusts that the certificate has not been forged. In particular, the client must assume that the public key K^+_{CA} indeed belongs to the associated certification authority. If in doubt, it should be possible to verify the validity of K^+_{CA} through another certificate coming from a different, possibly more trusted certification authority.

Such hierarchical **trust models** in which the highest-level certification authority must be trusted by everyone, are not uncommon. For example, **Privacy Enhanced Mail (PEM)** uses a three-level trust model in which lowest-level certification authorities can be authenticated by **Policy Certification Authorities (PCA)**, which in turn can be authenticated by the **Internet Policy Registration Authority (IPRA)**. If a user does not trust the IPRA, or does not think he can safely talk to the IPRA, there is no hope he will ever trust e-mail messages to be sent in a secure way when using PEM. More information on this model can be found in Kent (1993). Other trust models are discussed in Menezes et al. (1996).

Lifetime of Certificates

An important issue concerning certificates is their longevity. First let us consider the situation in which a certification authority hands out lifelong certificates. Essentially, what the certificate then states is that the public key will always be valid for the entity identified by the certificate. Clearly, such a statement is not what we want. If the private key of the identified entity is ever compromised, no unsuspecting client should ever be able to use the public key (let alone malicious clients). In that case, we need a mechanism to **revoke** the certificate by making it publicly-known that the certificate is no longer valid.

There are several ways to revoke a certificate. One common approach is with a **Certificate Revocation List** (**CRL**) published regularly by the certification authority. Whenever a client checks a certificate, it will have to check the CRL to see whether the certificate has been revoked or not. This means that the client will at least have to contact the certification authority each time a new CRL is published. Note that if a CRL is published daily, it also takes a day to revoke a certificate. Meanwhile, a compromised certificate can be falsely used until it is published on the next CRL. Consequently, the time between publishing CRLs cannot be too long. In addition, getting a CRL incurs some overhead.

An alternative approach is to restrict the lifetime of each certificate. In essence, this approach is analogous to handing out leases as we discussed in Chap. 6. The validity of a certificate automatically expires after some time. If for whatever reason the certificate should be revoked before it expires, the certification authority can still publish it on a CRL. However, this approach will still force clients to check the latest CRL whenever verifying a certificate. In other words, they will need to contact the certification authority or a trusted database containing the latest CRL.

A final extreme case is to reduce the lifetime of a certificate to nearly zero. In effect, this means that certificates are no longer used; instead, a client will always have to contact the certification authority to check the validity of a public key. As a consequence, the certification authority must be continuously online.

In practice, certificates are handed out with restricted lifetimes. In the case of Internet applications, the expiration time is often as much as a year (Stein, 1998). Such an approach requires that CRLs are published regularly, but that they are also inspected when certificates are checked. Practice indicates that client applications hardly ever consult CRLs and simply assume a certificate to be valid until it expires. In this respect, when it comes to Internet security in practice, there is still much room for improvement, unfortunately.

9.4.2 Secure Group Management

Many security systems make use of special services such as Key Distribution Centers (KDCs) or Certification Authorities (CAs). These services demonstrate a difficult problem in distributed systems. In the first place, they must be trusted. To enhance the trust in security services, it is necessary to provide a high degree of protection against all kinds of security threats. For example, as soon as a CA has been compromised, it becomes impossible to verify the validity of a public key, making the entire security system completely worthless.

On the other hand, it is also necessary that many security services offer high availability. For example, in the case of a KDC, each time two processes want to set up a secure channel, at least one of them will need to contact the KDC for a shared secret key. If the KDC is not available, secure communication cannot be established unless an alternative technique for key establishment is available, such as the Diffie-Hellman key exchange.

The solution to high availability is replication. On the other hand, replication makes a server more vulnerable to security attacks. We already discussed how secure group communication can take place by sharing a secret among the group members. In effect, no single group member is capable of compromising certificates, making the group itself highly secure. What remains to consider is how to actually manage a group of replicated servers. Reiter et al. (1994) propose the following solution.

The problem that needs to be solved is to ensure that when a process asks to join a group G, the integrity of the group is not compromised. A group G is assumed to use a secret key CK_G shared by all group members for encrypting group messages. In addition, it also uses a public/private key pair (K_G^+, K_G^-) for communication with nongroup members.

Whenever a process P wants to join a group G, it sends a join request JR identifying G and P, P's local time T, a generated *reply pad RP* and a generated secret key $K_{P,G}$. RP and $K_{P,G}$ are jointly encrypted using the group's public key K_G^+, as shown as message 1 in Fig. 9-35. The use of RP and $K_{P,G}$ is explained in more detail below. The join request JR is signed by P, and is sent along with a certificate containing P's public key. We have used the widely-applied notation $[M]_A$ to denote that message M has been signed by subject A.

When a group member Q receives such a join request, it first authenticates P, after which communication with the other group members takes place to see whether P can be admitted as a group member. Authentication of P takes place in the usual way by means of the certificate. The timestamp T is used to make sure that the certificate was still valid at the time it was sent. (Note that we need to be sure that the time has not been tampered with as well.) Group member Q verifies the signature of the certification authority and subsequently extracts P's public key from the certificate to check the validity of JR. At that point, a group-specific protocol is followed to see whether all group members agree on admitting P.

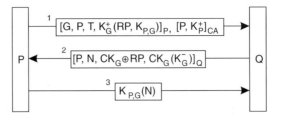

Figure 9-35. Securely admitting a new group member.

If P is allowed to join the group, Q returns a group admittance message GA, shown as message 2 in Fig. 9-35, identifying P and containing a nonce N. The reply pad RP is used to encrypt the group's communication key CK_G. In addition, P will also need the group's private key K_G^-, which is encrypted with CK_G. Message GA is subsequently signed by Q using key $K_{P,G}$.

Process P can now authenticate Q, because only a true group member can have discovered the secret key $K_{P,G}$. The nonce N in this protocol is not used for security; instead, when P sends back N encrypted with $K_{P,G}$ (message 3), Q then knows that P has received all the necessary keys, and has therefore now indeed joined the group.

Note that instead of using the reply pad RP, P and Q could also have encrypted CK_G using P's public key. However, because RP is used only once, namely for the encryption of the group's communication key in message GA, using RP is safer. If P's private key were ever to revealed, it would become possible to also reveal CK_G, which would compromise the secrecy of all group communication.

9.4.3 Authorization Management

Managing security in distributed systems is also concerned with managing access rights. So far, we have hardly touched upon the issue of how access rights are initially granted to users or groups of users, and how they are subsequently maintained in an unforgeable way. It is time to correct this omission.

In nondistributed systems, managing access rights is relatively easy. When a new user is added to the system, that user is given initial rights, for example, to create files and subdirectories in a specific directory, create processes, use CPU time, and so on. In other words, a complete account for a user is set up for one specific machine in which all rights have been specified in advance by the system administrators.

In a distributed system, matters are complicated by the fact that resources are spread across several machines. If the approach for nondistributed systems were to be followed, it would be necessary to create an account for each user on each machine. In essence, this is the approach followed in network operating systems.

in single machine

Matters can be simplified a bit by creating a single account on a central server. That server is consulted each time a user accesses certain resources or machines.

Capabilities and Attribute Certificates

A much better approach that has been widely applied in distributed systems is the use of capabilities. As we explained briefly above, a **capability** is an unforgeable data structure for a specific resource, specifying exactly the access rights that the holder of the capability has with respect to that resource. Different implementations of capabilities exist. Here, we briefly discuss the implementation as used in the Amoeba operating system (Tanenbaum et al., 1986).

Amoeba was one of the first object-based distributed systems. Its model of distributed objects is that of remote objects. In other words, an object resides at a server while clients are offered transparent access to that object by means of a proxy. To invoke an operation on an object, a client passes a capability to its local operating system, which then locates the server where the object resides and subsequently does an RPC to that server.

A capability is a 128-bit identifier, internally organized as shown in Fig. 9-36. The first 48 bits are initialized by the object's server when the object is created and effectively form a machine-independent identifier of the object's server, referred to as the **server port**. Amoeba uses broadcasting to locate the machine where the server is currently located.

48 bits	24 bits	8 bits	48 bits
Server port	Object	Rights	Check

Figure 9-36. A capability in Amoeba.

The next 24 bits are used to identify the object at the given server. Note that the server port together with the object identifier form a 72-bit systemwide unique identifier for every object in Amoeba. The next 8 bits are used to specify the access rights of the holder of the capability. Finally, the 48-bits *check* field is used to make a capability unforgeable, as we explain in the following pages.

When an object is created, its server picks a random *check* field and stores it both in the capability as well as internally in its own tables. All the right bits in a new capability are initially on, and it is this **owner capability** that is returned to the client. When the capability is sent back to the server in a request to perform an operation, the *check* field is verified.

To create a restricted capability, a client can pass a capability back to the server, along with a bit mask for the new rights. The server takes the original *check* field from its tables, XORs it with the new rights (which must be a subset of the rights in the capability), and then runs the result through a one-way function.

The server then creates a new capability, with the same value in the *object* field, but with the new rights bits in the *rights* field and the output of the one-way function in the *check* field. The new capability is then returned to the caller. The client may send this new capability to another process, if it wishes.

The method of generating restricted capabilities is illustrated in Fig. 9-37. In this example, the owner has turned off all the rights except one. For example, the restricted capability might allow the object to be read, but nothing else. The meaning of the *rights* field is different for each object type since the legal operations themselves also vary from object type to object type.

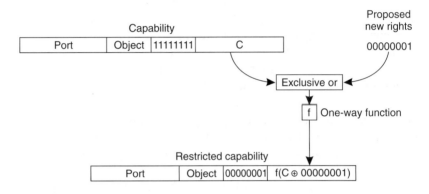

Figure 9-37. Generation of a restricted capability from an owner capability.

If all rights are on → it's owner → use the original random number.

When the restricted capability comes back to the server, the server sees from the *rights* field that it is not an *owner capability* because at least one bit is turned off. The server then fetches the original random number from its tables, XORs it with the *rights* field from the capability, and runs the result through the one-way function. If the result agrees with the *check* field, the capability is accepted as valid.

It should be obvious from this algorithm that a user who tries to add rights that he does not have will simply invalidate the capability. Inverting the *check* field in a restricted capability to get the argument (*C* XOR 00000001 in Fig. 9-37) is impossible because the function *f* is a one-way function. It is through this cryptographic technique that capabilities are protected from tampering. Note that *f* essentially does the same as computing a message digest as discussed earlier. Changing anything in the original message (like inverting a bit), will immediately be detected.

A generalization of capabilities that is sometimes used in modern distributed systems is the **attribute certificate**. Unlike the certificates discussed above that are used to verify the validity of a public key, attribute certificates are used to list certain *(attribute, value)*-pairs that apply to an identified entity. In particular, attribute certificates can be used to list the access rights that the holder of a certificate has with respect to the identified resource.

Like other certificates, attribute certificates are handed out by special certification authorities, usually called **attribute certification authorities**. Compared to Amoeba's capabilities, such an authority corresponds to an object's server. In general, however, the attribute certification authority and the server managing the entity for which a certificate has been created need not be the same. The access rights listed in a certificate are signed by the attribute certification authority.

Delegation

Now consider the following problem. A user wants to have a large file printed for which he has read-only access rights. In order not to bother others too much, the user sends a request to the print server, asking it to start printing the file no earlier than 2 o'clock in the morning. Instead of sending the entire file to the printer, the user passes the file name to the printer so that it can copy it to its spooling directory, if necessary, when actually needed.

Although this scheme seems to be perfectly in order, there is one major problem: the printer will generally not have the appropriate access permissions to the named file. In other words, if no special measures are taken, as soon as the print server wants to read the file in order to print it, the system will deny the server access to the file. This problem could have been solved if the user had temporarily **delegated** his access rights for the file to the print server.

Delegation of access rights is an important technique for implementing protection in computer systems and distributed systems, in particular. The basic idea is simple: by passing certain access rights from one process to another, it becomes easier to distribute work between several processes without adversely affecting the protection of resources. In the case of distributed systems, processes may run on different machines and even within different administrative domains as we discussed for Globus. Delegation can avoid much overhead as protection can often be handled locally.

There are several ways to implement delegation. A general approach as described in Neuman (1993), is to make use of a proxy. A **proxy** in the context of security in computer systems is a token that allows its owner to operate with the same or restricted rights and privileges as the subject that granted the token. (Note that this notion of a proxy is different from a proxy as a synonym for a client-side stub. Although we try to avoid overloading terms, we make an exception here as the term "proxy" in the definition above is too widely used to ignore.) A process can create a proxy with at best the same rights and privileges it has itself. If a process creates a new proxy based on one it currently has, the derived proxy will have at least the same restrictions as the original one, and possibly more.

Before considering a general scheme for delegation, consider the following two approaches. First, delegation is relatively simple if Alice knows everyone. If she wants to delegate rights to Bob, she merely needs to construct a certificate saying "Alice says Bob has rights R," such as $[A,B,R]_A$. If Bob wants to pass some of these rights to Charlie, he will ask Charlie to contact Alice and ask her for an appropriate certificate.

In a second simple case Alice can simply construct a certificate saying "The bearer of this certificate has rights R." However, in this case we need to protect the certificate against illegal copying, as is done with securely passing capabilities between processes. Neuman's scheme handles this case, as well as avoiding the issue that Alice needs to know everyone to whom rights need to be delegated.

A proxy in Neuman's scheme has two parts, as illustrated in Fig. 9-38. Let A be the process that created the proxy. The first part of the proxy is a set $C = \{R, S^+_{proxy}\}$, consisting of a set R of access rights that have been delegated by A, along with a publicly-known part of a secret that is used to authenticate the holder of the certificate. We will explain the use of S^+_{proxy} below. The certificate carries the signature $sig(A,C)$ of A, to protect it against modifications. The second part contains the other part of the secret, denoted as S^-_{proxy}. It is essential that S^-_{proxy} is protected against disclosure when delegating rights to another process.

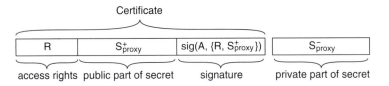

Figure 9-38. The general structure of a proxy as used for delegation.

Another way of looking at the proxy is as follows. If Alice wants to delegate some of her rights to Bob, she makes a list of rights (R) that Bob can exercise. By signing the list, she prevents Bob from tampering with it. However, having only a signed list of rights is often not enough. If Bob wants to exercise his rights, he may have to prove that he actually got the list from Alice and did not, for example, steal it from someone else. Therefore, Alice comes up with a very nasty question (S^+_{proxy}) that only she knows the answer to (S^-_{proxy}). Anyone can easily verify the correctness of the answer when given the question. The question is appended to the list before Alice adds her signature.

When delegating some of her rights, Alice gives the signed list of rights, along with the nasty question, to Bob. She also gives Bob the answer ensuring that no one can intercept it. Bob now has a list of rights, signed by Alice, which he can hand over to, say, Charlie, when necessary. Charlie will ask him the nasty question at the bottom of the list. If Bob knows the answer to it, Charlie will know for sure that Alice had indeed delegated the listed rights to Bob.

An important property of this scheme is that Alice need not be consulted. In fact, Bob may decide to pass on (some of) the rights on the list to Dave. In doing so, he will also tell Dave the answer to the question, so that Dave can prove the list was handed over to him by someone entitled to it. Alice never needs to know about Dave at all.

A protocol for delegating and exercising rights is shown in Fig. 9-39. Assume that Alice and Bob share a secret key $K_{A,B}$ that can be used for encrypting messages they send to each other. Then, Alice first sends Bob the certificate $C = \{R, S_{proxy}^{+}\}$, signed with $sig(A, C)$ (and denoted again as $[R, S_{proxy}^{+}]_A$). There is no need to encrypt this message: it can be sent as plaintext. Only the private part of the secret needs to be encrypted, shown as $K_{A,B}(S_{proxy}^{-})$ in message 1.

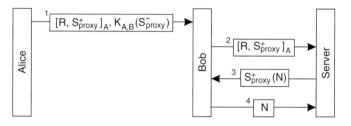

Figure 9-39. Using a proxy to delegate and prove ownership of access rights.

Now suppose that Bob wants an operation to be carried out at an object that resides at a specific server. Also, assume that Alice is authorized to have that operation carried out, and that she has delegated those rights to Bob. Therefore, Bob hands over his credentials to the server in the form of the signed certificate $[R, S_{proxy}^{+}]_A$.

At that point, the server will be able to verify that C has not been tampered with: any modification to the list of rights, or the nasty question will be noticed, because both have been jointly signed by Alice. However, the server does not know yet whether Bob is the rightful owner of the certificate. To verify this, the server must use the secret that came with C.

There are several ways to implement S_{proxy}^{+} and S_{proxy}^{-}. For example, assume S_{proxy}^{+} is a public key and S_{proxy}^{-} the corresponding private key. Z can then challenge Bob by sending him a nonce N, encrypted with S_{proxy}^{+}. By decrypting $S_{proxy}^{+}(N)$ and returning N, Bob proves he knows the secret and is thus the rightful holder of the certificate. There are other ways to implement secure delegation as well, but the basic idea is always the same: show you know a secret.

9.5 SUMMARY

Security plays an extremely important role in distributed systems. A distributed system should provide the mechanisms that allow a variety of different security policies to be enforced. Developing and properly applying those mechanisms generally makes security a difficult engineering exercise.

Three important issues can be distinguished. The first issue is that a distributed system should offer facilities to establish secure channels between processes. A secure channel, in principle, provides the means to mutually authenticate the communicating parties, and protect messages against tampering during their transmission. A secure channel generally also provides confidentiality so that no one but the communicating parties can read the messages that go through the channel.

An important design issue is whether to use only a symmetric cryptosystem (which is based on shared secret keys), or to combine it with a public-key system. Current practice shows the use of public-key cryptography for distributing short-term shared secret keys. The latter are known as session keys.

The second issue in secure distributed systems is access control, or authorization. Authorization deals with protecting resources in such a way that only processes that have the proper access rights can actual access and use those resources. Access control always take place after a process has been authenticated. Related to access control is preventing denial-of-service, which turns out to a difficult problem for systems that are accessible through the Internet.

There are two ways of implementing access control. First, each resource can maintain an access control list, listing exactly the access rights of each user or process. Alternatively, a process can carry a certificate stating precisely what its rights are for a particular set of resources. The main benefit of using certificates is that a process can easily pass its ticket to another process, that is, delegate its access rights. Certificates, however, have the drawback that they are often difficult to revoke.

Special attention is needed when dealing with access control in the case of mobile code. Besides being able to protect mobile code against a malicious host, it is generally more important to protect a host against malicious mobile code. Several proposals have been made, of which the sandbox is currently the most widely-applied one. However, sandboxes are rather restrictive, and more flexible approaches based on true protection domains have been devised as well.

The third issue in secure distributed systems concerns management. There are essentially two important subtopics: key management and authorization management. Key management includes the distribution of cryptographic keys, for which certificates as issued by trusted third parties play an important role. Important with respect to authorization management are attribute certificates and delegation.

PROBLEMS

1. Which mechanisms could a distributed system provide as security services to application developers that believe only in the end-to-end argument in system's design, as discussed in Chap. 6?

2. In the RISSC approach, can all security be concentrated on secure servers or not?

3. Suppose that you were asked to develop a distributed application that would allow teachers to set up exams. Give at least three statements that would be part of the security policy for such an application.

4. Would it be safe to join message 3 and message 4 in the authentication protocol shown in Fig. 9-12, into $K_{A,B}(R_B, R_A)$?

5. Why is it not necessary in Fig. 9-15 for the KDC to know for sure it was talking to Alice when it receives a request for a secret key that Alice can share with Bob?

6. What is wrong in implementing a nonce as a timestamp?

7. In message 2 of the Needham-Schroeder authentication protocol, the ticket is encrypted with the secret key shared between Alice and the KDC. Is this encryption necessary?

8. Can we safely adapt the authentication protocol shown in Fig. 9-19 such that message 3 consists only of R_B?

9. Devise a simple authentication protocol using signatures in a public-key cryptosystem.

10. Assume Alice wants to send a message m to Bob. Instead of encrypting m with Bob's public key K_B^+, she generates a session key $K_{A,B}$ and then sends $[K_{A,B}(m), K_B^+(K_{A,B})]$. Why is this scheme generally better? (*Hint:* consider performance issues.)

11. What is the role of the timestamp in message 6 in Fig. 9-23, and why does it need to be encrypted?

12. Complete Fig. 9-23 by adding the communication for authentication between Alice and Bob.

13. How can role changes be expressed in an access control matrix?

14. How are ACLs implemented in a UNIX file system?

15. How can an organization enforce the use of a Web proxy gateway and prevent its users to directly access external Web servers?

16. Referring to Fig. 9-31, to what extent does the use of Java object references as capabilities actually depend on the Java language?

17. Name three problems that will be encountered when developers of interfaces to local resources are required to insert calls to enable and disable privileges to protect against unauthorized access by mobile programs as explained in the text.

18. Name a few advantages and disadvantages of using centralized servers for key management.

19. The Diffie-Hellman key-exchange protocol can also be used to establish a shared secret key between three parties. Explain how.

20. There is no authentication in the Diffie-Hellman key-exchange protocol. By exploiting this property, a malicious third party, Chuck, can easily break into the key exchange taking place between Alice and Bob, and subsequently ruin the security. Explain how this would work.

21. Give a straightforward way how capabilities in Amoeba can be revoked.

22. Does it make sense to restrict the lifetime of a session key? If so, give an example how that could be established.

23. **(Lab assignment)** Install and configure a Kerberos v5 environment for a distributed system consisting of three different machines. One of these machines should be running the KDC. Make sure you can setup a (Kerberos) telnet connection between any two machines, but making use of only a single registered password at the KDC. Many of the details on running Kerberos are explained in Garman (2003).

10

DISTRIBUTED
OBJECT-BASED SYSTEMS

With this chapter, we switch from our discussion of principles to an examination of various paradigms that are used to organize distributed systems. The first paradigm consists of distributed objects. In distributed object-based systems, the notion of an object plays a key role in establishing distribution transparency. In principle, everything is treated as an object and clients are offered services and resources in the form of objects that they can invoke.

Distributed objects form an important paradigm because it is relatively easy to hide distribution aspects behind an object's interface. Furthermore, because an object can be virtually anything, it is also a powerful paradigm for building systems. In this chapter, we will take a look at how the principles of distributed systems are applied to a number of well-known object-based systems. In particular, we cover aspects of CORBA, Java-based systems, and Globe.

10.1 ARCHITECTURE

Object orientation forms an important paradigm in software development. Ever since its introduction, it has enjoyed a huge popularity. This popularity stems from the natural ability to build software into well-defined and more or less independent components. Developers could concentrate on implementing specific functionality independent from other developers.

Object orientation began to be used for developing distributed systems in the 1980s. Again, the notion of an independent object hosted by a remote server while attaining a high degree of distribution transparency formed a solid basis for developing a new generation of distributed systems. In this section, we will first take a deeper look into the general architecture of object-based distributed systems, after which we can see how specific principles have been deployed in these systems.

10.1.1 Distributed Objects

The key feature of an object is that it encapsulates data, called the **state**, and the operations on those data, called the **methods**. Methods are made available through an **interface**. It is important to understand that there is no "legal" way a process can access or manipulate the state of an object other than by invoking methods made available to it via an object's interface. An object may implement multiple interfaces. Likewise, given an interface definition, there may be several objects that offer an implementation for it.

This separation between interfaces and the objects implementing these interfaces is crucial for distributed systems. A strict separation allows us to place an interface at one machine, while the object itself resides on another machine. This organization, which is shown in Fig. 10-1, is commonly referred to as a **distributed object**.

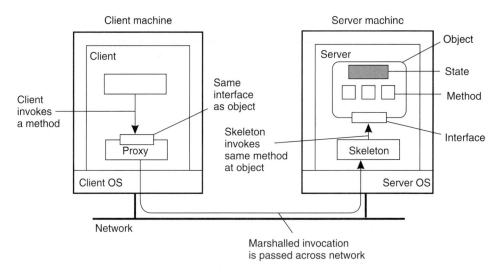

Figure 10-1. Common organization of a remote object with client-side proxy.

When a client **binds** to a distributed object, an implementation of the object's interface, called a **proxy**, is then loaded into the client's address space. A proxy is analogous to a client stub in RPC systems. The only thing it does is marshal method invocations into messages and unmarshal reply messages to return the result of the method invocation to the client. The actual object resides at a server machine, where it offers the same interface as it does on the client machine. Incoming invocation requests are first passed to a server stub, which unmarshals them to make method invocations at the object's interface at the server. The server stub is also responsible for marshaling replies and forwarding reply messages to the client-side proxy.

The server-side stub is often referred to as a **skeleton** as it provides the bare means for letting the server middleware access the user-defined objects. In practice, it often contains incomplete code in the form of a language-specific class that needs to be further specialized by the developer.

A characteristic, but somewhat counterintuitive feature of most distributed objects is that their state is *not* distributed: it resides at a single machine. Only the interfaces implemented by the object are made available on other machines. Such objects are also referred to as **remote objects**. In a general distributed object, the state itself may be physically distributed across multiple machines, but this distribution is also hidden from clients behind the object's interfaces.

Compile-Time versus Runtime Objects

Objects in distributed systems appear in many forms. The most obvious form is the one that is directly related to language-level objects such as those supported by Java, C++, or other object-oriented languages, which are referred to as compile-time objects. In this case, an object is defined as the instance of a class. A **class** is a description of an abstract type in terms of a module with data elements and operations on that data (Meyer, 1997).

Using compile-time objects in distributed systems often makes it much easier to build distributed applications. For example, in Java, an object can be fully defined by means of its class and the interfaces that the class implements. Compiling the class definition results in code that allows it to instantiate Java objects. The interfaces can be compiled into client-side and server-side stubs, allowing the Java objects to be invoked from a remote machine. A Java developer can be largely unaware of the distribution of objects: he sees only Java programming code.

The obvious drawback of compile-time objects is the dependency on a particular programming language. Therefore, an alternative way of constructing distributed objects is to do this explicitly during runtime. This approach is followed in many object-based distributed systems, as it is independent of the programming language in which distributed applications are written. In particular, an application may be constructed from objects written in multiple languages.

When dealing with runtime objects, how objects are actually implemented is basically left open. For example, a developer may choose to write a C library containing a number of functions that can all work on a common data file. The essence is how to let such an implementation appear to be an object whose methods can be invoked from a remote machine. A common approach is to use an **object adapter**, which acts as a *wrapper* around the implementation with the sole purpose to give it the appearance of an object. The term adapter is derived from a design pattern described in Gamma et al. (1994), which allows an interface to be converted into something that a client expects. An example object adapter is one that dynamically binds to the C library mentioned above and opens an associated data file representing an object's current state.

Object adapters play an important role in object-based distributed systems. To make wrapping as easy as possible, objects are solely defined in terms of the interfaces they implement. An implementation of an interface can then be registered at an adapter, which can subsequently make that interface available for (remote) invocations. The adapter will take care that invocation requests are carried out, and thus provide an image of remote objects to its clients. We return to the organization of object servers and adapters later in this chapter.

Persistent and Transient Objects

Besides the distinction between language-level objects and runtime objects, there is also a distinction between persistent and transient objects. A **persistent object** is one that continues to exist even if it is currently not contained in the address space of any server process. In other words, a persistent object is not dependent on its current server. In practice, this means that the server that is currently managing the persistent object, can store the object's state on secondary storage and then exit. Later, a newly started server can read the object's state from storage into its own address space, and handle invocation requests. In contrast, a **transient object** is an object that exists only as long as the server that is hosting the object. As soon as that server exits, the object ceases to exist as well. There used to be much controversy about having persistent objects; some people believe that transient objects are enough. To take the discussion away from middleware issues, most object-based distributed systems simply support both types.

10.1.2 Example: Enterprise Java Beans

The Java programming language and associated model has formed the foundation for numerous distributed systems and applications. Its popularity can be attributed to the straightforward support for object orientation, combined with the inherent support for remote method invocation. As we will discuss later in this chapter, Java provides a high degree of access transparency, making it easier to use than, for example, the combination of C with remote procedure calling.

Ever since its introduction, there has been a strong incentive to provide facilities that would ease the development of distributed applications. These facilities go well beyond language support, requiring a runtime environment that supports traditional multitiered client-server architectures. To this end, much work has been put into the development of **(Enterprise) Java Beans (EJB)**.

An EJB is essentially a Java object that is hosted by a special server offering different ways for remote clients to invoke that object. Crucial is that this server provides the support to separate application functionality from systems-oriented functionality. The latter includes functions for looking up objects, storing objects, letting objects be part of a transaction, and so on. How this separation can be realized is discussed below when we concentrate on object servers. How to develop EJBs is described in detail by Monson-Hafael et al. (2004). The specifications can be found in Sun Microsystems (2005a).

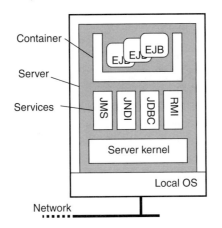

Figure 10-2. General architecture of an EJB server.

With this separation in mind, EJBs can be pictured as shown in Fig. 10-2. The important issue is that an EJB is embedded inside a container which effectively provides interfaces to underlying services that are implemented by the application server. The container can more or less automatically bind the EJB to these services, meaning that the correct references are readily available to a programmer. Typical services include those for remote method invocation (RMI), database access (JDBC), naming (JNDI), and messaging (JMS). Making use of these services is more or less automated, but does require that the programmer makes a distinction between four kinds of EJBs:

1. Stateless session beans

2. Stateful session beans

3. Entity beans

4. Message-driven beans

As its name suggests, a **stateless session bean** is a transient object that is invoked once, does its work, after which it discards any information it needed to perform the service it offered to a client. For example, a stateless session bean could be used to implement a service that lists the top-ranked books. In this case, the bean would typically consist of an SQL query that is submitted to an database. The results would be put into a special format that the client can handle, after which its work would have been completed and the listed books discarded.

In contrast, a **stateful session bean** maintains client-related state. The canonical example is a bean implementing an electronic shopping cart like those widely deployed for electronic commerce. In this case, a client would typically be able to put things in a cart, remove items, and use the cart to go to an electronic checkout. The bean, in turn, would typically access databases for getting current prices and information on number of items still in stock. However, its lifetime would still be limited, which is why it is referred to as a session bean: when the client is finished (possibly having invoked the object several times), the bean will automatically be destroyed.

An **entity bean** can be considered to be a long-lived persistent object. As such, an entity bean will generally be stored in a database, and likewise, will often also be part of distributed transactions. Typically, entity beans store information that may be needed a next time a specific client access the server. In settings for electronic commerce, an entity bean can be used to record customer information, for example, shipping address, billing address, credit card information, and so on. In these cases, when a client logs in, his associated entity bean will be restored and used for further processing.

Finally, **message-driven beans** are used to program objects that should react to incoming messages (and likewise, be able to send messages). Message-driven beans cannot be invoked directly by a client, but rather fit into a *publish-subscribe* way of communication, which we briefly discussed in Chap. 4. What it boils down to is that a message-driven bean is automatically called by the server when a specific message m is received, to which the server (or rather an application it is hosting) had previously subscribed. The bean contains application code for handling the message, after which the server simply discards it. Message-driven beans are thus seen to be stateless. We will return extensively to this type of communication in Chap. 13.

10.1.3 Example: Globe Distributed Shared Objects

Let us now take a look at a completely different type of object-based distributed system. **Globe** is a system in which scalability plays a central role. All aspects that deal with constructing a large-scale wide-area system that can support huge numbers of users and objects drive the design of Globe. Fundamental to this approach is the way objects are viewed. Like other object-based systems, objects in Globe are expected to encapsulate state and operations on that state.

An important difference with other object-based systems is that objects are also expected to encapsulate the implementation of policies that prescribe the distribution of an object's state across multiple machines. In other words, each object determines how its state will be distributed over its replicas. Each object also controls its own policies in other areas as well.

By and large, objects in Globe are put in charge as much as possible. For example, an object decides how, when, and where its state should be migrated. Also, an object decides if its state is to be replicated, and if so, how replication should take place. In addition, an object may also determine its security policy and implementation. Below, we describe how such encapsulation is achieved.

Object Model

Unlike most other object-based distributed systems, Globe does not adopt the remote-object model. Instead, objects in Globe can be physically distributed, meaning that the state of an object can be distributed and replicated across multiple processes. This organization is shown in Fig. 10-3, which shows an object that is distributed across four processes, each running on a different machine. Objects in Globe are referred to as **distributed shared objects**, to reflect that objects are normally shared between several processes. The object model originates from the distributed objects used in Orca as described in Bal (1989). Similar approaches have been followed for fragmented objects (Makpangou et al., 1994).

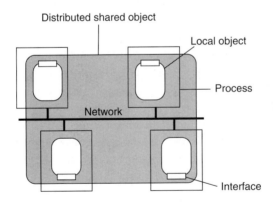

Figure 10-3. The organization of a Globe distributed shared object.

A process that is bound to a distributed shared object is offered a local implementation of the interfaces provided by that object. Such a local implementation is called a **local representative**, or simply **local object**. In principle, whether or not a local object has state is completely transparent to the bound process. All implementation details of an object are hidden behind the interfaces offered to a process. The only thing visible outside the local object are its methods.

Globe local objects come in two flavors. A **primitive local object** is a local object that does not contain any other local objects. In contrast, a **composite local object** is an object that is composed of multiple (possibly composite) local objects. Composition is used to construct a local object that is needed for implementing distributed shared objects. This local object is shown in Fig. 10-4 and consists of at least four subobjects.

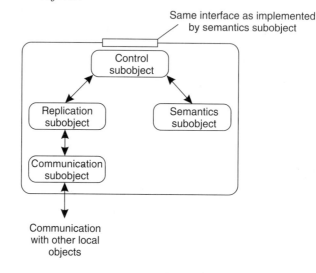

Figure 10-4. The general organization of a local object for distributed shared objects in Globe.

The **semantics subobject** implements the functionality provided by a distributed shared object. In essence, it corresponds to ordinary remote objects, similar in flavor to EJBs.

The **communication subobject** is used to provide a standard interface to the underlying network. This subobject offers a number of message-passing primitives for connection-oriented as well as connectionless communication. There are also more advanced communication subobjects available that implement multicasting interfaces. Communication subobjects can be used that implement reliable communication, while others offer only unreliable communication.

Crucial to virtually all distributed shared objects is the **replication subobject**. This subobject implements the actual distribution strategy for an object. As in the case of the communication subobject, its interface is standardized. The replication subobject is responsible for deciding exactly when a method as provided by the semantics subobject is to be carried out. For example, a replication subobject that implements active replication will ensure that all method invocations are carried out in the same order at each replica. In this case, the subobject will have to communicate with the replication subobjects in other local objects that comprise the distributed shared object.

The **control subobject** is used as an intermediate between the user-defined interfaces of the semantics subobject and the standardized interfaces of the replication subobject. In addition, it is responsible for exporting the interfaces of the semantics subobject to the process bound to the distributed shared object. All method invocations requested by that process are marshaled by the control subobject and passed to the replication subobject.

The replication subobject will eventually allow the control subobject to carry on with an invocation request and to return the results to the process. Likewise, invocation requests from remote processes are eventually passed to the control subobject as well. Such a request is then unmarshaled, after which the invocation is carried out by the control subobject, passing results back to the replication subobject.

10.2 PROCESSES

A key role in object-based distributed systems is played by object servers, that is, the server designed to host distributed objects. In the following, we first concentrate on general aspects of object servers, after which we will discuss the open-source JBoss server.

10.2.1 Object Servers

An object server is a server tailored to support distributed objects. The important difference between a general object server and other (more traditional) servers is that an object server by itself does not provide a specific service. Specific services are implemented by the objects that reside in the server. Essentially, the server provides only the means to invoke local objects, based on requests from remote clients. As a consequence, it is relatively easy to change services by simply adding and removing objects.

An object server thus acts as a place where objects live. An object consists of two parts: data representing its state and the code for executing its methods. Whether or not these parts are separated, or whether method implementations are shared by multiple objects, depends on the object server. Also, there are differences in the way an object server invokes its objects. For example, in a multithreaded server, each object may be assigned a separate thread, or a separate thread may be used for each invocation request. These and other issues are discussed next.

Alternatives for Invoking Objects

For an object to be invoked, the object server needs to know which code to execute, on which data it should operate, whether it should start a separate thread to take care of the invocation, and so on. A simple approach is to assume that all objects look alike and that there is only one way to invoke an object. Unfortunately, such an approach is generally inflexible and often unnecessarily constrains developers of distributed objects.

A much better approach is for a server to support different policies. Consider, for example, transient objects. Recall that a transient object is an object that exists only as long as its server exists, but possibly for a shorter period of time. An in-memory, read-only copy of a file could typically be implemented as a transient object. Likewise, a calculator could also be implemented as a transient object. A reasonable policy is to create a transient object at the first invocation request and to destroy it as soon as no clients are bound to it anymore.

The advantage of this approach is that a transient object will need a server's resources only as long as the object is really needed. The drawback is that an invocation may take some time to complete, because the object needs to be created first. Therefore, an alternative policy is sometimes to create all transient objects at the time the server is initialized, at the cost of consuming resources even when no client is making use of the object.

In a similar fashion, a server could follow the policy that each of its objects is placed in a memory segment of its own. In other words, objects share neither code nor data. Such a policy may be necessary when an object implementation does not separate code and data, or when objects need to be separated for security reasons. In the latter case, the server will need to provide special measures, or require support from the underlying operating system, to ensure that segment boundaries are not violated.

The alternative approach is to let objects at least share their code. For example, a database containing objects that belong to the same class can be efficiently implemented by loading the class implementation only once into the server. When a request for an object invocation comes in, the server need only fetch that object's state from the database and execute the requested method.

Likewise, there are many different policies with respect to threading. The simplest approach is to implement the server with only a single thread of control. Alternatively, the server may have several threads, one for each of its objects. Whenever an invocation request comes in for an object, the server passes the request to the thread responsible for that object. If the thread is currently busy, the request is temporarily queued.

The advantage of this approach is that objects are automatically protected against concurrent access: all invocations are serialized through the single thread associated with the object. Neat and simple. Of course, it is also possible to use a separate thread for each invocation request, requiring that objects should have already been protected against concurrent access. Independent of using a thread per object or thread per method is the choice of whether threads are created on demand or the server maintains a pool of threads. Generally there is no single best policy. Which one to use depends on whether threads are available, how much performance matters, and similar factors.

Object Adapter

Decisions on how to invoke an object are commonly referred to as **activation policies**, to emphasize that in many cases the object itself must first be brought into the server's address space (i.e., activated) before it can actually be invoked. What is needed then is a mechanism to group objects per policy. Such a mechanism is sometimes called an **object adapter**, or alternatively an **object wrapper**. An object adapter can best be thought of as software implementing a specific activation policy. The main issue, however, is that object adapters come as generic components to assist developers of distributed objects, and which need only to be configured for a specific policy.

An object adapter has one or more objects under its control. Because a server should be capable of simultaneously supporting objects that require different activation policies, several object adapters may reside in the same server at the same time. When an invocation request is delivered to the server, that request is first dispatched to the appropriate object adapter, as shown in Fig. 10-5.

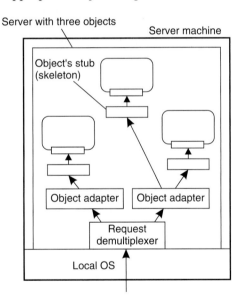

Figure 10-5. Organization of an object server supporting different activation policies.

An important observation is that object adapters are unaware of the specific interfaces of the objects they control. Otherwise, they could never be generic. The only issue that is important to an object adapter is that it can extract an object reference from an invocation request, and subsequently dispatch the request to the referenced object, but now following a specific activation policy. As is also o;-lustrated in Fig. 10-5, rather than passing the request directly to the object, an adapter hands an invocation request to the server-side stub of that object. The stub, also called a skeleton, is normally generated from the interface definitions of the object, unmarshals the request and invokes the appropriate method.

An object adapter can support different activation policies by simply configuring it at runtime. For example, in CORBA-compliant systems (OMG, 2004a), it is possible to specify whether an object should continue to exist after its associated adapter has stopped. Likewise, an adapter can be configured to generate object identifiers, or to let the application provide one. As a final example, an adapter can be configured to operate in single-threaded or multithreaded mode as we explained above.

As a side remark, note that although in Fig. 10-5 we have spoken about objects, we have said nothing about what these objects actually are. In particular, it should be stressed that as part of the implementation of such an object the server may (indirectly) access databases or call special library routines. The implementation details are hidden for the object adapter who communicates only with a skeleton. As such, the actual implementation may have nothing to do with what we often see with language-level (i.e., compile-time) objects. For this reason, a different terminology is generally adopted. A **servant** is the general term for a piece of code that forms the implementation of an object. In this light, a Java bean can be seen as nothing but just another kind of servant.

10.2.2 Example: The Ice Runtime System

Let us take a look at how distributed objects are handled in practice. We briefly consider the Ice distributed-object system, which has been partly developed in response to the intricacies of commercial object-based distributed systems (Henning, 2004). In this section, we concentrate on the core of an Ice object server and defer other parts of the system to later sections.

An object server in Ice is nothing but an ordinary process that simply starts with initializing the Ice runtime system (RTS). The basis of the runtime environment is formed by what is called a *communicator*. A communicator is a component that manages a number of basic resources, of which the most important one is formed by a pool of threads. Likewise, it will have associated dynamically allocated memory, and so on. In addition, a communicator provides the means for configuring the environment. For example, it is possible to specify maximum message lengths, maximum invocation retries, and so on.

Normally, an object server would have only a single communicator. However, when different applications need to be fully separated and protected from each other, a separate communicator (with possibly a different configuration) can be created within the same process. At the very least, such an approach would separate the different thread pools so that if one application has consumed all its threads, then this would not affect the other application.

A communicator can also be used to create an object adapter, such as shown in Fig. 10-6. We note that the code is simplified and incomplete. More examples and detailed information on Ice can be found in Henning and Spruiell (2005).

```
main(int argc, char* argv[]) {
    Ice::Communicator      ic;
    Ice::ObjectAdapter     adapter;
    Ice::Object            object;

    ic = Ice::initialize(argc, argv);
    adapter =
        ic->createObjectAdapterWithEnd Points( "MyAdapter","tcp -p 10000");
    object = new MyObject;
    adapter->add(object, objectID);
    adapter->activate();
    ic->waitForShutdown();
}
```

Figure 10-6. Example of creating an object server in Ice.

In this example, we start with creating and initializing the runtime environment. When that is done, an object adapter is created. In this case, it is instructed to listen for incoming TCP connections on port 10000. Note that the adapter is created in the context of the just created communicator. We are now in the position to create an object and to subsequently add that object to the adapter. Finally, the adapter is *activated*, meaning that, under the hood, a thread is activated that will start listening for incoming requests.

This code does not yet show much differentiation in activation policies. Policies can be changed by modifying the *properties* of an adapter. One family of properties is related to maintaining an adapter-specific set of threads that are used for handling incoming requests. For example, one can specify that there should always be only one thread, effectively serializing all accesses to objects that have been added to the adapter.

Again, note that we have not specified MyObject. Like before, this could be a simple C++ object, but also one that accesses databases and other external services that jointly implement an object. By registering MyObject with an adapter, such implementation details are completely hidden from clients, who now believe that they are invoking a remote object.

In the example above, an object is created as part of the application, after which it is added to an adapter. Effectively, this means that an adapter may need to support many objects at the same time, leading to potential scalability problems. An alternative solution is to dynamically load objects into memory when they are needed. To do this, Ice provides support for special objects known as *locators*. A locator is called when the adapter receives an incoming request for an object that has not been explicitly added. In that case, the request is forwarded to the locator, whose job is to further handle the request.

To make matters more concrete, suppose a locator is handed a request for an object of which the locator knows that its state is stored in a relational database system. Of course, there is no magic here: the locator has been programmed explicitly to handle such requests. In this case, the object's identifier may correspond to the key of a record in which that state is stored. The locator will then simply do a lookup on that key, fetch the state, and will then be able to further process the request.

There can be more than one locator added to an adapter. In that case, the adapter would keep track of which object identifiers would belong to the same locator. Using multiple locators allows supporting many objects by a single adapter. Of course, objects (or rather their state) would need to be loaded at runtime, but this dynamic behavior would possibly make the server itself relatively simple.

10.3 COMMUNICATION

We now draw our attention to the way communication is handled in object-based distributed systems. Not surprisingly, these systems generally offer the means for a remote client to invoke an object. This mechanism is largely based on remote procedure calls (RPCs), which we discussed extensively in Chap. 4. However, before this can happen, there are numerous issues that need to be dealt with.

10.3.1 Binding a Client to an Object

An interesting difference between traditional RPC systems and systems supporting distributed objects is that the latter generally provides systemwide object references. Such object references can be freely passed between processes on different machines, for example as parameters to method invocations. By hiding the actual implementation of an object reference, that is, making it opaque, and perhaps even using it as the only way to reference objects, distribution transparency is enhanced compared to traditional RPCs.

When a process holds an object reference, it must first bind to the referenced object before invoking any of its methods. Binding results in a proxy being placed in the process's address space, implementing an interface containing the methods the process can invoke. In many cases, binding is done automatically. When the underlying system is given an object reference, it needs a way to locate the server that manages the actual object, and place a proxy in the client's address space.

With **implicit binding**, the client is offered a simple mechanism that allows it to directly invoke methods using only a reference to an object. For example, C++

allows overloading the unary member selection operator ("$\rightarrow$") permitting us to introduce object references as if they were ordinary pointers as shown in Fig. 10-7(a). With implicit binding, the client is transparently bound to the object at the moment the reference is resolved to the actual object. In contrast, with **explicit binding**, the client should first call a special function to bind to the object before it can actually invoke its methods. Explicit binding generally returns a pointer to a proxy that is then become locally available, as shown in Fig. 10-7(b).

```
Distr_object* obj_ref;        // Declare a systemwide object reference
obj_ref = ...;                // Initialize the reference to a distrib. obj.
obj_ref→do_something( );      // Implicitly bind and invoke a method
```
                                (a)

```
Distr_object obj_ref;         // Declare a systemwide object reference
Local_object* obj_ptr;        // Declare a pointer to local objects
obj_ref = ...;                // Initialize the reference to a distrib. obj.
obj_ptr = bind(obj_ref);      // Explicitly bind and get ptr to local proxy
obj_ptr→do_something( );      // Invoke a method on the local proxy
```
                                (b)

Figure 10-7. (a) An example with implicit binding using only global references. (b) An example with explicit binding using global and local references.

Implementation of Object References

It is clear that an object reference must contain enough information to allow a client to bind to an object. A simple object reference would include the network address of the machine where the actual object resides, along with an end point identifying the server that manages the object, plus an indication of which object. Note that part of this information will be provided by an object adapter. However, there are a number of drawbacks to this scheme.

First, if the server's machine crashes and the server is assigned a different end point after recovery, all object references have become invalid. This problem can be solved as is done in DCE: have a local daemon per machine listen to a well-known end point and keep track of the server-to-end point assignments in an end point table. When binding a client to an object, we first ask the daemon for the server's current end point. This approach requires that we encode a server ID into the object reference that can be used as an index into the end point table. The server, in turn, is always required to register itself with the local daemon.

However, encoding the network address of the server's machine into an object reference is not always a good idea. The problem with this approach is that the server can never move to another machine without invalidating all the references to the objects it manages. An obvious solution is to expand the idea of a local daemon maintaining an end point table to a **location server** that keeps track of the machine where an object's server is currently running. An object reference would then contain the network address of the location server, along with a systemwide identifier for the server. Note that this solution comes close to implementing flat name spaces as we discussed in Chap. 5.

What we have tacitly assumed so far is that the client and server have somehow already been configured to use the same protocol stack. Not only does this mean that they use the same transport protocol, for example, TCP; furthermore it means that they use the same protocol for marshaling and unmarshaling parameters. They must also use the same protocol for setting up an initial connection, handle errors and flow control the same way, and so on.

We can safely drop this assumption provided we add more information in the object reference. Such information may include the identification of the protocol that is used to bind to an object and of those that are supported by the object's server. For example, a single server may simultaneously support data coming in over a TCP connection, as well as incoming UDP datagrams. It is then the client's responsibility to get a proxy implementation for at least one of the protocols identified in the object reference.

We can even take this approach one step further, and include an **implementation handle** in the object reference, which refers to a complete implementation of a proxy that the client can dynamically load when binding to the object. For example, an implementation handle could take the form of a URL pointing to an archive file, such as *ftp://ftp.clientware.org/proxies/java/proxy-v1.1a.zip*. The binding protocol would then only need to prescribe that such a file should be dynamically downloaded, unpacked, installed, and subsequently instantiated. The benefit of this approach is that the client need not worry about whether it has an implementation of a specific protocol available. In addition, it gives the object developer the freedom to design object-specific proxies. However, we do need to take special security measures to ensure the client that it can trust the downloaded code.

10.3.2 Static versus Dynamic Remote Method Invocations

After a client is bound to an object, it can invoke the object's methods through the proxy. Such a **remote method invocation**, or simply **RMI**, is very similar to an RPC when it comes to issues such as marshaling and parameter passing. An essential difference between an RMI and an RPC is that RMIs generally support systemwide object references as explained above. Also, it is not necessary to have only general-purpose client-side and server-side stubs available. Instead, we can more easily accommodate object-specific stubs as we also explained.

The usual way to provide RMI support is to specify the object's interfaces in an interface definition language, similar to the approach followed with RPCs.

Alternatively, we can make use of an object-based language such as Java, that will handle stub generation automatically. This approach of using predefined interface definitions is generally referred to as **static invocation**. Static invocations require that the interfaces of an object are known when the client application is being developed. It also implies that if interfaces change, then the client application must be recompiled before it can make use of the new interfaces.

As an alternative, method invocations can also be done in a more dynamic fashion. In particular, it is sometimes convenient to be able to *compose* a method invocation at runtime, also referred to as a **dynamic invocation**. The essential difference with static invocation is that an application selects at runtime which method it will invoke at a remote object. Dynamic invocation generally takes a form such as

    invoke(object, method, input_parameters, output_parameters);

where *object* identifies the distributed object, *method* is a parameter specifying exactly which method should be invoked, *input_parameters* is a data structure that holds the values of that method's input parameters, and *output_parameters* refers to a data structure where output values can be stored.

For example, consider appending an integer *int* to a file object *fobject*, for which the object provides the method append. In this case, a static invocation would take the form

    fobject.append(int)

whereas the dynamic invocation would look something like

    invoke(fobject, id(append), int)

where the operation *id(append)* returns an identifier for the method append.

To illustrate the usefulness of dynamic invocations, consider an object browser that is used to examine sets of objects. Assume that the browser supports remote object invocations. Such a browser is capable of binding to a distributed object and subsequently presenting the object's interface to its user. The user could then be asked to choose a method and provide values for its parameters, after which the browser can do the actual invocation. Typically, such an object browser should be developed to support any possible interface. Such an approach requires that interfaces can be inspected at runtime, and that method invocations can be dynamically constructed.

Another application of dynamic invocations is a batch processing service to which invocation requests can be handed along with a time when the invocation should be done. The service can be implemented by a queue of invocation requests, ordered by the time that invocations are to be done. The main loop of the service would simply wait until the next invocation is scheduled, remove the request from the queue, and call invoke as given above.

10.3.3 Parameter Passing

Because most RMI systems support systemwide object references, passing parameters in method invocations is generally less restricted than in the case of RPCs. However, there are some subtleties that can make RMIs trickier than one might initially expect, as we briefly discuss in the following pages.

Let us first consider the situation that there are only distributed objects. In other words, all objects in the system can be accessed from remote machines. In that case, we can consistently use object references as parameters in method invocations. References are passed by value, and thus copied from one machine to the other. When a process is given an object reference as the result of a method invocation, it can simply bind to the object referred to when needed later.

Unfortunately, using only distributed objects can be highly inefficient, especially when objects are small, such as integers, or worse yet, Booleans. Each invocation by a client that is not colocated in the same server as the object, generates a request between different address spaces or, even worse, between different machines. Therefore, references to remote objects and those to local objects are often treated differently.

When invoking a method with an object reference as parameter, that reference is copied and passed as a value parameter only when it refers to a remote object. In this case, the object is literally passed by reference. However, when the reference refers to a local object, that is an object in the same address space as the client, the referred object is copied as a whole and passed along with the invocation. In other words, the object is passed by value.

These two situations are illustrated in Fig. 10-8, which shows a client program running on machine A, and a server program on machine C. The client has a reference to a local object $O1$ that it uses as a parameter when calling the server program on machine C. In addition, it holds a reference to a remote object $O2$ residing at machine B, which is also used as a parameter. When calling the server, a copy of $O1$ is passed to the server on machine C, along with only a copy of the reference to $O2$.

Note that whether we are dealing with a reference to a local object or a reference to a remote object can be highly transparent, such as in Java. In Java, the distinction is visible only because local objects are essentially of a different data type than remote objects. Otherwise, both types of references are treated very much the same [see also Wollrath et al. (1996)]. On the other hand, when using conventional programming languages such as C, a reference to a local object can be as simple as a pointer, which can never be used to refer to a remote object.

The side effect of invoking a method with an object reference as parameter is that we may be *copying* an object. Obviously, hiding this aspect is unacceptable, so that we are consequently forced to make an explicit distinction between local and distributed objects. Clearly, this distinction not only violates distribution transparency, but also makes it harder to write distributed applications.

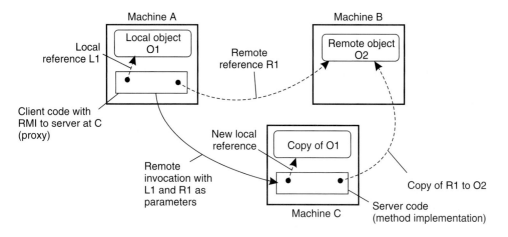

Figure 10-8. The situation when passing an object by reference or by value.

10.3.4 Example: Java RMI

In Java, distributed objects have been integrated into the language. An important goal was to keep as much of the semantics of nondistributed objects as possible. In other words, the Java language developers have aimed for a high degree of distribution transparency. However, as we shall see, Java's developers have also decided to make distribution apparent where a high degree of transparency was simply too inefficient, difficult, or impossible to realize.

The Java Distributed-Object Model

Java also adopts remote objects as the only form of distributed objects. Recall that a remote object is a distributed object whose state always resides on a single machine, but whose interfaces can be made available to remote processes. Interfaces are implemented in the usual way by means of a proxy, which offers exactly the same interfaces as the remote object. A proxy itself appears as a local object in the client's address space.

There are only a few, but subtle and important, differences between remote objects and local objects. First, cloning local or remote objects are different. Cloning a local object O results in a new object of the same type as O with exactly the same state. Cloning thus returns an exact copy of the object that is cloned. These semantics are hard to apply to a remote object. If we were to make an exact copy of a remote object, we would not only have to clone the actual object at its server, but also the proxy at each client that is currently bound to the remote object. Cloning a remote object is therefore an operation that can be executed only by the server. It results in an exact copy of the actual object in the server's address space.

Proxies of the actual object are thus not cloned. If a client at a remote machine wants access to the cloned object at the server, it will first have to bind to that object again.

Java Remote Object Invocation

As the distinction between local and remote objects is hardly visible at the language level, Java can also hide most of the differences during a remote method invocation. For example, any primitive or object type can be passed as a parameter to an RMI, provided only that the type can be marshaled. In Java terminology, this means that it must be **serializable**. Although, in principle, most objects can be serialized, serialization is not always allowed or possible. Typically, platform-dependent objects such as file descriptors and sockets, cannot be serialized.

The only distinction made between local and remote objects during an RMI is that local objects are passed by value (including large objects such as arrays), whereas remote objects are passed by reference. In other words, a local object is first copied after which the copy is used as parameter value. For a remote object, a reference to the object is passed as parameter instead of a copy of the object, as was also shown in Fig. 10-8.

In Java RMI, a reference to a remote object is essentially implemented as we explained in Sec. 10.3.3. Such a reference consists of the network address and end point of the server, as well as a local identifier for the actual object in the server's address space. That local identifier is used only by the server. As we also explained, a reference to a remote object also needs to encode the protocol stack that is used by a client and the server to communicate. To understand how such a stack is encoded in the case of Java RMI, it is important to realize that each object in Java is an instance of a class. A class, in turn, contains an implementation of one or more interfaces.

In essence, a remote object is built from two different classes. One class contains an implementation of server-side code, which we call the *server class*. This class contains an implementation of that part of the remote object that will be running on a server. In other words, it contains the description of the object's state, as well as an implementation of the methods that operate on that state. The server-side stub, that is, the skeleton, is generated from the interface specifications of the object.

The other class contains an implementation of the client-side code, which we call the *client class*. This class contains an implementation of a proxy. Like the skeleton, this class is also generated from the object's interface specification. In its simplest form, the only thing a proxy does is to convert each method call into a message that is sent to the server-side implementation of the remote object, and convert a reply message into the result if a method call. For each call, it sets up a connection with the server, which is subsequently torn down when the call is finished. For this purpose, the proxy needs the server's network address and end point as mentioned above. This information, along with the local identifier of the object at the server, is always stored as part of the state of a proxy.

Consequently, a proxy has all the information it needs to let a client invoke methods of the remote object. In Java, proxies are serializable. In other words, it is possible to marshal a proxy and send it as a series of bytes to another process, where it can be unmarshaled and used to invoke methods on the remote object. In other words, a proxy can be used as a reference to a remote object.

This approach is consistent with Java's way of integrating local and distributed objects. Recall that in an RMI, a local object is passed by making a copy of it, while a remote object is passed by means of a systemwide object reference. A proxy is treated as nothing else but a local object. Consequently, it is possible to pass a serializable proxy as parameter in an RMI. The side effect is that such a proxy can be used as a reference to the remote object.

In principle, when marshaling a proxy, its complete implementation, that is, all its state and code, is converted to a series of bytes. Marshaling the code like this is not very efficient and may lead to very large references. Therefore, when marshaling a proxy in Java, what actually happens is that an implementation handle is generated, specifying precisely which classes are needed to construct the proxy. Possibly, some of these classes first need to be downloaded from a remote site. The implementation handle replaces the marshaled code as part of a remote-object reference. In effect, references to remote objects in Java are in the order of a few hundred bytes.

This approach to referencing remote objects is highly flexible and is one of the distinguishing features of Java RMI (Waldo, 1998). In particular, it allows for object-specific solutions. For example, consider a remote object whose state changes only once in a while. We can turn such an object into a truly distributed object by copying the entire state to a client at binding time. Each time the client invokes a method, it operates on the local copy. To ensure consistency, each invocation also checks whether the state at the server has changed, in which case the local copy is refreshed. Likewise, methods that modify the state are forwarded to the server. The developer of the remote object will now have to implement only the necessary client-side code, and have it dynamically downloaded when the client binds to the object.

Being able to pass proxies as parameters works only because each process is executing the same Java virtual machine. In other words, each process is running in the same execution environment. A marshaled proxy is simply unmarshaled at the receiving side, after which its code can be executed. In contrast, in DCE for example, passing stubs is out of the question, as different processes may be running in execution environments that differ with respect to language, operating system, and hardware. Instead, a DCE process first needs to (dynamically) link in a locally-available stub that has been previously compiled specifically for the process's execution environment. By passing a reference to a stub as parameter in an RPC, it is possible to refer to objects across process boundaries.

10.3.5 Object-Based Messaging

Although RMI is the preferred way of handling communication in object-based distributed systems, messaging has also found its way as an important alternative. There are various object-based messaging systems available, and, as can be expected, offer very much the same functionality. In this section we will take a closer look at CORBA messaging, partly because it also provides an interesting way of combining method invocation and message-oriented communication.

CORBA is a well-known specification for distributed systems. Over the years, several implementations have come to existence, although it remains to be seen to what extent CORBA itself will ever become truly popular. However, independent of popularity, the CORBA specifications are comprehensive (which to many also means they are very complex). Recognizing the popularity of messaging systems, CORBA was quick to include a specification of a messaging service.

What makes messaging in CORBA different from other systems is its inherent object-based approach to communication. In particular, the designers of the messaging service needed to retain the model that all communication takes place by invoking an object. In the case of messaging, this design constraint resulted in two forms of asynchronous method invocations (in addition to other forms that were provided by CORBA as well).

An **asynchronous method invocation** is analogous to an asynchronous RPC: the caller continues after initiating the invocation without waiting for a result. In CORBA's **callback model**, a client provides an object that implements an interface containing callback methods. These methods can be called by the underlying communication system to pass the result of an asynchronous invocation. An important design issue is that asynchronous method invocations do not affect the original implementation of an object. In other words, it is the client's responsibility to transform the original synchronous invocation into an asynchronous one; the server is presented with a normal (synchronous) invocation request.

Constructing an asynchronous invocation is done in two steps. First, the original interface as implemented by the object is replaced by two new interfaces that are to be implemented by client-side software only. One interface contains the specification of methods that the client can call. None of these methods returns a value or has any output parameter. The second interface is the callback interface. For each operation in the original interface, it contains a method that will be called by the client's runtime system to pass the results of the associated method as called by the client.

As an example, consider an object implementing a simple interface with just one method:

    int add(in int i, in int j, out int k);

Assume that this method takes two nonnegative integers i and j and returns $i + j$ as output parameter k. The operation is assumed to return -1 if the operation did not complete successfully. Transforming the original (synchronous) method invocation into an asynchronous one with callbacks is achieved by first generating the following pair of method specifications (for our purposes, we choose convenient names instead of following the strict rules as specified in OMG (2004a):

```
void sendcb_add(in int i, in int j);          // Downcall by the client
void replycb_add(in int ret_val, in int k);   // Upcall to the client
```

In effect, all output parameters from the original method specification are removed from the method that is to be called by the client, and returned as input parameters of the callback operations. Likewise, if the original method specified a return value, that value is passed as an input parameter to the callback operation.

The second step consists of compiling the generated interfaces. As a result, the client is offered a stub that allows it to asynchronously invoke sendcb_add. However, the client will need to provide an implementation for the callback interface, in our example containing the method replycb_add. This last method is called by the client's local runtime system (RTS), resulting in an upcall to the client application. Note that these changes do not affect the server-side implementation of the object. Using this example, the callback model is summarized in Fig. 10-9.

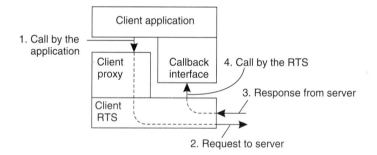

Figure 10-9. CORBA's callback model for asynchronous method invocation.

As an alternative to callbacks, CORBA provides a **polling model**. In this model, the client is offered a collection of operations to poll its local RTS for incoming results. As in the callback model, the client is responsible for transforming the original synchronous method invocations into asynchronous ones. Again, most of the work can be done by automatically deriving the appropriate method specifications from the original interface as implemented by the object.

Returning to our example, the method add will lead to the following two generated method specifications (again, we conveniently adopt our own naming conventions):

```
void sendpoll_add(in int i, in int j);            // Called by the client
void replypoll_add(out int ret_val, out int k);   // Also called by the client
```

The most important difference between the polling and callback models is that the method replypoll_add will have to be implemented by the client's RTS. This implementation can be automatically generated from interface specifications, just as the client-side stub is automatically generated as we explained for RPCs. The polling model is summarized in Fig. 10-10. Again, notice that the implementation of the object as it appears at the server's side does not have to be changed.

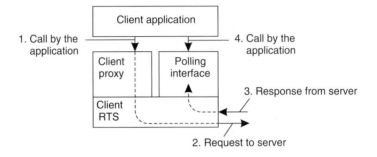

Figure 10-10. CORBA's polling model for asynchronous method invocation.

What is missing from the models described so far is that the messages sent between a client and a server, including the response to an asynchronous invocation, are stored by the underlying system in case the client or server is not yet running. Fortunately, most of the issues concerning such persistent communication do not affect the asynchronous invocation model discussed so far. What is needed is to set up a collection of message servers that will allow messages (be they invocation requests or responses), to be temporarily stored until their delivery can take place.

To this end, the CORBA specifications also include interface definitions for what are called **routers**, which are analogous to the message routers we discussed in Chap. 4, and which can be implemented, for example, using IBM's WebSphere queue managers.

Likewise, Java has its own **Java Messaging Service** (**JMS**) which is again very similar to what we have discussed before [see Sun Microsystems (2004a)]. We will return to messaging more extensively in Chap. 13 when we discuss the publish/subscribe paradigm.

10.4 NAMING

The interesting aspect of naming in object-based distributed systems evolves around the way that object references are supported. We already described these object references in the case of Java, where they effectively correspond to portable proxy implementations. However, this a language-dependent way of being able to refer to remote objects. Again taking CORBA as an example, let us see how basic naming can also be provided in a language and platform-independent way. We also discuss a completely different scheme, which is used in the Globe distributed system.

10.4.1 CORBA Object References

Fundamental to CORBA is the way its objects are referenced. When a client holds an object reference, it can invoke the methods implemented by the referenced object. It is important to distinguish the object reference that a client process uses to invoke a method, and the one implemented by the underlying RTS.

A process (be it client or server) can use only a language-specific implementation of an object reference. In most cases, this takes the form of a pointer to a local representation of the object. That reference cannot be passed from process *A* to process *B*, as it has meaning only within the address space of process *A*. Instead, process *A* will first have to marshal the pointer into a process-independent representation. The operation to do so is provided by its RTS. Once marshaled, the reference can be passed to process *B*, which can unmarshal it again. Note that processes *A* and *B* may be executing programs written in different languages.

In contrast, the underlying RTS will have its own language-independent representation of an object reference. This representation may even differ from the marshaled version it hands over to processes that want to exchange a reference. The important thing is that when a process refers to an object, its underlying RTS is implicitly passed enough information to know which object is actually being referenced. Such information is normally passed by the client and server-side stubs that are generated from the interface specifications of an object.

One of the problems that early versions of CORBA had was that each implementation could decide on how it represented an object reference. Consequently, if process *A* wanted to pass a reference to process *B* as described above, this would generally succeed only if both processes were using the same CORBA implementation. Otherwise, the marshaled version of the reference held by process *A* would be meaningless to the RTS used by process *B*.

Current CORBA systems all support the same language-independent representation of an object reference, which is called an **Interoperable Object Reference** or **IOR**. Whether or not a CORBA implementation uses IORs internally is not all that important. However, when passing an object reference between two different CORBA systems, it is passed as an IOR. An IOR contains all the information needed to identify an object. The general layout of an IOR is shown in Fig. 10-11, along with specific information for the communication protocol used in CORBA.

Each IOR starts with a repository identifier. This identifier is assigned to an interface so that it can be stored and looked up in an interface repository. It is used to retrieve information on an interface at runtime, and can assist in, for example,

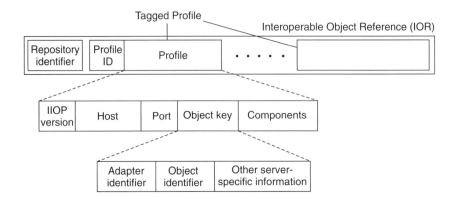

Figure 10-11. The organization of an IOR with specific information for IIOP.

type checking or dynamically constructing an invocation. Note that if this identifier is to be useful, both the client and server must have access to the same interface repository, or at least use the same identifier to identify interfaces.

The most important part of each IOR is formed by what are called **tagged profiles**. Each such profile contains the complete information to invoke an object. If the object server supports several protocols, information on each protocol can be included in a separate tagged profile. CORBA used the **Internet Inter-ORB Protocol (IIOP)** for communication between nodes. (An **ORB** or **Object Request Broker** is the name used by CORBA for their object-based runtime system.) IIOP is essentially a dedicated protocol for supported remote method invocations. Details on the profile used for IIOP are also shown in Fig. 10-11.

The IIOP profile is identified by a *ProfileID* field in the tagged profile. Its body consists of five fields. The *IIOP version* field identifies the version of IIOP that is used in this profile.

The *Host* field is a string identifying exactly on which host the object is located. The host can be specified either by means of a complete DNS domain name (such as *soling.cs.vu.nl*), or by using the string representation of that host's IP address, such as *130.37.24.11*.

The *Port* field contains the port number to which the object's server is listening for incoming requests.

The *Object key* field contains server-specific information for demultiplexing incoming requests to the appropriate object. For example, an object identifier generated by a CORBA object adapter will generally be part of such an object key. Also, this key will identify the specific adapter.

Finally, there is a *Components* field that optionally contains more information needed for properly invoking the referenced object. For example, this field may contain security information indicating how the reference should be handled, or what to do in the case the referenced server is (temporarily) unavailable.

10.4.2 Globe Object References

Let us now take a look at a different way of referencing objects. In Globe, each distributed shared object is assigned a globally unique object identifier (OID), which is a 256-bit string. A Globe OID is a true identifier as defined in Chap. 5. In other words, a Globe OID refers to at most one distributed shared object; it is never reused for another object; and each object has at most one OID.

Globe OIDs can be used only for comparing object references. For example, suppose processes *A* and *B* are each bound to a distributed shared object. Each process can request the OID of the object they are bound to. If and only if the two OIDs are the same, then *A* and *B* are considered to be bound to the same object.

Unlike CORBA references, Globe OIDs cannot be used to directly contact an object. Instead, to locate an object, it is necessary to look up a contact address for that object in a location service. This service returns a **contact address**, which is comparable to the location-dependent object references as used in CORBA and other distributed systems. Although Globe uses its own specific location service, in principle any of the location services discussed in Chap. 5 would do.

Ignoring some minor details, a contact address has two parts. The first one is an **address identifier** by which the location service can identify the proper leaf node to which insert or delete operations for the associated contact address are to forwarded. Recall that because contact addresses are location dependent, it is important to insert and delete them starting at an appropriate leaf node.

The second part consists of actual address information, but this information is completely opaque to the location service. To the location service, an address is just an array of bytes that can equally stand for an actual network address, a marshaled interface pointer, or even a complete marshaled proxy.

Two kinds of addresses are currently supported in Globe. A **stacked address** represents a layered protocol suite, where each layer is represented by the three-field record shown in Fig. 10-12.

Field	Description
Protocol identifier	A constant representing a (known) protocol
Protocol address	A protocol-specific address
Implementation handle	Reference to a file in a class repository

Figure 10-12. The representation of a protocol layer in a stacked contact address.

The *Protocol identifier* is a constant representing a known protocol. Typical protocol identifiers include *TCP*, *UDP*, and *IP*. The *Protocol address* field contains a protocol-specific address, such as TCP port number, or an IPv4 network address. Finally, an *Implementation handle* can be optionally provided to indicate where a default implementation for the protocol can be found. Typically, an implementation handle is represented as a URL.

The second type of contact address is an **instance address**, which consists of the two fields shown in Fig. 10-13. Again, the address contains an *implementation handle*, which is nothing but a reference to a file in a class repository where an implementation of a local object can be found. That local object should be loaded by the process that is currently binding to the object.

Field	Description
Implementation handle	Reference to a file in a class repository
Initialization string	String that is used to initialize an implementation

Figure 10-13. The representation of an instance contact address.

Loading follows a standard protocol, similar to class loading in Java. After the implementation has been loaded and the local object created, initialization takes place by passing the *initialization string* to the object. At that point, the object identifier has been completed resolved.

Note the difference in object referencing between CORBA and Globe, a difference which occurs frequently in distributed object-based systems. Where CORBA references contain exact information where to contact an object, Globe references require an additional lookup step to retrieve that information. This distinction also appears in systems such as Ice, where the CORBA equivalent is referred to as a *direct* reference, and the Globe equivalent as an *indirect* reference (Henning and Spruiell, 2005).

10.5 SYNCHRONIZATION

There are only a few issues regarding synchronization in distributed systems that are specific to dealing with distributed objects. In particular, the fact that implementation details are hidden behind interfaces may cause problems: when a process invokes a (remote) object, it has no knowledge whether that invocation will lead to invoking other objects. As a consequence, if an object is protected against concurrent accesses, we may have a cascading set of locks that the invoking process is unaware of, as sketched in Fig. 10-14(a).

In contrast, when dealing with data resources such as files or database tables that are protected by locks, the pattern for the control flow is actually visible to the process using those resources, as shown in Fig. 10-14(b). As a consequence, the process can also exert more control at runtime when things go wrong, such as giving up locks when it believes a deadlock has occurred. Note that transaction processing systems generally follow the pattern shown in Fig. 10-14(b).

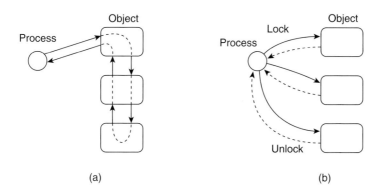

Figure 10-14. Differences in control flow for locking objects

In object-based distributed systems it is therefore important to know where and when synchronization takes place. An obvious location for synchronization is at the object server. If multiple invocation requests for the same object arrive, the server can decide to serialize those requests (and possibly keep a lock on an object when it needs to do a remote invocation itself).

However, letting the object server maintain locks complicates matters in the case that invoking clients crash. For this reason, locking can also be done at the client side, an approach that has been adopted in Java. Unfortunately, this scheme has its own drawbacks.

As we mentioned before, the difference between local and remote objects in Java is often difficult to make. Matters become more complicated when objects are protected by declaring its methods to be **synchronized**. If two processes simultaneously call a synchronized method, only one of the processes will proceed while the other will be blocked. In this way, we can ensure that access to an object's internal data is completely serialized. A process can also be blocked inside an object, waiting for some condition to become true.

Logically, blocking in a remote object is simple. Suppose that client A calls a synchronized method of a remote object. To make access to remote objects look always *exactly* the same as to local objects, it would be necessary to block A in the client-side stub that implements the object's interface and to which A has direct access. Likewise, another client on a different machine would need to be blocked locally as well before its request can be sent to the server. The consequence is that we need to synchronize different clients at different machines. As we discussed in Chap. 6, distributed synchronization can be fairly complex.

An alternative approach would be to allow blocking only at the server. In principle, this works fine, but problems arise when a client crashes while its invocation is being handled by the server. As we discussed in Chap. 8, we may require relatively sophisticated protocols to handle this situation, and which that may significantly affect the overall performance of remote method invocations.

Therefore, the designers of Java RMI have chosen to restrict blocking on remote objects only to the proxies (Wollrath et al., 1996). This means that threads in the same process will be prevented from concurrently accessing the same remote object, but threads in different processes will not. Obviously, these synchronization semantics are tricky: at the syntactic level (i.e., when reading source code) we may see a nice, clean design. Only when the distributed application is actually executed, unanticipated behavior may be observed that should have been dealt with at design time. Here we see a clear example where striving for distribution transparency is *not* the way to go.

10.6 CONSISTENCY AND REPLICATION

Many object-based distributed systems follow a traditional approach toward replicated objects, effectively treating them as containers of data with their own special operations. As a result, when we consider how replication is handled in systems supporting Java beans, or CORBA-compliant distributed systems, there is not really that much new to report other than what we have discussed in Chap. 7.

For this reason, we focus on a few particular topics regarding consistency and replication that are more profound in object-based distributed systems than others. We will first consider consistency and move to replicated invocations.

10.6.1 Entry Consistency

As we mentioned in Chap. 7, data-centric consistency for distributed objects comes naturally in the form of entry consistency. Recall that in this case, the goal is to group operations on shared data using synchronization variables (e.g., in the form of locks). As objects naturally combine data and the operations on that data, locking objects during an invocation serializes access and keeps them consistent.

Although conceptually associating a lock with an object is simple, it does not necessarily provide a proper solution when an object is replicated. There are two issues that need to be solved for implementing entry consistency. The first one is that we need a means to prevent concurrent execution of multiple invocations on the same object. In other words, when any method of an object is being executed, no other methods may be executed. This requirement ensures that access to the internal data of an object is indeed serialized. Simply using local locking mechanisms will ensure this serialization.

The second issue is that in the case of a replicated object, we need to ensure that all changes to the replicated state of the object are the same. In other words, we need to make sure that no two independent method invocations take place on different replicas at the same time. This requirement implies that we need to order invocations such that each replica sees all invocations in the same order. This requirement can generally be met in one of two ways: (1) using a primary-based approach or (2) using totally-ordered multicast to the replicas.

In many cases, designing replicated objects is done by first designing a single object, possibly protecting it against concurrent access through local locking, and subsequently replicating it. If we were to use a primary-based scheme, then additional effort from the application developer is needed to serialize object invocations. Therefore, it is often convenient to assume that the underlying middleware supports totally-ordered multicasting, as this would not require any changes at the clients, nor would it require additional programming effort from application developers. Of course, how the totally ordered multicasting is realized by the middleware should be transparent. For all the application may know, its implementation may use a primary-based scheme, but it could equally well be based on Lamport clocks.

However, even if the underlying middleware provides totally-ordered multicasting, more may be needed to guarantee orderly object invocation. The problem is one of granularity: although all replicas of an object server may receive invocation requests in the same order, we need to ensure that all threads in those servers process those requests in the correct order as well. The problem is sketched in Fig. 10-15.

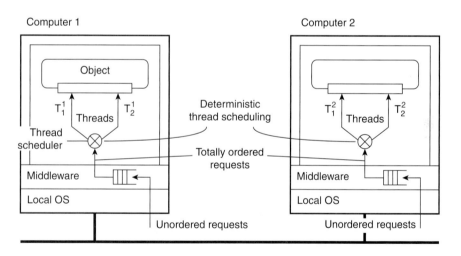

Figure 10-15. Deterministic thread scheduling for replicated object servers.

Multithreaded (object) servers simply pick up an incoming request, pass it on to an available thread, and wait for the next request to come in. The server's thread scheduler subsequently allocates the CPU to runnable threads. Of course, if the middleware has done its best to provide a total ordering for request delivery, the thread schedulers should operate in a deterministic fashion in order not to mix the ordering of method invocations on the same object. In other words, If threads

T_1^1 and T_1^2 from Fig. 10-15 handle the same incoming (replicated) invocation request, they should both be scheduled before T_2^1 and T_2^2, respectively.

Of course, simply scheduling *all* threads deterministically is not necessary. In principle, if we already have totally-ordered request delivery, we need only to ensure that all requests for the same replicated object are handled in the order they were delivered. Such an approach would allow invocations for different objects to be processed concurrently, and without further restrictions from the thread scheduler. Unfortunately, only few systems exist that support such concurrency.

One approach, described in Basile et al. (2002), ensures that threads sharing the same (local) lock are scheduled in the same order on every replica. At the basics lies a primary-based scheme in which one of the replica servers takes the lead in determining, for a specific lock, which thread goes first. An improvement that avoids frequent communication between servers is described in Basile et al. (2003). Note that threads that do not share a lock can thus operate concurrently on each server.

One drawback of this scheme is that it operates at the level of the underlying operating system, meaning that every lock needs to be managed. By providing application-level information, a huge improvement in performance can be made by identifying only those locks that are needed for serializing access to replicated objects (Taiani et al., 2005). We return to these issues when we discuss fault tolerance for Java.

Replication Frameworks

An interesting aspect of most distributed object-based systems is that by nature of the object technology it is often possible to make a clean separation between devising functionality and handling extra-functional issues such as replication. As we explained in Chap. 2, a powerful mechanism to accomplish this separation is formed by interceptors.

Babaoglu et al. (2004) describe a framework in which they use interceptors to replicate Java beans for J2EE servers. The idea is relatively simple: invocations to objects are intercepted at three different points, as also shown in Fig. 10-16:

1. At the client side just before the invocation is passed to the stub.

2. Inside the client's stub, where the interception forms part of the replication algorithm.

3. At the server side, just before the object is about to be invoked.

The first interception is needed when it turns out that the caller is replicated. In that case, synchronization with the other callers may be needed as we may be dealing with a replicated invocation as discussed before.

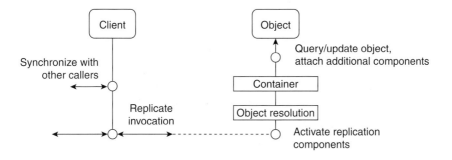

Figure 10-16. A general framework for separating replication algorithms from objects in an EJB environment.

Once it has been decided that the invocation can be carried out, the interceptor in the client-side stub can take decisions on where to be forward the request to, or possibly implement a fail-over mechanism when a replica cannot be reached.

Finally, the server-side interceptor handles the invocation. In fact, this interceptor is split into two. At the first point, just after the request has come in and before it is handed over to an adapter, the replication algorithm gets control. It can then analyze for whom the request is intended allowing it to activate, if necessary, any replication objects that it needs to carry out the replication. The second point is just before the invocation, allowing the replication algorithm to, for example, get and set attribute values of the replicated object.

The interesting aspect is that the framework can be set up independent of any replication algorithm, thus leading to a complete separation of object functionality and replication of objects.

10.6.2 Replicated Invocations

Another problem that needs to be solved is that of replicated invocations. Consider an object A calling another object B as shown in Fig. 10-17. Object B is assumed to call yet another object C. If B is replicated, each replica of B will, in principle, call C independently. The problem is that C is now called multiple times instead of only once. If the called method on C results in the transfer of $100,000, then clearly, someone is going to complain sooner or later.

There are not many general-purpose solutions to solve the problem of replicated invocations. One solution is to simply forbid it (Maassen et al., 2001), which makes sense when performance is at stake. However, when replicating for fault tolerance, the following solution proposed by Mazouni et al. (1995) may be deployed. Their solution is independent of the replication policy, that is, the exact details of how replicas are kept consistent. The essence is to provide a replication-aware communication layer on top of which (replicated) objects execute. When a replicated object B invokes another replicated object C, the invocation

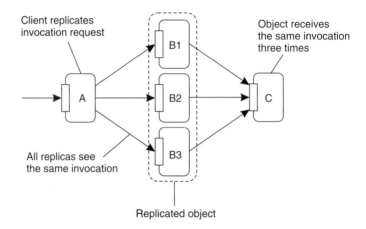

Figure 10-17. The problem of replicated method invocations.

request is first assigned the same, unique identifier by each replica of *B*. At that point, a coordinator of the replicas of *B* forwards its request to all the replicas of object *C*, while the other replicas of *B* hold back their copy of the invocation request, as shown in Fig. 10-18(a). The result is that only a single request is forwarded to each replica of *C*.

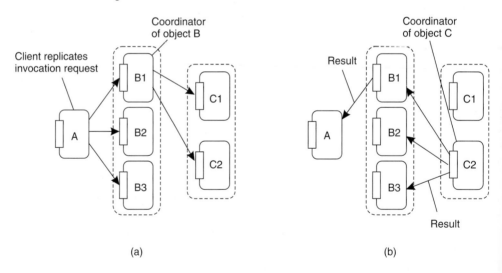

Figure 10-18. (a) Forwarding an invocation request from a replicated object to another replicated object. (b) Returning a reply from one replicated object to another.

The same mechanism is used to ensure that only a single reply message is returned to the replicas of *B*. This situation is shown in Fig. 10-18(b). A coordinator of the replicas of *C* notices it is dealing with a replicated reply message that has been generated by each replica of *C*. However, only the coordinator forwards that reply to the replicas of object *B*, while the other replicas of *C* hold back their copy of the reply message.

When a replica of *B* receives a reply message for an invocation request it had either forwarded to *C* or held back because it was not the coordinator, the reply is then handed to the actual object.

In essence, the scheme just described is based on using multicast communication, but in preventing that the same message is multicast by different replicas. As such, it is essentially a sender-based scheme. An alternative solution is to let a receiving replica detect multiple copies of incoming messages belonging to the same invocation, and to pass only one copy to its associated object. Details of this scheme are left as an exercise.

10.7 FAULT TOLERANCE

Like replication, fault tolerance in most distributed object-based systems use the same mechanisms as in other distributed systems, following the principles we discussed in Chap. 8. However, when it comes to standardization, CORBA arguably provides the most comprehensive specification.

10.7.1 Example: Fault-Tolerant CORBA

The basic approach for dealing with failures in CORBA is to replicate objects into **object groups**. Such a group consists of one or more identical copies of the same object. However, an object group can be referenced as if it were a single object. A group offers the same interface as the replicas it contains. In other words, replication is transparent to clients. Different replication strategies are supported, including primary-backup replication, active replication, and quorum-based replication. These strategies have all been discussed in Chap. 7. There are various other properties associated with object groups, the details of which can be found in OMG (2004a).

To provide replication and failure transparency as much as possible, object groups should not be distinguishable from normal CORBA objects, unless an application prefers otherwise. An important issue, in this respect, is how object groups are referenced. The approach followed is to use a special kind of IOR, called an **Interoperable Object Group Reference (IOGR)**. The key difference with a normal IOR is that an IOGR contains multiple references to *different* objects, notably replicas in the same object group. In contrast, an IOR may also contain multiple references, but all of them will refer to the *same* object, although possibly using a different access protocol.

Whenever a client passes an IOGR to its runtime system (RTS), that RTS attempts to bind to one of the referenced replicas. In the case of IIOP, the RTS may possibly use additional information it finds in one of the IIOP profiles of the IOGR. Such information can be stored in the *Components* field we discussed previously. For example, a specific IIOP profile may refer to the primary or a backup of an object group, as shown in Fig. 10-19, by means of the separate tags *TAG_PRIMARY* and *TAG_BACKUP*, respectively.

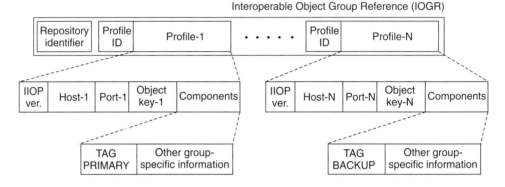

Figure 10-19. A possible organization of an IOGR for an object group having a primary and backups.

If binding to one of the replicas fails, the client RTS may continue by attempting to bind to another replica, thereby following any policy for next selecting a replica that it suits to best. To the client, the binding procedure is completely transparent; it appears as if the client is binding to a regular CORBA object.

An Example Architecture

To support object groups and to handle additional failure management, it is necessary to add components to CORBA. One possible architecture of a fault-tolerant version of CORBA is shown in Fig. 10-20. This architecture is derived from the Eternal system (Moser et al., 1998; and Narasimhan et al., 2000), which provides a fault tolerance infrastructure constructed on top of the Totem reliable group communication system (Moser et al., 1996).

There are several components that play an important role in this architecture. By far the most important one is the **replication manager**, which is responsible for creating and managing a group of replicated objects. In principle, there is only one replication manager, although it may be replicated for fault tolerance.

As we have stated, to a client there is no fundamental difference between an object group and any other type of CORBA object. To create an object group, a client simply invokes the normal create_object operation as offered, in this case,

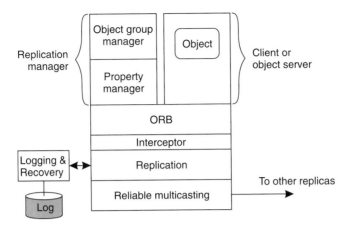

Figure 10-20. An example architecture of a fault-tolerant CORBA system.

by the replication manager, specifying the type of object to create. The client remains unaware of the fact that it is implicitly creating an object group. The number of replicas that are created when starting a new object group is normally determined by the system-dependent default value. The replica manager is also responsible for replacing a replica in the case of a failure, thereby ensuring that the number of replicas does not drop below a specified minimum.

The architecture also shows the use of message-level interceptors. In the case of the Eternal system, each invocation is intercepted and passed to a separate replication component that maintains the required consistency for an object group and which ensures that messages are logged to enable recovery.

Invocations are subsequently sent to the other group members using reliable, totally-ordered multicasting. In the case of active replication, an invocation request is passed to each replica object by handing it to that object's underlying runtime system. However, in the case of passive replication, an invocation request is passed only to the RTS of the primary, whereas the other servers only log the invocation request for recovery purposes. When the primary has completed the invocation, its state is then multicast to the backups.

This architecture is based on using interceptors. Alternative solutions exist as well, including those in which fault tolerance has been incorporated in the runtime system (potentially affecting interoperability), or in which special services are used on top of the RTS to provide fault tolerance. Besides these differences, practice shows that there are other problems not (yet) covered by the CORBA standard. As an example of one problem that occurs in practice, if replicas are created on different implementations, there is no guarantee that this approach will actually work. A review of the different approaches and an assessment of fault tolerance in CORBA is discussed in Felber and Narasimhan (2004).

10.7.2 Example: Fault-Tolerant Java

Considering the popularity of Java as a language and platform for developing distributed applications, some effort has also been into adding fault tolerance to the Java runtime system. An interesting approach is to ensure that the Java virtual machine can be used for active replication.

Active replication essentially dictates that the replica servers execute as deterministic finite-state machines (Schneider, 1990). An excellent candidate in Java to fulfill this role is the Java Virtual Machine (JVM). Unfortunately, the JVM is not deterministic at all. There are various causes for nondeterministic behavior, identified independently by Napper et al. (2003) and Friedman and Kama (2003):

1. JVM can execute native code, that is, code that is external to the JVM and provided to the latter through an interface. The JVM treats native code like a black box: it sees only the interface, but has no clue about the (potentially nondeterministic) behavior that a call causes. Therefore, in order to use the JVM for active replication, it is necessary to make sure that native code behaves in a deterministic way.

2. Input data may be subject to nondeterminism. For example, a shared variable that can be manipulated by multiple threads may change for different instances of the JVM as long as threads are allowed to operate concurrently. To control this behavior, shared data should at the very least be protected through locks. As it turned out, the Java runtime environment did not always adhere to this rule, despite its support for multithreading.

3. In the presence of failures, different JVMs will produce different output revealing that the machines have been replicated. This difference may cause problems when the JVMs need to brought back into the same state. Matters are simplified if one can assume that all output is idempotent (i.e., can simply be replayed), or is testable so that one can check whether output was produced before a crash or not. Note that this assumption is necessary in order to allow a replica server to decide whether or not it should re-execute an operation.

Practice shows that turning the JVM into a deterministic finite-state machine is by no means trivial. One problem that needs to be solved is the fact that replica servers may crash. One possible organization is to let the servers run according to a primary-backup scheme. In such a scheme, one server coordinates all actions that need to be performed, and from time to time instructs the backup to do the same. Careful coordination between primary and backup is required, of course.

Note that despite the fact that replica servers are organized in a primary-backup setting, we are still dealing with active replication: the replicas are kept up to date by letting each of them execute the same operations in the same order. However, to ensure the same nondeterministic behavior by all of the servers, the behavior of one server is taken as the one to follow.

In this setting, the approach followed by Friedman and Kama (2003) is to let the primary first execute the instructions of what is called a **frame**. A frame consists of the execution of several context switches and ends either because all threads are blocking for I/O to complete, or after a predefined number of context switches has taken place. Whenever a thread issues an I/O operation, the thread is blocked by the JVM put on hold. When a frame starts, the primary lets all I/O requests proceed, one after the other, and the results are sent to the other replicas. In this way, at least deterministic behavior with respect to I/O operations is enforced.

The problem with this scheme is easily seen: the primary is always ahead of the other replicas. There are two situations we need to consider. First, if a replica server other than the primary crashes, no real harm is done except that the degree of fault tolerance drops. On the other hand, when the primary crashes, we may find ourselves in a situation that data (or rather, operations) are lost.

To minimize the damage, the primary works on a per-frame basis. That is, it sends update information to the other replicas only after completion of its current frame. The effect of this approach is that when the primary is working on the k-th frame, that the other replica servers have all the information needed to process the frame preceding the k-th one. The damage can be limited by making frames small, at the price of more communication between the primary and the backups.

10.8 SECURITY

Obviously, security plays an important role in any distributed system and object-based ones are no exception. When considering most object-based distributed systems, the fact that distributed objects are remote objects immediately leads to a situation in which security architectures for distributed systems are very similar. In essence, each object is protected through standard authentication and authorization mechanisms, like the ones we discussed in Chap. 9.

To make clear how security can fit in specifically in an object-based distributed system, we shall discuss the security architecture for the Globe system. As we mentioned before, Globe supports truly distributed objects in which the state of a single object can be spread and replicated across multiple machines. Remote objects are just a special case of Globe objects. Therefore, by considering the Globe security architecture, we can also see how its approach can be equally applied to more traditional object-based distributed systems. After discussing Globe, we briefly take a look at security in traditional object-based systems.

10.8.1 Example: Globe

As we said, Globe is one of the few distributed object-based systems in which an object's state can be physically distributed and replicated across multiple machines. This approach also introduces specific security problems, which have led to an architecture as described in Popescu et al. (2002).

Overview

When we consider the general case of invoking a method on a remote object, there are at least two issues that are important from a security perspective: (1) is the caller invoking the correct object and (2) is the caller allowed to invoke that method. We refer to these two issues as **secure object binding** and **secure method invocation**, respectively. The former has everything to do with authentication, whereas the latter involves authorization. For Globe and other systems that support either replication or moving objects around, we have an additional problem, namely that of **platform security**. This kind of security comprises two issues. First, how can the platform to which a (local) object is copied be protected against any malicious code contained in the object, and secondly, how can the object be protected against a malicious replica server.

Being able to copy objects to other hosts also brings up another problem. Because the object server that is hosting a copy of an object need not always be fully trusted, there must be a mechanism that prevents that every replica server hosting an object from being allowed to also execute any of an object's methods. For example, an object's owner may want to restrict the execution of update methods to a small group of replica servers, whereas methods that only read the state of an object may be executed by any authenticated server. Enforcing such policies can be done through **reverse access control**, which we discuss in more detail below.

There are several mechanisms deployed in Globe to establish security. First, every Globe object has an associated public/private key pair, referred to as the **object key**. The basic idea is that anyone who has knowledge about an object's private key can set the access policies for users and servers. In addition, every replica has an associated **replica key**, which is also constructed as a public/private key pair. This key pair is generated by the object server currently hosting the specific replica. As we will see, the replica key is used to make sure that a specific replica is part of a given distributed shared object. Finally, each user is also assumed to have a unique public/private key pair, known as the **user key**.

These keys are used to set the various access rights in the form of certificates. Certificates are handed out per object. There are three types, as shown in Fig. 10-21. A **user certificate** is associated with a specific user and specifies exactly which methods that user is allowed to invoke. To this end, the certificate contains a bit string U with the same length as the number of methods available for the object. $U[i] = 1$ if and only if the user is allowed to invoke method M_i. Likewise, there is also a **replica certificate** that specifies, for a given replica server, which methods it is allowed to execute. It also has an associated bit string R, where $R[i] = i$ if and only if the server is allowed to execute method M_i.

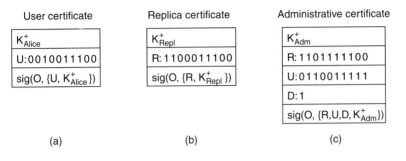

Figure 10-21. Certificates in Globe: (a) a user certificate, (b) a replica certificate, (c) an administrative certificate.

For example, the user certificate in Fig. 10-21(a) tells that Alice (who can be identified through her public key K_{Alice}^+), has the right to invoke methods M_2, M_5, M_6, and M_7 (note that we start indexing U at 0). Likewise, the replica certificate states that the server owning K_{Repl}^+ is allowed to execute methods M_0, M_1, M_5, M_6, and M_7.

An administrative certificate can be used by any authorized entity to issue user and replica certificates. In the case, the R and U bit strings specify for which methods and which entities a certificate can be created. Moreover, there is bit indicating whether an administrative entity can delegate (part of) its rights to someone else. Note that when Bob in his role as administrator creates a user certificate for Alice, he will sign that certificate with his own signature, not that of the object. As a consequence, Alice's certificate will need to be traced back to Bob's administrative certificate, and eventually to an administrative certificate signed with the object's private key.

Administrative certificates come in handy when considering that some Globe objects may be massively replicated. For example, an object's owner may want to manage only a relatively small set of permanent replicas, but delegate the creation of server-initiated replicas to the servers hosting those permanent replicas. In that case, the owner may decide to allow a permanent replica to install other replicas for read-only access by all users. Whenever Alice wants to invoke a read-only method, she will succeed (provided she is authorized). However, when wanting to invoke an update method, she will have to contact one of the permanent replicas, as none of the other replica servers is allowed to execute such methods.

As we explained, the binding process in Globe requires that an object identifier (OID) is resolved to a contact address. In principle, any system that supports flat names can be used for this purpose. To securely associate an object's public key to its OID, we simply compute the OID as a 160-bit secure hash of the public key. In this way, anyone can verify whether a given public key belongs to a given OID. These identifier are also known as **self-certifying names**, a concept pioneered in the Secure File System (Mazieres et al., 1999), which we will discuss in Chap. 11.

We can also check whether a replica *R* belongs to an object *O*. In that case, we merely need to inspect the replica certificate for *R*, and check who issued it. The signer may be an entity with administrative rights, in which case we need to inspect its administrative certificate. The bottom line is that we can construct a chain of certificates of which the last one is signed using the object's private key. In that case, we know that *R* is part of *O*.

To mutually protect objects and hosts against each other, techniques for mobile code, as described in Chap. 9 are deployed. Detecting that objects have been tampered with can be done with special auditing techniques which we will describe in Chap. 12.

Secure Method Invocation

Let us now look into the details of securely invoking a method of a Globe object. The complete path from requesting an invocation to actually executing the operation at a replica is sketched in Fig. 10-22. A total of 13 steps need to be executed in sequence, as shown in the figure and described in the following text.

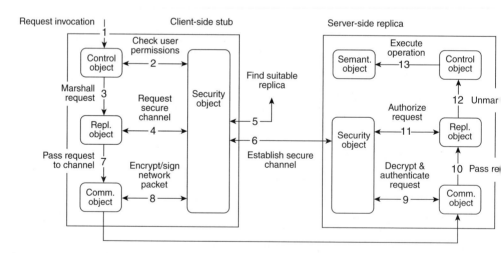

Figure 10-22. Secure method invocation in Globe.

1. First, an application issues a invocation request by locally calling the associated method, just like calling a procedure in an RPC.

2. The control subobject checks the user permissions with the information stored in the local security object. In this case, the security object should have a valid user certificate.

3. The request is marshaled and passed on.

4. The replication subobject requests the middleware to set up a secure channel to a suitable replica.

5. The security object first initiates a replica lookup. To achieve this goal, it could use any naming service that can look up replicas that have been specified to be able to execute certain methods. The Globe location service has been modified to handle such lookups (Ballintijn, 2003).

6. Once a suitable replica has been found, the security subobject can set up a secure channel with its peer, after which control is returned to the replication subobject. Note that part of this establishment requires that the replica proves it is allowed to carry out the requested invocation.

7. The request is now passed on to the communication subobject.

8. The subobject encrypts and signs the request so that it can pass through the channel.

9. After its receipt, the request is decrypted and authenticated.

10. The request is then simply passed on to the server-side replication subobject.

11. Authorization takes place: in this case the user certificate from the client-side stub has been passed to the replica so that we can verify that the request can indeed be carried out.

12. The request is then unmarshaled.

13. Finally, the operation can be executed.

Although this may seem to be a relatively large number of steps, the example shows how a secure method invocation can be broken down into small units, each unit being necessary to ensure that an authenticated client can carry out an authorized invocation at an authenticated replica. Virtually all object-based distributed systems follow these steps. The difference with Globe is that a suitable replica needs to be located, and that this replica needs to prove it may execute the method call. We leave such a proof as an exercise to the reader.

10.8.2 Security for Remote Objects

When using remote objects we often see that the object reference itself is implemented as a complete client-side stub, containing all the information that is needed to access the remote object. In its simplest form, the reference contains the exact contact address for the object and uses a standard marshaling and communication protocol to ship an invocation to the remote object.

However, in systems such as Java, the client-side stub (called a **proxy**) can be virtually anything. The basic idea is that the developer of a remote object also develops the proxy and subsequently registers the proxy with a directory service. When a client is looking for the object, it will eventually contact the directory service, retrieve the proxy, and install it. There are obviously some serious problems with this approach.

First, if the directory service is hijacked, then an attacker may be able to return a bogus proxy to the client. In effect, such a proxy may be able to compromise all communication between the client and the server hosting the remote object, damaging both of them.

Second, the client has no way to authenticate the server: it only has the proxy and all communication with the server necessarily goes through that proxy. This may be an undesirable situation, especially because the client now simply needs to trust the proxy that it will do its work correctly.

Likewise, it may be more difficult for the server to authenticate the client. Authentication may be necessary when sensitive information is sent to the client. Also, because client authentication is now tied to the proxy, we may also have the situation that an attacker is spoofing a client causing damage to the remote object.

Li et al. (2004b) describe a general security architecture that can be used to make remote object invocations safer. In their model, they assume that proxies are indeed provided by the developer of a remote object and registered with a directory service. This approach is followed in Java RMI, but also Jini (Sun Microsystems, 2005).

The first problem to solve is to authenticate a remote object. In their solution, Li and Mitchell propose a two-step approach. First, the proxy which is downloaded from a directory service is signed by the remote object allowing the client to verify its origin. The proxy, in turn, will authenticate the object using TLS with server authentication, as we discussed in Chap. 9. Note that it is the object developer's task to make sure that the proxy indeed properly authenticates the object. The client will have to rely on this behavior, but because it is capable of authenticating the proxy, relying on object authentication is at the same level as trusting the remote object to behave decently.

To authenticate the client, a separate authenticator is used. When a client is looking up the remote object, it will be directed to this authenticator from which it downloads an **authentication proxy**. This is a special proxy that offers an interface by which the client can have itself authenticated by the remote object. If this authentication succeeds, then the remote object (or actually, its object server) will pass on the actual proxy to the client. Note that this approach allows for authentication independent of the protocol used by the actual proxy, which is considered an important advantage.

Another important advantage of separating client authentication is that it is now possible to pass dedicated proxies to clients. For example, certain clients may be allowed to request only execution of read-only methods. In such a case, after authentication has taken place, the client will be handed a proxy that offers only such methods, and no other. More refined access control can easily be envisaged.

10.9 SUMMARY

Most object-based distributed systems use a remote-object model in which an object is hosted by server that allows remote clients to do method invocations. In many cases, these objects will be constructed at runtime, effectively meaning that their state, and possibly also code is loaded into an object server when a client does a remote invocation. Globe is a system in which truly distributed shared objects are supported. In this case, an object's state may be physically distributed and replicated across multiple machines.

To support distributed objects, it is important to separate functionality from extra-functional properties such as fault tolerance or scalability. To this end, advanced object servers have been developed for hosting objects. An object server provides many services to basic objects, including facilities for storing objects, or to ensure serialization of incoming requests. Another important role is providing the illusion to the outside world that a collection of data and procedures operating on that data correspond to the concept of an object. This role is implemented by means of object adapters.

When it comes to communication, the prevalent way to invoke an object is by means of a remote method invocation (RMI), which is very similar to an RPC. An important difference is that distributed objects generally provide a systemwide object reference, allowing a process to access an object from any machine. Global object reference solve many of the parameter-passing problems that hinder access transparency of RPCs.

There are many different ways in which these object references can be implemented, ranging from simple passive data structures describing precisely where a remote object can be contacted, to portable code that need simply be invoked by a client. The latter approach is now commonly adopted for Java RMI.

There are no special measures in most systems to handle object synchronization. An important exception is the way that synchronized Java methods are treated: the synchronization takes place only between clients running on the same machine. Clients running on different machines need to take special synchronization measures. These measures are not part of the Java language.

Entry consistency is an obvious consistency model for distributed objects and is (often implicitly) supported in many systems. It is obvious as we can naturally associate a separate lock for each object. One of the problems resulting from replicating objects are replicated invocations. This problem is more evident because objects tend to be treated as black boxes.

Fault tolerance in distributed object-based systems very much follows the approaches used for other distributed systems. One exception is formed by trying to make the Java virtual machine fault tolerant by letting it operate as a deterministic finite state machine. Then, by replicating a number of these machines, we obtain a natural way for providing fault tolerance.

Security for distributed objects evolves around the idea of supporting secure method invocation. A comprehensive example that generalizes these invocations to replicated objects is Globe. As it turns out, it is possible to cleanly separate policies from mechanisms. This is true for authentication as well as authorization. Special attention needs to be paid to systems in which the client is required to download a proxy from a directory service, as is commonly the case for Java.

PROBLEMS

1. We made a distinction between remote objects and distributed objects. What is the difference?

2. Why is it useful to define the interfaces of an object in an Interface Definition Language?

3. Some implementations of distributed-object middleware systems are entirely based on dynamic method invocations. Even static invocations are compiled to dynamic ones. What is the benefit of this approach?

4. Outline a simple protocol that implements at-most-once semantics for an object invocation.

5. Should the client and server-side objects for asynchronous method invocation be persistent?

6. In the text, we mentioned that an implementation of CORBA's asynchronous method invocation do not affect the server-side implementation of an object. Explain why this is the case.

7. Give an example in which the (inadvertent) use of callback mechanisms can easily lead to an unwanted situation.

8. Is it possible for an object to have more than one servant?

9. Is it possible to have system-specific implementations of CORBA object references while still being able to exchange references with other CORBA-based systems?

10. How can we authenticate the contact addresses returned by a lookup service for secure Globe objects?

11. What is the key difference between object references in CORBA and those in Globe?

12. Consider Globe. Outline a simple protocol by which a secure channel is set up between a user proxy (which has access to the Alice's private key) and a replica that we know for certain can execute a given method.

13. Give an example implementation of an object reference that allows a client to bind to a transient remote object.

14. Java and other languages support exceptions, which are raised when an error occurs. How would you implement exceptions in RPCs and RMIs?

15. How would you incorporate persistent asynchronous communication into a model of communication based on RMIs to remote objects?

16. Consider a distributed object-based system that supports object replication, in which *all* method invocations are totally ordered. Also, assume that an object invocation is atomic (e.g., because every object is automatically locked when invoked). Does such a system provide entry consistency? What about sequential consistency?

17. Describe a receiver-based scheme for dealing with replicated invocations, as mentioned in the text.

11

DISTRIBUTED FILE SYSTEMS

Considering that sharing data is fundamental to distributed systems, it is not surprising that distributed file systems form the basis for many distributed applications. Distributed file systems allow multiple processes to share data over long periods of time in a secure and reliable way. As such, they have been used as the basic layer for distributed systems and applications. In this chapter, we consider distributed file systems as a paradigm for general-purpose distributed systems.

11.1 ARCHITECTURE

We start our discussion on distributed file systems by looking at how they are generally organized. Most systems are built following a traditional client-server architecture, but fully decentralized solutions exist as well. In the following, we will take a look at both kinds of organizations.

11.1.1 Client-Server Architectures

Many distributed files systems are organized along the lines of client-server architectures, with Sun Microsystem's **Network File System (NFS)** being one of the most widely-deployed ones for UNIX-based systems. We will take NFS as a canonical example for server-based distributed file systems throughout this chapter. In particular, we concentrate on NFSv3, the widely-used third version of NFS

(Callaghan, 2000) and NFSv4, the most recent, fourth version (Shepler et al., 2003). We will discuss the differences between them as well.

The basic idea behind NFS is that each file server provides a standardized view of its local file system. In other words, it should not matter how that local file system is implemented; each NFS server supports the same model. This approach has been adopted for other distributed files systems as well. NFS comes with a communication protocol that allows clients to access the files stored on a server, thus allowing a heterogeneous collection of processes, possibly running on different operating systems and machines, to share a common file system.

The model underlying NFS and similar systems is that of a **remote file service**. In this model, clients are offered transparent access to a file system that is managed by a remote server. However, clients are normally unaware of the actual location of files. Instead, they are offered an interface to a file system that is similar to the interface offered by a conventional local file system. In particular, the client is offered only an interface containing various file operations, but the server is responsible for implementing those operations. This model is therefore also referred to as the **remote access model**. It is shown in Fig. 11-1(a).

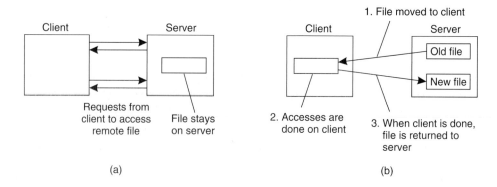

Figure 11-1. (a) The remote access model. (b) The upload/download model.

In contrast, in the **upload/download model** a client accesses a file locally after having downloaded it from the server, as shown in Fig. 11-1(b). When the client is finished with the file, it is uploaded back to the server again so that it can be used by another client. The Internet's FTP service can be used this way when a client downloads a complete file, modifies it, and then puts it back.

NFS has been implemented for a large number of different operating systems, although the UNIX-based versions are predominant. For virtually all modern UNIX systems, NFS is generally implemented following the layered architecture shown in Fig. 11-2.

A client accesses the file system using the system calls provided by its local operating system. However, the local UNIX file system interface is replaced by an

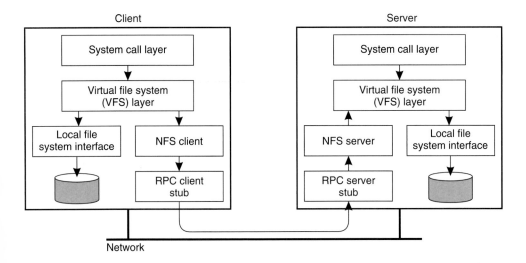

Figure 11-2. The basic NFS architecture for UNIX systems.

interface to the **Virtual File System** (**VFS**), which by now is a de facto standard for interfacing to different (distributed) file systems (Kleiman, 1986). Virtually all modern operating systems provide VFS, and not doing so more or less forces developers to largely reimplement huge of an operating system when adopting a new file-system structure. With NFS, operations on the VFS interface are either passed to a local file system, or passed to a separate component known as the **NFS client**, which takes care of handling access to files stored at a remote server. In NFS, all client-server communication is done through RPCs. The NFS client implements the NFS file system operations as RPCs to the server. Note that the operations offered by the VFS interface can be different from those offered by the NFS client. The whole idea of the VFS is to hide the differences between various file systems.

On the server side, we see a similar organization. The **NFS server** is responsible for handling incoming client requests. The RPC stub unmarshals requests and the NFS server converts them to regular VFS file operations that are subsequently passed to the VFS layer. Again, the VFS is responsible for implementing a local file system in which the actual files are stored.

An important advantage of this scheme is that NFS is largely independent of local file systems. In principle, it really does not matter whether the operating system at the client or server implements a UNIX file system, a Windows 2000 file system, or even an old MS-DOS file system. The only important issue is that these file systems are compliant with the file system model offered by NFS. For example, MS-DOS with its short file names cannot be used to implement an NFS server in a fully transparent way.

File System Model

The file system model offered by NFS is almost the same as the one offered by UNIX-based systems. Files are treated as uninterpreted sequences of bytes. They are hierarchically organized into a naming graph in which nodes represent directories and files. NFS also supports hard links as well as symbolic links, like any UNIX file system. Files are named, but are otherwise accessed by means of a UNIX-like **file handle**, which we discuss in detail below. In other words, to access a file, a client must first look up its name in a naming service and obtain the associated file handle. Furthermore, each file has a number of attributes whose values can be looked up and changed. We return to file naming in detail later in this chapter.

Fig. 11-3 shows the general file operations supported by NFS versions 3 and 4, respectively. The create operation is used to create a file, but has somewhat different meanings in NFSv3 and NFSv4. In version 3, the operation is used for creating regular files. Special files are created using separate operations. The link operation is used to create hard links. Symlink is used to create symbolic links. Mkdir is used to create subdirectories. Special files, such as device files, sockets, and named pipes are created by means of the mknod operation.

This situation is changed completely in NFSv4, where create is used for creating *nonregular* files, which include symbolic links, directories, and special files. Hard links are still created using a separate link operation, but regular files are created by means of the open operation, which is new to NFS and is a major deviation from the approach to file handling in older versions. Up until version 4, NFS was designed to allow its file servers to be stateless. For reasons we discuss later in this chapter, this design criterion has been abandoned in NFSv4, in which it is assumed that servers will generally maintain state between operations on the same file.

The operation rename is used to change the name of an existing file the same as in UNIX.

Files are deleted by means of the remove operation. In version 4, this operation is used to remove any kind of file. In previous versions, a separate rmdir operation was needed to remove a subdirectory. A file is removed by its name and has the effect that the number of hard links to it is decreased by one. If the number of links drops to zero, the file may be destroyed.

Version 4 allows clients to open and close (regular) files. Opening a nonexisting file has the side effect that a new file is created. To open a file, a client provides a name, along with various values for attributes. For example, a client may specify that a file should be opened for write access. After a file has been successfully opened, a client can access that file by means of its file handle. That handle is also used to close the file, by which the client tells the server that it will no longer need to have access to the file. The server, in turn, can release any state it maintained to provide that client access to the file.

Operation	v3	v4	Description
Create	Yes	No	Create a regular file
Create	No	Yes	Create a nonregular file
Link	Yes	Yes	Create a hard link to a file
Symlink	Yes	No	Create a symbolic link to a file
Mkdir	Yes	No	Create a subdirectory in a given directory
Mknod	Yes	No	Create a special file
Rename	Yes	Yes	Change the name of a file
Remove	Yes	Yes	Remove a file from a file system
Rmdir	Yes	No	Remove an empty subdirectory from a directory
Open	No	Yes	Open a file
Close	No	Yes	Close a file
Lookup	Yes	Yes	Look up a file by means of a file name
Readdir	Yes	Yes	Read the entries in a directory
Readlink	Yes	Yes	Read the path name stored in a symbolic link
Getattr	Yes	Yes	Get the attribute values for a file
Setattr	Yes	Yes	Set one or more attribute values for a file
Read	Yes	Yes	Read the data contained in a file
Write	Yes	Yes	Write data to a file

Figure 11-3. An incomplete list of file system operations supported by NFS.

The lookup operation is used to look up a file handle for a given path name. In NFSv3, the lookup operation will not resolve a name beyond a mount point. (Recall from Chap. 5 that a mount point is a directory that essentially represents a link to a subdirectory in a *foreign* name space.) For example, assume that the name */remote/vu* refers to a mount point in a naming graph. When resolving the name */remote/vu/mbox*, the lookup operation in NFSv3 will return the file handle for the mount point */remote/vu* along with the remainder of the path name (i.e., *mbox*). The client is then required to explicitly mount the file system that is needed to complete the name lookup. A file system in this context is the collection of files, attributes, directories, and data blocks that are jointly implemented as a logical block device (Tanenbaum and Woodhull, 2006).

In version 4, matters have been simplified. In this case, lookup will attempt to resolve the entire name, even if this means crossing mount points. Note that this approach is possible only if a file system has already been mounted at mount points. The client is able to detect that a mount point has been crossed by inspecting the file system identifier that is later returned when the lookup completes.

There is a separate operation readdir to read the entries in a directory. This operation returns a list of *(name, file handle)* pairs along with attribute values that the client requested. The client can also specify how many entries should be returned. The operation returns an offset that can be used in a subsequent call to readdir in order to read the next series of entries.

Operation readlink is used to read the data associated with a symbolic link. Normally, this data corresponds to a path name that can be subsequently looked up. Note that the lookup operation cannot handle symbolic links. Instead, when a symbolic link is reached, name resolution stops and the client is required to first call readlink to find out where name resolution should continue.

Files have various attributes associated with them. Again, there are important differences between NFS version 3 and 4, which we discuss in detail later. Typical attributes include the type of the file (telling whether we are dealing with a directory, a symbolic link, a special file, etc.), the file length, the identifier of the file system that contains the file, and the last time the file was modified. File attributes can be read and set using the operations getattr and setattr, respectively.

Finally, there are operations for reading data from a file, and writing data to a file. Reading data by means of the operation read is completely straightforward. The client specifies the offset and the number of bytes to be read. The client is returned the actual number of bytes that have been read, along with additional status information (e.g., whether the end-of-file has been reached).

Writing data to a file is done using the write operation. The client again specifies the position in the file where writing should start, the number of bytes to be written, and the data. In addition, it can instruct the server to ensure that all data are to be written to stable storage (we discussed stable storage in Chap. 8). NFS servers are required to support storage devices that can survive power supply failures, operating system failures, and hardware failures.

11.1.2 Cluster-Based Distributed File Systems

NFS is a typical example for many distributed file systems, which are generally organized according to a traditional client-server architecture. This architecture is often enhanced for server clusters with a few differences.

Considering that server clusters are often used for parallel applications, it is not surprising that their associated file systems are adjusted accordingly. One well-known technique is to deploy **file-striping techniques**, by which a single file is distributed across multiple servers. The basic idea is simple: by distributing a large file across multiple servers, it becomes possible to fetch different parts in parallel. Of course, such an organization works well only if the application is organized in such a way that parallel data access makes sense. This generally requires that the data as stored in the file have a very regular structure, for example, a (dense) matrix.

For general-purpose applications, or those with irregular or many different types of data structures, file striping may not be an effective tool. In those cases, it is often more convenient to partition the file system as a whole and simply store

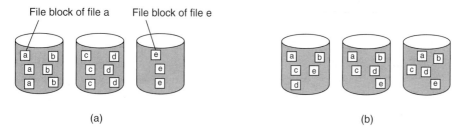

(a) (b)

Figure 11-4. The difference between (a) distributing whole files across several servers and (b) striping files for parallel access.

different files on different servers, but not to partition a single file across multiple servers. The difference between these two approaches is shown in Fig. 11-4.

More interesting are the cases of organizing a distributed file system for very large data centers such as those used by companies like Amazon and Google. These companies offer services to Web clients resulting in reads and updates to a massive number of files distributed across literally tens of thousands of computers [see also Barroso et al. (2003)]. In such environments, the traditional assumptions concerning distributed file systems no longer hold. For example, we can expect that at any single moment there will be a computer malfunctioning.

To address these problems, Google, for example, has developed its own **Google file system** (**GFS**), of which the design is described in Ghemawat et al. (2003). Google files tend to be very large, commonly ranging up to multiple gigabytes, where each one contains lots of smaller objects. Moreover, updates to files usually take place by appending data rather than overwriting parts of a file. These observations, along with the fact that server failures are the norm rather than the exception, lead to constructing clusters of servers as shown in Fig. 11-5.

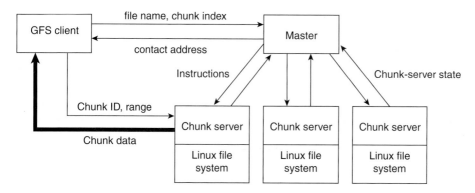

Figure 11-5. The organization of a Google cluster of servers.

Each GFS cluster consists of a single master along with multiple **chunk servers**. Each GFS file is divided into chunks of 64 Mbyte each, after which these chunks are distributed across what are called chunk servers. An important observation is that a GFS master is contacted only for metadata information. In particular, a GFS client passes a file name and chunk index to the master, expecting a contact address for the chunk. The contact address contains all the information to access the correct chunk server to obtain the required file chunk.

To this end, the GFS master essentially maintains a name space, along with a mapping from file name to chunks. Each chunk has an associated identifier that will allow a chunk server to lookup it up. In addition, the master keeps track of where a chunk is located. Chunks are replicated to handle failures, but no more than that. An interesting feature is that the GFS master does not attempt to keep an accurate account of chunk locations. Instead, it occasionally contacts the chunk servers to see which chunks they have stored.

The advantage of this scheme is simplicity. Note that the master is in control of allocating chunks to chunk servers. In addition, the chunk servers keep an account of what they have stored. As a consequence, once the master has obtained chunk locations, it has an accurate picture of where data is stored. However, matters would become complicated if this view had to be consistent all the time. For example, every time a chunk server crashes or when a server is added, the master would need to be informed. Instead, it is much simpler to refresh its information from the current set of chunk servers through polling. GFS clients simply get to know which chunk servers the master believes is storing the requested data. Because chunks are replicated anyway, there is a high probability that a chunk is available on at least one of the chunk servers.

not consistent all the time.

Why does this scheme scale? An important design issue is that the master is largely in control, but that it does not form a bottleneck due to all the work it needs to do. Two important types of measures have been taken to accommodate scalability.

First, and by far the most important one, is that the bulk of the actual work is done by chunk servers. When a client needs to access data, it contacts the master to find out which chunk servers hold that data. After that, it communicates only with the chunk servers. Chunks are replicated according to a primary-backup scheme. When the client is performing an update operation, it contacts the nearest chunk server holding that data, and pushes its updates to that server. This server will push the update to the next closest one holding the data, and so on. Once all updates have been propagated, the client will contact the primary chunk server, who will then assign a sequence number to the update operation and pass it on to the backups. Meanwhile, the master is kept out of the loop.

Second, the (hierarchical) name space for files is implemented using a simple single-level table, in which path names are mapped to metadata (such as the equivalent of inodes in traditional file systems). Moreover, this entire table is kept in main memory, along with the mapping of files to chunks. Updates on these data are logged to persistent storage. When the log becomes too large, a checkpoint is made by which the main-memory data is stored in such a way that it can be immediately mapped back into main memory. As a consequence, the intensity of I/O of a GFS master is strongly reduced.

This organization allows a single master to control a few hundred chunk servers, which is a considerable size for a single cluster. By subsequently organizing a service such as Google into smaller services that are mapped onto clusters, it is not hard to imagine that a huge collection of clusters can be made to work together.

11.1.3 Symmetric Architectures

Of course, fully symmetric organizations that are based on peer-to-peer technology also exist. All current proposals use a DHT-based system for distributing data, combined with a key-based lookup mechanism. An important difference is whether they build a file system on top of a distributed storage layer, or whether whole files are stored on the participating nodes.

An example of the first type of file system is Ivy, a distributed file system that is built using a Chord DHT-based system. Ivy is described in Muthitacharoen et al. (2002). Their system essentially consists of three separate layers as shown in Fig. 11-6. The lowest layer is formed by a Chord system providing basic decentralized lookup facilities. In the middle is a fully distributed block-oriented storage layer. Finally, on top there is a layer implementing an NFS-like file system.

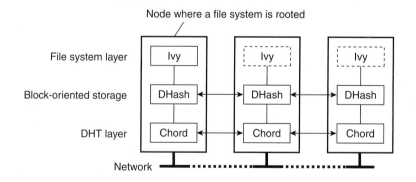

Figure 11-6. The organization of the Ivy distributed file system.

Data storage in Ivy is realized by a Chord-based, block-oriented distributed storage system called **DHash** (Dabek et al., 2001). In essence, DHash is quite simple. It only knows about data blocks, each block typically having a size of 8 KB. Ivy uses two kinds of data blocks. A **content-hash block** has an associated key, which is computed as the secure hash of the block's content. In this way, whenever a block is looked up, a client can immediately verify whether the correct block has been looked up, or that another or corrupted version is returned.

Furthermore, Ivy also makes use of **public-key blocks**, which are blocks having a public key as lookup key, and whose content has been signed with the associated private key.

To increase availability, DHash replicates every block B to the k immediate successors of the server responsible for storing B. In addition, looked up blocks are also cached along the route that the lookup request followed.

Files are implemented as a separate data structure on top of DHash. To achieve this goal, each user maintains a log of operations it carries out on files. For simplicity, we assume that there is only a single user per node so that each node will have its own log. A log is a linked list of immutable records, where each record contains all the information related to an operation on the Ivy file system. Each node appends records only to its own, local, log. Only a log's head is mutable, and points to the most recently appended record. Each record is stored in a separate content-hash block, whereas a log's head is kept in a public-key block.

There are different types of records, roughly corresponding to the different operations supported by NFS. For example, when performing an update operation on a file, a *write* record is created, containing the file's identifier along with the offset for the pile pointer and the data that is being written. Likewise, there are records for creating files (i.e., adding a new inode), manipulating directories, etc.

To create a new file system, a node simply creates a new log along with a new inode that will serve as the root. Ivy deploys what is known as an **NFS loopback server** which is just a local user-level server that accepts NFS requests from local clients. In the case of Ivy, this NFS server supports mounting the newly created file system allowing applications to access it as any other NFS file system.

When performing a read operation, the local Ivy NFS server makes a pass over the log, collecting data from those records that represent write operations on the same block of data, allowing it to retrieve the most recently stored values. Note that because each record is stored as a DHash block, multiple lookups across the overlay network may be needed to retrieve the relevant values.

Instead of using a separate block-oriented storage layer, alternative designs propose to distribute whole files instead of data blocks. The developers of Kosha (Butt et al. 2004) propose to distribute files at a specific directory level. In their approach, each node has a mount point named */kosha* containing the files that are to be distributed using a DHT-based system. Distributing files at directory level 1 means that all files in a subdirectory */kosha/a* will be stored at the same node. Likewise, distribution at level 2 implies that all files stored in subdirectory */kosha/a/aa* are stored at the same node. Taking a level-1 distribution as an example, the node responsible for storing files under */kosha/a* is found by computing the hash of *a* and taking that as the key in a lookup.

The potential drawback of this approach is that a node may run out of disk space to store all the files contained in the subdirectory that it is responsible for. Again, a simple solution is found in placing a branch of that subdirectory on another node and creating a symbolic link to where the branch is now stored.

11.2 PROCESSES

When it comes to processes, distributed file systems have no unusual properties. In many cases, there will be different types of cooperating processes: storage servers and file managers, just as we described above for the various organizations.

The most interesting aspect concerning file system processes is whether or not they should be stateless. NFS is a good example illustrating the trade-offs. One of its long-lasting distinguishing features (compared to other distributed file systems), was the fact that servers were stateless. In other words, the NFS protocol did not require that servers maintained any client state. This approach was followed in versions 2 and 3, but has been abandoned for version 4.

The primary advantage of the stateless approach is simplicity. For example, when a stateless server crashes, there is essentially no need to enter a recovery phase to bring the server to a previous state. However, as we explained in Chap. 8, we still need to take into account that the client cannot be given any guarantees whether or not a request has actually been carried out.

The stateless approach in the NFS protocol could not always be fully followed in practical implementations. For example, locking a file cannot easily be done by a stateless server. In the case of NFS, a separate lock manager is used to handle this situation. Likewise, certain authentication protocols require that the server maintains state on its clients. Nevertheless, NFS servers could generally be designed in such a way that only very little information on clients needed to be maintained. For the most part, the scheme worked adequately.

Starting with version 4, the stateless approach was abandoned, although the new protocol is designed in such a way that a server does not need to maintain much information about its clients. Besides those just mentioned, there are other reasons to choose for a stateful approach. An important reason is that NFS version 4 is expected to also work across wide-area networks. This requires that clients can make effective use of caches, in turn requiring an efficient cache consistency protocol. Such protocols often work best in collaboration with a server that maintains some information on files as used by its clients. For example, a server may associate a lease with each file it hands out to a client, promising to give the client exclusive read and write access until the lease expires or is refreshed. We return to such issues later in this chapter.

The most apparent difference with the previous versions is the support for the open operation. In addition, NFS supports callback procedures by which a server can do an RPC to a client. Clearly, callbacks also require a server to keep track of its clients.

Similar reasoning has affected the design of other distributed file systems. By and large, it turns out that maintaining a fully stateless design can be quite difficult, often leading to building stateful solutions as an enhancement, such as is the case with NFS file locking.

11.3 COMMUNICATION

As with processes, there is nothing particularly special or unusual about communication in distributed file systems. Many of them are based on remote procedure calls (RPCs), although some interesting enhancements have been made to support special cases. The main reason for choosing an RPC mechanism is to make the system independent from underlying operating systems, networks, and transport protocols.

11.3.1 RPCs in NFS

For example, in NFS, all communication between a client and server proceeds along the **Open Network Computing RPC (ONC RPC)** protocol, which is formally defined in Srinivasan (1995a), along with a standard for representing marshaled data (Srinivasan, 1995b). ONC RPC is similar to other RPC systems as we discussed in Chap. 4.

Every NFS operation can be implemented as a single remote procedure call to a file server. In fact, up until NFSv4, the client was made responsible for making the server's life as easy as possible by keeping requests relatively simple. For example, in order to read data from a file for the first time, a client normally first had to look up the file handle using the lookup operation, after which it could issue a read request, as shown in Fig. 11-7(a).

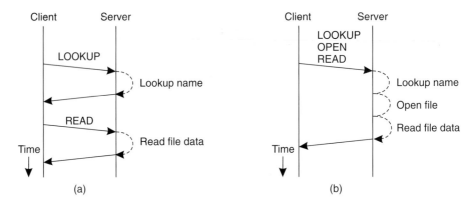

Figure 11-7. (a) Reading data from a file in NFS version 3. (b) Reading data using a compound procedure in version 4.

This approach required two successive RPCs. The drawback became apparent when considering the use of NFS in a wide-area system. In that case, the extra latency of a second RPC led to performance degradation. To circumvent such problems, NFSv4 supports **compound procedures** by which several RPCs can be grouped into a single request, as shown in Fig. 11-7(b).

In our example, the client combines the lookup and read request into a single RPC. In the case of version 4, it is also necessary to open the file before reading can take place. After the file handle has been looked up, it is passed to the open operation, after which the server continues with the read operation. The overall effect in this example is that only two messages need to be exchanged between the client and server.

There are no transactional semantics associated with compound procedures. The operations grouped together in a compound procedure are simply handled in the order as requested. If there are concurrent operations from other clients, then no measures are taken to avoid conflicts. If an operation fails for whatever reason, then no further operations in the compound procedure are executed, and the results found so far are returned to the client. For example, if lookup fails, a succeeding open is not even attempted.

11.3.2 The RPC2 Subsystem

Another interesting enhancement to RPCs has been developed as part of the Coda file system (Kistler and Satyanarayanan, 1992). **RPC2** is a package that offers reliable RPCs on top of the (unreliable) UDP protocol. Each time a remote procedure is called, the RPC2 client code starts a new thread that sends an invocation request to the server and subsequently blocks until it receives an answer. As request processing may take an arbitrary time to complete, the server regularly sends back messages to the client to let it know it is still working on the request. If the server dies, sooner or later this thread will notice that the messages have ceased and report back failure to the calling application.

An interesting aspect of RPC2 is its support for side effects. A **side effect** is a mechanism by which the client and server can communicate using an application-specific protocol. Consider, for example, a client opening a file at a video server. What is needed in this case is that the client and server set up a continuous data stream with an isochronous transmission mode. In other words, data transfer from the server to the client is guaranteed to be within a minimum and maximum end-to-end delay.

RPC2 allows the client and the server to set up a separate connection for transferring the video data to the client on time. Connection setup is done as a side effect of an RPC call to the server. For this purpose, the RPC2 runtime system provides an interface of side-effect routines that is to be implemented by the application developer. For example, there are routines for setting up a connection and routines for transferring data. These routines are automatically called by the RPC2 runtime system at the client and server, respectively, but their implementation is otherwise completely independent of RPC2. This principle of side effects is shown in Fig. 11-8.

Another feature of RPC2 that makes it different from other RPC systems is its support for multicasting. An important design issue in Coda is that servers keep

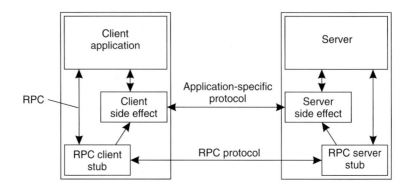

Figure 11-8. Side effects in Coda's RPC2 system.

track of which clients have a local copy of a file. When a file is modified, a server invalidates local copies by notifying the appropriate clients through an RPC. Clearly, if a server can notify only one client at a time, invalidating all clients may take some time, as illustrated in Fig. 11-9(a).

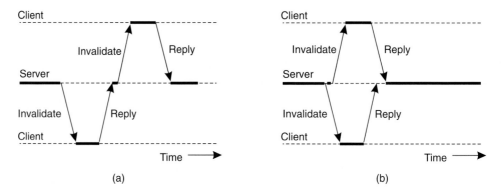

Figure 11-9. (a) Sending an invalidation message one at a time. (b) Sending invalidation messages in parallel.

The problem is caused by the fact that an RPC may occasionally fail. Invalidating files in a strict sequential order may be delayed considerably because the server cannot reach a possibly crashed client, but will give up on that client only after a relatively long expiration time. Meanwhile, other clients will still be reading from their local copies.

An alternative (and better) solution is shown in Fig. 11-9(b). Here, instead of invalidating each copy one by one, the server sends an invalidation message to all clients at the same time. As a consequence, all nonfailing clients are notified in the same time as it would take to do an immediate RPC. Also, the server notices within the usual expiration time that certain clients are failing to respond to the RPC, and can declare such clients as being crashed.

Parallel RPCs are implemented by means of the **MultiRPC** system, which is part of the RPC2 package (Satyanarayanan and Siegel, 1990). An important aspect of MultiRPC is that the parallel invocation of RPCs is fully transparent to the callee. In other words, the receiver of a MultiRPC call cannot distinguish that call from a normal RPC. At the caller's side, parallel execution is also largely transparent. For example, the semantics of MultiRPC in the presence of failures are much the same as that of a normal RPC. Likewise, the side-effect mechanisms can be used in the same way as before.

MultiRPC is implemented by essentially executing multiple RPCs in parallel. This means that the caller explicitly sends an RPC request to each recipient. However, instead of immediately waiting for a response, it defers blocking until all requests have been sent. In other words, the caller invokes a number of one-way RPCs, after which it blocks until all responses have been received from the non-failing recipients. An alternative approach to parallel execution of RPCs in MultiRPC is provided by setting up a multicast group, and sending an RPC to all group members using IP multicast.

11.3.3 File-Oriented Communication in Plan 9

Finally, it is worth mentioning a completely different approach to handling communication in distributed file systems. **Plan 9** (Pike et al., 1995). is not so much a distributed file system, but rather a *file-based distributed system*. All resources are accessed in the same way, namely with file-like syntax and operations, including even resources such as processes and network interfaces. This idea is inherited from UNIX, which also attempts to offer file-like interfaces to resources, but it has been exploited much further and more consistently in Plan 9. To illustrate, network interfaces are represented by a file system, in this case consisting of a collection of special files. This approach is similar to UNIX, although network interfaces in UNIX are represented by files and not file systems. (Note that a file system in this context is again the logical block device containing all the data and metadata that comprise a collection of files.) In Plan 9, for example, an individual TCP connection is represented by a subdirectory consisting of the files shown in Fig. 11-10.

The file *ctl* is used to send control commands to the connection. For example, to open a telnet session to a machine with IP address 192.31.231.42 using port 23, requires that the sender writes the text string "connect 192.31.231.42!23" to file *ctl*. The receiver would previously have written the string "announce 23" to its own *ctl* file, indicating that it can accept incoming session requests.

The *data* file is used to exchange data by simply performing read and write operations. These operations follow the usual UNIX semantics for file operations.

File	Description
ctl	Used to write protocol-specific control commands
data	Used to read and write data
listen	Used to accept incoming connection setup requests
local	Provides information on the caller's side of the connection
remote	Provides information on the other side of the connection
status	Provides diagnostic information on the current status of the connection

Figure 11-10. Files associated with a single TCP connection in Plan 9.

For example, to write data to a connection, a process simply invokes the operation

    res = write(fd, buf, nbytes);

where *fd* is the file descriptor returned after opening the data file, *buf* is a pointer to a buffer containing the data to be written, and *nbytes* is the number of bytes that should be extracted from the buffer. The number of bytes actually written is returned and stored in the variable *res*.

The file *listen* is used to wait for connection setup requests. After a process has announced its willingness to accept new connections, it can do a blocking read on file *listen*. If a request comes in, the call returns a file descriptor to a new *ctl* file corresponding to a newly-created connection directory. It is thus seen how a completely file-oriented approach toward communication can be realized.

11.4 NAMING

Naming arguably plays an important role in distributed file systems. In virtually all cases, names are organized in a hierarchical name space like those we discussed in Chap. 5. In the following we will again consider NFS as a representative for how naming is often handled in distributed file systems.

11.4.1 Naming in NFS

Location transparency: File name ↛ location

The fundamental idea underlying the NFS naming model is to provide clients complete transparent access to a remote file system as maintained by a server. This transparency is achieved by letting a client be able to mount a remote file system into its own local file system, as shown in Fig. 11-11.

Instead of mounting an entire file system, NFS allows clients to mount only part of a file system, as also shown in Fig. 11-11. A server is said to **export** a directory when it makes that directory and its entries available to clients. An exported directory can be mounted into a client's local name space.

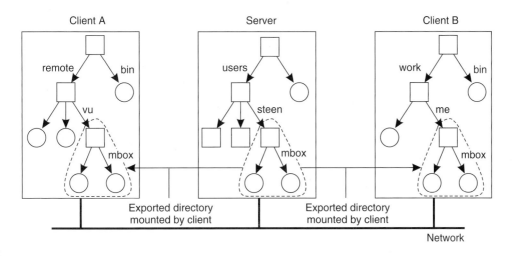

Figure 11-11. Mounting (part of) a remote file system in NFS.

This design approach has a serious implication: in principle, users do not share name spaces. As shown in Fig. 11-11, the file named */remote/vu/mbox* at client *A* is named */work/me/mbox* at client *B*. A file's name therefore depends on how clients organize their own local name space, and where exported directories are mounted. The drawback of this approach in a distributed file system is that sharing files becomes much harder. For example, Alice cannot tell Bob about a file using the name she assigned to that file, for that name may have a completely different meaning in Bob's name space of files.

There are several ways to solve this problem, but the most common one is to provide each client with a name space that is partly standardized. For example, each client may be using the local directory */usr/bin* to mount a file system containing a standard collection of programs that are available to everyone. Likewise, the directory */local* may be used as a standard to mount a local file system that is located on the client's host.

An NFS server can itself mount directories that are exported by other servers. However, it is not allowed to export those directories to its own clients. Instead, a client will have to explicitly mount such a directory from the server that maintains it, as shown in Fig. 11-12. This restriction comes partly from simplicity. If a server could export a directory that it mounted from another server, it would have to return special file handles that include an identifier for a server. NFS does not support such file handles.

To explain this point in more detail, assume that server *A* hosts a file system *FS_A* from which it exports the directory */packages*. This directory contains a subdirectory */draw* that acts as a mount point for a file system *FS_B* that is exported by server *B* and mounted by *A*. Let *A* also export */packages/draw* to its own clients,

Nested export not supported

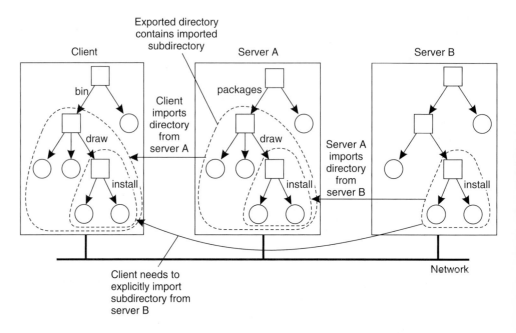

Figure 11-12. Mounting nested directories from multiple servers in NFS.

and assume that a client has mounted */packages* into its local directory */bin* as shown in Fig. 11-12.

If name resolution is iterative (as is the case in NFSv3), then to resolve the name */bin/draw/install*, the client contacts server *A* when it has locally resolved */bin* and requests *A* to return a file handle for directory */draw*. In that case, server *A* should return a file handle that includes an identifier for server *B*, for only *B* can resolve the rest of the path name, in this case */install*. As we have said, this kind of name resolution is not supported by NFS.

Name resolution in NFSv3 (and earlier versions) is strictly iterative in the sense that only a single file name at a time can be looked up. In other words, resolving a name such as */bin/draw/install* requires three separate calls to the NFS server. Moreover, the client is fully responsible for implementing the resolution of a path name. NFSv4 also supports recursive name lookups. In this case, a client can pass a complete path name to a server and request that server to resolve it.

There is another peculiarity with NFS name lookups that has been solved with version 4. Consider a file server hosting several file systems. With the strict iterative name resolution in version 3, whenever a lookup was done for a directory on which another file system was mounted, the lookup would return the file handle of the directory. Subsequently reading that directory would return its *original* content, not that of the root directory of the mounted file system.

To explain, assume that in our previous example that both file systems FS_A and FS_B are hosted by a single server. If the client has mounted */packages* into its local directory */bin*, then looking up the file name *draw* at the server would return the file handle for *draw*. A subsequent call to the server for listing the directory entries of *draw* by means of readdir would then return the list of directory entries that were *originally* stored in FS_A in subdirectory */packages/draw*. Only if the client had also mounted file system FS_B, would it be possible to properly resolve the path name *draw/install* relative to */bin*.

NFSv4 solves this problem by allowing lookups to cross mount points at a server. In particular, lookup returns the file handle of the *mounted* directory instead of that of the original directory. The client can detect that the lookup has crossed a mount point by inspecting the file system identifier of the looked up file. If required, the client can locally mount that file system as well.

File Handles

A file handle is a reference to a file within a file system. It is independent of the name of the file it refers to. A file handle is created by the server that is hosting the file system and is unique with respect to all file systems exported by the server. It is created when the file is created. The client is kept ignorant of the actual content of a file handle; it is completely opaque. File handles were 32 bytes in NFS version 2, but were variable up to 64 bytes in version 3 and 128 bytes in version 4. Of course, the length of a file handle is not opaque.

Ideally, a file handle is implemented as a true identifier for a file relative to a file system. For one thing, this means that as long as the file exists, it should have one and the same file handle. This persistence requirement allows a client to store a file handle locally once the associated file has been looked up by means of its name. One benefit is performance: as most file operations require a file handle instead of a name, the client can avoid having to look up a name repeatedly before every file operation. Another benefit of this approach is that the client can now *can use even name* access the file independent of its (current) names.   *name independent ∈ is changed*

Because a file handle can be locally stored by a client, it is also important that a server does not reuse a file handle after deleting a file. Otherwise, a client may mistakenly access the wrong file when it uses its locally stored file handle.

Note that the combination of iterative name lookups and not letting a lookup operation allow crossing a mount point introduces a problem with getting an initial file handle. In order to access files in a remote file system, a client will need to provide the server with a file handle of the directory where the lookup should take place, along with the name of the file or directory that is to be resolved. NFSv3 solves this problem through a separate mount protocol, by which a client actually mounts a remote file system. After mounting, the client is passed back the **root file handle** of the mounted file system, which it can subsequently use as a starting point for looking up names.

In NFSv4, this problem is solved by providing a separate operation putrootfh that tells the server to solve all file names relative to the root file handle of the file system it manages. The root file handle can be used to look up any other file handle in the server's file system. This approach has the additional benefit that there is no need for a separate mount protocol. Instead, mounting can be integrated into the regular protocol for looking up files. A client can simply mount a remote file system by requesting the server to resolve names relative to the file system's root file handle using putrootfh.

Automounting

As we mentioned, the NFS naming model essentially provides users with their own name space. Sharing in this model may become difficult if users name the same file differently. One solution to this problem is to provide each user with a local name space that is partly standardized, and subsequently mounting remote file systems the same for each user.

Another problem with the NFS naming model has to do with deciding when a remote file system should be mounted. Consider a large system with thousands of users. Assume that each user has a local directory /home that is used to mount the home directories of other users. For example, Alice's home directory may be locally available to her as /home/alice, although the actual files are stored on a remote server. This directory can be automatically mounted when Alice logs into her workstation. In addition, she may have access to Bob's public files by accessing Bob's directory through /home/bob.

The question, however, is whether Bob's home directory should also be mounted automatically when Alice logs in. The benefit of this approach would be that the whole business of mounting file systems would be transparent to Alice. However, if this policy were followed for every user, logging in could incur a lot of communication and administrative overhead. In addition, it would require that all users are known in advance. A much better approach is to transparently mount another user's home directory on demand, that is, when it is first needed.

On-demand mounting of a remote file system (or actually an exported directory) is handled in NFS by an **automounter**, which runs as a separate process on the client's machine. The principle underlying an automounter is relatively simple. Consider a simple automounter implemented as a user-level NFS server on a UNIX operating system. For alternative implementations, see Callaghan (2000).

Assume that for each user, the home directories of all users are available through the local directory /home, as described above. When a client machine boots, the automounter starts with mounting this directory. The effect of this local mount is that whenever a program attempts to access /home, the UNIX kernel will forward a lookup operation to the NFS client, which in this case, will forward the request to the automounter in its role as NFS server, as shown in Fig. 11-13.

[handwritten margin note: drawback: of "mount all @ once logged in"]

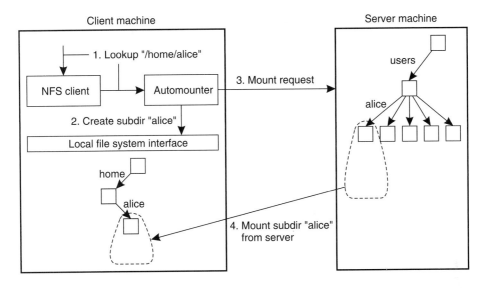

Figure 11-13. A simple automounter for NFS.

For example, suppose that Alice logs in. The login program will attempt to read the directory */home/alice* to find information such as login scripts. The automounter will thus receive the request to look up subdirectory */home/alice*, for which reason it first creates a subdirectory */alice* in */home*. It then looks up the NFS server that exports Alice's home directory to subsequently mount that directory in */home/alice*. At that point, the login program can proceed.

The problem with this approach is that the automounter will have to be involved in all file operations to guarantee transparency. If a referenced file is not locally available because the corresponding file system has not yet been mounted, the automounter will have to know. In particular, it will need to handle all read and write requests, even for file systems that have already been mounted. This approach may incur a large performance problem. It would be better to have the auto mounter only mount/unmount directories, but otherwise stay out of the loop.

A simple solution is to let the automounter mount directories in a special subdirectory, and install a symbolic link to each mounted directory. This approach is shown in Fig. 11-14.

In our example, the user home directories are mounted as subdirectories of */tmp_mnt*. When Alice logs in, the automounter mounts her home directory in */tmp_mnt/home/alice* and creates a symbolic link */home/alice* that refers to that subdirectory. In this case, whenever Alice executes a command such as

ls –l /home/alice

the NFS server that exports Alice's home directory is contacted directly without further involvement of the automounter.

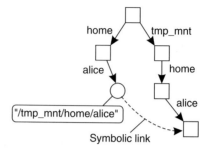

Figure 11-14. Using symbolic links with automounting.

11.4.2 Constructing a Global Name Space

Large distributed systems are commonly constructed by gluing together various legacy systems into one whole. When it comes to offering shared access to files, having a global name space is about the minimal glue that one would like to have. At present, file systems are mostly opened for sharing by using primitive means such as access through FTP. This approach, for example, is generally used in Grid computing.

More sophisticated approaches are followed by truly wide-area distributed file systems, but these often require modifications to operating system kernels in order to be adopted. Therefore, researchers have been looking for approaches to integrate existing file systems into a single, global name space but using only user-level solutions. One such system, simply called **Global Name Space Service** (**GNS**) is proposed by Anderson et al. (2004).

GNS does not provide interfaces to access files. Instead, it merely provides the means to set up a global name space in which several existing name spaces have been merged. To this end, a GNS client maintains a virtual tree in which each node is either a directory or a **junction**. A junction is a special node that indicates that name resolution is to be taken over by another process, and as such bears some resemblance with a mount point in traditional file system. There are five different types of junctions, as shown in Fig. 11-15.

A GNS junction simply refers to another GNS instance, which is just another virtual tree hosted at possibly another process. The two logical junctions contain information that is needed to contact a location service. The latter will provide the contact address for accessing a file system and a file, respectively. A physical file-system name refers to a file system at another server, and corresponds largely to a contact address that a logical junction would need. For example, a URL such as *ftp://ftp.cs.vu.nl/pub* would contain all the information to access files at the indicated FTP server. Analogously, a URL such as *http//www.cs.vu.nl/index.htm* is a typical example of a physical file name.

Junction	Description
GNS junction	Refers to another GNS instance
Logical file-system name	Reference to subtree to be looked up in a location service
Logical file name	Reference to a file to be looked up in a location service
Physical file-system name	Reference to directly remote-accessible subtree
Physical file name	Reference to directly remote-accessible file

Figure 11-15. Junctions in GNS.

Obviously, a junction should contain all the information needed to continue name resolution. There are many ways of doing this, but considering that there are so many different file systems, each specific junction will require its own implementation. Fortunately, there are also many common ways of accessing remote files, including protocols for communicating with NFS servers, FTP servers, and Windows-based machines (notably CIFS).

GNS has the advantage of decoupling the naming of files from their actual location. In no way does a virtual tree relate to where files and directories are physically placed. In addition, by using a location service it is also possible to move files around without rendering their names unresolvable. In that case, the new physical location needs to be registered at the location service. Note that this is completely the same as what we have discussed in Chap. 5.

11.5 SYNCHRONIZATION

Let us now continue our discussion by focusing on synchronization issues in distributed file systems. There are various issues that require our attention. In the first place, synchronization for file systems would not be an issue if files were not shared. However, in a distributed system, the semantics of file sharing becomes a bit tricky when performance issues are at stake. To this end, different solutions have been proposed of which we discuss the most important ones next.

11.5.1 Semantics of File Sharing

When two or more users share the same file at the same time, it is necessary to define the semantics of reading and writing precisely to avoid problems. In single-processor systems that permit processes to share files, such as UNIX, the semantics normally state that when a read operation follows a write operation, the read returns the value just written, as shown in Fig. 11-16(a). Similarly, when two writes happen in quick succession, followed by a read, the value read is the value stored by the last write. In effect, the system enforces an absolute time ordering on all operations and always returns the most recent value. We will refer to this model as **UNIX semantics**. This model is easy to understand and straightforward to implement.

absolute-time ordering

① only one server.
②process sequentially.

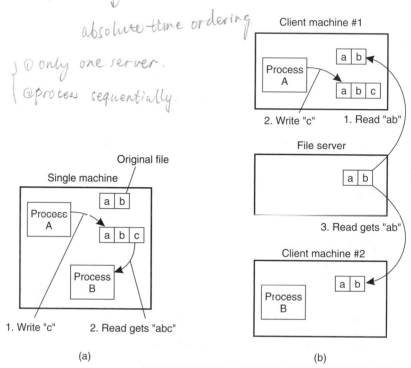

Figure 11-16. (a) On a single processor, when a read follows a write, the value returned by the read is the value just written. (b) In a distributed system with caching, obsolete values may be returned.

In a distributed system, UNIX semantics can be achieved easily as long as there is only one file server and clients do not cache files. All reads and writes go directly to the file server, which processes them strictly sequentially. This approach gives UNIX semantics (except for the minor problem that network delays may cause a read that occurred a microsecond after a write to arrive at the server first and thus gets the old value).

In practice, however, the performance of a distributed system in which all file requests must go to a single server is frequently poor. This problem is often solved by allowing clients to maintain local copies of heavily-used files in their private (local) caches. Although we will discuss the details of file caching below, for the moment it is sufficient to point out that if a client locally modifies a cached file and shortly thereafter another client reads the file from the server, the second client will get an obsolete file, as illustrated in Fig. 11-16(b).

One way out of this difficulty is to propagate all changes to cached files back to the server immediately. Although conceptually simple, this approach is inefficient. An alternative solution is to relax the semantics of file sharing. Instead of requiring a read to see the effects of all previous writes, one can have a new rule that says: "Changes to an open file are initially visible only to the process (or possibly machine) that modified the file. Only when the file is closed are the changes made visible to other processes (or machines)." The adoption of such a rule does not change what happens in Fig. 11-16(b), but it does redefine the actual behavior (B getting the original value of the file) as being the correct one. When A closes the file, it sends a copy to the server, so that subsequent reads get the new value, as required.

This rule is widely-implemented and is known as **session semantics**. Most distributed file systems implement session semantics. This means that although in theory they follow the remote access model of Fig. 11-1(a), most implementations make use of local caches, effectively implementing the upload/download model of Fig. 11-1(b).

Using session semantics raises the question of what happens if two or more clients are simultaneously caching and modifying the same file. One solution is to say that as each file is closed in turn, its value is sent back to the server, so the final result depends on whose close request is most recently processed by the server. A less pleasant, but easier to implement alternative is to say that the final result is one of the candidates, but leave the choice of which one unspecified.

A completely different approach to the semantics of file sharing in a distributed system is to make all files immutable. There is thus no way to open a file for writing. In effect, the only operations on files are create and read.

What is possible is to create an entirely new file and enter it into the directory system under the name of a previous existing file, which now becomes inaccessible (at least under that name). Thus although it becomes impossible to modify the file x, it remains possible to replace x by a new file atomically. In other words, although *files* cannot be updated, *directories* can be. Once we have decided that files cannot be changed at all, the problem of how to deal with two processes, one of which is writing on a file and the other of which is reading it, just disappears, greatly simplifying the design.

What does remain is the problem of what happens when two processes try to replace the same file at the same time. As with session semantics, the best solution here seems to be to allow one of the new files to replace the old one, either the last one or nondeterministically.

A somewhat stickier problem is what to do if a file is replaced while another process is busy reading it. One solution is to somehow arrange for the reader to continue using the old file, even if it is no longer in any directory, analogous to the way UNIX allows a process that has a file open to continue using it, even after it has been deleted from all directories. Another solution is to detect that the file has changed and make subsequent attempts to read from it fail.

atomic transaction

A fourth way to deal with shared files in a distributed system is to use atom\%ic transactions. To summarize briefly, to access a file or a group of files, a process first executes some type of BEGIN_TRANSACTION primitive to signal that what follows must be executed indivisibly. Then come system calls to read and write one or more files. When the requested work has been completed, an END_TRANSACTION primitive is executed. The key property of this method is that the system guarantees that all the calls contained within the transaction will be carried out in order, without any interference from other, concurrent transactions. If two or more transactions start up at the same time, the system ensures that the final result is the same as if they were all run in some (undefined) sequential order.

In Fig. 11-17 we summarize the four approaches we have discussed for dealing with shared files in a distributed system.

Method	Comment
UNIX semantics	Every operation on a file is instantly visible to all processes
Session semantics	No changes are visible to other processes until the file is closed
Immutable files	No updates are possible; simplifies sharing and replication
Transactions	All changes occur atomically

Figure 11-17. Four ways of dealing with the shared files in a distributed system.

NFS V1–V3: lock manager. (a separate server from file.
V4: locks integrated in file system.

11.5.2 File Locking

Notably in client-server architectures with stateless servers, we need additional facilities for synchronizing access to shared files. The traditional way of doing this is to make use of a lock manager. Without exception, a lock manager follows the centralized locking scheme as we discussed in Chap. 6.

However, matters are not as simple as we just sketched. Although a central lock manager is generally deployed, the complexity in locking comes from the need to allow concurrent access to the same file. For this reason, a great number of different locks exist, and moreover, the granularity of locks may also differ. Let us consider NFSv4 again.

Conceptually, file locking in NFSv4 is simple. There are essentially only four operations related to locking, as shown in Fig. 11-18. NFSv4 distinguishes read locks from write locks. Multiple clients can simultaneously access the same part of a file provided they only read data. A write lock is needed to obtain exclusive access to modify part of a file.

Operation lock is used to request a read or write lock on a consecutive range of bytes in a file. It is a nonblocking operation; if the lock cannot be granted due to another conflicting lock, the client gets back an error message and has to poll the server at a later time. There is no automatic retry. Alternatively, the client can

Operation	Description
Lock	Create a lock for a range of bytes
Lockt	Test whether a conflicting lock has been granted
Locku	Remove a lock from a range of bytes
Renew	Renew the lease on a specified lock

Figure 11-18. NFSv4 operations related to file locking.

request to be put on a FIFO-ordered list maintained by the server. As soon as the conflicting lock has been removed, the server will grant the next lock to the client at the top of the list, provided it polls the server before a certain time expires. This approach prevents the server from having to notify clients, while still being fair to clients whose lock request could not be granted because grants are made in FIFO order.

The lockt operation is used to test whether a conflicting lock exists. For example, a client can test whether there are any read locks granted on a specific range of bytes in a file, before requesting a write lock for those bytes. In the case of a conflict, the requesting client is informed exactly who is causing the conflict and on which range of bytes. It can be implemented more efficiently than lock, because there is no need to attempt to open a file.

Removing a lock from a file is done by means of the locku operation.

Locks are granted for a specific time (determined by the server). In other words, they have an associated lease. Unless a client renews the lease on a lock it has been granted, the server will automatically remove it. This approach is followed for other server-provided resources as well and helps in recovery after failures. Using the renew operation, a client requests the server to renew the lease on its lock (and, in fact, other resources as well).

In addition to these operations, there is also an implicit way to lock a file, referred to as **share reservation**. Share reservation is completely independent from locking, and can be used to implement NFS for Windows-based systems. When a client opens a file, it specifies the type of access it requires (namely *READ*, *WRITE*, or *BOTH*), and which type of access the server should deny other clients (*NONE*, *READ*, *WRITE*, or *BOTH*). If the server cannot meet the client's requirements, the open operation will fail for that client. In Fig. 11-19 we show exactly what happens when a new client opens a file that has already been successfully opened by another client. For an already opened file, we distinguish two different state variables. The access state specifies how the file is currently being accessed by the current client. The denial state specifies what accesses by new clients are not permitted.

In Fig. 11-19(a), we show what happens when a client tries to open a file requesting a specific type of access, given the current denial state of that file.

Current file denial state

Request access		NONE	READ	WRITE	BOTH
	READ	Succeed	Fail	Succeed	Fail
	WRITE	Succeed	Succeed	Fail	Fail
	BOTH	Succeed	Fail	Fail	Fail

(a)

Requested file denial state

Current access state		NONE	READ	WRITE	BOTH
	READ	Succeed	Fail	Succeed	Fail
	WRITE	Succeed	Succeed	Fail	Fail
	BOTH	Succeed	Fail	Fail	Fail

(b)

when the file ← is being accessed, the corresponding type of operation can not be disallowed by others

Figure 11-19. The result of an open operation with share reservations in NFS.
(a) When the client requests shared access given the current denial state.
(b) When the client requests a denial state given the current file access state.

Likewise, Fig. 11-19(b) shows the result of opening a file that is currently being accessed by another client, but now requesting certain access types to be disallowed.

NFSv4 is by no means an exception when it comes to offering synchronization mechanisms for shared files. In fact, it is by now accepted that any simple set of primitives such as only complete-file locking, reflects poor design. Complexity in locking schemes comes mostly from the fact that a fine granularity of locking is required to allow for concurrent access to shared files. Some attempts to reduce complexity while keeping performance have been taken [see, e.g., Burns et al. (2001)], but the situation remains somewhat unsatisfactory. In the end, we may be looking at completely redesigning our applications for scalability rather than trying to patch situations that come from wanting to share data the way we did in nondistributed systems.

11.5.3 Sharing Files in Coda

The session semantics in NFS dictate that the last process that closes a file will have its changes propagated to the server; any updates in concurrent, but earlier sessions will be lost. A somewhat more subtle approach can also be taken. To accommodate file sharing, the Coda file system (Kistler and Satyanaryanan, 1992) uses a special allocation scheme that bears some similarities to share reservations in NFS. To understand how the scheme works, the following is important. When a client successfully opens a file f, an entire copy of f is transferred to the client's machine. The server records that the client has a copy of *f*. So far, this approach is similar to open delegation in NFS.

Now suppose client *A* has opened file *f* for writing. When another client *B* wants to open *f* as well, it will fail. This failure is caused by the fact that the server has recorded that client *A* might have already modified *f*. On the other hand, had client *A* opened *f* for reading, an attempt by client *B* to get a copy from the server for reading would succeed. An attempt by *B* to open for writing would succeed as well.

Now consider what happens when several copies of *f* have been stored locally at various clients. Given what we have just said, only one client will be able to modify *f*. If this client modifies *f* and subsequently closes the file, the file will be transferred back to the server. However, every other client may proceed to read its *read old version* local copy despite the fact that the copy is actually outdated.

The reason for this apparently inconsistent behavior is that a session is treated as a transaction in Coda. Consider Fig. 11-20, which shows the time line for two processes, *A* and *B*. Assume *A* has opened *f* for reading, leading to session S_A. Client *B* has opened *f* for writing, shown as session S_B.

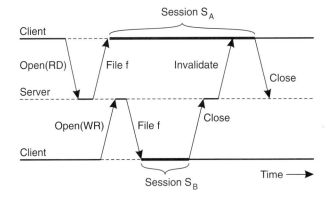

Figure 11-20. The transactional behavior in sharing files in Coda.

When *B* closes session S_B, it transfers the updated version of *f* to the server, which will then send an invalidation message to *A*. *A* will now know that it is reading from an older version of *f*. However, from a transactional point of view, this really does not matter because session S_A could be considered to have been scheduled before session S_B.

11.6 CONSISTENCY AND REPLICATION *hide latency*

Caching and replication play an important role in distributed file systems, most notably when they are designed to operate over wide-area networks. In what follows, we will take a look at various aspects related to client-side caching of file data, as well as the replication of file servers. Also, we consider the role of replication in peer-to-peer file-sharing systems.

11.6.1 Client-Side Caching

To see how client-side caching is deployed in practice, we return to our example systems NFS and Coda.

Caching in NFS

Caching in NFSv3 has been mainly left outside of the protocol. This approach has led to the implementation of different caching policies, most of which never guaranteed consistency. At best, cached data could be stale for a few seconds compared to the data stored at a server. However, implementations also exist that allowed cached data to be stale for 30 seconds without the client knowing. This state of affairs is less than desirable.

NFSv4 solves some of these consistency problems, but essentially still leaves cache consistency to be handled in an implementation-dependent way. The general caching model that is assumed by NFS is shown in Fig. 11-21. Each client can have a memory cache that contains data previously read from the server. In addition, there may also be a disk cache that is added as an extension to the memory cache, using the same consistency parameters.

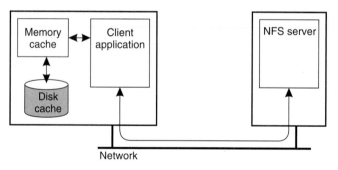

Figure 11-21. Client-side caching in NFS.

Typically, clients cache file data, attributes, file handles, and directories. Different strategies exist to handle consistency of the cached data, cached attributes, and so on. Let us first take a look at caching file data.

NFSv4 supports two different approaches for caching file data. The simplest approach is when a client opens a file and caches the data it obtains from the server as the result of various read operations. In addition, write operations can be carried out in the cache as well. When the client closes the file, NFS requires that if modifications have taken place, the cached data must be flushed back to the server. This approach corresponds to implementing session semantics as discussed earlier.

Once (part of) a file has been cached, a client can keep its data in the cache even after closing the file. Also, several clients on the same machine can share a single cache. NFS requires that whenever a client opens a previously closed file that has been (partly) cached, the client must immediately revalidate the cached data. Revalidation takes place by checking when the file was last modified and invalidating the cache in case it contains stale data.

In NFSv4 a server may delegate some of its rights to a client when a file is opened. **Open delegation** takes place when the client machine is allowed to locally handle open and close operations from other clients on the same machine. Normally, the server is in charge of checking whether opening a file should succeed or not, for example, because share reservations need to be taken into account. With open delegation, the client machine is sometimes allowed to make such decisions, avoiding the need to contact the server.

For example, if a server has delegated the opening of a file to a client that requested write permissions, file locking requests from other clients on the same machine can also be handled locally. The server will still handle locking requests from clients on other machines, by simply denying those clients access to the file. Note that this scheme does not work in the case of delegating a file to a client that requested only read permissions. In that case, whenever another local client wants to have write permissions, it will have to contact the server; it is not possible to handle the request locally.

An important consequence of delegating a file to a client is that the server needs to be able to recall the delegation, for example, when another client on a different machine needs to obtain access rights to the file. Recalling a delegation requires that the server can do a callback to the client, as illustrated in Fig. 11-22.

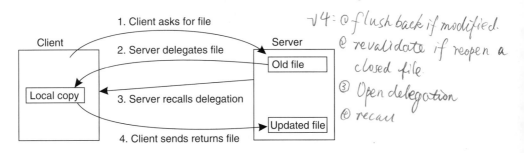

Figure 11-22. Using the NFSv4 callback mechanism to recall file delegation.

A callback is implemented in NFS using its underlying RPC mechanisms. Note, however, that callbacks require that the server keeps track of clients to which it has delegated a file. Here, we see another example where an NFS server can no longer be implemented in a stateless manner. Note, however, that the combination of delegation and stateful servers may lead to various problems in the presence of client and server failures. For example, what should a server do when it had delegated a file to a now unresponsive client? As we discuss shortly, leases will generally form an adequate practical solution.

Clients can also cache attribute values, but are largely left on their own when it comes to keeping cached values consistent. In particular, attribute values of the same file cached by two different clients may be different unless the clients keep these attributes mutually consistent. Modifications to an attribute value should be immediately forwarded to the server, thus following a write-through cache coherence policy.

A similar approach is followed for caching file handles (or rather, the name-to-file handle mapping) and directories. To mitigate the effects of inconsistencies, NFS uses leases on cached attributes, file handles, and directories. After some time has elapsed, cache entries are thus automatically invalidated and revalidation is needed before they are used again.

Client-Side Caching in Coda

Client-side caching is crucial to the operation of Coda for two reasons. First, caching is done to achieve scalability. Second, caching provides a higher degree of fault tolerance as the client becomes less dependent on the availability of the server. For these two reasons, clients in Coda always cache entire files. In other words, when a file is opened for either reading or writing, an entire copy of the file is transferred to the client, where it is subsequently cached.

Unlike many other distributed file systems, cache coherence in Coda is maintained by means of callbacks. We already came across this phenomenon when discussing file-sharing semantics. For each file, the server from which a client had fetched the file keeps track of which clients have a copy of that file cached locally. A server is said to record a **callback promise** for a client. When a client updates its local copy of the file for the first time, it notifies the server, which, in turn, sends an invalidation message to the other clients. Such an invalidation message is called a **callback break**, because the server will then discard the callback promise it held for the client it just sent an invalidation.

The interesting aspect of this scheme is that as long as a client knows it has an outstanding callback promise at the server, it can safely access the file locally. In particular, suppose a client opens a file and finds it is still in its cache. It can then use that file provided the server still has a callback promise on the file for that client. The client will have to check with the server if that promise still holds. If so, there is no need to transfer the file from the server to the client again.

This approach is illustrated in Fig. 11-23, which is an extension of Fig. 11-20. When client A starts session S_A, the server records a callback promise. The same happens when B starts session S_B. However, when B closes S_B, the server breaks its promise to callback client A by sending A a callback break. Note that due to the transactional semantics of Coda, when client A closes session S_A, nothing special happens; the closing is simply accepted as one would expect.

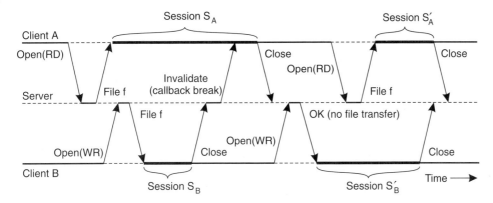

Figure 11-23. The use of local copies when opening a session in Coda.

The consequence is that when A later wants to open session S_A', it will find its local copy of f to be invalid, so that it will have to fetch the latest version from the server. On the other hand, when B opens session S_B', it will notice that the server still has an outstanding callback promise implying that B can simply re-use the local copy it still has from session S_B.

Client-Side Caching for Portable Devices

One important development for many distributed systems is that many storage devices can no longer be assumed to be permanently connected to the system through a network. Instead, users have various types of storage devices that are semi-permanently connected, for example, through cradles or docking stations. Typical examples include PDAs, laptop devices, but also portable multimedia devices such as movie and audio players.

In most cases, an explicit upload/download model is used for maintaining files on portable storage devices. Matters can be simplified if the storage device is viewed as part of a distributed file system. In that case, whenever a file needs to be accessed, it may be fetched from the local device or over the connection to the rest of the system. These two cases need to be distinguished.

Tolia et al. (2004) propose to take a very simple approach by storing locally a cryptographic hash of the data contained in files. These hashes are stored on the portable device and used to redirect requests for associated content. For example, when a directory listing is stored locally, instead of storing the data of each listed file, only the computed has is stored. Then, when a file is fetched, the system will first check whether the file is locally available and up-to-date. Note that a stale file will have a different hash than the one stored in the directory listing. If the file is locally available, it can be returned to the client, otherwise a data transfer will need to take place.

Obviously, when a device is disconnected it will be impossible to transfer any data. Various techniques exist to ensure with high probability that likely to-be-used files are indeed stored locally on the device. Compared to the on-demand data transfer approach inherent to most caching schemes, in these cases we would need to deploy file-prefetching techniques. However, for many portable storage devices, we can expect that the user will use special programs to pre-install files on the device.

11.6.2 Server-Side Replication

In contrast to client-side caching, server-side replication in distributed file systems is less common. Of course, replication is applied when availability is at stake, but from a performance perspective it makes more sense to deploy caches in which a whole file, or otherwise large parts of it, are made locally available to a client. An important reason why client-side caching is so popular is that practice shows that file sharing is relatively rare. When sharing takes place, it is often only for reading data, in which case caching is an excellent solution.

Another problem with server-side replication for performance is that a combination of a high degree of replication and a low read/write ratio may actually degrade performance. This is easy to understand when realizing that every update operation needs to be carried out at every replica. In other words, for an N-fold replicated file, a single update request will lead to an N-fold increase of update operations. Moreover, concurrent updates need to be synchronized, leading to more communication and further performance reduction.

For these reasons, file servers are generally replicated only for fault tolerance. In the following, we illustrate this type of replication for the Coda file system.

Server Replication in Coda

Coda allows file servers to be replicated. As we mentioned, the unit of replication is a collection of files called a **volume**. In essence, a volume corresponds to a UNIX disk partition, that is, a traditional file system like the ones directly supported by operating systems, although volumes are generally much smaller. The collection of Coda servers that have a copy of a volume, are known as that volume's **Volume Storage Group**, or simply **VSG**. In the presence of failures, a client may not have access to all servers in a volume's VSG. A client's **Accessible Volume Storage Group** (**AVSG**) for a volume consists of those servers in that volume's VSG that the client can contact at the moment. If the AVSG is empty, the client is said to be **disconnected**.

Coda uses a replicated-write protocol to maintain consistency of a replicated volume. In particular, it uses a variant of Read-One, Write-All (ROWA), which was explained in Chap. 7. When a client needs to read a file, it contacts one of the members in its AVSG of the volume to which that file belongs. However, when closing a session on an updated file, the client transfers it in parallel to each member in the AVSG. This parallel transfer is accomplished by means of MultiRPC as explained before.

This scheme works fine as long as there are no failures, that is, for each client, that client's AVSG of a volume is the same as its VSG. However, in the presence of failures, things may go wrong. Consider a volume that is replicated across three servers S_1, S_2, and S_3. For client A, assume its AVSG covers servers S_1 and S_2 whereas client B has access only to server S_3, as shown in Fig. 11-24.

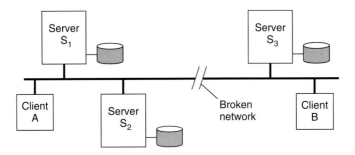

Figure 11-24. Two clients with a different AVSG for the same replicated file.

Coda uses an optimistic strategy for file replication. In particular, both A and B will be allowed to open a file, f, for writing, update their respective copies, and transfer their copy back to the members in their AVSG. Obviously, there will be different versions of f stored in the VSG. The question is how this inconsistency can be detected and resolved.

The solution adopted by Coda is deploying a versioning scheme. In particular, a server S_i in a VSG maintains a **Coda version vector** $CVV_i(f)$ for each file f contained in that VSG. If $CVV_i(f)[j] = k$, thenserver S_i knows that server S_j has seen at least version k of file f. $CVV_i(f)[i]$ is the number of the current version of f stored at server S_i. An update of f at server S_i will lead to an increment of $CVV_i(f)[i]$. Note that version vectors are completely analogous to the vector timestamps discussed in Chap. 6.

Returning to our three-server example, $CVV_i(f)$ is initially equal to $[1,1,1]$ for each server S_i. When client A reads f from one of the servers in its AVSG, say S_1, it also receives $CVV_1(f)$. After updating f, client A multicasts f to each server in its AVSG, that is, S_1 and S_2. Both servers will then record that their respective copy has been updated, but not that of S_3. In other words,

$$CVV_1(f) = CVV_2(f) = [2,2,1]$$

Meanwhile, client B will be allowed to open a session in which it receives a copy of f from server S_3, and subsequently update f as well. When closing its session and transferring the update to S_3, server S_3 will update its version vector to $CVV_3(f)=[1,1,2]$.

When the partition is healed, the three servers will need to reintegrate their copies of f. By comparing their version vectors, they will notice that a conflict has occurred that needs to be repaired. In many cases, conflict resolution can be automated in an application-dependent way, as discussed in Kumar and Satyanarayanan (1995). However, there are also many cases in which users will have to assist in resolving a conflict manually, especially when different users have changed the same part of the same file in different ways.

11.6.3 Replication in Peer-to-Peer File Systems

Let us now examine replication in peer-to-peer file-sharing systems. Here, replication also plays an important role, notably for speeding up search and lookup requests, but also to balance load between nodes. An important property in these systems is that virtually all files are read only. Updates consist only in the form of adding files to the system. A distinction should be made between unstructured and structured peer-to-peer systems.

Unstructured Peer-to-Peer Systems

Fundamental to unstructured peer-to-peer systems is that looking up data boils down to *searching* that data in the network. Effectively, this means that a node will simply have to, for example, broadcast a search query to its neighbors, from where the query may be forwarded, and so on. Obviously, searching through broadcasting is generally not a good idea, and special measures need to be taken to avoid performance problems. Searching in peer-to-peer systems is discussed extensively in Risson and Moors (2006).

Independent of the way broadcasting is limited, it should be clear that if files are replicated, searching becomes easier and faster. One extreme is to replicate a file at all nodes, which would imply that searching for any file can be done entirely local. However, given that nodes have a limited capacity, full replication is out of the question. The problem is then to find an optimal replication strategy, where optimality is defined by the number of different nodes that need to process a specific query before a file is found.

Cohen and Shenker (2002) have examined this problem, assuming that file replication can be controlled. In other words, assuming that nodes in an unstructured peer-to-peer system can be instructed to hold copies of files, what is then the best allocation of file copies to nodes?

Let us consider two extremes. One policy is to uniformly distribute n copies of each file across the entire network. This policy ignores that different files may have different request rates, that is, that some files are more popular than others. As an alternative, another policy is to replicate files according to how often they are searched for: the more popular a file is, the more replicas we create and distribute across the overlay.

As a side remark, note that this last policy may make it very expensive to locate unpopular files. Strange as this may seem, such searches may prove to be increasingly important from an economic point of view. The reasoning is simple: with the Internet allowing fast and easy access to tons of information, exploiting niche markets suddenly becomes attractive. So, if you are interested in getting the right equipment for, let's say a recumbent bicycle, the Internet is the place to go to provided its search facilities will allow you to efficiently discover the appropriate seller.

Quite surprisingly, it turns out that the uniform and the popular policy perform just as good when looking at the average number of nodes that need to be queried. The distribution of queries is the same in both cases, and such that the distribution of documents in the popular policy follows the distribution of queries. Moreover, it turns out that any allocation "between" these two is better. Obtaining such an allocation is doable, but not trivial.

Replication in unstructured peer-to-peer systems happens naturally when users download files from others and subsequently make them available to the community. Controlling these networks is very difficult in practice, except when parts are controlled by a single organization. Moreover, as indicated by studies conducted on BitTorrent, there is also an important social factor when it comes to replicating files and making them available (Pouwelse et al., 2005). For example, some people show altruistic behavior, or simply continue to make files no longer available than strictly necessary after they have completed their download. The question comes to mind whether systems can be devised that exploit this behavior.

Structured Peer-to-Peer Systems

Considering the efficiency of lookup operations in structured peer-to-peer systems, replication is primarily deployed to balance the load between the nodes. We already encountered in Chap. 5 how a "structured" form of replication, as exploited by Ramasubramanian and Sirer (2004b) could even reduce the average lookup steps to $O(1)$. However, when it comes to load balancing, different approaches need to be explored.

One commonly applied method is to simply replicate a file along the path that a query has followed from source to destination. This replication policy will have the effect that most replicas will be placed close to the node responsible for storing the file, and will thus indeed offload that node when there is a high request rate. However, such a replication policy does not take the load of other nodes into account, and may thus easily lead to an imbalanced system.

To address these problems, Gopalakrishnan et al. (2004) propose a different scheme that takes the current load of nodes along the query route into account. The principal idea is to store replicas at the source node of a query, and to cache pointers to such replicas in nodes along the query route from source to destination. More specifically, when a query from node P to Q is routed through node R, R will check whether any of *its* files should be offloaded to P. It does so by simply looking at its own query load. If R is serving too many lookup requests for files it is currently storing in comparison to the load imposed on P, it can ask P to install copies of R's most requested files. This principle is sketched in Fig. 11-25.

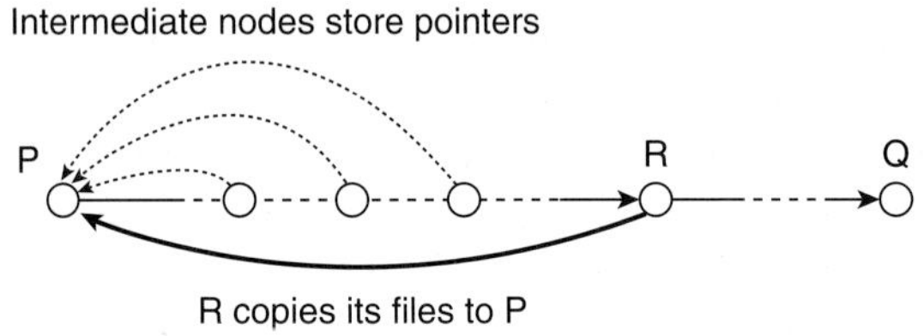

Figure 11-25. Balancing load in a peer-to-peer system by replication.

If P can accept file f from R, each node visited on the route from P to R will install a pointer for f to P, indicating that a replica of f can be found at P.

Clearly, disseminating information on where replicas are stored is important for this scheme to work. Therefore, when routing a query through the overlay, a node may also pass on information concerning the replicas it is hosting. This information may then lead to further installment of pointers, allowing nodes to take informed decisions of redirecting requests to nodes that hold a replica of a requested file. These pointers are placed in a limited-size cache and are replaced following a simple least-recently used policy (i.e., cached pointers referring to files that are never asked for, will be removed quickly).

11.6.4 File Replication in Grid Systems

As our last subject concerning replication of files, let us consider what happens in Grid computing. Naturally, performance plays a crucial role in this area as many Grid applications are highly compute-intensive. In addition, we see that applications often also need to process vast amounts of data. As a result, much effort has been put into replicating files to where applications are being executed. The means to do so, however, are (somewhat) surprisingly simple.

A key observation is that in many Grid applications data are read only. Data are often produced from sensors, or from other applications, but rarely updated or otherwise modified after they are produced and stored. As a result, data replication can be applied in abundance, and this is exactly what happens.

Unfortunately, the size of the data sets are sometimes so enormous that special measures need to be taken to avoid that data providers (i.e., those machine storing data sets) become overloaded due to the amount of data they need to transfer over the network. On the other hand, because much of the data is heavily replicated, balancing the load for retrieving copies is less of an issue.

Replication in Grid systems mainly evolves around the problem of locating the best sources to copy data from. This problem can be solved by special **replica location services**, very similar to the location services we discussed for naming systems. One obvious approach that has been developed for the Globus toolkit is to use a DHT-based system such as Chord for decentralized lookup of replicas (Cai et al., 2004). In this case, a client passes a file name to any node of the service, where it is converted to a key and subsequently looked up. The information returned to the client contains contact addresses for the requested files.

To keep matters simple, located files are subsequently downloaded from various sites using an FTP-like protocol, after which the client can register its own replicas with the replication location service. This architecture is described in more detail in Chervenak et al. (2005), but the approach is fairly straightforward.

11.7 FAULT TOLERANCE

Fault tolerance in distributed file systems is handled according to the principles we discussed in Chap. 8. As we already mentioned, in many cases, replication is deployed to create fault-tolerant server groups. In this section, we will therefore concentrate on some special issues in fault tolerance for distributed file systems.

11.7.1 Handling Byzantine Failures

One of the problems that is often ignored when dealing with fault tolerance is that servers may exhibit arbitrary failures. In other words, most systems do not consider the Byzantine failures we discussed in Chap. 8. Besides complexity, the reason for ignoring these type of failures has to do with the strong assumptions that need to be made regarding the execution environment. Notably, it must be assumed that communication delays are bounded.

In practical settings, such an assumption is not realistic. For this reason, Castro and Liskov (2002) have devised a solution for handling Byzantine failures that can also operate in networks such as the Internet. We discuss this protocol here, as it can (and has been) directly applied to distributed file systems, notably an NFS-based system. Of course, there are other applications as well. The basic idea is to deploy active replication by constructing a collection of finite state machines and to have the nonfaulty processes in this collection execute operations in the same order. Assuming that at most k processes fail at once, a client sends an operation to the entire group and accepts an answer that is returned by at least $k + 1$ different processes.

To achieve protection against Byzantine failures, the server group must consist of at least $3k + 1$ processes. The difficult part in achieving this protection is to ensure that nonfaulty processes execute all operations in the same order. A simple means to achieve this goal is to assign a coordinator that simply serializes all operations by attaching a sequence number to each request. The problem, of course, is that the coordinator may fail.

It is with failing coordinators that the problems start. Very much like with virtual synchrony, processes go through a series of views, where in each view the members agree on the nonfaulty processes, and initiate a view change when the current master appears to be failing. This latter can be detected if we assume that sequence numbers are handed out one after the other, so that a gap, or a timeout for an operation may indicate that something is wrong. Note that processes may falsely conclude that a new view needs to be installed. However, this will not affect the correctness of the system.

An important part of the protocol relies on the fact that requests can be correctly ordered. To this end, a quorum mechanism is used: whenever a process receives a request to execute operation o with number n in view v, it sends this to all other processes, and waits until it has received a confirmation from at least $2k$ others that have seen the same request. In this way, we obtain a quorum of size $2k + 1$ for the request. Such a confirmation is called a **quorum certificate**. In essence, it tells us that a sufficiently large number of processes have stored the same request and that it is thus safe to proceed.

The whole protocol consists of five phases, shown in Fig. 11-26.

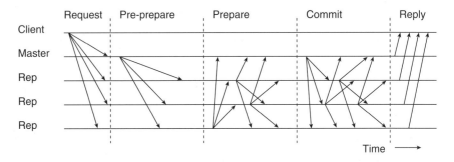

Figure 11-26. The different phases in Byzantine fault tolerance.

During the first phase, a client sends a request to the entire server group. Once the master has received the request, it multicasts a sequence number in a *pre-prepare phase* so that the associated operation will be properly ordered. At that point, the slave replicas need to ensure that the master's sequence number is accepted by a quorum, provided that each of them accepts the master's proposal. Therefore, if a slave accepts the proposed sequence number, it multicasts this acceptance to the others. During the *commit* phase, agreement has been reached and all processes inform each other and execute the operation, after which the client can finally see the result.

When considering the various phases, it may seem that after the *prepare* phase, all processes should have agreed on the same ordering of requests. However, this is true only within the same view: if there was a need to change to a new view, different processes may have the same sequence number for different operations, but which were assigned in different views. For this reason, we need the *commit* phase as well, in which each process now tells the others that it has stored the request in its local log, and for the current view. As a consequence, even if there is a need to recover from a crash, a process will know exactly which sequence number had been assigned, and during which view.

Again, a committed operation can be executed as soon as a nonfaulty process has seen the same $2k$ commit messages (and they should match its own intentions). Again, we now have a quorum of $2k + 1$ for executing the operation. Of course, pending operations with lower sequence numbers should be executed first.

Changing to a new view essentially follows the view changes for virtual synchrony as described in Chap. 8. In this case, a process needs to send information on the pre-prepared messages that it knows of, as well as the received prepared messages from the previous view. We will skip further details here.

The protocol has been implemented for an NFS-based file system, along with various important optimizations and carefully crafted data structures, of which the details can be found in Castro and Liskov (2002). A description of a wrapper that will allow the incorporation of Byzantine fault tolerance with legacy applications can be found in Castro et al. (2003).

11.7.2 High Availability in Peer-to-Peer Systems

An issue that has received special attention is ensuring availability in peer-to-peer systems. On the one hand, it would seem that by simply replicating files, availability is easy to guarantee. The problem, however, is that the unavailability of nodes is so high that this simple reasoning no longer holds. As we explained in Chap. 8, the key solution to high availability is redundancy. When it comes to files, there are essentially two different methods to realize redundancy: replication and erasure coding.

Erasure coding is a well-known technique by which a file is partitioned into m fragments which are subsequently recoded into $n > m$ fragments. The crucial issue in this coding scheme is that any set of m encoded fragments is sufficient to reconstruct the original file. In this case, the redundancy factor is equal to $r_{ec}=n/m$. Assuming an average node availability of a, and a required file unavailability of ε, we need to guarantee that at least m fragments are available, that is:

$$1 - \varepsilon = \sum_{i=m}^{n} \begin{bmatrix} n \\ i \end{bmatrix} a^i (1-a)^{n-i}$$

If we compare this to replicating files, we see that file unavailability is completely dictated by the probability that all its r_{rep} replicas are unavailable. If we assume that node departures are independent and identically distributed, we have

$$1 - \varepsilon = 1 - (1 - a)^{r_{rep}}$$

Applying some algebraic manipulations and approximations, we can express the difference between replication and erasure coding by considering the ratio r_{rep}/r_{ec} in its relation to the availability a of nodes. This relation is shown in Fig. 11-27, for which we have set $m = 5$ [see also Bhagwan et al. (2004) and Rodrigues and Liskov (2005)].

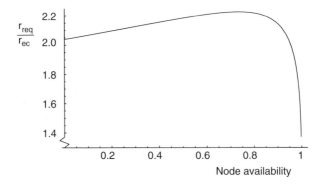

Figure 11-27. The ratio r_{rep}/r_{ec} as a function of node availability a.

What we see from this figure is that under all circumstances, erasure coding requires less redundancy than simply replicating files. In other words, replicating files for increasing availability in peer-to-peer networks in which nodes regularly come and go is less efficient from a storage perspective than using erasure coding techniques.

One may argue that these savings in storage are not really an issue anymore as disk capacity is often overwhelming. However, when realizing that maintaining redundancy will impose communication, then lower redundancy is going to save bandwidth usage. This performance gain is notably important when the nodes correspond to user machines connected to the Internet through asymmetric DSL or cable lines, where outgoing links often have a capacity of only a few hundred Kbps.

11.8 SECURITY

Many of the security principles that we discussed in Chap. 9 are directly applied to distributed file systems. Security in distributed file systems organized along a client-server architecture is to have the servers handle authentication and access control. This is a straightforward way of dealing with security, an approach that has been adopted, for example, in systems such as NFS.

In such cases, it is common to have a separate authentication service, such as Kerberos, while the file servers simply handle authorization. A major drawback of this scheme is that it requires centralized administration of users, which may severely hinder scalability. In the following, we first briefly discuss security in NFS as an example of the traditional approach, after which we pay attention to alternative approaches.

11.8.1 Security in NFS

As we mentioned before, the basic idea behind NFS is that a remote file system should be presented to clients as if it were a local file system. In this light, it should come as no surprise that security in NFS mainly focuses on the communication between a client and a server. Secure communication means that a secure channel between the two should be set up as we discussed in Chap. 9.

In addition to secure RPCs, it is necessary to control file accesses. which are handled by means of access control file attributes in NFS. A file server is in charge of verifying the access rights of its clients, as we will explain below. Combined with secure RPCs, the NFS security architecture is shown in Fig. 11-28.

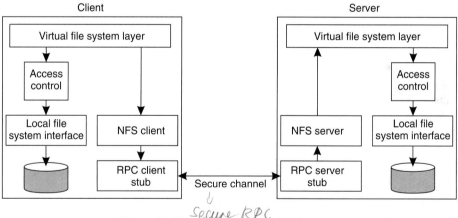

Figure 11-28. The NFS security architecture.

Secure RPCs

Because NFS is layered on top of an RPC system, setting up a secure channel in NFS boils down to establishing secure RPCs. Up until NFSv4, a secure RPC meant that only authentication was taken care of. There were three ways for doing authentication. We will now examine each one in turn.

The most widely-used method, one that actually hardly does any authentication, is known as system authentication. In this UNIX-based method, a client simply passes its effective user ID and group ID to the server, along with a list of groups it claims to be a member of. This information is sent to the server as unsigned plaintext. In other words, the server has no way at all of verifying whether the claimed user and group identifiers are actually associated with the sender. In essence, the server assumes that the client has passed a proper login procedure, and that it can trust the client's machine.

The second authentication method in older NFS versions uses Diffie-Hellman key exchange to establish a session key, leading to what is called **secure NFS**. We explained how Diffie-Hellman key exchange works in Chap. 9. This approach is much better than system authentication, but is more complex, for which reason it is implemented less frequently. Diffie-Hellman can be viewed as a public-key cryptosystem. Initially, there was no way to securely distribute a server's public key, but this was later corrected with the introduction of a secure name service. A point of criticism has always been the use of relatively small public keys, which are only 192 bits in NFS. It has been shown that breaking a Diffie-Hellman system with such short keys is nearly trivial (Lamacchia and Odlyzko, 1991).

The third authentication protocol is Kerberos, which we also described in Chap. 9.

With the introduction of NFSv4, security is enhanced by the support for RPCSEC_GSS. **RPCSEC_GSS** is a general security framework that can support a myriad of security mechanism for setting up secure channels (Eisler et al., 1997). In particular, it not only provides the hooks for different authentication systems, but also supports message integrity and confidentiality, two features that were not supported in older versions of NFS.

RPCSEC_GSS is based on a standard interface for security services, namely **GSS-API**, which is fully described in Linn (1997). The RPCSEC_GSS is layered on top of this interface, leading to the organization shown in Fig. 11-29.

For NFSv4, RPCSEC_GSS should be configured with support for Kerberos V5. In addition, the system must also support a method known as **LIPKEY**, described in Eisler (2000). LIPKEY is a public-key system that allows clients to be authenticated using a password while servers can be authenticated using a public key.

The important aspect of secure RPC in NFS is that the designers have chosen not to provide their own security mechanisms, but only to provide a standard way for handling security. As a consequence, proven security mechanisms, such as Kerberos, can be incorporated into an NFS implementation without affecting other parts of the system. Also, if an existing security mechanisms turns out to be flawed (such as in the case of Diffie-Hellman when using small keys), it can easily be replaced.

It should be noted that because RPCSEC_GSS is implemented as part of the RPC layer that underlies the NFS protocols, it can also be used for older versions

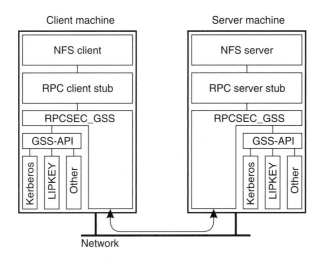

Figure 11-29. Secure RPC in NFSv4.

of NFS. However, this adaptation to the RPC layer became available only with the introduction of NFSv4.

Access Control

Authorization in NFS is analogous to secure RPC: it provides the mechanisms but does not specify any particular policy. Access control is supported by means of the *ACL* file attribute. This attribute is a list of access control entries, where each entry specifies the access rights for a specific user or group. Many of the operations that NFS distinguishes with respect to access control are relatively straightforward and include those for reading, writing, and executing files, manipulating file attributes, listing directories, and so on.

Noteworthy is also the synchronize operation that essentially tells whether a process that is colocated with a server can directly access a file, bypassing the NFS protocol for improved performance. The NFS model for access control has much richer semantics than most UNIX models. This difference comes from the requirements that NFS should be able to interoperate with Windows systems. The underlying thought is that it is much easier to fit the UNIX model of access control to that of Windows, then the other way around.

Another aspect that makes access control different from file systems such as in UNIX, is that access can be specified for different users and different groups. Traditionally, access to a file is specified for a single user (the owner of the file), a single group of users (e.g., members of a project team), and for everyone else. NFS has many different kinds of users and processes, as shown in Fig. 11-30.

Type of user	Description
Owner	The owner of a file
Group	The group of users associated with a file
Everyone	Any user or process
Interactive	Any process accessing the file from an interactive terminal
Network	Any process accessing the file via the network
Dialup	Any process accessing the file through a dialup connection to the server
Batch	Any process accessing the file as part of batch job
Anonymous	Anyone accessing the file without authentication
Authenticated	Any authenticated user or process
Service	Any system-defined service process

Figure 11-30. The various kinds of users and processes distinguished by NFS with respect to access control.

11.8.2 Decentralized Authentication

One of the main problems with systems such as NFS is that in order to properly handle authentication, it is necessary that users are registered through a central system administration. A solution to this problem is provided by using the **Secure File Systems (SFS)** in combination with decentralized authentication servers. The basic idea, described in full detail in Kaminsky et al. (2003) is quite simple. What other systems lack is the possibility for a user to specify that a *remote* user has certain privileges on his files. In virtually all cases, users must be globally known to all authentication servers. A simpler approach would be to let Alice specify that "Bob, whose details can be found at *X*," has certain privileges. The authentication server that handles Alice's credentials could then contact server *X* to get information on Bob.

An important problem to solve is to have Alice's server know for sure it is dealing with Bob's authentication server. This problem can be solved using self-certifying names, a concept introduced in SFS (Mazières et al., 1999) aimed at separating key management from file-system security. The overall organization of SFS is shown in Fig. 11-31. To ensure portability across a wide range of machines, SFS has been integrated with various NFSv3 components. On the client machine, there are three different components, not counting the user's program. The NFS client is used as an interface to user programs, and exchanges information with an **SFS client**. The latter appears to the NFS client as being just another NFS server.

The SFS client is responsible for setting up a secure channel with an SFS server. It is also responsible for communicating with a locally-available **SFS user agent**, which is a program that automatically handles user authentication. SFS

Client machine   Server machine

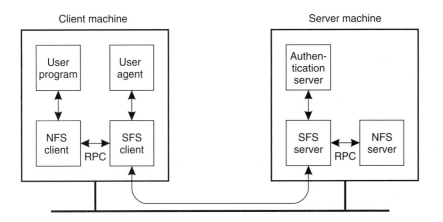

Figure 11-31. The organization of SFS.

does not prescribe how user authentication should take place. In correspondence with its design goals, SFS separates such matters and uses different agents for different user-authentication protocols.

On the server side there are also three components. The NFS server is again used for portability reasons. This server communicates with the **SFS server** which operates as an NFS client to the NFS server. The SFS server forms the core process of SFS. This process is responsible for handling file requests from SFS clients. Analogous to the SFS agent, an SFS server communicates with a separate authentication server to handle user authentication.

What makes SFS unique in comparison to other distributed file systems is its organization of its name space. SFS provides a global name space that is rooted in a directory called */sfs*. An SFS client allows its users to create symbolic links within this name space. More importantly, SFS uses **self-certifying pathnames** to name its files. Such a pathname essentially carries all the information to authenticate the SFS server that is providing the file named by the pathname. A self-certifying pathname consists of three parts, as shown in Fig. 11-32.

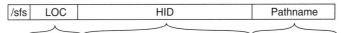

Figure 11-32. A self-certifying pathname in SFS.

The first part of the name consists of a location *LOC*, which is either a DNS domain name identifying the SFS server, or its corresponding IP address. SFS assumes that each server S has a public key K_S^+. The second part of a self-certifying pathname is a host identifier HID that is computed by taking a cryptographic hash H over the server's location and its public key:

$$HID=H(LOC,K_S^+)$$

HID is represented by a 32-digit number in base 32. The third part is formed by the local pathname on the SFS server under which the file is actually stored.

Whenever a client accesses an SFS server, it can authenticate that server by simply asking it for its public key. Using the well-known hash function H, the client can then compute HID and verify it against the value found in the pathname. If the two match, the client knows it is talking to the server bearing the name as found in the location.

How does this approach separate key management from file system security? The problem that SFS solves is that obtaining a server's public key can be completely separated from file system security issues. One approach to getting the server's key is letting a client contact the server and requesting the key as described above. However, it is also possible to locally store a collection of keys, for example by system administrators. In this case, there is no need to contact a server. Instead, when resolving a pathname, the server's key is looked up locally after which the host ID can be verified using the location part of the path name.

To simplify matters, naming transparency can be achieved by using symbolic links. For example, assume a client wants to access a file named

/sfs/sfs.cs.vu.nl:ag62hty4wior450hdh63u62i4f0kqere/home/steen/mbox

To hide the host ID, a user can create a symbolic link

/sfs/vucs → */sfs/sfs.cs.vu.nl:ag62hty4wior450hdh63u62i4f0kqere*

and subsequently use only the pathname */sfs/vucs/home/steen/mbox*. Resolution of that name will automatically expand to the full SFS pathname, and using the public key found locally, authenticate the SFS server named *sfs.vu.cs.nl*.

In a similar fashion, SFS can be supported by certification authorities. Typically, such an authority would maintain links to the SFS servers for which it is acting. As an example, consider an SFS certification authority *CA* that runs the SFS server named

/sfs/sfs.certsfs.com:kty83pad72qmbna9uefdppioq7053jux

Assuming the client has already installed a symbolic link

/certsfs → */sfs/sfs.certsfs.com:kty83pad72qmbna9uefdppioq7053jux*,

the certification authority could use another symbolic link

/vucs → */sfs/sfs.vu.cs.nl:ag62hty4wior450hdh63u62i4f0kqere*

that points to the SFS server *sfs.vu.cs.nl*. In this case, a client can simply refer to

/certsfs/vucs/home/steen/mbox knowing that it is accessing a file server whose public key has been certified by the certification authority *CA*.

Returning to our problem of decentralized authentication, it should now be clear that we have all the mechanisms in place to avoid requiring Bob to be registered at Alice's authentication server. Instead, the latter can simply contact Bob's server provided it is given a name. That name already contains a public key so that Alice's server can verify the identity of Bob's server. After that, Alice's server can accept Bob's privileges as indicated by Alice. As said, the details of this scheme can be found in Kaminsky et al. (2003).

11.8.3 Secure Peer-to-Peer File-Sharing Systems

So far, we have discussed distributed file systems that were relatively easy to secure. Traditional systems either use straightforward authentication and access control mechanisms extended with secure communication, or we can leverage traditional authentication to a completely decentralized scheme. However, matters become complicated when dealing with fully decentralized systems that rely on collaboration, such as in peer-to-peer file-sharing systems.

Secure Lookups in DHT-Based Systems

There are various issues to deal with (Castro et al., 2002a; and Wallach, 2002). Let us consider DHT-based systems. In this case, we need to rely on secure lookup operations, which essentially boil down to a need for secure routing. This means that when a nonfaulty node looks up a key k, its request is indeed forwarded to the node responsible for the data associated with k, or a node storing a copy of that data. Secure routing requires that three issues are dealt with:

1. Nodes are assigned identifiers in a secure way.

2. Routing tables are securely maintained.

3. Lookup requests are securely forwarded between nodes.

When nodes are not securely assigned their identifier, we may face the problem that a malicious node can assign itself an ID so that all lookups for specific keys will be directed to itself, or forwarded along the route that it is part of. This situation becomes more serious when nodes can team up, effectively allowing a group to form a huge "sink" for many lookup requests. Likewise, without secure identifier assignment, a single node may also be able to assign itself *many* identifiers, also known as a **Sybil attack**, creating the same effect (Douceur, 2002).

More general than the Sybil attack is an attack by which a malicious node controls so many of a nonfaulty node's neighbors, that it becomes virtually impossible for correct nodes to operate properly. This phenomenon is also known as an

eclipse attack, and is analyzed in Singh et al. (2006). Defending yourself against such an attack is difficult. One reasonable solution is to constrain the number of incoming edges for each node. In this way, an attacker can have only a limited number of correct nodes pointing to it. To also prevent an attacker from taking over all incoming links to correct nodes, the number of outgoing links should also be constrained [see also Singh et al. (2004)]. Problematic in all these cases is that a centralized authority is needed for handing out node identifiers. Obviously, such an authority goes against the decentralized nature of peer-to-peer systems.

When routing tables can be filled in with alternative nodes, as is often the case when optimizing for network proximity, an attacker can easily convince a node to point to malicious nodes. Note that this problem does not occur when there are strong constraints on filling routing table entries, such as in the case of Chord. The solution, therefore, is to mix choosing alternatives with a more constrained filling of tables [of which details are described in Castro et al. (2002a)].

Finally, to defend against message-forwarding attacks, a node may simply forward messages along several routes. One way to do this is to initiate a lookup from different source nodes.

Secure Collaborative Storage

However, the mere fact that nodes are required to collaborate introduces more problems. For example, collaboration may dictate that nodes should offer about the same amount of storage that they use from others. Enforcing this policy can be quite tricky. One solution is to a apply a secure trading of storage, as for Samsara, as described in Cox and Noble (2003).

The idea is quite simple: when a server P wants to store one of its files f on another server Q, it makes storage available of a size equal to that of f, and reserves that space exclusively for Q. In other words, Q now has an outstanding **claim** at A, as shown in Fig. 11-33.

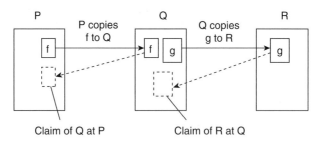

Figure 11-33. The principle of storage claims in the Samsara peer-to-peer system.

To make this scheme work, each participant reserves an amount of storage and divides that into equal-sized chunks. Each chunk consists of incompressible data. In Samsara, chunk c_i consists of a 160-bit hash value h_i computed over a secret passphrase W concatenated with the number i. Now assume that claims are handed out in units of 256 bytes. In that case, the first claim is computed by taking the first 12 chunks along with the first 16 bytes of next chunk. These chunks are concatenated and encrypted using a private key K. In general, claim C_j is computed as

$$C_j = K(h_k, h_{k+1}, \dots, h_{k+11}, h_{k+12}[0], \dots, h_{k+12}[15])$$

where $k=j\times13$. Whenever P wants to make use of storage at Q, Q returns a collection of claims that P is now forced to store. Of course, Q need never store its own claims. Instead, it can compute when needed.

The trick now is that once in a while, Q may want to check whether P is still storing its claims. If P cannot prove that it is doing so, Q can simply discard P's data. One blunt way of letting P prove it still has the claims is returning copies to Q. Obviously, this will waste a lot of bandwidth. Assume that Q had handed out claims $C_{j_1}, \dots, C_{j_k}$ to P. In that case, Q passes a 160-bit string d to P, and requests it to compute the 160-bit hash d_1 of d concatenated with C_{j_1}. This hash is then to be concatenated with C_{j_2}, producing a hash value d_2, and so on. In the end, P need only return d_n to prove it still holds all the claims.

Of course, Q may also want to replicate its files to another node, say R. In doing so, it will have to hold claims for R. However, if Q is running out of storage, but has claimed storage at P, it may decide to pass those claims to R instead. This principle works as follows.

Assume that P is holding a claim C_Q for Q, and Q is supposed to hold a claim C_R for R. Because there is no restriction on what Q can store at P, Q might as well decide to store C_R at P. Then, whenever R wants to check whether Q is still holding its claim, Q will pass a value d to Q and request it to compute the hash of d concatenated with C_R. To do so, Q simply passes d on to P, requests P to compute the hash, and returns the result to R. If it turns out that P is no longer holding the claim, Q will be punished by R, and Q, in turn, can punish P by removing stored data.

11.9 SUMMARY

Distributed file systems form an important paradigm for building distributed systems. They are generally organized according to the client-server model, with client-side caching and support for server replication to meet scalability requirements. In addition, caching and replication are needed to achieve high availability. More recently, symmetric architectures such as those in peer-to-peer file-sharing systems have emerged. In these cases, an important issue is whether whole files or data blocks are distributed.

Instead of building a distributed file system directly on top of the transport layer it is common practice to assume the existence of an RPC layer, so that all operations can be simply expressed as RPCs to a file server instead of having to use primitive message-passing operations. Some variants of RPC have been developed, such as the MultiRPC provided in Coda, which allows a number of servers to be called in parallel.

What makes distributed file systems different from nondistributed file systems is the semantics of sharing files. Ideally, a file system allows a client to always read the data that have most recently been written to a file. These UNIX file-sharing semantics are very hard to implement efficiently in a distributed system. NFS supports a weaker form known as session semantics, by which the final version of a file is determined by the last client that closes a file, which it had previously opened for writing. In Coda, file sharing adheres to transactional semantics in the sense that reading clients will only get to see the most recent updates if they reopen a file. Transactional semantics in Coda do not cover all the ACID properties of regular transactions. In the case that a file server stays in control of all operations, actual UNIX semantics can be provided, although scalability is then an issue. In all cases, it is necessary to allow concurrent updates on files, which brings relatively intricate locking and reservation schemes into play.

To achieve acceptable performance, distributed file systems generally allow clients to cache an entire file. This whole-file caching approach is supported, for example, in NFS, although it is also possible to store only very large chunks of a file. Once a file has been opened and (partly) transferred to the client, all operations are carried out locally. Updates are flushed to the server when the file is closed again.

Replication also plays an important role in peer-to-peer systems, although matters are strongly simplified because files are generally read-only. More important in these systems is trying to reach acceptable load balance, as naive replication schemes can easily lead to hot spots holding many files and thus become potential bottlenecks.

Fault tolerance is usually dealt with using traditional methods. However, it is also possible to build file systems that can deal with Byzantine failures, even when the system as a whole is running on the Internet. In this case, by assuming reasonable timeouts and initiating new server groups (possibly based on false failure detection), practical solutions can be built. Notably for distributed file systems, one should consider to apply erasure coding techniques to reduce the overall replication factor when aiming for only high availability.

Security is of paramount importance for any distributed system, including file systems. NFS hardly provides any security mechanisms itself, but instead implements standardized interfaces that allow different existing security systems to be used, such as, for example Kerberos. SFS is different in the sense it allows file names to include information on the file server's public key. This approach simplifies key management in large-scale systems. In effect, SFS distributes a key by including it in the name of a file. SFS can be used to implement a decentralized authentication scheme. Achieving security in peer-to-peer file-sharing systems is difficult, partly because of the assumed collaborative nature in which nodes will always tend to act selfish. Also, making lookups secure turns out to be a difficult problem that actually requires a central authority for handing out node identifiers.

PROBLEMS

1. Is a file server implementing NFS version 3 required to be stateless?

2. Explain whether or not NFS is to be considered a distributed file system.

3. Despite that GFS scales well, it could be argued that the master is still a potential bottleneck. What would be a reasonable alternative to replace it?

4. Using RPC2's side effects is convenient for continuous data streams. Give another example in which it makes sense to use an application-specific protocol next to RPC.

5. NFS does not provide a global, shared name space. Is there a way to mimic such a name space?

6. Give a simple extension to the NFS lookup operation that would allow iterative name lookup in combination with a server exporting directories that it mounted from another server.

7. In UNIX-based operating systems, opening a file using a file handle can be done only in the kernel. Give a possible implementation of an NFS file handle for a user-level NFS server for a UNIX system.

8. Using an automounter that installs symbolic links as described in the text makes it harder to hide the fact that mounting is transparent. Why?

9. Suppose that the current denial state of a file in NFS is *WRITE*. Is it possible that another client can first successfully open that file and then request a write lock?

10. Taking into account cache coherence as discussed in Chap. 7, which kind of cache-coherence protocol does NFS implement?

11. Does NFS implement entry consistency?

12. We stated that NFS implements the remote access model to file handling. It can be argued that it also supports the upload/download model. Explain why.

13. In NFS, attributes are cached using a write-through cache coherence policy. Is it necessary to forward all attributes changes immediately?

14. What calling semantics does RPC2 provide in the presence of failures?

15. Explain how Coda solves read-write conflicts on a file that is shared between multiple readers and only a single writer.

16. Using self-certifying path names, is a client always ensured it is communicating with a nonmalicious server?

17. (**Lab assignment**) One of the easiest ways for building a UNIX-based distributed system, is to couple a number of machines by means of NFS. For this assignment, you are to connect two file systems on different computers by means of NFS. In particular, install an NFS server on one machine such that various parts of its file system are automatically mounted when the first machine boots.

18. (**Lab assignment**) To integrate UNIX-based machines with Windows clients, one can make use of Samba servers. Extend the previous assignment by making a UNIX-based system available to a Windows client, by installing and configuring a Samba server. At the same time, the file system should remain accessible through NFS.

12

DISTRIBUTED
WEB-BASED SYSTEMS

The World Wide Web (**WWW**) can be viewed as a huge distributed system consisting of millions of clients and servers for accessing linked documents. Servers maintain collections of documents, while clients provide users an easy-to-use interface for presenting and accessing those documents.

The Web started as a project at CERN, the European Particle Physics Laboratory in Geneva, to let its large and geographically dispersed group of researchers access shared documents using a simple hypertext system. A document could be anything that could be displayed on a user's computer terminal, such as personal notes, reports, figures, blueprints, drawings, and so on. By linking documents to each other, it became easy to integrate documents from different projects into a new document without the necessity for centralized changes. The only thing needed was to construct a document providing links to other relevant documents [see also Berners-Lee et al. (1994)].

The Web gradually grew slowly to sites other than high-energy physics, but popularity sharply increased when graphical user interfaces became available, notably Mosaic (Vetter et al., 1994). Mosaic provided an easy-to-use interface to present and access documents by merely clicking a mouse button. A document was fetched from a server, transferred to a client, and presented on the screen. To a user, there was conceptually no difference between a document stored locally or in another part of the world. In this sense, distribution was transparent.

Since 1994, Web developments have been initiated by the World Wide Web Consortium, a collaboration between CERN and M.I.T. This consortium is responsible for standardizing protocols, improving interoperability, and further enhancing the capabilities of the Web. In addition, we see many new developments take place outside this consortium, not always leading to the compability one would hope for. By now, the Web is more than just a simple document-based system. Notably with the introduction of Web services we are seeing a huge distributed system emerging in which **services** rather than just documents are being used, composed, and offered to any user or machine that can find use of them.

In this chapter we will take a closer look at this rapidly growing and pervasive system. Considering that the Web itself is so young and that so much as changed in such a short time, our description can only be a snapshot of its current state. However, as we shall see, many concepts underlying Web technology are based on the principles discussed in the first part of this book. Also, we will see that for many concepts, there is still much room for improvement.

12.1 ARCHITECTURE

The architecture of Web-based distributed systems is not fundamentally different from other distributed systems. However, it is interesting to see how the initial idea of supporting distributed documents has evolved since its inception in 1990s. Documents turned from being purely static and passive to dynamically generated containing all kinds of active elements. Furthermore, in recent years, many organizations have begun supporting services instead of just documents. In the following, we discuss the architectural impacts of these shifts.

12.1.1 Traditional Web-Based Systems

Unlike many of the distributed systems we have been discussing so far, Web-based distributed systems are relatively new. In this sense, it is somewhat difficult to talk about traditional Web-based systems, although there is a clear distinction between the systems that were available at the beginning and those that are used today.

Many Web-based systems are still organized as relatively simple client-server architectures. The core of a Web site is formed by a process that has access to a local file system storing documents. The simplest way to refer to a document is by means of a reference called a **Uniform Resource Locator** (**URL**). It specifies where a document is located, often by embedding the DNS name of its associated server along with a file name by which the server can look up the document in its local file system. Furthermore, a URL specifies the application-level protocol for transferring the document across the network. There are several different protocols available, as we explain below.

A client interacts with Web servers through a special application known as a **browser**. A browser is responsible for properly displaying a document. Also, a browser accepts input from a user mostly by letting the user select a reference to another document, which it then subsequently fetches and displays. The communication between a browser and Web server is standardized: they both adhere to the **HyperText Transfer Protocol** (**HTTP**) which we will discuss below. This leads to the overall organization shown in Fig. 12-1.

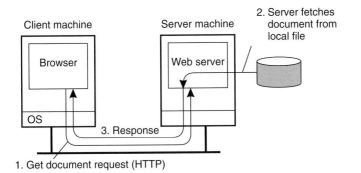

Figure 12-1. The overall organization of a traditional Web site.

The Web has evolved considerably since its introduction. By now, there is a wealth of methods and tools to produce information that can be processed by Web clients and Web servers. In the following, we will go into detail on how the Web acts as a distributed system. However, we skip most of the methods and tools used to construct Web documents, as they often have no direct relationship to the distributed nature of the Web. A good introduction on how to build Web-based applications can be found in Sebesta (2006).

Web Documents

Fundamental to the Web is that virtually all information comes in the form of a document. The concept of a document is to be taken in its broadest sense: not only can it contain plain text, but a document may also include all kinds of dynamic features such as audio, video, animations and so on. In many cases, special helper applications are needed to make a document "come to life." Such interpreters will typically be integrated with a user's browser.

Most documents can be roughly divided into two parts: a main part that at the very least acts as a template for the second part, which consists of many different bits and pieces that jointly constitute the document that is displayed in a browser. The main part is generally written in a **markup language**, very similar to the type of languages that are used in word-processing systems. The most widely-used markup language in the Web is **HTML**, which is an acronym for **HyperText**

Markup Language. As its name suggests, HTML allows the embedding of links to other documents. When activating such links in a browser, the referenced document will be fetched from its associated server.

Another, increasingly important markup language is the **Extensible Markup Language** (**XML**) which, as its name suggests, provides much more flexibility in defining what a document should look like. The major difference between HTML and XML is that the latter includes the definitions of the elements that mark up a document. In other words, it is a meta-markup language. This approach provides a lot of flexibility when it comes to specifying exactly what a document looks like: there is no need to stick to a single model as dictated by a fixed markup language such as HTML.

HTML and XML can also include all kinds of tags that refer to **embedded documents**, that is, references to files that should be included to make a document complete. It can be argued that the embedded documents turn a Web document into something active. Especially when considering that an embedded document can be a complete program that is executed on-the-fly as part of displaying information, it is not hard to imagine the kind of things that can be done.

Embedded documents come in all sorts and flavors. This immediately raises an issue how browsers can be equipped to handle the different file formats and ways to interpret embedded documents. Essentially, we need only two things: a way of specifying the type of an embedded document, and a way of allowing a browser to handle data of a specific type.

Each (embedded) document has an associated **MIME type**. MIME stands for **Multipurpose Internet Mail Exchange** and, as its name suggests, was originally developed to provide information on the content of a message body that was sent as part of electronic mail. MIME distinguishes various types of message contents. These types are also used in the WWW, but it is noted that standardization is difficult with new data formats showing up almost daily.

MIME makes a distinction between top-level types and subtypes. Some common top-level types are shown in Fig. 12-2 and include types for text, image, audio, and video. There is a special *application* type that indicates that the document contains data that are related to a specific application. In practice, only that application will be able to transform the document into something that can be understood by a human.

The *multipart* type is used for composite documents, that is, documents that consists of several parts where each part will again have its own associated top-level type.

For each top-level type, there may be several subtypes available, of which some are also shown in Fig. 12-2. The type of a document is then represented as a combination of top-level type and subtype, such as, for example, *application/PDF*. In this case, it is expected that a separate application is needed for processing the document, which is represented in PDF. Many subtypes are experimental, meaning that a special format is used requiring its own application at the

Type	Subtype	Description
Text	Plain	Unformatted text
	HTML	Text including HTML markup commands
	XML	Text including XML markup commands
Image	GIF	Still image in GIF format
	JPEG	Still image in JPEG format
Audio	Basic	Audio, 8-bit PCM sampled at 8000 Hz
	Tone	A specific audible tone
Video	MPEG	Movie in MPEG format
	Pointer	Representation of a pointer device for presentations
Application	Octet-stream	An uninterpreted byte sequence
	Postscript	A printable document in Postscript
	PDF	A printable document in PDF
Multipart	Mixed	Independent parts in the specified order
	Parallel	Parts must be viewed simultaneously

Figure 12-2. Six top-level MIME types and some common subtypes.

user's side. In practice, it is the Web server who will provide this application, either as a separate program that will run aside a browser, or as a so-called **plug-in** that can be installed as part of the browser.

This (changing) variety of document types forces browsers to be extensible. To this end, some standardization has taken place to allow plug-ins adhering to certain interfaces to be easily integrated in a browser. When certain types become popular enough, they are often shipped with browsers or their updates. We return to this issue below when discussing client-side software.

Multitiered Architectures

The combination of HTML (or any other markup language such as XML) with scripting provides a powerful means for expressing documents. However, we have hardly discussed where documents are actually processed, and what kind of processing takes place. The WWW started out as the relatively simple two-tiered client-server system shown previously in Fig. 12-1. By now, this simple architecture has been extended with numerous components to support the advanced type of documents we just described.

One of the first enhancements to the basic architecture was support for simple user interaction by means of the **Common Gateway Interface** or simply **CGI**. CGI defines a standard way by which a Web server can execute a program taking user data as input. Usually, user data come from an HTML form; it specifies the program that is to be executed at the server side, along with parameter values that are filled in by the user. Once the form has been completed, the program's name and collected parameter values are sent to the server, as shown in Fig. 12-3.

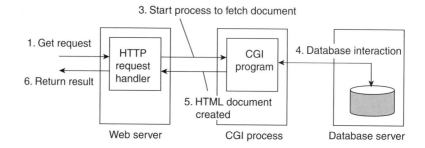

Figure 12-3. The principle of using server-side CGI programs.

When the server sees the request, it starts the program named in the request and passes it the parameter values. At that point, the program simply does its work and generally returns the results in the form of a document that is sent back to the user's browser to be displayed.

CGI programs can be as sophisticated as a developer wants. For example, as shown in Fig. 12-3, many programs operate on a database local to the Web server. After processing the data, the program generates an HTML document and returns that document to the server. The server will then pass the document to the client. An interesting observation is that to the server, it appears as if it is asking the CGI program to fetch a document. In other words, the server does nothing but delegate the fetching of a document to an external program.

The main task of a server used to be handling client requests by simply fetching documents. With CGI programs, fetching a document could be delegated in such a way that the server would remain unaware of whether a document had been generated on the fly, or actually read from the local file system. Note that we have just described a two-tiered organization of server-side software.

However, servers nowadays do much more than just fetching documents. One of the most important enhancements is that servers can also process a document before passing it to the client. In particular, a document may contain a **server-side script**, which is executed by the server when the document has been fetched locally. The result of executing a script is sent along with the rest of the document to the client. The script itself is not sent. In other words, using a server-side script changes a document by essentially replacing the script with the results of its execution.

As server-side processing of Web documents increasingly requires more flexibility, it should come as no surprise that many Web sites are now organized as a three-tiered architecture consisting of a Web server, an application server, and a database. The Web server is the traditional Web server that we had before; the application server runs all kinds of programs that may or may not access the third tier, consisting of a database. For example, a server may accept a customer's query, search its database of matching products, and then construct a clickable Web page listing the products found. In many cases the server is responsible for running Java programs, called **servlets**, that maintain things like shopping carts, implement recommendations, keep lists of favorite items, and so on.

This three-tiered organization introduces a problem, however: a decrease in performance. Although from an architectural point of view it makes sense to distinguish three tiers, practice shows that the application server and database are potential bottlenecks. Notably improving database performance can turn out to be a nasty problem. We will return to this issue below when discussing caching and replication as solutions to performance problems.

12.1.2 Web Services

So far, we have implicitly assumed that the client-side software of a Web-based system consists of a browser that acts as the interface to a user. This assumption is no longer universally true anymore. There is a rapidly growing group of Web-based systems that are offering general services to remote applications without immediate interactions from end users. This organization leads to the concept of **Web services** (Alonso et al., 2004).

Web Services Fundamentals

Simply stated, a Web service is nothing but a traditional service (e.g., a naming service, a weather-reporting service, an electronic supplier, etc.) that is made available over the Internet. What makes a Web service special is that it adheres to a collection of standards that will allow it to be *discovered* and accessed over the Internet by client applications that follow those standards as well. It should come as no surprise then, that those standards form the core of Web services architecture [see also Booth et al. (2004)].

The principle of providing and using a Web service is quite simple, and is shown in Fig. 12-4. The basic idea is that some client application can call upon the services as provided by a server application. Standardization takes place with respect to how those services are described such that they can be looked up by a client application. In addition, we need to ensure that service call proceeds along the rules set by the server application. Note that this principle is no different from what is needed to realize a remote procedure call.

An important component in the Web services architecture is formed by a directory service storing service descriptions. This service adheres to the **Universal Description, Discovery and Integration** standard (**UDDI**). As its name suggests, UDDI prescribes the layout of a database containing service descriptions that will allow Web service clients to browse for relevant services.

Operations in Web Service Arch:

○Publish = provide service ~~des~~ *description⟶ interface & implementation*

○Find = requestor Look up a service retrieves a description.

○Bind = requestor invokes an interaction with the service at runtime.

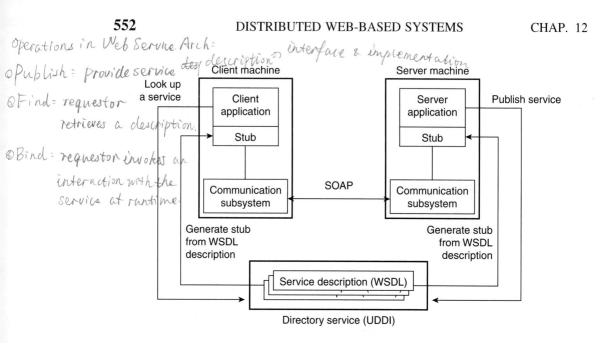

Figure 12-4. The principle of a Web service.

define the interface of service.

Services are described by means of the **Web Services Definition Language (WSDL)** which is a formal language very much the same as the interface definition languages used to support RPC-based communication. A WSDL description contains the precise definitions of the interfaces provided by a service, that is, procedure specification, data types, the (logical) location of services, etc. An important issue of a WSDL description is that can be automatically translated to client-side and server-side stubs, again, analogous to the generation of stubs in ordinary RPC-based systems.

Finally, a core element of a Web service is the specification of how communication takes place. To this end, the **Simple Object Access Protocol (SOAP)** is used, which is essentially a framework in which much of the communication between two processes can be standardized. We will discuss SOAP in detail below, where it will also become clear that calling the framework simple is not really justified.

Web Services Composition and Coordination

The architecture described so far is relatively straightforward: a service is implemented by means of an application and its invocation takes place according to a specific standard. Of course, the application itself may be complex and, in fact, its components may be completely distributed across a local-area network. In such cases, the Web service is most likely implemented by means of an internal proxy or daemon that interacts with the various components constituting the distributed application. In that case, all the principles we have discussed so far can be readily applied as we have discussed.

In the model so far, a Web service is offered in the form of a single invocation. In practice, much more complex invocation structures need to take place before a service can be considered as completed. For example, take an electronic bookstore. Ordering a book requires selecting a book, paying, and ensuring its delivery. From a service perspective, the actual service should be modeled as a transaction consisting of multiple steps that need to be carried out in a specific order. In other words, we are dealing with a **complex service** that is built from a number of basic services.

Complexity increases when considering Web services that are offered by combining Web services from different providers. A typical example is devising a Web-based shop. Most shops consist roughly of three parts: a first part by which the goods that a client requires are selected, a second one that handles the payment of those goods, and a third one that takes care of shipping and subsequent tracking of goods. In order to set up such a shop, a provider may want to make use of a electronic bank service that can handle payment, but also a special delivery service that handles the shipping of goods. In this way, a provider can concentrate on its core business, namely the offering of goods.

In these scenarios it is important that a customer sees a coherent service: namely a shop where he can select, pay, and rely on proper delivery. However, internally we need to deal with a situation in which possibly three different organizations need to act in a coordinated way. Providing proper support for such **composite services** forms an essential element of Web services. There are at least two classes of problems that need to be solved. First, how can the coordination between Web services, possibly from different organizations, take place? Second, how can services be easily composed?

Coordination among Web services is tackled through **coordination protocols**. Such a protocol prescribes the various steps that need to take place for (composite) service to succeed. The issue, of course, is to *enforce* the parties taking part in such protocol take the correct steps at the right moment. There are various ways to achieve this; the simplest is to have a single coordinator that controls the messages exchanged between the participating parties.

However, although various solutions exist, from the Web services perspective it is important to standardize the commonalities in coordination protocols. For one, it is important that when a party wants to participate in a specific protocol, that it knows with which other process(es) it should communicate. In addition, it may very well be that a process is involved in multiple coordination protocols at the same time. Therefore, identifying the instance of a protocol is important as well. Finally, a process should know which role it is to fulfill.

These issues are standardized in what is known as **Web Services Coordination** (Frend et al., 2005). From an architectural point of view, it defines a separate service for handling coordination protocols. The coordination of a protocol is part of this service. Processes can register themselves as participating in the coordination so that their peers know about them.

To make matters concrete, consider a coordination service for variants of the two-phase protocol (2PC) we discussed in Chap. 8. The whole idea is that such a service would implement the coordinator for various protocol instances. One obvious implementation is that a single process plays the role of coordinator for multiple protocol instances. An alternative is that have each coordinator be implemented by a separate thread.

A process can request the activation of a specific protocol. At that point, it will essentially be returned an identifier that it can pass to other processes for registering as participants in the newly-created protocol instance. Of course, all participating processes will be required to implement the specific interfaces of the protocol that the coordination service is supporting. Once all participants have registered, the coordinator can send the *VOTE_REQUEST*, *COMMIT*, and other messages that are part of the 2PC protocol to the participants when needed.

It is not difficult to see that due to the commonality in, for example, 2PC protocols, standardization of interfaces and messages to exchange will make it much easier to compose and coordinate Web services. The actual work that needs to be done is not very difficult. In this respect, the added value of a coordination service is to be sought entirely in the standardization.

Clearly, a coordination service already offers facilities for composing a Web service out of other services. There is only one potential problem: how the service is composed is public. In many cases, this is not a desirable property, as it would allow any competitor to set up exactly the same composite service. What is needed, therefore, are facilities for setting up private coordinators. We will not go into any details here, as they do not touch upon the principles of service composition in Web-based systems. Also, this type of composition is still very much in flux (and may continue to be so for a long time). The interested reader is referred to (Alonso et al., 2004).

12.2 PROCESSES

We now turn to the most important processes used in Web-based systems and their internal organization.

12.2.1 Clients

a web client

The most important Web client is a piece of software called a **Web browser**, which enables a user to navigate through Web pages by fetching those pages from servers and subsequently displaying them on the user's screen. A browser typically provides an interface by which hyperlinks are displayed in such a way that the user can easily select them through a single mouse click.

Web browsers used to be simple programs, but that was long ago. Logically, they consist of several components, shown in Fig. 12-5 [see also Grosskurth and Godfrey (2005)].

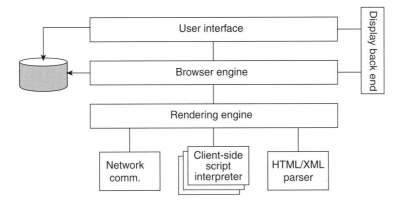

Figure 12-5. The logical components of a Web browser.

An important aspect of Web browsers is that they should (ideally) be platform independent. This goal is often achieved by making use of standard graphical libraries, shown as the display back end, along with standard networking libraries.

The core of a browser is formed by the browser engine and the rendering engine. The latter contains all the code for properly displaying documents as we explained before. This rendering at the very least requires parsing HTML or XML, but may also require script interpretation. In most case, there is only an interpreter for Javascript included, but in theory other interpreters may be included as well. The browser engine provides the mechanisms for an end user to go over a document, select parts of it, activate hyperlinks, etc.

One of the problems that Web browser designers have to face is that a browser should be easily extensible so that it, in principle, can support any type of document that is returned by a server. The approach followed in most cases is to offer facilities for what are known as plug-ins. As mentioned before, a **plug-in** is a small program that can be dynamically loaded into a browser for handling a specific document type. The latter is generally given as a MIME type. A plug-in should be locally available, possibly after being specifically transferred by a user from a remote server. Plug-ins normally offer a standard interface to the browser and, likewise, expect a standard interface from the browser. Logically, they form an extension of the rendering engine shown in Fig. 12-5.

Another client-side process that is often used is a **Web proxy** (Luotonen and Altis, 1994). Originally, such a process was used to allow a browser to handle application-level protocols other than HTTP, as shown in Fig. 12-6. For example, to transfer a file from an FTP server, the browser can issue an HTTP request to a local FTP proxy, which will then fetch the file and return it embedded as HTTP.

Figure 12-6. Using a Web proxy when the browser does not speak FTP.

By now, most Web browsers are capable of supporting a variety of protocols, or can otherwise be dynamically extended to do so, and for that reason do not need proxies. However, proxies are still used for other reasons. For example, a proxy can be configured for filtering requests and responses (bringing it close to an application-level firewall), logging, compression, but most of all caching. We return to proxy caching below. A widely-used Web proxy is **Squid**, which has been developed as an open-source project. Detailed information on Squid can be found in Wessels (2004).

12.2.2 The Apache Web Server

By far the most popular Web server is Apache, which is estimated to be used to host approximately 70% of all Web sites. Apache is a complex piece of software, and with the numerous enhancements to the types of documents that are now offered in the Web, it is important that the server is highly configurable and extensible, and at the same time largely independent of specific platforms.

Making the server platform independent is realized by essentially providing its own basic runtime environment, which is then subsequently implemented for different operating systems. This runtime environment, known as the **Apache Portable Runtime** (**APR**), is a library that provides a platform-independent interface for file handling, networking, locking, threads, and so on. When extending Apache (as we will discuss shortly), portability is largely guaranteed provided that only calls to the APR are made and that calls to platform-specific libraries are avoided.

As we said, Apache is tailored not only to provide flexibility (in the sense that it can be configured to considerable detail), but also that it is relatively easy to extend its functionality. For example, later in this chapter we will discuss adaptive replication in Globule, a home-brew content delivery network developed in the authors' group at the Vrije Universiteit Amsterdam. Globule is implemented as an extension to Apache, based on the APR, but also largely independent of other extensions developed for Apache.

From a certain perspective, Apache can be considered as a completely general server tailored to produce a response to an incoming request. Of course, there are all kinds of hidden dependencies and assumptions by which Apache turns out to be primarily suited for handling requests for Web documents. For example, as we mentioned, Web browsers and servers use HTTP as their communication protocol. HTTP is virtually always implemented on top of TCP, for which reason the core of Apache assumes that all incoming requests adhere to a TCP-based connection-oriented way of communication. Requests based on, for example, UDP cannot be properly handled without modifying the Apache core.

However, the Apache core makes few assumptions on how incoming requests should be handled. Its overall organization is shown in Fig. 12-7. Fundamental to this organization is the concept of a **hook**, which is nothing but a placeholder for a specific group of functions. The Apache core assumes that requests are processed in a number of phases, each phase consisting of a few hooks. Each hook thus represents a group of similar actions that need to be executed as part of processing a request.

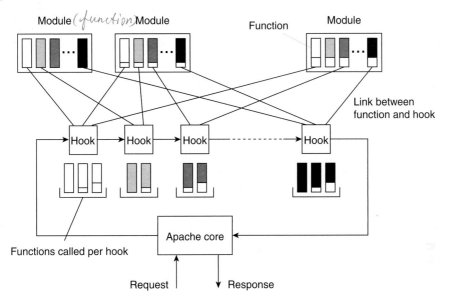

Figure 12-7. The general organization of the Apache Web server.

For example, there is a hook to translate a URL to a local file name. Such a translation will almost certainly need to be done when processing a request. Likewise, there is a hook for writing information to a log, a hook for checking a client's identification, a hook for checking access rights, and a hook for checking which MIME type the request is related to (e.g., to make sure that the request can be properly handled). As shown in Fig. 12-7, the hooks are processed in a predetermined order. It is here that we explicitly see that Apache enforces a specific flow of control concerning the processing of requests.

The functions associated with a hook are all provided by separate **modules**. Although in principle a developer could change the set of hooks that will be processed by Apache, it is far more common to write modules containing the functions that need to be called as part of processing the standard hooks provided by unmodified Apache. The underlying principle is fairly straightforward. Every hook can contain a set of functions that each should match a specific function prototype (i.e., list of parameters and return type). A module developer will write functions for specific hooks. When compiling Apache, the developer specifies which function should be added to which hook. The latter is shown in Fig. 12-7 as the various links between functions and hooks.

Because there may be tens of modules, each hook will generally contain several functions. Normally, modules are considered to be mutual independent, so that functions in the same hook will be executed in some arbitrary order. However, Apache can also handle module dependencies by letting a developer specify an ordering in which functions from different modules should be processed. By and large, the result is a Web server that is extremely versatile. Detailed information on configuring Apache, as well as a good introduction to how it can be extended can be found in Laurie and Laurie (2002).

12.2.3 Web Server Clusters

An important problem related to the client-server nature of the Web is that a Web server can easily become overloaded. A practical solution employed in many designs is to simply replicate a server on a cluster of servers and use a separate mechanism, such as a front end, to redirect client requests to one of the replicas. This principle is shown in Fig. 12-8, and is an example of horizontal distribution as we discussed in Chap. 2.

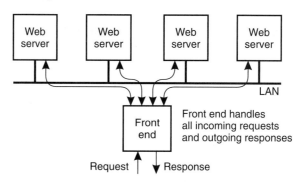

Figure 12-8. The principle of using a server cluster in combination with a front end to implement a Web service.

A crucial aspect of this organization is the design of the front end, as it can become a serious performance bottleneck, what will all the traffic passing through it. In general, a distinction is made between front ends operating as transport-layer switches, and those that operate at the level of the application layer.

Whenever a client issues an HTTP request, it sets up a TCP connection to the server. A transport-layer switch simply passes the data sent along the TCP connection to one of the servers, depending on some measurement of the server's load. The response from that server is returned to the switch, which will then forward it to the requesting client. As an optimization, the switch and servers can *⇒ Transport* collaborate in implementing a **TCP handoff**, as we discussed in Chap. 3. The *level.* main drawback of a transport-layer switch is that the switch cannot take into account the content of the HTTP request that is sent along the TCP connection. At best, it can only base its redirection decisions on server loads.

As a general rule, a better approach is to deploy **content-aware request distribution**, by which the front end first inspects an incoming HTTP request, and then decides which server it should forward that request to. Content-aware distri- *⇒ Application* bution has several advantages. For example, if the front end always forwards re- *level.* quests for the same document to the same server, that server may be able to effectively cache the document resulting in higher response times. In addition, it is possible to actually distribute the collection of documents among the servers instead of having to replicate each document for each server. This approach makes more efficient use of the available storage capacity and allows using dedicated servers to handle special documents such as audio or video.

A problem with content-aware distribution is that the front end needs to do a lot of work. Ideally, one would like to have the efficiency of TCP handoff and the functionality of content-aware distribution. What we need to do is distribute the work of the front end, and combine that with a transport-layer switch, as proposed in Aron et al. (2000). In combination with TCP handoff, the front end has two tasks. First, when a request initially comes in, it must decide which server will handle the rest of the communication with the client. Second, the front end should forward the client's TCP messages associated with the handed-off TCP connection.

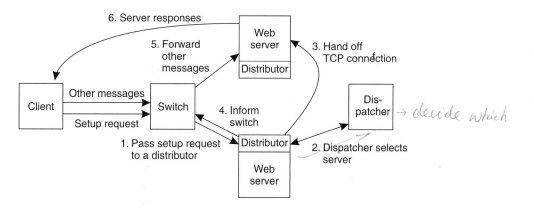

Figure 12-9. A scalable content-aware cluster of Web servers.

These two tasks can be distributed as shown in Fig. 12-9. The dispatcher is responsible for deciding to which server a TCP connection should be handed off; a distributor monitors incoming TCP traffic for a handed-off connection. The switch is used to forward TCP messages to a distributor. When a client first contacts the Web service, its TCP connection setup message is forwarded to a distributor, which in turn contacts the dispatcher to let it decide to which server the connection should be handed off. At that point, the switch is notified that it should send all further TCP messages for that connection to the selected server.

There are various other alternatives and further refinements for setting up Web server clusters. For example, instead of using any kind of front end, it is also possible to use **round-robin DNS** by which a single domain name is associated with multiple IP addresses. In this case, when resolving the host name of a Web site, a client browser would receive a list of multiple addresses, each address corresponding to one of the Web servers. Normally, browsers choose the first address on the list. However, what a popular DNS server such as **BIND** does is circulate the entries of the list it returns (Albitz and Liu, 2001). As a consequence, we obtain a simple distribution of requests over the servers in the cluster.

Finally, it is also possible not to use any sort of intermediate but simply to give each Web server with the same IP address. In that case, we do need to assume that the servers are all connected through a single broadcast LAN. What will happen is that when an HTTP request arrives, the IP router connected to that LAN will simply forward it to all servers, who then run the same distributed algorithm to deterministically decide which of them will handle the request.

The different ways of organizing Web clusters and alternatives like the ones we discussed above, are described in an excellent survey by Cardellini et al., (2002). The interested reader is referred to their paper for further details and references.

12.3 COMMUNICATION

When it comes to Web-based distributed systems, there are only a few communication protocols that are used. First, for traditional Web systems, HTTP is the standard protocol for exchanging messages. Second, when considering Web services, SOAP is the default way for message exchange. Both protocols will be discussed in a fair amount of detail in this section.

12.3.1 Hypertext Transfer Protocol

All communication in the Web between clients and servers is based on the **Hypertext Transfer Protocol (HTTP)**. HTTP is a relatively simple client-server protocol; a client sends a request message to a server and waits for a response message. An important property of HTTP is that it is stateless. In other words, it does not have any concept of open connection and does not require a server to maintain information on its clients. HTTP is described in Fielding et al. (1999).

HTTP Connections

HTTP is based on TCP. Whenever a client issues a request to a server, it first sets up a TCP connection to the server and then sends its request message on that connection. The same connection is used for receiving the response. By using TCP as its underlying protocol, HTTP need not be concerned about lost requests and responses. A client and server may simply assume that their messages make it to the other side. If things do go wrong, for example, the connection is broken or a time-out occurs an error is reported. However, in general, no attempt is made to recover from the failure.

One of the problems with the first versions of HTTP was its inefficient use of TCP connections. Each Web document is constructed from a collection of different files from the same server. To properly display a document, it is necessary that these files are also transferred to the client. Each of these files is, in principle, just another document for which the client can issue a separate request to the server where they are stored.

In HTTP version 1.0 and older, each request to a server required setting up a separate connection, as shown in Fig. 12-10(a). When the server had responded, the connection was broken down again. Such connections are referred to as being **nonpersistent**. A major drawback of nonpersistent connections is that it is relatively costly to set up a TCP connection. As a consequence, the time it can take to transfer an entire document with all its elements to a client may be considerable.

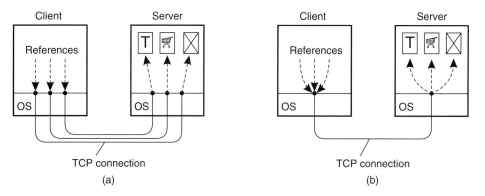

Figure 12-10. (a) Using nonpersistent connections. (b) Using persistent connections.

Note that HTTP does not preclude that a client sets up several connections simultaneously to the same server. This approach is often used to hide latency caused by the connection setup time, and to transfer data in parallel from the server to the client. Many browsers use this approach to improve performance.

Another approach that is followed in HTTP version 1.1 is to make use of a **persistent connection**, which can be used to issue several requests (and their respective responses), without the need for a separate connection for each *(request, response)*-pair. To further improve performance, a client can issue several requests in a row without waiting for the response to the first request (also referred to as **pipelining**). Using persistent connections is illustrated in Fig. 12-10(b).

HTTP Methods

HTTP has been designed as a general-purpose client-server protocol oriented toward the transfer of documents in both directions. A client can request each of these operations to be carried out at the server by sending a request message containing the operation desired to the server. A list of the most commonly used request messages is given in Fig. 12-11.

Operation	Description
Head	Request to return the header of a document
Get	Request to return a document to the client
Put	Request to store a document
Post	Provide data that are to be added to a document (collection)
Delete	Request to delete a document

Figure 12-11. Operations supported by HTTP.

HTTP assumes that each document may have associated metadata, which are stored in a separate header that is sent along with a request or response. The head operation is submitted to the server when a client does not want the actual document, but rather only its associated metadata. For example, using the head operation will return the time the referred document was modified. This operation can be used to verify the validity of the document as cached by the client. It can also be used to check whether a document exists, without having to actually transfer the document.

The most important operation is get. This operation is used to actually fetch a document from the server and return it to the requesting client. It is also possible to specify that a document should be returned only if it has been modified after a specific time. Also, HTTP allows documents to have associated **tags**, (character strings) and to fetch a document only if it matches certain tags.

The put operation is the opposite of the get operation. A client can request a server to store a document under a given name (which is sent along with the request). Of course, a server will in general not blindly execute put operations, but will only accept such requests from authorized clients. How these security issues are dealt with is discussed later.

The operation post is somewhat similar to storing a document, except that a client will request data to be added to a document or collection of documents. A typical example is posting an article to a news group. The distinguishing feature, compared to a put operation is that a post operation tells to which group of documents an article should be "added." The article is sent along with the request. In contrast, a put operation carries a document and the name under which the server is requested to store that document.

Finally, the delete operation is used to request a server to remove the document that is named in the message sent to the server. Again, whether or not deletion actually takes place depends on various security measures. It may even be the case that the server itself does not have the proper permissions to delete the referred document. After all, the server is just a user process.

HTTP Messages

All communication between a client and server takes place through messages. HTTP recognizes only request and response messages. A request message consists of three parts, as shown in Fig. 12-12(a). The **request line** is mandatory and identifies the operation that the client wants the server to carry out along with a reference to the document associated with that request. A separate field is used to identify the version of HTTP the client is expecting. We explain the additional message headers below.

A response message starts with a **status line** containing a version number and also a three-digit status code, as shown in Fig. 12-12(b). The code is briefly explained with a textual phrase that is sent along as part of the status line. For example, status code 200 indicates that a request could be honored, and has the associated phrase "OK." Other frequently used codes are:

400 (Bad Request)
403 (Forbidden)
404 (Not Found).

A request or response message may contain additional headers. For example, if a client has requested a post operation for a read-only document, the server will respond with a message having status code 405 ("Method Not Allowed") along with an *Allow* message header specifying the permitted operations (e.g., head and get). As another example, a client may be interested only in a document if it has not been modified since some time T. In that case, the client's get request is augmented with an *If-Modified-Since* message header specifying value T.

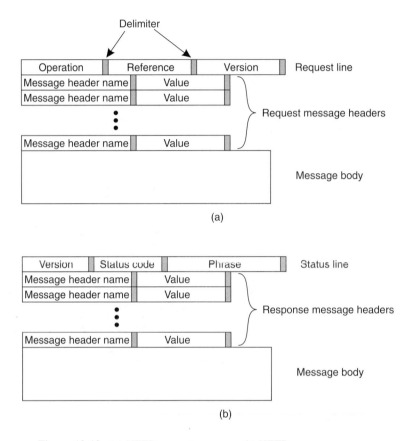

Figure 12-12. (a) HTTP request message. (b) HTTP response message.

Fig. 12-13 shows a number of valid message headers that can be sent along with a request or response. Most of the headers are self-explanatory, so we will not discuss every one of them.

There are various message headers that the client can send to the server explaining what it is able to accept as response. For example, a client may be able to accept responses that have been compressed using the *gzip* compression program available on most Windows and UNIX machines. In that case, the client will send an *Accept-Encoding* message header along with its request, with its content containing "Accept-Encoding:gzip." Likewise, an *Accept* message header can be used to specify, for example, that only HTML Web pages may be returned.

There are two message headers for security, but as we discuss later in this section, Web security is usually handled with a separate transport-layer protocol.

The *Location* and *Referer* message header are used to **redirect** a client to another document (note that "Referer" is misspelled in the specification). Redirecting corresponds to the use of forwarding pointers for locating a document, as

Header	Source	Contents
Accept	Client	The type of documents the client can handle
Accept-Charset	Client	The character sets are acceptable for the client
Accept-Encoding	Client	The document encodings the client can handle
Accept-Language	Client	The natural language the client can handle
Authorization	Client	A list of the client's credentials
WWW-Authenticate	Server	Security challenge the client should respond to
Date	Both	Date and time the message was sent
ETag	Server	The tags associated with the returned document
Expires	Server	The time for how long the response remains valid
From	Client	The client's e-mail address
Host	Client	The DNS name of the document's server
If-Match	Client	The tags the document should have
If-None-Match	Client	The tags the document should not have
If-Modified-Since	Client	Tells the server to return a document only if it has been modified since the specified time
If-Unmodified-Since	Client	Tells the server to return a document only if it has not been modified since the specified time
Last-Modified	Server	The time the returned document was last modified
Location	Server	A document reference to which the client should redirect its request
Referer	Client	Refers to client's most recently requested document
Upgrade	Both	The application protocol the sender wants to switch to
Warning	Both	Information about the status of the data in the message

Figure 12-13. Some HTTP message headers.

explained in Chap. 5. When a client issues a request for document *D*, the server may possibly respond with a *Location* message header, specifying that the client should reissue the request, but now for document *D′*. When using the reference to *D′*, the client can add a *Referer* message header containing the reference to *D* to indicate what caused the redirection. In general, this message header is used to indicate the client's most recently requested document.

The *Upgrade* message header is used to switch to another protocol. For example, client and server may use HTTP/1.1 initially only to have a generic way of setting up a connection. The server may immediately respond with telling the client that it wants to continue communication with a secure version of HTTP, such as SHTTP (Rescorla and Schiffman, 1999). In that case, the server will send an *Upgrade* message header with content "Upgrade:SHTTP."

12.3.2 Simple Object Access Protocol

Where HTTP is the standard communication protocol for traditional Web-based distributed systems, the **Simple Object Access Protocol** (**SOAP**) forms the standard for communication with Web services (Gudgin et al., 2003). SOAP has made HTTP even more important than it already was: most SOAP communications are implemented through HTTP. SOAP by itself is not a difficult protocol. Its main purpose is to provide a relatively simple means to let different parties who may know very little of each other be able to communicate. In other words, the protocol is designed with the assumption that two communicating parties have very little common knowledge.

Based on this assumption, it should come as no surprise that SOAP messages are largely based on XML. Recall that XML is a meta-markup language, meaning that an XML description includes the definition of the elements that are used to describe a document. In practice, this means that the definition of the syntax as used for a message is part of that message. Providing this syntax allows a receiver to parse very different types of messages. Of course, the *meaning* of a message is still left undefined, and thus also what actions to take when a message comes in. If the receiver cannot make any sense out of the contents of a message, no progress can be made.

A SOAP message generally consists of two parts, which are jointly put inside what is called a **SOAP envelope**. The body contains the actual message, whereas the header is optional, containing information relevant for nodes along the path from sender to receiver. Typically, such nodes consist of the various processes in a multitiered implementation of a Web service. Everything in the envelope is expressed in XML, that is, the header and the body.

Strange as it may seem, a SOAP envelope does not contain the address of the recipient. Instead, SOAP explicitly assumes that the recipient is specified by the protocol that is used to transfer messages. To this end, SOAP specifies **bindings** to underlying transfer protocols. At present, two such bindings exist: one to HTTP and one to SMTP, the Internet mail-transfer protocol. So, for example, when a SOAP message is bound to HTTP, the recipient will be specified in the form of a URL, whereas a binding to SMTP will specify the recipient in the form of an e-mail address.

These two different types of bindings also indicate two different styles of interactions. The first, most common one, is the **conversational exchange style**. In this style, two parties essentially exchange structured documents. For example, such a document may contain a complete purchase order as one would fill in when electronically booking a flight. The response to such an order could be a confirmation document, now containing an order number, flight information, a seat reservation, and perhaps also a bar code that needs to be scanned when boarding.

In contrast, an **RPC-style exchange** adheres closer to the traditional request-response behavior when invoking a Web service. In this case, the SOAP message will identify explicitly the procedure to be called, and also provide a list of parameter values as input to that call. Likewise, the response will be a formal message containing the response to the call.

Typically, an RPC-style exchange is supported by a binding to HTTP, whereas a conversational style message will be bound to either SMTP or HTTP. However, in practice, most SOAP messages are sent over HTTP.

An important observation is that, although XML makes it much easier to use a general parser because syntax definitions are now part of a message, the XML syntax itself is extremely verbose. As a result, parsing XML messages in practice often introduces a serious performance bottleneck (Allman, 2003). In this respect, it is somewhat surprising that improving XML performance receives relatively little attention, although solutions are underway (see, e.g., Kostoulas et al., 2006).

```
<env:Envelope xmlns:env="http://www.w3.org/2003/05/soap-envelope">
    <env:Header>
        <n:alertcontrol xmlns:n="http://example.org/alertcontrol">
            <n:priority>1</n:priority>
            <n:expires>2001-06-22T14:00:00-05:00</n:expires>
        </n:alertcontrol>
    </env:Header>
    <env:Body>
        <m:alert xmlns:m="http://example.org/alert">
            <m:msg>Pick up Mary at school at 2pm</m:msg>
        </m:alert>
    </env:Body>
</env:Envelope>
```

Figure 12-14. An example of an XML-based SOAP message.

What is equally surprising is that many people believe that XML specifications can be conveniently read by human beings. The example shown in Fig. 12-14 is taken from the official SOAP specification (Gudgin et al., 2003). Discovering what this SOAP message conveys requires some searching, and it is not hard to imagine that obscurity in general may come as a natural by-product of using XML. The question then comes to mind, whether the text-based approach as followed for XML has been the right one: no one can conveniently read XML documents, and parsers are severely slowed down.

12.4 NAMING

The Web uses a single naming system to refer to documents. The names used are called **Uniform Resource Identifiers** or simply **URI**s (Berners-Lee et al., 2005). URIs come in two forms. A **Uniform Resource Locator** (**URL**) is a URI that identifies a document by including information on how and where to access the document. In other words, a URL is a location-dependent reference to a document. In contrast, a **Uniform Resource Name (URN)** acts as true identifier as discussed in Chap. 5. A URN is used as a globally unique, location-independent, and persistent reference to a document.

The actual syntax of a URI is determined by its associated **scheme**. The name of a scheme is part of the URI. Many different schemes have been defined, and in the following we will mention a few of them along with examples of their associated URIs. The *http* scheme is the best known, but it is not the only one. We should also note that the difference between URL and URN is gradually diminishing. Instead, it is now common to simply define URI name spaces [see also Daigle et al. (2002)].

In the case of URLs, we see that they often contain information on how and where to access a document. How to access a document is generally reflected by the name of the scheme that is part of the URL, such as *http*, *ftp*, or *telnet*. Where a document is located is embedded in a URL by means of the DNS name of the server to which an access request can be sent, although an IP address can also be used. The number of the port on which the server will be listening for such requests is also part of the URL; when left out, a default port is used. Finally, a URL also contains the name of the document to be looked up by that server, leading to the general structures shown in Fig. 12-15.

Scheme	Host name	Pathname
http ://	www.cs.vu.nl	/home/steen/mbox

(a)

Scheme	Host name	Port	Pathname
http ://	www.cs.vu.nl :	80	/home/steen/mbox

(b)

Scheme	Host name	Port	Pathname
http ://	130.37.24.11 :	80	/home/steen/mbox

(c)

Figure 12-15. Often-used structures for URLs. (a) Using only a DNS name. (b) Combining a DNS name with a port number. (c) Combining an IP address with a port number.

Resolving a URL such as those shown in Fig. 12-15 is straightforward. If the server is referred to by its DNS name, that name will need to be resolved to the server's IP address. Using the port number contained in the URL, the client can then contact the server using the protocol named by the scheme, and pass it the document's name that forms the last part of the URL.

Name	Used for	Example
http	HTTP	http://www.cs.vu.nl:80/globe
mailto	E-mail	mailto:steen@cs.vu.nl
ftp	FTP	ftp://ftp.cs.vu.nl/pub/minix/README
file	Local file	file:/edu/book/work/chp/11/11
data	Inline data	data:text/plain;charset=iso-8859-7,%e1%e2%e3
telnet	Remote login	telnet://flits.cs.vu.nl
tel	Telephone	tel:+31201234567
modem	Modem	modem:+31201234567;type=v32

Figure 12-16. Examples of URIs.

Although URLs are still commonplace in the Web, various separate URI name spaces have been proposed for other kinds of Web resources. Fig. 12-16 shows a number of examples of URIs. The *http* URI is used to transfer documents using HTTP as we explained above. Likewise, there is an *ftp* URI for file transfer using FTP.

An immediate form of documents is supported by *data* URIs (Masinter, 1998). In such a URI, the document itself is embedded in the URI, similar to embedding the data of a file in an inode (Mullender and Tanenbaum, 1984). The example shows a URI containing plain text for the Greek character string αβγ.

URIs are often used as well for purposes other than referring to a document. For example, a *telnet* URI is used for setting up a telnet session to a server. There are also URIs for telephone-based communication as described in Schulzrinne (2005). The *tel* URI as shown in Fig. 12-16 essentially embeds only a telephone number and simply lets the client to establish a call across the telephone network. In this case, the client will typically be a telephone. The *modem* URI can be used to set up a modem-based connection with another computer. In the example, the URI states that the remote modem should adhere to the ITU-T V32 standard.

12.5 SYNCHRONIZATION

Synchronization has not been much of an issue for most traditional Web-based systems for two reasons. First, the strict client-server organization of the Web, in which servers never exchange information with other servers (or clients with other clients) means that there is nothing much to synchronize. Second, the Web can be considered as being a read-mostly system. Updates are generally done by a single person or entity, and hardly ever introduce write-write conflicts.

However, things are changing. For example, there is an increasing demand to provide support for collaborative authoring of Web documents. In other words, the Web should provide support for concurrent updates of documents by a group of collaborating users or processes. Likewise, with the introduction of Web services, we are now seeing a need for servers to synchronize with each other and that their actions are coordinated. We already discussed coordination in Web services above. We therefore briefly pay some attention to synchronization for collaborative maintenance of Web documents.

Distributed authoring of Web documents is handled through a separate protocol, namely **WebDAV** (Goland et al., 1999). WebDAV stands for **Web Distributed Authoring and Versioning** and provides a simple means to lock a shared document, and to create, delete, copy, and move documents from remote Web servers. We briefly describe synchronization as supported in WebDAV. An overview of how WebDAV can be used in a practical setting is provided in Kim et al. (2004).

To synchronize concurrent access to a shared document, WebDAV supports a simple locking mechanism. There are two types of write locks. An exclusive write lock can be assigned to a single client, and will prevent any other client from modifying the shared document while it is locked. There is also a shared write lock, which allows multiple clients to simultaneously update the document. Because locking takes place at the granularity of an entire document, shared write locks are convenient when clients modify different parts of the same document. However, the clients, themselves, will need to take care that no write-write conflicts occur.

Assigning a lock is done by passing a lock token to the requesting client. The server registers which client currently has the lock token. Whenever the client wants to modify the document, it sends an HTTP post request to the server, along with the lock token. The token shows that the client has write-access to the document, for which reason the server will carry out the request.

An important design issue is that there is no need to maintain a connection between the client and the server while holding the lock. The client can simply disconnect from the server after acquiring the lock, and reconnect to the server when sending an HTTP request.

Note that when a client holding a lock token crashes, the server will one way or the other have to reclaim the lock. WebDAV does not specify how servers should handle these and similar situations, but leaves that open to specific implementations. The reasoning is that the best solution will depend on the type of documents that WebDAV is being used for. The reason for this approach is that there is no general way to solve the problem of orphan locks in a clean way.

12.6 CONSISTENCY AND REPLICATION

Perhaps one of the most important systems-oriented developments in Web-based distributed systems is ensuring that access to Web documents meets stringent performance and availability requirements. These requirements have led to numerous proposals for caching and replicating Web content, of which various ones will be discussed in this section. Where the original schemes (which are still largely deployed) have been targeted toward supporting static content, much effort is also being put into support dynamic content, that is, supporting documents that are generated as the result of a request, as well as those containing scripts and such. An excellent and complete picture of Web caching and replication is provided by Rabinovich and Spatscheck (2002).

12.6.1 Web Proxy Caching

Client-side caching generally occurs at two places. In the first place, most browsers are equipped with a simple caching facility. Whenever a document is fetched it is stored in the browser's cache from where it is loaded the next time. Clients can generally configure caching by indicating when consistency checking should take place, as we explain for the general case below.

In the second place, a client's site often runs a Web proxy. As we explained, a Web proxy accepts requests from local clients and passes these to Web servers. When a response comes in, the result is passed to the client. The advantage of this approach is that the proxy can cache the result and return that result to another client, if necessary. In other words, a Web proxy can implement a shared cache.

In addition to caching at browsers and proxies, it is also possible to place caches that cover a region, or even a country, thus leading to **hierarchical caches**. Such schemes are mainly used to reduce network traffic, but have the disadvantage of potentially incurring a higher latency compared to using nonhierarchical schemes. This higher latency is caused by the need for the client to check multiple caches rather than just one in the nonhierarchical scheme. However, this higher latency is strongly related to the popularity of a document: for popular documents, the chance of finding a copy in a cache closer to the client is higher than for a unpopular document.

As an alternative to building hierarchical caches, one can also organize caches for cooperative deployment as shown in Fig. 12-17. In **cooperative caching** or **distributed caching**, whenever a cache miss occurs at a Web proxy, the proxy first checks a number of neighboring proxies to see if one of them contains the requested document. If such a check fails, the proxy forwards the request to the Web server responsible for the document. This scheme is primarily deployed with Web caches belonging to the same organization or institution that are colocated in the same LAN. It is interesting to note that a study by Wolman et al. (1999) shows that cooperative caching may be effective for only relatively small groups of clients (in the order of tens of thousands of users). However, such groups can also be serviced by using a single proxy cache, which is much cheaper in terms of communication and resource usage.

A comparison between hierarchical and cooperative caching by Rodriguez et al. (2001) makes clear that there are various trade-offs to make. For example,

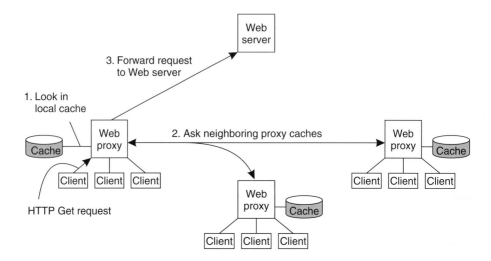

Figure 12-17. The principle of cooperative caching.

because cooperative caches are generally connected through high-speed links, the transmission time needed to fetch a document is much lower than for a hierarchical cache. Also, as is to be expected, storage requirements are less strict for cooperative caches than hierarchical ones. Also, they find that expected latencies for hierarchical caches are lower than for distributed caches.

Different cache-consistency protocols have been deployed in the Web. To guarantee that a document returned from the cache is consistent, some Web proxies first send a conditional HTTP get request to the server with an additional *If-Modified-Since* request header, specifying the last modification time associated with the cached document. Only if the document has been changed since that time, will the server return the entire document. Otherwise, the Web proxy can simply return its cached version to the requesting local client. Following the terminology introduced in Chap. 7, this corresponds to a pull-based protocol.

Unfortunately, this strategy requires that the proxy contacts a server for each request. To improve performance at the cost of weaker consistency, the widely-used Squid Web proxy (Wessels, 2004) assigns an expiration time T_{expire} that depends on how long ago the document was last modified when it is cached. In particular, if $T_{last\_modified}$ is the last modification time of a document (as recorded by its owner), and T_{cached} is the time it was cached, then

$$T_{expire} = \alpha(T_{cached} - T_{last\_modified}) + T_{cached}$$

with $\alpha = 0.2$ (this value has been derived from practical experience). Until T_{expire}, the document is considered valid and the proxy will not contact the server. After the expiration time, the proxy requests the server to send a fresh copy, unless it had not been modified. In other words, when $\alpha = 0$, the strategy is the same as the previous one we discussed.

Note that documents that have not been modified for a long time will not be checked for modifications as soon as recently modified documents. The obvious drawback is that a proxy may return an invalid document, that is, a document that is older than the current version stored at the server. Worse yet, there is no way for the client to detect the fact that it just received an obsolete document.

As an alternative to the pull-based protocol is that the server notifies proxies that a document has been modified by sending an invalidation. The problem with this approach for Web proxies is that the server may need to keep track of a large number of proxies, inevitably leading to a scalability problem. However, by combining leases and invalidations, Cao and Liu (1998) show that the state to be maintained at the server can be kept within acceptable bounds. Note that this state is largely dictated by the expiration times set for leases: the lower, the less caches a server needs to keep track of. Nevertheless, invalidation protocols for Web proxy caches are hardly ever applied.

A comparison of Web caching consistency policies can be found in Cao and Oszu (2002). Their conclusion is that letting the server send invalidations can outperform any other method in terms of bandwidth and perceived client latency, while maintaining cached documents consistent with those at the origin server. These findings hold for access patterns as often observed for electronic commerce applications.

Another problem with Web proxy caches is that they can be used only for static documents, that is, documents that are not generated on-the-fly by Web servers as the response to a client's request. These dynamically generated documents are often unique in the sense that the same request from a client will presumably lead to a different response the next time. For example, many documents contain advertisements (called **banners**) which change for every request made. We return to this situation below when we discuss caching and replication for Web applications.

Finally, we should also mention that much research has been conducted to find out what the best cache replacement strategies are. Numerous proposals exist, but by-and-large, simple replacement strategies such as evicting the least recently used object work well enough. An in-depth survey of replacement strategies is presented in Podling and Boszormenyi (2003).

12.6.2 Replication for Web Hosting Systems

As the importance of the Web continues to increase as a vehicle for organizations to present themselves and to directly interact with end users, we see a shift between maintaining the content of a Web site and making sure that the site is easily and continuously accessible. This distinction has paved the way for **content delivery networks (CDNs)**. The main idea underlying these CDNs is that they act as a Web hosting service, providing an infrastructure for distributing and replicating the Web documents of multiple sites across the Internet. The size of the infrastructure can be impressive. For example, as of 2006, Akamai is reported to have over 18,000 servers spread across 70 countries.

The sheer size of a CDN requires that hosted documents are automatically distributed and replicated, leading to the architecture of a self-managing system as we discussed in Chap. 2. In most cases, a large-scale CDN is organized along the lines of a feedback-control loop, as shown in Fig. 12-18 and which is described extensively in Sivasubramanian et al. (2004b).

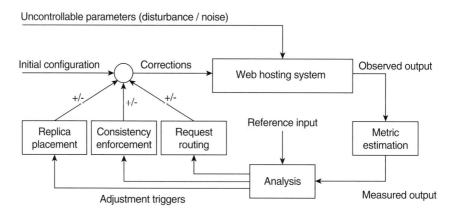

Figure 12-18. The general organization of a CDN as a feedback-control system (adapted from Sivasubramanian et al., 2004b).

There are essentially three different kinds of aspects related to replication in Web hosting systems: metric estimation, adaptation triggering, and taking appropriate measures. The latter can be subdivided into replica placement decisions, consistency enforcement, and client-request routing. In the following, we briefly pay attention to each these.

Metric Estimation

An interesting aspect of CDNs is that they need to make a trade-off between many aspects when it comes to hosting replicated content. For example, access times for a document may be optimal if a document is massively replicated, but at the same time this incurs a financial cost, as well as a cost in terms of bandwidth usage for disseminating updates. By and large, there are many proposals for estimating how well a CDN is performing. These proposals can be grouped into several classes.

First, there are *latency metrics*, by which the time is measured for an action, for example, fetching a document, to take place. Trivial as this may seem, estimating latencies becomes difficult when, for example, a process deciding on

the placement of replicas needs to know the delay between a client and some remote server. Typically, an algorithm globally positioning nodes as discussed in
Chap. 6 will need to be deployed.

Instead of estimating latency, it may be more important to measure the available bandwidth between two nodes. This information is particularly important
when large documents need to be transferred, as in that case the responsiveness of
the system is largely dictated by the time that a document can be transferred.
There are various tools for measuring available bandwidth, but in all cases it turns
out that accurate measurements can be difficult to attain. Further information can
be found in Strauss et al. (2003).

Another class consists of *spatial metrics* which mainly consist of measuring
the distance between nodes in terms of the number of network-level routing hops,
or hops between autonomous systems. Again, determining the number of hops between two arbitrary nodes can be very difficult, and may also not even correlate
with latency (Huffaker et al., 2002). Moreover, simply looking at routing tables is
not going to work when low-level techniques such as **multi-protocol label
switching** (**MPLS**) are deployed. MPLS circumvents network-level routing by
using virtual-circuit techniques to immediately and efficiently forward packets to
their destination [see also Guichard et al. (2005)]. Packets may thus follow completely different routes than advertised in the tables of network-level routers.

A third class is formed by *network usage* metrics which most often entails
consumed bandwidth. Computing consumed bandwidth in terms of the number of
bytes to transfer is generally easy. However, to do this correctly, we need to take
into account how often the document is read, how often it is updated, and how
often it is replicated. We leave this as an exercise to the reader.

Consistency metrics tell us to what extent a replica is deviating from its master copy. We already discussed extensively how consistency can be measured in
the context of continuous consistency in Chap. 7 (Yu and Vahdat, 2002).

Finally, *financial* metrics form another class for measuring how well a CDN *case dependent*
is doing. Although not technical at all, considering that most CDN operate on a
commercial basis, it is clear that in many cases financial metrics will be decisive.
Moreover, the financial metrics are closely related to the actual infrastructure of
the Internet. For example, most commercial CDNs place servers at the edge of the
Internet, meaning that they hire capacity from ISPs directly servicing end users.
At this point, business models become intertwined with technological issues, an
area that is not at all well understood. There is only few material available on the
relation between financial performance and technological issues (Janiga et al.,
2001).

From these examples it should become clear that simply measuring the performance of a CDN, or even estimating its performance may by itself be an
extremely complex task. In practice, for commercial CDNs the issue that really
counts is whether they can meet the service-level agreements that have been made
with customers. These agreements are often formulated simply in terms of how

quickly customers are to be serviced. It is then up to the CDN to make sure that these agreements are met.

Adaptation Triggering

Another question that needs to be addressed is when and how adaptations are to be triggered. A simple model is to periodically estimate metrics and subsequently take measures as needed. This approach is often seen in practice. Special processes located at the servers collect information and periodically check for changes.

A major drawback of periodic evaluation is that sudden changes may be missed. One type of sudden change that is receiving considerable attention is that of flash crowds. A **flash crowd** is a sudden burst in requests for a specific Web document. In many cases, these type of bursts can bring down an entire service, in turn causing a cascade of service outages as witnessed during several events in the recent history of the Internet.

Handling flash crowds is difficult. A very expensive solution is to massively replicate a Web site and as soon as request rates start to rapidly increase, requests should be redirected to the replicas to offload the master copy. This type of over-provisioning is obviously not the way to go. Instead, what is needed is a **flash-crowd predictor** that will provide a server enough time to dynamically install replicas of Web documents, after which it can redirect requests when the going gets tough. One of the problems with attempting to predict flash crowds is that they can be so very different. Fig. 12-19 shows access traces for four different Web sites that suffered from a flash crowd. As a point of reference, Fig. 12-19(a) shows regular access traces spanning two days. There are also some very strong peaks, but otherwise there is nothing shocking going on. In contrast, Fig. 12-19(b) shows a two-day trace with four sudden flash crowds. There is still some regularity, which may be discovered after a while so that measures can be taken. However, the damage may be been done before reaching that point.

Fig. 12-19(c) shows a trace spanning six days with at least two flash crowds. In this case, any predictor is going to have a serious problem, as it turns out that both increases in request rate are almost instantaneously. Finally, Fig. 12-19(d) shows a situation in which the first peak should probably cause no adaptations, but the second obviously should. This situation turns out to be the type of behavior that can be dealt with quite well through runtime analysis.

One promising method to predict flash crowds is using a simple linear extrapolation technique. Baryshikov et al. (2005) propose to continuously measure the number of requests to a document during a specific time interval $[t - W, t)$, where W is the **window size**. The interval itself is divided into small slots, where for each slot the number of requests are counted. Then, by applying simple linear regression, we can fit a curve f_t expressing the number of accesses as a function of time. By extrapolating the curve to time instances beyond t, we obtain a

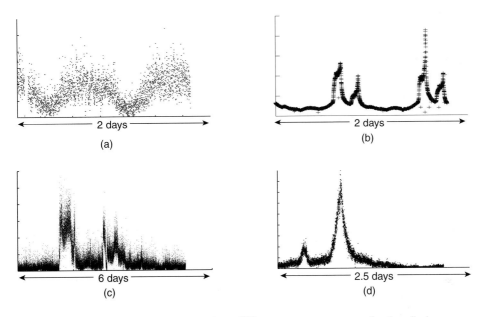

Figure 12-19. One normal and three different access patterns reflecting flash-crowd behavior (adapted from Baryshnikov et al., 2005).

prediction for the number of requests. If the number of requests are predicted to exceed a given threshold, an alarm is raised.

This method works remarkably well for multple access patterns. Unfortunately, the window size as well as determining what the alarm threshold are supposed to be depends highly on the Web server traffic. In practice, this means that much manual fine tuning is needed to configure an ideal predictor for a specific site. It is yet unknown how flash-crowd predictors can be automatically configured.

Adjustment Measures

As mentioned, there are essentially only three (related) measures that can be taken to change the behavior of a Web hosting service: changing the placement of replicas, changing consistency enforcement, and deciding on how and when to redirect client requests. We already discussed the first two measures extensively in Chap. 7. Client-request redirection deserves some more attention. Before we discuss some of the trade-offs, let us first consider how consistency and replication are dealt with in a practical setting by considering the Akamai situation (Leighton and Lewin, 2000; and Dilley et al., 2002).

The basic idea is that each Web document consists of a main HTML (or XML) page in which several other documents such as images, video, and audio have been embedded. To display the entire document, it is necessary that the embedded documents are fetched by the user's browser as well. The assumption is that these embedded documents rarely change, for which reason it makes sense to cache or replicate them.

Each embedded document is normally referenced through a URL. However, in Akamai's CDN, such a URL is modified such that it refers to a **virtual ghost**, which is a reference to an actual server in the CDN. The URL also contains the host name of the origin server for reasons we explain next. The modified URL is resolved as follows, as is also shown in Fig. 12-20.

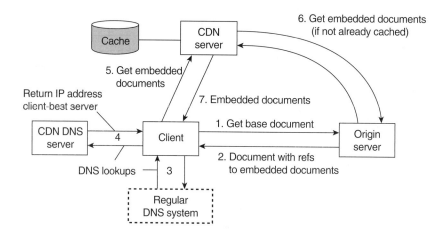

Figure 12-20. The principal working of the Akamai CDN.

The name of the virtual ghost includes a DNS name such as *ghosting.com*, which is resolved by the regular DNS naming system to a CDN DNS server (the result of step 3). Each such DNS server keeps track of servers close to the client. To this end, any of the proximity metrics we have discussed previously could be used. In effect, the CDN DNS servers redirects the client to a replica server best for that client (step 4), which could mean the closest one, the least-loaded one, or a combination of several such metrics (the actual redirection policy is proprietary).

Finally, the client forwards the request for the embedded document to the selected CDN server. If this server does not yet have the document, it fetches it from the original Web server (shown as step 6), caches it locally, and subsequently passes it to the client. If the document was already in the CDN server's cache, it can be returned forthwith. Note that in order to fetch the embedded document, the replica server must be able to send a request to the origin server, for which reason its host name is also contained in the embedded document's URL.

An interesting aspect of this scheme is the simplicity by which consistency of documents can be enforced. Clearly, whenever a main document is changed, a client will always be able to fetch it from the origin server. In the case of embedded documents, a different approach needs to be followed as these documents are, in principle, fetched from a nearby replica server. To this end, a URL for an embedded document not only refers to a special host name that eventually leads to a CDN DNS server, but also contains a unique identifier that is changed every time the embedded document changes. In effect, this identifier changes the name of the embedded document. As a consequence, when the client is redirected to a specific CDN server, that server will not find the named document in its cache and will thus fetch it from the origin server. The old document will eventually be evicted from the server's cache as it is no longer referenced.

This example already shows the importance of client-request redirection. In principle, by properly redirecting clients, a CDN can stay in control when it comes to client-perceived performance, but also taking into account global system performance by, for example, avoiding that requests are sent to heavily loaded servers. These so-called **adaptive redirection policies** can be applied when information on the system's current behavior is provided to the processes that take redirection decisions. This brings us partly back to the metric estimation techniques discussed previously.

Besides the different policies, an important issue is whether request redirection is transparent to the client or not. In essence, there are only three redirection techniques: TCP handoff, DNS redirection, and HTTP redirection. We already discussed TCP handoff. This technique is applicable only for server clusters and does not scale to wide-area networks.

DNS redirection is a transparent mechanism by which the client can be kept completely unaware of where documents are located. Akamai's two-level redirection is one example of this technique. We can also directly deploy DNS to return one of several addresses as we discussed before. Note, however, that DNS redirection can be applied only to an entire site: the name of individual documents does not fit into the DNS name space.

HTTP redirection, finally, is a nontransparent mechanism. When a client requests a specific document, it may be given an alternative URL as part of an HTTP response message to which it is then redirected. An important observation is that this URL is visible to the client's browser. In fact, the user may decide to bookmark the referral URL, potentially rendering the redirection policy useless.

12.6.3 Replication of Web Applications

Up to this point we have mainly concentrated on caching and replicating static Web content. In practice, we see that the Web is increasingly offering more dynamically generated content, but that it is also expanding toward offering services that can be called by remote applications. Also in these situations we see that caching and replication can help considerably in improving the overall performance, although the methods to reach such improvements are more subtle than what we discussed so far [see also Conti et al. (2005)].

When considering improving performance of Web applications through caching and replication, matters are complicated by the fact that several solutions can be deployed, with no single one standing out as the best. Let us consider the edge-server situation as sketched in Fig. 12-21. In this case, we assume a CDN in which each hosted site has an origin server that acts as the authoritative site for all read and update operations. An edge server is used to handle client requests, and has the ability to store (partial) information as also kept at an origin server.

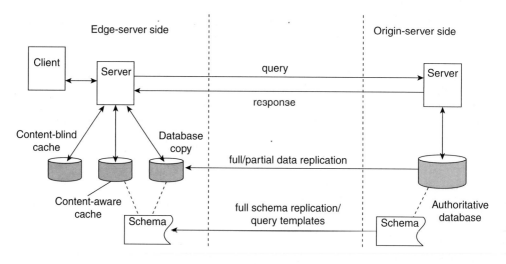

Figure 12-21. Alternatives for caching and replication with Web applications.

Recall that in an edge-server architecture, Web clients request data through an edge server, which, in turn, gets its information from the origin server associated with the specific Web site referred to by the client. As also shown in Fig. 12-21, we assume that the origin server consists of a database from which responses are dynamically created. Although we have shown only a single Web server, it is common to organize each server according to a multitiered architecture as we discussed before. An edge server can now be roughly organized along the following lines.

First, to improve performance, we can decide to apply full replication of the data stored at the origin server. This scheme works well whenever the update ratio is low and when queries require an extensive database search. As mentioned above, we assume that all updates are carried out at the origin server, which takes responsibility for keeping the replicas and the edge servers in a consistent state. Read operations can thus take place at the edge servers. Here we see that replicating for performance will fail when the update ratio is high, as each update will incur communication over a wide-area network to bring the replicas into a consistent state. As shown in Sivasubramanian et al. (2004a), the read/update ratio is the determining factor to what extent the origin database in a wide-area setting should be replicated.

Another case for full replication is when queries are generally complex. In the case of a relational database, this means that a query requires that multiple tables need to be searched and processed, as is generally the case with a join operation. Opposed to complex queries are simple ones that generally require access to only a single table in order to produce a response. In the latter case, **partial replication** by which only a subset of the data is stored at the edge server may suffice.

The problem with partial replication is that it may be very difficult to manually decide which data is needed at the edge server. Sivasubramanian et al. (2005) propose to handle this automatically by replicating records according to the same principle that Globule replicates its Web pages. As we discussed in Chap. 2, this means that an origin server analyzes access traces for data records on which it subsequently bases its decision on where to place records. Recall that in Globule, decision-making was driven by taking the cost into account for executing read and update operations once data was in place (and possibly replicated). Costs are expressed in a simple linear function:

$$cost = (w_1 \times m_1) + (w_2 \times m_2) + \cdots + (w_n \times m_n)$$

with m_k being a performance metric (such as consumed bandwidth) and $w_k > 0$ the relative weight indicating how important that metric is.

An alternative to partial replication is to make use of **content-aware caches**. The basic idea in this case is that an edge server maintains a local database that is now tailored to the type of queries that can be handled at the origin server. To explain, in a full-fledged database system a query will operate on a database in which the data has been organized into tables such that, for example, redundancy is minimized. Such databases are also said to be **normalized**.

In such databases, any query that adheres to the data schema can, in principle, be processed, although perhaps at considerable costs. With content-aware caches, an edge server maintains a database that is organized according to the structure of queries. What this means is that queries are assumed to adhere to a limited number of templates, effectively meaning that the different kinds of queries that can be processed is restricted. In these cases, whenever a query is received, the edge server matches the query against the available templates, and subsequently looks in its local database to compose a response, if possible. If the requested data is not available, the query is forwarded to the origin server after which the response is cached before returning it to the client.

In effect, what the edge server is doing is checking whether a query can be answered with the data that is stored locally. This is also referred to as a **query containment check**. Note that such data was stored locally as responses to previously issued queries. This approach works best when queries tend to be repeated.

Part of the complexity of content-aware caching comes from the fact that the data at the edge server needs to be kept consistent. To this end, the origin server needs to know which records are associated with which templates, so that any update of a record, or any update of a table, can be properly addressed by, for example, sending an invalidation message to the appropriate edge servers. Another source of complexity comes from the fact that queries still need to be processed at edge servers. In other words, there is nonnegligible computational power needed to handle queries. Considering that databases often form a performance bottleneck in Web servers, alternative solutions may be needed. Finally, caching results from queries that span multiple tables (i.e., when queries are complex) such that a query containment check can be carried out effectively is not trivial. The reason is that the organization of the results may be very different from the organization of the tables on which the query operated.

These observations lead us to a third solution, namely **content-blind caching**, described in detail by Sivasubramanian et al. (2006). The idea of content-blind caching is extremely simple: when a client submits a query to an edge server, the server first computes a unique hash value for that query. Using this hash value, it subsequently looks in its cache whether it has processed this query before. If not, the query is forwarded to the origin and the result is cached before returning it to the client. If the query had been processed before, the previously cached result is returned to the client.

The main advantage of this scheme is the reduced computational effort that is required from an edge server in comparison to the database approaches described above. However, content-blind caching can be wasteful in terms of storage as the caches may contain much more redundant data in comparison to content-aware caching or database replication. Note that such redundancy also complicates the process of keeping the cache up to date as the origin server may need to keep an accurate account of which updates can potentially affect cached query results. These problems can be alleviated when assuming that queries can match only a limited set of predefined templates as we discussed above.

Obviously, these techniques can be equally well deployed for the upcoming generation of Web services, but there is still much research needed before stable solutions can be identified.

12.7 FAULT TOLERANCE

Fault tolerance in the Web-based distributed systems is mainly achieved through client-side caching and server replication. No special methods are incorporated in, for example, HTTP to assist fault tolerance or recovery. Note, however, that high availability in the Web is achieved through redundancy that makes use of generally available techniques in crucial services such as DNS. as an example we mentioned before, DNS allows several addresses to be returned as the result of a name lookup. In traditional Web-based systems, fault tolerance can be relatively easy to achieve considering the stateless design of servers, along with the often static nature of the provided content.

When it comes to Web services, similar observations hold: hardly any new or special techniques are introduced to deal with faults (Birman, 2005). However, it should be clear that problems of masking failures and recoveries can be more severe. For example, Web services support wide-area distributed transactions and solutions will definitely have to deal with failing participating services or unreliable communication.

Even more important is that in the case of Web services we may easily be dealing with complex calling graphs. Note that in many Web-based systems computing follows a simple two-tiered client-server calling convention. This means that a client calls a server, which then computes a response without the need of additional external services. As said, fault tolerance can often be achieved by simply replicating the server or relying partly on result caching.

This situation no longer holds for Web services. In many cases, we are now dealing with multitiered solutions in which servers also act as clients. Applying replication to servers means that callers and callees need to handle replicated invocations, just as in the case of replicated objects as we discussed back in Chap. 10.

Problems are aggravated for services that have been designed to handle Byzantine failures. Replication of components plays a crucial role here, but so does the protocol that clients execute. In addition, we now have to face the situation that a Byzantine fault-tolerant (**BFT**) service may need to act as a client of another nonreplicated service. A solution to this problem is proposed in Merideth et al. (2005) that is based on the BFT system proposed by Castro and Liskov (2002), which we discussed in Chap. 11.

There are three issues that need to be handled. First, clients of a BFT service should see that service as just another Web service. In particular, this means that the internal replication of that service should be hidden from the client, along with a proper processing of responses. For example, a client needs to collect $k + 1$ identical answers from up to $2k + 1$ responses, assuming that the BFT service is designed to handle at most k failing processes. Typically, this type of response processing can be hidden away in client-side stubs, which can be automatically generated from WSDL specifications.

Second, a BFT service should guarantee internal consistency when acting as a client. In particular, it needs to handle the case that the external service it is calling upon returns different answers to different replicas. This could happen, for example, when the external service itself is failing for whatever reason. As a result, the replicas may need to run an additional agreement protocol as an extension to the protocols they are already executing to provide Byzantine fault tolerance. After executing this protocol, they can send their answers back to the client.

Finally, external services should also treat a BFT service acting as a client, as a single entity. In particular, a service cannot simply accept a request coming from a single replica, but can proceed only when it has received at least $k + 1$ identical requests from different replicas.

These three situations lead to three different pieces of software that need to be integrated into toolkits for developing Web services. Details and performance evaluations can be found in Merideth et al. (2005).

12.8 SECURITY

Considering the open nature of the Internet, devising a security architecture that protects clients and servers against various attacks is crucially important. Most of the security issues in the Web deal with setting up a secure channel between a client and server. The predominant approach for setting up a secure channel in the Web is to use the **Secure Socket Layer** (**SSL**), originally implemented by Netscape. Although SSL has never been formally standardized, most Web clients and servers nevertheless support it. An update of SSL has been formally laid down in RFC 2246 and RFC 3546, now referred to as the **Transport Layer Security** (**TLS**) protocol (Dierks and Allen, 1996; and Blake-Wilson et al., 2003).

As shown in Fig. 12-22, TLS is an application-independent security protocol that is logically layered on top of a transport protocol. For reasons of simplicity, TLS (and SSL) implementations are usually based on TCP. TLS can support a variety of higher-level protocols, including HTTP, as we discuss below. For example, it is possible to implement secure versions of FTP or Telnet using TLS.

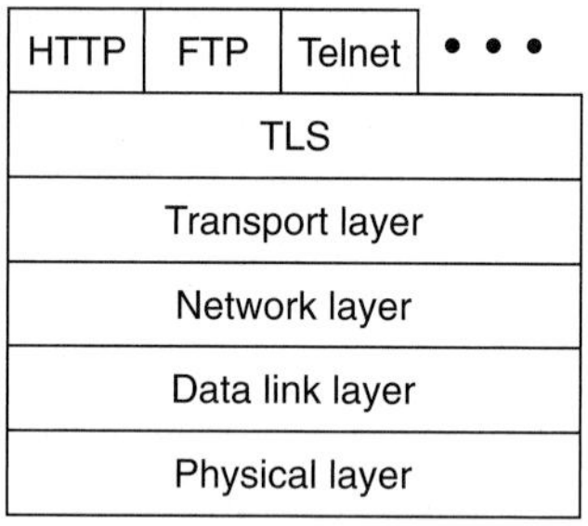

HTTP	FTP	Telnet	• • •
TLS			
Transport layer			
Network layer			
Data link layer			
Physical layer			

Figure 12-22. The position of TLS in the Internet protocol stack.

TLS itself is organized into two layers. The core of the protocol is formed by the **TLS record protocol layer**, which implements a secure channel between a client and server. The exact characteristics of the channel are determined during its setup, but may include message fragmentation and compression, which are applied in conjunction with message authentication, integrity, and confidentiality.

Setting up a secure channel proceeds in two phases, as shown in Fig. 12-23. First, the client informs the server of the cryptographic algorithms it can handle, as well as any compression methods it supports. The actual choice is always made by the server, which reports its choice back to the client. These first two messages shown in Fig. 12-23.

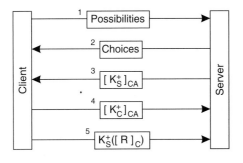

Figure 12-23. TLS with mutual authentication.

In the second phase, authentication takes place. The server is always required to authenticate itself, for which reason it passes the client a certificate containing its public key signed by a certification authority *CA*. If the server requires that the client be authenticated, the client will have to send a certificate to the server as well, shown as message 4 in Fig. 12-23.

The client generates a random number that will be used by both sides for constructing a session key, and sends this number to the server, encrypted with the server's public key. In addition, if client authentication is required, the client signs the number with its private key, leading to message 5 in Fig. 12-23. (In reality, a separate message is sent with a scrambled and signed version of the random number, establishing the same effect.) At that point, the server can verify the identity of the client, after which the secure channel has been set up.

12.9 SUMMARY

It can be argued that Web-based distributed systems have made networked applications popular with end users. Using the notion of a Web document as the means for exchanging information comes close to the way people often communicate in office environments and other settings. Everyone understands what a paper document is, so extending this concept to electronic documents is quite logical for most people.

The hypertext support as provided to Web end users has been of paramount importance to the Web's popularity. In addition, end users generally see a simple client-server architecture in which documents are simply fetched from a specific site. However, modern Web sites are organized along multitiered architectures in which a final component is merely responsible for generating HTML or XML pages as responses that can be displayed at the client.

Replacing the end user with an application has brought us Web services. From a technological point of view, Web services by themselves are generally not spectacular, although they are still in their infancy. What is important, however, is that very different services need to be discovered and be accessible to authorized clients. As a result, huge efforts are spent on standardization of service descriptions, communications, directories, and various interactions. Again, each standard by itself does not represent particularly new insights, but being a standard contributes to the expansion of Web services.

Processes in the Web are tailored to handling HTTP requests, of which the Apache Web server is a canonical example. Apache has proven to be a versatile vehicle for handling HTTP-based systems, but can also be easily extended to facilitate specific needs such as replication.

As the Web operates over the Internet, much attention has been paid to improving performance through caching and replication. More or less standard techniques have been developed for client-side caching, but when it comes to replication considerable advances have been made. Notably when replication of Web applications is at stake, it turns out that different solutions will need to co-exist for attaining optimal performance.

Both fault tolerance and security are generally handled using standard techniques that have since long been applied for many other types of distributed systems.

PROBLEMS

1. To what extent is e-mail part of the Web's document model?

2. In many cases, Web sites are designed to be accessed by users. However, when it comes to Web services, we see that Web sites become dependent on each other. Considering the three-tiered architecture of Fig. 12-3, where would you expect to see the dependency occur?

3. The Web uses a file-based approach to documents by which a client first fetches a file before it is opened and displayed. What is the consequence of this approach for multimedia files?

4. One could argue that from an technological point of view Web services do not address any new issues. What is the compelling argument to consider Web services important?

5. What would be the main advantage of using the distributed server discussed in Chap. 3 to implement a Web server cluster, in comparison to the way the such clusters are organized as shown in Fig. 12-9. What is an obvious disadvantage?

6. Why do persistent connections generally improve performance compared to nonpersistent connections?

7. SOAP is often said to adhere to RPC semantics. Is this really true?

8. Explain the difference between a plug-in, an applet, a servlet, and a CGI program.

9. In WebDAV, is it sufficient for a client to show only the lock token to the server in order to obtain write permissions?

10. Instead of letting a Web proxy compute an expiration time for a document, a server could do this instead. What would be the benefit of such an approach?

11. With Web pages becoming highly personalized (because they can be dynamically generated on a per-client basis on demand), one could argue that Web caches will soon all be obsolete. Yet, this is most likely not going to happen any time in the immediate future. Explain why.

12. Does the Akamai CDN follow a pull-based or push-based distribution protocol?

13. Outline a simple scheme by which an Akamai CDN server can find out that a cached embedded document is stale without checking the document's validity at the original server.

14. Would it make sense to associate a replication strategy with each Web document separately, as opposed to using one or only a few global strategies?

15. Assume that a nonreplicated document of size s bytes is requested r times per second. If the document is replicated to k different servers, and assuming that updates are propagated separately to each replica, when will replication be cheaper than when the document is not replicated?

16. Consider a Web site experiencing a flash crowd. What could be an appropriate measure to take in order to ensure that clients are still serviced well?

17. There are, in principle, three different techniques for redirecting clients to servers: TCP handoff, DNS-based redirection, and HTTP-based redirection. What are the main advantages and disadvantages of each technique?

18. Give an example in which a query containment check as performed by an edge server supporting content-aware caching will return successfully.

19. (**Lab assignment**) Set up a simple Web-based system by installing and configuring the Apache Web server for your local machine such that it can be accessed from a local browser. If you have multiple computers in a local-area network, make sure that the server can be accessed from any browser on that network.

20. (**Lab assignment**) WebDAV is supported by the Apache Web server and allows multiple users to share files for reading and writing over the Internet. Install and configure

Apache for a WebDAV-enabled directory in a local-area network. Test the configuration by using a WebDAV client.

13

DISTRIBUTED
COORDINATION-BASED SYSTEMS

In the previous chapters we took a look at different approaches to distributed systems, in each chapter focusing on a single data type as the basis for distribution. The data type, being either an object, file, or (Web) document, has its origins in nondistributed systems. It is adapted for distributed systems in such a way that many issues about distribution can be made transparent to users and developers.

In this chapter we consider a generation of distributed systems that assume that the various components of a system are inherently distributed and that the real problem in developing such systems lies in coordinating the activities of different components. In other words, instead of concentrating on the transparent distribution of components, emphasis lies on the coordination of activities between those components.

We will see that some aspects of coordination have already been touched upon in the previous chapters, especially when considering event-based systems. As it turns out, many conventional distributed systems are gradually incorporating mechanisms that play a key role in coordination-based systems.

Before taking a look at practical examples of systems, we give a brief introduction to the notion of coordination in distributed systems.

13.1 INTRODUCTION TO COORDINATION MODELS

Key to the approach followed in coordination-based systems is the clean separation between computation and coordination. If we view a distributed system as a collection of (possibly multithreaded) processes, then the computing part of a distributed system is formed by the processes, each concerned with a specific computational activity, which in principle, is carried out independently from the activities of other processes.

In this model, the coordination part of a distributed system handles the communication and cooperation between processes. It forms the glue that binds the activities performed by processes into a whole (Gelernter and Carriero, 1992). In distributed coordination-based systems, the focus is on how coordination between the processes takes place.

Cabri et al. (2000) provide a taxonomy of coordination models for mobile agents that can be applied equally to many other types of distributed systems. Adapting their terminology to distributed systems in general, we make a distinction between models along two different dimensions, temporal and referential, as shown in Fig. 13-1.

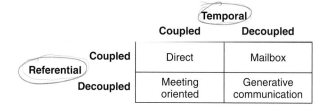

Figure 13-1. A taxonomy of coordination models (adapted from Cabri et al., 2000).

When processes are temporally and referentially coupled, coordination takes place in a direct way, referred to as **direct coordination**. The referential coupling generally appears in the form of explicit referencing in communication. For example, a process can communicate only if it knows the name or identifier of the other processes it wants to exchange information with. Temporal coupling means that processes that are communicating will both have to be up and running. This coupling is analogous to the transient message-oriented communication we discussed in Chap. 4.

A different type of coordination occurs when processes are temporally decoupled, but referentially coupled, which we refer to as **mailbox coordination**. In this case, there is no need for two communicating processes to execute at the same time in order to let communication take place. Instead, communication takes place by putting messages in a (possibly shared) mailbox. This situation is analogous to persistent message-oriented communication as described in Chap. 4. It is necessary to explicitly address the mailbox that will hold the messages that are to be exchanged. Consequently, there is a referential coupling.

The combination of referentially decoupled and temporally coupled systems form the group of models for **meeting-oriented coordination**. In referentially decoupled systems, processes do not know each other explicitly. In other words, when a process wants to coordinate its activities with other processes, it cannot directly refer to another process. Instead, there is a concept of a meeting in which processes temporarily group together to coordinate their activities. The model prescribes that the meeting processes are executing at the same time.

Meeting-based systems are often implemented by means of events, like the ones supported by object-based distributed systems. In this chapter, we discuss another mechanism for implementing meetings, namely **publish/subscribe systems**. In these systems, processes can subscribe to messages containing information on specific subjects, while other processes produce (i.e., publish) such messages. Most publish/subscribe systems require that communicating processes are active at the same time; hence there is a temporal coupling. However, the communicating processes may otherwise remain anonymous.

The most widely-known coordination model is the combination of referentially and temporally decoupled processes, exemplified by **generative communication** as introduced in the Linda programming system by Gelernter (1985). The key idea in generative communication is that a collection of independent processes make use of a shared persistent dataspace of tuples. **Tuples** are tagged data records consisting of a number (but possibly zero) typed fields. Processes can put any type of record into the shared dataspace (i.e., they generate communication records). Unlike the case with blackboards, there is no need to agree in advance on the structure of tuples. Only the tag is used to distinguish between tuples representing different kinds of information.

An interesting feature of these shared dataspaces is that they implement an associative search mechanism for tuples. In other words, when a process wants to extract a tuple from the dataspace, it essentially specifies (some of) the values of the fields it is interested in. Any tuple that matches that specification is then removed from the dataspace and passed to the process. If no match could be found, the process can choose to block until there is a matching tuple. We defer the details on this coordination model to later when discussing concrete systems.

We note that generative communication and shared dataspaces are often also considered to be forms of publish/subscribe systems. In what follows, we shall adopt this commonality as well. A good overview of publish/subscribe systems (and taking a rather broad perspective) can be found in Eugster et al. (2003). In this chapter we take the approach that in these systems there is at least referential decoupling between processes, but preferably also temporal decoupling.

13.2 ARCHITECTURES

An important aspect of coordination-based systems is that communication takes place by describing the characteristics of data items that are to be exchanged. As a consequence, naming plays a crucial role. We return to naming later in this chapter, but for now the important issue is that in many cases, data items are not explicitly identified by senders and receivers.

13.2.1 Overall Approach

Let us first assume that data items are described by a series of **attributes**. A data item is said to be **published** when it is made available for other processes to read. To that end, a **subscription** needs to be passed to the middleware, containing a description of the data items that the subscriber is interested in. Such a description typically consists of some (*attribute, value*) pairs, possibly combined with (*attribute, range*) pairs. In the latter case, the specified attribute is expected to take on values within a specified range. Descriptions can sometimes be given using all kinds of predicates formulated over the attributes, very similar in nature to SQL-like queries in the case of relational databases. We will come across these types of descriptors later in this chapter.

We are now confronted with a situation in which subscriptions need to be **matched** against data items, as shown in Fig. 13-2. When matching succeeds, there are two possible scenarios. In the first case, the middleware may decide to forward the published data to its current set of subscribers, that is, processes with a matching subscription. As an alternative, the middleware can also forward a **notification** at which point subscribers can execute a read operation to retrieve the published data item.

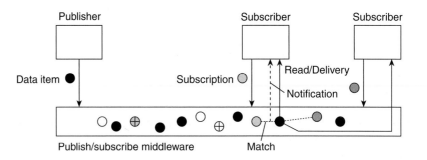

Figure 13-2. The principle of exchanging data items between publishers and subscribers.

In those cases in which data items are immediately forwarded to subscribers, the middleware will generally not offer storage of data. Storage is either explicitly handled by a separate service, or is the responsibility of subscribers. In other words, we have a referentially decoupled, but temporally coupled system.

This situation is different when notifications are sent so that subscribers need to explicitly read the published data. Necessarily, the middleware will have to store data items. In these situations there are additional operations for data management. It is also possible to attach a lease to a data item such that when the lease expires that the data item is automatically deleted.

In the model described so far, we have assumed that there is a fixed set of n attributes $a_1, \ldots, a_n$ that is used to describe data items. In particular, each published data item is assumed to have an associated vector $<(a_1, v_1), \ldots, (a_n, v_n)>$ of (*attribute, value*) pairs. In many coordination-based systems, this assumption is false. Instead, what happens is that **events** are published, which can be viewed as data items with only a single specified attribute.

Events complicate the processing of subscriptions. To illustrate, consider a subscription such as "notify when room R4.20 is unoccupied and the door is unlocked." Typically, a distributed system supporting such subscriptions can be implemented by placing independent sensors for monitoring room occupancy (e.g., motion sensors) and those for registering the status of a door lock. Following the approach sketched so far, we would need to *compose* such primitive events into a publishable data item to which processes can then subscribe. Event composition turns out to be a difficult task, notably when the primitive events are generated from sources dispersed across the distributed system.

Clearly, in coordination-based systems such as these, the crucial issue is the efficient and scalable implementation of matching subscriptions to data items, along with the construction of relevant data items. From the outside, a coordination approach provides lots of potential for building very large-scale distributed systems due to the strong decoupling of processes. On the other hand, as we shall see next, devising scalable implementations without losing this independence is not a trivial exercise.

13.2.2 Traditional Architectures

The simplest solution for matching data items against subscriptions is to have a centralized client-server architecture. This is a typical solution currently adopted by many publish/subscribe systems, including IBM's WebSphere (IBM, 2005c) and popular implementations for Sun's JMS (Sun Microsystems, 2004a). Likewise, implementations for the more elaborate generative communication models such as Jini (Sun Microsystems, 2005b) and JavaSpaces (Freeman et al., 1999) are mostly based on central servers. Let us take a look at two typical examples.

Example: Jini and JavaSpaces

Jini is a distributed system that consists of a mixture of different but related elements. It is strongly related to the Java programming language, although many of its principles can be implemented equally well in other languages. An important part of the system is formed by a coordination model for generative communication. Jini provides temporal and referential decoupling of processes through a coordination system called **JavaSpaces** (Freeman et al., 1999), derived from Linda. A JavaSpace is a shared dataspace that stores tuples representing a typed set of references to Java objects. Multiple JavaSpaces may coexist in a single Jini system.

Tuples are stored in serialized form. In other words, whenever a process wants to store a tuple, that tuple is first marshaled, implying that all its fields are marshaled as well. As a consequence, when a tuple contains two different fields that refer to the same object, the tuple as stored in a JavaSpace implementation will hold two marshaled copies of that object.

A tuple is put into a JavaSpace by means of a write operation, which first marshals the tuple before storing it. Each time the write operation is called on a tuple, another marshaled copy of that tuple is stored in the JavaSpace, as shown in Fig. 13-3. We will refer to each marshaled copy as a **tuple instance**.

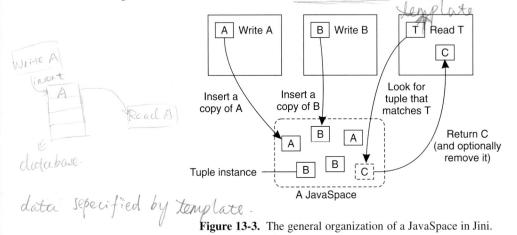

Figure 13-3. The general organization of a JavaSpace in Jini.

The interesting aspect of generative communication in Jini is the way that tuple instances are read from a JavaSpace. To read a tuple instance, a process provides another tuple that it uses as a **template** for matching tuple instances as stored in a JavaSpace. Like any other tuple, a template tuple is a typed set of object references. Only tuple instances of the same type as the template can be read from a JavaSpace. A field in the template tuple either contains a reference to an actual object or contains the value *NULL*. For example, consider the class

```
class public Tuple implements Entry {
    public Integer id, value;
    public Tuple(Integer id, Integer value){this.id = id; this.value = value}
}
```

Then a template declared as

```
Tuple template = new Tuple(null, new Integer(42))
```

will match the tuple

```
Tuple item = new Tuple("MyName", new Integer(42))
```

To match a tuple instance in a JavaSpace against a template tuple, the latter is marshaled as usual, including its *NULL* fields. For each tuple instance of the same type as the template, a field-by-field comparison is made with the template tuple.

Two fields match if they both have a copy of the same reference or if the field in the template tuple is *NULL*. A tuple instance matches a template tuple if there is a pairwise matching of their respective fields.

When a tuple instance is found that matches the template tuple provided as part of a read operation, that tuple instance is unmarshaled and returned to the reading process. There is also a take operation that additionally removes the tuple instance from the JavaSpace. Both operations block the caller until a matching tuple is found. It is possible to specify a maximum blocking time. In addition, there are variants that simply return immediately if no matching tuple existed.

Processes that make use of JavaSpaces need not coexist at the same time. In fact, if a JavaSpace is implemented using persistent storage, a complete Jini system can be brought down and later restarted without losing any tuples.

Although Jini does not support it, it should be clear that having a central server allows subscriptions to be fairly elaborate. For example, at the moment two nonnull fields match if they are identical. However, realizing that each field represents an object, matching could also be evaluated by executing an object-specific comparison operator [see also Picco et al. (2005)]. In fact, if such an operator can be overridden by an application, more-or-less arbitrary comparison semantics can be implemented. It is important to note that such comparisons may require an extensive search through currently stored data items. Such searches cannot be easily efficiently implemented in a distributed way. It is exactly for this reason that when elaborate matching rules are supported we will generally see only centralized implementations.

Another advantage of having a centralized implementation is that it becomes easier to implement synchronization primitives. For example, the fact that a process can block until a suitable data item is published, and then subsequently execute a destructive read by which the matching tuple is removed, offers facilities for process synchronization without processes needing to know each other. Again, synchronization in decentralized systems is inherently difficult as we also discussed in Chap. 6. We will return to synchronization below.

Example: TIB/Rendezvous

An alternative solution to using central servers is to immediately disseminate published data items to the appropriate subscribers using multicasting. This principle is used in **TIB/Rendezvous**, of which the basic architecture is shown in Fig. 13-4 (TIBCO, 2005) In this approach, a data item is a message tagged with a compound keyword describing its content, such as *news.comp.os.books*. A subscriber provides (parts of) a keyword, or indicating the messages it wants to receive, such as *news.comp.*.books*. These keywords are said to indicate the **subject** of a message.

Fundamental to its implementation is the use of broadcasting common in local-area networks, although it also uses more efficient communication facilities

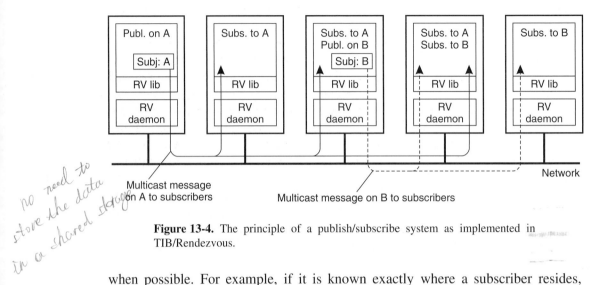

no need to store the data in a shared storage

Figure 13-4. The principle of a publish/subscribe system as implemented in TIB/Rendezvous.

when possible. For example, if it is known exactly where a subscriber resides, point-to-point messages will generally be used. Each host on such a network will run a **rendezvous daemon**, which takes care that messages are sent and delivered according to their subject. Whenever a message is published, it is multicast to each host on the network running a rendezvous daemon. Typically, multicasting is implemented using the facilities offered by the underlying network, such as IP-multicasting or hardware broadcasting.

Processes that subscribe to a subject pass their subscription to their local daemon. The daemon constructs a table of (*process, subject*), entries and whenever a message on subject *S* arrives, the daemon simply checks in its table for local subscribers, and forwards the message to each one. If there are no subscribers for *S*, the message is discarded immediately.

When using multicasting as is done in TIB/Rendezvous, there is no reason why subscriptions cannot be elaborate and be more than string comparison as is currently the case. The crucial observation here is that because messages are forwarded to every node anyway, the potentially complex matching of published data against subscriptions can be done entirely locally without further network communication. However, as we shall discuss later, simple comparison rules are required whenever matching across wide-area networks is needed.

13.2.3 Peer-to-Peer Architectures

only subscriber should recv it.

The traditional architectures followed by most coordination-based systems suffer from scalability problems (although their commercial vendors will state otherwise). Obviously, having a central server for matching subscriptions to published data cannot scale beyond a few hundred clients. Likewise, using multicasting requires special measures to extend beyond the realm of local-area networks.

Moreover, if scalability is to be guaranteed, further restrictions on describing subscriptions and data items may be necessary.

Much research has been spent on realizing coordination-based systems using peer-to-peer technology. Straightforward implementations exist for those cases in which keywords are used, as these can be hashed to unique identifiers for published data. This approach has also been used for mapping (*attribute, value*) pairs to identifiers. In these cases, matching reduces to a straightforward lookup of an identifier, which can be efficiently implemented in a DHT-based system. This approach works well for the more conventional publish/subscribe systems as illustrated by Tam and Jacobsen (2003), but also for generative communication (Busi et al., 2004).

Matters become complicated for more elaborate matching schemes. Notoriously difficult are the cases in which ranges need to be supported and only very few proposals exist. In the following, we discuss one such proposal, devised by one of the authors and his colleagues (Voulgaris et al., 2006).

Example: A Gossip-Based Publish/Subscribe System

Consider a publish/subscribe system in which data items can be described by means of N attributes $a_1, \ldots, a_N$ whose value can be directly mapped to a floating-point number. Such values include, for example, floats, integers, enumerations, booleans, and strings. A subscription s takes the form of a tuple of (*attribute, value/range*) pairs, such as

$$s = <a_1 \rightarrow 3.0, a_4 \rightarrow [0.0, 0.5)>$$

In this example, s specifies that a_1 should be equal to 3.0, and a_4 should lie in the interval [0.0, 0.5). Other attributes are allowed to take on any value. For clarity, assume that every node i enters only one subscription s_i.

Note that each subscription s_i actually specifies a subset S_i in the N-dimensional space of floating-point numbers. Such a subset is also called a hyperspace. For the system as a whole, only published data whose description falls in the union $\mathbf{S} = \cup S_i$ of these hyperspaces is of interest. The whole idea is to automatically partition $\mathbf{S}$ into M disjoint hyperspaces $\mathbf{S}_1, \ldots, \mathbf{S}_M$ such that each falls completely in one of the subscription hyperspaces S_i, and together they cover all subscriptions. More formally, we have that:

$$(\mathbf{S}_m \cap S_i \neq \varnothing) \Rightarrow (\mathbf{S}_m \subseteq S_i)$$

Moreover, the system keeps M minimal in the sense that there is no partitioning with fewer parts $\mathbf{S}_m$. The whole idea is to register, for each hyperspace $\mathbf{S}_m$, exactly those nodes i for which $\mathbf{S}_m \subseteq S_i$. In that case, when a data item is published, the system need merely find the $\mathbf{S}_m$ to which that item belongs, from which point it can forward the item to the associated nodes.

To this end, nodes regularly exchange subscriptions using an epidemic proto-col. If two nodes i and j notice that their respective subscriptions intersect, that is $S_{ij} \equiv S_i \cap S_j \neq \emptyset$ they will record this fact and keep references to each other. If they discover a third node k with $S_{ijk} \equiv S_{ij} \cap S_k \neq \emptyset$, the three of them will con-nect to each other so that a data item d from S_{ijk} can be efficiently disseminated. Note that if $S_{ij} - S_{ijk} \neq \emptyset$, nodes i and j will maintain their mutual references, but now associate it strictly with $S_{ij} - S_{ijk}$.

In essence, what we are seeking is a means to cluster nodes into M different groups, such that nodes i and j belong to the same group if and only if their sub-scriptions S_i and S_j intersect. Moreover, nodes in the same group should be organ-ized into an overlay network that will allow efficient dissemination of a data item in the hyperspace associated with that group. This situation for a single attribute is sketched in Fig. 13-5.

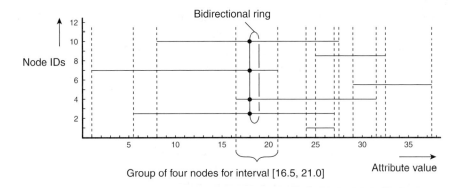

Figure 13-5. Grouping nodes for supporting range queries in a peer-to-peer publish/subscribe system.

Here, we see a total of seven nodes in which the horizontal line for node i indicates its range of interest for the value of the single attribute. Also shown is the grouping of nodes into disjoint ranges of interests for values of the attribute. For example, nodes 3, 4, 7, and 10 will be grouped together representing the inter-val [16.5, 21.0]. Any data item with a value in this range should be disseminated to only these four nodes.

To construct these groups, the nodes are organized into a gossip-based un-structured network. Each node maintains a list of references to other neighbors (i.e., a **partial view**), which it periodically exchanges with one of its neighbors as described in Chap. 2. Such an exchange will allow a node to learn about random other nodes in the system. Every node keeps track of the nodes it discovers with overlapping interests (i.e., with an intersecting subscription).

At a certain moment, every node i will generally have references to other nodes with overlapping interests. As part of exchanging information with a node j, node i orders these nodes by their identifiers and selects the one with the lowest identifier $i_1 > j$, such that its subscription overlaps with that of node j, that is, $S_{j,i_1} \equiv S_{i_1} \cap S_j \neq \varnothing$.

The next one to be selected is $i_2 > i_1$ such that its subscription also overlaps with that of j, but only if it contains elements not yet covered by node i_1. In other words, we should have that $S_{j,i_1,i_2} \equiv (S_{i_2} - S_{j,i_1}) \cap S_j \neq \varnothing$. This process is repeated until all nodes that have an overlapping interest with node i have been inspected, leading to an ordered list $i_1 < i_2 < \cdots < i_n$. Note that a node i_k is in this list because it covers a region R of common interest to node i and j not yet jointly covered by nodes with a lower identifier than i_k. In effect, node i_k is the *first* node that node j should forward a data item to that falls in this unique region R. This procedure can be expanded to let node i construct a bidirectional ring. Such a ring is also shown in Fig. 13-5.

Whenever a data item d is published, it is disseminated as quickly as possible to *any* node that is interested in it. As it turns out, with the information available at every node finding a node i interested in d is simple. From there on, node i need simply forward d along the ring of subscribers for the particular range that d falls into. To speed up dissemination, short-cuts are maintained for each ring as well. Details can be found in Voulgaris et al. (2006).

Discussion

An approach somewhat similar to this gossip-based solution in the sense that it attempts to find a partitioning of the space covered by the attribute's values, but which uses a DHT-based system is described in Gupta et al. (2004). In another proposal described in Bharambe (2004), each attribute a_i is handled by a separate process P_i, which in turn partitions the range of its attribute across multiple processes. When a data item d is published, it is forwarded to each P_i, where it is subsequently stored at the process responsible for the d's value of a_i.

All these approaches are illustrative for the complexity when mapping a nontrivial publish/subscribe system to a peer-to-peer network. In essence, this complexity comes from the fact that supporting search in attribute-based naming systems is inherently difficult to establish in a decentralized fashion. We will again come across these difficulties when discussing replication.

13.2.4 Mobility and Coordination

A topic that has received considerable attention in the literature is how to combine publish/subscribe solutions with node mobility. In many cases, it is assumed that there is a fixed basic infrastructure with access points for mobile nodes. Under these assumptions, the issue becomes how to ensure that published messages are not delivered more than once to a subscriber who switches access points. One practical solution to this problem is to let subscribers keep track of the messages they have already received and simply discard duplicates. Alternative, but more intricate solutions comprise routers that keep track of which messages have been sent to which subscribers (see, e.g., Caporuscio et al., 2003).

Example: Lime

In the case of generative communication, several solutions have been proposed to operate a shared dataspace in which (some of) the nodes are mobile. A canonical example in this case is Lime (Murphy et al., 2001), which strongly resembles the JavaSpace model we discussed previously.

In Lime, each process has its own associated dataspace, but when processes are in each other's proximity such that they are connected, their dataspaces become shared. Theoretically, being connected can mean that there is a route in a joint underlying network that allows two processes to exchange data. In practice, however, it either means that two processes are temporarily located on the same physical host, or their respective hosts can communicate with each other through a (single hop) wireless link. Formally, the processes should be member of the same group and use the same group communication protocol.

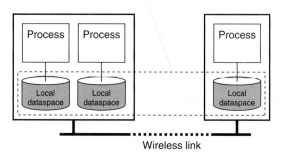

Figure 13-6. Transient sharing of local dataspaces in Lime.

The local dataspaces of connected processes form a transiently shared dataspace that will allow processes to exchange tuples, as shown in Fig. 13-6. For example, when a process P executes a write operation, the associated tuple is stored in the process's local dataspace. In principle, it stays there until there is a matching take operation, possibly from another process that is now in the same group as P. In this way, the fact that we are actually dealing with a completely distributed shared dataspace is transparent for participating processes. However, Lime also allows breaking this transparency by specifying exactly for whom a tuple is intended. Likewise, read and take operations can have an additional parameter specifying from which process a tuple is expected.

To better control how tuples are distributed, dataspaces can carry out what are known as **reactions**. A reaction specifies an action to be executed when a tuple matching a given template is found in the local dataspace. Each time a dataspace changes, an executable reaction is selected at random, often leading to a further modification of the dataspace. Reactions span the current shared dataspace, but there are several restrictions to ensure that they can be executed efficiently. For example, in the case of weak reactions, it is only guaranteed that the associated actions are eventually executed, provided the matching data is still accessible.

The idea of reactions has been taken a step further in TOTA, where each tuple has an associated code fragment telling exactly how that tuple should be moved between dataspaces, possibly also including transformations (Mamei and Zambonelli, 2004).

13.3 PROCESSES

There is nothing really special about the processes used in publish/subscribe systems. In most cases, efficient mechanisms need to be deployed for searching in a potentially large collection of data. The main problem is devising schemes that work well in distributed environments. We return to this issue below when discussing consistency and replication.

13.4 COMMUNICATION

Communication in many publish/subscribe systems is relatively simple. For example, in virtually every Java-based system, all communication proceeds through remote method invocations. One important problem that needs to be handled when publish/subscribe systems are spread across a wide-area system is that published data should reach only the relevant subscribers. As we described above, using a self-organizing method by which nodes in a peer-to-peer system are automatically clustered, after which dissemination takes place per cluster is one solution. An alternative solution is to deploy content-based routing.

13.4.1 Content-Based Routing

In **content-based routing**, the system is assumed to be built on top of a point-to-point network in which messages are explicitly routed between nodes. Crucial in this setup is that routers can take routing decisions by considering the content of a message. More precisely, it is assumed that each message carries a description of its content, and that this description can be used to cut-off routes for which it is known that they do not lead to receivers interested in that message.

A practical approach toward content-based routing is proposed in Carzaniga et al. (2004). Consider a publish/subscribe system consisting of N servers to which clients (i.e., applications) can send messages, or from which they can read incoming messages. We assume that in order to read messages, an application will have previously provided the server with a description of the kind of data it is interested in. The server, in turn, will notify the application when relevant data has arrived.

Carzaniga et al. propose a two-layered routing scheme in which the lowest layer consists of a shared broadcast tree connecting the N servers. There are various ways for setting up such a tree, ranging from network-level multicast support to application-level multicast trees as we discussed in Chap. 4. Here, we also assume that such a tree has been set up with the N servers as end nodes, along with a collection of intermediate nodes forming the routers. Note that the distinction between a server and a router is only a logical one: a single machine may host both kinds of processes.

Consider first two extremes for content-based routing, assuming we need to support only simple subject-based publish/subscribe in which each message is tagged with a unique (noncompound) keyword. One extreme solution is to send each published message to every server, and subsequently let the server check whether any of its clients had subscribed to the subject of that message. In essence, this is the approach followed in TIB/Rendezvous.

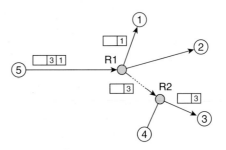

Figure 13-7. Naive content-based routing.

The other extreme solution is to let every server broadcast its subscriptions to all other servers. As a result, every server will be able to compile a list of (*subject, destination*) pairs. Then, whenever an application submits a message on subject *s*, its associated server prepends the destination servers to that message. When the message reaches a router, the latter can use the list to decide on the paths that the message should follow, as shown in Fig. 13-7.

Taking this last approach as our starting point, we can refine the capabilities of routers for deciding where to forward messages to. To that end, each server broadcasts its subscription across the network so that routers can compose **routing filters**. For example, assume that node 3 in Fig. 13-7 subscribes to messages for which an attribute *a* lies in the range [0,3], but that node 4 wants messages with $a \in [2,5]$. In this case, router R_2 will create a routing filter as a table with an entry for each of its outgoing links (in this case three: one to node 3, one to node 4, and one toward router R_1), as shown in Fig. 13-8.

Interface	Filter
To node 3	$a \in [0,3]$
To node 4	$a \in [2,5]$
Toward router R_1	(unspecified)

Figure 13-8. A partially filled routing table.

More interesting is what happens at router R_1. In this example, the subscriptions from nodes 3 and 4 dictate that any message with a lying in the interval $[0,3] \cup [2,5] = [0,5]$ should be forwarded along the path to router R_2, and this is precisely the information that R_1 will store in its table. It is not difficult to imagine that more intricate subscription compositions can be supported.

This simple example also illustrates that whenever a node leaves the system, or when it is no longer interested in specific messages, it should cancel its subscription and essentially broadcast this information to all routers. This cancellation, in turn, may lead to adjusting various routing filters. Late adjustments will at worst lead to unnecessary traffic as messages may be forwarded along paths for which there are no longer subscribers. Nevertheless, timely adjustments are needed to keep performance at an acceptable level.

One of the problems with content-based routing is that although the principle of composing routing filters is simple, identifying the links along which an incoming message must be forwarded can be compute-intensive. The computational complexity comes from the implementation of matching attribute values to subscriptions, which essentially boils down to an entry-by-entry comparison. How this comparison can be done efficiently is described in Carzaniga et al. (2003).

13.4.2 Supporting Composite Subscriptions

The examples so far form relatively simple extensions to routing tables. These extensions suffice when subscriptions take the form of vectors of (*attribute, value/range*) pairs. However, there is often a need for more sophisticated expressions of subscriptions. For example, it may be convenient to express **compositions** of subscriptions in which a process specifies in a single subscription that it is interested in very different types of data items. To illustrate, a process may want to see data items on stocks from IBM *and* data on their revenues, but sending data items of only one kind is not useful.

To handle subscription compositions, Li and Jacobsen (2005) proposed to design routers analogous to rule databases. In effect, subscriptions are transformed into rules stating under which conditions published data should be forwarded, and along which outgoing links. It is not difficult to imagine that this may lead to content-based routing schemes that are far more advanced than the routing filters described above. Supporting subscription composition is strongly related to naming issues in coordination-based systems, which we discuss next.

13.5 NAMING

Let us now pay some more attention to naming in coordination-based systems. So far, we have mostly assumed that every published data item has an associated vector of n (*attribute, value*) pairs and that processes can subscribe to data items by specifying predicates over these attribute values. In general, this naming scheme can be readily applied, although systems differ with respect to attribute types, values, and the predicates that can be used.

For example, with JavaSpaces we saw that essentially only comparison for equality is supported, although this can be relatively easily extended in application-specific ways. Likewise, many commercial publish/subscribe systems support only rather primitive string-comparison operators.

One of the problems we already mentioned is that in many cases we cannot simply assume that every data item is tagged with values for all attributes. In particular, we will see that a data item has only one associated (*attribute, value*) pair, in which case it is also referred to as an **event**. Support for subscribing to events, and notably composite events largely dictates the discussion on naming issues in publish/subscribe systems. What we have discussed so far should be considered as the more primitive means for supporting coordination in distributed systems. We now address in more depth events and event composition.

When dealing with composite events, we need to take two different issues into account. The first one is to describe compositions. Such descriptions form the basis for subscriptions. The second issue is how to collect (primitive) events and subsequently match them to subscriptions. Pietzuch et al. (2003) have proposed a general framework for event composition in distributed systems. We take this framework as the basis for our discussion.

13.5.1 Describing Composite Events

Let us first consider some examples of composite events to give a better idea of the complexity that we may need to deal with. Fig. 13-9 shows examples of increasingly complex composite events. In this example, R4.20 could be an air-conditioned and secured computer room.

The first two subscriptions are relatively easy. S_1 is an example that can be handled by a primitive discrete event, whereas S_2 is a simple composition of two discrete events. Subscription S_3 is more complex as it requires that the system can also report time-related events. Matters are further complicated if subscriptions

Ex.	Description
S1	Notify when room R4.20 is unoccupied
S2	Notify when R4.20 is unoccupied and the door is unlocked
S3	Notify when R4.20 is unoccupied for 10 seconds while the door is unlocked
S4	Notify when the temperature in R4.20 rises more than 1 degree per 30 minutes
S5	Notify when the average temperature in R4.20 is more than 20 degrees in the past 30 minutes

Figure 13-9. Examples of events in a distributed system.

involve aggregated values required for computing gradients (S_4) or averages (S_5). Note that in the case of S_5 we are requiring a continuous monitoring of the system in order to send notifications on time.

The basic idea behind an event-composition language for distributed systems is to enable the formulation of subscriptions in terms of primitive events. In their framework, Pietzuch et al. provide a relatively simple language for an extended type of finite-state machine (FSM). The extensions allow for the specification of sojourn times in states, as well as the generation of new (composite) events. The precise details of their language are not important for our discussion here. What is important is that subscriptions can be translated into FSMs.

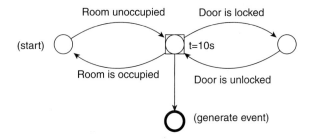

Figure 13-10. The finite state machine for subscription S3 from Fig. 13-9.

To give an example, Fig. 13-10 shows the FSM for subscription S_3 from Fig. 13-9. The special case is given by the timed state, indicated by the label "$t = 10s$" which specifies that a transition to the final state is made if the door is not locked within 10 seconds.

Much more complex subscriptions can be described. An important aspect is that these FSMs can often be decomposed into smaller FSMs that communicate by passing events to each other. Note that such an event communication would normally trigger a state transition at the FSM for which that event is intended. For example, assume that we want to automatically turn off the lights in room R4.20

after 2 seconds when we are certain that nobody is there anymore (and the door is locked). In that case, we can reuse the FSM from Fig. 13-10 if we let it generate an event for a second FSM that will trigger the lighting, as shown in Fig. 13-11

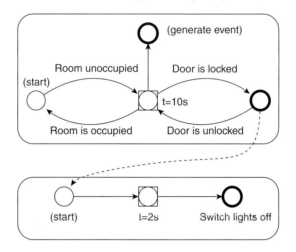

Figure 13-11. Two coupled FSMs.

The important observation here is that these two FSMs can be implemented as separate processes in the distributed system. In this case, the FSM for controlling the lighting will subscribe to the composed event that is triggered when R4.20 is unoccupied and the door is locked. This leads to distributed detectors which we discuss next.

13.5.2 Matching Events and Subscriptions

Now consider a publish/subscribe system supporting composite events. Every subscription is provided in the form of an expression that can be translated into a finite state machine (FSM). State transitions are essentially triggered by primitive events that take place, such as leaving a room or locking a door.

To match events and subscriptions, we can follow a simple, naive implementation in which every subscriber runs a process implementing the finite state machine associated with its subscription. In that case, all the primitive events that are relevant for a specific subscription will have to be forwarded to the subscriber. Obviously, this will generally not be very efficient.

A much better approach is to consider the complete collection of subscriptions, and decompose subscriptions into communicating finite state machines, such that some of these FSMs are shared between different subscriptions. An example of this sharing was shown in Fig. 13-11. This approach toward handling subscriptions leads to what are known as **distributed event detectors**. Note that a distribution of event detectors is similar in nature to the distributed resolution of names in various naming systems. Primitive events lead to state transitions in relatively simple finite state machines, in turn triggering the generation of composite events. The latter can then lead to state transitions in other FSMs, again possibly leading to further event generation. Of course, events translate to messages that are sent over the network to processes that subscribed to them.

Besides optimizing through sharing, breaking down subscriptions into communicating FSMs also has the potential advantage of optimizing network usage. Consider again the events related to monitoring the computer room we described above. Assuming that there only processes interested in the composite events, it makes sense to compose these events close to the computer room. Such a placement will prevent having to send the primitive events across the network. Moreover, when considering Fig. 13-9, we see that we may only need to send the alarm when noticing that the room is unoccupied for 10 seconds while the door is unlocked. Such an event will generally occur rarely in comparison to, for example, (un)locking the door.

Decomposing subscriptions into distributed event detectors, and subsequently optimally placing them across a distributed system is still subject to much research. For example, the last word on subscription languages has not been said, and especially the trade-off between expressiveness and efficiency of implementations will attract a lot of attention. In most cases, the more expressive a language is, the more unlikely there will be an efficient distributed implementation. Current proposals such as by Demers et al. (2006) and by Liu and Jacobsen (2004) confirm this. It will take some years before we see these techniques being applied to commercial publish/subscribe systems.

13.6 SYNCHRONIZATION

Synchronization in coordination-based systems is generally restricted to systems supporting generative communication. Matters are relatively straightforward when only a single server is used. In that case, processes can be simply blocked until tuples become available, but it is also simpler to remove them. Matters become complicated when the shared dataspace is replicated and distributed across multiple servers, as we describe next.

13.7 CONSISTENCY AND REPLICATION

Replication plays a key role in the scalability of coordination-based systems, and notably those for generative communication. In the following, we first consider some standard approaches as have been explored in a number of systems such as JavaSpaces. Next, we describe some recent results that allow for the dynamic and automatic placement of tuples depending on their access patterns.

13.7.1 Static Approaches

The distributed implementation of a system supporting generative communication frequently requires special attention. We concentrate on possible distributed implementations of a JavaSpace server, that is, an implementation by which the collection of tuple instances may be distributed and replicated across several machines. An overview of implementation techniques for tuple-based runtime systems is given by Rowstron (2001).

General Considerations

An efficient distributed implementation of a JavaSpace has to solve two problems:

1. How to simulate associative addressing without massive searching.

2. How to distribute tuple instances among machines and locate them later.

The key to both problems is to observe that each tuple is a typed data structure. Splitting the tuple space into subspaces, each of whose tuples is of the same type simplifies programming and makes certain optimizations possible. For example, because tuples are typed, it becomes possible to determine at compile time which subspace a call to a write, read, or take operates on. This partitioning means that only a fraction of the set of tuple instances has to be searched.

In addition, each subspace can be organized as a hash table using (part of) its i-th tuple field as the hash key. Recall that every field in a tuple instance is a marshaled reference to an object. JavaSpaces does not prescribe how marshaling should be done. Therefore, an implementation may decide to marshal a reference in such a way that the first few bytes are used as an identifier of the type of the object that is being marshaled. A call to a write, read, or take operation can then be executed by computing the hash function of the ith field to find the position in the table where the tuple instance belongs. Knowing the subspace and table position eliminates all searching. Of course, if the ith field of a read or take operation is *NULL*, hashing is not possible, so a complete search of the subspace is generally needed. By carefully choosing the field to hash on, however, searching can often be avoided.

Additional optimizations are also used. For example, the hashing scheme described above distributes the tuples of a given subspace into bins to restrict searching to a single bin. It is possible to place different bins on different machines, both to spread the load more widely and to take advantage of locality. If the hashing function is the type identifier modulo the number of machines, the number of bins scales linearly with the system size [see also Bjornson (1993)].

Javaspace full replication, non-scalable.

On a network of computers, the best choice depends on the communication architecture. If reliable broadcasting is available, a serious candidate is to replicate all the subspaces in full on all machines, as shown in Fig. 13-12. When a write is done, the new tuple instance is broadcast and entered into the appropriate subspace on each machine. To do a read or take operation, the local subspace is searched. However, since successful completion of a take requires removing the tuple instance from the JavaSpace, a delete protocol is required to remove it from all machines. To prevent race conditions and deadlocks, a two-phase commit protocol can be used.

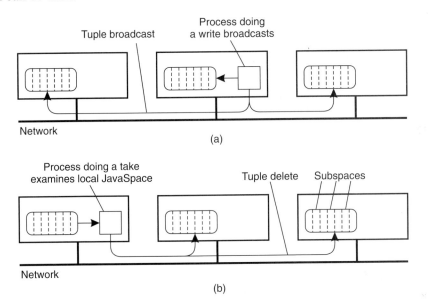

Figure 13-12. A JavaSpace can be replicated on all machines. The dotted lines show the partitioning of the JavaSpace into subspaces. (a) Tuples are broadcast on write. (b) reads are local, but the removing an instance when calling take must be broadcast.

This design is straightforward, but may not scale well as the system grows in the number of tuple instances and the size of the network. For example, implementing this scheme across a wide-area network is prohibitively expensive.

The inverse design is to do writes locally, storing the tuple instance only on the machine that generated it, as shown in Fig. 13-13. To do a read or take, a process must broadcast the template tuple. Each recipient then checks to see if it has a match, sending back a reply if it does.

If the tuple instance is not present, or if the broadcast is not received at the machine holding the tuple, the requesting machine retransmits the broadcast request ad infinitum, increasing the interval between broadcasts until a suitable tuple instance materializes and the request can be satisfied. If two or more tuple

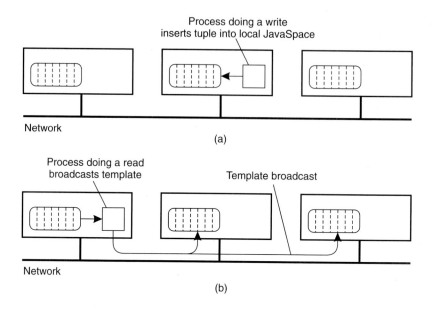

Figure 13-13. Nonreplicated JavaSpace. (a) A write is done locally. (b) A read or take requires the template tuple to be broadcast in order to find a tuple instance.

instances are sent, they are treated like local writes and the instances are effectively moved from the machines that had them to the one doing the request. In fact, the runtime system can even move tuples around on its own to balance the load. Carriero and Gelernter (1986) used this method for implementing the Linda tuple space on a LAN.

These two methods can be combined to produce a system with partial replication. As a simple example, imagine that all the machines logically form a rectangular grid, as shown in Fig. 13-14. When a process on a machine *A* wants to do a write, it broadcasts (or sends by point-to-point message) the tuple to all machines in its row of the grid. When a process on a machine *B* wants to read or take a tuple instance, it broadcasts the template tuple to all machines in its column. Due to the geometry, there will always be exactly one machine that sees both the tuple instance and the template tuple (*C* in this example), and that machine makes the match and sends the tuple instance to the process requesting for it. This approach is similar to using quorum-based replication as we discussed in Chap. 7.

The implementations we have discussed so far have serious scalability problems caused by the fact that multicasting is needed either to insert a tuple into a tuple space, or to remove one. Wide-area implementations of tuple spaces do not exist. At best, several *different* tuple spaces can coexist in a single system, where each tuple space itself is implemented on a single server or on a local-area network. This approach is used, for example, in PageSpaces (Ciancarini et al., 1998)

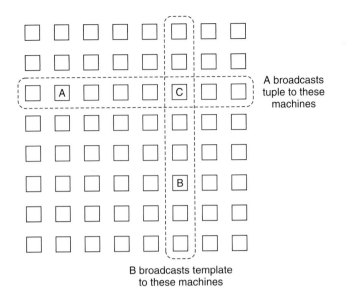

A broadcasts
tuple to these
machines

B broadcasts template
to these machines

Figure 13-14. Partial broadcasting of tuples and template tuples.

and WCL (Rowstron and Wray, 1998). In WCL, each tuple-space server is responsible for an entire tuple space. In other words, a process will always be directed to exactly one server. However, it is possible to migrate a tuple space to a different server to enhance performance. How to develop an efficient wide-area implementation of tuple spaces is still an open question.

13.7.2 Dynamic Replication

Replication in coordination-based systems has generally been restricted to static policies for parallel applications like those discussed above. In commercial applications, we also see relatively simple schemes in which entire dataspaces or otherwise statically predefined parts of a data set are subject to a single policy (GigaSpaces, 2005). Inspired by the fine-grained replication of Web documents in Globule, performance improvements can also be achieved when differentiating replication between the different kinds of data stored in a dataspace. This differentiation is supported by GSpace, which we briefly discuss in this section.

GSpace Overview

GSpace is a distributed coordination-based system that is built on top of Java-Spaces (Russello et al., 2004, 2006). Distribution and replication of tuples in GSpace is done for two different reasons: improving performance and availability. A key element in this approach is the separation of concerns: tuples that need to be replicated for availability may need to follow a different strategy than those for which performance is at stake. For this reason, the architecture of GSpace has been set up to support a variety of replication policies, and such that different tuples may follow different policies.

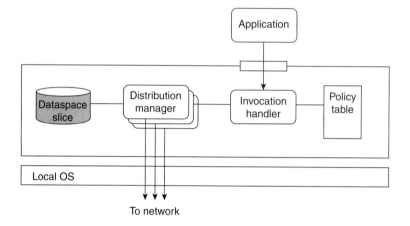

Figure 13-15. Internal organization of a GSpace kernel.

The principal working is relatively simple. Every application is offered an interface with a read, write, and take interface, similar to what is offered by Java-Spaces. However, every call is picked up by a local invocation handler which looks up the policy that should be followed for the specific call. A policy is selected based on the type and content of the tuple/template that is passed as part of the call. Every policy is identified by a template, similar to the way that templates are used to select tuples in other Java-based shared dataspaces as we discussed previously.

The result of this selection is a reference to a distribution manager, which implements the same interface, but now does it according to a specific replication policy. For example, if a master/slave policy has been implemented, a read operation may be implemented by immediately reading a tuple from the locally available dataspace. Likewise, a write operation may require that the distribution manager forwards the update to the master node and awaits an acknowledgment before performing the operation locally.

Finally, every GSpace kernel has a local dataspace, called a slice, which is implemented as a full-fledged, nondistributed version of JavaSpaces.

In this architecture (of which some components are not shown for clarity), policy descriptors can be added at runtime, and likewise, distribution managers can be changed as well. This setup allows for a fine-grained tuning of the distribution and replication of tuples, and as is shown in Russello et al. (2004), such fine-tuning allows for much higher performance than is achievable with any fixed, global strategy that is applied to all tuples in a dataspace.

Adaptive Replication

However, the most important aspect with systems such as GSpace is that replication management is automated. In other words, rather than letting the application developer figure out which combination of policies is the best, it is better to let the system monitor access patterns and behavior and subsequently adopt policies as necessary.

To this end, GSpace follows the same approach as in Globule: it continuously measures consumed network bandwidth, latency, and memory usage and depending on which of these metrics is considered most important, places tuples on different nodes and chooses the most appropriate way to keep replicas consistent. The evaluation of which policy is the best for a given tuple is done by means of a central coordinator which simply collects traces from the nodes that constitute the GSpace system.

An interesting aspect is that from time to time we may need to switch from one replication policy to another. There are several ways in which such a transition can take place. As GSpace aims to separate mechanisms from policies as best as possible, it can also handle different **transition policies**. The default case is to temporarily freeze all operations for a specific type of tuple, remove all replicas and reinsert the tuple into the shared dataspace but now following the newly selected replication policy. However, depending on the new replication policy, a different way of making the transition may be possible (and cheaper). For example, when switching from no replication to master/slave replication, one approach could be to lazily copy tuples to the slaves when they are first accessed.

13.8 FAULT TOLERANCE

When considering that fault tolerance is fundamental to any distributed system, it is somewhat surprising how relatively little attention has been paid to fault tolerance in coordination-based systems, including basic publish/subscribe systems as well as those supporting generative communication. In most cases, attention focuses on ensuring efficient reliability of data delivery, which essentially boils down to guaranteeing reliable communication. When the middleware is also expected to store data items, as is the case with generative communication, some effort is paid to reliable storage. Let us take a closer look at these two cases.

13.8.1 Reliable Publish-Subscribe Communication

In coordination-based systems where published data items are matched only against live subscribers, reliable communication plays a crucial role. In this case, fault tolerance is most often implemented through the implementation of reliable multicast systems that underly the actual publish/subscribe software. There are several issues that are generally taken care of. First, independent of the way that content-based routing takes place, a reliable multicast channel is set up. Second, process fault tolerance needs to be handled. Let us take a look how these matters are addressed in TIB/Rendezvous.

Example: Fault Tolerance in TIB/Rendezvous

TIB/Rendezvous assumes that the communication facilities of the underlying network are inherently unreliable. To compensate for this unreliability, whenever a rendezvous daemon publishes a message to other daemons, it will keep that message for at least 60 seconds. When publishing a message, a daemon attaches a (subject independent) sequence number to that message. A receiving daemon can detect it is missing a message by looking at sequence numbers (recall that messages are delivered to all daemons). When a message has been missed, the publishing daemon is requested to retransmit the message.

This form of reliable communication cannot prevent that messages may still be lost. For example, if a receiving daemon requests a retransmission of a message that has been published more than 60 seconds ago, the publishing daemon will generally not be able to help recover this lost message. Under normal circumstances, the publishing and subscribing applications will be notified that a communication error has occurred. Error handling is then left to the applications to deal with.

Much of the reliability of communication in TIB/Rendezvous is based on the reliability offered by the underlying network. TIB/Rendezvous also provides reliable multicasting using (unreliable) IP multicasting as its underlying communication means. The scheme followed in TIB/Rendezvous is a transport-level multicast protocol known as **Pragmatic General Multicast** (**PGM**), which is described in Speakman et al. (2001). We will discuss PGM briefly.

PGM does not provide hard guarantees that when a message is multicast it will eventually be delivered to each receiver. Fig. 13-16(a) shows a situation in which a message has been multicast along a tree, but it has not been delivered to two receivers. PGM relies on receivers detecting that they have missed messages for which they will send a retransmission request (i.e., a NAK) to the sender. This request is sent along the reverse path in the multicast tree rooted at the sender, as shown in Fig. 13-16(b). Whenever a retransmission request reaches an intermediate node, that node may possibly have cached the requested message, at which point it will handle the retransmission. Otherwise, the node simply forwards the NAK to the next node toward the sender. The sender is ultimately responsible for retransmitting a message.

PGM takes several measures to provide a scalable solution to reliable multicasting. First, if an intermediate node receives several retransmission requests for exactly the same message, only one retransmission request is forwarded toward

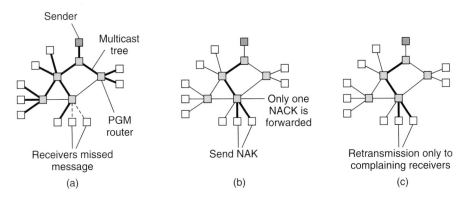

Figure 13-16. The principle of PGM. (a) A message is sent along a multicast tree. (b) A router will pass only a single NAK for each message. (c) A message is retransmitted only to receivers that have asked for it.

the sender. In this way, an attempt is made to ensure that only a single NAK reaches the sender, so that a feedback implosion is avoided. We already came a-cross this problem in Chap. 8 when discussing scalability issues in reliable multi-casting.

A second measure taken by PGM is to remember the path through which a NAK traverses from receivers to the sender, as is shown in Fig. 13-16(c). When the sender finally retransmits the requested message, PGM takes care that the message is multicast only to those receivers that had requested retransmission. Consequently, receivers to which the message had been successfully delivered are not bothered by retransmissions for which they have no use.

Besides the basic reliability scheme and reliable multicasting through PGM, TIB/Rendezvous provides further reliability by means of **certified message delivery**. In this case, a process uses a special communication channel for send-ing or receiving messages. The channel has an associated facility, called a **ledger**, for keeping track of sent and received certified messages. A process that wants to receive certified messages registers itself with the sender of such messages. In effect, registration allows the channel to handle further reliability issues for which the rendezvous daemons provide no support. Most of these issues are hidden from applications and are handled by the channel's implementation.

When a ledger is implemented as a file, it becomes possible to provide reli-able message delivery even in the presence of process failures. For example, when a receiving process crashes, all messages it misses until it recovers again are stored in a sender's ledger. Upon recovery, the receiver simply contacts the ledger and requests the missed messages to be retransmitted.

To enable the masking of process failures, TIB/Rendezvous provides a simple means to automatically activate or deactivate processes. In this context, an active process normally responds to all incoming messages, while an inactive one does not. An inactive process is a running process that can handle only special events as we explain shortly.

Processes can be organized into a group, with each process having a unique rank associated with it. The rank of a process is determined by its (manually assigned) weight, but no two processes in the same group may have the same rank. For each group, TIB/Rendezvous will attempt to have a group-specific number of processes active, called the group's **active goal**. In many cases, the active goal is set to one so that all communication with a group reduces to a primary-based protocol as discussed in Chap. 7.

An active process regularly sends a message to all other members in the group to announce that it is still up and running. Whenever such a **heartbeat message** is missing, the middleware will automatically activate the highest-ranked process that is currently inactive. Activation is accomplished by a callback to an action operation that each group member is expected to implement. Likewise, when a previously crashed process recovers again and becomes active, the lowest-ranked currently active process will be automatically deactivated.

To keep consistent with the active processes, special measures need to be taken by an inactive process before it can become active. A simple approach is to let an inactive process subscribe to the same messages as any other group member. An incoming message is processed as usual, but no reactions are ever published. Note that this scheme is akin to active replication.

13.8.2 Fault Tolerance in Shared Dataspaces

When dealing with generative communication, matters become more complicated. As also noted in Tolksdorf and Rowstron (2000), as soon as fault tolerance needs to be incorporated in shared dataspaces, solutions can often become so inefficient that only centralized implementations are feasible. In such cases, traditional solutions are applied, notably using a central server that is backed up in using a simple primary-backup protocol, in combination with checkpointing.

An alternative is to deploy replication more aggressively by placing copies of data items across the various machines. This approach has been adopted in GSpace, essentially deploying the same mechanisms it uses for improving performance through replication. To this end, each node computes its availability, which is then used in computing the availability of a single (replicated) data item (Russello et al., 2006).

To compute its availability, a node regularly writes a timestamp to persistent storage, allowing it to compute the time when it is up, and the time when it was down. More precisely, availability is computed in terms of the **mean time to failure** (**MTTF**) and the **mean time to repair** (**MTTR**):

$$Availability\ node = \frac{MTTF}{MTTF+MTTR}$$

To compute *MTTF* and *MTTR*, a node simply looks at the logged timestamps, as shown in Fig. 13-17. This will allow it to compute the averages for the time between failures, leading to an availability of:

$$Availability\ node = \frac{\sum_{k=1}^{n} (T_k^{start} - T_{k-1}^{end})}{\sum_{k=1}^{n} (T_k^{start} - T_{k-1}^{end}) + \sum_{k=1}^{n} (T_k^{end} - T_k^{start})}$$

Note that it is necessary to regularly log timestamps and that T_k^{start} can be taken only as a best estimate of when a crash occurred. However, the thus computed availability will be pessimistic, as the actual time that a node crashed for the kth time will be slightly later than T_k^{start}. Also, instead of taking averages since the beginning, it is also possible to take only the last N crashes into account.

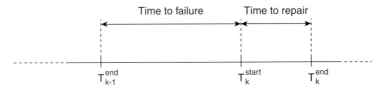

Figure 13-17. The time line of a node experiencing failures.

In GSpace, each type of data item has an associated primary node that is responsible for computing that type's availability. Given that a data item is replicated across m nodes, its availability is computed by considering the availability a_i of each of the m nodes leading to:

$$Availability\ data\ item = 1 - \prod_{k=1}^{m} (1 - a_i)$$

By simply taking the availability of a data item into account, as well as those of all nodes, the primary can compute an optimal placement for a data item that will satisfy the availability requirements for a data item. In addition, it can also take other factors into account, such as bandwidth usage and CPU loads. Note that placement may change over time if these factors fluctuate.

13.9 SECURITY

Security in coordination-based systems poses a difficult problem. On the one hand we have stated that processes should be referentially decoupled, but on the other hand we should also ensure the integrity and confidentiality of data. This security is normally implemented through secure (multicast) channels, which effectively require that senders and receivers can authenticate each other. Such authentication violates referential decoupling.

To solve this problem there are different approaches. One common approach is to set up a network of brokers that handle the processing of data and subscriptions. Client processes will then contact the brokers, who then take care of authentication and authorization. Note that such an approach does require that the clients trust the brokers. However, as we shall see later, by differentiating between types of brokers, it is not necessary that a client has to trust *all* brokers comprising the system.

By nature of data coordination, authorization naturally translates to confidentiality issues. We will now take a closer look at these issues, following the discussion as presented in Wang et al. (2002).

13.9.1 Confidentiality

One important difference between many distributed systems and coordination-based ones is that in order to provide efficiency, the middleware needs to inspect the content of published data. Without being able to do so, the middleware can essentially only flood data to all potential subscribers. This poses the problem of **information confidentiality** which refers to the fact that it is sometimes important to disallow the middleware to inspect published data. This problem can be circumvented through end-to-end encryption; the routing substrate only sees source and destination addresses.

If published data items are structured in the sense that every item contains multiple fields, it is possible to deploy partial secrecy. For example, data regarding real estate may need to be shipped between agents of the same office with branches at different locations, but without revealing the exact address of the property. To allow for content-based routing, the address field could be encrypted, while the description of the property could be published in the clear. To this end, Khurana and Koleva (2006) propose to use a per-field encryption scheme as introduced in Bertino and Ferrari (2002). In this case, the agents belonging to the same branch would share the secret key for decrypting the address field. Of course, this violates referential decoupling, but we will discuss a potential solution to this problem later.

More problematic is the case when none of the fields may be disclosed to the middleware in plaintext. The only solution that remains is that content-based routing takes place on the encrypted data. As routers get to see only encrypted data, possibly on a per-field basis, subscriptions will need to be encoded in such a way that partial matching can take place. Note that a partial match is the basis that a router uses to decide which outgoing link a published data item should be forwarded on.

This problem comes very close to querying and searching through encrypted data, something clearly next to impossible to achieve. As it turns out, maintaining a high degree of secrecy while still offering reasonable performance is known to be very difficult (Kantarcioglu and Clifton, 2005). One of the problems is that if per-field encryption is used, it becomes much easier to find out what the data is all about.

Having to work on encrypted data also brings up the issue of **subscription confidentiality**, which refers to the fact that subscriptions may not be disclosed to the middleware either. In the case of subject-based addressing schemes, one solution is to simply use per-field encryption and apply matching on a strict field-by-field basis. Partial matching can be accommodated in the case of compound keywords, which can be represented as encrypted sets of their constituents. A subscriber would then send encrypted forms of such constituents and let the routers check for set membership, as also suggested by Raiciu and Rosenblum (2005). As it turns out, it is even possible to support range queries, provided an efficient scheme can be devised for representing intervals. A potential solution is discussed in Li et al. (2004a).

Finally, **publication confidentiality** is also an issue. In this case, we are touching upon the more traditional access control mechanisms in which certain processes should not even be allowed to see certain messages. In such cases, publishers may want to explicitly restrict the group of possible subscribers. In many cases, this control can be exerted out-of-band at the level of the publishing and subscribing applications. However, it may convenient that the middleware offers a service to handle such access control.

Decoupling Publishers from Subscribers

If it is necessary to protect data and subscriptions from the middleware, Khurana and Koleva (2006) propose to make use of a special accounting service (AS), which essentially sits between clients (publishers and subscribers) and the actual publish/subscribe middleware. The basic idea is to decouple publishers from subscribers while still providing information confidentiality. In their scheme, subscribers register their interest in specific data items, which are subsequently routed as usual. The data items are assumed to contain fields that have been encrypted. To allow for decryption, once a message should be delivered to a subscriber, the router passes it to the accounting service where it is *transformed* into a message that only the subscriber can decrypt. This scheme is shown in Fig. 13-18.

A publisher registers itself at any node of the publish/subscribe network, that is, at a broker. The broker forwards the registration information to the accounting service which then generates a public key to be used by the publisher, and which is signed by the AS. Of course, the AS keeps the associated private key to itself. When a subscriber registers, it provides an encryption key that is forwarded by the broker. It is necessary to go through a separate authentication phase to ensure that only legitimate subscribers register. For example, brokers should generally not be allowed to subscribe for published data.

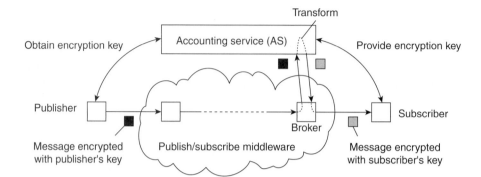

Figure 13-18. Decoupling publishers from subscribers using an additional trusted service.

Ignoring many details, when a data item is published, its critical fields will have been encrypted by the publisher. When the data item arrives at a broker who wishes to pass it on to a subscriber, the former requests the AS to transform the message by first decrypting it, and then encrypt it with the key provided by the subscriber. In this way, the brokers will never get to know about content that should be kept secret, while at the same time, publishers and subscribers need not share key information.

Of course, it is crucial that accounting service itself can scale. Various measures can be taken, but one reasonable approach is to introduce realms in a similar way that Kerberos does. In this case, messages in transmission may need to be transformed by re-encrypting them using the public key of a foreign accounting service. For details, we refer the interested reader to (Khurana and Koleva, 2006).

13.9.2 Secure Shared Dataspaces

Very little work has been done when it comes to making shared dataspaces secure. A common approach is to simply encrypt the fields of data items and let matching take place only when decryption succeeds and content matches with a subscription. This approach is described in Vitek et al. (2003). One of the major problems with this approach is that keys may need to be shared between publishers and subscribers, or that the decryption keys of the publishers should be known to authorized subscribers.

Of course, if the shared dataspace is trusted (i.e., the processes implementing the dataspace are allowed to see the content of tuples), matters become much simpler. Considering that most implementations make use of only a single server, extending that server with authentication and authorization mechanisms is often the approach followed in practice.

13.10 SUMMARY

Coordination-based distributed systems play an important role in building distributed applications. Most of these systems focus on referential uncoupling of processes, meaning that processes need not explicitly refer to each other to enable communication. In addition, it is also possible to provide temporal decoupling by which processes do not have to coexist in order to communicate.

An important group of coordination-based systems is formed by those systems that follow the publish/subscribe paradigm as is done in TIB/Rendezvous. In this model, messages do not carry the address of their receiver(s), but instead are addressed by a subject. Processes that wish to receive messages should subscribe to a specific subject; the middleware will take care that messages are routed from publishers to subscribers.

More sophisticated are the systems in which subscribers can formulate predicates over the attributes of published data items. In such cases, we are dealing with content-based publish/subscribe systems. For efficiency, it is important that routers can install filters such that published data is forwarded only across those outgoing links for which it is known that there are subscribers.

Another group of coordination-based systems uses generative communication, which takes place by means of a shared dataspace of tuples. A tuple is a typed data structure similar to a record. To read a tuple from a tuple space, a process specifies what it is looking for by providing a template tuple. A tuple that matches that template is then selected and returned to the requesting process. If no match could be found, the process blocks.

Coordination-based systems are different from many other distributed systems in that they concentrate fully on providing a convenient way for processes to communicate without knowing each other in advance. Also, communication may continue in an anonymous way. The main advantage of this approach is flexibility as it becomes easier to extend or change a system while it continues to operate.

The principles of distributed systems as discussed in the first part of the book apply equally well to coordination-based systems, although caching and replication play a less prominent role in current implementations. In addition, naming is strongly related to attribute-based searching as supported by directory services. Problematic is the support for security, as it essentially violates the decoupling between publishers and subscribers. Problems are further aggravated when the middleware should be shielded from the content of published data, making it much more difficult to provide efficient solutions.

PROBLEMS

1. What type of coordination model would you classify the message-queuing systems discussed in Chap. 4?

2. Outline an implementation of a publish/subscribe system based on a message-queuing system like that of IBM WebSphere.

3. Explain why decentralized coordination-based systems have inherent scalability problems.

4. To what is a subject name in TIB/Rendezvous actually resolved, and how does name resolution take place?

5. Outline a simple implementation for totally-ordered message delivery in a TIB/Rendezvous system.

6. In content-based routing such as used in the Siena system, which we described in the text, we may be confronted with a serious management problem. Which problem is that?

7. Assume a process is replicated in a TIB/Rendezvous system. Give two solutions to avoid so that messages from this replicated process are not published more than once.

8. To what extent do we need totally-ordered multicasting when processes are replicated in a TIB/Rendezvous system?

9. Describe a simple scheme for PGM that will allow receivers to detect missing messages, even the last one in a series.

10. How could a coordination model based on generative communication be implemented in TIB/Rendezvous?

11. A lease period in Jini is always specified as a duration and not as an absolute time at which the lease expires. Why is this done?

12. What are the most important scalability problems in Jini?

13. Consider a distributed implementation of a JavaSpace in which tuples are replicated a-cross several machines. Give a protocol to delete a tuple such that race conditions are avoided when two processes try to delete the same tuple.

14. Suppose that a transaction T in Jini requires a lock on an object that is currently locked by another transaction T'. Explain what happens.

15. Suppose that a Jini client caches the tuple it obtained from a JavaSpace so that it can avoid having to go to the JavaSpace the next time. Does this caching make any sense?

16. Answer the previous question, but now for the case that a client caches the results returned by a lookup service.

17. Outline a simple implementation of a fault-tolerant JavaSpace.

18. In some subject-based publish/subscribe systems, secure solutions are sought in end-to-end encryption beteen publishers and subscribers. However, this approach may violate the initial design goals of coordination-based systems. How?

14

READING LIST
AND BIBLIOGRAPHY

In the previous 13 chapters we have touched upon a variety of topics. This chapter is intended as an aid to readers interested in pursuing their study of distributed systems further. Section 13.1 is a list of suggested readings. Section 13.2 is an alphabetical bibliography of all books and articles cited in this book.

14.1 SUGGESTIONS FOR FURTHER READING

14.1.1 Introduction and General Works

Coulouris et al., *Distributed Systems—Concepts and Design*

A good general text on distributed systems. Its coverage is similar to the material found in this book, but is organized completely different. There is much material on distributed transactions, along with some older material on distributed shared memory systems.

Foster and Kesselman, *The Grid 2: Blueprint for a New Computing Infrastructure*

This is the second edition of a book in which many Grid experts highlight various issues of large-scale Grid computing. The book covers all the important topics, including many examples on current and future applications.

Neuman, "Scale in Distributed Systems"

One of the few papers that provides a systematic overview on the issue of scale in distributed systems. It takes a look at caching, replication, and distribution as scaling techniques, and provides a number of rule-of-thumbs to applying these techniques for designing large-scale systems.

Silberschatz et al., *Applied Operating System Concepts*

A general textbook on operating systems including material on distributed systems with an emphasis on file systems and distributed coordination.

Verissimo and Rodrigues, *Distributed Systems for Systems Architects*

An advanced reading on distributed systems, basically covering the same material as in this book. Relatively more emphasis is put on fault tolerance and real-time distributed systems. Attention is also paid to management of distributed systems.

Zhao and Guibas, *Wireless Sensor Networks*

Many books on (wireless) sensor networks describe these systems from a net-working approach. This book takes a more systems perspective, which makes it an attractive read for those interested in distributed systems. The book gives a good coverage of wireless sensor networks.

14.1.2 Architecture

Babaoglu et al., *Self-star Properties in Complex Information Systems*

Much has been said about self-* systems, but not always with the degree of substance that would be preferred. This book contains a collection of papers from authors with a variety of backgrounds that consider how self-* aspects find their way into modern computer systems.

Bass et al., *Software Architecture in Practice*

This widely used book gives an excellent practical introduction and overview on software architecture. Although the focus is not specifically toward distributed systems, it provides an excellent basis for understanding the various ways that complex software systems can be organized.

Hellerstein et al., *Feedback Control of Computing Systems*

For those readers with some mathematical background, this book provides a thorough treatment on how feedback control loops can be applied to (distributed) computer systems. As such, it forms an alternative basis for much of the research on self-* and autonomic computing systems.

Lua et al., "A Survey and Comparison of Peer-to-Peer Overlay Network Schemes"

An excellent survey of modern peer-to-peer systems, covering structured as well as unstructured networks. This paper forms a good introduction for those wanting to get deeper into the subject but do not really know where to start.

Oram, *Peer-to-Peer: Harnessing the Power of Disruptive Technologies*

This book bundles a number of papers on the first generation of peer-to-peer networks. It covers various projects as well as important issues such as security, trust, and accountability. Despite the fact that peer-to-peer technology has made a lot of progress, this book is still valuable for understanding many of the basic issues that needed to be addressed.

White et al., "An Architectural Approach to Autonomic Computing"

Written by the technical people behind the idea of autonomic computing, this short paper gives a high-level overview of the requirements that need to be met for self-* systems.

14.1.3 Processes

Andrews, *Foundations of Multithreaded, Parallel, and Distributed Programming*

If you ever need a thorough introduction to programming parallel and distributed systems, this is the book to look for.

Lewis and Berg, *Multithreaded Programming with Pthreads*

Pthreads form the POSIX standard for implementing threads for operating systems and are widely supported by UNIX-based systems. Although the authors concentrate on Pthreads, this book provides a good introduction to thread programming in general. As such, it forms a solid basis for developing multithreaded clients and servers.

Schmidt et al., *Pattern-Oriented Software Architecture—Patterns for Concurrent and Networked Objects*

Researchers have also looked at common design patterns in distributed systems. These patterns can ease the development of distributed systems as they allow programmers to concentrate more on system-specific issues. In this book, design patterns are discussed for service access, event handling, synchronization, and concurrency.

Smith and Nair, *Virtual Machines: Versatile Platforms for Systems and Processes*

These authors have also published a brief overview of virtualization in the May 2005 issue of *Computer*, but this book goes into many of the (often intricate) details of virtual machines. As we have mentioned in the text, virtual machines are becoming increasingly important for distributed systems. This book forms an excellent introduction into the subject.

Stevens and Rago, *Advanced Programming in the UNIX Environment*
    If there is ever a need to purchase a single volume on programming on UNIX systems, this is the book to consider. Like other books written by the late Richard Stevens, this volume contains a wealth of detailed information on how to develop servers and other types of programs. This second edition has been extended by Rago, who is also well known for books on similar topics.

14.1.4 Communication

Birrell and Nelson, "Implementing Remote Procedure Calls"
    A classical paper on the design and implementation of one of the first remote procedure call systems.

Hohpe and Woolf, *Enterprise Integration Patterns*
    Like other material on design patterns this book provides high-level overviews on how to construct messaging solutions. The book forms an excellent read for those wanting to design message-oriented solutions, and covers a wealth of patterns that can be followed during the design phase.

Peterson and Davie, *Computer Networks, A Systems Approach*
    An alternative textbook to computer networks which takes a somewhat similar approach as this book by considering a number of principles and how they apply to networking.

Steinmetz and Nahrstedt, *Multimedia Systems*
    A good textbook (although poorly copyedited) covering many aspects of (distributed) systems for multimedia processing, together forming a fine introduction into the subject.

14.1.5 Naming

Albitz and Liu, *DNS and BIND*
    BIND is a publicly available and widely-used implementation of a DNS server. In this book, all the details are discussed on setting up a DNS domain using BIND. As such, it provides a lot of practical information on the largest distributed naming service in use today.

Balakrishnan et al., "Looking up Data in P2P Systems"

An easy-to-read and good introduction into lookup mechanisms in peer-to-peer systems. Only a few details are provided on the actual working of these mechanisms, but forming a good starting-point for further reading.

Balakrishnan et al., "A Layered Naming Architecture for the Internet"

In this paper, the authors argue to combine structured naming with flat naming, thereby distinguishing three different levels: (1) human-friendly names which are to be mapped to service identifiers, (2) the service identifiers which are to be mapped to end point identifiers that uniquely identify a host, and (3) the end points that are to be mapped to network addresses. Of course, for those parts that only identifiers are used, one can conveniently use a DHT-based system.

Loshin, *Big Book of Lightweight Directory Access Protocol (LDAP) RFCs*

LDAP-based systems are widely used in distributed systems. The ultimate source for LDAP services are the RFCs as published by the IETF. Loshin has collected all the relevant ones in a single volume, making it the comprehensive source for designing and implementing LDAP services.

Needham, "Names"

An easy-to-read and excellent article on the role of names in distributed systems. Emphasis is on naming systems as discussed in Section 5.3, using DEC's GNS as an example.

Pitoura and Samaras, "Locating Objects in Mobile Computing"

This article can be used as a comprehensive introduction to location services. The authors discuss various kinds of location services, including those used in telecommunications systems. The article has an extensive list of references that can be used as starting point for further reading.

Saltzer, "Naming and Binding Objects"

Although written in 1978 and focused on nondistributed systems, this paper should be the starting point for any research on naming. The author provides an excellent treatment on the relation between names and objects, and, in particular, what it takes to resolve a name to a referenced object. Separate attention is paid to the concept of closure mechanisms.

14.1.6 Synchronization

Guerraoui and Rodrigues, *Introduction to Reliable Distributed Programming*

A somewhat misleading title for a book that largely concentrates on distributed algorithms that achieve reliability. The book has accompanying software that allows many of the theoretical descriptions to be tested in practice.

Lynch, *Distributed Algorithms*

Using a single framework, the book describes many different kinds of distributed algorithms. Three different timing models are considered: simple synchronous models, asynchronous models without any timing assumptions, and partially synchronous models, which come close to real systems. Once you get used to the theoretical notation, you will find this book containing many useful algorithms.

Raynal and Singhal, "Logical Time: Capturing Causality in Distributed Systems"

This paper describes in relatively simple terms three types of logical clocks: scalar time (i.e., Lamport timestamps), vector time, and matrix time. In addition, the paper describes various implementations that have been used in a number of practical and experimental distributed systems.

Tel, *Introduction to Distributed Algorithms*

An alternative introductory textbook for distributed algorithms, which concentrates solely on solutions for message-passing systems. Although quite theoretical, in many cases the reader can quite easily construct solutions for real systems.

14.1.7 Consistency and Replication

Adve and Gharachorloo, "Shared Memory Consistency Models: A Tutorial"

Until recently, there have been many groups developing distributed systems in which the physically dispersed memories where joined together into a single virtual address space, leading to what are known as distributed shared memory systems. Various memory consistency models have been designed for these systems and form the basis for the models discussed in Chap. 7. This paper provides an excellent introduction into these memory consistency models.

Gray et al., "The Dangers of Replication and a Solution"

The paper discusses the trade-off between replication implementing sequential consistency models (called eager replication) and lazy replication. Both forms of replication are formulated for transactions. The problem with eager replication is its poor scalability, whereas lazy replication may easily lead to difficult or impossible conflict resolutions. The authors propose a hybrid scheme.

Saito and Shapiro, "Optimistic Replication"

The presents presents a taxonomy of optimistic replication algorithms as used for weak consistency models. It describes an alternative way of looking at replication and its associated consistency protocols. An interesting issue is the discussion on scalability of various solutions. The paper also includes a large number of useful references.

Sivasubramanian et al., "Replication for Web Hosting Systems"

In this paper, the authors discuss the many aspects that need to be addressed to handle replication for Web hosting systems, including replica placement, consistency protocols, and routing requests to the best replica. The paper also includes an extensive list of relevant material.

Wiesmann et al., "Understanding Replication in Databases and Distributed Systems"

Traditionally, there has been a difference between dealing with replication in distributed databases and in general-purpose distributed systems. In databases, the main reason for replication used to be to improve performance. In general-purpose distributed, replication has often been done for improving fault tolerance. The papers presents a framework that allows solutions from these two areas to be more easily compared.

14.1.8 Fault Tolerance

Marcus and Stern, *Blueprints for High Availability*

There are many issues to be considered when developing (distributed) systems for high availability. The authors of this book take a pragmatic approach and touch upon many of the technical and nontechnical issues.

Birman, *Reliable Distributed Systems*

Written by an authority in the field, this book contains a wealth of information on the pitfalls of developing highly dependable distributed systems. The author provides many examples from academia and industry to illustrate what can go wrong and what can be done about it. The covers a wide variety of topics, including client/server computing, Web services, object-based systems (CORBA), and also peer-to-peer systems.

Cristian and Fetzer, The Timed Asynchronous Distributed System Model"

The paper discusses a more realistic model for distributed systems other than the pure synchronous or asynchronous cases. Two important assumptions are that services are complete within a specific time interval, and that communication is unreliable and subject to performance failures. The paper demonstrates the applicability of this model for capturing important properties of real distributed systems.

Guerraoui and Schiper, "Software-Based Replication for Fault Tolerance"

A brief and clear overview on how replication in distributed systems can be applied for improving fault tolerance. Discusses primary-backup replication as well as active replication, and relates replication to group communication.

Jalote, *Fault Tolerance in Distributed Systems*

One of the few textbooks entirely directed toward fault tolerance in distributed systems. The book covers reliable broadcasting, recovery, replication, and process resilience. There is a separate chapter on software design faults.

14.1.9 Security

Anderson, *Security Engineering: A Guide to Building Dependable Distributed Systems*

One of the very few books that successfully aims at covering the whole security area. The book discusses the basics such as passwords, access control, and cryptography. Security is tightly coupled to application domains, and security in several domains is discussed: the military, banking, medical systems, among others. Finally, social, organizational, and political aspects are discussed as well. A great starting point for further reading and research.

Bishop, *Computer Security: Art and Science*

Although this book is not specifically written for distributed systems, it contains a wealth of information of general issues for computer security, including many of the topics discussed in Chap. 9. Furthermore, there is material on security policies, assurance, evaluation, and many implementation issues.

Blaze et al, "The Role of Trust Management in Distributed Systems Security"

The paper argues that large-scale distributed systems should be able to grant access to a resource using a simpler approach than current ones. In particular, if the set of credentials accompanying a request is known to comply with a local security policy, the request should be granted. In other words, authorization should take place without separating authentication and access control. The paper explains this model and shows how it can be implemented.

Kaufman et al., *Network Security*

This authoritative and frequently witty book is the first place to look for an introduction to network security. Secret and public key algorithms and protocols, message hashes, authentication, Kerberos, and e-mail are all explained at length. The best parts are the interauthor (and even intra-author) discussions, labeled by subscripts, as in: "I_2 could not get me$_1$ to be very specific ... "

Menezes at al., *Handbook of Applied Cryptography*

The title says it all. The book provides the necessary mathematical background to understand the many different cryptographic solutions for encryption, hashing, and so on. Separate chapters are devoted to authentication, digital signatures, key establishment, and key management.

Rafaeli and Hutchison, *A Survey of Key Management for Secure Group Communication*

The title says it all. The authors discuss various schemes that can be used in those systems where process groups need to communicate and interact in a secure way. The paper concentrates on the means to manage and distribute keys.

Schneier, *Secrets and Lies*

By the same author as *Applied Cryptography*, this book focuses on explaining security issues for nontechnical people. An important observation is that security is not just a technological issue. In fact, what can be learned from reading this book is that perhaps most of the security-related risks have to do with humans and the way we organize things. As such, it supplements much of the material we presented in Chap. 8.

14.1.10 Distributed Object-Based Systems

Emmerich, *Engineering Distributed Objects*

An excellent book devoted entirely to remote-object technology, paying specific attention to CORBA, DCOM, and Java RMI. As such, it provides a good basis for comparing these three popular object models. In addition, material is presented on designing systems using remote objects, handling different forms of communication, locating objects, persistence, transactions, and security.

Fleury and Reverbel, "The JBoss Extensible Server"

Many Web applications are based on the JBoss J2EE object server. In this paper, the original developers of that server outline the underlying principles and general design.

Henning, "The Rise and Fall of CORBA"

Written by an expert on CORBA development (but who has come to other insights), this article contains strong arguments against the use of CORBA. Most salient is the fact that Henning believes that CORBA is simply too complex and that it does not make the lives of developers of distributed systems any easier.

Henning and Vinoski, *Advanced CORBA Programming with C++*

If you need material on programming CORBA, and in the meantime learning a lot on what CORBA means in practice, this book will be your choice. Written by two people involved in specifying and developing CORBA systems, the book is full of practical and technical details without being limited to to a specific CORBA implementation.

14.1.11 Distributed File Systems

Blanco et al., "A Survey of Data Management in Peer-to-Peer Systems"
An extensive survey, covering many important peer-to-peer systems. The authors describe data management issues including data integration, query processing, and data consistency. Pate, *UNIX Filesystems: Evolution, Design, and Implementation*
This book describes many of the filesystems that have been developed for UNIX systems, but also contains a separate chapter on distributed file systems. It gives an overview of the various NFS versions, as well as filesystems for server clusters.

Satyanarayanan, "The Evolution of Coda"
Coda is an important distributed files system for supporting mobile users. In particular, it has advanced features for supporting what are known as disconnected operations, by which a user can continue to work on his own set of files without having contact with the main servers. This article describes how the system has evolved over the years as new requirements surfaced.

Zhu et al., "Hibernator: Helping Disk Arrays Sleep through the Winter"
Data centers use an incredible number of disks to get their work done. Obviously, this requires a vast amount of energy. This paper describes various techniques how energy consumption can be brought down by, for example, distinguishing hot data from data that is not accessed so often.

14.1.12 Distributed Web-Based Systems

Alonso et al., *Web Services: Concepts, Architectures and Applications*
The popularity and intricacy of Web services has led to an endless stream of documents, too many that can be characterized only as garbage. In contrast, this is one of those very few books that gives a crystal-clear description of what Web services are all about. Highly recommended as an introduction to the novice, an overview for those who have read too much of the garbage, and an example for those producing the garbage.

Chappell, *Understanding .NET*
The approach that Microsoft has taken to support the development of Web services, is to combine many of their existing techniques into a single framework, along with adding a number of new features. The result is called .NET. This approach has caused much confusion on what this framework actually is. David Chappell does a good job of explaining matters.

Fielding, "Principled Design of the Modern Web Architecture"
From the chief designer of the Apache Web server, this paper discusses a general approach on how to organize Web applications such that they can make best use of the current set of protocols.

Podling and Boszormenyi, "A Survey of Web Cache Replacement Strategies"
We have barely touched upon the work that needs to be done when Web caches become full. This paper gives an excellent overview on the choices that can be made to evict content from caches when they fill up.

Rabinovich and Spatscheck, *Web Caching and Replication*
An excellent book that provides an overview as well as many details on content distribution in the Web.

Sebesta, *Programming the World Wide Web*
We have barely touched upon the actual development of Web applications, which generally involves using a myriad of tools and techniques. This book provides a comprehensive overview and forms a good starting point for developing Web sites.

14.1.13 Distributed Coordination-Based Systems

Cabri et al., "Uncoupling Coordination: Tuple-based Models for Mobility"
The authors give a good overview of Linda-like systems that can operate in mobile, distributed environments. This paper also shows that there is still a lot of research being conducted in a field that was initiated more than 15 years ago.

Pietzuch and Bacon, "Hermes: A Distrib. Event-Based Middleware Architecture"
Hermes is a distributed publish/subscribe system developed at Cambridge University, UK. It has been used as the basis for many experiments in large-scale event-based systems, including security. This paper describes the basic organization of Hermes.

Wells et al., "Linda Implementations in Java for Concurrent Systems"
For those interested in modern implementations of tuple spaces in Java, this paper provides a good overview. It is more or less focused on computing instead of general tuple-space applications, but nevertheless demonstrates the various tradeoffs that need to be made when performance is at stake.

Zhao et al., "Subscription Propagation in Highly-Available Publish/Subscribe Middleware"
Although a fairly technical article, this paper gives a good idea of some of the issues that play a role when availability is an important design criterion in

publish/subscribe systems. In particular, the authors consider how subscription updates can be propagated when routing paths have been made redundant to achieve high availability. It is not hard to imagine that, for example, out-of-order message delivery can easily occur. Such cases need to be dealt with.

14.2 ALPHABETICAL BIBLIOGRAPHY

ABADI, M. and NEEDHAM, R.: "Prudent Engineering Practice for Cryptographic Protocols." *IEEE Trans. Softw. Eng.*, (22)1:6-15, Jan. 1996. Cited on page 400.

ABDULLAHI, S. and RINGWOOD, G.: "Garbage Collecting the Internet: A Survey of Distributed Garbage Collection." *ACM Comput. Surv.*, (30)3:330-373, Sept. 1998. Cited on page 186.

ABERER, K. and HAUSWIRTH, M.: "Peer-to-Peer Systems." In Singh, M. (ed.), *The Practical Handbook of Internet Computing*, chapter 35. Boca Raton, FL: CRC Press, 2005. Cited on page 15.

ABERER, K., ALIMA, L. O., GHODSI, A., GIRDZIJAUSKAS, S., HAUSWIRTH, M., and HARIDI, S.: "The Essence of P2P: A Reference Architecture for Overlay Networks." *Proc. Fifth Int'l Conf. Peer-to-Peer Comput.*, (Konstanz, Germany). Los Alamitos, CA: IEEE Computer Society Press, 2005. pp. 11-20. Cited on page 44.

ADAR, E. and HUBERMAN, B. A.: "Free Riding on Gnutella." Hewlett Packard, Information Dynamics Lab, Jan. 2000. Cited on page 53.

AIYER, A., ALVISI, L., CLEMENT, A., DAHLIN, M., and MARTIN, J.-P.: "BAR Fault Tolerance for Cooperative Services." *Proc. 20th Symp. Operating System Principles*, (Brighton, UK). New York, NY: ACM Press, 2005. pp. 45-58. Cited on page 335.

AKYILDIZ, I. F., SU, W., SANKARASUBRAMANIAM, Y., and CAYIRCI, E.: "A Survey on Sensor Networks." *IEEE Commun. Mag.*, (40)8:102-114, Aug. 2002. Cited on page 28.

AKYILDIZ, I. F., WANG, X., and WANG, W.: "Wireless Mesh Networks: A Survey." *Comp. Netw.*, (47)4:445-487, Mar. 2005. Cited on page 28.

ALBITZ, P. and LIU, C.: *DNS and BIND*. Sebastopol, CA: O'Reilly & Associates, 4th ed., 2001. Cited on pages 210, 560, 626.

ALLEN, R. and LOWE-NORRIS, A.: *Windows 2000 Active Directory*. Sebastopol, CA: O'Reilly & Associates, 2nd ed., 2003. Cited on page 221.

ALLMAN, M.: "An Evaluation of XML-RPC." *Perf. Eval. Rev.*, (30)4:2-11, Mar. 2003. Cited on page 567.

ALONSO, G., CASATI, F., KUNO, H., and MACHIRAJU, V.: *Web Services: Concepts, Architectures and Applications*. Berlin: Springer-Verlag, 2004. Cited on pages 20, 551, 554, 632.

ALVISI, L. and MARZULLO, K.: "Message Logging: Pessimistic, Optimistic, Causal, and Optimal." *IEEE Trans. Softw. Eng.*, (24)2:149-159, Feb. 1998. Cited on pages 370, 371.

AMAR, L., BARAK, A., and SHILOH, A.: "The MOSIX Direct File System Access Method for Supporting Scalable Cluster File Systems." *Cluster Comput.*, (7)2:141-150, Apr. 2004. Cited on page 18.

ANDERSON, O. T., LUAN, L., EVERHART, C., PEREIRA, M., SARKAR, R., and XU, J.: "Global Namespace for Files." *IBM Syst. J.*, (43)4:702-722, Apr. 2004. Cited on page 512.

ANDERSON, R.: *Security Engineering – A Guide to Building Dependable Distributed Systems*. New York: John Wiley, 2001. Cited on page 630.

ANDERSON, T., BERSHAD, B., LAZOWSKA, E., and LEVY, H.: "Scheduler Activations: Efficient Kernel Support for the User-Level Management of Parallelism." *Proc. 13th Symp. Operating System Principles*. New York, NY: ACM Press, 1991. pp. 95-109. Cited on page 75.

ANDREWS, G.: *Foundations of Multithreaded, Parallel, and Distributed Programming*. Reading, MA: Addison-Wesley, 2000. Cited on pages 232, 625.

ANDROUTSELLIS-THEOTOKIS, S. and SPINELLIS, D.: "A Survey of Peer-to-Peer Content Distribution Technologies." *ACM Comput. Surv.*, (36)4:335-371, Dec. 2004. Cited on page 44.

ARAUJO, F. and RODRIGUES, L.: "Survey on Position-Based Routing." Technical Report MINEMA TR-01, University of Lisbon, Oct. 2005. Cited on page 261.

ARKILLS, B.: *LDAP Directories Explained: An Introduction and Analysis*. Reading, MA: Addison-Wesley, 2003. Cited on page 218.

ARON, M., SANDERS, D., DRUSCHEL, P., and ZWAENEPOEL, W.: "Scalable Content-aware Request Distribution in Cluster-based Network Servers." *Proc. USENIX Ann. Techn. Conf.* USENIX, 2000. pp. 323-336. Cited on page 559.

ATTIYA, H. and WELCH, J.: *Distributed Computing Fundamentals, Simulations, and Advanced Topics*. New York: John Wiley, 2nd ed., 2004. Cited on page 232.

AVIZIENIS, A., LAPRIE, J.-C., RANDELL, B., and LANDWEHR, C.: "Basic Concepts and Taxonomy of Dependable and Secure Computing." *IEEE Trans. Depend. Secure Comput.*, (1)1:11-33, Jan. 2004. Cited on page 323.

AWADALLAH, A. and ROSENBLUM, M.: "The vMatrix: A Network of Virtual Machine Monitors for Dynamic Content Distribution." *Proc. Seventh Web Caching Workshop*, (Boulder, CO), 2002. Cited on page 80.

AWADALLAH, A. and ROSENBLUM, M.: "The vMatrix: Server Switching." *Proc. Tenth Workshop on Future Trends in Distributed Computing Systems*, (Suzhou, China). Los Alamitos, CA: IEEE Computer Society Press, 2004. pp. 110-118. Cited on page 94.

BABAOGLU, O., JELASITY, M., MONTRESOR, A., FETZER, C., LEONARDI, S., VAN MOORSEL, A., and VAN STEEN, M. (eds.): *Self-star Properties in Complex Information Systems*, vol. 3460 of *Lect. Notes Comp. Sc.*. Berlin: Springer-Verlag, 2005. Cited on pages 59, 624.

BABAOGLU, O. and TOUEG, S.: "Non-Blocking Atomic Commitment." In Mullender, S. (ed.), *Distributed Systems*, pp. 147-168. Wokingham: Addison-Wesley, 2nd ed., 1993. Cited on page 359.

BABCOCK, B., BABU, S., DATAR, M., MOTWANI, R., and WIDOM, J.: "Models and Issues in Data Stream Systems." *Proc. 21st Symp. on Principles of Distributed Computing*, (Monterey, CA). New York, NY: ACM Press, 2002. pp. 1-16. Cited on page 158.

BAL, H.: *The Shared Data-Object Model as a Paradigm for Programming Distributed Systems*. Ph.D.. Thesis, Vrije Universiteit, Amsterdam, 1989. Cited on page 449.

BALAKRISHNAN, H., KAASHOEK, M. F., KARGER, D., MORRIS, R., and STOICA, I.: "Looking up Data in P2P Systems." *Commun. ACM*, (46)2:43-48, Feb. 2003. Cited on pages 44, 188, 627.

BALAKRISHNAN, H., LAKSHMINARAYANAN, K., RATNASAMY, S., SHENKER, S., STOICA, I., and WALFISH, M.: "A Layered Naming Architecture for the Internet." *Proc. SIGCOMM*, (Portland, OR). New York, NY: ACM Press, 2004. pp. 343-352. Cited on page 626.

BALAZINSKA, M., BALAKRISHNAN, H., and KARGER, D.: "INS/Twine: A Scalable Peer-to-Peer Architecture for Intentional Resource Discovery." *Proc. First Int'l Conf. Pervasive Computing*, vol. 2414 of *Lect. Notes Comp. Sc.*, (Zurich, Switzerland). Berlin: Springer-Verlag, 2002. pp. 195-210. Cited on pages 222, 223.

BALLINTIJN, G.: *Locating Objects in a Wide-area System*. Ph.D. thesis, Vrije Universiteit Amsterdam, 2003. Cited on pages 192, 485.

BARATTO, R. A., NIEH, J., and KIM, L.: "THINC: A Remote Display Architecture for Thin-Client Computing." *Proc. 20th Symp. Operating System Principles*, (Brighton, UK). New York, NY: ACM Press, 2005. pp. 277-290. Cited on pages 85, 86.

BARBORAK, M., MALEK, M., and DAHBURA, A.: "The Consensus Problem in Fault-Tolerant Computing." *ACM Comput. Surv.*, (25)2:171-220, June 1993. Cited on page 335.

BARHAM, P., DRAGOVIC, B., FRASER, K., HAND, S., HARRIS, T., HO, A., NEUGEBAR, R., PRATT, I., and WARFIELD, A.: "Xen and the Art of Virtualization." *Proc. 19th Symp. Operating System Principles*, (Bolton Landing, NY). New York, NY: ACM Press, 2003. pp. 164-177. Cited on page 81.

BARKER, W.: "Recommendation for the Triple Data Encryption Algorithm (TDEA) Block Cipher." NIST Special Publication 800-67, May 2004. Cited on page 393.

BARRON, D.: *Pascal – The Language and its Implementation*. New York: John Wiley, 1981. Cited on page 110.

BARROSO, L., DEAM, J., and HOLZE, U.: "Web Search for a Planet: The Google Cluster Architecture." *IEEE Micro*, (23)2:21-28, Mar. 2003. Cited on page 497.

BARYSHNIKOV, Y., COFFMAN, E. G., PIERRE, G., RUBENSTEIN, D., SQUILLANTE, M., and YIMWADSANA, T.: "Predictability of Web-Server Traffic Congestion." *Proc. Tenth Web Caching Workshop*, (Sophia Antipolis, France). IEEE, 2005. pp. 97-103. Cited on page 576.

BASILE, C., KALBARCZYK, Z., and IYER, R. K.: "A Preemptive Deterministic Scheduling Algorithm for Multithreaded Replicas." *Proc. Int'l Conf. Dependable Systems and Networks*, (San Francisco, CA). Los Alamitos, CA: IEEE Computer Society Press, 2003. pp. 149-158. Cited on page 474.

BASILE, C., WHISNANT, K., KALBARCZYK, Z., and IYER, R. K.: "Loose Synchronization of Multithreaded Replicas." *Proc. 21st Symp. on Reliable Distributed Systems*, (Osaka, Japan). Los Alamitos, CA: IEEE Computer Society Press, 2002. pp. 250-255. Cited on page 474.

BASS, L., CLEMENTS, P., and KAZMAN, R.: *Software Architecture in Practice.* Reading, MA: Addison-Wesley, 2nd ed., 2003. Cited on pages 34, 35, 36, 624.

BAVIER, A., BOWMAN, M., CHUN, B., CULLER, D., KARLIN, S., MUIR, S., PETERSON, L., ROSCOE, T., SPALINK, T., and WAWRZONIAK, M.: "Operating System Support for Planetary-Scale Network Services." *Proc. First Symp. Networked Systems Design and Impl.*, (San Francisco, CA). Berkeley, CA: USENIX, 2004. pp. 245-266. Cited on pages 99, 102.

BERNERS-LEE, T., CAILLIAU, R., NIELSON, H. F., and SECRET, A.: "The World-Wide Web." *Commun. ACM*, (37)8:76-82, Aug. 1994. Cited on page 545.

BERNERS-LEE, T., FIELDING, R., and MASINTER, L.: "Uniform Resource Identifiers (URI): Generic Syntax." RFC 3986, Jan. 2005. Cited on page 567.

BERNSTEIN, P.: "Middleware: A Model for Distributed System Services." *Commun. ACM*, (39)2:87-98, Feb. 1996. Cited on page 20.

BERNSTEIN, P., HADZILACOS, V., and GOODMAN, N.: *Concurrency Control and Recovery in Database Systems.* Reading, MA: Addison-Wesley, 1987. Cited on pages 355, 363.

BERSHAD, B., ZEKAUSKAS, M., and SAWDON, W.: "The Midway Distributed Shared Memory System." *Proc. COMPCON*. IEEE, 1993. pp. 528-537. Cited on page 286.

BERTINO, E. and FERRARI, E.: "Secure and Selective Dissemination of XML Documents." *ACM Trans. Inf. Syst. Sec.*, (5)3:290–331, 2002. Cited on page 618.

BHAGWAN, R., TATI, K., CHENG, Y., SAVAGE, S., and VOELKER, G. M.: "Total Recall: Systems Support for Automated Availability Management." *Proc. First Symp. Networked Systems Design and Impl.*, (San Francisco, CA). Berkeley, CA: USENIX, 2004. pp. 337-350. Cited on page 532.

BHARAMBE, A. R., AGRAWAL, M., and SESHAN, S.: "Mercury: Supporting Scalable Multi-Attribute Range Queries." *Proc. SIGCOMM*, (Portland, OR). New York, NY: ACM Press, 2004. pp. 353-366. Cited on pages 225, 599.

BIRMAN, K.: *Reliable Distributed Systems: Technologies, Web Services, and Applications.* Berlin: Springer-Verlag, 2005. Cited on pages 90, 335, 582, 629.

BIRMAN, K.: "A Response to Cheriton and Skeen's Criticism of Causal and Totally Ordered Communication." *Oper. Syst. Rev.*, (28)1:11-21, Jan. 1994. Cited on page 251.

BIRMAN, K. and JOSEPH, T.: "Reliable Communication in the Presence of Failures." *ACM Trans. Comp. Syst.*, (5)1:47-76, Feb. 1987. Cited on page 350.

BIRMAN, K., SCHIPER, A., and STEPHENSON, P.: "Lightweight Causal and Atomic Group Multicast." *ACM Trans. Comp. Syst.*, (9)3:272-314, Aug. 1991. Cited on page 353.

BIRMAN, K. and VAN RENESSE, R. (eds.): *Reliable Distributed Computing with the Isis Toolkit.* Los Alamitos, CA: IEEE Computer Society Press, 1994. Cited on page 251.

BIRRELL, A. and NELSON, B.: "Implementing Remote Procedure Calls." *ACM Trans. Comp. Syst.*, (2)1:39-59, Feb. 1984. Cited on pages 126, 626.

BISHOP, M.: *Computer Security: Art and Science.* Reading, MA: Addison-Wesley, 2003. Cited on pages 385, 630.

BJORNSON, R.: *Linda on Distributed Memory Multicomputers.* Ph.D. Thesis, Yale University, Department of Computer Science, 1993. Cited on page 608.

BLACK, A. and ARTSY, Y.: "Implementing Location Independent Invocation." *IEEE Trans. Par. Distr. Syst.*, (1)1:107-119, Jan. 1990. Cited on page 186.

BLAIR, G., COULSON, G., and GRACE, P.: "Research Directions in Reflective Middleware: the Lancaster Experience." *Proc. Third Workshop Reflective & Adaptive Middleware*, (Toronto, Canada). New York, NY: ACM Press, 2004. pp. 262-267. Cited on page 58.

BLAIR, G. and STEFANI, J.-B.: *Open Distributed Processing and Multimedia.* Reading, MA: Addison-Wesley, 1998. Cited on pages 8, 165.

BLAKE-WILSON, S., NYSTROM, M., HOPWOOD, D., MIKKELSEN, J., and WRIGHT, T.: "Transport Layer Security (TLS) Extensions." RFC 3546, June 2003. Cited on page 584.

BLANCO, R., AHMED, N., HADALLER, D., SUNG, L. G. A., LI, H., and SOLIMAN, M. A.: "A Survey of Data Management in Peer-to-Peer Systems." Technical Report CS-2006-18, University of Waterloo, Canada, June 2006. Cited on page 632.

BLAZE, M., FEIGENBAUM, J., IOANNIDIS, J., and KEROMYTIS, A.: "The Role of Trust Management in Distributed Systems Security." In Vitek, J. and Jensen, C. (eds.), *Secure Internet Programming: Security Issues for Mobile and Distributed Objects*, vol. 1603 of *Lect. Notes Comp. Sc.*, pp. 185-210. Berlin: Springer-Verlag, 1999. Cited on page 630.

BLAZE, M.: *Caching in Large-Scale Distributed File Systems.* Ph.D. thesis, Department of Computer Science, Princeton University, Jan. 1993. Cited on page 301.

BONNET, P., GEHRKE, J., and SESHADRI, P.: "Towards Sensor Database Systems." *Proc. Second Int'l Conf. Mobile Data Mgt.*, vol. 1987 of *Lect. Notes Comp. Sc.*, (Hong Kong, China). Berlin: Springer-Verlag, 2002. pp. 3-14. Cited on page 29.

BOOTH, D., HAAS, H., MCCABE, F., NEWCOMER, E., CHAMPION, M., FERRIS, C., and ORCHARD, D.: "Web Services Architecture." W3C Working Group Note, Feb. 2004. Cited on page 551.

BOUCHENAK, S., BOYER, F., HAGIMONT, D., KRAKOWIAK, S., MOS, A., DE PALMA3, N., QUEMA3, V., and STEFANI, J.-B.: "Architecture-Based Autonomous Repair Management: An Application to J2EE Clusters." *Proc. 24th Symp. on Reliable Distributed Systems*, (Orlando, FL). Los Alamitos, CA: IEEE Computer Society Press, 2005. pp. 13-24. Cited on page 65.

BREWER, E.: "Lessons from Giant-Scale Services." *IEEE Internet Comput.*, (5)4:46-55, July 2001. Cited on page 98.

BRUNETON, E., COUPAYE, T., LECLERCQ, M., QUEMA, V., and STEFANI, J.-B.: "An Open Component Model and Its Support in Java." *Proc. Seventh Int'l Symp. Component-based Softw. Eng.*, vol. 3054 of *Lect. Notes Comp. Sc.*, (Edinburgh, UK). Berlin: Springer-Verlag, 2004. pp. 7-22. Cited on page 65.

BUDHIJARA, N., MARZULLO, K., SCHNEIDER, F., and TOUEG, S.: "The Primary-Backup Approach." In Mullender, S. (ed.), *Distributed Systems*, pp. 199-216. Wokingham: Addison-Wesley, 2nd ed., 1993. Cited on page 308.

BUDHIRAJA, N. and MARZULLO, K.: "Tradeoffs in Implementing Primary-Backup Protocols." Technical Report TR 92-1307, Department of Computer Science, Cornell University, 1992. Cited on page 309.

BURNS, R. C., REES, R. M., STOCKMEYER, L. J., and LONG, D. D. E.: "Scalable Session Locking for a Distributed File System." *Cluster Computing*, (4)4:295-306, Oct. 2001. Cited on page 518.

BUSI, N., MONTRESOR, A., and ZAVATTARO, G.: "Data-driven Coordination in Peer-to-Peer Information Systems." *Int'l J. Coop. Inf. Syst.*, (13)1:63-89, Mar. 2004. Cited on page 597.

BUTT, A. R., JOHNSON, T. A., ZHENG, Y., and HU, Y. C.: "Kosha: A Peer-to-Peer Enhancement for the Network File System." *Proc. Int'l Conf. Supercomputing*, (Washington, DC). Los Alamitos, CA: IEEE Computer Society Press, 2004. pp. 51-61. Cited on page 500.

CABRI, G., FERRARI, L., LEONARDI, L., MAMEI, M., and ZAMBONELLI, F.: "Uncoupling Coordination: Tuple-based Models for Mobility." In Bellavista, Paolo and Corradi, Antonio (eds.), *The Handbook of Mobile Middleware*. London, UK: CRC Press, 2006. Cited on page 633.

CABRI, G., LEONARDI, L., and ZAMBONELLI, F.: "Mobile-Agent Coordination Models for Internet Applications." *IEEE Computer*, (33)2:82-89, Feb. 2000. Cited on page 590.

CAI, M., CHERVENAK, A., and FRANK, M.: "A Peer-to-Peer Replica Location Service Based on A Distributed Hash Table." *Proc. High Perf. Comput., Netw., & Storage Conf.*, (Pittsburgh, PA). New York, NY: ACM Press, 2004. pp. 56-67. Cited on page 529.

CALLAGHAN, B.: *NFS Illustrated*. Reading, MA: Addison-Wesley, 2000. Cited on pages 492, 510.

CANDEA, G., BROWN, A. B., FOX, A., and PATTERSON, D.: "Recovery-Oriented Computing: Building Multitier Dependability." *IEEE Computer*, (37)11:60-67, Nov. 2004a. Cited on page 372.

CANDEA, G., KAWAMOTO, S., FUJIKI, Y., FRIEDMAN, G., and FOX, A.: "Microreboot: A Technique for Cheap Recovery." *Proc. Sixth Symp. on Operating System Design and Implementation*, (San Francisco, CA). Berkeley, CA: USENIX, 2004b. pp. 31-44. Cited on page 372.

CANDEA, G., KICIMAN, E., KAWAMOTO, S., and FOX, A.: "Autonomous Recovery in Componentized Internet Applications." *Cluster Comput.*, (9)2:175-190, Feb. 2006. Cited on page 372.

CANTIN, J., LIPASTI, M., and SMITH, J.: "The Complexity of Verifying Memory Coherence and Consistency." *IEEE Trans. Par. Distr. Syst.*, (16)7:663-671, July 2005. Cited on page 288.

CAO, L. and OSZU, T.: "Evaluation of Strong Consistency Web Caching Techniques." *World Wide Web*, (5)2:95-123, June 2002. Cited on page 573.

CAO, P. and LIU, C.: "Maintaining Strong Cache Consistency in the World Wide Web." *IEEE Trans. Comp.*, (47)4:445-457, Apr. 1998. Cited on page 573.

CAPORUSCIO, M., CARZANIGA, A., and WOLF, A. L.: "Design and Evaluation of a Support Service for Mobile, Wireless Publish/Subscribe Applications." *IEEE Trans. Softw. Eng.*, (29)12:1059-1071, Dec. 2003. Cited on page 600.

CARDELLINI, V., CASALICCHIO, E., COLAJANNI, M., and YU, P.: "The State of the Art in Locally Distributed Web-Server Systems." *ACM Comput. Surv.*, (34)2:263-311, June 2002. Cited on page 560.

CARRIERO, N. and GELERNTER, D.: "The S/Net's Linda Kernel." *ACM Trans. Comp. Syst.*, (32)2:110-129, May 1986. Cited on page 609.

CARZANIGA, A., RUTHERFORD, M. J., and WOLF, A. L.: "A Routing Scheme for Content-Based Networking." *Proc. 23rd INFOCOM Conf.*, (Hong Kong, China). Los Alamitos, CA: IEEE Computer Society Press, 2004. Cited on page 601.

CARZANIGA, A. and WOLF, A. L.: "Forwarding in a Content-based Network." *Proc. SIGCOMM*, (Karlsruhe, Germany). New York, NY: ACM Press, 2003. pp. 163-174. Cited on page 603.

CASTRO, M., DRUSCHEL, P., GANESH, A., ROWSTRON, A., and WALLACH, D. S.: "Secure Routing for Structured Peer-to-Peer Overlay Networks." *Proc. Fifth Symp. on Operating System Design and Implementation*, (Boston, MA). New York, NY: ACM Press, 2002a. pp. 299-314. Cited on pages 539, 540.

CASTRO, M., DRUSCHEL, P., HU, Y. C., and ROWSTRON, A.: "Topology-aware Routing in Structured Peer-to-Peer Overlay Networks." Technical Report MSR-TR-2002-82, Microsoft Research, Cambridge, UK, June 2002b. Cited on page 190.

CASTRO, M., RODRIGUES, R., and LISKOV, B.: "BASE: Using Abstraction to Improve Fault Tolerance." *ACM Trans. Comp. Syst.*, (21)3:236-269, Aug. 2003. Cited on page 531.

CASTRO, M., COSTA, M., and ROWSTRON, A.: "Debunking Some Myths about Structured and Unstructured Overlays." *Proc. Second Symp. Networked Systems Design and Impl.*, (Boston, MA). Berkeley, CA: USENIX, 2005. Cited on page 49.

CASTRO, M., DRUSCHEL, P., KERMARREC, A.-M., and ROWSTRON, A.: "Scribe: A Large-Scale and Decentralized Application-Level Multicast Infrastructure." *IEEE J. Selected Areas Commun.*, (20)8:100-110, Oct. 2002. Cited on page 167.

CASTRO, M. and LISKOV, B.: "Practical Byzantine Fault Tolerance and Proactive Recovery." *ACM Trans. Comp. Syst.*, (20)4:398-461, Nov. 2002. Cited on pages 529, 531, 583.

CHAPPELL, D.: *Understanding .NET.* Reading, MA: Addison-Wesley, 2002. Cited on page 632.

CHERITON, D. and MANN, T.: "Decentralizing a Global Naming Service for Improved Performance and Fault Tolerance." *ACM Trans. Comp. Syst.*, (7)2:147-183, May 1989. Cited on page 203.

CHERITON, D. and SKEEN, D.: "Understanding the Limitations of Causally and Totally Ordered Communication." *Proc. 14th Symp. Operating System Principles.* ACM, 1993. pp. 44-57. Cited on page 251.

CHERVENAK, A., SCHULER, R., KESSELMAN, C., KORANDA, S., and MOE, B.: "Wide Area Data Replication for Scientific Collaborations." *Proc. Sixth Int'l Workshop on Grid Computing*, (Seattle, WA). New York, NY: ACM Press, 2005. Cited on page 529.

CHERVENAK, A., FOSTER, I., KESSELMAN, C., SALISBURY, C., and TUECKE, S.: "The Data Grid: Towards an Architecture for the Distributed Management and Analysis of Large Scientific Datasets." *J. Netw. Comp. App.*, (23)3:187-200, July 2000. Cited on page 380.

CHESWICK, W. and BELLOVIN, S.: *Firewalls and Internet Security.* Reading, MA: Addison-Wesley, 2nd ed., 2000. Cited on page 418.

CHOW, R. and JOHNSON, T.: *Distributed Operating Systems and Algorithms.* Reading, MA: Addison-Wesley, 1997. Cited on pages 363, 366.

CHUN, B. and SPALINK, T.: "Slice Creation and Management." Technical Report PDN-03-013, PlanetLab Consortium, July 2003. Cited on page 101.

CIANCARINI, P., TOLKSDORF, R., VITALI, F., and KNOCHE, A.: "Coordinating Multi-agent Applications on the WWW: A Reference Architecture." *IEEE Trans. Softw. Eng.*, (24)5:362-375, May 1998. Cited on page 610.

CLARK, C., FRASER, K., HAND, S., HANSEN, J. G., JUL, E., LIMPACH, C., PRATT, I., and WARFIELD, A.: "Live Migration of Virtual Machines." *Proc. Second Symp. Networked Systems Design and Impl.*, (Boston, MA). Berkeley, CA: USENIX, 2005. Cited on page 111.

CLARK, D.: "The Design Philosophy of the DARPA Internet Protocols." *Proc. SIGCOMM*, (Austin, TX). New York, NY: ACM Press, 1989. pp. 106-114. Cited on page 91.

CLEMENT, L., HATELY, A., VON RIEGEN, C., and ROGERS, T.: "Universal Description, Discovery and Integration (UDDI)." Technical Report, OASIS UDDI, 2004. Cited on page 222.

COHEN, B.: "Incentives Build Robustness in Bittorrent." *Proc. First Workshop on Economics of Peer-to-Peer Systems*, (Berkeley, CA), 2003. Cited on page 53.

COHEN, D.: "On Holy Wars and a Plea for Peace." *IEEE Computer*, (14)10:48-54, Oct. 1981. Cited on page 131.

COHEN, E. and SHENKER, S.: "Replication Strategies in Unstructured Peer-to-Peer Networks." *Proc. SIGCOMM*, (Pittsburgh, PA). New York, NY: ACM Press, 2002. pp. 177-190. Cited on page 526.

COMER, D.: *Internetworking with TCP/IP, Volume I: Principles, Protocols, and Architecture.* Upper Saddle River, NJ: Prentice Hall, 5th ed., 2006. Cited on page 121.

CONTI, M., GREGORI, E., and LAPENNA, W.: "Content Delivery Policies in Replicated Web Services: Client-Side vs. Server-Side." *Cluster Comput.,* (8)47-60, Jan. 2005. Cited on page 579.

COPPERSMITH, D.: "The Data Encryption Standard (DES) and its Strength Against Attacks." *IBM J. Research and Development,* (38)3:243-250, May 1994. Cited on page 394.

COULOURIS, G., DOLLIMORE, J., and KINDBERG, T.: *Distributed Systems, Concepts and Design.* Reading, MA: Addison-Wesley, 4th ed., 2005. Cited on page 623.

COX, L. and NOBLE, B.: "Samsara: Honor Among Thieves in Peer-to-Peer Storage." *Proc. 19th Symp. Operating System Principles,* (Bolton Landing, NY). New York, NY: ACM Press, 2003. pp. 120-131. Cited on page 540.

COYLER, A., BLAIR, G., and RASHID, A.: "Managing Complexity In Middleware." *Proc. Second AOSD Workshop on Aspects, Components, and Patterns for Infrastructure Software,* 2003. Cited on page 58.

CRESPO, A. and GARCIA-MOILINA, H.: "Semantic Overlay Networks for P2P Systems." Technical Report, Stanford University, Department of Computer Science, 2003. Cited on page 225.

CRISTIAN, F.: "Probabilistic Clock Synchronization." *Distributed Computing,* (3)146-158, 1989. Cited on page 240.

CRISTIAN, F.: "Understanding Fault-Tolerant Distributed Systems." *Commun. ACM,* (34)2:56-78, Feb. 1991. Cited on page 324.

CRISTIAN, F. and FETZER, C.: "The Timed Asynchronous Distributed System Model." *IEEE Trans. Par. Distr. Syst.,* (10)6:642-657, June 1999. Cited on page 629.

CROWLEY, C.: *Operating Systems, A Design-Oriented Approach.* Chicago: Irwin, 1997. Cited on page 197.

DABEK, F., COX, R., KAASHOEK, F., and MORRIS, R.: "Vivaldi: A Decentralized Network Coordinate System." *Proc. SIGCOMM,* (Portland, OR). New York, NY: ACM Press, 2004a. Cited on page 263.

DABEK, F., KAASHOEK, M. F., KARGER, D., MORRIS, R., and STOICA, I.: "Wide-area Cooperative Storage with CFS." *Proc. 18th Symp. Operating System Principles.* ACM, 2001. Cited on page 499.

DABEK, F., LI, J., SIT, E., ROBERTSON, J., KAASHOEK, M. F., and MORRIS, R.: "Designing a dht for low latency and high throughput." *Proc. First Symp. Networked Systems Design and Impl.,* (San Francisco, CA). Berkeley, CA: USENIX, 2004b. pp. 85-98. Cited on page 191.

DAIGLE, L., VAN GULIK, D., IANNELLA, R., and FALTSTROM, P.: "Uniform Resource Names (URN) Namespace Definition Mechanisms." RFC 3406, Oct. 2002. Cited on page 568.

DAVIE, B., CHARNY, A., BENNET, J., BENSON, K., BOUDEC, J. L., COURTNEY, W., S.DAVARI, FIROIU, V., and STILIADIS, D.: "An Expedited Forwarding PHB (Per-Hop Behavior)." RFC 3246, Mar. 2002. Cited on page 161.

DAY, J. and ZIMMERMAN, H.: "The OSI Reference Model." *Proceedings of the IEEE*, (71)12:1334-1340, Dec. 1983. Cited on page 117.

DEERING, S., ESTRIN, D., FARINACCI, D., JACOBSON, V., LIU, C.-G., and WEI, L.: "The PIM Architecture for Wide-Area Multicast Routing." *IEEE/ACM Trans. Netw.*, (4)2:153-162, Apr. 1996. Cited on page 183.

DEERING, S. and CHERITON, D.: "Multicast Routing in Datagram Internetworks and Extended LANs." *ACM Trans. Comp. Syst.*, (8)2:85-110, May 1990. Cited on page 183.

DEMERS, A., GEHRKE, J., HONG, M., RIEDEWALD, M., and WHITE, W.: "Towards Expressive Publish/Subscribe Systems." *Proc. Tenth Int'l Conf. on Extended Database Technology*, (Munich, Germany), 2006. Cited on page 607.

DEMERS, A., GREENE, D., HAUSER, C., IRISH, W., LARSON, J., SHENKER, S., STURGIS, H., SWINEHART, D., and TERRY, D.: "Epidemic Algorithms for Replicated Database Maintenance." *Proc. Sixth Symp. on Principles of Distributed Computing*, (Vancouver). ACM, 1987. pp. 1-12. Cited on pages 170, 172.

DEUTSCH, P., SCHOULTZ, R., FALTSTROM, P., and WEIDER, C.: "Architecture of the WHOIS++ Service." RFC 1835, Aug. 1995. Cited on page 63.

D\'FAGO, X., SHIPER, A., and URB{´A}N, P.: "Total Order Broadcast and Multicast Algorithms: Taxonomy and Survey." *ACM Comput. Surv.*, (36)4:372-421, Dec. 2004. Cited on page 344.

DIAO, Y., HELLERSTEIN, J., PAREKH, S., GRIFFITH, R., KAISER, G., and PHUNG, D.: "A Control Theory Foundation for Self-Managing Computing Systems." *IEEE J. Selected Areas Commun.*, (23)12:2213-2222, Dec. 2005. Cited on page 60.

DIERKS, T. and ALLEN, C.: "The Transport Layer Security Protocol." RFC 2246, Jan. 1996. Cited on page 584.

DIFFIE, W. and HELLMAN, M.: "New Directions in Cryptography." *IEEE Trans. Information Theory*, (IT-22)6:644-654, Nov. 1976. Cited on page 429.

DILLEY, J., MAGGS, B., PARIKH, J., PROKOP, H., SITARAMAN, R., and WEIHL, B.: "Globally Distributed Content Delivery." *IEEE Internet Comput.*, (6)5:50-58, Sept. 2002. Cited on page 577.

DIOT, C., LEVINE, B., LYLES, B., KASSEM, H., and BALENSIEFEN, D.: "Deployment Issues for the IP Multicast Service and Architecture." *IEEE Network*, (14)1:78-88, Jan. 2000. Cited on page 166.

DOORN, J. H. and RIVERO, L. C. (eds.): *Database Integrity: Challenges and Solutions.* Hershey, PA: Idea Group, 2002. Cited on page 384.

DOUCEUR, J. R.: "The Sybil Attack." *Proc. First Int'l Workshop on Peer-to-Peer Systems*, vol. 2429 of *Lect. Notes Comp. Sc.* Berlin: Springer-Verlag, 2002. pp. 251-260. Cited on page 539.

DUBOIS, M., SCHEURICH, C., and BRIGGS, F.: "Synchronization, Coherence, and Event Ordering in Multiprocessors." *IEEE Computer*, (21)2:9-21, Feb. 1988. Cited on page 283.

DUNAGAN, J., HARVEY, N. J. A., JONES, M. B., KOSTIC, D., THEIMER, M., and WOLMAN, A.: "FUSE: Lightweight Guaranteed Distributed Failure Notification." *Proc. Sixth Symp. on Operating System Design and Implementation*, (San Francisco, CA). Berkeley, CA: USENIX, 2004. Cited on page 336.

DUVVURI, V., SHENOY, P., and TEWARI, R.: "Adaptive Leases: A Strong Consistency Mechanism for the World Wide Web." *IEEE Trans. Know. Data Eng.*, (15)5:1266-1276, Sept. 2003. Cited on page 304.

EDDON, G. and EDDON, H.: *Inside Distributed COM*. Redmond, WA: Microsoft Press, 1998. Cited on page 136.

EISLER, M.: "LIPKEY - A Low Infrastructure Public Key Mechanism Using SPKM." RFC 2847, June 2000. Cited on page 534.

EISLER, M., CHIU, A., and LING, L.: "RPCSEC_GSS Protocol Specification." RFC 2203, Sept. 1997. Cited on page 534.

ELNOZAHY, E. N. and PLANK, J. S.: "Checkpointing for Peta-Scale Systems: A Look into the Future of Practical Rollback-Recovery." *IEEE Trans. Depend. Secure Comput.*, (1)2:97-108, Apr. 2004. Cited on page 368.

ELNOZAHY, E., ALVISI, L., WANG, Y.-M., and JOHNSON, D.: "A Survey of Rollback-Recovery Protocols in Message-Passing Systems." *ACM Comput. Surv.*, (34)3:375-408, Sept. 2002. Cited on pages 366, 372.

ELSON, J., GIROD, L., and ESTRIN, D.: "Fine-Grained Network Time Synchronization using Reference Broadcasts." *Proc. Fifth Symp. on Operating System Design and Implementation*, (Boston, MA). New York, NY: ACM Press, 2002. pp. 147-163. Cited on page 242.

EMMERICH, W.: *Engineering Distributed Objects*. New York: John Wiley, 2000. Cited on page 631.

EUGSTER, P., FELBER, P., GUERRAOUI, R., and KERMARREC, A.-M.: "The Many Faces of Publish/Subscribe." *ACM Comput. Surv.*, (35)2:114-131, June 2003. Cited on pages 35, 591.

EUGSTER, P., GUERRAOUI, R., KERMARREC, A.-M., and MASSOULI´E, L.: "Epidemic Information Dissemination in Distributed Systems." *IEEE Computer*, (37)5:60-67, May 2004. Cited on page 170.

FARMER, W. M., GUTTMAN, J. D., and SWARUP, V.: "Security for Mobile Agents: Issues and Requirements." *Proc. 19th National Information Systems Security Conf.*, 1996. pp. 591-597. Cited on page 421.

FELBER, P. and NARASIMHAN, P.: "Experiences, Strategies, and Challenges in Building Fault-Tolerant CORBA Systems." *IEEE Computer*, (53)5:497-511, May 2004. Cited on page 479.

FERGUSON, N. and SCHNEIER, B.: *Practical Cryptography*. New York: John Wiley, 2003. Cited on pages 391, 400.

FIELDING, R., GETTYS, J., MOGUL, J., FRYSTYK, H., MASINTER, L., LEACH, P., and BERNERS-LEE, T.: "Hypertext Transfer Protocol – HTTP/1.1." RFC 2616, June 1999. Cited on pages 122, 560.

FIELDING, R. T. and TAYLOR, R. N.: "Principled Design of the Modern Web Architecture." *ACM Trans. Internet Techn.*, (2)2:115–150, 2002. Cited on page 633.

FILMAN, R. E., ELRAD, T., CLARKE, S., and AKSIT, M. (eds.): *Aspect-Oriented Software Development.* Reading, MA: Addison-Wesley, 2005. Cited on page 57.

FISCHER, M., LYNCH, N., and PATTERSON, M.: "Impossibility of Distributed Consensus with one Faulty Processor." *J. ACM*, (32)2:374-382, Apr. 1985. Cited on page 334.

FLEURY, M. and REVERBEL, F.: "The JBoss Extensible Server." *Proc. Middleware 2003*, vol. 2672 of *Lect. Notes Comp. Sc.*, (Rio de Janeiro, Brazil). Berlin: Springer-Verlag, 2003. pp. 344 - 373. Cited on page 631.

FLOYD, S., JACOBSON, V., MCCANNE, S., LIU, C.-G., and ZHANG, L.: "A Reliable Multicast Framework for Light-weight Sessions and Application Level Framing." *IEEE/ACM Trans. Netw.*, (5)6:784-803, Dec. 1997. Cited on pages 345, 346.

FOSTER, I. and KESSELMAN, C.: *The Grid 2: Blueprint for a New Computing Infrastructure.* San Mateo, CA: Morgan Kaufman, 2nd ed., 2003. Cited on pages 380, 623.

FOSTER, I., KESSELMAN, C., TSUDIK, G., and TUECKE, S.: "A Security Architecture for Computational Grids." *Proc. Fifth Conf. Computer and Communications Security.* ACM, 1998. pp. 83-92. Cited on pages 380, 382, 383.

FOSTER, I., KESSELMAN, C., and TUECKE, S.: "The Anatomy of the Grid, Enabling Scalable Virtual Organizations." *Journal of Supercomputer Applications*, (15)3:200-222, Fall 2001. Cited on page 19.

FOSTER, I., KISHIMOTO, H., and SAVVA, A.: "The Open Grid Services Architecture, Version 1.0." GGF Informational Document GFD-I.030, Jan. 2005. Cited on page 20.

FOWLER, R.: *Decentralized Object Finding Using Forwarding Addresses.* Ph.D. Thesis, University of Washington, Seattle, 1985. Cited on page 184.

FRANKLIN, M. J., CAREY, M. J., and LIVNY, M.: "Transactional Client-Server Cache Consistency: Alternatives and Performance." *ACM Trans. Database Syst.*, (22)3:315-363, Sept. 1997. Cited on pages 313, 314.

FREEMAN, E., HUPFER, S., and ARNOLD, K.: *JavaSpaces, Principles, Patterns and Practice.* Reading, MA: Addison-Wesley, 1999. Cited on page 593.

FREUND, R.: "Web Services Coordination, Version 1.0, Feb. 2005. Cited on page 553.

FRIEDMAN, R. and KAMA, A.: "Transparent Fault-Tolerant Java Virtual Machine." *Proc. 22nd Symp. on Reliable Distributed Systems*, (Florence, Italy). IEEE Computer Society Press: IEEE Computer Society Press, 2003. pp. 319-328. Cited on pages 480, 481.

FUGGETTA, A., PICCO, G. P., and VIGNA, G.: "Understanding Code Mobility." *IEEE Trans. Softw. Eng.*, (24)5:342-361, May 1998. Cited on page 105.

GAMMA, E., HELM, R., JOHNSON, R., and VLISSIDES, J.: *Design Patterns, Elements of Reusable Object-Oriented Software.* Reading, MA: Addison-Wesley, 1994. Cited on pages 418, 446.

GARBACKI, P., EPEMA, D., and VAN STEEN, M.: "A Two-Level Semantic Caching Scheme for Super-Peer Networks." *Proc. Tenth Web Caching Workshop*, (Sophia Antipolis, France). IEEE, 2005. Cited on page 51.

GARCIA-MOLINA, H.: "Elections in a Distributed Computing System." *IEEE Trans. Comp.*, (31)1:48-59, Jan. 1982. Cited on page 264.

GARMAN, J.: *Kerberos: The Definitive Guide.* Sebastopol, CA: O'Reilly & Associates, 2003. Cited on pages 411, 442.

GELERNTER, D.: "Generative Communication in Linda." *ACM Trans. Prog. Lang. Syst.*, (7)1:80-112, 1985. Cited on page 591.

GELERNTER, D. and CARRIERO, N.: "Coordination Languages and their Significance." *Commun. ACM*, (35)2:96-107, Feb. 1992. Cited on page 590.

GHEMAWAT, S., GOBIOFF, H., and LEUNG, S.-T.: "The Google File System." *Proc. 19th Symp. Operating System Principles*, (Bolton Landing, NY). New York, NY: ACM Press, 2003. pp. 29-43. Cited on page 497.

GIFFORD, D.: "Weighted Voting for Replicated Data." *Proc. Seventh Symp. Operating System Principles*. ACM, 1979. pp. 150-162. Cited on page 311.

GIGASPACES: *GigaSpaces Cache 5.0 Documentation.* New York, NY, 2005. Cited on page 611.

GIL, T. M. and POLETTO, M.: "MULTOPS: a Data-Structure for Bandwidth Attack Detection." *Proc. Tenth USENIX Security Symp.*, (Washington, DC). Berkeley, CA: USENIX, 2001. pp. 23-38. Cited on page 427.

GLADNEY, H.: "Access Control for Large Collections." *ACM Trans. Inf. Syst.*, (15)2:154-194, Apr. 1997. Cited on page 418.

GOLAND, Y., WHITEHEAD, E., FAIZI, A., CARTER, S., and JENSEN, D.: "HTTP Extensions for Distributed Authoring – WEBDAV." RFC 2518, Feb. 1999. Cited on page 569.

GOLLMANN, D.: *Computer Security.* New York: John Wiley, 2nd ed., 2006. Cited on page 384.

GONG, L. and SCHEMERS, R.: "Implementing Protection Domains in the Java Development Kit 1.2." *Proc. Symp. Network and Distributed System Security*. Internet Society, 1998. pp. 125-134. Cited on page 426.

GOPALAKRISHNAN, V., SILAGHI, B., BHATTACHARJEE, B., and KELEHER, P.: "Adaptive Replication in Peer-to-Peer Systems." *Proc. 24th Int'l Conf. on Distributed Computing Systems*, (Tokyo). Los Alamitos, CA: IEEE Computer Society Press, 2004. pp. 360-369. Cited on page 527.

GRAY, C. and CHERITON, D.: "Leases: An Efficient Fault-Tolerant Mechanism for Distributed File Cache Consistency." *Proc. 12th Symp. Operating System Principles*, (Litchfield Park, AZ). New York, NY: ACM Press, 1989. pp. 202-210. Cited on page 304.

GRAY, J., HELLAND, P., O'NEIL, P., and SASHNA, D.: "The Dangers of Replication and a Solution." *Proc. SIGMOD Int'l Conf. on Management Of Data*. ACM, 1996. pp. 173-182. Cited on pages 276, 628.

GRAY, J. and REUTER, A.: *Transaction Processing: Concepts and Techniques.* San Mateo, CA: Morgan Kaufman, 1993. Cited on page 21.

GRAY, J.: "Notes on Database Operating Systems." In Bayer, R., Graham, R., and Seegmuller, G. (eds.), *Operating Systems: An Advanced Course*, vol. 60 of *Lect. Notes Comp. Sc.*, pp. 393-481. Berlin: Springer-Verlag, 1978. Cited on page 355.

GRIMM, R., DAVIS, J., LEMAR, E., MACBETH, A., SWANSON, S., ANDERSON, T., BERSHAD, B., BORRIELLO, G., GRIBBLE, S., and WETHERALL, D.: "System Support for Pervasive Applications." *ACM Trans. Comp. Syst.*, (22)4:421-486, Nov. 2004. Cited on page 25.

GROPP, W., HUSS-LEDERMAN, S., LUMSDAINE, A., LUSK, E., NITZBERG, B., SAPHIR, W., and SNIR, M.: *MPI: The Complete Reference – The MPI-2 Extensions.* Cambridge, MA: MIT Press, 1998a. Cited on page 145.

GROPP, W., LUSK, E., and SKJELLUM, A.: *Using MPI, Portable Parallel Programming with the Message-Passing Interface.* Cambridge, MA: MIT Press, 2nd ed., 1998b. Cited on page 145.

GROSSKURTH, A. and GODFREY, M. W.: "A Reference Architecture for Web Browsers." *Proc. 21st Int'l Conf. Softw. Mainten.*, (Budapest, Hungary). Los Alamitos, CA: IEEE Computer Society Press, 2005. pp. 661-664. Cited on page 554.

GUDGIN, M., HADLEY, M., MENDELSOHN, N., MOREAU, J.-J., and NIELSEN, H. F.: "SOAP Version 1.2." W3C Recommendation, June 2003. Cited on pages 565, 567.

GUERRAOUI, R. and RODRIGUES, L.: *Introduction to Reliable Distributed Programming.* Berlin: Springer-Verlag, 2006. Cited on pages 232, 627.

GUERRAOUI, R. and SCHIPER, A.: "Software-Based Replication for Fault Tolerance." *IEEE Computer*, (30)4:68-74, Apr. 1997. Cited on pages 328, 629.

GUICHARD, J., FAUCHEUR, F. L., and VASSEUR, J.-P.: *Definitive MPLS Network Designs.* Indianapolis, IN: Cisco Press, 2005. Cited on page 575.

GULBRANDSEN, A., VIXIE, P., and ESIBOV, L.: "A dns rr for specifying the location of services (dns srv)." RFC 2782, Feb. 2000. Cited on page 211.

GUPTA, A., SAHIN, O. D., AGRAWAL, D., and ABBADI, A. E.: "Meghdoot: Content-Based Publish/Subscribe over P2P Networks." *Proc. Middleware 2004*, vol. 3231 of *Lect. Notes Comp. Sc.*, (Toronto, Canada). Berlin: Springer-Verlag, 2004. pp. 254-273. Cited on page 599.

GUSELLA, R. and ZATTI, S.: "The Accuracy of the Clock Synchronization Achieved by TEMPO in Berkeley UNIX 4.3BSD." *IEEE Trans. Softw. Eng.*, (15)7:847-853, July 1989. Cited on page 241.

HADZILACOS, V. and TOUEG, S.: "Fault-Tolerant Broadcasts and Related Problems." In Mullender, S. (ed.), *Distributed Systems*, pp. 97-145. Wokingham: Addison-Wesley, 2nd ed., 1993. Cited on pages 324, 352.

HALSALL, F.: *Multimedia Communications: Applications, Networks, Protocols and Standards.* Reading, MA: Addison-Wesley, 2001. Cited on pages 157, 160.

HANDURUKANDE, S., KERMARREC, A.-M., FESSANT, F. L., and MASSOULIE, L.: "Exploiting Semantic Clustering in the eDonkey P2P network." *Proc. 11th SIGOPS European Workshop*, (Leuven, Belgium). New York, NY: ACM Press, 2004. Cited on page 226.

HELDER, D. A. and JAMIN, S.: "End-Host Multicast Communication Using Switch-Trees Protocols." *Proc. Second Int'l Symp. Cluster Comput. & Grid*, (Berlin, Germany). Los Alamitos, CA: IEEE Computer Society Press, 2002. pp. 419-424. Cited on page 169.

HELLERSTEIN, J. L., DIAO, Y., PAREKH, S., and TILBURY, D. M.: *Feedback Control of Computing Systems*. New York: John Wiley, 2004. Cited on pages 60, 624.

HENNING, M.: "A New Approach to Object-Oriented Middleware." *IEEE Internet Comput.*, (8)1:66-75, Jan. 2004. Cited on page 454.

HENNING, M.: "The Rise and Fall of CORBA." *ACM Queue*, (4)5, 2006. Cited on page 631.

HENNING, M. and SPRUIELL, M.: *Distributed Programming with Ice*. ZeroC Inc., Brisbane, Australia, May 2005. Cited on pages 455, 470.

HENNING, M. and VINOSKI, S.: *Advanced CORBA Programming with C++*. Reading, MA: Addison-Wesley, 1999. Cited on page 631.

HOCHSTETLER, S. and BERINGER, B.: "Linux Clustering with CSM and GPFS." Technical Report SG24-6601-02, International Technical Support Organization, IBM, Austin, TX, Jan. 2004. Cited on page 98.

HOHPE, G. and WOOLF, B.: *Enterprise Integration Patterns: Designing, Building, and Deploying Messaging Solutions*. Reading, MA: Addison-Wesley, 2004. Cited on pages 152, 626.

HOROWITZ, M. and LUNT, S.: "FTP Security Extensions." RFC 2228, Oct. 1997. Cited on page 122.

HOWES, T.: "The String Representation of LDAP Search Filters." RFC 2254, Dec. 1997. Cited on page 221.

HUA CHU, Y., RAO, S. G., SESHAN, S., and ZHANG, H.: "A Case for End System Multicast." *IEEE J. Selected Areas Commun.*, (20)8:1456-1471, Oct. 2002. Cited on page 168.

HUFFAKER, B., FOMENKOV, M., PLUMMER, D. J., MOORE, D., and CLAFFY, K.: "Distance Metrics in the Internet." *Proc. Int'l Telecommun. Symp.*, (Natal RN, Brazil). Los Alamitos, CA: IEEE Computer Society Press, 2002. Cited on page 575.

HUNT, G., NAHUM, E., and TRACEY, J.: "Enabling Content-Based Load Distribution for Scalable Services." Technical Report, IBM T.J. Watson Research Center, May 1997. Cited on page 94.

HUTTO, P. and AHAMAD, M.: "Slow Memory: Weakening Consistency to Enhance Concurrency in Distributed Shared Memories." *Proc. Tenth Int'l Conf. on Distributed Computing Systems*. IEEE, 1990. pp. 302-311. Cited on page 284.

IBM: *WebSphere MQ Application Programming Guide*, May 2005a. Cited on page 152.

IBM: *WebSphere MQ Intercommunication*, May 2005b. Cited on page 152.

IBM: *WebSphere MQ Publish/Subscribe User's Guide*, May 2005c. Cited on page 593.

IBM: *WebSphere MQ System Administration*, May 2005d. Cited on page 152.

ISO: "Open Distributed Processing Reference Model." International Standard ISO/IEC IS 10746, 1995. Cited on page 5.

JAEGER, T., PRAKASH, A., LIEDTKE, J., and ISLAM, N.: "Flexible Control of Downloaded Executable Content." *ACM Trans. Inf. Syst. Sec.*, (2)2:177-228, May 1999. Cited on page 426.

JALOTE, P.: *Fault Tolerance in Distributed Systems*. Englewood Cliffs, NJ: Prentice Hall, 1994. Cited on pages 312, 322, 630.

JANIC, M.: *Multicast in Network and Application Layer*. Ph.d. Thesis, Delft University of Technology, The Netherlands, Oct. 2005. Cited on page 166.

JANIGA, M. J., DIBNER, G., and GOVERNALI, F. J.: "Internet Infrastructure: Content Delivery." Goldman Sachs Global Equity Research, Apr. 2001. Cited on page 575.

JELASITY, M., GUERRAOUI, R., KERMARREC, A.-M., and VAN STEEN, M.: "The Peer Sampling Service: Experimental Evaluation of Unstructured Gossip-Based Implementations." *Proc. Middleware 2004*, vol. 3231 of *Lect. Notes Comp. Sc.*, (Toronto, Canada). Berlin: Springer-Verlag, 2004. pp. 79-98. Cited on page 47.

JELASITY, M., VOULGARIS, S., GUERRAOUI, R., KERMARREC, A.-M., and VAN STEEN, M.: "Gossip-based Peer Sampling." Technical Report, Vrije Universiteit, Department of Computer Science, Sept. 2005a. Cited on pages 47, 49, 171, 226.

JELASITY, M. and BABAOGLU, O.: "T-Man: Gossip-based Overlay Topology Management." *Proc. Third Int'l Workshop Eng. Self-Organising App.*, (Utrecht, The Netherlands), 2005. Cited on pages 49, 50.

JELASITY, M., MONTRESOR, A., and BABAOGLU, O.: "Gossip-based Aggregation in Large Dynamic Networks." *ACM Trans. Comp. Syst.*, (23)3:219-252, Aug. 2005b. Cited on page 173.

JIN, J. and NAHRSTEDT, K.: "QoS Specification Languages for Distributed Multimedia Applications: A Survey and Taxonomy." *IEEE Multimedia*, (11)3:74-87, July 2004. Cited on page 160.

JING, J., HELAL, A., and ELMAGARMID, A.: "Client-Server Computing in Mobile Environments." *ACM Comput. Surv.*, (31)2:117-157, June 1999. Cited on page 41.

JOHNSON, B.: "An Introduction to the Design and Analysis of Fault-Tolerant Systems." In Pradhan, D.K. (ed.), *Fault-Tolerant Computer System Design*, pp. 1-87. Upper Saddle River, NJ: Prentice Hall, 1995. Cited on page 326.

JOHNSON, D., PERKINS, C., and ARKKO, J.: "Mobility Support for IPv6." RFC 3775, June 2004. Cited on page 186.

JOSEPH, J., ERNEST, M., and FELLENSTEIN, C.: "Evolution of grid computing architecture and grid adoption models." *IBM Syst. J.*, (43)4:624-645, Apr. 2004. Cited on page 20.

JUL, E., LEVY, H., HUTCHINSON, N., and BLACK, A.: "Fine-Grained Mobility in the Emerald System." *ACM Trans. Comp. Syst.*, (6)1:109-133, Feb. 1988. Cited on page 186.

JUNG, J., SIT, E., BALAKRISHNAN, H., and MORRIS, R.: "DNS Performance and the Effectiveness of Caching." *IEEE/ACM Trans. Netw.*, (10)5:589 - 603, Oct. 2002. Cited on page 216.

KAHN, D.: *The Codebreakers*. New York: Macmillan, 1967. Cited on page 391.

KAMINSKY, M., SAVVIDES, G., MAZIhRES, D., and KAASHOEK, M. F.: "Decentralized User Authentication in a Global File System." *Proc. 19th Symp. Operating System Principles*, (Bolton Landing, NY). New York, NY: ACM Press, 2003. pp. 60-73. Cited on pages 535, 538.

KANTARCIOGLU, M. and CLIFTON, C.: "Security Issues in Querying Encrypted Data." *Proc. 19th Conf. Data & Appl. Security*, vol. 3654 of *Lect. Notes Comp. Sc.*, (Storrs, CT). Berlin: Springer-Verlag, 2005. pp. 325-337. Cited on page 618.

KARNIK, N. and TRIPATHI, A.: "Security in the Ajanta Mobile Agent System." *Software – Practice & Experience*, (31)4:301-329, Apr. 2001. Cited on page 421.

KASERA, S., KUROSE, J., and TOWSLEY, D.: "Scalable Reliable Multicast Using Multiple Multicast Groups." *Proc. Int'l Conf. Measurements and Modeling of Computer Systems*. ACM, 1997. pp. 64-74. Cited on page 346.

KATZ, E., BUTLER, M., and MCGRATH, R.: "A Scalable HTTP Server: The NCSA Prototype." *Comp. Netw. & ISDN Syst.*, (27)2:155-164, Sept. 1994. Cited on page 76.

KAUFMAN, C., PERLMAN, R., and SPECINER, M.: *Network Security: Private Communication in a Public World*. Englewood Cliffs, NJ: Prentice Hall, 2nd ed., 2003. Cited on pages 400, 630.

KENT, S.: "Internet Privacy Enhanced Mail." *Commun. ACM*, (36)8:48-60, Aug. 1993. Cited on page 431.

KEPHART, J. O. and CHESS, D. M.: "The Vision of Autonomic Computing." *IEEE Computer*, (36)1:41-50, Jan. 2003. Cited on page 59.

KHOSHAFIAN, S. and BUCKIEWICZ, M.: *Introduction to Groupware, Workflow, and Workgroup Computing*. New York: John Wiley, 1995. Cited on page 151.

KHURANA, H. and KOLEVA, R.: "Scalable Security and Accounting Services for Content-Based Publish Subscribe Systems." *Int'l J. E-Business Res.*, (2), 2006. Cited on pages 618, 619, 620.

KIM, S., PAN, K., SINDERSON, E., and WHITEHEAD, J.: "Architecture and Data Model of a WebDAV-based Collaborative System." *Proc. Collaborative Techn. Symp.\fR, (San Diego, CA), 2004. pp. 48-55. Cited on page 570.*

KISTLER, J. and SATYANARYANAN, M.: "Disconnected Operation in the Coda File System." *ACM Trans. Comp. Syst.*, (10)1:3-25, Feb. 1992. Cited on pages 503, 518.

KLEIMAN, S.: "Vnodes: an Architecture for Multiple File System Types in UNIX." *Proc. Summer Techn. Conf.* USENIX, 1986. pp. 238-247. Cited on page 493.

KOHL, J., NEUMAN, B., and T'SO, T.: "The Evolution of the Kerberos Authentication System." In Brazier, F. and Johansen, D. (eds.), *Distributed Open Systems*, pp. 78-94. Los Alamitos, CA: IEEE Computer Society Press, 1994. Cited on page 411.

KON, F., COSTA, F., CAMPBELL, R., and BLAIR, G.: "The Case for Reflective Middleware." *Commun. ACM*, (45)6:33-38, June 2002. Cited on page 57.

KOPETZ, H. and VERISSIMO, P.: "Real Time and Dependability Concepts." In Mullender, S. (ed.), *Distributed Systems*, pp. 411-446. Wokingham: Addison-Wesley, 2nd ed., 1993. Cited on page 322.

KOSTOULAS, M. G., MATSA, M., MENDELSOHN, N., PERKINS, E., HEIFETS, A., and MERCALDI, M.: "XML Screamer: An Integrated Approach to High Performance XML Parsing, Validation and Deserialization." *Proc. 15th Int'l WWW Conf.*, (Edinburgh, Scotland). New York, NY: ACM Press, 2006. Cited on page 567.

KUMAR, P. and SATYANARAYANAN, M.: "Flexible and Safe Resolution of File Conflicts." *Proc. Winter Techn. Conf.* USENIX, 1995. pp. 95-106. Cited on page 526.

LAI, A. and NIEH, J.: "Limits of Wide-Area Thin-Client Computing." *Proc. Int'l Conf. Measurements and Modeling of Computer Systems*, (Marina Del Rey, CA). New York, NY: ACM Press, 2002. pp. 228-239. Cited on page 84.

LAMACCHIA, B. and ODLYZKO, A.: "Computation of Discrete Logarithms in Prime Fields." *Designs, Codes, and Cryptography*, (1)1:47-62, May 1991. Cited on page 534.

LAMPORT, L.: "Time, Clocks, and the Ordering of Events in a Distributed System." *Commun. ACM*, (21)7:558-565, July 1978. Cited on page 244.

LAMPORT, L.: "How to Make a Multiprocessor Computer that Correctly Executes Multiprocessor Programs." *IEEE Trans. Comp.*, (C-29)9:690-691, Sept. 1979. Cited on page 282.

LAMPORT, L., SHOSTAK, R., and PAESE, M.: "Byzantine Generals Problem." *ACM Trans. Prog. Lang. Syst.*, (4)3:382-401, July 1982. Cited on pages 326, 332, 334.

LAMPSON, B., ABADI, M., BURROWS, M., and WOBBER, E.: "Authentication in Distributed Systems: Theory and Practice." *ACM Trans. Comp. Syst.*, (10)4:265-310, Nov. 1992. Cited on page 397.

LAPRIE, J.-C.: "Dependability – Its Attributes, Impairments and Means." In Randell, B., Laprie, J.-C., Kopetz, H., and Littlewood, B. (eds.), *Predictably Dependable Computing Systems*, pp. 3-24. Berlin: Springer-Verlag, 1995. Cited on page 378.

LAURIE, B. and LAURIE, P.: *Apache: The Definitive Guide*. Sebastopol, CA: O'Reilly & Associates, 3rd ed., 2002. Cited on page 558.

LEFF, A. and RAYFIELD, J. T.: "Alternative Edge-server Architectures for Enterprise JavaBeans Applications." *Proc. Middleware 2004*, vol. 3231 of *Lect. Notes Comp. Sc.*, (Toronto, Canada). Berlin: Springer-Verlag, 2004. pp. 195-211. Cited on page 52.

LEIGHTON, F. and LEWIN, D.: "Global Hosting System." United States Patent, Number 6,108,703, Aug. 2000. Cited on page 577.

LEVIEN, R. (ed.): *Signposts in Cyberspace: The Domain Name System and Internet Navigation*. Washington, DC: National Academic Research Council, 2005. Cited on page 210.

LEVINE, B. and GARCIA-LUNA-ACEVES, J.: "A Comparison of Reliable Multicast Protocols." *ACM Multimedia Systems Journal*, (6)5:334-348, 1998. Cited on page 345.

LEWIS, B. and BERG, D. J.: *Multithreaded Programming with Pthreads.* Englewood Cliffs, NJ: Prentice Hall, 2nd ed., 1998. Cited on pages 70, 625.

LI, G. and JACOBSEN, H.-A.: "Composite Subscriptions in Content-Based Publish/Subscribe Systems." *Proc. Middleware 2005*, vol. 3790 of *Lect. Notes Comp. Sc.,* (Grenoble, France). Berlin: Springer-Verlag, 2005. pp. 249-269. Cited on page 603.

LI, J., LU, C., and SHI, W.: "An Efficient Scheme for Preserving Confidentiality in Content-Based Publish-Subscribe Systems." Technical Report GIT-CC-04-01, Georgia Institute of Technology, College of Computing, 2004a. Cited on page 619.

LI, N., MITCHELL, J. C., and TONG, D.: "Securing Java RMI-based Distributed Applications." *Proc. 20th Ann. Computer Security Application Conf.,* (Tucson, AZ). ACSA, 2004b. Cited on page 486.

LILJA, D.: "Cache Coherence in Large-Scale Shared-Memory Multiprocessors: Issues and Comparisons." *ACM Comput. Surv.,* (25)3:303-338, Sept. 1993. Cited on page 313.

LIN, M.-J. and MARZULLO, K.: "Directional Gossip: Gossip in a Wide-Area Network." In *Proc. Third European Dependable Computing Conf.,* vol. 1667 of *Lect. Notes Comp. Sc.,* pp. 364-379. Berlin: Springer-Verlag, Sept. 1999. Cited on page 172.

LIN, S.-D., LIAN, Q., CHEN, M., , and ZHANG, Z.: "A Practical Distributed Mutual Exclusion Protocol in Dynamic Peer-to-Peer Systems." *Proc. Third Int'l Workshop on Peer-to-Peer Systems,* vol. 3279 of *Lect. Notes Comp. Sc.,* (La Jolla, CA). Berlin: Springer-Verlag, 2004. pp. 11-21. Cited on pages 254, 255.

LING, B. C., KICIMAN, E., and FOX, A.: "Session State: Beyond Soft State." *Proc. First Symp. Networked Systems Design and Impl.,* (San Francisco, CA). Berkeley, CA: USENIX, 2004. pp. 295-308. Cited on page 91.

LINN, J.: "Generic Security Service Application Program Interface, version 2." RFC 2078, Jan. 1997. Cited on page 534.

LIU, C.-G., ESTRIN, D., SHENKER, S., and ZHANG, L.: "Local Error Recovery in SRM: Comparison of Two Approaches." *IEEE/ACM Trans. Netw.,* (6)6:686-699, Dec. 1998. Cited on page 346.

LIU, H. and JACOBSEN, H.-A.: "Modeling Uncertainties in Publish/Subscribe Systems." *Proc. 20th Int'l Conf. Data Engineering,* (Boston, MA). Los Alamitos, CA: IEEE Computer Society Press, 2004. pp. 510-522. Cited on page 607.

LO, V., ZHOU, D., LIU, Y., GauthierDickey, C., and LI, J.: "Scalable Supernode Selection in Peer-to-Peer Overlay Networks." *Proc. Second Hot Topics in Peer-to-Peer Systems,* (La Jolla, CA), 2005. Cited on page 269.

LOSHIN, P. (ed.): *Big Book of Lightweight Directory Access Protocol (LDAP) RFCs.* San Mateo, CA: Morgan Kaufman, 2000. Cited on page 627.

LUA, E. K., CROWCROFT, J., PIAS, M., SHARMA, R., and LIM, S.: "A Survey and Comparison of Peer-to-Peer Overlay Network Schemes." *IEEE Communications Surveys & Tutorials,* (7)2:22-73, Apr. 2005. Cited on pages 15, 44, 625.

LUI, J., MISRA, V., and RUBENSTEIN, D.: "On the Robustness of Soft State Protocols." *Proc. 12th Int'l Conf. on Network Protocols,* (Berlin, Germany). Los Alamitos, CA: IEEE Computer Society Press, 2004. pp. 50-60. Cited on page 91.

LUOTONEN, A. and ALTIS, K.: "World-Wide Web Proxies." *Comp. Netw. & ISDN Syst.*, (27)2:1845-1855, 1994. Cited on page 555.

LYNCH, N.: *Distributed Algorithms.* San Mateo, CA: Morgan Kaufman, 1996. Cited on pages 232, 263, 628.

MAASSEN, J., KIELMANN, T., and BAL, H. E.: "Parallel Application Experience with Replicated Method Invocation." *Conc. & Comput.: Prac. Exp.*, (13)8-9:681-712, 2001. Cited on page 475.

MACGREGOR, R., DURBIN, D., OWLETT, J., and YEOMANS, A.: *Java Network Security.* Upper Saddle River, NJ: Prentice Hall, 1998. Cited on page 422.

MADDEN, S. R., FRANKLIN, M. J., HELLERSTEIN, J. M., and HONG, W.: "TinyDB: An Acquisitional Query Processing System for Sensor Networks." *ACM Trans. Database Syst.*, (30)1:122-173, 2005. Cited on page 30.

MAKPANGOU, M., GOURHANT, Y., LE NARZUL, J.-P., and SHAPIRO, M.: "Fragmented Objects for Distributed Abstractions." In Casavant, T. and Singhal, M. (eds.), *Readings in Distributed Computing Systems*, pp. 170-186. Los Alamitos, CA: IEEE Computer Society Press, 1994. Cited on page 449.

MALKHI, D. and REITER, M.: "Secure Execution of Java Applets using a Remote Playground." *IEEE Trans. Softw. Eng.*, (26)12:1197-1209, Dec. 2000. Cited on page 424.

MAMEI, M. and ZAMBONELLI, F.: "Programming Pervasive and Mobile Computing Applications with the TOTA Middleware." *Proc. Second Int'l Conf. Pervasive Computing and Communications (PerCom)*, (Orlando, FL). Los Alamitos, CA: IEEE Computer Society Press, 2004. pp. 263-273. Cited on page 601.

MANOLA, F. and MILLER, E.: "RDF Primer." W3C Recommendation, Feb. 2004. Cited on page 218.

MARCUS, E. and STERN, H.: *Blueprints for High Availability.* New York: John Wiley, 2nd ed., 2003. Cited on page 629.

MASCOLO, C., CAPRA, L., and EMMERICH, W.: "Principles of Mobile Computing Middleware." In Mahmoud, Qusay H. (ed.), *Middleware for Communications*, chapter 12. New York: John Wiley, 2004. Cited on page 25.

MASINTER, L.: "The Data URL Scheme." RFC 2397, Aug. 1998. Cited on page 568.

MAZIERES, D., KAMINSKY, M., KAASHOEK, M., and WITCHEL, E.: "Separating Key Management from File System Security." *Proc. 17th Symp. Operating System Principles.* ACM, 1999. pp. 124-139. Cited on pages 484, 536.

MAZOUNI, K., GARBINATO, B., and GUERRAOUI, R.: "Building Reliable Client-Server Software Using Actively Replicated Objects." In Graham, I., Magnusson, B., Meyer, B., and Nerson, J.-M (eds.), *Technology of Object Oriented Languages and Systems*, pp. 37-53. Englewood Cliffs, NJ: Prentice Hall, 1995. Cited on page 475.

MCKINLEY, P., SADJADI, S., KASTEN, E., and CHENG, B.: "Composing Adaptive Software." *IEEE Computer*, (37)7:56-64, Jan. 2004. Cited on page 57.

MEHTA, N., MEDVIDOVIC, N., and PHADKE, S.: "Towards A Taxonomy Of Software Connectors." *Proc. 22nd Int'l Conf. on Software Engineering*, (Limerick, Ireland). New York, NY: ACM Press, 2000. pp. 178-187. Cited on page 34.

MENEZES, A. J., VAN OORSCHOT, P. C., and VANSTONE, S. A.: *Handbook of Applied Cryptography*. Boca Raton: CRC Press, 3rd ed., 1996. Cited on pages 391, 430, 431, 630.

MERIDETH, M. G., IYENGAR, A., MIKALSEN, T., TAI, S., ROUVELLOU, I., and NARASIMHAN, P.: "Thema: Byzantine-Fault-Tolerant Middleware for Web-Service Applications." *Proc. 24th Symp. on Reliable Distributed Systems*, (Orlando, FL). Los Alamitos, CA: IEEE Computer Society Press, 2005. pp. 131-142. Cited on page 583.

MEYER, B.: *Object-Oriented Software Construction*. Englewood Cliffs, NJ: Prentice Hall, 2nd ed., 1997. Cited on page 445.

MILLER, B. N., KONSTAN, J. A., and RIEDL, J.: "PocketLens: Toward a Personal Recommender System." *ACM Trans. Inf. Syst.*, (22)3:437–476, July 2004. Cited on page 27.

MILLS, D. L.: *Computer Network Time Synchronization: The Network Time Protocol*. Boca Raton, FL: CRC Press, 2006. Cited on page 241.

MILLS, D. L.: "Network Time Protocol (version 3): Specification, Implementation, and Analysis." RFC 1305, July 1992. Cited on page 241.

MILOJICIC, D., DOUGLIS, F., PAINDAVEINE, Y., WHEELER, R., and ZHOU, S.: "Process Migration." *ACM Comput. Surv.*, (32)3:241-299, Sept. 2000. Cited on page 103.

MIN, S. L. and BAER, J.-L.: "Design and Analysis of a Scalable Cache Coherence Scheme Based on Clocks and Timestamps." *IEEE Trans. Par. Distr. Syst.*, (3)1:25-44, Jan. 1992. Cited on page 313.

MIRKOVIC, J., DIETRICH, S., and ANDPETER REIHER, D. D.: *Internet Denial of Service: Attack and Defense Mechanisms*. Englewood Cliffs, NJ: Prentice Hall, 2005. Cited on page 428.

MIRKOVIC, J. and REIHER, P.: "A Taxonomy of DDoS Attack and DDoS Defense Mechanisms." *ACM Comp. Commun. Rev.*, (34)2:39–53, Apr. 2004. Cited on page 428.

MOCKAPETRIS, P.: "Domain Names - Concepts and Facilities." RFC 1034, Nov. 1987. Cited on pages 203, 210.

MONSON-HAEFEL, R., BURKE, B., and LABOUREY, S.: *Enterprise Java Beans*. Sebastopol, CA: O'Reilly & Associates, 4th ed., 2004. Cited on page 447.

MOSER, L., MELLIAR-SMITH, P., AGARWAL, D., BUDHIA, R., and LINGLEY-PAPADOPOULOS, C.: "Totem: A Fault-Tolerant Multicast Group Communication System." *Commun. ACM*, (39)4:54-63, Apr. 1996. Cited on page 478.

MOSER, L., MELLIOR-SMITH, P., and NARASIMHAN, P.: "Consistent Object Replication in the Eternal System." *Theory and Practice of Object Systems*, (4)2:81-92, 1998. Cited on page 478.

MULLENDER, S. and TANENBAUM, A.: "Immediate Files." *Software – Practice & Experience*, (14)3:365-368, 1984. Cited on page 568.

MUNTZ, D. and HONEYMAN, P.: "Multi-level Caching in Distributed File Systems." *Proc. Winter Techn. Conf.* USENIX, 1992. pp. 305-313. Cited on page 301.

MURPHY, A., PICCO, G., and ROMAN, G.-C.: "Lime: A Middleware for Physical and Logical Mobility." *Proc. 21st Int'l Conf. on Distr. Computing Systems*, (Phoenix, AZ). Los Alamitos, CA: IEEE Computer Society Press, 2001. pp. 524-533. Cited on page 600.

MUTHITACHAROEN, A., MORRIS, R., GIL, T., and CHEN, B.: "Ivy: A Read/Write Peer-to-Peer File System." *Proc. Fifth Symp. on Operating System Design and Implementation*, (Boston, MA). New York, NY: ACM Press, 2002. pp. 31-44. Cited on page 499.

NAPPER, J., ALVISI, L., and VIN, H. M.: "A Fault-Tolerant Java Virtual Machine." *Proc. Int'l Conf. Dependable Systems and Networks*, (San Francisco, CA). Los Alamitos, CA: IEEE Computer Society Press, 2003. pp. 425-434. Cited on page 480.

NARASIMHAN, P., MOSER, L., and MELLIAR-SMITH, P.: "The Eternal System." In Urban, J. and Dasgupta, P. (eds.), *Encyclopedia of Distributed Computing*. Dordrecht, The Netherlands: Kluwer Academic Publishers, 2000. Cited on page 478.

NAYATE, A., DAHLIN, M., and IYENGAR, A.: "Transparent Information Dissemination." *Proc. Middleware 2004*, vol. 3231 of *Lect. Notes Comp. Sc.*, (Toronto, Canada). Berlin: Springer-Verlag, 2004. pp. 212-231. Cited on page 52.

NEEDHAM, R. and SCHROEDER, M.: "Using Encryption for Authentication in Large Networks of Computers." *Commun. ACM*, (21)12:993-999, Dec. 1978. Cited on page 402.

NEEDHAM, R.: "Names." In Mullender, S. (ed.), *Distributed Systems*, pp. 315-327. Wokingham: Addison-Wesley, 2nd ed., 1993. Cited on page 627.

NELSON, B.: *Remote Procedure Call*. Ph.D. Thesis, Carnegie-Mellon University, 1981. Cited on page 342.

NEUMAN, B.: "Scale in Distributed Systems." In Casavant, T. and Singhal, M. (eds.), *Readings in Distributed Computing Systems*, pp. 463-489. Los Alamitos, CA: IEEE Computer Society Press, 1994. Cited on pages 9, 12, 624.

NEUMAN, B.: "Proxy-Based Authorization and Accounting for Distributed Systems." *Proc. 13th Int'l Conf. on Distributed Computing Systems*. IEEE, 1993. pp. 283-291. Cited on page 437.

NEUMAN, C., YU, T., HARTMAN, S., and RAEBURN, K.: "The Kerberos Network Authentication Service." RFC 4120, July 2005. Cited on page 411.

NEUMANN, P.: "Architectures and Formal Representations for Secure Systems." Technical Report, Computer Science Laboratory, SRI International, Menlo Park, CA, Oct. 1995. Cited on page 388.

NG, E. and ZHANG, H.: "Predicting Internet Network Distance with Coordinates-Based Approaches." *Proc. 21st INFOCOM Conf.*, (New York, NY). Los Alamitos, CA: IEEE Computer Society Press, 2002. Cited on page 262.

NIEMELA, E. and LATVAKOSKI, J.: "Survey of Requirements and Solutions for Ubiquitous Software." *Proc. Third Int'l Conf. Mobile & Ubiq. Multimedia*, (College Park, MY), 2004. pp. 71–78. Cited on page 25.

NOBLE, B., FLEIS, B., and KIM, M.: "A Case for Fluid Replication." *Proc. NetStore'99*, 1999. Cited on page 301.

OBRACZKA, K.: "Multicast Transport Protocols: A Survey and Taxonomy." *IEEE Commun. Mag.*, (36)1:94-102, Jan. 1998. Cited on page 166.

OMG: "The Common Object Request Broker: Core Specification, revision 3.0.3." OMG Document formal/04-03-12, Object Management Group, Framingham, MA, Mar. 2004a. Cited on pages 54, 454, 465, 477.

OMG: "UML 2.0 Superstructure Specification." OMG Document ptc/04-10-02, Object Management Group, Framingham, MA, Oct. 2004b. Cited on page 34.

OPPENHEIMER, D., ALBRECHT, J., PATTERSON, D., and VAHDAT, A.: "Design and Implementation Tradeoffs for Wide-Area Resource Discovery." *Proc. 14th Int'l Symp. on High Performance Distributed Computing*, (Research Triangle Park, NC). Los Alamitos, CA: IEEE Computer Society Press, 2005. Cited on page 224.

ORAM, A. (ed.): *Peer-to-Peer: Harnessing the Power of Disruptive Technologies*. Sebastopol, CA: O'Reilly & Associates, 2001. Cited on pages 15, 625.

OZSU, T. and VALDURIEZ, P.: *Principles of Distributed Database Systems*. Upper Saddle River, NJ: Prentice Hall, 2nd ed., 1999. Cited on pages 43, 298.

PAI, V., ARON, M., BANGA, G., SVENDSEN, M., DRUSCHEL, P., ZWAENEPOEL, W., and NAHUM, E.: "Locality-Aware Request Distribution in Cluster-Based Network Servers." *Proc. Eighth Int'l Conf. Architectural Support for Programming Languages and Operating Systems*, (San Jose, CA). New York, NY: ACM Press, 1998. pp. 205-216. Cited on page 94.

PANZIERI, F. and SHRIVASTAVA, S.: "Rajdoot: A Remote Procedure Call Mechanism with Orphan Detection and Killing." *IEEE Trans. Softw. Eng.*, (14)1:30-37, Jan. 1988. Cited on page 342.

PARTRIDGE, C., MENDEZ, T., and MILLIKEN, W.: "Host Anycasting Service." RFC 1546, Nov. 1993. Cited on page 228.

PATE, S.: *UNIX Filesystems: Evolution, Design, and Implementation*. New York: John Wiley, 2003. Cited on page 631.

PEASE, M., SHOSTAK, R., and LAMPORT, L.: "Reaching Agreement in the Presence of Faults." *J. ACM*, (27)2:228-234, Apr. 1980. Cited on page 326.

PERKINS, C., HODSON, O., and HARDMAN, V.: "A Survey of Packet Loss Recovery Techniques for Streaming Audio." *IEEE Network*, (12)5:40-48, Sept. 1998. Cited on page 162.

PETERSON, L. and DAVIE, B.: *Computer Networks, A Systems Approach*. San Mateo, CA: Morgan Kaufman, 3rd ed., 2003. Cited on page 626.

PETERSON, L., BAVIER, A., FIUCZYNSKI, M., MUIR, S., and ROSCOE, T.: "Towards a Comprehensive PlanetLab Architecture." Technical Report PDN-05-030, PlanetLab Consortium, June 2005. Cited on page 99.

PFLEEGER, C.: *Security in Computing*. Upper Saddle River, NJ: Prentice Hall, 3rd ed., 2003. Cited on pages 378, 394.

PICCO, G., BALZAROTTI, D., and COSTA, P.: "LighTS: A Lightweight, Customizable Tuple Space Supporting Context-Aware Applications." *Proc. Symp. Applied Computing*, (Santa Fe, NM). New York, NY: ACM Press, 2005. pp. 413-419. Cited on page 595.

PIERRE, G. and VAN STEEN, M.: "Globule: A Collaborative Content Delivery Network." *IEEE Commun. Mag.*, (44)8, Aug. 2006. Cited on pages 54, 63.

PIERRE, G., VAN STEEN, M., and TANENBAUM, A.: "Dynamically Selecting Optimal Distribution Strategies for Web Documents." *IEEE Trans. Comp.*, (51)6:637-651, June 2002. Cited on page 64.

PIETZUCH, P. R. and BACON, J. M.: "Hermes: A Distributed Event-Based Middleware Architecture." *Proc. Workshop on Distributed Event-Based Systems*, (Vienna, Austria). Los Alamitos, CA: IEEE Computer Society Press, 2002. Cited on page 633.

PIKE, R., PRESOTTO, D., DORWARD, S., FLANDRENA, B., THOMPSON, K., TRICKEY, H., and WINTERBOTTOM, P.: "Plan 9 from Bell Labs." *Computing Systems*, (8)3:221-254, Summer 1995. Cited on pages 197, 505.

PINZARI, G.: "NX X Protocol Compression." Technical Report D-309/3-NXP-DOC, NoMachine, Rome, Italy, Sept. 2003. Cited on page 84.

PITOURA, E. and SAMARAS, G.: "Locating Objects in Mobile Computing." *IEEE Trans. Know. Data Eng.*, (13)4:571-592, July 2001. Cited on pages 192, 627.

PLAINFOSSE, D. and SHAPIRO, M.: "A Survey of Distributed Garbage Collection Techniques." In *Proc. Int'l Workshop on Memory Management*, vol. 986 of *Lect. Notes Comp. Sc.*, pp. 211-249. Berlin: Springer-Verlag, Sept. 1995. Cited on page 186.

PLUMMER, D.: "Ethernet Address Resolution Protocol." RFC 826, Nov. 1982. Cited on page 183.

PODLING, S. and BOSZORMENYI, L.: "A Survey of Web Cache Replacement Strategies." *ACM Comput. Surv.*, (35)4:374-398, Dec. 2003. Cited on pages 573, 632.

POPESCU, B., VAN STEEN, M., and TANENBAUM, A.: "A Security Architecture for Object-Based Distributed Systems." *Proc. 18th Ann. Computer Security Application Conf.*, (Las Vegas, NA). ACSA, 2002. Cited on page 482.

POSTEL, J.: "Simple Mail Transfer Protocol." RFC 821, Aug. 1982. Cited on page 151.

POSTEL, J. and REYNOLDS, J.: "File Transfer Protocol." RFC 995, Oct. 1985. Cited on page 122.

POTZL, H., ANDERSON, M., and STEINBRINK, B.: "Linux-VServer: Resource Efficient Context Isolation." *Free Software Magazine*, no. 5, June 2005. Cited on page 103.

POUWELSE, J., GARBACKI, P., EPEMA, D., and SIPS, H.: "A Measurement Study of the BitTorrent Peer-to-Peer File-Sharing System." Technical Report PDS-2004-003, Technical University Delft, Apr. 2004. Cited on page 53.

POUWELSE, J. A., GARBACKI, P., EPEMA, D. H. J., and SIPS, H. J.: "The Bittorrent P2P File-Sharing System: Measurements and Analysis." *Proc. Fourth Int'l Workshop on Peer-to-Peer Systems*, vol. 3640 of *Lect. Notes Comp. Sc.*, (Ithaca, NY). Berlin: Springer-Verlag, 2005. pp. 205-216. Cited on page 527.

QIN, F., TUCEK, J., SUNDARESAN, J., and ZHOU, Y.: "Rx: Treating Bugs as Allergies - A Safe Method to Survive Software Failures." *Proc. 20th Symp. Operating System Principles*, (Brighton, UK). New York, NY: ACM Press, 2005. pp. 235-248. Cited on page 372.

QIU, L., PADMANABHAN, V., and VOELKER, G.: "On the Placement of Web Server Replicas." *Proc. 20th INFOCOM Conf.*, (Anchorage (AK)). Los Alamitos, CA: IEEE Computer Society Press, 2001. pp. 1587-1596. Cited on pages 296, 297.

RABINOVICH, M. and SPASTSCHECK, O.: *Web Caching and Replication.* Reading, MA: Addison-Wesley, 2002. Cited on pages 52, 570, 633.

RABINOVICH, M., RABINOVICH, I., RAJARAMAN, R., and AGGARWAL, A.: "A Dynamic Object Replication and Migration Protocol for an Internet Hosting Service." *Proc. 19th Int'l Conf. on Distributed Computing Systems.* IEEE, 1999. pp. 101-113. Cited on page 299.

RADIA, S.: *Names, Contexts, and Closure Mechanisms in Distributed Computing Environments.* Ph.D. Thesis, University of Waterloo, Ontario, 1989. Cited on page 198.

RADOSLAVOV, P., GOVINDAN, R., and ESTRIN, D.: "Topology-Informed Internet Replica Placement." *Proc. Sixth Web Caching Workshop*, (Boston, MA). Amsterdam: North-Holland, 2001. Cited on page 296.

RAFAELI, S. and HUTCHISON, D.: "A Survey of Key Management for Secure Group Communication." *ACM Comput. Surv.*, (35)3:309-329, Sept. 2003. Cited on page 631.

RAICIU, C. and ROSENBLUM, D.: "Enabling Confidentiality in Content-Based Publish/Subscribe Infrastructures." Technical Report RN/05/30, Department of Computer Science, University College London, 2005. Cited on page 619.

RAMANATHAN, P., SHIN, K., and BUTLER, R.: "Fault-Tolerant Clock Synchronization in Distributed Systems." *IEEE Computer*, (23)10:33-42, Oct. 1990. Cited on page 238.

RAMASUBRAMANIAN, V. and SIRER, E. G.: "The Design and Implementation of a Next Generation Name Service for the Internet." *Proc. SIGCOMM*, (Portland, OR). New York, NY: ACM Press, 2004a. Cited on page 215.

RAMASUBRAMANIAN, V. and SIRER, E. G.: "Beehive: O(1) Lookup Performance for Power-Law Query Distributions in Peer-to-Peer Overlays." *Proc. First Symp. Networked Systems Design and Impl.*, (San Francisco, CA). Berkeley, CA: USENIX, 2004b. pp. 99-112. Cited on pages 216, 527.

RATNASAMY, S., FRANCIS, P., HANDLEY, M., KARP, R., and SCHENKER, S.: "A Scalable Content-Addressable Network." *Proc. SIGCOMM*. ACM, 2001. pp. 161-172. Cited on page 45.

RAYNAL, M. and SINGHAL, M.: "Logical Time: Capturing Causality in Distributed Systems." *IEEE Computer*, (29)2:49-56, Feb. 1996. Cited on pages 246, 628.

REITER, M.: "How to Securely Replicate Services." *ACM Trans. Prog. Lang. Syst.*, (16)3:986-1009, May 1994. Cited on pages 409, 411.

REITER, M., BIRMAN, K., and VAN RENESSE, R.: "A Security Architecture for Fault-Tolerant Systems." *ACM Trans. Comp. Syst.*, (12)4:340-371, Nov. 1994. Cited on page 433.

RESCORLA, E. and SCHIFFMAN, A.: "The Secure HyperText Transfer Protocol." RFC 2660, Aug. 1999. Cited on page 565.

REYNOLDS, J. and POSTEL, J.: "Assigned Numbers." RFC 1700, Oct. 1994. Cited on page 89.

RICART, G. and AGRAWALA, A.: "An Optimal Algorithm for Mutual Exclusion in Computer Networks." *Commun. ACM*, (24)1:9-17, Jan. 1981. Cited on page 255.

RISSON, J. and MOORS, T.: "Survey of Research towards Robust Peer-to-Peer Networks: Search Methods." *Comp. Netw.*, (50), 2006. Cited on pages 47, 226.

RIVEST, R.: "The MD5 Message Digest Algorithm." RFC 1321, Apr. 1992. Cited on page 395.

RIVEST, R., SHAMIR, A., and ADLEMAN, L.: "A Method for Obtaining Digital Signatures and Public-key Cryptosystems." *Commun. ACM*, (21)2:120-126, Feb. 1978. Cited on page 394.

RIZZO, L.: "Effective Erasure Codes for Reliable Computer Communication Protocols." *ACM Comp. Commun. Rev.*, (27)2:24-36, Apr. 1997. Cited on page 364.

RODRIGUES, L., FONSECA, H., and VERISSIMO, P.: "Totally Ordered Multicast in Large-Scale Systems." *Proc. 16th Int'l Conf. on Distributed Computing Systems*. IEEE, 1996. pp. 503-510. Cited on page 311.

RODRIGUES, R. and LISKOV, B.: "High Availability in DHTs: Erasure Coding vs. Replication." *Proc. Fourth Int'l Workshop on Peer-to-Peer Systems*, (Ithaca, NY), 2005. Cited on page 532.

RODRIGUEZ, P., SPANNER, C., and BIERSACK, E.: "Analysis of Web Caching Architecture: Hierarchical and Distributed Caching." *IEEE/ACM Trans. Netw.*, (21)4:404-418, Aug. 2001. Cited on page 571.

ROSENBLUM, M. and GARFINKEL, T.: "Virtual Machine Monitors: Current Technology and Future Trends." *IEEE Computer*, (38)5:39-47, May 2005. Cited on page 82.

ROUSSOS, G., MARSH, A. J., and MAGLAVERA, S.: "Enabling Pervasive Computing with Smart Phones." *IEEE Pervasive Comput.*, (4)2:20-26, Apr. 2005. Cited on page 25.

ROWSTRON, A.: "Run-time Systems for Coordination." In Omicini, A., Zambonelli, F., Klusch, M., and Tolksdorf, R. (eds.), *Coordination of Internet Agents: Models, Technologies and Applications*, pp. 78-96. Berlin: Springer-Verlag, 2001. Cited on page 607.

ROWSTRON, A. and DRUSCHEL, P.: "Pastry: Scalable, Distributed Object Location and Routing for Large-Scale Peer-to-Peer Systems." *Proc. Middleware 2001*, vol. 2218 of *Lect. Notes Comp. Sc.* Berlin: Springer-Verlag, 2001. pp. 329-350. Cited on pages 167, 191, 216.

ROWSTRON, A. and WRAY, S.: "A Run-Time System for WCL." In Bal, H., Belkhouche, B., and Cardelli, L. (eds.), *Internet Programming Languages*, vol. 1686 of *Lect. Notes Comp. Sc.*, pp. 78-96. Berlin: Springer-Verlag, 1998. Cited on page 610.

RUSSELLO, G., CHAUDRON, M., and VAN STEEN, M.: "Adapting Strategies for Distributing Data in Shared Data Space." *Proc. Int'l Symp. Distr. Objects & Appl. (DOA)*, vol. 3291 of *Lect. Notes Comp. Sc.*, (Agia Napa, Cyprus). Berlin: Springer-Verlag, 2004. pp. 1225-1242. Cited on pages 611, 612.

RUSSELLO, G., CHAUDRON, M., VAN STEEN, M., and BOKHAROUSS, I.: "Dynamically Adapting Tuple Replication for Managing Availability in a Shared Data Space." *Sc. Comp. Programming*, (63), 2006. Cited on pages 611, 616.

SADJADI, S. and MCKINLEY, P.: "A Survey of Adaptive Middleware." Technical Report MSU-CSE-03-35, Michigan State University, Computer Science and Engineering, Dec. 2003. Cited on page 55.

SAITO, Y. and SHAPIRO, M.: "Optimistic Replication." *ACM Comput. Surv.*, (37)1:42-81, Mar. 2005. Cited on page 628.

SALTZER, J. and SCHROEDER, M.: "The Protection of Information in Computer Systems." *Proceedings of the IEEE*, (63)9:1278-1308, Sept. 1975. Cited on page 416.

SALTZER, J.: "Naming and Binding Objects." In Bayer, R., Graham, R., and Seegmuller, G. (eds.), *Operating Systems: An Advanced Course*, vol. 60 of *Lect. Notes Comp. Sc.*, pp. 99-208. Berlin: Springer-Verlag, 1978. Cited on page 627.

SALTZER, J., REED, D., and CLARK, D.: "End-to-End Arguments in System Design." *ACM Trans. Comp. Syst.*, (2)4:277-288, Nov. 1984. Cited on page 252.

SANDHU, R. S., COYNE, E. J., FEINSTEIN, H. L., and YOUMAN, C. E.: "Role-Based Access Control Models." *IEEE Computer*, (29)2:38-47, Feb. 1996. Cited on page 417.

SAROIU, S., GUMMADI, P. K., and GRIBBLE, S. D.: "Measuring and Analyzing the Characteristics of Napster and Gnutella Hosts." *ACM Multimedia Syst.*, (9)2:170-184, Aug. 2003. Cited on page 53.

SATYANARAYANAN, M.: "The Evolution of Coda." *ACM Trans. Comp. Syst.*, (20)2:85-124, May 2002. Cited on page 632.

SATYANARAYANAN, M. and SIEGEL, E.: "Parallel Communication in a Large Distributed System." *IEEE Trans. Comp.*, (39)3:328-348, Mar. 1990. Cited on page 505.

SAXENA, P. and RAI, J.: "A Survey of Permission-based Distributed Mutual Exclusion Algorithms." *Computer Standards and Interfaces*, (25)2:159-181, May 2003. Cited on page 252.

SCHMIDT, D., STAL, M., ROHNERT, H., and BUSCHMANN, F.: *Pattern-Oriented Software Architecture – Patterns for Concurrent and Networked Objects*. New York: John Wiley, 2000. Cited on pages 55, 625.

SCHNEIDER, F.: "Implementing Fault-Tolerant Services Using the State Machine Approach: A Tutorial." *ACM Comput. Surv.*, (22)4:299-320, Dec. 1990. Cited on pages 248, 303, 480.

SCHNEIER, B.: *Applied Cryptography*. New York: John Wiley, 2nd ed., 1996. Cited on pages 391, 411.

SCHNEIER, B.: *Secrets and Lies*. New York: John Wiley, 2000. Cited on pages 391, 630.

SCHULZRINNE, H.: "The tel URI for Telephone Numbers." RFC 3966, Jan. 2005. Cited on page 569.

SCHULZRINNE, H., CASNER, S., FREDERICK, R., and JACOBSON, V.: "RTP: A Transport Protocol for Real-Time Applications." RFC 3550, July 2003. Cited on page 121.

SEBESTA, R.: *Programming the World Wide Web.* Reading, MA: Addison-Wesley, 3rd ed., 2006. Cited on pages 547, 633.

SHAPIRO, M., DICKMAN, P., and PLAINFOSSE, D.: "SSP Chains: Robust, Distributed References Supporting Acyclic Garbage Collection." Technical Report 1799, INRIA, Rocquencourt, France, Nov. 1992. Cited on page 184.

SHAW, M. and CLEMENTS, P.: "A Field Guide to Boxology: Preliminary Classification of Architectural Styles for Software Systems." *Proc. 21st Int'l Comp. Softw. & Appl. Conf.*, 1997. pp. 6-13. Cited on page 34.

SHEPLER, S., CALLAGHAN, B., ROBINSON, D., THURLOW, R., BEAME, C., EISLER, M., and NOVECK, D.: "Network File System (NFS) Version 4 Protocol." RFC 3530, Apr. 2003. Cited on pages 201, 492.

SHETH, A. P. and LARSON, J. A.: "Federated Database Systems for Managing Distributed, Heterogeneous, and Autonomous Databases." *ACM Comput. Surv.*, (22)3:183-236, Sept. 1990. Cited on page 299.

SHOOMAN, M. L.: *Reliability of Computer Systems and Networks: Fault Tolerance, Analysis, and Design.* New York: John Wiley, 2002. Cited on page 322.

SILBERSCHATZ, A., GALVIN, P., and GAGNE, G.: *Operating System Concepts.* New York: John Wiley, 7th ed., 2005. Cited on pages 197, 624.

SINGH, A., CASTRO, M., DRUSCHEL, P., and ROWSTRON, A.: "Defending Against Eclipse Attacks on Overlay Networks." *Proc. 11th SIGOPS European Workshop*, (Leuven, Belgium). New York, NY: ACM Press, 2004. pp. 115-120. Cited on page 539.

SINGH, A., NGAN, T.-W., DRUSCHEL, P., and WALLACH, D. S.: "Eclipse Attacks on Overlay Networks: Threats and Defenses." *Proc. 25th INFOCOM Conf.*, (Barcelona, Spain). Los Alamitos, CA: IEEE Computer Society Press, 2006. Cited on page 539.

SINGHAL, M. and SHIVARATRI, N.: *Advanced Concepts in Operating Systems: Distributed, Database, and Multiprocessor Operating Systems.* New York: McGraw-Hill, 1994. Cited on page 364.

SIVASUBRAMANIAN, S., PIERRE, G., and VAN STEEN, M.: "Replicating Web Applications On-Demand." *Proc. First Int'l Conf. Services Comput.*, (Shanghai, China). Los Alamitos, CA: IEEE Computer Society Press, 2004a. pp. 227-236. Cited on page 580.

SIVASUBRAMANIAN, S., PIERRE, G., VAN STEEN, M., and ALONSO, G.: "GlobeCBC: Content-blind Result Caching for Dynamic Web Applications." Technical Report, Vrije Universiteit, Department of Computer Science, Jan. 2006. Cited on page 582.

SIVASUBRAMANIAN, S., SZYMANIAK, M., PIERRE, G., and VAN STEEN, M.: "Replication for Web Hosting Systems." *ACM Comput. Surv.*, (36)3:1-44, Sept. 2004b. Cited on pages 299, 573, 629.

SIVASUBRAMANIAN, S., ALONSO, G., PIERRE, G., and VAN STEEN, M.: "GlobeDB: Autonomic Data Replication for Web Applications." *Proc. 14th Int'l WWW Conf.*, (Chiba, Japan). New York, NY: ACM Press, 2005. pp. 33-42. Cited on page 581.

SIVRIKAYA, F. and YENER, B.: "Time Synchronization in Sensor Networks: A Survey." *IEEE Network*, (18)4:45-50, July 2004. Cited on page 242.

SKEEN, D.: "Nonblocking Commit Protocols." *Proc. SIGMOD Int'l Conf. on Management Of Data*. ACM, 1981. pp. 133-142. Cited on page 359.

SKEEN, D. and STONEBRAKER, M.: "A Formal Model of Crash Recovery in a Distributed System." *IEEE Trans. Softw. Eng.*, (SE-9)3:219-228, Mar. 1983. Cited on page 361.

SMITH, J. and NAIR, R.: "The Architecture of Virtual Machines." *IEEE Computer*, (38)5:32-38, May 2005. Cited on pages 80, 81.

SMITH, J. and NAIR, R.: *Virtual Machines: Versatile Platforms for Systems and Processes*. San Mateo, CA: Morgan Kaufman, 2005. Cited on page 625.

SNIR, M., OTTO, S., HUSS-LEDERMAN, S., WALKER, D., and DONGARRA, J.: *MPI: The Complete Reference – The MPI Core*. Cambridge, MA: MIT Press, 1998. Cited on page 145.

SPEAKMAN, T., CROWCROFT, J., GEMMELL, J., FARINACCI, D., LIN, S., LESHCHINER, D., LUBY, M., MONTGOMERY, T., RIZZO, L., TWEEDLY, A., BHASKAR, N., EDMONSTONE, R., SUMANASEKERA, R., and VICISANO, L.: "PGM Reliable Transport Protocol Specification." RFC 3208, Dec. 2001. Cited on page 614.

SPECHT, S. M. and LEE, R. B.: "Distributed Denial of Service: Taxonomies of Attacks, Tools, and Countermeasures." *Proc. Int'l Workshop on Security in Parallel and Distributed Systems*, (San Francisco, CA), 2004. pp. 543-550. Cited on page 427.

SPECTOR, A.: "Performing Remote Operations Efficiently on a Local Computer Network." *Commun. ACM*, (25)4:246-260, Apr. 1982. Cited on page 339.

SRINIVASAN, R.: "RPC: Remote Procedure Call Protocol Specification Version 2." RFC 1831, Aug. 1995a. Cited on page 502.

SRINIVASAN, R.: "XDR: External Data Representation Standard." RFC 1832, Aug. 1995b. Cited on page 502.

SRIPANIDKULCHAI, K., MAGGS, B., and ZHANG, H.: "Efficient Content Location Using Interest-Based Locality in Peer-to-Peer Systems." *Proc. 22nd INFOCOM Conf.*, (San Francisco, CA). Los Alamitos, CA: IEEE Computer Society Press, 2003. Cited on page 225.

STEIN, L.: *Web Security, A Step-by-Step Reference Guide*. Reading, MA: Addison-Wesley, 1998. Cited on page 432.

STEINDER, M. and SETHI, A.: "A Survey of Fault Localization Techniques in Computer Networks." *Sc. Comp. Programming*, (53)165-194, May 2004. Cited on page 372.

STEINER, J., NEUMAN, C., and SCHILLER, J.: "Kerberos: An Authentication Service for Open Network Systems." *Proc. Winter Techn. Conf.* USENIX, 1988. pp. 191-202. Cited on page 411.

STEINMETZ, R.: "Human Perception of Jitter and Media Synchronization." *IEEE J. Selected Areas Commun.*, (14)1:61-72, Jan. 1996. Cited on page 163.

STEINMETZ, R. and NAHRSTEDT, K.: *Multimedia Systems*. Berlin: Springer-Verlag, 2004. Cited on pages 93, 157, 160, 626.

STEVENS, W.: *UNIX Network Programming – Networking APIs: Sockets and XTI*. Englewood Cliffs, NJ: Prentice Hall, 2nd ed., 1998. Cited on pages 76, 142.

STEVENS, W.: *UNIX Network Programming – Interprocess Communication*. Englewood Cliffs, NJ: Prentice Hall, 2nd ed., 1999. Cited on pages 70, 136.

STEVENS, W. and RAGO, S.: *Advanced Programming in the UNIX Environment*. Reading, MA: Addison-Wesley, 2nd ed., 2005. Cited on pages 72, 626.

STOICA, I., MORRIS, R., LIBEN-NOWELL, D., KARGER, D. R., KAASHOEK, M. F., DABEK, F., and BALAKRISHNAN, H.: "Chord: A Scalable Peer-to-peer Lookup Protocol for Internet Applications." *IEEE/ACM Trans. Netw.*, (11)1:17-32, Feb. 2003. Cited on pages 44, 188.

STOJMENOVIC, I.: "Position-based Routing in Ad Hoc Networks." *IEEE Commun. Mag.*, (40)7:128-134, July 2002. Cited on page 261.

STRAUSS, J., KATABI, D., and KAASHOEK, F.: "A Measurement Study of Available Bandwidth Estimation Tools." *Proc. Third Internet Measurement Conf.*, (Miami Beach, FL, USA). New York, NY: ACM Press, 2003. pp. 39–44. Cited on page 575.

SUGERMAN, J., VENKITACHALAM, G., and LIM, B.-H.: "Virtualizing I/O Devices on VMware Workstation s Hosted Virtual Machine Monitor." *Proc. USENIX Ann. Techn. Conf.*, (Boston, MA). Berkeley, CA: USENIX, 2001. pp. 1-14. Cited on page 81.

SUN MICROSYSTEMS: *Java Message Service, Version 1.1*. Sun Microsystems, Mountain Ciew, Calif., Apr. 2004a. cited on pages 466, 593.

SUN MICROSYSTEMS: *Java Remote Method Invocation Specification, JDK 1.5*. Sun Microsystems, Mountain View, Calif., 2004b. Cited on page 122.

SUN MICROSYSTEMS: *EJB 3.0 Simplified API*. Sun Microsystems, Mountain View, Calif., Aug. 2005a. Cited on page 447.

SUN MICROSYSTEMS: *Jini Technology Starter Kit, Version 2.1*, Oct. 2005b. Cited on pages 486, 593.

SUNDARARAMAN, B., BUY, U., and KSHEMKALYANI, A. D.: "Clock Synchronization for Wireless Sensor Networks: A Survey." *Ad-Hoc Networks*, (3)3:281-323, May 2005. Cited on page 242.

SZYMANIAK, M., PIERRE, G., and VAN STEEN, M.: "Scalable Cooperative Latency Estimation." *Proc. Tenth Int'l Conf. Parallel and Distributed Systems*, (Newport Beach, CA). Los Alamitos, CA: IEEE Computer Society Press, 2004. pp. 367-376. Cited on page 263.

SZYMANIAK, M., PIERRE, G., and VAN STEEN, M.: "A Single-Homed Ad hoc Distributed Server." Technical Report IR-CS-013, Vrije Universiteit, Department of Computer Science, Mar. 2005. Cited on page 96.

SZYMANIAK, M., PIERRE, G., and VAN STEEN, M.: "Latency-driven replica placement." *IPSJ Digital Courier*, (2), 2006. Cited on page 297.

TAIANI, F., FABRE, J.-C., and KILLIJIAN, M.-O.: "A Multi-Level Meta-Object Protocol for Fault-Tolerance in Complex Architectures." *Proc. Int'l Conf. Dependable Systems and Networks*, (Yokohama, Japan). Los Alamitos, CA: IEEE Computer Society Press, 2005. pp. 270-279. Cited on page 474.

TAM, D., AZIMI, R., and JACOBSEN, H.-A.: "Building Content-Based Publish/Subscribe Systems with Distributed Hash Tables." *Proc. First Int'l Workshop on Databases, Information Systems and Peer-to-Peer Computing*, vol. 2944 of *Lect. Notes Comp. Sc.*, (Berlin, Germany). Berlin: Springer-Verlag, 2003. pp. 138-152. Cited on page 597.

TAN, S.-W., WATERS, G., and CRAWFORD, J.: "A Survey and Performance Evaluation of Scalable Tree-based Application Layer Multicast Protocols." Technical Report 9-03, University of Kent, UK, July 2003. Cited on page 169.

TANENBAUM, A.: *Computer Networks*. Upper Saddle River, NJ: Prentice Hall, 4th ed., 2003. Cited on pages 117, 336.

TANENBAUM, A., MULLENDER, S., and VAN RENESSE, R.: "Using Sparse Capabilities in a Distributed Operating System." *Proc. Sixth Int'l Conf. on Distributed Computing Systems*. IEEE, 1986. pp. 558-563. Cited on page 435.

TANENBAUM, A., VAN RENESSE, R., VAN STAVEREN, H., SHARP, G., MULLENDER, S., JANSEN, J., and VAN ROSSUM, G.: "Experiences with the Amoeba Distributed Operating System." *Commun. ACM*, (33)12:46-63, Dec. 1990. Cited on page 415.

TANENBAUM, A. and WOODHULL, A.: *Operating Systems, Design and Implementation*. Englewood Cliffs, NJ: Prentice Hall, 3rd ed., 2006. Cited on pages 197, 495.

TANISCH, P.: "Atomic Commit in Concurrent Computing." *IEEE Concurrency*, (8)4:34-41, Oct. 2000. Cited on page 355.

TARTALJA, I. and MILUTINOVIC, V.: "Classifying Software-Based Cache Coherence Solutions." *IEEE Softw.*, (14)3:90-101, May 1997. Cited on page 313.

TEL, G.: *Introduction to Distributed Algorithms*. Cambridge, UK: Cambridge University Press, 2nd ed., 2000. Cited on pages 232, 263, 628.

TERRY, D., DEMERS, A., PETERSEN, K., SPREITZER, M., THEIMER, M., and WELSH, B.: "Session Guarantees for Weakly Consistent Replicated Data." *Proc. Third Int'l Conf. on Parallel and Distributed Information Systems*, (Austin, TX). Los Alamitos, CA: IEEE Computer Society Press, 1994. pp. 140-149. Cited on pages 290, 293, 295.

TERRY, D., PETERSEN, K., SPREITZER, M., and THEIMER, M.: "The Case for Non-transparent Replication: Examples from Bayou." *IEEE Data Engineering*, (21)4:12-20, Dec. 1998. Cited on page 290.

THOMAS, R.: "A Majority Consensus Approach to Concurrency Control for Multiple Copy Databases." *ACM Trans. Database Syst.*, (4)2:180-209, June 1979. Cited on page 311.

TIBCO: *TIB/Rendezvous Concepts, Release 7.4*. TIBCO Software Inc., Palo Alto, CA, July 2005. Cited on pages 54, 595.

TOLIA, N., HARKES, J., KOZUCH, M., and SATYANARAYAN, M.: "Integrating Portable and Distributed Storage." *Proc. Third USENIX Conf. File and Storage Techn.*, (Boston, MA). Berkeley, CA: USENIX, 2004. Cited on page 523.

TOLKSDORF, R. and ROWSTRON, A.: "Evaluating Fault Tolerance Methods for Large-scale Linda-like systems." *Proc. Int'l Conf. on Parallel and Distributed Processing Techniques and Applications*, vol. 2, (Las Vegas, NV), 2000. pp. 793-800. Cited on page 616.

TOWSLEY, D., KUROSE, J., and PINGALI, S.: "A Comparison of Sender-Initiated and Receiver-Initiated Reliable Multicast Protocols." *IEEE J. Selected Areas Commun.*, (15)3:398-407, Apr. 1997. Cited on page 345.

TRIPATHI, A., KARNIK, N., VORA, M., AHMED, T., and SINGH, R.: "Mobile Agent Programming in Ajanta." *Proc. 19th Int'l Conf. on Distributed Computing Systems*. IEEE, 1999. pp. 190-197. Cited on page 422.

TUREK, J. and SHASHA, S.: "The Many Faces of Consensus in Distributed Systems." *IEEE Computer*, (25)6:8-17, June 1992. Cited on pages 332, 335.

UMAR, A.: *Object-Oriented Client/Server Internet Environments*. Upper Saddle River, NJ: Prentice Hall, 1997. Cited on page 41.

UPnP Forum: "UPnP Device Architecture Version 1.0.1, Dec. 2003. Cited on page 26.

VAN RENESSE, R., BIRMAN, K., and VOGELS, W.: "Astrolabe: A Robust and Scalable Technology for Distributed System Monitoring, Management, and Data Mining." *ACM Trans. Comp. Syst.*, (21)2:164-206, May 2003. Cited on page 61.

VAN STEEN, M., HAUCK, F., HOMBURG, P., and TANENBAUM, A.: "Locating Objects in Wide-Area Systems." *IEEE Commun.*, (36)1:104-109, Jan. 1998. Cited on page 192.

VASUDEVAN, S., KUROSE, J. F., and TOWSLEY, D. F.: "Design and Analysis of a Leader Election Algorithm for Mobile Ad Hoc Networks." *Proc. 12th Int'l Conf. on Network Protocols*, (Berlin, Germany). Los Alamitos, CA: IEEE Computer Society Press, 2004. pp. 350-360. Cited on pages 267, 268.

VEIGA, L. and FERREIRA, P.: "Asynchronous Complete Distributed Garbage Collection." *Proc. 19th Int'l Parallel & Distributed Processing Symp.*, (Denver, CO). Los Alamitos, CA: IEEE Computer Society Press, 2005. Cited on page 186.

VELAZQUEZ, M.: "A Survey of Distributed Mutual Exclusion Algorithms." Technical Report CS-93-116, University of Colorado at Boulder, Sept. 1993. Cited on page 252.

VERISSIMO, P. and RODRIGUES, L.: *Distributed Systems for Systems Architects*. Dordrecht, The Netherlands: Kluwer Academic Publishers, 2001. Cited on page 624.

VETTER, R., SPELL, C., and WARD, C.: "Mosaic and the World-Wide Web." *IEEE Computer*, (27)10:49-57, Oct. 1994. Cited on page 545.

VITEK, J., BRYCE, C., and ORIOL, M.: "Coordinating Processes with Secure Spaces." *Sc. Comp. Programming*, (46)1-2, 2003. Cited on page 620.

VOGELS, W.: "Tracking Service Availability in Long Running Business Activities." *Proc. First Int'l Conf. Service Oriented Comput.*, vol. 2910 of *Lect. Notes Comp. Sc.*, (Trento, Italy). Berlin: Springer-Verlag, 2003. pp. 395-408. Cited on page 336.

VOULGARIS, S. and VAN STEEN, M.: "Epidemic-style Management of Semantic Overlays for Content-Based Searching." *Proc. 11th Int'l Conf. Parallel and Distributed Computing (Euro-Par)*, vol. 3648 of *Lect. Notes Comp. Sc.*, (Lisbon, Portugal). Berlin: Springer-Verlag, 2005. pp. 1143-1152. Cited on page 226.

VOULGARIS, S., RIVI°ERE, E., KERMARREC, A.-M., and VAN STEEN, M.: "Sub-2-Sub: Self-Organizing Content-Based Publish and Subscribe for Dynamic and Large Scale Collaborative Networks." *Proc. Fifth Int'l Workshop on Peer-to-Peer Systems*, (Santa Barbara, CA), 2006. Cited on page 597.

VOYDOCK, V. and KENT, S.: "Security Mechanisms in High-Level Network Protocols." *ACM Comput. Surv.*, (15)2:135-171, June 1983. Cited on page 397.

WAH, B. W., SU, X., and LIN, D.: "A Survey of Error-Concealment Schemes for Real-Time Audio and Video Transmissions over the Internet." *Proc. Int'l Symp. Multimedia Softw. Eng.*, (Taipei, Taiwan). Los Alamitos, CA: IEEE Computer Society Press, 2000. pp. 17-24. Cited on page 162.

WAHBE, R., LUCCO, S., ANDERSON, T., and GRAHAM, S.: "Efficient Software-based Fault Isolation." *Proc. 14th Symp. Operating System Principles*. ACM, 1993. pp. 203-216. Cited on page 422.

WALDO, J.: "Remote Procedure Calls and Java Remote Method Invocation." *IEEE Concurrency*, (6)3:5-7, July 1998. Cited on page 463.

WALFISH, M., BALAKRISHNAN, H., , and SHENKER, S.: "Untangling the Web from DNS." *Proc. First Symp. Networked Systems Design and Impl.*, (San Francisco, CA). Berkeley, CA: USENIX, 2004. pp. 225-238. Cited on page 215.

WALLACH, D.: "A Survey of Peer-to-Peer Security Issues." *Proc. Int'l Symp. Softw. Security*, vol. 2609 of *Lect. Notes Comp. Sc.*, (Tokyo, Japan). Berlin: Springer-Verlag, 2002. pp. 42-57. Cited on page 539.

WALLACH, D., BALFANZ, D., DEAN, D., and FELTEN, E.: "Extensible Security Architectures for Java." *Proc. 16th Symp. Operating System Principles*. ACM, 1997. pp. 116-128. Cited on pages 424, 426.

WANG, C., CARZANIGA, A., EVANS, D., and WOLF, A. L.: "Security Issues and Requirements for Internet-Scale Publish-Subscribe Systems." *Proc. 35th Hawaii Int'l Conf. System Sciences*, vol. 9. IEEE, 2002. pp. 303-310. Cited on page 618.

WANG, H., LO, M. K., and WANG, C.: "Consumer Privacy Concerns about Internet Marketing." *Commun. ACM*, (41)3:63-70, Mar. 1998. Cited on page 4.

WATTS, D. J.: *Small Worlds, The Dynamics of Networks between Order and Randomness.* Princeton, NJ: Princeton University Press, 1999. Cited on page 226.

WELLS, G., CHALMERS, A., and CLAYTON, P.: "Linda Implementations in Java for Concurrent Systems." *Conc. & Comput.: Prac. Exp.*, (16)10:1005-1022, Aug. 2004. Cited on page 633.

WESSELS, D.: *Squid: The Definitive Guide.* Sebastopol, CA: O'Reilly & Associates, 2004. Cited on pages 556, 572.

WHITE, S. R., HANSON, J. E., WHALLEY, I., CHESS, D. M., , and KEPHART, J. O.: "An Architectural Approach to Autonomic Computing." *Proc. First Int'l Conf. Autonomic Comput.*, (New York, NY). Los Alamitos, CA: IEEE Computer Society Press, 2004. pp. 2-9. Cited on page 625.

WIERINGA, R. and DE JONGE, W.: "Object Identifiers, Keys, and Surrogates–Object Identifiers Revisited." *Theory and Practice of Object Systems*, (1)2:101-114, 1995. Cited on page 181.

WIESMANN, M., PEDONE, F., SCHIPER, A., KEMME, B., and ALONSO, G.: "Understanding Replication in Databases and Distributed Systems." *Proc. 20th Int'l Conf. on Distributed Computing Systems*. IEEE, 2000. pp. 264-274. Cited on page 276.

WOLLRATH, A., RIGGS, R., and WALDO, J.: "A Distributed Object Model for the Java System." *Computing Systems*, (9)4:265-290, Fall 1996. Cited on pages 460, 472.

WOLMAN, A., VOELKER, G., SHARMA, N., CARDWELL, N., KARLIN, A., and LEVY, H.: "On the Scale and Performance of Cooperative Web Proxy Caching." *Proc. 17th Symp. Operating System Principles*. ACM, 1999. pp. 16-31. Cited on page 571.

WU, D., HOU, Y., ZHU, W., ZHANG, Y., and PEHA, J.: "Streaming Video over the Internet: Approaches and Directions." *IEEE Trans. Circuits & Syst. Video Techn.*, (11)1:1-20, Feb. 2001. Cited on page 159.

YANG, B. and GARCIA-MOLINA, H.: "Designing a Super-Peer Network." *Proc. 19th Int'l Conf. Data Engineering*, (Bangalore, India). Los Alamitos, CA: IEEE Computer Society Press, 2003. pp. 49-60. Cited on page 51.

YANG, M., ZHANG, Z., LI, X., and DAI, Y.: "An Empirical Study of Free-Riding Behavior in the Maze P2P File-Sharing System." *Proc. Fourth Int'l Workshop on Peer-to-Peer Systems*, Lect. Notes Comp. Sc., (Ithaca, NY). Berlin: Springer-Verlag, 2005. Cited on page 53.

YELLIN, D.: "Competitive Algorithms for the Dynamic Selection of Component Implementations." *IBM Syst. J.*, (42)1:85-97, Jan. 2003. Cited on page 58.

YU, H. and VAHDAT, A.: "Efficient Numerical Error Bounding for Replicated Network Services." In Abbadi, Amr El, Brodie, Michael L., Chakravarthy, Sharma, Dayal, Umeshwar, Kamel, Nabil, Schlageter, Gunter, and Whang, Kyu-Young (eds.), *Proc.26th Int'l Conf. Very Large Data Bases*, (Cairo, Egypt). San Mateo, CA: Morgan Kaufman, 2000. pp. 123-133. Cited on page 306.

YU, H. and VAHDAT, A.: "Design and Evaluation of a Conit-Based Continuous Consistency Model for Replicated Services." *ACM Trans. Comp. Syst.*, (20)3:239–282, 2002. Cited on pages 277, 279, 575.

ZHANG, C. and JACOBSEN, H.-A.: "Resolving Feature Convolution in Middleware Systems." *Proc. 19th OOPSLA*, (Vancouver, Canada). New York, NY: ACM Press, 2004. pp. 188-205. Cited on page 58.

ZHAO, B., HUANG, L., STRIBLING, J., RHEA, S., JOSEPH, A., and KUBIATOWICZ, J.: "Tapestry: A Resilient Global-Scale Overlay for Service Deployment." *IEEE J. Selected Areas Commun.*, (22)1:41-53, Jan. 2004. Cited on page 216.

ZHAO, F. and GUIBAS, L.: *Wireless Sensor Networks*. San Mateo, CA: Morgan Kaufman, 2004. Cited on pages 28, 624.

ZHAO, Y., STURMAN, D., and BHOLA, S.: "Subscription Propagation in Highly-Available Publish/Subscribe Middleware." *Proc. Middleware 2004*, vol. 3231 of *Lect. Notes Comp. Sc.*, (Toronto, Canada). Berlin: Springer-Verlag, 2004. pp. 274-293. Cited on page 633.

ZHU, Q., CHEN, Z., TAN, L., ZHOU, Y., KEETON, K., and WILKES, J.: "Hibernator: Helping Disk Arrays Sleep through the Winter." *Proc. 20th Symp. Operating System Prin.*, (Brighton, UK). New York, NY: ACM Press, 2005. pp. 177-190. Cited on page 632.

ZHUANG, S. Q., GEELS, D., STOICA, I., and KATZ, R. H.: "On Failure Detection Algorithms in Overlay Networks." *Proc. 24th INFOCOM Conf.*, (Miami, FL). Los Alamitos, CA: IEEE Computer Society Press, 2005. Cited on page 335.

ZOGG, J.-M.: "GPS Basics." Technical Report GPS-X-02007, UBlox, Mar. 2002. Cited on page 236.

ZWICKY, E., COOPER, S., CHAPMAN, D., and RUSSELL, D.: *Building Internet Firewalls*. Sebastopol, CA: O'Reilly & Associates, 2nd ed., 2000. Cited on page 418.

INDEX

B

Dynamo:

① Consistent hashing (virtual nodes)
- partitioning.
- incremental scalability
- number of Vnode according to physical infrastructure

② Vector clocks with reconciliation during reads. → <node, counter> for every version of every obj
- high availability for write
- version size decouple from update rates

⎡ - modification → immutable version of data
⎢ - syntatic reconciliation (choose latest)
⎢ - semantic rec (collapse)
⎣ - truncate when reach threshold.

③ Sloppy Quorum (first N healthy rather than highest N).
Hinted Handoff (send to other node, kept hintedly, sent back when recovery
- temporary failure

④ Merkle tree (anti-entropy).
— permanent failure

hash of data

⑤ Membership & Failure Detection
↳ gossip-based. | ① membership ② partitioning & placement
External Discovery: seeds.
↳ decentralised. local notion of failure.

Assumptions and Requirements

Query Model:
- operate on single data items.
- data stored as binary obj identified by key
- small obj (<1MB)

ACID
- Eventual consistency.
- no isolation guarantee.
- Durability

Efficiency
- Low latency (99.9th percentile of requests)
- High throughput

Operation
- Internal no-hostile.
integrity & security.